Lecture Notes of the Institute for Computer Sciences, Social Informatics and Telecommunications Engineering 305

More information about this series at http://www.springer.com/series/8197

Songqing Chen · Kim-Kwang Raymond Choo ·
Xinwen Fu · Wenjing Lou ·
Aziz Mohaisen (Eds.)

Security and Privacy in Communication Networks

15th EAI International Conference, SecureComm 2019
Orlando, FL, USA, October 23–25, 2019
Proceedings, Part II

 Springer

Editors
Songqing Chen (iD)
George Mason University
Fairfax, VA, USA

Kim-Kwang Raymond Choo (iD)
The University of Texas at San Antonio
San Antonio, TX, USA

Xinwen Fu (iD)
Boston University
Lowell, MA, USA

Wenjing Lou
Virginia Tech
Blacksburg, VA, USA

Aziz Mohaisen (iD)
University of Central Florida
Orlando, FL, USA

ISSN 1867-8211 ISSN 1867-822X (electronic)
Lecture Notes of the Institute for Computer Sciences, Social Informatics
and Telecommunications Engineering
ISBN 978-3-030-37230-9 ISBN 978-3-030-37231-6 (eBook)
https://doi.org/10.1007/978-3-030-37231-6

This Springer imprint is published by the registered company Springer Nature Switzerland AG
The registered company address is: Gewerbestrasse 11, 6330 Cham, Switzerland

Preface

The importance of ensuring security and privacy in communications networks is recognized by both the research and practitioner community. This is, for example, evidenced by the establishment of the U.S. Cyber Command as a unified combatant command in May 2018. This is also the focus of the 15th EAI International Conference on Security and Privacy in Communication Networks (SecureComm 2019).

This proceedings contains 56 papers, which were selected from 149 submissions (i.e. acceptance rate of 37.6%) from universities, national laboratories, and the private sector from across the USA as well as other countries in Europe and Asia. All the submissions went through an extensive review process by internationally-recognized experts in cybersecurity.

Any successful conference requires the contributions of different stakeholder groups and individuals, who have selfishly volunteered their time and energy in disseminating the call for papers, submitting their research findings, participating in the peer reviews and discussions, etc. First and foremost, we would like to offer our gratitude to the entire Organizing Committee for guiding the entire process of the conference. We are also deeply grateful to all the Technical Program Committee members for their time and efforts in reading, commenting, debating, and finally selecting the papers. We also thank all the external reviewers for assisting the Technical Program Committee in their particular areas of expertise as well as all the authors, participants, and session chairs for their valuable contributions. Support from the Steering Committee and EAI staff members was also crucial in ensuring the success of the conference. It has been a great privilege to be working with such a large group of dedicated and talented individuals.

We hope that you found the discussions and interactions at SecureComm 2019 intellectually stimulating, as well as enjoyed what Orlando, FL, had to offer. Enjoy the proceedings!

September 2019

Xinwen Fu
Kim-Kwang Raymond Choo
Aziz Mohaisen
Wenjing Lou

Organization

Steering Committee

Imrich Chlamtac	University of Trento, Italy
Guofei Gu	Texas A&M University, USA
Peng Liu	Pennsylvania State University, USA
Sencun Zhu	Pennsylvania State University, USA

Organizing Committee

General Chairs

Xinwen Fu	University of Central Florida, USA
Kim-Kwang Raymond Choo	The University of Texas at San Antonio, USA

TPC Chair and Co-chairs

Aziz Mohaisen	University of Central Florida, USA
Wenjing Lou	Virginia Tech, USA

Sponsorship and Exhibit Chair

Qing Yang	University of North Texas, USA

Local Chairs

Clay Posey	University of Central Florida, USA
Cliff C. Zou	University of Central Florida, USA

Workshops Chairs

Kaiqi Xiong	University of South Florida, USA
Liang Xiao	Xiamen University, China

Publicity and Social Media Chairs

Yao Liu	University of South Florida, USA
Zhen Ling	Southeast University, China

Publications Chairs

Songqing Chen	George Mason University, USA
Houbing Song	Embry-Riddle Aeronautical University, USA

Web Chairs

Bryan Pearson	University of Central Florida, USA
Yue Zhang	University of Central Florida, USA

Panels Chairs

Simon (Xinming) Ou	University of South Florida, USA
Craig A. Shue	Worcester Polytechnic Institute, USA

Demos Chair

Song Han	University of Connecticut, USA

Tutorials Chair

Yong Guan	Iowa State University, USA

Technical Program Committee

Amro Awad	University of Central Florida, USA
Kai Bu	Zhejiang University, China
Yinzhi Cao	Johns Hopkins University, USA
Eric Chan-Tin	Loyola University Chicago, USA
Kai Chen	Chinese Academy of Sciences, China
Yu Chen	Binghamton University - SUNY, USA
Sherman S. M. Chow	The Chinese University of Hong Kong, Hong Kong, China
Jun Dai	California State University, Sacramento, USA
Karim Elish	Florida Polytechnic University, USA
Birhanu Eshete	University of Michigan, USA
Debin Gao	Singapore Management University, Singapore
Le Guan	University of Georgia, USA
Yong Guan	Iowa State University, USA
Yongzhong He	Beijing Jiaotong University, China
Murtuza Jadliwala	The University of Texas at San Antonio, USA
George Kesidis	Pennsylvania State University, USA
Joongheon Kim	Chung-Ang University, South Korea
Hyoungshick Kim	Sungkyunkwan University, South Korea
Gokhan Kul	Delaware State University, USA
Laurent L. Njilla	Air Force Research Laboratory, USA
Yingjiu Li	Singapore Management University, Singapore
Jingqiang Lin	Chinese Academy of Sciences, China
Zhiqiang Lin	The Ohio State University, USA
Yao Liu	University of South Florida, USA
Javier Lopez	UMA, Spain
Wenjing Lou	Virginia Tech, USA
Rongxing Lu	University of New Brunswick, Canada

Ashraf Matrawy	Carleton University, Canada
Aziz Mohaisen	University of Central Florida, USA
Vaibhav Rastogi	Northwestern University, USA
Sankardas Roy	Bowling Green State University, USA
Pierangela Samarati	University of Milan, Italy
Mohamed Shehab	UNC Charlotte, USA
Seungwon Shin	KAIST, South Korea
Houbing Song	Embry-Riddle Aeronautical University, USA
Jeffrey Spaulding	Niagara University, USA
Martin Strohmeier	University of Oxford, UK
Wenhai Sun	Purdue University, USA
Qiang Tang	New Jersey Institute of Technology, USA
A. Selcuk Uluagac	Florida International University, USA
Eugene Vasserman	Kansas State University, USA
Cong Wang	City University of Hong Kong Shenzhen Research Institute, Hong Kong, China
Huihui Wang	Jacksonville University, USA
Qian Wang	Wuhan University, China
An Wang	Case Western Reserve University, USA
Edgar Weippl	SBA Research, Austria
Susanne Wetzel	Stevens Institute of Technology, USA
Dinghao Wu	Pennsylvania State University, USA
Mengjun Xie	The University of Tennessee at Chattanooga, USA
Fengyuan Xu	Nanjing University, China
Shouhuai Xu	The University of Texas at San Antonio, USA
Shucheng Yu	Stevens Institute of Technology, USA
Jiawei Yuan	Embry-Riddle Aeronautical University, USA
Xingliang Yuan	Monash University, Australia
Fareed Zaffar	LUMS University, Pakistan
Xiao Zhang	Palo Alto Networks, USA
Junjie Zhang	Wright State University, USA
Kuan Zhang	University of Nebraska-Lincoln, USA
Wensheng Zhang	Iowa State University, USA
Yuan Zhang	Nanjing University, China
Hong-Sheng Zhou	Virginia Commonwealth University, USA
Cliff Zou	University of Central Florida, USA

Contents – Part II

Blockchains and IoT

Security and Analytics

Machine Learning, Privately

Better Clouds

ATCS Workshop

Contents – Part I

Catching Malware

Machine Learning

Everything Traffic Security

Deep Analytics

TL;DR Hazard: A Comprehensive Study of Levelsquatting Scams

Kun Du[1], Hao Yang[1], Zhou Li[2], Haixin Duan[3(✉)], Shuang Hao[4], Baojun Liu[1],
Yuxiao Ye[1,4], Mingxuan Liu[1], Xiaodong Su[4], Guang Liu[4], Zhifeng Geng[4],
Zaifeng Zhang[5], and Jinjin Liang[5]

[1] Tsinghua University, Beijing, China
{dk15,yang-h16,lbj15,liumx18}@mails.tsinghua.edu.cn
[2] University of California, Irvine, USA
zhou.li@uci.edu
[3] Tsinghua University, Beijing National Research Center
for Information Science and Technology, Beijing, China
duanhx@tsinghua.edu.cn
[4] University of Texas at Dallas, Richardson, USA
shao@utdallas.edu, yeyuxiao@outlook.com,
suxiaodong.sxd@gmail.com, lg2001607@163.com, zhifeng.geng@qq.com
[5] Network security Research Lab at Qihoo 360, Beijing, China
zhangzaifeng@360.cn, liangjinjin@360.cn

Abstract. In this paper, we present a large-scale analysis about an emerging new type of domain-name fraud, which we call *levelsquatting*. Unlike existing frauds that impersonate well-known brand names (like google.com) by using similar second-level domain names, adversaries here embed brand name in the subdomain section, deceiving users especially mobile users who do not pay attention to the entire domain names.

First, we develop a detection system, LDS, based on passive DNS data and webpage content. Using LDS, we successfully detect 817,681 levelsquatting domains. Second, we perform detailed characterization on levelsquatting scams. Existing blacklists are less effective against levelsquatting domains, with only around 4% of domains reported by Virus-Total and PhishTank respectively. In particular, we find a number of levelsquatting domains impersonate well-known search engines. So far, Baidu security team has acknowledged our findings and removed these domains from its search result. Finally, we analyze how levelsquatting domain names are displayed in different browsers. We find 2 mobile browsers (Firefox and UC) and 1 desktop browser (Internet Explorer) that can confuse users when showing levelsquatting domain names in the address bar.

In summary, our study sheds light to the emerging levelsquatting fraud and we believe new approaches are needed to mitigate this type of fraud.

Keywords: LDS · DNS · Levelsquatting

© ICST Institute for Computer Sciences, Social Informatics and Telecommunications Engineering 2019
Published by Springer Nature Switzerland AG 2019. All Rights Reserved
S. Chen et al. (Eds.): SecureComm 2019, LNICST 305, pp. 3–25, 2019.
https://doi.org/10.1007/978-3-030-37231-6_1

1   Introduction

Fast-paced reading is favored in the Internet age. Lengthy articles are less likely to be read and often receive comments like *TL;DR* (short for *Too long; didn't read*) [1]. While impatience to long text may leave valuable information overlooked, negligence to a long domain name can lead to much worse consequences.

As a real-world example, Fig. 1 shows a phishing website with a long domain name, mails.tsinghua.edu.cn.locale.rebornplasticsurgery.com, displayed in IE browser's address bar with default settings. The domain name is so lengthy that only the subdomain mails.tsinghua.edu.cn can be displayed, which is identical to the authentic login domain name of Tsinghua university. A user can be deceived to put her login credential when visiting this website.

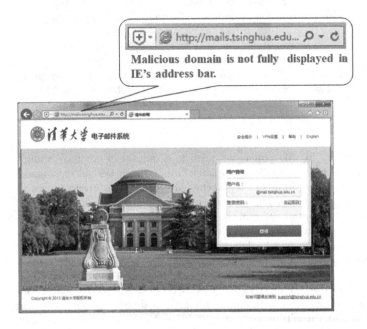

Fig. 1. An example of Levelsquatting domain displayed in IE.

We term this type of fraud as *levelsquatting*. Adversaries here create domains by using its *subdomain* section to impersonate a *brand domain*. Levelsquatting scams bring cybercriminals several benefits: (1) This type of attack is more deceptive (compared to traditional domain squatting), since the displayed part of the domain name can have quite legitimate looking in both desktop and mobile browsers; (2) Adversaries can create subdomains to impersonate arbitrary brand domains. If they use e2LDs(effective second level domain names) for the same purpose, they have to find ones not registered yet. and (3) Adversaries can leverage mechanisms of name servers that controlled by themselves, like wildcard DNS, to manage a large pool of levelsquatting concurrently. In this work, we perform the first large-scale analysis to understand this type of fraud.

Finding levelsquatting Domains. To discover levelsquatting domains, we have developed a system named called LDS (Levelsquatting Detection System), which monitors large volume of *passive DNS data* and identifies levelsquatting. LDS first searches for the levelsquatting candidates by matching a list of popular domain names. Then for each candidate, it collects WHOIS information, page content, visual appearance, and performs a three-stage detection procedure. After sampling and manually verification, we confirm LDS can work effectively. As described in Sect. 3, LDS achieves the precision of 96.9% on a sample of our dataset.

Discoveries. The amount of levelsquatting domains discovered by LDS is 817,681, which enable us to conduct a comprehensive study of levelsquatting scams. We highlight our findings below.

(1) We find a new type of attack that impersonates search engines. For example, the domain www.baidu.com.baidu-service.com has identical appearance as Baidu and it can even returns meaningful search results when being queried. The goal of adversaries here is to insert illegal ads, *e.g.*, gamble promotions, in the returned results. In total, we find 13,331 fake search-engine websites. We report them to Baidu security team, and all of them have been confirmed malicious.

(2) While a levelsquatting domain can be created by adding a subdomain record into the DNS zone file, we find *wildcard DNS record* is used more often for management ease: 517,839 (63.33%) levelsquatting FQDNs (fully qualified domain names referring to absolute domain names) or 41,389 (64.55%) e2LDs have wildcard DNS records.

(3) The effectiveness of blacklists regarding levelsquatting is very limited. We check the identified levelsquatting domains on PhishTank[1] and VirusTotal[2]. Only around 4% of the them have been captured by VirusTotal and Phish-Tank respectively.

(4) We conjecture that the rise of levelsquatting attack is attributed to the problematic design of modern browsers. In fact, we investigate and show that some mobile browsers (*e.g.*, Firefox and UC) and desktop browsers (*e.g.*, Internet Explorer 9 on Windows 7) fail to display levelsquatting FQDNs correctly, making users vulnerable to this fraud. As a result, we suggest these browser manufacturers to adjust their UI and highlight the e2LD section.

In summary, our work makes the following contributions.

(1) We perform the first large-scale study of levelsquatting fraud using a detection system LDS we developed.

---

[1] https://www.phishtank.com/.
[2] https://www.virustotal.com/.

(2) We make an in-depth measurement study of the identified levelsquatting domains.

(3) We check levelsquatting on PC and mobile browsers and find several visual issues that can confuse users. We suggest browser manufactures to fix those issues and highlight the e2LD section more clearly.

2   Background

In this section, we first give a brief overview of existing methods for subdomain creation. Then we define levelsquatting and describe the scope of this study. Finally, we survey existing attacks against brand names that have been extensively studied and compare them with levelsquatting.

Subdomain Creation. In this work, we consider a domain name as *FQDN*, its right part offered by registrar (*e.g.*, GoDaddy[3]) as *e2LD* and its left part as *subdomain*. To learn whether a domain is managed by a registrar, we check if it is one level under an effective top-level domain (eTLD) (*e.g.*, .com and .co.uk)[4], an approach commonly used by existing works [4].

There are three types of DNS records that can create subdomain, A, AAAA and CNAME records. The first two associate a subdomain with an IP v4/v6 address, *e.g.*, <b.example.com A 93.184.216.34>. CNAME specifies the alias of another canonical domain, *e.g.*, <www.example.com CNAME example.com>. Additionally, the owner can specify a *wildcard* record, by filling the subdomain part with a character *, which will capture DNS requests to any subdomain not specified in the zone file.

Levelsquatting. A registrar usually enforces no extra restriction on subdomain creation, if the whole domain name complies with the IETF standard [5]. Such loose policy unfortunately allows attackers to create a subdomain impersonating a well-known brand without any hurdle. We name such fraud domains as *levelsquatting* domains. More concretely, it contains a well-known brand (*e.g.*, google.com) in its *subdomain* section, while the e2LD section does not belong to the brand owner.

Whether a domain is created for levelsquatting depends on its similarity to a known brand in both its subdomain and e2LD sections. For the subdomain section, we assume attackers: (1) use the exact brand name without any typo (*e.g.*, go0gle.com.example.com is excluded); (2) keep the entire e2LD section of the targeted brand within the subdomain section (*e.g.*, google.example.com is excluded); (3) target a brand's FQDN as well in addition to its e2LD (*e.g.*, accounts.google.com.example.com is included). We choose these criteria to reduce the computation overhead (*e.g.*, finding all brand typos is computationally expensive) while achieve good coverage.

Comparison to Domain-Squatting. Previous studies have revealed many tricks adopted by adversaries to impersonate a brand. *Domain-squatting* is

---

[3] https://www.godaddy.com/.

[4] We use the public suffix list provided by https://publicsuffix.org/ to match eTLD.

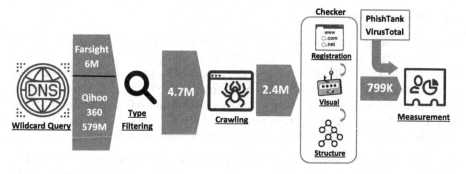

Fig. 2. Processing flow of LDS. The number in the figure refers to the number of records remained after each filtering step.

arguably the most popular approach. In this approach, adversaries *buy an e2LD* that looks similar to a brand domain and fool users who cannot distinguish the difference. This can be done through typo-squatting [6], bit-squatting [7], homophone-squatting [8], homograph-squatting [9] and *etc.* A recent work by Kintis *et al.* covers combo-squatting, in which case attackers combine brand name with one or more phrases (*e.g.*, youtube-live.com) and register the e2LD [10]. Despite the high similarity, these approaches will fail if the user is careful enough when reviewing the domain name.

However, a recent attack called *punycode scam* takes one step further to erase the visual difference. Punycode is a way to represent a Unicode letter using ASCII character set. But many Unicode letters look almost the same as ASCII letters (*e.g.*, Cyrillic "a" and Latin "a"). They can be abused to construct scam domains looking exactly the same as brand domains [11,12].

All approaches listed above require attackers to *buy* e2LDs *similar* to the targeted brand. The monetary cost is still non-negligible and the choices are usually limited. In comparison, creating levelsquatting domain needs virtually *zero* cost and the choices are *unlimited*. Moreover, when the domain is displayed in a defective browser, discerning the difference is much more difficult.

3 Finding levelsquatting Domains

While levelsquatting domains are spotted in wild occasionally [2], there is no systematic study measuring the scale and characterizing the purpose. A large volume of samples is essential to yield meaningful insights into this phenomenon, but so far the coverage from public sources is still limited (see Sect. 5.2 for more details). To overcome the issue of data scarcity, we build an system named LDS (Levelsquatting Detection System) to automatically discover scam levelsquatting domains. At high level, LDS selects candidate domains from passive DNS data and identifies scam ones based on the combination of registration-, structural- and visual-analysis. Below we first give an overview of LDS and then dive into the details of each component.

3.1 System Overview

The top challenge we need to address here is how to discover a large amount of levelsquatting domains efficiently. Although some registrars (*e.g.*, VeriSign) have published zone files they managed, subdomains are not included. Whether a subdomain exists can be learned through issuing DNS query, but enumerating all subdomains is impossible. Our solution, on the other hand, is to examine the domain resolutions logged by passive DNS collectors. We scan two passive DNS datasets offered by Farsight[5] and Qihoo 360[6] in this research.

Brand Selection. Although any brand may be subjected to levelsquatting attack, impersonating well-known brands accords with the best interest of attackers. In this study, we select e2LD from Alexa top 10 K list[7] (named Dom_{Alexa}) for detection. This dataset yields a decent coverage of web categories (46 categories labeled by Alexa[8] are included). Next, we construct a list of wildcard strings (*e.g.*, `*.google.com.*`) and submit them to passive DNS service. In the end, we obtain a corpus of 586,197,541 DNS logs. We filter logs matching A, AAAA and CNAME in record type and extract domain names. We collect 4,735,289 domains as candidates (named Dom_{All}).

Design and Data Collection. Through an initial exploration on a small subset within Dom_{All}, we gain three insights about levelsquatting domains. First, many of them have been leveraged to deliver phishing content with similar visual appearances to the targeted brand domains [13]. Second, attackers prefer to use off-the-shelf website template to reduce development cost [14,15], introducing irregular similarity among pages of levelsquatting domains. Third, registration information of levelsquatting e2LD and brand e2LD are usually irrelevant. Motivated by these insights, we build a crawler infrastructure to query WHOIS information from registrars, download homepage and capture screenshots for each domain in Dom_{All}.

We obtain 2,473,809 valid pages from Dom_{All} and we label this set as Dom_{Sus}. We notice that almost half of Dom_{All} become expired during our research. This is because adversaries here prefer to e2LD with short lifetime to reduce their cost, illustrated by previous work [15]. Every domain in Dom_{Sus} is examined by a detection component based on registration-, structural-, and visual-features and the alarmed domain is considered as levelsquatting (the set is named Dom_{LD}). Figure 2 illustrates the processing flow and the implementation details are elaborated in the following chapter.

3.2 Implementation of Checkers

We develop three checkers to exam each domain in Dom_{Sus}. All these three checkers are sequential. At the high level, a domain is labeled *suspicious* if registration

---

[5] https://www.dnsdb.info/.

[6] https://www.passivedns.cn/.

[7] http://s3.amazonaws.com/alexa-static/top-1m.csv.zip.

[8] https://www.alexa.com/topsites/category.

information mismatches correspondent brand domain in Dom_{Alexa}. Structural and visual representation check similarity between Dom_{Sus} or Dom_{Alexa}. We consider a domain as levelsquatting if two checkers alarm. The details of each checker is elaborated below.

Registration Checker. We query public WHOIS servers to obtain registration information for e2LDs in Dom_{Sus} and Dom_{Alexa}. Though a levelsquatting domain can pretend by manipulating the subdomain section, faking registration information is not always feasible. In fact, not all the WHOIS fields can be controlled by attackers, *e.g.*, register email and registration date. Although adversaries can utilize "Domain Privacy Protection" service to hide their tracks, they cannot rely on brand domain use the same service.

From WHOIS servers, we obtain 58,372 and 10,000 valid records for e2LDs in Dom_{Sus} and Dom_{Alexa}[9]. For every WHOIS record associated with Dom_{Sus}, we extract email address, telephone number, creation date, expiration date, and match them with Dom_{Alexa}. The domains having zero overlap will be further inspected by the structural- and visual- checker.

Structural Checker. As the second step, we inspect the homepage under each domain. On one hand, malicious pages tend to share the same structure due to the use of web templates. On the other hand, when a malicious page is designed for phishing, its structure should resemble to the brand domain. As a result, we compare each page structural similarity in Dom_{Sus} and Dom_{Alexa} by using "Page Compare library"[10].

Visual Checker. In this step, we aim to determine whether the levelsquatting domain runs a phishing page mimicking one in Dom_{Alexa}. We look into the visual similarity between them. As the first step, our crawler launches a browser instance and visit homepages in Dom_{Alexa} and Dom_{Sus} by using selenium library[11]. We take a screen shot for each domain. Then we check structural similarity between each image in Dom_{Sus} and Dom_{Alexa} by using skimage[12].

By using both structural and visual checkers, we can filter out non-malicious levelsquatting domains. Similar to our approach, DeltaPhish [19], also exploits the structural and visual similarity to detect phishing pages. Though DeltaPhish extracted more features, it relies on a pre-labeled training dataset and the computation is more time-consuming. Our approach is training-free and more efficient.

4   Evaluation

The Precision of LDS. LDS detects 817,681 levelsquatting FQDNs (Dom_{LD}) and we want to learn how accurate the result is. In the beginning, we use "query"

---

[9] We are not able to obtain WHOIS records for all e2LDs within Dom_{Sus} because they have become expired when we queried.

[10] https://github.com/TeamHG-Memex/page-compare.

[11] https://www.seleniumhq.org/.

[12] https://scikit-image.org/.

mode of VirusTotal API[13] to get URL report for every detected levelsquatting FQDN and use the number of alarms to determine whether it is scam. But it turns out that most of the domains are not even been submitted to VirusTotal (more details in Sect. 5.2). Therefore, we have to resort to manual verification. However, manually confirming all of them within a reasonable time is impossible. As an alternative, we sample FQDNs randomly and validate them for 10 rounds. We calculate precision rate for each round and consider the average value as the true precision rate.

In each round, we first sample 1,000 results and check whether the FQDN is used for phishing, *e.g.*, stealing login credentials. For the remaining ones, our validation rules focus on the strategies adopted by attackers. In particular, we first compare two pages crawled by common browser user-agent and spider user-agent strings, determining if cloaking performed, which is widely used for Blackhat SEO. Then we follow the method proposed by Wang *et al.* [17] to find cloaking pages: if there is no similarity in visual effect or page structures between two pages, the domain is labeled as cloaking. Next, we go through the page content and check if it is used to promote illegal business like porn, gamble or fake shops. We also examine e2LD's WHOIS information and consider it a true positive when the domain is recently registered by a non-authoritative party. After 10 rounds calculation, we get the system precision rate is 96.9%.

Analysis of False Positives. We conservatively treat the false positives rate 3.1%. But a close look suggests none of them is absolutely innocent. Among these 310 domains, 178 of them show regional news, but none of their sources are well known and the same content/page structure are found, which indicate they might serve spun content for spam purposes [18]. The other 132 domains all display a message showing that the domain is expired. However, when we revisited them one month later, 118 of them showed more than 2 ads about lottery and porn. We speculate these domains might be purchased later by attackers or just use expired pages occasionally to avoid detection.

5   Measurement

In this section, we present our analysis about levelsquatting domains. We first describe the dataset we use. Then, we evaluate how effective the current defense stands against levelsquatting and how popular levelsquatting is used for scam activities. Next we examine the statistics of the lexical features, including the popularity of different prefixes in subdomains. Finally, we take a deep look into the infrastructure behind levelsquatting domains.

5.1   Datasets

To enrich the diversity of the levelsquatting domains, in addition to the 799,893 domains captured by LDS, we also acquire data from PhishTank and VirusTotal. The summary is listed in Table 1.

---

[13] The "query" mode retrieves the prior scanning result of a URL that *has been submitted* to VirusTotal by another user.

PhishTank (DS_{PT}). Levelsquatting is supposed to be used a lot for phishing attacks. As a result, we download all URLs submitted to PhishTank between May 2016 to July 2017, with 1,025,336 records in total, and search for levelsquatting FQDNs. We use the same check algorithm described in Sect. 3 and get 14,387 levelsquatting FQDNs in the end.

VirusTotal (DS_{VT}). Another data source is VirusTotal, a well-known public service offering URL and file scanning. We download the feed from February to April, 2017, accounting for 160,399,466 URLs in total. After filtering, we obtain 3,528 levelsquatting FQDNs (all of them are alarmed by *at least two* blacklists).

Combining the three datasets, we obtain 817,681 unique levelsquatting FQDNs (we name the entire set DS_{All}), mapped to 64,124 e2LDs. The overlap of the three datasets is small: only 127 FQDNs or 40 e2LDs from DS_{LDS} are also contained in DS_{PT} and DS_{VT}.

Table 1. Summary of datasets.

Notation	Source	Period	# FQDNs	# e2LDs
DS_{LDS}	LDS	03.2017-04.2017	799,893	58,988
DS_{PT}	PhishTank	05.2016-07.2017	14,387	3,887
DS_{VT}	VirusTotal	02.2017-04.2017	3,528	1,289
$DS_{Overlapped}$	–	–	127	40
Sum (DS_{All})	–	–	817,681	64,124

5.2 Impact of Levelsquatting

Blacklist is a common first-line defense against malicious URLs, but according to our study, its coverage on levelsquatting domains is quite limited. Our conclusion comes from a coverage test on VirusTotal: we queried all 817,681 FQDNs from DS_{LDS} using VirusTotal API under "query" mode, and found only 39,249 are alarmed, accounting for 4.80% of DS_{LDS}. It turns out that most of the domains (618,374, 75.63%) are not even submitted to VirusTotal.

Although levelsquatting has been observed in the wild as an attack vector for phishing, whether it has become a popular option for the phishing purpose is unclear yet. The answers seems negative: 332,007 distinct FQDNs (covering 1,025,336 URLs) are obtained from PhishTank but DS_{PT} only has 14,387 (4.33% of 332,007) FQDNs. As another supporting evidence, most of the domains recorded by PhishTank are short, each of which in average consists of only 2.83 levels.

Prefix. Attackers are free to add prefixes in front of a brand, in order to impersonate a specific brand domain. To learn their preference, we have extracted all prefixes and counted the number of appearance among DS_{All}. Top 15 prefixes with their occupied percentage are shown in Fig. 3. Among them, www. is chosen

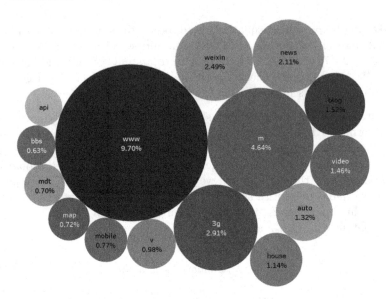

Fig. 3. Top 15 prefix keywords.

most frequently (79,338 or 9.70% of DS_{All}). The top 15 prefixes show up 31.09% of all levelsquatting domains. Prefix known to be associated with mobile services, like `m.`, `3g.` and `weixin.` (representing WeChat, the top mobile chat app in China), are ranked highly, suggesting that attackers actively exploit the display vulnerabilities in mobile devices (discussed in Sect. 7).

5.3   Infrastructure

Levelsquatting domains serve as the gateway to attackers' infrastructure. For better understanding, we first look into the IP addresses and registrants behind, then we analyze domains with wildcard DNS record, distribution in new gTLD and HTTPS certificates they deployed.

IP Addresses. We performed DNS queries on all levelsquatting FQDNs in DS_{All} to obtain their IP addresses by using pydig[14]. In total, 710,347 (86.87%) requests returned valid results and 54,118 IPs were obtained. We show the top 10 IP addresses that levelsquatting domains prefer in Table 2. From this table we can see that the top 10 servers host more than 38% of total levelsquatting domains.

Registrants. We are interested in who actually control the levelsquatting domains. Hence we select WHOIS records of domains in DS_{All} and obtain 58,372 valid records in total. By grouping the domains with registrant email addresses, we find that 23.41% of them are under 10 email addresses. We list these registrants in Table 3. We search email addresses for relevant information, find that

---

[14] https://github.com/shuque/pydig.

Table 2. Top 10 IP addresses of malicious levelsquatting domains.

No.	IP	ASN	Location	Count of levelsquatting FQDNs	Percentage
1	69.172.201.153	AS19324	US	76,387	9.34%
2	185.53.179.8	AS61969	Europe	48,932	5.98%
3	199.59.242.150	AS395082	US	35,327	4.32%
4	202.181.24.196	AS55933	Australia	34,395	4.21%
5	205.178.189.131	AS19871	US	31,238	3.82%
6	52.33.196.199	AS16509	US	23,994	2.93%
7	72.52.4.122	AS32787	US	21532	2.63%
8	93.46.8.89	AS12874	Italy	17,328	2.12%
9	72.52.4.119	AS32787	US	13,551	1.66%
10	118.193.172.49	AS58879	HK	10,689	1.31%
Total	–	–	–	313,373	38.32%

Table 3. Top 10 registrant emails.

No.	Email	Count of Levelsquatting e2LDs	Percentage
1	yu****@yinsibaohu.aliyun.com	3,328	5.19%
2	yuming****@163.com	2,985	4.66%
3	4645468b********@privacy.everdns.com	1,633	2.55%
4	zz****@sina.com	1,397	2.18%
5	28***@qq.com	1,255	1.96%
6	c138e837********@privacy.everdns.com	1,231	1.92%
7	xiaosh********@163.com	989	1.54%
8	ljj********@gmail.com	751	1.17%
9	whoisa****@west263.com	730	1.14%
10	zr**@qq.com	712	1.11%
Total	–	15,011	23.41%

many of them belong to professional domain brokers who own massive amount of domains. Similar observations were also described in previous works looking into the underground economy [3] and blackhat SEO [15].

Registration Dates. Next, we examine the registration dates of the levelsquatting e2LDs. Figure 4 illustrates the ECDF of registration dates, which shows that more than 59.27% of domains were registered after 2016. Previous studies suggest recent registration date is an indicator of domains owned by attackers [21,22], and our result suggests that hijacking reputable e2LD and adding subdomains under its zone file are not popular, since reputable e2LDs tend to

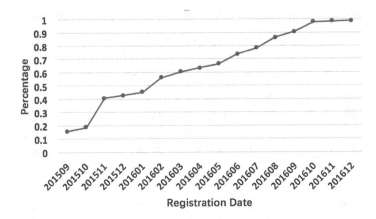

Fig. 4. ECDF of registration dates.

Table 4. Top 10 new gTLDs in levelsquatting e2LDs.

No.	New gTLD	Count	Percentage of new gTLD domains	Percentage of all e2LDs
1	.top	3,868	20.92%	6.03%
2	.win	3,034	16.41%	4.73%
3	.pw	2,672	14.45%	4.17%
4	.info	2,254	12.19%	3.52%
5	.bid	1,862	10.07%	2.90%
6	.loan	1,213	6.56%	1.89%
7	.party	1,021	5.52%	1.59%
8	.racing	893	4.83%	1.39%
9	.faith	586	3.17%	0.91%
10	.date	313	1.69%	0.49%
Total	–	17,716	95.83%	27.63%

have a long registration lifetime (*e.g.*, `google.com` has been registered for more than 20 years). Instead, creating e2LD or compromising newly registered e2LD is more popular.

Wildcard DNS. While LDS has detected 817,681 unique levelsquatting FQDNs, they are mapped to only 64,124 e2LDs. We suspect there may be many wildcard DNS records among them. To verify this assessment, we probe all 64,124 e2LDs using the same method proposed by Du *et al.* [15]. In essence, for an e2LD like `example.com`, we first try to resolve the IP address of `*.example.com`. The e2LD is considered to support wildcard DNS if there is a valid response. Otherwise, we issue two queries with random subdomain names, like `aaa.example.com` and `bbb.example.com`. If the two responses are matched, the e2LD is considered to support wildcard DNS as well. In the end, we discovered 41,389 e2LDs (64.55% of 64,124) contain wildcard DNS records, suggesting this configuration is widely used by adversaries.

Abuse of New gTLD Domains. Previous studies [15] discovered that there is an increasing tendency of registering malicious domains under new gTLDs, like .top. We want to learn whether new gTLD is also favored by levelsquatting attackers. As such, we use the new gTLD list published by ICANN [23] to filter the e2LDs in DS_{All}. It turns out a prominent ratio of e2LDs (17,716, 27.63% of 64,124) are under new gTLDs, which aligns with the discovery of previous works. We think the the major reason is that most new gTLDs are cheap and lack of maintenance. We show the top 10 new gTLDs abused in Table 4.

SSL Certificates. Deploying SSL certificates and supporting HTTPs connection is a growing trend for site administrators. To make malicious sites, especially phishing sites more convincing to visitors, SSL certificates are also used by attackers [24]. For levelsquatting domains, the motivation is the same but our measurement result shows that they have not seriously considered this option. We ran port scan with ZMap[15] over all DS_{All} and find that only 587 of them provide certificates. By comparison, a study [25] showed that already 70% of Alexa Top One Million sites provide SSL certificates. We download all these 587 certifications and extracted the issuers. Only **six** issuers are found. **All** of them can provide free SSL certification with 30-day period or even longer. We believe this is the main reason that these issuers are selected (Table 5).

Table 5. SSL Certification issuers and domain count.

No.	Certification Issuer	Charge	Count	Percentage
1	RapidSSL SHA256 CA - G3	30 days free	276	47.02%
2	Let's Encrypt Authority X3	Free	207	35.26%
3	WoSign CA Free SSL Certificate G2	Free	40	6.81%
4	GlobalSign Organization Validation CA - G2	30 days free	26	4.43%
5	Cybertrust Japan Public CA G3	30 days free	23	3.92%
6	Amazon	12 month free	15	2.56%
Total	–	–	**587**	**100%**

6   Characterization

In this section, we take a closer look into the business behind levelsquatting domains and their targeted brands, to get a better understanding of how they serve attackers' operations.

---

[15] https://github.com/zmap/zmap.

6.1 Types of Malicious Activities

LDS is able to classify levelsquatting domains into two categories: phishing and non-phishing. In order to learn more finer-grained categorical information, *e.g.*, the business operated behind the domain, we extract more features from the associated pages and run another classification procedure. Specifically, we randomly sampled 10,000 pages from DS_{All} first and manually labeled them into 5 categories, including porn, lottery, phishing, blackhat SEO, malware-delivery to prepare the training dataset. Then, the texts from title and href tags of each page are extracted and we use a deep-learning algorithm, CNN (Convolutional Neural Network) to build the classification model [26]. We choose CNN because it has been applied to similar tasks like sentence and text classification, and achieved many successes [27,28]. After the training step, we use CNN model to classify all DS_{All} pages. The result on levelsquatting FQDNs are shown in Fig. 5. It turns out most of the levelsquatting domains were used for porn (42.59%) and lottery (34.42%).

Since the purposes of phishing sites are not always identical, we run the same CNN-based approach to obtain sub-categories under the phishing category. The statistics of the associated FQDNs are shown in Fig. 6. It turns out the majority (94.89%) of FQDNs attempts to impersonate well-known sites of web portals, finance, advertisements and search-engine. Below we elaborate each category.

Fake Web Portals. The sites here are developed to help attackers gain high search rankings illicitly (*i.e.*, blackhat SEO). Attackers crawl content from reputable web portals and update everyday. Because the ranking algorithm favors sites with high dynamics and meaningful content, attackers' sites will gain relatively high score. In the mean time, blackhat SEO keywords and malicious URLs are embedded into the copied content. As a result, querying blackhat SEO keywords in search engines will lead to malicious URLs with higher possibilities [15].

Fake Financial Sites. This is a classic type of phishing sites. Their goal is to steal users' credentials by impersonating the login pages of other sites, especially bank websites. These sites make themselves look almost the same as bank sites, stock buying and selling sites, to allure users to submit their bank card number and password.

Fake Advertisements. These sites promote products by exaggerating their effects. For instance, fake weight-losing products are frequently seen. Their common strategy is to crawl the content from reputable shopping sites like www.amazon.com and replace some of the contents with fake advertisements.

Fake Search Engine. This is a *new* type of blackhat SEO that never reported before and we will show more details in Sect. 6.3. They pretend to be a valid search-engine site. A search query will be forwarded to the authentic site and the returned results would be mixed with illegal ads. As it is fully functional, users would prone to trust the returned results and click the illegal ads.

No.	Type	Count	Percentage
1	Porn	348,233	42.59%
2	Lottery	281,425	34.42%
3	Phishing	137,388	16.80%
4	Blackhat SEO	40,316	4.93%
5	Malware delivery	2,893	0.35%
6	Others	7,426	0.91%
Total	-	817,681	100%

No.	Type	Count	Percentage
1	Fake web portal	45,783	33.32%
2	Fake finance	41,322	30.08%
3	Fake advertisement	29,925	21.78%
4	Fake search engine	13,331	9.70%
5	Fake domain Parking	1,937	1.41%
Total	-	132,298	96.30%

Fig. 5. Levelsquatting FQDN categories.   **Fig. 6.** Phishing FQDN sub-categories.

6.2 Visiting Strategies

A user could make a mistake when typing a domain name and visit a typo-squatting site accidentally, but it's not possible to type a levelsquatting domain name by mistake. So we wonder how these levelsquatting domains visited by users and who are their referrers.

Although it is straightforward to trace forward from a levelsquatting domain to its destination by following redirection and hyperlink, tracing *backward* is very challenging. A levelsquatting domain can also be embedded in webpage and many other media like email. Unfortunately, without data shared by service providers like email servers, finding the origin is impossible. We focus on websites that link to levelsquatting domains as we can leverage search engine, whose indexed pages are open to public, to find website origin. To this end, we queried all FQDNs in DS_{All} using Baidu and downloaded the first 3 result pages for each. We choose Baidu because Baidu allows us to run automated query without being blocked. In the end, we find only 80,159 queries returning at least one result, suggesting most of them are referred by other channels rather than websites.

The next step is to find pages in the search result that point to levelsquatting FQDNs. Instead of directly crawling, we choose to analyze its *short description* and look for FQDN in DS_{All}. To notice, short description of search result has been used for detecting promotional-infection in [20]. In the end, we found 298,370 search results satisfying this criteria. Interestingly, more than 27% of the results point to forums zhidao.baidu.com and zhihu.com (Chinese versions of Quora). We report these content to Baidu Security Team and all are removed now.

Here we give a real-world example showing how a visitor reaches a levelsquatting domain from the website referral, and illustrate it in Fig. 7. The attacker first posts a thread on zhidao.baidu.com which advertises a link pointing to pan.baidu.com. vrd579.com, a levelsquatting domain impersonating pan.baidu.com, Baidu's cloud-drive service. The thread tops the search result when a user queries "nude picture of Arena of Valor characters" (translated from Chinese). When user follows the search result and the link in the post by mobile, she will land on the levelsquatting site while only "pan.baidu.com" will be shown in her browser address bar, which will induce her to input her password or download malicious apps.

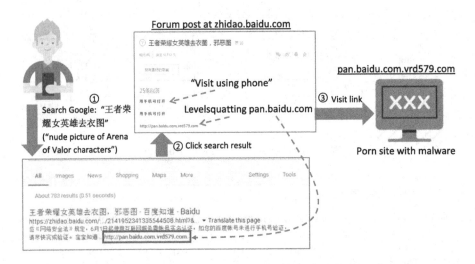

Fig. 7. An example showing how a visitor reaches a levelsquatting domain.

One may wonder if such search poisoning attack is only effective against Baidu. To examine this argument, we evaluated Google by sampling 10,000 domains in DS_{All} and querying them through our proxy pool. It turns out more than 85% levelsquatting domains were also indexed by Google.

6.3 An Example of Fake Search Engine

As pointed out in Sect. 6.1, during the course of our study, we have discovered a *new* type of phishing attack impersonating search engines. The fake search-engine site copies content from authentic site, but when a user searches a term, illegal ads are inserted ahead of the original search results. Figure 8 shows the returned page of www.baidu.com.baidu-service.com (impersonating Baidu search) when querying "abc." The first item is an advertisement pointing to a lottery site 8f.com, which is not allowed in Baidu's search result because it's not permitted by the Chinese government. We count the number of levelsquatting domains under this category and find the top three are also the three leading search engines in China: Baidu, 360 search and Sogou. The fake sites count is 4,583, 3,950 and 2,318 seperately.

7 Browser UI Vulnerabilities

When the length of a domain name exceeds the visible area of browser's address bar, a part of the domain name will not be displayed. A user could mis-recognize the domain in this case. Browser vendors should carefully design the address bar to either leave enough space for domain name or notify users when part of the

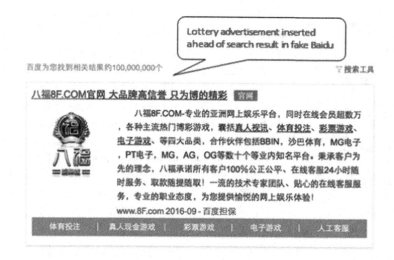

Fig. 8. Fake Baidu search result.

domain, especially the e2LD section, is hidden. Unfortunately, not all browsers follow these design principles.

We first examine how a lengthy domain is displayed on mobile browsers. Five representative mobile browsers are tested through visiting mails.tsinghua.edu.cn.locale.rebornplasticsurgery.com in an Android phone. Figure 9 shows the corresponding address bars. UC browser[16] is the most vulnerable as the domain name is entirely hidden in address bar. Similarly, Firefox only shows a few extra letters. Chrome and Safari perform better as more letters are displayed. We recommend Firefox and UC Browser to redesign the address bar for allowing better visibility. A work published recently [29] also pointed out that many mobile browsers fail to display levelsquatting domain name in a secured manner, which resonates with our findings. The desktop browsers are expected to be immune from this vulnerability, given that their UI has much larger visible area. We test 8 popular desktop browser and find only IE 9 partially displays as shown in Fig. 10.

8 Discussion

Limitations. The criteria we enforce on the brand selection rule out potential levelsquatting domains that include typos (*e.g.*, go0gle.com.example.com) or overlap with only part of brand e2LDs (*e.g.*, google.example.com). The major reason is that finding true positives under these cases requires a lot more web crawling and queries against passive DNS. Besides, we argue that these domains are less likely to be created by attackers who have absolute freedom to fill the subdomain section with anything they like.

---

[16] http://www.ucweb.com/.

Mobile (Resolution: 720x1280)	
Browser Version	**Address Bar**
Firefox 64.0.2	← → ⊕ mails.tsinghua ⬛ C ② ⋮
Chrome 71.0.3578.99	tsinghua.edu.cn.locale.rebornplasticsurgery.com ① ⋮
Opera 49.2.2361	mails.tsinghua.edu.cn.locale.rebornplasticsurgery.com
Safari with WebKit 605.1.15	mails.tsinghua.edu.cn.locale.rebornplasticsurː ↻
UCBrowser 12.2.6.1133	⊙ 清华邮箱 G ˅ Search ○

Fig. 9. Address bar of mobile browsers.

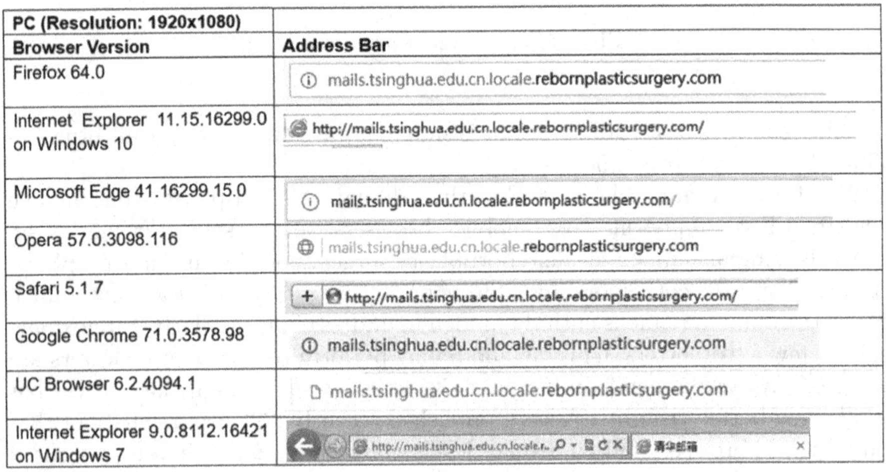

PC (Resolution: 1920x1080)	
Browser Version	**Address Bar**
Firefox 64.0	ⓘ mails.tsinghua.edu.cn.locale.**rebornplasticsurgery.com**
Internet Explorer 11.15.16299.0 on Windows 10	⊜ http://mails.tsinghua.edu.cn.locale.rebornplasticsurgery.com/
Microsoft Edge 41.16299.15.0	ⓘ mails.tsinghua.edu.cn.locale.rebornplasticsurgery.com/
Opera 57.0.3098.116	⊕ mails.tsinghua.edu.cn.locale.**rebornplasticsurgery.com**
Safari 5.1.7	+ ◉ http://mails.tsinghua.edu.cn.locale.rebornplasticsurgery.com/
Google Chrome 71.0.3578.98	ⓘ mails.tsinghua.edu.cn.locale.rebornplasticsurgery.com
UC Browser 6.2.4094.1	◻ mails.tsinghua.edu.cn.locale.rebornplasticsurgery.com
Internet Explorer 9.0.8112.16421 on Windows 7	← ◉ http://mails.tsinghua.edu.cn.locale.r.. ♀ ˅ ⊠ C × ◉ 清华邮箱 ×

Fig. 10. Address bar of desktop browsers.

Knowing the design of LDS, attackers could adjust their strategies to avoid detection. For instance, they could target less popular brand domains (*i.e.*, beyond Alexa top 10K) or change the page content to reduce the structure and visual similarity. These issues could be addressed when running other detection systems at the same time.

The majority of domain names inspected by LDS come from the passive DNS managed Qihoo 360. For this data, as far as we know, most of the logs are retrieved by DNS resolvers located in China. Thus, our measurement results could have certain bias towards one region, mainly about business categories and targeted brands (*e.g.*, Baidu has the most impersonators as shown in our result).

Suggestions to Browser Manufactures. We recommend browser companies to leave more space in the address bar. For example, a scroll bar could be activated when the domain overflows the display region to allow user to see the full name. Another way is to highlight the e2LD part in the address bar.

Suggestions to Users. A domain name should be reviewed more carefully when it is lengthy or covers the entire region of the address bar. The entire domain name should be inspected, not only the beginning section. If the e2LD section is suspicious or never seen before, the domain should be avoided.

Suggestions to Registrars. We suggest registrars to adjust their policy to limit the length and depth of a subdomain, given that normal domains rarely have so many characters or levels. Alternatively, registrars can enforce a rule to forbid a domain owner to create a subdomain with multiple levels at one shot.

Responsible Disclosure. We have reported 4,583 fake search-engine sites impersonating Baidu search and 38,275 pages embedding `baidu.com` in the subdomain section to Baidu security team. All of them have been confirmed malicious. In addition, the posts under `zhidao.baidu.com` backlinked by the malicious pages are all removed.

Regarding the browser UI vulnerabilities, we have contacted several browser vendors including Baidu browser[17] and 360 security browser[18] which have the similar issue as UC browser. Their security teams have acknowledged our findings and have fixed in the current browsers.

9   Related Work

Domain-squatting. Various domain-squatting attacks have been discovered and studied before, including typo-squatting [6], bit-squatting [7], homophone-squatting [8], homograph-squatting [9], combosquatting [10] and etc. Attackers under these scenarios all need to *buy* an e2LD and create domains *similar* to the brand domain. They can be thwarted when the owner actively registers adjacent domains or by detection mechanisms based on domain-name similarity [6, 30–32]. However, such methods fail to defend from levelsquatting attack since the subdomain can be arbitrarily created by attackers under any e2LD not controlled by brand owners.

Domain Abuse. Understanding how attackers register and use domains is essential for detecting malicious domains. Previous works have extensively studied attackers' strategies and patterns in domain registration [34–36]. Their studies show attackers' preferences of registrars with loose regulations. In [29], authors focused UI vulnerabilities in mobile browsers and gave a systematic measurement on security vulnerabilities in them.

Our work leverages passive DNS data, registration data and visual similarity to discover levelsquatting domains. Passive DNS data has been extensively leveraged for detecting botnet and spam domains [37–40]. Recently, the data from domain registrars has shown potential in detecting domain abuse at the

---

[17] https://liulanqi.baidu.com/.
[18] http://se.360.cn/.

early stage [21,41]. We leverage similarity-based approach to detect phishing levelsquatting domains, which aligns with previous works in this area [13,42,43].

We compared our work with [44], which studied how adversaries use subdomains created under the *compromised* e2LDs for malign purposes. In our work, we focus on the attack that utilizes subdomains created to impersonate reputable domains. Attackers only need to buy a cheap domain name and create reputable prefix purposefully, and they do not need to compromise legitimate domains.

Underground Economy. Our study shows that levelsquatting is extensively used by the underground economy to deceive web users. This "dark" community has been investigated by many researchers in order to gain better understanding about its operational model and build effective defense. On this topic, Levchenko et al. [16] revealed the infrastructure and strategies used for email spam. Nektarios et al. [45] studied how illicit drug trade was facilitated through search-redirection attack. Many of the underground transactions happen at anonymous marketplace. Its scale and operational model were studied by Nicolas *et al.* [46], and Barratt *et al.* [47].

10 Conclusion

In this work, we present a study about the phenomenon of levelsquatting, which exploits visual vulnerabilities of browsers to defraud web users. In order to obtain sufficient amount of data, we have developed a system named LDS, which examines a large volume of passive DNS data and applies three different checkers to detect levelsquatting domains. In the end we have identified 817,681 malicious FQDNs with an accuracy of 96.9%.

Based on the data produced by LDS and obtained from VirusTotal and PhishTank, we carried out a comprehensive study to understand the impact of this threat and the strategies used by attackers. Our study has already revealed several unique insights, like prefixes favored by attackers. We also discovered a new type of phishing attack against search-engine. Furthermore, we analyze how levelsquatting domain name is displayed in mobile and desktop browsers and find 3 browsers (2 mobile and 1 desktop) display domain names in a misleading way. We have reported our findings to Baidu security team and 360 security, receiving very positive feedback.

Our study shows that attackers are constantly exploiting the weakness of domain ecosystem and inventing new attack vectors. In the future, we will continue the research regarding domain abuse with a focus on its impact and the new trend.

Acknowledgments. We thank anonymous reviewers for their insightful comments. This work is supported in part by the National Natural Science Foundation of China (U1836213, U1636204) and the BNRist Network and Software Security Research Program (Grant No. BNR2019TD01004).

References

1. What Is TLDR? (2017). https://www.lifewire.com/what-is-tldr-2483633
2. How scammers use sub-domains (2016). http://easykey.uk/computer-safety/how-scammers-use-sub-domains
3. Yang, H., et al.: How to learn klingon without a dictionary: detection and measurement of black keywords used by the underground economy. In: 2017 IEEE Symposium on Security and Privacy (SP). IEEE (2017)
4. Marchal, S., François, J., State, R., Engel, T.: Proactive discovery of phishing related domain names. In: Balzarotti, D., Stolfo, S.J., Cova, M. (eds.) RAID 2012. LNCS, vol. 7462, pp. 190–209. Springer, Heidelberg (2012). https://doi.org/10.1007/978-3-642-33338-5_10
5. DOMAIN NAMES - IMPLEMENTATION AND SPECIFICATION (1987). https://tools.ietf.org/html/rfc1035
6. Wang, Y.-M., et al.: Strider typo-patrol: discovery and analysis of systematic typosquatting. In: SRUTI, vol. 6, No. 31-36 p. 2 (2006)
7. Nikiforakis, N., et al.: Bitsquatting: exploiting bit-flips for fun, or profit?. In: Proceedings of The 22nd International Conference on World Wide Web. ACM (2013)
8. Wiener, S.: Grass-mud horses to victory: the phonological constraints of subversive puns. In: Proceedings of the 23rd North American Conference on Chinese Linguistics, vol. 1 (2011)
9. Holgers, T., Watson, D.E., Gribble, S.D.: Cutting through the confusion: a measurement study of homograph attacks. In: USENIX Annual Technical Conference, General Track (2006)
10. Kintis, P., et al.: Hiding in plain sight: a longitudinal study of combosquatting abuse. In: Proceedings of the 2017 ACM SIGSAC Conference on Computer and Communications Security. ACM (2017)
11. Phishing with 'punycode' - when foreign letters spell English words (2017). https://nakedsecurity.sophos.com/2017/04/19/phishing-with-punycode-when-foreign-letters-spell-english-words/
12. Liu, B., et al.: A reexamination of internationalized domain names: the good, the bad and the ugly. In: 48th Annual IEEE/IFIP International Conference on Dependable Systems and Networks (2018)
13. Maurer, M.-E., Herzner, D.: Using visual website similarity for phishing detection and reporting. In: CHI 2012 Extended Abstracts on Human Factors in Computing Systems. ACM (2012)
14. Levchenko, K., Pitsillidis, A., Chachra, N., et al.: Click trajectories: end-to-end analysis of the spam value chain. In: 2011 IEEE Symposium on Security and Privacy, pp. 431–446. IEEE (2011)
15. Du, K., et al.: The ever-changing labyrinth: a large-scale analysis of wildcard DNS powered Blackhat SEO. In: 25th USENIX Security Symposium (USENIX Security 16) (2016)
16. Levchenko, K., et al.: Click trajectories: end-to-end analysis of the spam value chain. In: 2011 IEEE Symposium on Security and Privacy. IEEE (2011)
17. Wang, D.Y., Savage, S., Voelker, G.M.: Cloak and dagger: dynamics of web search cloaking. In: Proceedings of the 18th ACM Conference on Computer and Communications Security. ACM (2011)
18. Zhang, Q., Wang, D.Y., Voelker, G.M.: DSpin: detecting automatically spun content on the web. In: NDSS (2014)

19. Foley, S.N., Gollmann, D., Snekkenes, E. (eds.): DeltaPhish: detecting phishing webpages in compromised websites. ESORICS 2017. LNCS, vol. 10492, pp. 370–388. Springer, Cham (2017). https://doi.org/10.1007/978-3-319-66402-6_22
20. Liao, X., et al.: Seeking nonsense, looking for trouble: efficient promotional-infection detection through semantic inconsistency search. In: 2016 IEEE Symposium on Security and Privacy (SP). IEEE (2016)
21. Hao, S., et al.: PREDATOR: proactive recognition and elimination of domain abuse at time-of-registration. In: Proceedings of the 2016 ACM SIGSAC Conference on Computer and Communications Security. ACM (2016)
22. Li, Z., et al.: Knowing your enemy: understanding and detecting malicious web advertising. In: Proceedings of the 2012 ACM Conference on Computer and Communications Security. ACM (2012)
23. new gTLD Statistics by Top-Level Domains (2016). https://ntldstats.com/tld
24. Nagunwa, T.: Behind identity theft and fraud in cyberspace: the current landscape of phishing vectors. Int. J. Cyber-Secur. Digital Forensics (IJCSDF) 3(1), 72–83 (2014)
25. TLS Certificates from the Top Million Sites (2016). https://adamcaudill.com/2016/09/23/tls-certificates-top-million-sites/
26. Kim, Y.: Convolutional neural networks for sentence classification. arXiv preprint arXiv:1408.5882 (2014)
27. Kalchbrenner, N., Grefenstette, E., Blunsom, P.: A convolutional neural network for modelling sentences. arXiv preprint arXiv:1404.2188 (2014)
28. Liu, P., Qiu, X., Huang, X.: Recurrent neural network for text classification with multi-task learning. arXiv preprint arXiv:1605.05101 (2016)
29. Luo, M., et al.: Hindsight: understanding the evolution of UI vulnerabilities in mobile browsers. In: Proceedings of the 2017 ACM SIGSAC Conference on Computer and Communications Security. ACM (2017)
30. Chen, G., et al.: Combating typo-squatting for safer browsing. In: 2009 International Conference on Advanced Information Networking and Applications Workshops. IEEE (2009)
31. Banerjee, A., Rahman, M.S., Faloutsos, M.: SUT: quantifying and mitigating url typosquatting. Comput. Netw. 55(13), 3001–3014 (2011)
32. Linari, A. et al.: Typo-Squatting: The Curse"of Popularity (2009)
33. Agten, P., et al.: Seven months' worth of mistakes: a longitudinal study of typosquatting abuse. In: NDSS (2015)
34. Shuang, H., Feamster, N., Pandrangi, R.: Monitoring the initial DNS behavior of malicious domains. In: Proceedings of the 2011 ACM SIGCOMM Conference on Internet Measurement Conference. ACM (2011)
35. Coull, S.E., et al.: Understanding domain registration abuses. Comput. secur. 31(7), 806–815 (2012)
36. Anderson, D.S., et al.: Spamscatter: characterizing internet scam hosting infrastructure. Diss. University of California, San Diego (2007)
37. Antonakakis, M., et al.: Building a dynamic reputation system for DNS. In: USENIX security symposium (2010)
38. Antonakakis, M., et al.: From throw-away traffic to bots: detecting the rise of DGA-based malware. In: Presented as part of the 21st USENIX Security Symposium (USENIX Security 12) (2012)
39. Bilge, L., et al.: EXPOSURE: finding malicious domains using passive DNS analysis. In: NDSS (2011)
40. Antonakakis, M., et al.: Detecting Malware Domains at the Upper DNS Hierarchy. In: USENIX Security Symposium, vol. 11 (2011)

41. Lever, C., et al.: Domain-Z: 28 registrations later measuring the exploitation of residual trust in domains. In: 2016 IEEE Symposium on Security and Privacy (SP). IEEE (2016)
42. Garera, S., et al.: A framework for detection and measurement of phishing attacks. In: Proceedings of the 2007 ACM Workshop on Recurring Malcode. ACM (2007)
43. Medvet, E., Kirda, E., Kruegel, C.: Visual-similarity-based phishing detection. In: Proceedings of the 4th International Conference on Security and Privacy in Communication Netowrks. ACM (2008)
44. Liu, D., et al.: Don't let one rotten apple spoil the whole barrel: towards automated detection of shadowed domains. In: Proceedings of the 2017 ACM SIGSAC Conference on Computer and Communications Security. ACM (2017)
45. Leontiadis, N., Moore, T., Christin, N.: Measuring and analyzing search-redirection attacks in the illicit online prescription drug trade. In: USENIX Security Symposium, vol. 11 (2011)
46. Christin, N.: Traveling the silk road: a measurement analysis of a large anonymous online marketplace. In: Proceedings of the 22nd International Conference on World Wide Web. ACM (2013)
47. Barratt, M.J., Ferris, J.A., Winstock, A.R.: Use of Silk Road, the online drug marketplace, in the United Kingdom. Australia and the United States. Addiction **109**(5), 774–783 (2014)

Account Lockouts: Characterizing and Preventing Account Denial-of-Service Attacks

Yu Liu[1], Matthew R. Squires[1], Curtis R. Taylor[1,2], Robert J. Walls[1], and Craig A. Shue[1(✉)]

[1] Worcester Polytechnic Institute, Worcester, MA 10609, USA
{ylu25,mrsquires,crtaylor,rjwalls,cshue}@wpi.edu
[2] Oak Ridge National Laboratory, Oak Ridge, TN 37830, USA

Abstract. To stymie password guessing attacks, many systems lock an account after a given number of failed authentication attempts, preventing access even if proper credentials are later provided. Combined with the proliferation of single sign-on providers, adversaries can use relatively few resources to launch large-scale application-level denial-of-service attacks against targeted user accounts by deliberately providing incorrect credentials across multiple authentication attempts.

In this paper, we measure the extent to which this vulnerability exists in production systems. We focus on Microsoft services, which are used in many organizations, to identify exposed authentication points. We measure 2,066 organizations and found between 58% and 77% of organizations expose authentication portals that are vulnerable to account lockout attacks. Such attacks can be completely successful with only 13 KBytes/s of attack traffic. We then propose and evaluate a set of lockout bypass mechanisms for legitimate users. Our performance and security evaluation shows these solutions are effective while introducing little overhead to the network and systems.

Keywords: Account lockout · Denial-of-Service (DoS) attack · Single Sign-On · Middleboxes · Measurement

1 Introduction

In an attempt to gain unauthorized access to a system, attackers may try to guess the credentials associated with a legitimate user's account. These attackers may vary in sophistication, from brute-forcing passwords on default usernames to using a list of known usernames at an organization and lists of most commonly used passwords. Prior analysis of password data sets has shown that end-users often select weak passwords that are vulnerable to such attacks [37]. Further, many organizations consider usability and memorability to be key goals in username generation. As a result, usernames are often generated that match email addresses and use parts of a user's real name [38].

© ICST Institute for Computer Sciences, Social Informatics and Telecommunications Engineering 2019
Published by Springer Nature Switzerland AG 2019. All Rights Reserved
S. Chen et al. (Eds.): SecureComm 2019, LNICST 305, pp. 26–46, 2019.
https://doi.org/10.1007/978-3-030-37231-6_2

Given this threat, many systems implement an account lockout mechanism in which all authentication attempts are denied after a certain number of failed attempts in a predetermined time window. NIST, which sets standards for US government systems, recommends an attempt threshold of 100 attempts or less with a lockout period of between 30 s and 60 min [2]. The SANS institute recommends a threshold of five attempts with a 30 min lockout period [30]. To be PCI compliant, which is required for organizations handling consumer payment information, accounts must be locked out for 30 min after six failed attempts [26].

This account lockout mechanism can be used by attackers to create a denial-of-service (DoS) attack that prevents legitimate users from gaining access to their accounts [22]. Such an attack is easy to launch: an attacker can issue authentication attempts at a rate that would keep an account perpetually locked. With the aforementioned thresholds, such an attack would consume minimal attacker bandwidth and computational resources. Even if simple IP address blocking is used for repeated failed attempts, an attacker could use a network of compromised machines to distribute the attempts.

With the deployment of single-sign-on (SSO) services, account lockouts can transform from a simple nuisance to a crippling attack. Recent work has explored web-based SSO systems and the relationships between identity providers that authenticate users and other websites, called relying parties, that use those identity providers to authenticate their own users [10]. In one example, a single identity provider was used by 42, 232 relying parties. Further, recent reports [28] estimate that Active Directory—Microsoft's prominent SSO identity provider— is used in more than 90% of companies in the Fortune 1000. With an account lockout attack on a single identity provider, a targeted user could be denied access to thousands of other services.

In this paper, we ask two key research questions: *To what extent are organizations vulnerable to account lockout attacks? What countermeasures can be effectively deployed to address these attacks in a way that supports even legacy systems and devices?* Given its widespread deployment and integral nature at organizations, we focus our investigation on Microsoft's Active Directory service. In doing so, we make the following contributions:

1. **Vulnerability Measurements:** We examine 2,066 organizations, including Fortune 1000 companies and universities, to determine the extent to which attackers can systematically identify vulnerable authentication portals and lock accounts. We find that roughly 58% of the universities and roughly 77% of the companies examined expose a vulnerable authentication portal. Lockouts targeting these portals can potentially deny users access to thousands of applications [23].
2. **A Suite of Proposed Countermeasures:** Rather than relying on changes to Active Directory, we propose countermeasures that can be deployed immediately on legacy architectures. The suite of options, based on the concept of distinct authentication pools, includes mechanisms that work across devices with end-user involvement to completely transparent options, such as those using web browsers or modified home routers.

3. **Evaluation of the Countermeasures:** We evaluate the security effectiveness and performance of the proposed countermeasures. We find that each has clear availability advantages while introducing minimal performance costs. Notably, we find that existing authentication mechanisms—such as multifactor authentication—are insufficient to stop account lockout attacks because the root problem lies with the lockout policy, not the mechanism.

2 Background and Related Work

The combination of a username and password is a ubiquitous method of user authentication. Attackers try to obtain such sensitive information to infiltrate computer systems. The sophistication of theses attempts vary. The most basic attack, a brute force attack, exhaustively enumerates all possible character combinations until a valid sequence allows access. The success rate of brute force attacks is dependent upon the underlying strength of user passwords [39].

Other approaches are more sophisticated and use information about end-user behavior to increase success rates [12]. Dictionary attacks, for example, form the password guesses by using a large database of popular passwords or words in a targeted language's dictionary. Prior research has found that many end-users select passwords that could easily be discovered by a dictionary attack [37]. Further, discovered passwords from a compromised service may be used to guess passwords for the same user at other sites due to password reuse [14].

To combat password guessing attacks, standard bodies recommend account lockout thresholds [2,26,30]. After a specified number of failed login attempts, the account lockout approach denies access to a given account even if valid credentials are provided [8]. This simple mechanism makes brute force password guessing infeasible and limits the rate at which attackers can make attempts using dictionaries. Unfortunately, account lockouts provide a natural avenue for denial-of-service attacks: an adversary can simply make numerous failed authentication attempts for a given username, causing the account to lock, and thereby preventing the legitimate account user from authenticating, as shown in Fig. 1.

Other techniques attempt to limit malicious authentication attempts without using a lockout. A common approach is a form of automated Turing test before each login attempt that will purportedly distinguish a human from an automated adversary. A prominent approach is the CAPTCHA [27], which requires a user to decode an image or audio signal in a way that is challenging for computers to do. Such approaches may help deter dictionary attacks, but they do impose usability costs upon users [3]. Unfortunately, with innovations in machine learning, some previously-effective CAPTCHAs may be defeated automatically [36]. Further, hardware or legacy systems may be unable to support CAPTCHAs.

Aura et al. [4] propose the use of client-side puzzles to defend against denial-of-service (DoS) attacks by slowing the attack rate. Each time the client makes a request to the server, it is asked to solve a cryptographic puzzle provided by the server. These puzzles must require significant client effort to solve and are unpredictable. The verification of the result should be inexpensive. Dean et al. [6]

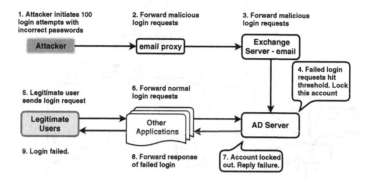

Fig. 1. In an account lockout attack, the attacker selects a username and tries to authenticate with invalid passwords. Each failed attempt causes the server to increment the failed attempt counter for that specific account. When the legitimate user attempts to authenticate, the account may already be locked.

incorporate cryptographic puzzles into the TLS protocol to protect servers from DoS attacks. Koh et al. [15] evaluated a high performance puzzle algorithm.

Unfortunately, puzzle-based defenses may not be compatible with some existing systems and applications. For example, the use of a CAPTCHA may not be feasible when logging into a legacy video conferencing system. Some prior versions of mail software, such as Outlook 2010, not support tools like CAPTCHAs when authenticating. Similar limitations may occur for Skype for Business and applications without a browser-based interface.

2.1   Other Application-Layer Availability Attacks

Most denial-of-service (DoS) availability attacks target a bottleneck resource and overwhelm it to prevent legitimate user access. Network-based flooding attacks, for example, attempt to saturate the bottleneck bandwidth between the Internet and a targeted victim. Application-layer DoS attacks exploit a bottleneck in the host software to deny access. Moore et al. [24] describe an application-layer threat between an HTTP sever and a backend database resource. The account lockout attack is a variant of an application-level availability attack [22].

Source IP address filtering tries to mitigate a DoS attack by blocking the machines originating the attack. Unfortunately, modern attackers have botnets with millions of machines. By strategically cycling the attack machines, IP blacklisting techniques can be rendered useless since an attacker would have a large supply of previously-unseen machines that could trigger a lockout.

2.2   Active Directory (AD)

Active Directory (AD) is a service from Microsoft for managing user accounts and system resources belonging to an organization. It groups users, workstations, servers, and policies and organizes them into hierarchies that facilitate

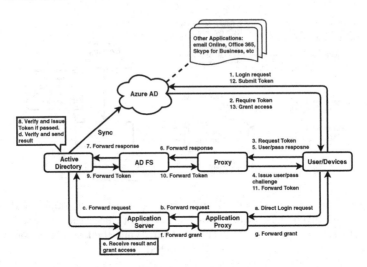

Fig. 2. This diagram depicts the components and interactions between an on-site AD domain controller, an Azure AD domain controller, and the ADFS connector.

management. This service allows user management to be logically centralized by an organization in a set of domain controllers. Application servers may authenticate users via these domain controllers rather than managing accounts and passwords locally, as shown in Fig. 2. For example, Microsoft's email server, Exchange, uses an AD server for authentication.

Organizations may host their AD domain controllers on-site, host them in the cloud through Microsoft's Azure AD service, or use a hybrid of both options. The Azure AD service is essential for Microsoft-hosted online services like Office 365 and Skype for Business Online. Those Azure-based services communicate directly with the Azure AD domain controllers rather than using the on-premise servers. In hybrid deployments, on-site AD domain controllers may configure a unidirectional synchronization channel with the Azure AD servers. For the purposes of account lockouts, an account locked by an on-site domain controller will result in a lock in all domain controllers and, depending upon the configured settings, may propagate to Azure domain controllers. In contrast, an account locked by an Azure domain controller will not propagate to on-site domain controllers.

Microsoft also provides an Active Directory Federation Services (ADFS) interface for applications to interact with Active Directory when they cannot use the integrated Windows authentication service. ADFS has its own account lockout mechanism, but that lockout only affects ADFS services.

For an attacker to maximize the impact of an account lockout, the best option would be to target a service that authenticates to an on-site domain controller, if such a domain controller exists, in addition to targeting an Azure AD domain controller. An account lockout in ADFS or in an Azure AD domain controller may result in a lockout that affects only a subset of the organization's services.

However, in some attack scenarios, a subset may be acceptable to an attacker if it includes a critical service the attacker wishes to make unavailable.

2.3 Middleboxes for Security

Middleboxes, such as firewalls, intrusion detection systems, and proxies, have regularly been used for security purposes in the enterprise. Recent techniques have leveraged the cloud for enterprise security [31].

Other work has extended middlebox techniques to residential networks, including for whole-home proxies [35], validating TLS connections [34], and verifying IoT device communication [16]. As demonstrated by Taylor et al. [33], these residential middleboxes are feasible in countries like the United States since most residential users are within 50 ms of a public cloud data center, causing middleboxes to only incur minor latency costs.

Our work shows how middleboxes can address account lockouts on an enterprise network in a backwards-compatible manner. We further show that middleboxes at the home (e.g. via a modified home router) can further enable robust account lockout protections.

3 System Overview

Active Directory is inherently flexible and scalable, which can lead to deployments that vary greatly in terms of complexity and redundancy. In the simplest case, an Active Directory setup involves a primary domain controller, one or more dependent application servers, and a set of client machines that wish to use the application server. Organizations may deploy other infrastructure, such as secondary domain controllers, proxy servers, and middleboxes, to support legacy systems or to achieve resiliency or security goals. Such infrastructure has little impact on the account lockout threat and we omit it for simplicity.

3.1 Assumptions and Threat Model

In the context of this work, the goal of the adversary is to deny a legitimate user access to services and resources through an account lockout attack. These adversaries may perform reconnaissance on an organization ahead of an attack to obtain email addresses, usernames, or to locate public-facing authentication portals. With the availability of botnets, an adversary may have significant computational and network resources. These resources afford the attacker significant flexibility in devising her attack strategy. For example, the attacker may send a high-volume of authentication requests from geographically-diverse machines and rapidly switch between IP addresses to avoid IP-based blacklisting.

This work does not consider attempts to compromise the Active Directory server, its dependent servers, or other hardware such as the organization's switches and routers. If these servers fall under the control of the adversary, it would be impossible for an organization to guarantee the accuracy of a user's identity or the availability of authentication services. Similarly, we assume an adversary lacks valid user credentials.

The defender's goal is to provide legitimate users with the ability to authenticate even under an ongoing lockout attack. For our proposed countermeasures, we assume that the organization's IT staff can insert one or more middleboxes into an organization's infrastructure, but they cannot modify the Active Directory server or the services that authenticate against Active Directory.

4   Characterizing the Account Lockout Problem

In this section, we explore the following research questions:

1. Can attackers feasibly exploit public authentication portals to launch account lockouts? With the help of a cooperating organization, we use only public data to effect an account lockout on a test account in a production environment using Microsoft's Active Directory service. Since that organization follows industry best practices and standards, this experiment is likely representative of many other organizations.
2. Can attackers automatically discover organizations' authentication portals for lockout attacks? Using an Internet measurement study, we show that authentication portals can be easily discovered by attackers.

4.1   Case Study: Identifying the Attack Surface in Production

We contacted a multinational organization with over 5,000 employees that uses Active Directory extensively and gained their approval to assess the impact of account lockouts across their environment. This organization used Active Directory for authentication for the vast majority of their IT services. From this case study, we created an Internet measurement strategy to characterize the risks at other organizations to determine the broader applicability of our findings.

Our partnering organization made an Active Directory administrator available to provide feedback on our tests, but the organization required anonymity as part of their participation. The organization created a test account for our use which was modeled after a standard employee account at the organization. The organization set a secure password on the account and ensured it was not shared with the authors performing the authentication attempts.

In our testing, we independently gathered information that was available publicly without use of organizational insider knowledge. In our experiments, we found that the organization used `mail.[organization domain]` to forward to a themed Outlook Web App (OWA) portal, which is a Microsoft-provided interface for web-based email. Since the portal used IP addresses that were not associated with Microsoft, we determine that the OWA portal was not Azure-hosted and thus was not using an Azure AD server for authentication.

With many Office 365 services, Microsoft provides a centralized authentication portal that leverages the user's email address to determine the appropriate Azure AD server to use to process the authentication. That authentication page compares the host portion of the email address to its list of registered organization domains. Accordingly, we went to the Office 365 authentication page [21] and entered a randomly constructed username, followed by the '@' character, and then the organization's domain name. The website redirected to the organization's account authentication page, where we were prompted to enter a password. This interface appeared to be Azure-hosted, indicating that login attempts would be directed to an Azure AD server. Account lockouts generated on this service would likely only affect services authenticating against the Azure AD server while not affecting user access via the OWA page we previously discovered.

We then examined Skype for Business (SFB, formerly known as Microsoft Lync). Based on Microsoft's documentation, the `lyncdiscover.[organization domain]` host name is typically used for this service. We performed a `CNAME` query on that host and the response indicated that the organization was not using an Azure-hosted SFB service. We then performed a DNS `A` record query, which returned a valid IP address that is not associated with Microsoft's Azure data centers, which suggests that the organization uses an on-site SFB service.

4.2   Case Study: Testing Account Lockouts in Production

After identifying the attack surfaces of the measured organization, we began testing account lockouts. Microsoft's documentation for Windows Server 2012 [17] and 2016 [18] recommends an account lockout of 10 attempts with a lockout period of 15 min. For Azure's AD service, Microsoft's documentation indicates a threshold of 10 attempts with a 1 min lockout period. The most generous lockout policy was suggested by NIST with up to 100 attempts and a lockout period as short as 30 s. Based on these thresholds, we created an attack that would try authenticating as our test account with randomly-generated passwords around 200 times per minute. This attack is relatively low bandwidth at only 13 KBytes/s, which poses little burden on the attacker or on the organization's infrastructure. However, under the most conservative guidance, the attack would keep the targeted account perpetually locked.

We first targeted our attack at the organization's OWA portal. Our organization contact confirmed that the attack caused the account to be locked at the organization, preventing the account from logging into the organization's resources for the duration of the attack. We discontinued the attack and the organization contact removed the account lockout.

We next performed an attack targeted at SFB. Using the fake account, we use a tool provided by an open source project on Github named `lyncsmash` [25]. It provides an option to discover the SFB servers and an option to launch an account lockout attack. We manually went to the URL found in the tool, entered the username supplied by the organization, and entered an inaccurate password 10 times. Our organization contact then confirmed that the account was locked. We note that the `lyncsmash` tool can automate these attempts.

In these tests, we used the same source IP address for each query. While a simple IP rate limit or blacklist would stop our attack, an actual attacker could easily perform the attempts using a botnet to ensure no IP address queried more than once. This would easily keep the account locked without an obvious defense. The measured organization's contact confirmed that the organization lacks a mechanism to combat such account lockouts.

4.3   Characterizing the Risk with Internet Measurements

While our partner organization was vulnerable to an account lockout attack, we now focus on determining the extent to which other organizations are likewise vulnerable. We begin by making non-invasive measurements of the public-facing infrastructure of a set of organizations. While we focus on Active Directory in this work, most organizations avoid directly exposing their AD servers to the public for security reasons. However, in many cases, these organizations expose their application servers to boost productivity. To allow employees to access their email outside the office, these organizations may expose Exchange email servers or website interfaces, such as the popular Outlook Web App (OWA) that Microsoft provides. Unified messaging services, like Microsoft Skype for Business (SFB), allow employees, customers, and partners to instant message, call, and join video conferences remotely. In some cases, the devices joining these calls may be mobile phones or dedicated video conferencing hardware.

Given the popularity of email and unified messaging, our measurement study focuses on determining the extent to which authentication portals for Microsoft-specific email and messaging servers are exposed publicly since we know such servers must use an AD server for authentication. We perform our measurements by using a list of domains associated with the Fortune 1000 companies [11] and with 1,066 universities [32]. We focus on these organizations because their domains can be easily obtained. Further, these larger organizations likely have need for centralized authentication services like Active Directory.

Using our list of domains, we perform a DNS MX record lookup on the provided domain to determine the identity of the organization's public SMTP server. The host names of the SMTP servers provide some insight into the underlying infrastructure. For example, host names ending with .protection.outlook.com are indicative of an organization using Microsoft's cloud-hosted email service. Since these organizations necessarily use Active Directory in Microsoft's Azure cloud, these servers can be used to initiate an account lockout for all Azure-hosted solutions at the organization. Other MX records may indicate that the mail server is located on-site at the organization or is hosted by another provider.

Our second measurement uses information related to email auto-discovery [19]. We issue CNAME queries for the host autodiscover associated with the organization's domain (e.g., autodiscover.example.com). In some cases, the CNAME result was autodiscover.outlook.com, indicating the mail services use Microsoft's Azure-hosted Exchange server. In the case when another host name was returned, the mail server was not Azure-hosted. We then issued a web request on port 80 or 443 to the host name returned in the CNAME record. In some cases, the server required valid credentials to proceed. In some cases, the credentials would be validated by an Active Directory server, enabling the account lockout attack. However, in other cases, the authentication credentials

Table 1. Our measurement study results show the majority of each group uses Microsoft services and has at least one exposed authentication portal, enabling account lockout attacks. The final column shows unique organizations vulnerable, even if an organization has multiple exposed attack surfaces.

Organizations	Exchange email		Skype for business		Extent vulnerable
	On-site	Azure-hosted	On-site	Azure-hosted	
Fortune 1000	190	339	360	345	765 (76.5%)
Universities	126	416	124	395	616 (57.8%)

could be independent of a user account (e.g., a username and password shared across the organization for relatively weak protection).

The discovered mail server's default web page could reveal information about the infrastructure. In some cases, the servers presented a default or themed version of Microsoft's Outlook Web Application (OWA) page, which is commonly associated with an on-premises Exchange server. When web servers return 403 forbidden, it means there could be a portal which requires authentication. We simply append "/owa" or "/autodiscover" and we found half of them redirect to an OWA login page. In other cases, the web server returned pages containing the string "Microsoft Corporation" indicating this server runs Microsoft's software. These authentication portals provide an avenue for the account lockout attack.

Some domains did not use an auto-discovery service or did not provide an obvious account authentication page. For these domains, we issued an A record DNS query for the `mail` host name associated with the domain (e.g., `mail.example.com`), which follows the examples provided in Microsoft's documentation for configuring mail servers. We found that nearly half of organizations provide such a server for their employees to authenticate, though few of them used a default interface such as OWA or Microsoft's Azure-hosted email portal.

We next focused our measurements on the Skype for Business (SFB) service. Microsoft's SFB client automatically searches for an organization's servers using a mechanism similar to email auto-discovery. For all the Fortune 1000 and university domains, we perform a `CNAME` DNS query on the `lyncdiscover` host associated with the organization (e.g., `lyncdiscover.example.com`), which can reveal which organizations use SFB services. We also query for `dialin.example.com` and `meet.example.com`, which are other commonly used SFB host names. When organizations use Microsoft's Azure hosted systems, the `CNAME` query returns an answer associated with the `webdir.online.lync.com` host name. For all the non-Azure responses, we performed a A record DNS query to obtain the IP address of the on-site SFB service.

In Table 1, we show the result of the measurements. Roughly 77% of companies and 58% of universities had servers that would be affected by some form of account lockout attack. For organizations that use Azure-hosted services, an account lockout attack targeted at these servers would affect other services that consult the Azure Active Directory server, but they would not affect services that communicate with an on-site Active Directory server because the uni-directional Azure AD server connection with an on-site AD server does provide the capability to share this information. However, attacks against services that communicate to a non-Azure AD server would affect all services, since non-Azure AD servers propagate an account lockout organization-wide, including to the Azure AD server. Accordingly, attackers looking for the biggest impact may target non-Azure AD servers when possible.

5   Discussion of Potential Countermeasures

Our measurements demonstrate that account lockout attacks can be crippling for an organization and that many large organizations are vulnerable to these attacks. However, there are a variety of mechanisms that may be effective at mitigating such attacks. Each method has strengths and limitations in terms of ease of deployment, legacy compatibility, visibility and impact on end-users. We discuss potential methods and implemented two of them, one which modifies a residential router and another that leverages user provided secret information, to show to what extent we can prevent account lockout attacks.

Countermeasure: Private Usernames. An account lockout attack requires knowledge of the target username. In practice, gaining this knowledge is often trivial. For example, Alice's username might be `alice` and her email address may be `alice@example.com`. Intuitively, if the username becomes harder to guess then lockout attacks become commensurately harder for the attacker to execute. Private usernames offer tangible benefits. The approach is backwards-compatible with all existing infrastructure, it avoids lockout attempts on the username, and incurs no additional computational overheads or infrastructure. However, the approach may sacrifice end-user convenience for this computational efficiency. In particular, end-users will now need to manage multiple identifiers and know when to enter their private username and when to use their public email address. Further, organizations may need to reconsider how access control systems and resource sharing will work when a username is intended to be kept private from an employee's coworkers. Finally, transitioning to a private username schema may be prohibitively disruptive for organizations that have a large number of users and legacy systems.

Countermeasure: Multi-factor Authentication. Another countermeasure is to ask the user to provide additional secret information as part of a multi-factor authentication (MFA) scheme, such as biometrics, hardware tokens, or one-time pass codes that are transmitted via a smartphone application. MFA-based approaches are effective at distinguishing legitimate users from attackers, assuming the attacker has not compromised all the factors. Further, they are widely deployed so users are already familiar with the process and the usability cost is relatively low compared to the security benefits. Unfortunately, multi-factor schemes alone cannot solve the problem of account lockouts. Intuitively, this problem is not necessarily a limitation of multi-factor authentication but of the lockout policies themselves. In other words, most lockout polices only account for the *number* of failed attempts and not the *kind* of information used in the attempt. Consider Active Directory's multi-factor authentication interface; this workflow allows a username and password to be used in conjunction with a second factor verification via smartphone application or text message. Failed authentication attempts still lead to an account lockout as the second factor is only used if the provided username and password are valid. In short, the second factor does not influence the server's decision to lockout an account.

Countermeasure: Observed Characteristics. The above approaches rely on the user to provide private information as proof. An orthogonal approach is for the authenticating server to use historical information related to the user's behavior or observable connection characteristics. For example, Eriksson et al. [9] studied geographic detection based on IP addresses. The primary limitation of such approaches is they must be tuned carefully to balance between false negatives (allowing an attacker to authenticate) and false positives (preventing a legitimate user from authenticating).

5.1   Distinct Authentication Pools

The goal of this work is to incorporate and augment existing authentication approaches. Our proposed countermeasures are based on the following observations. First, existing authentication mechanisms fail to stop account lockout attacks because the problem lies with the lockout policy not the mechanism. Second, account lockout policies should base lockout decisions on the totality of information rather than a simple boolean log of attempts. Third, the proliferation of legacy systems means that organizations are more likely to adopt defenses (at least in the short term) that do not require changes to the end-user software or existing authentication servers.

We codify these observations into a proposed authentication scheme based on *distinct authentication pools*. This scheme is designed to leverage historical activity, network proximity, and secondary credentials to maintain separate authentication risk pools with their own lockout thresholds and failed authentication attempt counts, as shown in Fig. 3. Each pool maintains a separate counter and threshold which can be configured to meet different security requirements. To make authentication pools immediately applicable to existing systems, we use security middleboxes to implement the key functionality without requiring changes to the services or Active Directory servers. Importantly, this scheme allows a user to authenticate even if there is an on-going lockout attack.

We also propose and implement two novel, and orthogonal, authentication mechanisms to serve as the basis for two of the authentication pools. The first is a token-based mechanism that transparently authenticates requests originating from a user's residential network. The second proposed mechanism leverages a user-supplied credential that effectively turns a public username into a private username. We discuss the design of both mechanisms below.

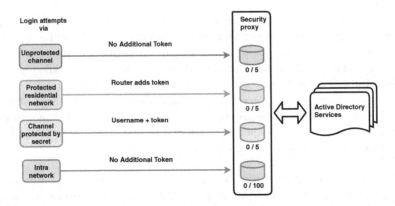

Fig. 3. With a security middlebox or proxy, an organization can create separate authentication thresholds and authentication attempt counts based on factors that may indicate the user's legitimacy. This diagram depicts four authentication pools based on the presence of tokens, manual authenticators, and on-site presence. The proxy can send commands to help account management in Active Directory, such as unlocking an account, restoring the original account lock state, and checking the account status. (Color figure online)

5.2   Protecting Requests from Residential Networks

Many existing web-based authentication systems leverage HTTP cookies to determine if a user is currently logged in or has logged in successfully in the past. The pool proxy server could validate cookie values and place users with valid cookies in a pool that is separate from users that do not present such cookies. Unfortunately, such an approach is limited to web-based authentication. Instead, we propose leveraging an approach from the TCP Fast Open (TFO) standard [5]. In essence, an authentication server orders the client or a middlebox to store a cookie, allowing that client or middlebox to prove it previously logged in successfully when trying to authenticate again in the future. Like the original TFO standard, the cookie we introduce would not be an authoritative authenticator and it would not be resistant to a man-in-the-middle attack. However, it does provide sufficient evidence to put a client in a separate authentication risk pool.

The authentication pool proxies can be implemented using the TLS "peek and splice" technique [29], in which the proxy is on the route to the protected application servers and has the private TLS keys associated with each server. This allows the proxy to decrypt the traffic, extract the username, and validate tokens and cookie values. If a token is present, the proxy server can then issue commands to the Active Directory server to determine whether the account is locked out, and if so, temporarily lift the lock. It can then re-encrypt the request with the tokens extracted and send it to the application server to process the authentication attempt. Once the authentication result is sent back to the proxy, it can re-lock the account, if it was previously locked.

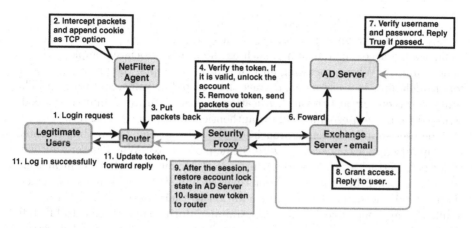

Fig. 4. With a residential middlebox, tokens can be automatically supplied and stored by examining packets to and from application servers.

In our implementation, to check if an account is locked and obtain the number of failed authentication attempts, the proxy speaks the LDAP protocol with the AD server. Using the `python-ldap` library [7], the security proxy checks the account status via the `ldap.search()` function on the `badPwdCount` attribute with administrator privileges. To unlock the account, the proxy server uses the `ldap.modify_s()` function and sets value of `lockoutTime` to 0. Finally, to restore the failed authentication attempts, the proxy server can use an invalid password to send the same number of prior authentication attempts.

For cookies using TCP options, the process can proceed in a fashion similar to TCP Fast Open (see Fig. 4). Organizations can provide some employees with a modified router that will act as a middlebox that manages TCP cookies for the user. When the user accesses the organization's servers, the router checks to see if it has a cookie for the destination. If so, it adds the cookie as a TCP option with the request. The security proxy can then extract the cookie and perform the appropriate account unlocking operations before sending the request to the application server. Upon receiving a positive authentication response from the application server, the security proxy can generate a cookie value and insert it as a TCP option. The user's router will then extract the cookie, store it locally, and then forward the response to the user.

5.3 Supporting Private Usernames

A token can also be user-supplied. The secret code can be shared via email, on an employee's badge, or in new employee orientation materials. When a user supplies the username for authentication, they can insert a delimiter followed by a non-public value that the proxy device can detect (e.g., `username+code`). The non-public value can be arbitrary set by the proxy administrator and changed if it was ever learned by an adversary and used in an account lockout attack.

Each account should have unique secret token used for login. Since the value is only used to circumvent a lockout attack, the value could be one the user could readily access or remember, such as the user's associated employee ID or badge number. When processing authentication attempts, the proxy can search for the delimiter in a username, extract the non-public value, and verify it. The proxy can then forward the authentication request with the delimiter and code stripped from the username field for authentication by the AD server.

The user-supplied token approach has the value of being easily implemented and supported in legacy systems with the help of a proxy. When a user's account is not being attacked, they need not provide the token since the default authentication pool will be unlocked. After their account is locked due to an attack, the user only needs to type a short addition to their username to gain access. While this approach does require user training, during support calls to IT staff, the helpdesk staff can quickly remind users of the override. Finally, when setting up automated clients, such as email programs or smartphone applications, the user can choose to enter the token to ensure continued access during attacks without incurring any inconvenience. The user-supplied token avoids the complications of legacy usernames and access control that are associated with the private username approach while attaining similar benefits.

6   Evaluation of the Authentication Pools System

For our evaluation, we consider both the security effectiveness and the performance of using authentication pools. We focus on the two authentication mechanisms proposed in the preceding section: (1) authenticating requests from residential networks and (2) providing support for private usernames with tokens.

6.1   Implementation and Experimental Setup

For our baseline experiments, we configured a Windows Server 2016 Standard server to run the Active Directory service on a virtual machine with two cores and 8 GB of RAM. We configured an Exchange 2010 server on another Windows Server 2016 Standard VM with two cores and 8 GB of RAM. The Exchange server used the Active Directory server VM for authentication and the POP3 service for checking emails. To test the proposed countermeasures, we implemented two different middleboxes: the authentication pool proxy and the residential router. Our client is another Ubuntu 16.04 server VM that runs a POP3 Python script client that attempts to use our Exchange email server. While the deployed enterprise configurations will differ from our experimental setup, we believe this setup is sufficient for evaluating the security and performance characteristics.

The pool proxy implementation supports both the TLS "peek and splice" and the private username authentication mechanisms described in the preceding section. We use an Ubuntu virtual machine with 2 cores and 4096 MB of RAM and the `tcpproxy` library [13], which allows the interception and modification of packets. The `tcpproxy` library provides the functionality to wrap normal socket communication into TLS protected communication when a private key is imported. The pool proxy uses a copy of the Exchange server's private key. The decrypted payload contains the account information. However, when `tcpproxy` uses SSL-wrapped sockets, it only provides the decrypted packet payload without network or transport layer headers. Using the `libnetfilter_queue` library and the `iptables` tool, the pool proxy intercepts the packets and extracts any TCP options from the packet headers before forwarding, to `tcpproxy` to see any token TCP options. If they are present, as shown by the green line in Fig. 3, the proxy switches the request to a separate authentication pool.

To support private usernames, the pool proxy also checks each username for a + character and extracts the subsequent code. If the code is valid, the system recognizes the connection as associated with the blue line in Fig. 3. When the verification of a security token succeeds, the security proxy issues commands to the AD domain controller to unlock the account if additional attempts are permitted for that pool group. After the credential verification completes at the domain controller, the security proxy sends commands to restore the account lock status. When the TCP option is used, the security proxy generates a new token and appends it to the reply packet as a TCP option. The router can thus extract the new token and store it for future use.

For the residential router, we use an Ubuntu 16.04 server VM configured with single core and 2048 MB of RAM. We then created a C program that uses the Linux `libnetfilter_queue` library and `iptables` to intercept traffic to and from the residential network. The program is designed in a fashion to allow it to be ported to commodity router hardware. The program uses the packet's destination address to determine if it is a known organizational application server. If so, supplies any associated token as a TCP option. The program also looks at the packet's source address to determine if it is an application server, and if so, the program looks for TCP options containing a token. If one is found, the router stores it for future out-bound packets and removes the option before sending the packet towards its destination. In Fig. 4, we provide a diagram of this process.

6.2 Security Effectiveness

Using a methodology similar to our measurements in Sect. 4.2, we create a tool that emulates an attacker trying to trigger an account lockout. We use a Python script with the `poplib` library [1] to create a POP3 client. That script initiates 100 authentication attempts in rapid succession. Even with the relatively permissive NIST guidance, that volume triggered a lockout.

We unlocked the account and reset the failed attempt counter to zero. We then replicated this process using web requests to the Outlook Web Application (OWA) interface on the Exchange server manually. The outcome was the same: the legitimate user was unable to authenticate to either OWA or POP3 because the account was locked in AD.

We note that the account lockout through the OWA portal may be affected by credential caching in Microsoft's Internet Information Services (IIS). A parameter, `UserTokenTTL`, defines how long the IIS server should cache

Table 2. Our security evaluation determined the effectiveness of the TCP option and embedded code countermeasures. Across 20 trials, both approaches correctly allow legitimate requests and deny malicious attempts.

	Router TCP option		Username + secret	
	Token valid	Token invalid	Token valid	Token invalid
Allows access	20	0	20	0
Denies access	0	20	0	20

authentication tokens. The default cache flush delay is 15 min [20]. With that default, an attacker has 15 min to make unlimited password guess attempts. During that attack, the failed authentication attempts counter increases. After it hits the threshold, access via services like POP3 is denied because the account is locked, but the cached credential still allows a user to authenticate via the OWA portal. In effect, this delays the account lockout attack from affecting the OWA portal, but still allows an account lock to propagate throughout the rest of the organization. After the cache period ends, the account will also be locked on the OWA portal. Accordingly, this caching does not ultimately affect the attack's success.

For the residential router mechanism, we primed the router by performing a legitimate authentication attempt. We then cleared the account lock status and authentication attempt counts. We then ran the attacker script without presenting a token value. However, when the legitimate user attempted to login, the router supplied the previously obtained token and the security proxy correctly unlocked the account temporarily to process the request before re-locking it. We found that the legitimate user was able to authenticate without impediment despite the ongoing attack.

We repeated the TCP option process with an adversary that tried to forge TCP tokens, by supplying random values. As expected with the low likelihood of guessing a 10-byte token value, we found that adversary never generated a correct token. The security proxy accordingly ignored these tokens and the attacker remained locked out. However, when the legitimate user attempted to authenticate, the proxy recognized the token and properly allowed the attempt. Finally, we repeated these experiments using the user-supplied tokens. The legitimate user provided a username of the format `username+token` when attempting to authenticate. In our first experiment, the attacker did not provide tokens and in our second, the attacker attempted to guess tokens randomly. As with the TCP-option experiments, we found the attacker was unable to unlock the account while the legitimate user had unimpeded access to authenticate. In Table 2, we show the numerical results of our experiments. In each experiment, we conducted 20 separate trials and the results were consistent.

6.3   Performance Evaluation

To determine the performance impact of the approach, we use end-to-end timings. We measured the amount of time required to complete an authentication

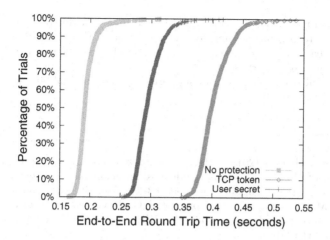

Fig. 5. We evaluate and compare end to end delay among three cases: red line shows without any middlebox or proxy, green line shows inserting tokens via TCP option and blue line shows username + secret token (Color figure online)

request using the `time.time()` function, provided by Python, in the legitimate client's script. We measured the timing without our countermeasures implemented and with them in place. This allows us to determine the sum of all overheads present in the system. We show the results in Fig. 5.

When comparing our the two authentication mechanisms, we found that the TCP option countermeasure added around 180 ms of latency while the user-supplied token added 80 ms of latency, compared to the same system without a countermeasure present. These overheads are so small they are unlikely to be perceived by an end-user. We believe the user secret scenario is faster in our implementation because it does not need to examine TCP options, extract tokens or append TCP tokens.

Based on these results, we find our countermeasures provide effective security benefits without introducing noticeable latency.

7   Conclusion

In this work, we explored the extent to which organizations are vulnerable to account lockouts and the impact that the lockouts could have. Looking only at the deployments of Microsoft Active Directory, we found that the majority of top companies and universities had an exposed authentication portal that would enable an attacker to launch an account lockout. Through our experiments with a partnering organization, we demonstrated the feasibility of such an attack in a production environment. We then introduced a suite of counter-measures and compared the benefits. We found that both user-supplied tokens and middlebox-added tokens would be effective and would add no perceptible delays or performance overheads.

Acknowledgements. The authors would like to thank the anonymous organization for allowing us to test our account lockout approach on their infrastructure and for providing feedback on the effectiveness of the account lockout approach when targeting different authentication portals.

This material is based upon work supported by the National Science Foundation under Grant No. 1651540.

References

1. POP3 protocol client (2018). https://docs.python.org/3/library/poplib.html
2. 800-63B, N.S.P.: Digital identity guidelines, authentication and lifecycle management (2018). https://pages.nist.gov/800-63-3/sp800-63b.html#throttle
3. Alsaleh, M., Mannan, M., van Oorschot, P.C.: Revisiting defenses against large-scale online password guessing attacks. IEEE Trans. Dependable Sec. Comput. **9**(1), 128–141 (2012)
4. Aura, T., Nikander, P., Leiwo, J.: DOS-resistant authentication with client puzzles. In: Christianson, B., Malcolm, J.A., Crispo, B., Roe, M. (eds.) Security Protocols 2000. LNCS, vol. 2133, pp. 170–177. Springer, Heidelberg (2001). https://doi.org/10.1007/3-540-44810-1_22
5. Cheng, Y., Chu, J., Radhakrishnan, S., Jain, A.: TCP Fast Open (2014). https://tools.ietf.org/html/rfc7413
6. Dean, D., Stubblefield, A.: Using client puzzles to protect TLS. In: USENIX Security Symposium, vol. 42 (2001)
7. Dufresne, J.: Python-ldap on github (2017). https://github.com/python-ldap/python-ldap/blob/python-ldap-3.2.0/Doc/index.rst
8. Durinovic-Johri, S., Wirth, P.E.: Access control system with lockout. US Patent 5,699,514 (1997)
9. Eriksson, B., Barford, P., Sommers, J., Nowak, R.: A learning-based approach for IP geolocation. In: Krishnamurthy, A., Plattner, B. (eds.) PAM 2010. LNCS, vol. 6032, pp. 171–180. Springer, Heidelberg (2010). https://doi.org/10.1007/978-3-642-12334-4_18
10. Ghasemisharif, M., Ramesh, A., Checkoway, S., Kanich, C., Polakis, J.: O single sign-off, where art thou? An empirical analysis of single sign-on account hijacking and session management on the web. In: USENIX Security Symposium, pp. 1475–1492 (2018)
11. Harvard University: Registrars of fortune 1000 companies - raw data. https://cyber.harvard.edu/archived_content/people/edelman/fortune-registrars/fortune-list.html
12. Herley, C., Florêncio, D.: Protecting financial institutions from brute-force attacks. In: Jajodia, S., Samarati, P., Cimato, S. (eds.) SEC 2008. ITIFIP, vol. 278, pp. 681–685. Springer, Boston (2008). https://doi.org/10.1007/978-0-387-09699-5_45
13. ickerwx: tcpproxy on github (2018). https://github.com/ickerwx/tcpproxy
14. Ives, B., Walsh, K.R., Schneider, H.: The domino effect of password reuse. Commun. ACM **47**(4), 75–78 (2004)
15. Koh, J.Y., Ming, J.T.C., Niyato, D.: Rate limiting client puzzle schemes for denial-of-service mitigation. In: 2013 IEEE Wireless Communications and Networking Conference (WCNC), pp. 1848–1853. IEEE (2013)
16. Liu, Y., Taylor, C.R., Shue, C.A.: Authenticating endpoints and vetting connections in residential networks. In: International Conference on Computing, Networking and Communications (ICNC), pp. 136–140 (2019)

17. Margosis, A.: Security baselines for Windows 8.1, Windows server 2012 R2 and Internet Explorer 11 (2014). https://blogs.technet.microsoft.com/secguide/2014/08/13/security-baselines-for-windows-8-1-windows-server-2012-r2-and-internet-explorer-11-final/
18. Margosis, A.: Security baseline for Windows 10 (2018). https://blogs.technet.microsoft.com/secguide/2016/10/17/security-baseline-for-windows-10-v1607-anniversary-edition-and-windows-server-2016/
19. Microsoft: Autodiscover for exchange (2015). https://docs.microsoft.com/en-us/exchange/client-developer/exchange-web-services/autodiscover-for-exchange
20. Microsoft Support: Changing the default interval for user tokens in IIS (2018). https://support.microsoft.com/en-us/help/152526/changing-the-default-interval-for-user-tokens-in-iis
21. Microsoft Support: Office365 login page (2019). https://login.microsoftonline.com/
22. MITRE Corporation: CWE-645: overly restrictive account lockout mechanism (2019). https://cwe.mitre.org/data/definitions/645.html
23. Monica, A.D., Baldwin, M., Cai, S., Casey, C.: Thousands of apps, one identity (2016). https://docs.microsoft.com/en-us/enterprise-mobility-security/solutions/thousands-apps-one-identity
24. Moore, D., Shannon, C., Brown, D.J., Voelker, G.M., Savage, S.: Inferring internet denial-of-service activity. ACM Trans. Comput. Syst. **24**(2), 115–139 (2006)
25. nyxgeek: Lyncsmash. https://github.com/nyxgeek/lyncsmash
26. PCIPolicyPortal: PCI compliance password requirements: best practices to know (2015). http://pcipolicyportal.com/blog/pci-compliance-password-requirements-best-practices-know/
27. Pope, C., Kaur, K.: Is it human or computer? Defending e-commerce with captchas. IT Prof. **7**(2), 43–49 (2005)
28. Pylon Technology News: Active directory in today's regulatory environment (2014). https://pylontechnology.com/active-directory-todays-regulatory-environment/
29. Rousskov, A.: Feature: SslBump peek and Splice (2019). https://wiki.squid-cache.org/Features/SslPeekAndSplice
30. SANS Institute: Top 10 mistakes on windows internal networks (2003). https://www.sans.org/reading-room/whitepapers/windows/top-10-mistakes-windows-internal-networks-1016
31. Sherry, J., Hasan, S., Scott, C., Krishnamurthy, A., Ratnasamy, S., Sekar, V.: Making middleboxes someone else's problem: network processing as a cloud service. ACM SIGCOMM Comput. Commun. Rev. **42**(4), 13–24 (2012)
32. Standford University: Alphabetic list of us universities and domains (1996). http://doors.stanford.edu/~sr/universities.html
33. Taylor, C.R., Guo, T., Shue, C.A., Najd, M.E.: On the feasibility of cloud-based SDN controllers for residential networks. In: IEEE Conference on Network Function Virtualization and Software Defined Networks (NFV-SDN), pp. 1–6 (2017)
34. Taylor, C.R., Shue, C.A.: Validating security protocols with cloud-based middleboxes. In: IEEE Conference on Communications and Network Security, pp. 261–269 (2016)
35. Taylor, C.R., Shue, C.A., Najd, M.E.: Whole home proxies: bringing enterprise-grade security to residential networks. In: IEEE International Conference on Communications (ICC), pp. 1–6 (2016)
36. Wang, Y., Huang, Y., Zheng, W., Zhou, Z., Liu, D., Lu, M.: Combining convolutional neural network and self-adaptive algorithm to defeat synthetic multi-digit text-based CAPTCHA. In: IEEE International Conference on Industrial Technology (ICIT), pp. 980–985. IEEE (2017)

37. Weir, M., Aggarwal, S., Collins, M., Stern, H.: Testing metrics for password creation policies by attacking large sets of revealed passwords. In: ACM Conference on Computer and Communications Security (CCS), pp. 162–175. ACM (2010)
38. Witty, R.J., Allan, A.: Best practices in user ID formation (2003). https://www.bus.umich.edu/kresgepublic/journals/gartner/research/117900/117943/117943.html
39. Yan, J., Blackwell, A., Anderson, R., Grant, A.: Password memorability and security: empirical results. IEEE Secur. Priv. **2**(5), 25–31 (2004)

Application Transiency: Towards a Fair Trade of Personal Information for Application Services

Raquel Alvarez[⊠], Jake Levenson, Ryan Sheatsley, and Patrick McDaniel

Pennsylvania State University, State College, PA 16802, USA
{rva5120,jml6407,rms5643}@psu.edu, mcdaniel@cse.psu.edu,
http://siis.cse.psu.edu/

Abstract. Smartphone users are offered a plethora of applications providing services, such as games and entertainment. In 2018, 94% of applications on Google Play were advertised as "free". However, many of these applications obtain undefined amounts of personal information from unaware users. In this paper, we introduce *transiency*: a privacy-enhancing feature that prevents applications from running unless explicitly opened by the user. Transient applications can only collect sensitive user information while they are being used, and remain disabled otherwise. We show that a transient app would not be able to detect a sensitive user activity, such as a daily commute to work, unless it was used during the activity. We define characteristics of transient applications and find that, of the top 100 free apps on Google Play, 88 could be made transient. By allowing the user to decide when to allow an app to collect their data, we move towards a fair trade of personal information for application services.

Keywords: Mobile privacy · Android

1 Introduction

In 2018, over 2.6 million apps were available on the Google Play market, of which 94% were advertised as "free" [42]. Users can request a ride from apps like Uber or Lyft, share pictures on Facebook, or send money to a friend through Venmo. While these applications are advertised as free, they present a hidden cost: privacy. The effects of smartphones on user privacy have been widely studied since their commercialization in 2007 [5,7,8,12,28–30,32–37]. Recently, the private preferences and habits of millions of Facebook users were misused for political purposes [39]. Many studies also show that users *do* care about their privacy [14,15,20]. A study by Oates et al. found that users have mental models of what privacy means to them [23]. However, platforms can fail to provide them with intuitive options to control application behaviors [14,16,22]. Many users think of

---

Supported by NSF.

S. Chen et al. (Eds.): SecureComm 2019, LNICST 305, pp. 47–66, 2019.
https://doi.org/10.1007/978-3-030-37231-6_3

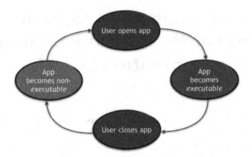

Fig. 1. Application transiency gives users control over when an application has access to sensitive information. A more fair trade is achieved since the user gets to decide whether their personal information is worth the privacy cost for the application service. We propose a new model in which the intuition of applications no longer running after being closed is realized.

closing physical barriers, such as doors and curtains, as an analogy to enabling privacy. By allowing all applications to constantly run in the background even after they are closed, smartphone application models don't adhere to common user privacy expectations.

Android controls user privacy through permissions that protect sensitive device resources. While permissions prevent applications from accessing arbitrary resources, studies have shown that permission models do not match user expectations on when and why sensitive data is being accessed [4,25]. Here, the authors showed that the context in which a resource is accessed matters, and that users prefer to deny access to resources that do not contribute to the functionality of the app. This led to recent work on helping users make educated decisions when granting permissions [10,11,13,24]. Recently, with Android 9.0, apps are no longer allowed background access to the camera and microphone. However, other sensitive resources (e.g., text messages) are still available to applications at any time, given that they were granted the permission once. Some studies have addressed this by sandboxing applications [8,9]. For example, Narain et al. fed crafted fake location data to protect the real location of users. In this paper, we show that smartphones can be designed to provide a fair trade of personal information in exchange for application services. We introduce *transiency*: a privacy-enhancing feature that prevents applications from running unless explicitly opened by the user. Transiency ensures that applications can only collect sensitive information when expected, as shown in Fig. 1. Therefore, users can now decide if application services are worth revealing their personal information for. We make the following contributions:

– We define transiency and efficiently integrate it into Android. This enforces a fair trade of personal information for application services.
– We define criteria for transient applications, and find that 88 of the top 100 free apps on Google Play (total of 105 ranked apps) should be treated as transient.

– We provide a case study to show the impact of treating applications as transient in terms of data collection. We find that we can prevent apps from detecting activity patterns by treating them as transient.

2 Background

In this section, we define technical details of Android relevant to the implementation of transiency.

2.1 Android OS Overview

The Android operating system is built on top of the Linux kernel, which is used to interact with the hardware functionality of smartphone devices, such as cameras and microphones. The main executable programs on Android devices are *applications*, which are developed in Java and built using the Application Framework. For more information about the architecture details of applications, refer to [1,44,46–48]. Below we describe in more detail some of the relevant architecture components to enforce application transiency.

Application Execution Flow. Applications exist in the system as Android Packages (APKs). APKs contain the necessary information to be executed by the Android Runtime (ART) [46]. In order for an application to be executed correctly, Android expects APKs to be available and readable by the system.

Background Processes. Android applications are designed to off-load large tasks that may potentially block the user interface (UI) to be run in the background. Logging the current location of the user to a server is an example of a task that would be executed in the background. In 2018, Votipka et al. performed an extensive user study in which they gained insights about what users think of background processes [14]. The results showed that users tend to understand the need for background processes while they interact with the UI. However, users were less comfortable with background processes not tied to foreground activities.

Permissions. Android uses permissions to protect applications from accessing device resources. Permissions are divided into two categories: *normal* and *dangerous*. Normal permissions are granted by default, but dangerous permissions must be granted by the user. Dangerous permissions protect access to sensitive resources, such as camera, microphone, text messages, call logs, calendar, etc.

Opening and Closing Applications. In order to open an application, Android defines a specific type of application that displays the available options to the user: *launcher*. The launcher app can be opened by pressing the "Home" button on the mobile device. Once open, a user can close an application by removing it from the "Recents Screen", as suggested by Google Support [51] (see Fig. 2). However, it is worth noting that closing an application does not prevent the application from running in the background and exercising the previously authorized access to sensitive resources.

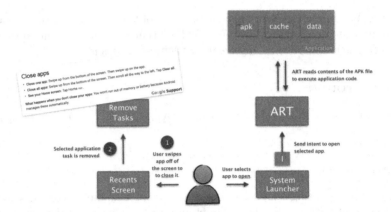

Fig. 2. Users can open apps by pressing the "Home" button and invoking the launcher app. To close applications, the user can swipe it off the screen. While closing an application is the terminology used by Google, the behavior is not equivalent to the application no longer running. Android allows applications to separate their user interfaces into *tasks*, which the user can terminate. However, while tasks can be terminated by the user, the application is still allowed to run on the background.

2.2   Sensitive Resource Access Control

Android protects access to valuable sensitive resources using *access control* policies [2,3]. The goal of these policies is to prevent applications from compromising user privacy. These policies ensure that applications only access sensitive resources allowed by the user. On the context of access control, applications (*subjects*) may or may not be authorized to access (*action*) sensitive system resources (*objects*). Android handles *authentication* and *authorization* as follows:

Authentication. At installation time, applications are given User IDs (UIDs) and are treated as users of the system. UIDs give applications an identity, which is used by Android to identify the application's set of authorized access.

Authorization. Android provides an interface for applications to prompt the user for access to sensitive resources. As mentioned previously, *dangerous permissions* must be granted by the user for an application to be able to access a resource such as GPS data. Android keeps track of the authorized access to sensitive resources for each application. Once the user grants permission, the application is free to exercise this right both when running in the foreground and background. However, as of Android 9.0, applications cannot access the microphone and camera resources while running in the background [54].

While permissions serve as a policy that allows users to explicitly grant access to sensitive resources, research has shown that this model places an unrealistic expectation on users [4,25]. Applications don't always provide clear privacy policies justifying the requested access [28], which presents an *information asymmetry* problem. By granting access to a sensitive resource, the user is not necessarily

giving their consent since they were not fully disclosed the information necessary to make that decision. This inequality inspired the solution presented in
this work.

3 Application Transiency Design Goals

In order to implement transiency, we define security, privacy, and usability
requirements.

- **Security Goals.** We *trust* that the OS faithfully implements and enforces
  application transiency. We consider any other party that may tamper with
  the transient state of an application to be a *threat*.
- **Privacy Goals.** We enforce that applications are not capable of running
  unless they were explicitly opened by the user. This guarantees that applications cannot access personal information unless they are being used.
- **Usability Goals.** Enforcing transiency should be intuitive and seamless to
  the user. This guarantees user privacy when expected, without affecting user
  experience.

4 Application Transiency Implementation

We expand the sensitive resource access control policy of permissions to provide
an intuitive interface where users can control their privacy. We propose a new
authorization protocol, in which users grant/revoke applications the right to
execute by opening/closing them. We address the goals described in the previous
section in our implementation of application transiency. Figure 3 provides an
implementation overview.

4.1 Enforcing Transiency

To enforce transiency, the user must be the only one who can execute an application. Otherwise, a closed application may attempt to execute code that accesses
sensitive user data. We solve this problem by leveraging access control used by
the OS to protect files on Android. Specifically, we revoke read access to APKs
if they are not explicitly open (shown in Fig. 3, step 13). Once revoked, if the
ART unit attempts to read the APK for any other reason aside from user intent,
it will fail. Conversely, when a user opens an application, our implementation
will restore the read permission before the ART attempts to read the APK file,
as shown in Fig. 3, steps 1–6.

Transiency is implemented at the OS level, as a system library only accessible
to applications/processes with a system UID (which is 0). Transiency can be
realized in the form of a "private-mode" system launcher. The system launcher,
when running on private-mode, uses the "swipping off the Recents screen" event
as the cue to stop the application from running. A user could select "private-
mode" from the Settings app (which is where most users expect to find interfaces

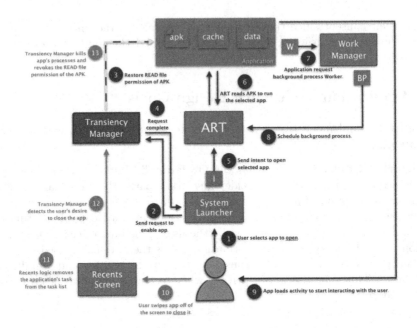

Fig. 3. An overview of the implementation of application transiency. Steps in blue, 1–9, correspond to the event of a user turning privacy off by opening the application. Steps in burgundy, 10–13, correspond to the event of a user turning privacy on by closing the application. **I** corresponds to the intent sent by the launcher to start an application, **W** corresponds to the Worker object specified by the application to perform a task in the background, and **BP** corresponds to a background process being scheduled by the Work Manager API for the requesting application [53]. In this diagram, we depict an application that, when opened by a user, requests a background process to perform some task and then loads the activity to interact with the user. Once the user is finished interacting with the application, they can close it by swiping it off the screen. Opening the application causes the Transiency Manager to restore the READ permission of the APK file to the system. Closing the application causes the Transiency Manager to revoke the READ permission to prevent execution. (Color figure online)

to change/enable/disable features, as pointed out by Lei et al.). In addition, malicious 3rd party applications cannot leverage the library functionality to perform attacks such as DoS (since each app is given a UID depending on the key used to sign the application, so only apps signed with manufacturer/system keys are given the UID 0).

This solution is efficient because revoking and restoring the read permission from the APK file causes a negligible overhead. In addition, enforcing transiency does not require a re-design of the system architecture to support it.

4.2 Making Transiency Intuitive

To meet the usability requirements defined in the previous section, we designed our implementation of transiency to meet user expectations of privacy. As pointed out by Oates et al. in 2018, for most users, regardless of demographics and technical experience, barriers are seen as the most common conceptual metaphor of privacy. Many related privacy with closing doors, locks, or curtains. This study served as an inspiration on our design to find a mapping from the mental models of what privacy means to users, to features in Android that can make this a reality.

Closing Doors. One of the common occurrences for most users was turning on privacy by closing a door or a curtain. Inspired by this, we equate closing an application to enabling privacy. Closing an application on Android refers to the action of selecting the "Recents" UI and swiping the application off of the screen [51, 52]. However, closing an application does not mean it is no longer running. Applications have the option to schedule background processes that will cause them to run again, unknown to the user. Therefore, the current application model does not meet the potential user expectations of privacy. For this reason, we chose the event of closing an application as the defining moment of turning on privacy. By closing the application, the user is guaranteed that the application will not run. This prevents applications from reading sensitive information when the user is not aware.

Opening Doors. Analogous to closing doors, we use opening doors to disable privacy. Android devices have a launcher application that is invoked when the "Home" button is pressed. This launcher application displays all installed and launchable applications on the system. A user can then touch one of the application icons to open it. Once an application is open, it can access sensitive information.

By enforcing transiency through opening and closing applications, we give the user an intuitive interface to better manage their privacy. This guides users towards a fair trade of sensitive information for application services.

4.3 Applying Transiency to Popular Applications

In this section, we analyze the behavior of popular applications when they are treated as transient and non-transient on the current Android architecture. We generalize these behaviors and define three main application functionalities that would require non-transiency.

Instagram is an application that displays user-generated content and allows users to communicate through comments and private messages. When treated as transient, Instagram no longer sends real-time notifications to the user. However, transiency does not prevent Instagram from displaying user-generated content. We therefore recommend that Instagram be treated as transient.

Subway Surfers is a game in which users can connect with other friends to form a network. When treated as transient, Subway Surfers no longer sends real-time notifications, but the user can still play the game as expected. Since transiency does not prevent the user from playing the game, we recommend that Subway Surfers be treated as transient.

Spotify offers users a music streaming platform. Treating Spotify as transient does not affect core functionality of the app. Therefore, we can recommend treating Spotify as transient.

Uber is a ride-sharing service app connecting riders with drivers. Treating Uber as transient does not affect the functionality of the app, since users can keep the application open for the duration of the ride. Therefore, we recommend treating Uber as transient.

While the user actively engages with the applications above, there exist other types of applications that passively interact with the user. We describe examples of those below:

Facebook Messenger is an app that enables users to communicate via phone calls, video calls and messages. When treated as transient, Facebook Messenger only notifies users in real-time when the app is open. However, keeping Facebook Messenger open at all times is not ideal for performance. Therefore, we recommend treating this application as non-transient.

Gmail provides an interface to read and send emails to other users. Gmail also loses the ability to notify the user in real-time when treated as transient. Therefore, we recommend treating Gmail as non-transient. Likewise, instant messaging applications have the same non-transiency requirements.

Step Counter gives a count of the approximate number of steps taken by the user. The app cannot use the sensors on the phone to constantly measure the amount of steps taken by the user in real-time unless the application is open. Therefore, we recommend treating the app as non-transient.

Clean Master offers users tools to clean files, a notification with a button to remove all other notifications, and other features such as taking a picture with the front-camera when the login passcode to unlock the screen is entered wrong. When treated as transient, this application cannot perform some of its core functionality, like taking pictures of the user that entered the wrong passcode, if the app is closed. We therefore recommend treating Clean Master as non-transient.

After analyzing these applications, we can generalize their behaviors to broadly describe non-transiency classification guidelines.

Recommended Classification Guidelines. Based on our analysis of the behavior of popular applications when they are treated as transient, we define three main functionalities to generalize when applications should not be treated as transient:

A. *The application provides real-time communication such as calling, messaging or receiving time-sensitive information.* This functionality enables real-time communication and exchange of information, such as Gmail. A user expects text messages to arrive at a reasonable time after the sender sent them, which requires the application to have real-time access to the network to retrieve messages intended for the user.

B. *The application requires real-time access to sensors to collect information and report it to the user.* This includes applications with functionality that depends on real-time information collected by device sensors, such as the Step Counter app. An application that reports the number of steps taken by the user depends on real-time information measured by device sensors. The user expects to see an accurate number of steps when they open the app, therefore the application cannot be transient.

C. *The application depends on real-time system state or other applications to provide its functionality.* Some applications may need to be aware of system events to function. For example, the Clean Master app.

While it is possible to analyze applications manually to determine their classification, it can be a time consuming task given that Google Play had a total of 2.6 million available applications in December 2018 [42]. We therefore explore methods to automate the process in the next section.

Automating Classification. To simplify the task of classifying apps, we explored using Google Play categories to recommend what applications should be transient and non-transient. To do this, we looked for categories on Google Play that would match the description of each of our A-C categories based on functionality. Below are our categories mapped to Google Play categories:

A - Communication: Applications in the Communication category depend on real-time delivery of content to the user. Some of these applications include WhatsApp and Facebook Messenger. Therefore, we mapped Communication to A.

B - Health & Fitness: Some applications in the Health & Fitness category depend on reading sensors that measure physical activities of a user, which makes this a non-transient category. An examples of these apps is Step Counter.

C - Tools: Applications in this category depend on real-time sensor and system information to report to the user. Analyzing current popular applications in the Tools category, we found that most applications were related to changing system settings, such as WiFi.

We selected three categories where each covered one of the three cases in which transiency would affect the primary functionality of an application. We evaluate the accuracy of this automated classification method by comparing it to the manual classification of the top 100 free apps on Google Play, which is described in Sect. 5.2.

4.4   Android Implementation: Transiency Launcher

To test our design, we develop a system launcher that implements application transiency.[1] We design the launcher to test the performance and usability of treating applications as transient on the current Android architecture. Figure 4 shows an overview of the architecture of this launcher.

UI. Our transiency launcher has a simple main activity that displays the list of installed and launchable applications on the system. Each entry on the list corresponds to an application, and the user can select an entry from the list to open the application selected. The launcher is invoked when the user presses the "Home" button.

Backend. Our launcher has a database that keeps track of the installed applications and their transient/non-transient classification. For testing purposes, we manually saved a list of names of applications treated as non-transient, which was decided following the criteria described in Sect. 4.3. When the user wants to open an application treated as transient, the launcher executes chmod through a shell to change the permissions of the application's APK to be readable by the system. The launcher then sends an intent to start the main activity of the selected application. If the user chooses to open a non-transient application,

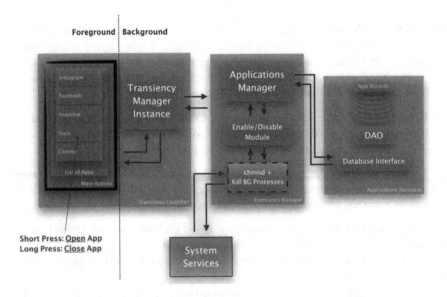

Fig. 4. Overview of the architecture of the transiency launcher. This launcher uses chmod to revoke/restore read permissions of the APK file to control when applications can collect user information. The Transiency Manager API can be used by our launcher to enable/disable the applications.

---

[1] Source code: https://github.com/rva5120/TransientLauncher.

the launcher sends the intent directly, as the APK permissions are not modified for non-transient applications. When the user long presses an entry to close an application, the launcher will execute chmod through a shell to change the permissions of the application's APK to no longer be readable by the system.

5 Evaluation

In this section, we will evaluate the classification and characterization of applications currently available on the market.

5.1 Characterization of Market Applications

We now evaluate the concept of application transiency by applying it to the top 100 free apps on Google Play. We analyzed these applications manually, and classified them according to the criteria defined in Sect. 4.3.

Classification Statistics. After manual classification, the top 100 free apps on Google Play (total of 105 apps) consisted of 88 transient and 17 non-transient, see Fig. 5.

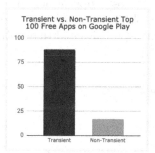

Fig. 5. Manual classification of transient/non-transient applications of the top 100 free apps on Google Play (total of 105 ranked apps), as of February 11th of 2019.

Characterization of Transient Applications. We find that over 50% of transient applications belong to the Games Google Play category, as shown in Fig. 6 (left). Our criteria led to all games being classified as transient. All games request the INTERNET permission, over 17% request the ACCESS_FINE_ LOCATION permission, and over 12% request the RECORD_AUDIO permission, see Fig. 7 (left). As we will see in Sect. 6, applications that request the INTERNET permission can also approximate the location of the device, therefore, most games can approximate location as well. By treating gaming applications as transient, we prevent them from recording audio in the background (if the device is running Android 8.0 and below) and collecting location data constantly when the user is not expecting it.

Transient applications in other categories also requested CAMERA and READ or WRITE_EXTERNAL_STORAGE permissions, which allows applications to take pictures in the background (for devices running Android 8.0 and below) and accessing pictures and other files. It is also worth noting that applications like Netflix and Facebook request the Activity Recognition permission. When these apps are not treated as transient, they can collect information about the user's physical activity. In addition, Facebook also requests the ACCESS_FINE_ LOCATION permission, which would allow the app to map certain routines such as commonly walked paths or commonly driven roads. However, if we treat apps like Facebook as transient, we can prevent the association of physical activity data with its corresponding user profile. Linking this kind of sensitive data together can pose physical dangers to users, as shown by [27].

Characterization of Non-transient Applications. During our analysis, we found that only 17 apps needed to be treated as non-transient. Out of the total 17, 5 belong to the Communication category (as shown in Fig. 6 (right)). This was not surprising, since applications in the Communication category are expected to need real-time access to network resources to allow users to communicate in real-time.

Non-transient applications also requested the INTERNET permission, and over 88% of them request READ and WRITE_EXTERNAL_STORAGE (see Fig. 7 (right)). We find that most applications also request ACCESS_FINE_ LOCATION and CAMERA. While these are expected based on the functionality provided by the applications, we also find that both Antivirus Free 2019 and

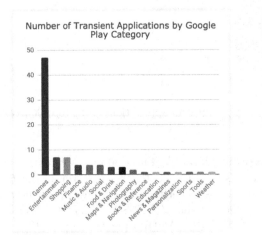
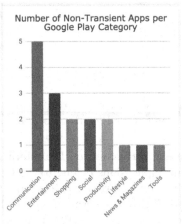

Fig. 6. Manual classification of applications grouped by Google Play category. Left: number of transient applications in each category, with Games being the category with the most transient apps with 47 (53.4% of all transient apps). Right: number of non-transient applications in each category, with Communications being the category with most non-transient apps with 5 (29.4% of all non-transient apps).

Super Cleaner requested access to the Activity Recognition API. This seems unusual, as a user may not expect for an antivirus application to need their physical activity to perform its functionality.

5.2 Classification Through Google Play Categories

Classifying apps using Google Play categories yields an accuracy of 88.57%, where 93 out of 105 apps were classified correctly compared to our manual classification. Our automatic classification method is less accurate when classifying applications that were manually labeled as non-transient. As expected, some applications place themselves under other categories. For example, TextNow, which enables communication among users, is categorized as Social. This may be caused by the fact that very popular applications like Facebook are in the Social category, so TextNow may be seen by more users and be more likely to get downloaded if it is in the Social category. However, since we label Social to be a transient category, communication apps that choose to be in the Social category will get misclassified and lose their non-transient privileges. Other communication apps, like Tinder, are also misclassified. Tinder is placed in the Dating category, which is expected since it enables communication between users with the purpose of dating.

Other examples of misclassified non-transient apps include IN Launcher, Bitmoji, Super Speed Cleaner and Antivirus Free 2019. Based on functionality, we would consider these apps to be Tools, which would grant them the privilege of

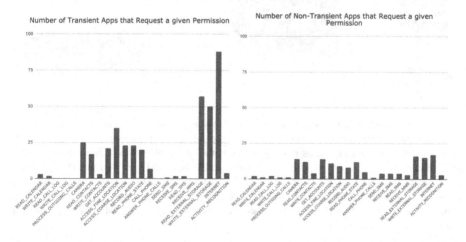

Fig. 7. Number of applications that request dangerous permissions, the INTERNET permission, and the Activity Recognition API permission of the top 100 free apps on Google Play. On the left, we see that all transient applications request the INTERNET permission, and over 25% of them request GPS location information. On the right, we see that all non-transient applications are likely to request INTERNET and location permissions as well.

being non-transient. However, they categorize themselves as Entertainment (for IN Launcher and Bitmoji) and Productivity (for Speed Cleaner and Antivirus Free 2019).

5.3 Implementation Performance

There is no visual delay when opening an application through a regular launcher vs our transiency launcher, which incurres an overhead of 0.02 ms. This performance overhead, which is added by the extra instructions executed to revoke/restore read permissions of the APK file, is negligible.

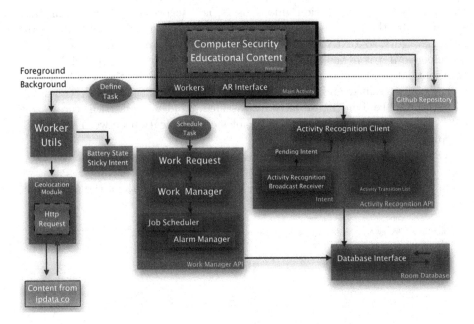

Fig. 8. Overview of the architecture of the Metis app. This app provides a user interface in which users can read weekly tutorials to learn about computer security. However, in the background, Metis is performing some data collection to learn more about your daily patterns, such as where you work, and when and how you get there. Metis only needs the INTERNET and ACTIVITY_RECOGNITION permissions, which are granted by default, to achieve its data collection goals. This makes Metis a good candidate to show that transiency is necessary to prevent apps from collecting data when users are not expecting it.

6   Case Study: Measuring Impact of Transiency on Data Collection

To show the kind of impact that treating applications as transient would have on sensitive data collection, we develop the Metis app. Figure 8 shows the overall architecture of Metis.[2]

6.1   Metis, the Knowledge Sharing App

Metis is an application that gives users a weekly article about computer security topics. The Metis UI is a simple webview object that displays the contents of a webpage hosted on a Github repository. The app displays a blog-style article with content to read. While looking like an innocent educational app in the foreground, Metis performs sensitive data collection in the background. The data collection strategy is inspired by the recent work of Chatterjee et al., in which they studied market applications that contribute to intimate partner violence. We focus on finding device resources that would reveal sensitive information without the user knowing or expecting it. We find that the INTERNET and the ACTIVITY_RECOGNITION permissions are good candidates for our purpose.

INTERNET. Metis, since it must request a webpage from Github to display its contents, needs to request the INTERNET permission. We find that we could *approximate the user's location by connecting to a geo-locating website*, such as Ipdata.co [40]. In addition to an approximate location, Ipdata.co reveals other potentially sensitive information: whether the user is on WiFi/cellular network, and the organization providing the IP. The figure below shows the information given by querying the API of Ipdata.co:

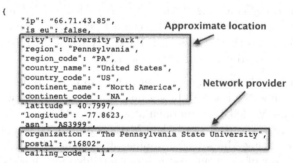

ACTIVITY_RECOGNITION. We use the approximate location information and combine it with the information available from the Activity Recognition API [49]. By requesting the normal ACTIVITY_RECOGNITION permission, we are able to setup Metis to *receive physical activity changes of the user*. For example, if the user starts walking or driving, Metis will receive a broadcast. This allows us to *recognize patterns of driving to and from work*, for example.

---

[2] Source code: https://github.com/rva5120/Metis_v2.

6.2   Data Collection: Transient vs. Non-transient

We compare the amount of data collected by Metis when it is treated as transient vs. non-transient.

Experiment. We run Metis on a rooted device with the transiency launcher described in Sect. 4.4 installed. We install two versions of Metis: Metis-T (treated as a transient application), and Metis-NT (treated as a non-transient application). We run this experiment for 1 day. Starting around 9 AM, we opened both applications. A few seconds later, we close both applications. Then, around 10:20 AM, we open both applications and leave them open. Below are the results captured until 12:30 PM by both apps.

Feb 26 2019
NA, NA 12:12:25–12:12:25 N/A NOT_CHARGING
State College, PA 12:24:35–12:24:35 The Pennsylvania State University NOT_CHARGING

Feb 26 2019
IN_VEHICLE 09:20:43–09:30:52
WALKING 09:30:52–09:30:52
STILL 09:50:06–09:50:06
WALKING 12:12:25–12:12:25
STILL 12:24:35–12:24:35

Feb 26 2019
Bellefonte, PA 10:23:45–12:27:53 The Pennsylvania State University NOT_CHARGING
Feb 26 2019
WALKING 12:11:27–12:11:27
STILL 12:14:39–10:27:53

Fig. 9. Results of running Metis-NT.   **Fig. 10.** Results of running Metis-T.

Metis-NT Results. The non-transient version of Metis is able to capture that we possibly commuted to work in the morning around 9:20 AM, which took around 10 min (see Fig. 9). It was detected that we walked for another 20 min, although during the experiment we walked for about 8 min. However, Metis-NT may not have received the "transition to STILL broadcast" until 9:50, so it records that we walked for longer than we actually did. Metis-NT also ran a background process around 12:24 PM where it recorded the geo-location received by Ipdata.co. In this case, Metis-NT detected that we were on a Pennsylvania State University network in University Park, PA which was the correct City, Region and University during our experiment.

Metis-T Results. Metis-T, on the other hand, is unable to detect the drive to work in the morning (see Fig. 10). It was only able to detect the walking activity around 12 because we left the app open after 10:20 AM.

Transiency has an impact over when Metis is able to collect sensitive information. By preventing Metis from running after being closed, we are able to preserve the privacy of an event that was not intended for Metis to detect. Also, transiency can have a major impact on protecting users by treating applications found by [27] as transient.

7   Discussion

By implementing transiency, we learn that most applications do not need the privilege of running constantly to provide their applications services. To prevent their execution while closed, we also explore the idea of installing and uninstalling applications. Installing an application every time the user opens it safely meets the privacy requirements, since the application is not able to execute code. However, it added too much overhead to the overall user experience. Also, uninstalling apps required users to interact with the application as if it was the first time they opened it. For example, a user would have to login every time they opened the app, which may cause an inconvenience. Therefore, we discarded this idea.

One of the main limitations of transiency for the current Android implementation is the inability to support notifications. In the future, it would be worth exploring what modifications can be made to the notifications API to be able to support transient notifications. Transient notifications would give applications the ability to ask the user for permission to run for a clearly specified purpose, implemented by a fine-grained API that does not allow the application to violate users' expectation of privacy.

We also observed that some applications already display a transient behavior. For example, Spotify will only play music while the application is open. If the user closes the application, music will stop playing. PrivateRide [6] is another example of an application that was re-designed to respect user privacy. These apps show that it is possible to design applications that provide useful functionalities without abusing privacy.

Lastly, we find that another benefit of transiency was addressing that users forget or find it inconvenient to delete unused applications [38]. If applications are treated as transient by default, users can rest assured that installing an application is not equivalent to giving it the privilege of running unconstrained.

8   Future Work

The classification of applications as either transient and non-transient provided was intended as a coarse approximation of the applications that could be treated as transient. In so doing, shed light in the likely impact of transiency on a real system. However, the system used by Google to categorize applications based on functionality is an imperfect medium to perform this analysis. As future work, we plan on incorporating the methods and findings of studies like AWare [7] and Turtle Guard [10] (which extensibly studied usability and contextual cues) to provide a more fine-grained classification methodology.

9   Conclusion

Throughout this paper, we explored the idea of enforcing transiency, which disables apps that were not explicitly opened by the user. Currently, Android applications can collect sensitive information even if they are not being used. Privacy is still an ongoing problem, which starts with the lack of control users have over the amount of information applications can collect. Transiency solves this issue intuitively, moving towards a fair trade of personal information in exchange for application services.

Acknowledgements. Thank you to Kim, Cookie, Bon Bon, and all the SIIS labers for the much needed support on my first paper journey. This material is based upon work supported by the National Science Foundation under Grant No. NS-1564105. Any opinions, findings, and conclusions or recommendations expressed in this material are those of the author(s) and do not necessarily reflect the views of the National Science Foundation.

References

1. Elenkov, N.: Android Security Internals. No Starch Press, San Francisco (2015)
2. Stamp, M.: Information Security Principles and Practice. Wiley, Hoboken (2011)
3. Jaeger, T.: Operating System Security. Morgan & Claypool Publishers, San Rafael (2008)
4. Nissenbaum, H.: Privacy as Contextual Integrity. Washington Law Review (2004)
5. Enck, W., et al.: TaintDroid: an information-flow tracking system for realt ime privacy monitoring on smartphones. In: OSDI (2010)
6. Pham, A., et al.: PrivateRide: a privacy-enhanced ride-hailing service. In: Proceedings of the 17th Privacy Enhancing Technologies Symposium (2018)
7. Petracca, G., et al.: AWare: preventing abuse of privacy-sensitive sensors via operation bindings. In: Proceedings of the 26th USENIX Security Symposium. USENIX Security (2017)
8. Narain, S., Noubir, G.: Mitigating location privacy attacks on mobile devices using dynamic app sandboxing. In: Procededings of the 19th Privacy Enhancing Technologies Symposium (PETS) (2019)
9. Zhou, Y., Zhang, X., Jiang, X., Freeh, V.W.: Taming information-stealing smartphone applications (on Android). In: McCune, J.M., Balacheff, B., Perrig, A., Sadeghi, A.-R., Sasse, A., Beres, Y. (eds.) Trust 2011. LNCS, vol. 6740, pp. 93–107. Springer, Heidelberg (2011). https://doi.org/10.1007/978-3-642-21599-5_7
10. Tsai, L., et al.: Turtle guard: helping Android users apply contextual privacy preferences. In: Proceedings of the 26th USENIX Security Symposium (2017)
11. Liu, B., et al.: Follow my recommendations: a personalized privacy assistant for mobile app permissions (2016)
12. Hornyack, P., Han, S., Jung, J., Schechter, S., Wetheral, D.: These aren't the droids you're looking for: retrofitting Android to protect data from imperious applications. In: CCS (2011)
13. Wijesekera, P., et al.: The feasibility of dynamically granted permissions: aligning mobile privacy with user preferences. In: NDSS (2017)
14. Votipka, D., Rabin, S.M., Micinski, K., Gilray, T., Mazurek, M.M., Foster, J.S.: User comfort with Android background resource accesses in different contexts. In: Proceedings of the 14th Symposium on Usable Privacy and Security (2018)
15. Egelman, S., Felt, A.P., Wagner, D.: Choice architecture and smartphone privacy: there's a price for that. In: Böhme, R. (ed.) The Economics of Information Security and Privacy, pp. 211–236. Springer, Heidelberg (2013). https://doi.org/10.1007/978-3-642-39498-0_10
16. Felt, A.P., Egelman, S., Wagner, D.: I've got 99 problems, but vibration ain't one: a survey of smartphone users' concerns. In: 2nd Annual ACM CCS Workshop on Security and Privacy in Smartphones and Mobile Devices (2012)
17. Felt, A.P., Ha, E., Egelman, S., Haney, A., Chin, E., Wagner, D.: Android permissions: user attention, comprehension, and behavior. In: Proceedings of the 8th Symposium on Usable Privacy and Security (SOUPS) (2012)

18. Bonné, B., Peddinti, S.T., Bilogrevic, I., Taft, N.: Exploring decision making with Android's runtime permission dialogs using in-context surveys. In: Proceedings of the 13th Symposium on Usable Privacy and Security (SOUPS) (2017)
19. Pu, Y., Grossklags, J.: Valuating friends' privacy: does anonymity of sharing personal data matter? In: Proceedings of the 13th Symposium on Usable Privacy and Security (SOUPS) (2017)
20. Tsai, J., Egelman, S., Cranor, L., Acquisti, A.: The effect of online privacy information on purchasing behavior: an experimental study. In: 6th Workshop on the Economics of Information Security (2007)
21. Samat, S., Acquisti, A.: Format vs. content: the impact of risk and presentation on disclosure decisions. In: Proceedings of the 13th Symposium on Usable Privacy and Security (SOUPS) (2017)
22. Rao, A., Schaub, F., Sadeh, N., Acquisti, A., Kang, R.: Expecting the unexpected: understanding mismatched privacy expectations online. In: Proceedings of the 12th Symposium on Usable Privacy and Security (SOUPS) (2016)
23. Oates, M., et al.: Turtles, locks, and bathrooms: understanding mental models of privacy through illustration. In: Proceedings of the 18th Privacy Enhancing Technologies Symposium (PETS) (2018)
24. Ismail, Q., Ahmed, T., Caine, K., Kapadia, A., Reiter, M.: To permit or not to permit, that is the usability question: crowdsourcing mobile apps' privacy permission settings. In: Proceedings of the 18th Privacy Enhancing Technologies Symposium (PETS) (2017)
25. Wijesekera, P., Baokar, A., Hosseini, A., Egelman, S., Wagner, D., Beznosov, K.: Android permissions remystified: a field study on contextual integrity. In: Proceedings of the 24th USENIX Security Symposium (2015)
26. Felt, A.P., Chin, E., Hanna, S., Song, D., Wagner, D.: Android permissions dymistified. In: CCS (2011)
27. Chatterjee, R., et al.: The spyware used in intimate partner violence. In: IEEE Symposium on Security and Privacy (2018)
28. Bowers, J., Reaves, B., Sherman, I.N., Traynor, P., Butler, K.: Regulators, mount up! analysis of privacy policies for mobile money services. In: Proceedings of the 13th Symposium on Usable Privacy and Security (SOUPS) (2017)
29. Das, A., Borisov, N., Chou, E.: Every move you make: exploring practical issues in smartphone motion sensor fingerprinting and countermeasures. In: Proceedings of the 18th Privacy Enhancing Technologies Symposium (PETS) (2018)
30. Reyes, I., et al.: Won't somebody think of the children? examining COPPA compliance at scale. In: Proceedings of the 18th Privacy Enhancing Technologies Symposium (2018)
31. Venkatadri, G., Lucherini, E., Sapiezynski, P., Mislove, A.: Investigating sources of PII used in Facebook's targeted advertising. In: Proceedings of the 19th Privacy Enhancing Technologies Symposium (2019)
32. Foppe, L., Martin, J., Mayberry, T., Rye, E.C., Brown, L.: Exploiting TLS client authentication for widespread user tracking (2018)
33. Bashir, M.A., Wilson, C.: Diffusion of user tracking data in the online advertising ecosystem. In: Proceedings of the 18th Privacy Enhancing Technologies Symposium (2018)
34. Lifshits, P., et al.: Power to peep-all: inference attacks by malicious batteries on mobile devices. In: Proceedings of the 18th Privacy Enhancing Technologies Symposium (2018)

35. Eskandari, M., Ahmad, M., Oliveira, A.S., Crispo, B.: Analyzing remote server locations for personal data transfers in mobile apps. In: Proceedings of the 17th Privacy Enhancing Technologies Symposium (2017)
36. Brookman, J., Rouge, P., Alva, A., Yeung, C.: Cross-device tracking: measurement and disclosures. In: Proceedings of the 17th Privacy Enhancing Technologies Symposium (2017)
37. Zhou, X., et al.: Identity, location. inferring your secrets from Android public resources. In: CCS, Disease and More (2013)
38. Park, H., Eun, J., Lee, J.: Why do smartphone users hesitate to delete unused apps? In: MobileHCI (2018)
39. Senate: Testimony of Mark Zuckerberg. https://www.judiciary.senate.gov/imo/media/doc/04-10-18%20Zuckerberg%20Testimony.pdf. Accessed Feb 2019
40. https://ipdata.co/ . Accessed Feb 2019
41. Statista: Distribution of free and paid Android apps (2019). https://www.statista.com/statistics/266211/distribution-of-free-and-paid-android-apps/
42. Statista: Number of Available Applications in the Google Play Store (2019). https://www.statista.com/statistics/266210/number-of-available-applications-in-the-google-play-store/
43. Statista: Number of Paying Spotify Subscribers. https://www.statista.com/statistics/244995/number-of-paying-spotify-subscribers/
44. Google (2019). https://developer.android.com/
45. Google (2019). https://developer.android.com/guide/components/fundamentals
46. Google (2019). https://source.android.com/
47. Google: Codelabs (2019). https://codelabs.developers.google.com/
48. Google: Android Open Source Code (2019). https://source.android.com/
49. Google: Activity Recognition API (2019). https://developers.google.com/location-context/activity-recognition/
50. IPData.co (2019). https://ipdata.co/
51. Google: Google Answers. https://support.google.com/android/answer/9079646?hl=en. Accessed Feb 2019
52. Google: The Recents UI (2019). https://developer.android.com/guide/components/activities/recents
53. Google: Work Manager API (2019). https://developer.android.com/reference/androidx/work/WorkManager
54. Google: Android 9.0 Behavior Changes (2019). https://developer.android.com/about/versions/pie/android-9.0-changes-all

CustomPro: Network Protocol Customization Through Cross-Host Feature Analysis

Yurong Chen$^{(\boxtimes)}$, Tian Lan, and Guru Venkataramani

George Washington University, Washington, USA
{gabrielchen,tlan,guruv}@gwu.edu

Abstract. The implementations of network protocols are often "bloated" due to various users' needs and complex environment for deployment. The continual expansion of program features contribute to not only growing complexity but also increased the attack surface, making the maintenance of network protocol security very challenging. Existing works try to mitigate program bloat by source-code level static analysis (such as tainting and slicing) or dynamic techniques such as binary reuse. While source code is not always available for the former technique, the latter suffers from limited code coverage because of the incomplete input space. In this paper, we propose CustomPro, a new approach for automated customization of network protocols. We adopt whole system emulation, dynamic tainting and symbolic execution to identify desired code from the original program binaries, then leverage binary rewriting techniques to create a customized program binary that only contains the desired functionalities. We implement a prototype of CustomPro and evaluate its feasibility using OpenSSL (a widely used SSL implementation) and Mosquitto (an IoT messaging protocol implementation). The results show that CustomPro is able to create functional program binaries with only desired features and significantly reduce the potential attack surface by targeting and eliminating unwanted protocol features.

Keywords: Program customization · Binary rewriting · Cross-host tainting

1 Introduction

Recently, network protocols have frequently become targets of cyber attacks. Even protocols that are carefully designed to enhance the security of communications (such as OpenSSL) can be exploited and leveraged, posing severe threats (such as information leakage and DoS attacks) to online users [2,11]. Network protocols are vulnerable due to a number of reasons: (a) The users' requirements of network hosts are typically various. In order to satisfy such requirements,

© ICST Institute for Computer Sciences, Social Informatics and Telecommunications Engineering 2019
Published by Springer Nature Switzerland AG 2019. All Rights Reserved
S. Chen et al. (Eds.): SecureComm 2019, LNICST 305, pp. 67–85, 2019.
https://doi.org/10.1007/978-3-030-37231-6_4

network protocol designs contain complex logic/checking and more-than-enough features. Furthermore, the changing environment also leads to continuous expansion of the existing program code base, known as the feature creep problem [20]. (b) Even standardized protocols may have a variety of different implementations and specifications, in accordance with heterogeneous system/user requirements (especially in IoT systems). Such inconsistency weighs on the feature creep issue and makes the management of protocol implementations much more difficult and the network connections prone to attacks. Feature creep has caused real-world problems. The protocol Simple Network Management Protocol (SNMP) contains the trap communication feature and the OpenSSL contains heartbeat. Both features have low utilization and could be removed without affecting the major functionalities. Unfortunately, they are included in the program and cause serious security threats such as denial of service attack and leakage of sensitive information.

Debloaing, a technique that removes undesired part from the code base to generate a customized program, has been proposed to mitigate the issue of feature creep. Some debloating techniques work only with source code, by performing static analysis such as tainting and slicing [19,20] to identify and eliminate unnecessary code. However, source code is not always available to users. Static analysis such as identifying function bodies in the program binaries could be extremely difficult and inaccurate [1]. On the other hand, other works that can produce customized program directly from the original program binaries, through dynamic binary reusing techniques. The downside of dynamic binary reuse is that it can only "mimic" a limited portion of the desired functionalities in the original program, because of the incomplete input feeding [3,23,35,46,47].

In this paper, we propose a new approach, CustomPro, for automated customization of network protocols, which is to discovering and rewriting network protocol functionalities/features from program binaries based on users' needs. CustomPro is able to trim the original program to a customized version that only contain desired components, thus greatly reducing the attack surface and chances of future exploitation. We define a program *feature* as a collection of basic blocks, which uniquely represent an independent, well-contained capability of the program. CustomPro consists in feature identification and rewriting modules. The key steps of feature identification in CustomPro are as follows. (1) We utilize whole system emulation to monitor and dump the needed information about protocol program execution, such as executed instructions, processor states and memory layout. (2) Packet tainting is used to mark the packets as taint source to identify different features. The intuition here is that different functionalities in the protocols are typically associated with and triggered by packets. Furthermore, since packets are transmitted across multiple hosts, we also propagate the taint across hosts to track the information flow and program executions [31,45]. (3) Since dynamic tainting depends on the given inputs, it may not be able to achieve high code coverage, thus can only identify limited portion of protocol features. To this end, *we combine tainting and symbolic execution to compensate for the incompleteness of dynamic analysis.* Symbolic execution will help discover more code relevant to the target features, while the tainting module can

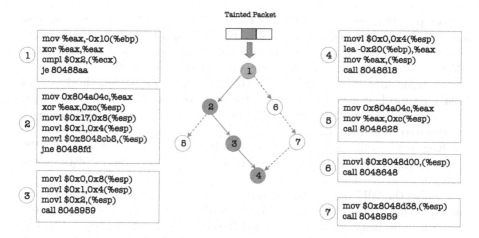

Fig. 1. Feature identification by combining tainting and symbolic execution

give hints to the symbolic execution engine to only explore "valuable" branches and avoid path explosion.

The feature rewriting module takes the output of feature identification module to perform binary rewriting, then produces a customized program binary. The undesired basic blocks are replaced with NOP instructions and Custom-Pro also takes care of the calling instructions to redirect such function calls, forcing the program to exit once the undesired features are executed. We apply CustomPro to popular protocol implementations such as OpenSSL and MQTT to remove the insecure features such as *heartbeat* (in OpenSSL) and *will* (in MQTT).

This work makes the following major contributions:

- We propose an automated framework CustomPro, that can customize network protocol implementations with only program binaries. Given the user's need, CustomPro produces a customized version of the original program to eliminate unnecessary code while keeping the desired features functional.
- We propose a feature identification mechanism that utilizes dynamic cross-host tainting and guided symbolic execution. The tainting information helps to identify relevant code and provide guidance to symbolic execution to avoid redundant path exploration.
- We evaluate CustomPro using popular protocol implementations such as OpenSSL and Mosquitto. The experimental results show that CustomPro is able to effectively customize software binaries, producing light-weight program binaries that eliminate potential vulnerabilities.

2   Motivation

The attacks against network systems through the vulnerabilties in protocols have never ceased and are often followed by severe consequences. *Heartbleed* [11] exposes private information such as server private keys to the Internet through a simple *Heartbeat* feature in OpenSSL. Nearly half a million certificates were exposed and over 199,500 sites are still vulnerable as of the time Jan. 2017, which is over three years after the bug was reported [21]. KRACK [36], or key reinstallation attack, a replay attack that leverages the vulnerable design in WAP2 protocol, can be exploited to gradually obtain the full keychain used for encrypting the traffic under a WIFI environment. The handshake messages are replayed by MITM (Man In The Middle) such that the end node will be deceived to reinstall the key that is already in use. The same key value will be used repeatedly for encryption, resulting in repeated occurrences of the same message.

Finally, the 2017 data breach on credit reporting agency Equifax had 146.6 million people expose their names and dates of birth, and 145.5 of those expose their Social Security Numbers and/or driver's license numbers, across US, UK and Canada [13]. The attack was believed to exploit the CVE-2017-5638, which is a flaw in the Apache Strut framework. This vulnerability was discovered and reported more than two months before the data breach happened.

The key takeaways from these attacks are as follows:

- Network Protocols are a critical link in the chain of network security.
- Patching solutions can't keep up. Patches can come late while the exploits have already led to large-scale disaster. Even after a patch is released, there is no guarantee that all vulnerable entities in the network will apply the patch soon enough, leaving some of them vulnerable for a longer time.
- Hardening the security of network protocols is very different from that of single-host and offline software systems, since protocols often contain a significant amount of features and operate in a fully distributed environment. Any effective solution must harden all of the entities collectively along with their corresponding binary code modules.

Software customization, an approach to extract desired parts and/or remove undesired ones from a target program, has been applied to reduce the attack surface and improve program security [19,20]. In this paper, we leverage customization to (1) remove wanted program features to reduce attack surface (or the risk of being attacked), e.g., protect the program from zero-day exploits; and (2) prevent the network from being exploited via known vulnerabilities before patches becomes available. However, previous customization techniques often remove unused functions from program source code, which is not always available especially for COTS and legacy programs. To this end, CustomPro develops protocol customization that only requires only program binary for customization. Moreover, in practice it is often hard (if possible at all) to identify all functions/code related to target protocol features from only several seed functions [20]. Network protocols such as SSL handshake often implement complex state machines where different states are convoluted together and even spread across different hosts, linked by only network packets. In CustomPro, we utilize a cross-host, dynamic tainting technique to track exchanged packets and trace program executions, in order to discover the code segments related to target protocol features. CustomPro rewrites the static binary based on the user needs. It further applies symbolic execution to identify any additional code belonging to the target features that were not captured during dynamic analysis.

We utilize the example shown in Fig. 1 to illustrate our key idea. The feature identification starts from a tainted packet or tainted fields in a packet. The taint will propagate through basic blocks of the binary code. In this example, there are two features F_a and F_b, starting from node 2 and 6 respectively. Suppose that a user wants to keep feature F_a and remove F_b. The basic blocks represented by shaded nodes (1,2,3,4) are tainted in the current execution path, i.e., $1 \rightarrow 2 \rightarrow 3 \rightarrow 4$, discovering code blocks (1,2,3,4).

However, another execution path $1 \rightarrow 2 \rightarrow 5$ also belonging to F_a has not been identified due to limited coverage of dynamic analysis. Hence, we perform symbolic execution starting from the node 2 to explore the possibility of any other execution paths of F_a, which eventually leads to discovery node 5.

Assumptions and Scope: We assume that the packet format of a target protocol is known beforehand and the feature-related fields can be identified. In practice, packet formats can always be identified either through protocol specifications or using reverse engineering techniques described in prior work [4,8,9,25]. We also assume that some (limited number of) test inputs are provided to trigger the target features and serve as starting point for our analysis. These inputs can be easily obtained from system tracing, packet sniffing, and/or fuzzing. The scope of this work is to customize a given implementation of network protocols with only access to program binaries.

3   System Overview

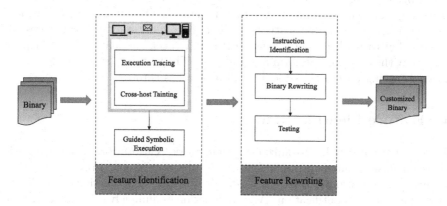

Fig. 2. CustomPro system diagram

We formally define protocol features and problem statement as follows:

Feature: A program feature is defined as a set of basic blocks – denoted by $F_i = \{f_i^1, f_i^2, ..., f_i^n\} \subseteq \mathcal{F}$ – which uniquely represent an independent, well-contained operation, utility, or capability of the program. A feature at the binary level may not always correspond to a software module at the source level. We use $\mathcal{T} = \{F_i, \forall i\}$ to denote the set of all available features in the program.

Problem Statement: The goal of CustomPro is that, for a given program binary and test cases invoking different program features, and user's customization requirement (i.e., a set of desire features $\hat{\mathcal{T}} \subseteq \mathcal{T}$), it will produce a modified binary that contains the minimum set of basic blocks/functions to satisfy the user's customization requirement and to support all desired features in $\hat{\mathcal{T}}$.

The design of CustomPro is depicted in Fig. 2. The requirement for customization is provided by users (which features to keep and which to remove). The feature identification module will take such requirement as well as the program binary to identify relevant code, after which the feature rewriting part modifies the original program binary based in the result of feature identification.

The feature identification module is explained in Sect. 4. Through program tracing, cross-host tainting and guided symbolic execution(**GSE**), CustomPro is able to find the program instructions that are necessary to perform the desired features. The discovered instructions can come from two sources: 1. Execution tracing and tainting form the basis of feature identification, in which executed program instructions are logged and those related to target features are tainted. 2. With the information above, GSE performs a light-weight search for additional code blocks that are also related to the target feature but not executed in the test runs. The feature identification module then combines and passes the collectively identified instructions (that are related to the target features) to the feature rewriting module.

Section 5 explains the details of feature rewriting module. The original program binary is modified according to the user's requirement. In order to verify the soundness of the customized program, program fuzzing is performed after rewriting. Fuzzing can check if the undesired features are indeed removed and also verify that the remaining features are functional. Once unexpected behaviors happen, i.e., the undesired features are not thoroughly removed or the desired features fail to work properly, CustomPro will check the feature identification part to fix the error and perform rewrite again. The feature identification/rewriting and fuzzing form a closed loop until no error is thrown.

4   Feature Identification

As a feature-oriented customization framework, CustomPro discovers basic blocks that are related to target features in program binary. Previous work for feature customization [20] requires users to provide seed functions in order to start the feature identification. A seed function is uniquely associated with a certain feature, and is used to bootstrap the program analysis such as tainting and slicing, in order to identify code that is related to the target feature. However, it is difficult for users to gain knowledge about the seed functions especially when the program source code is not available. CustomPro instead associate protocol features with network packets, and let users to choose the target network services/functionalities to start the feature identification. In particular, CustomPro's feature identification module performs program execution tracing, cross-host tainting and symbolic execution to discover the relationships between features and their corresponding code.

4.1 Execution Tracing

CustomPro starts with test inputs that trigger the target features, during which all code related to the target features are captured and identified dynamically. To this end, we employ dynamic program analysis to discover the code and other runtime information related to the target features. We run the program inside a whole system emulator-TEMU [44], where the instructions get executed will be logged and tainted instructions are labeled. The taint propagation mechanism will identify all code related to certain packets/fields. In fact, during the program execution, other runtime information such as operand values and CPU register values are also inspected and logged. These values are used later for a symbolic execution as described in Sect. 4.3.

Network protocols typically involve executions on multiple network entities with different roles, such as servers and clients. We execute all relevant entities on the guest OS inside TEMU, and implement a cross-host tainting mechanism to propagate taints between multiple entities. As will be described in Sect. 4.2, we piggyback taint information onto existing network packet, which requires the modification of both sender and receiver entities.

4.2 Cross-Host Packet Tainting

Not all of the logged instructions are related to the target features. One intuitive approach to identify relevant instructions is tainting. However, whole-packet-level tainting may fail to achieve the granularity needed to extract the code of the target feature. For example, in *ClientHello* message of SSL protocol, there could be undesired extensions such as *HeartBeats* along with other necessary fields. If the customization requirement is to remove heartbeat feature, packet-level tainting cannot distinguish *HeartBeats* from other features embeded in the same packet.

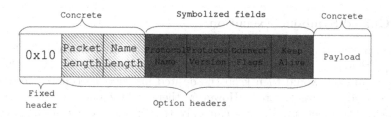

Fig. 3. Field symbolization in tainted fields

In CustomPro, we apply muti-tag, field-level tainting to label instructions according to the features they belong to. In particular, we classify tainted instructions into two sets: (1) $\mathcal{K}$: code related to desired features and will be kept in the customized binary and (2) $\mathcal{R}$: code related to undesired features and will be removed after customization. Note that untainted code will not be removed from the original binary since they are related to program initialization or state transitions. In addition, the instructions in $\mathcal{K}$ and $\mathcal{R}$ will be utilized during partial symbolic execution to identify any missing code blacks. The details will be explained in Sect. 4.3.

The tainting engine in TEMU maintains the taint tags in shadow memory. In our case, the shadow memory will track the taint status of every byte in NIC buffer. When the taint source and tag are specified at the packet (i.e., which fields are tainted and which tag each field gets), the corresponding memory location is tainted. The taint then will be propagated along with data flow such as read, DMA (Direct Memory Access), table lookups and arithmetic operations. By default, TEMU will taint the whole packet if it satifies the user-defined filters such as TCP packet and UDP packet. For a finer-grained tainting, we instrument the tainting engine in TEMU to enable field tainting on packets. The target fields are identified through their offsets in the packets.

In order to track the data flow across different hosts, CustomPro also implement a cross-host tainting mechanism [45] to transmit taint information in the network. This is essential for protocols that contain state machines on both server and client sides. Take SSL handshake process as an example, when the server is listening to incoming connections, it stays at a state ready to read *ClientHello*. After the *ClientHello* message is received and processed, the server will go into another state such as replying *ServerHello*, renegotiation or error state depending on the result of processing *ClientHello*. Suppose a *ServerHello* is sent to the server side, the client will change its state to reading the *ServerHello*. Such iterations extend the scope of data flow from one individual host to multiple hosts across the network, while the status of one execution depends on the executions on all other hosts in the protocol. To enable cross-host tainting, we piggyback taint information onto each packet flight. The taint information contains an offset table that indicates which bytes in the current packet are tainted and which labels are used to taint them, allowing the taints to be extracted and processed at the recipient.

4.3   Guided Symbolic Execution

By utilizing tainting, CustomPro now can map each instruction to its feature, on all participating entities of the protocol. To customize the binary, a straightforward approach would then keep the desired instructions (related to desired features) and remove the rest. However, there is still one limitation to this approach: The given test inputs can only trigger specific execution paths in the binary code, which may not provide a full coverage of the target feature execution.

To this end, after tracing and tainting, we take the execution traces and tainting information as the input to perform guided symbolic execution (**GSE**), in order to discover any additional code blocks that are related to the target features/fields. Symbolic execution is usually resource-consuming in terms of memory and CPU circles. To trim the searching space of symbolic execution, we (i) leverage the tainting results as well as the runtime information from execution tracing, to limit the number of locations that require symbolic execution and (ii) infer conditions from execution logs to further concretize certain variables as well as to limit the value ranges of certain symbolized fields. In particular, our solution is summarized as follows. (a) We leverage GSE to symbolize only the variables (i.e., registers and memory locations) that are tainted during execution and belong to the set $\mathcal{K}$ as mentioned in 4.2, because the operands of tainted instructions in set $\mathcal{K}$ contain or point to variables that are related to the desired packet fields. (b) During monitored execution, we take snapshots of the system states, e.g., when tainting starts (such as when the first tainted byte in the NIC is accessed by the program). This will dump the value of registers and process memory layout. The value of variables that we are not interested in will be passed into GSE to concretize as variables as possible. (c) Available packet format information may further limited the range of certain variables, in which case we can apply such conditions to reduce the search space of those symbolic variables. In particular, as shown in Fig. 3 (assume that this is a tainted packet), we only symbolize part of the header fields and skip the payload. The fields marked by dark gray will be symbolized while the unshaded fields will keep their concrete values. The hatched area are concrete fields that can help limit the range of symbolized fields. For example, the packet length fields can help set boundaries for the total length of other symbolized fields. Given other specifications of the protocol (such as the min/max/enum value of certain fields), we can further trim the searching space of GSE to accelerate the code exploration.

While dynamic tracing can precisely locate the basic blocks that get executed, it is easy to see that through one iteration of tracing and tainting, we can only identify the code blocks that process specific network packets and belong to only one execution path of the target feature. There are potentially other execution paths and branches that are also related to the same type of operation but not taken in particular runs. On the other hand, symbolic execution can be employed to explore more paths/branches, providing better code coverage . However, without properly trimming the searching space, it is often faced with a path explosion problem and could easily incur prohibitive overhead in practice. This can be illustrated by reusing the example in Fig. 1. At node 1, the format of packet is checked and either feature F_a or F_b will be invoked. Without symbolic execution, only one single path $(1 \rightarrow 2 \rightarrow 3 \rightarrow 4)$ is considered as the code related to F_a. After customization, the new binary containing only the identified execution path will not be able to process any packet inputs that will lead to node 5. And if symbolic execution is applied without the tainting information, it will start exploration from node 1 and try to symbolically execute all possible paths from there. Significant CPU and memory resources can be required to explore redundant paths such as $1 \rightarrow 6 \rightarrow 7 \rightarrow 4$. Hence, we combine tainting and symbolic execution in CustomPro, by leveraging the tainted variables (such as registers and memory locations) from instruction tracing to guide symbolic execution. We will fix the value in the packet that indicates the feature F_a and symbolize other relevant fields, to explore the code only belonging to feature F_a.

If the input to feature identification contains multiple types of packets that cannot be executed during one execution, CustomPro will process the packet individually, then merge the basic blocks discovered from each iteration. Finally, CustomPro combines the addresses obtained from execution tracing, tainting and GSE to identify a set of instructions that should be kept during binary rewriting. All the basic blocks from 1 to 5 in Fig. 1 can be discovered by feature identification module, and will be kept in the customized program binary.

5   Feature Rewriting

Feature rewriting consists of three main steps: instruction identification, binary rewriting and verification, as explained in this section.

5.1   Instruction Identification

The static binary rewriting needs the information of instruction addresses in order to identify the target basic blocks. CustomPro locates the static instructions based on their offsets from the entry point. The offsets are pre-calculated from the runtime instruction traces, by subtract the runtime entry point address from the actual runtime addresses of target instructions.

To increase the coverage of the identified code, CustomPro cumulatively perform code discovering for different inputs, then get the union of all the target code. The intuition here is that limited execution traces may not reach all branches related to the target features. Let $\hat{\mathcal{F}}$ be a set of target program features for rewriting. If the constituent basic blocks of each feature $F_i \in \hat{\mathcal{F}}$ can be successfully identified, we can simply create a superset of their constituent basic blocks, i.e., $\hat{F} = \cup F_i$. Binary rewriting techniques are developed next to create a customized program by retaining only the features in $\hat{F}$.

5.2   Binary Rewriting

CustomPro implements a static binary rewriting module using DynInst. In particular, it utilizes the PatchAPI in DynInst to modify program binaries in basic block level based on the CFG analysis. Binary rewriting in CustomPro contains two parts:

- In order to prevent the basic blocks being called, CustomPro change the calling instructions to redirect the call, such that once the call site is reached, the program will exit.

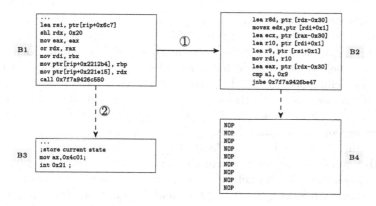

Fig. 4. An illustrative example of implementing feature rewriting on OpenSSL.

- To prevent the unwanted basic blocks from being executed through malicious operations such as Return-Oriented Programming (ROP), CustomPro replaces the such basic blocks with "NOP" (except for the shared code and data segments).

The solution is illustrated in Fig. 4. The original control flow is from basic block B_1 to B_2 via a "call" instruction as arrow 1 indicates. If B_2 is the target to be removed, CustomPro will change the call site in B_1 and redirect it to B_3(an exit point) as Arrow 2 indicates. In addition to the instrumentation of control flow, CustomPro will also replace B_2 with "NOP"s to prevent invoking the removed features (and feature-related blocks) at runtime, e.g., through ROP [30].

5.3   Verification

After the customized binary is generated, CustomPro contains a fuzzing engine to verify the correctness and soundness of customization. The fuzzing engine will generate inputs by categories, i.e., inputs that trigger desired or undesired features. In particular, the set $\mathcal{D}$ denotes benign inputs that invoke the desired features in customized program, and $\mathcal{E}$ denotes the vulnerable inputs that involve at least one of the eliminated features. If a benign input causes a crash, we will perform feature identification using this input and find out the necessary instructions to be added to the customized binary. On the other hand, if the vulnerable input fail to cause a program exit, we'll further examine the execution trace and add control flow redirection at proper locations. The verification process and above-mentioned feature identification/modification are performed iteratively to improve the correctness of program customization.

6   Implementation

We implement a prototype of CustomPro and describe the some core components here.

The cross-host tainting module is implemented in the system emulator. (1) By default, the whole-system emulator TEMU only supports single-host whole packet tainting. CustomPro enhances the tainting module to enable finer-grained tainting, i.e., field tainting, such that CustomPro can trace the code that is only related to specific packet fields. In particular, we modify the plugin of TEMU, "tracecap" to taint packet by the offsets of target field. (2) Also, we instrument syscalls such as $open(), read(), write(), connect(), recv() and send()$, so that the taint information can be passed among multiple hosts.

Later, the binary analysis tool Angr [32] is used to perform symbolic execution with the help of the taint information. The start location of symbolic execution is where the filed/packet get first tainted, and the termination point of symbolic execution is set to be the end of "main()" function. The tainting information helps Angr avoids irrelevant execution paths, but focus on the variables that are tainted. We utilize "ins_addr" member in "history.actions" to dump the instructions explored by Angr, then combine them with the instructions that are identified by tainting.

DynInst is used to perform static binary rewriting. The PatchAPI removed functions/basic blocks by replacing them with NOPs, and remove them from CFG list. We also replace the function calling instructions with program exit.

7   Evaluation

In this section, we evaluate the effect of feature customization on two real-world protocol implementations: OpenSSL and Mosquitto. We choose four features from OpenSSL, namely, *heartbeat, client certificate request, renegotiation, encrypt-then-MAC(ETM)*. Since the handshake of SSL protocol is a state machine-based process, and each feature involves the implementation on both client and server, we customize both sides of OpenSSL to eliminate each one of the four target features at one time. Mosquitto implements the MQTT protocol (an IoT messaging protocol) which involves three different entities in a message iteration: broker, publisher and subscriber. After the subscriber sign up for a certain topic, the publisher sends message related to that topic to the subscriber. The broker serves as a middle man and receives all message updates from the publisher then decides which subscribers the messages should be sent to, with respect to the message topics. We choose three features from mosquitto broker and publisher to build different customized versions of the protocol.

Experiment Setup: Our experiments are conducted on a 2.80 GHz Intel Xeon(R) CPU E5-2680 20-core server with 16 GB of main memory. The operating system is Ubuntu 14.04 LTS. To evaluate the feature customization on OpenSSL and Mosquitto, we first run the default program to get the number of runtime and static instructions with all target features included. The runtime instructions include all instructions that get executed, excluding dynamic library functions such as glibc code. We further filter out the library code based on the runtime addresses of instructions and mapping information from the */proc/PID/maps*. It is obvious that runtime instructions contain duplicated instructions, as the same basic block in the program binary can be executed multiple times. Hence, we also collect the number of (unique) instructions in the static program binary that are executed during runtime.

7.1   Customizing OpenSSL

OpenSSL is an open-source software that implements SSL/TLS protocols. We use OpenSSL version 1.0.1 for evaluation (the latest version still containing the *Heartbleed* bug). We first collect the number of runtime and static instructions from the default program by running the default *s_server* and *s_client*. Our experiments show that server executes 130212 runtime instructions and 111595 static instructions, while the client side executes 124151 runtime instructions and 111123 static instructions. We remove one of the four target features one-at-a-time to analyze how many instructions are involved in each feature.

HeartBeat: It is one of the well-known bugs in OpenSSL is CVE-2014-0160, namely, *Heartbleed*, which could be exploited by adversaries to steal sensitive data from the SSL server. Heartbleed is rooted in the feature *HeartBeat* in SSL, an extension designed to make sure that each end of the communication is still alive by sending a number of data and expecting the same message being echoed back. However, the receiver of the heartbeat request, rather than checking the actual size of the *HeartBeat* payload, simply allocates a memory buffer with the size declared in the length field of the received packet. If a *HeartBeat* request message is shorter than the claimed value, then extra content will be sent back (up to 64 KB) and revealed, containing sensitive memory content from the server. The *HeartBeat* feature can be automatically removed using CustomPro to produce customized program binaries that cannot generate or process *HeartBeat* packets, while other features are still intact. In practice, this provides system administrators with a swift, automatically-generated fix through program customization, without the need or time-overhead to perform full system analyze and patch construction. Our experiments show that 658 static instructions are removed from server and 636 instructions are removed from client.

ETM: Similar to heartbeat, the feature encrypt-then-mac (**ETM**) is also an extension in the process of handshake. After encrypting the plaintext, a MAC(message authentication code) of the ciphertext is calculated and appended to the end of ciphertext. The ETM helps to verify the integrity of the cipher-text. A bug related to ETM has been reported in CVE-2017-3733, where the program will crash if the ETM is defined in the process of renegotiation while it is not in the original handshake (or vice-versa). CustomPro can eliminate such vulnerability by removing the ETM feature from both client (793 instructions removed) and server sides (643 instructions removed) in an automated fashion.

Renegotiation: An interesting case in our study of customizing OpenSSL is about the feature renegotiation. Renegotiation is a feature that enables the connection to change some parameters without establishing a new SSL session so as to save resources. The vulnerabilities about renegotiation reported in CVE database (such as CVE-2009-3555 and CVE-2015-0291) cause the MIIT attack

Table 1. Number of instructions remaining in OpenSSL by removing different features

Removed feature	# Inst remaining in server		# Inst remaining in client	
	Dynamic	Static	Dynamic	Static
HeartBeat	128953	110937	111123	110487
ClientCertificate	121167	103214	107341	95025
Encrypt-then-MAC	128651	110952	122541	110330
Renegotiation	128953	110937	111123	105487

and DoS. However, as CustomPro taint and discover target instructions through the packets/fields, we cannot distinguish the feature renegotiation since the renegotiation request will basically result in another handshake (initialized by a hello request). As shown in Table 1, the customized version of either client or server is the same as the original one.

7.2   Customizing MQTT

Message Queuing Telemetry Transport (MQTT) is a protocol using a certain topic to subscribe and publish message which is always used in internet of things (IOT). There are three entities in MQTT communications, e.g., broker, publisher and subscriber. The subscriber signs up for a topic via broker, in order to receive messages published by publisher (and through the broker). The MQTT packets contain three fields that include *fix header, variable length header*, and *payload*. The fix header consists of control header and packet length. The variable length header is used when some extra program features are enabled. In this paper, we perform feature customization on Mosquitto ver 1.5.

Table 2. Number of instructions in Mosquitto after removing unwanted features

# Inst	Removed features		
	Publisher: insecure	Publisher: publishing file	Broker: loading config
Dynamic	1213	1172	8229
Static	1117	1069	7192

We run the default Mosquitto broker, subscriber and publisher with all three target features. The numbers of runtime instructions in broker, subscriber and publisher are 8937, 1117 and 1235, respectively. The numbers of static instructions in broker, subscriber and publisher are 7717, 1022 and 1132, respectively. Table 2 shows number of instructions after removing target features.

Among those removed features, some are particularly security concerning. The option "insecure" let subscriber and publisher skip the verification of the server hostname, which means a malicious third party could gain the access to the MQTT communication. The feature "publish file" is a feature that allows the publisher to send files (instead of message updates to subscribers), potentially offering a mechanism for malicious code injection.

8 Discussion

In this section, we discuss some limitations of our CustomPro framework, which will be considered as possible directions for future work.

Limitation of Tainting: During the feature identification, CustomPro utilizes the dynamic cross-host tainting to track the information flow among hosts. However, the tainting currently only work in a "forward" manner, i.e., the relevant code can only be tainted after the packet is identified and tainted. The taint information flow forward along with the program execution. However, the code that is related to generating the packets cannot be tainted in this way. Additional "backward" tainting module needs to be implemented to address this issue. However, this is only needed when the first packet is generated, because the following packets will all contain the initial taint information (which are provided by our across-host taint propagation), as they are always triggered by some incoming packets from other protocol entities. Hence, one possible future work is to leverage static backward tainting to identify code that generates the first packet, and improve protocol customization.

Limitation of Rewriting: Currently, CustomPro does not work on obfuscated/encrypted binaries since it relies on the correct static instruction address/offset. Also, instead of replacing instructions with NOPs and program crash, as a future work, we plan to silent undesired feature invocations and let the program continue execution, such that the (execution of) desired features will not be interrupted by unexpected invocations to undesired features.

9 Related Work

Vulnerability Discovery and Program Customization: Program bloating introduces more code as well as more bugs. Extensive works have focused on bug hunting in programs as such dynamic tainting [10,37] program customization [6,7,19,20,22,40], symbolic execution [28,34,42], fuzzing [26], learning-based approaches [24,38,41,42], hardware-assisted profiling and analysis [5,43] and malware/botnet analysis [12,14–18]. In this paper we leverage the tainting information to guide the symbolic execution. Pure symbolic execution has the problem of path explosion and different techniques have been studied to improve the efficiency of symbolic execution. StraightTaint [28] combines "incomplete" taint propagation and symbolic execution to improve the runtime tainting performance (by lightweight logging) while still keep necessary information for offline analysis. Driller [34] combines symbolic execution and fuzzing to quickly bypass the magic number checking. The intuition is that symbolic execution can efficiently figure out the conditions of entering different compartment of the code, while fuzzing can help inside each program compartment such that symbolic execution will not get stuck.

De-bloating: Specifically, in order to mitigate the problem of program feature creep, de-bloating techniques have been proposed [6,19,20,29,39]. Yufei Jiang et al. utilize program slicing and data analysis to identify the code that is related to the target feature at source code lelve [20]. In particular, they discover and delete code that has dependencies with its return value, parameter and call site. Similarly, Jred [19] aims to remove unused methods in JAVA program and libraries by analyzing the program call graph. It operates at IR level, i.e., the JAVA bytecode is lifted into Soot IR. After trimming, IR is transformed into Java bytecode to produce a light-weight program. CustomPro customizes program binaries in a more automated way by identifying relevant packets.

Binary Reuse: Binary reusing refers to the line of works that aims to extract useful components/functions from the program binaries through static and/or dynamic analysis [35,46,47]. CPR [23] tries to reconstruct the program binaries from dynamic instruction traces and memory dump, while Juan Caballero et al. identify self-contained code fragment from binary with the help of both static disassembling and dynamic execution monitoring. A chain of binary tools have been widely used to analyze binary code for different purposes, such as binary CFG analysis, vulnerability detection and binary rewriting. Specifically, binary rewriting tools such as DynInst [33] and Pin [27] are able to perform binary modification either statically or dynamically. In this paper, we employ DynInst to perform basic-block modification of program features. In feature identification module, we use TEMU [44] to emulate a system where the web servers are launched then monitored. TEMU also contains a tainting plugin ("trace-cap") that can taint the instructions from network packets. Angr [32] is used to perform symbolic execution together with the tainting information obtained through tracecap.

10   Conclusion

We design and evaluate a binary customization framework, CustomPro, for customizing network protocols. CustomPro aims to generate customized program binaries with *just-enough* features and can satisfy a broad array of customization requirements. Feature identification and feature rewriting are two major modules of CustomPro, for discovering the target features using program tracing and tainting-based symbolic execution, and for modifying the program features through binary instrumentation to obtain a customized program. Our experiment results demonstrate that CustomPro is able to effectively achieve the customization objectives in terms of obtaining an instrumented binary with the necessary functionalities and reducing the corresponding attack surface.

Acknowledgment. We thank the reviewers for their valuable opinions. This work was supported by the US Office of Naval Research (ONR) under Award N00014-17-1-2786 and N00014-15-1-2210. Any opinions, findings, conclusions, or recommendations expressed in this article are those of the authors, and do not necessarily reflect those of ONR.

References

1. Bao, T., Burket J., Woo M., Turner R., Brumley, D.: Byteweight: learning to recognize functions in binary code. USENIX, Byteweight (2014)
2. Basin, D., Cremers, C., Miyazaki, K., Radomirovic, S., Watanabe, D.: Improving the security of cryptographic protocol standards. IEEE Secur. Priv. **13**(3), 24–31 (2015)
3. Caballero, J., Johnson, N.M., McCamant, S., Song, D.: Binary code extraction and interface identification for security applications. Technical report, CL University Berkeley Department of Electrical Engineering and Computer Science (2009)
4. Caballero, J., Poosankam, P., Kreibich, C., Song, D.: Dispatcher: enabling active botnet infiltration using automatic protocol reverse-engineering. In: Proceedings of the 16th ACM Conference on Computer and Communications Security, pp. 621–634. ACM (2009)
5. Chen, J., Venkataramani, G., Huang, H.H.: Repram: re-cycling pram faulty blocks for extended lifetime. In IEEE/IFIP International Conference on Dependable Systems and Networks (DSN 2012), pp. 1–12. IEEE (2012)
6. Chen, Y., Lan, T., Venkataramani, G.: Damgate: dynamic adaptive multi-feature gating in program binaries. In: Proceedings of the 2017 Workshop on Forming an Ecosystem Around Software Transformation, pp. 23–29. ACM (2017)
7. Chen, Y., Sun, S., Lan, T., Venkataramani, G.: Toss: tailoring online server systems through binary feature customization. In: Proceedings of the 2018 Workshop on Forming an Ecosystem Around Software Transformation, pp. 1–7. ACM (2018)
8. Comparetti, P.M., Wondracek, G., Kruegel, C., Kirda, E.: Prospex: protocol specification extraction. In: 2009 30th IEEE Symposium on Security and Privacy, pp. 110–125. IEEE (2009)
9. Cui, W., Kannan, J., Wang, H.J.: Discoverer: automatic protocol reverse engineering from network traces. In: USENIX Security Symposium, pp. 1–14 (2007)
10. Doudalis, I., Clause, J., Venkataramani, G., Prvulovic, M., Orso, A.: Effective and efficient memory protection using dynamic tainting. IEEE Trans. Comput. **61**(1), 87–100 (2012)
11. Durumeric, Z., et al.: The matter of heartbleed. In: Proceedings of the 2014 Conference on Internet Measurement Conference, pp. 475–488. ACM (2014)
12. Feng, B., Li, Q., Ji, Y., Guo, D., Meng, X.: Stopping the cyberattack in the early stage: assessing the security risks of social network users. Secur. Commun. Netw. **2019**, 14 (2019)
13. Gressin, S.: The equifax data breach: what to do (2017)
14. He, Y., Li, Q., Cao, J., Ji, Y., Guo, D.: Understanding socialbot behavior on end hosts. Int. J. Distrib. Sensor Netw. **13**(2), 1550147717694170 (2017)
15. Ji, Y., He, Y., Jiang, X., Li, Q.: Towards social botnet behavior detecting in the end host. In: 2014 20th IEEE International Conference on Parallel and Distributed Systems (ICPADS), pp. 320–327. IEEE (2014)
16. Ji, Y., He, Y., Li, Q., Guo, D.: Botcatch: a behavior and signature correlated bot detection approach. In: 2013 IEEE 10th International Conference on High Performance Computing and Communications & 2013 IEEE International Conference on Embedded and Ubiquitous Computing (HPCC_EUC), pp. 1634–1639. IEEE (2013)
17. Ji, Y., He, Y., Zhu, D., Li, Q., Guo, D.: A multitiprocess mechanism of evading behavior-based bot detection approaches. In: Huang, X., Zhou, J. (eds.) ISPEC 2014. LNCS, vol. 8434, pp. 75–89. Springer, Cham (2014). https://doi.org/10.1007/978-3-319-06320-1_7

18. Ji, Y., Li, Q., He, Y., Guo, D.: Botcatch: leveraging signature and behavior for bot detection. Secur. Commun. Netw. **8**(6), 952–969 (2015)
19. Jiang, Y., Wu, D., Liu, P.: Jred: program customization and bloatware mitigation based on static analysis. In: Computer Software and Applications Conference (COMPSAC), 2016 IEEE 40th Annual, vol. 1, pp. 12–21. IEEE (2016)
20. Jiang, Y., Zhang, C., Wu, D., Liu, P.: Feature-based software customization: preliminary analysis, formalization, and methods. In: 2016 IEEE 17th International Symposium on High Assurance Systems Engineering (HASE), pp. 122–131. IEEE (2016)
21. Khandelwal, S.: Over 199, 500 websites are still vulnerable to heartbleed openssl bug (2017)
22. Kroes, T., et al.: Binrec: attack surface reduction through dynamic binary recovery. In: Proceedings of the 2018 Workshop on Forming an Ecosystem Around Software Transformation, pp. 8–13. ACM (2018)
23. Kwon, Y., Wang, W., Zheng, Y., Zhang, X., Xu, D.: Cpr: cross platform binary code reuse via platform independent trace program. In: Proceedings of the 26th ACM SIGSOFT International Symposium on Software Testing and Analysis, pp. 158–169. ACM (2017)
24. Li, Y., Yao, F., Lan, T., Venkataramani, G.: Sarre: semantics-aware rule recommendation and enforcement for event paths on android. IEEE Trans. Inf. Forensics Secur. **11**(12), 2748–2762 (2016)
25. Lim, J., Reps, T., Liblit, B.: Extracting output formats from executables. In: 2006 13th Working Conference on Reverse Engineering, pp. 167–178. IEEE (2006)
26. Liu, X., Li, X., Prajapati, R., Wu, D.: Deepfuzz: automatic generation of syntax valid c programs for fuzz testing. In: Proceedings of the AAAI Conference on Artificial Intelligence (2019)
27. Luk, C.-K.: et al.: Pin: building customized program analysis tools with dynamic instrumentation. In ACM SIGPLAN notices, vol. 40, pp. 190–200. ACM (2005)
28. Ming, J., Wu, D., Wang, J., Xiao, G., Peng, L.: Straighttaint: decoupled offline symbolic taint analysis. In: 2016 31st IEEE/ACM International Conference on Automated Software Engineering (ASE), pp. 308–319. IEEE (2016)
29. Mitchell, N., Sevitsky, G.: The causes of bloat, the limits of health. In: ACM SIGPLAN Notices, vol. 42, pp. 245–260. ACM (2007)
30. Prandini, M., Ramilli, M.: Return-oriented programming. IEEE Secur. Priv. **10**(6), 84–87 (2012)
31. Ramachandran, A., Mundada, Y., Tariq, M.B., Feamster, N.: Securing enterprise networks using traffic tainting. Georgia Inst. Technol., Atlanta, GA, USA, Techniocal Report GTCS-09-15 (2009)
32. Shoshitaishvili, Y., et al.: Sok: (state of) the art of war: offensive techniques in binary analysis. In: 2016 IEEE Symposium on Security and Privacy (SP), pp. 138–157. IEEE (2016)
33. Open Source. Dyninst: an application program interface (api) for runtime code generation. http://www.dyninst.org (2016)
34. Stephens, N., Grosen, J., Salls, C., Dutcher, A., Wang, R., Corbetta, J., Shoshitaishvili, Y., Kruegel, C., Vigna, G.: Driller: Augmenting fuzzing through selective symbolic execution. NDSS **16**, 1–16 (2016)
35. van der Veen, V., et al.: A tough call: mitigating advanced code-reuse attacks at the binary level. In: 2016 IEEE Symposium on Security and Privacy (SP), pp. 934–953. IEEE (2016)

36. Vanhoef, M., Piessens, F.: Key reinstallation attacks: forcing nonce reuse in wpa2. In: Proceedings of the 2017 ACM SIGSAC Conference on Computer and Communications Security, pp. 1313–1328. ACM (2017)
37. Venkataramani, G., Doudalis, I., Solihin, Y., Prvulovic, M.: Memtracker: an accelerator for memory debugging and monitoring. ACM Trans. Archit. Code Optimization (TACO) 6(2), 5 (2009)
38. Wang, S., Wang, P., Wu, D.: Semantics-aware machine learning for function recognition in binary code. In: 2017 IEEE International Conference on Software Maintenance and Evolution (ICSME), pp. 388–398. IEEE (2017)
39. Xu, G., Mitchell, N., Arnold, M., Rountev, A., Sevitsky, G.: Software bloat analysis: finding, removing, and preventing performance problems in modern large-scale object-oriented applications. In: Proceedings of the FSE/SDP Workshop on Future of Software Engineering Research, pp. 421–426. ACM (2010)
40. Xue, H., Chen, Y., Venkataramani, G., Lan, T., Jin, G., Li, J.: Morph: enhancing system security through interactive customization of application and communication protocol features. In: Proceedings of the 2018 ACM SIGSAC Conference on Computer and Communications Security, pp. 2315–2317. ACM (2018)
41. Xue, H., Chen, Y., Yao, F., Li, Y., Lan, T., Venkataramani, G.: SIMBER: eliminating redundant memory bound checks via statistical inference. In: De Capitani di Vimercati, S., Martinelli, F. (eds.) SEC 2017. IAICT, vol. 502, pp. 413–426. Springer, Cham (2017). https://doi.org/10.1007/978-3-319-58469-0_28
42. Yao, F., Li, Y., Chen, Y., Xue, H., Lan, T., Venkataramani, G.: Statsym: vulnerable path discovery through statistics-guided symbolic execution. In: 2017 47th Annual IEEE/IFIP International Conference on Dependable Systems and Networks (DSN), pp. 109–120. IEEE (2017)
43. Yao, F., Venkataramani, G., Doroslovački, M.: Covert timing channels exploiting non-uniform memory access based architectures. In: Proceedings of the on Great Lakes Symposium on VLSI 2017, pp. 155–160. ACM (2017)
44. Yin, H., Song, D.: Temu: The bitblaze dynamic analysis component (2008)
45. Zavou, A., Portokalidis, G., Keromytis, A.: Taint-exchange: a generic system for cross-process and cross-host taint tracking. Adv. Inf. Comput. Secur. 7038, 113–128 (2011)
46. Zeng, J., Fu, Y., Miller, K.A., Lin, Z., Zhang, X., Xu, D.: Obfuscation resilient binary code reuse through trace-oriented programming. In: Proceedings of the 2013 ACM SIGSAC Conference on Computer & Communications Security, pp. 487–498. ACM (2013)
47. Zhang, P., Li, J., Skaletsky, A., Etzion, O.: Apparatus, system, and method of dynamic binary translation with translation reuse, November 24 2009. US Patent 7,624,384

Systematic Theory

On the Security of TRNGs Based on Multiple Ring Oscillators

Xinying Wu[1,2,3], Yuan Ma[1,2,3], Jing Yang[1,2,3], Tianyu Chen[1,2(✉)], and Jingqiang Lin[1,2,3]

[1] Data Assurance and Communications Security Research Center, Chinese Academy of Sciences, Beijing, China
[2] State Key Laboratory of Information Security, Institute of Information Engineering, Chinese Academy of Sciences, Beijing, China
[3] School of Cyber Security, University of Chinese Academy of Sciences, Beijing, China
{wuxinying,mayuan,yangjing,chentianyu,linjingqiang}@iie.ac.cn

Abstract. True random number generator (TRNG) is essential for the implementation of cryptographic applications, such as digital signature algorithms and security protocols. The quality of generated sequences would directly influence the security of the cryptographic application. Furthermore, in order to enhance the generation rate of random numbers, a TRNG based on multiple ring oscillators (ROs), i.e., MRO-TRNG for short, has been proposed by Sunar *et al.* There exist potential risks threatening the security of the MRO-TRNG, like pseudo-randomness and phase interlock. For MRO-TRNG, experimental observation and statistical test results have been well investigated. However, these methods cannot distinguish the pseudo-randomness. The concept of entropy is used to quantify the amount of randomness. As far as we know, there is no entropy estimation method for MRO-TRNGs. In this regard, this paper provides an entropy estimation method to analyze the security of MRO-TRNG based on the method for oscillator-based TRNG, and calculates a lower bound of entropy. The theoretical results are verified through Matlab simulations and FPGA experiments. The conclusions can further guide the setting of design parameters (i.e., number of ROs, sampling frequency, *etc.*) to generate outputs with sufficient entropy.

Keywords: True random number generator · Multiple ring oscillators · Entropy estimation · Pseudo-randomness

1 Introduction

Random number generator (RNG) is a fundamental security module for many cryptographic systems. Its output, which is called random number, is often used in cryptographic algorithms, security protocols, *etc.* Generally, RNGs can be divided into two classes: true RNGs (TRNGs) and pseudo RNGs (PRNGs). In

S. Chen et al. (Eds.): SecureComm 2019, LNICST 305, pp. 89–107, 2019.
https://doi.org/10.1007/978-3-030-37231-6_5

practice, a TRNG usually generates a short bit string (seed) as the input of a PRNG, and the PRNG untilizes the seed to generate a long sequence by its stretch function. It is therefore crucial to guarantee the security of TRNGs.

Oscillator-based TRNG is one of the most commonly used structures in generating random number, whose entropy source is jitter caused by circuit noise. However, due to the small scale of the jitter within a signal period, conventional sampling methods cannot efficiently collect sufficient amount of jitter accumulation in a short time. In order to enhance the generation rate of random number, Sunar et al. [13] proposed a generation structure with multiple ROs (multiple-ROs) which increased the probability of sampling jitter events. In this paper, this type of TRNG is referred to as MRO-TRNG.

Since MRO-TRNG was proposed, there have been controversies over its structure, though the generation rate of random numbers can be quite high (dozens of Mbps or higher). The points are centered on two defects of the structure, the pseudo-randomness and phase interlock phenomenon. Pseudo-randomness is, in some situations, sequences generated by MRO-TRNG to exhibit statistical randomness, even if there is no jitter in the design [3]. Phase interlock is a circuit phenomenon between two or more ROs. They have nearly the same frequency with their phase difference fixed (i.e., locked). The phase interlock degrades the quality of the TRNG output [17]. The above indicated defects have been confirmed by simulation and hardware experiments. Bochard [3] discovered that in the absence of jitter, more than 18 ROs with slightly different frequencies can produce pseudo-random sequences, which are able to pass statistical tests (NIST SP 800-22 [12] and FIPS 140-2 [11]). Yoo et al. [17] found that in the hardware implementation, the oscillating signal of MRO-TRNG might have the phase interlock phenomenon through the variation of the location of ROs. This phenomenon can result in the randomness of the output sequence significantly lower than expected. Bochard [3] observed phase interlock phenomenon when the frequencies of ROs are close enough.

Therefore, the security evaluation of MRO-TRNG is a valuable issue. Statistical test is a common method to assess the quality of the RNGs. The commonly used statistical test suites include NIST SP 800-22 [12], NIST SP 800-90B [14], FIPS 140-2 [11], DIEHARD [10] and TestU01 [7]. Statistical tests are black-box tests. It assumes RNG is a black-box and evaluates the statistical properties of the output sequences. However, applying only the black-box statistical tests cannot assess the true randomness in the output of MRO-TRNG, and experimental observation is not sufficient enough to analyze the security of the structure. As the measurement of undeterministic behavior, entropy can be used to effectively quantify the true randomness of a TRNG. The standards ISO 18031 [4] and the AIS 31 [5] recommend guiding the design and testing of RNG by using entropy estimation. The entropy estimation is based on a stochastic model that is established for a specific TRNG structure. Compared with the statistical tests, the entropy estimation is a white-box test which can avoid the influence of pseudo-randomness.

On the security analysis of the MRO-TRNG, we propose an entropy estimation method for calculating the entropy of the output produced by MRO-TRNG, which provides a lower bound of (shannon) entropy. The proposed entropy estimation has been verified through simulation. On the basis of this theoretical method, we also implement a theoretically secure MRO-TRNG structure in FPGA platform, and the entropy of output is sufficient.

In summary, we make the following contributions.

- We propose an entropy estimation method for MRO-TRNG structure to analyze the security of MRO-TRNG for the first time. The entropy estimation method calculates a lower bound of entropy and minimum entropy. Even if there exists pseudo-randomness, the generated sequence can be guaranteed with sufficient true randomness according to our entropy estimation method.
- We verify the security of entropy estimation model through Matlab simulation. Besides, we simulate jitter-free MRO-TRNG to analyse the pseudo-randomness.
- In FPGA hardware platform, we implement a MRO-TRNG design. At a high sampling frequency (nearly 10 MHz), the output sequence can always pass the NIST SP 800-22 statistical test. However, according to the entropy estimation method, only when the sampling frequency is no higher than 5 MHz, the entropy of the output can be guaranteed no lower than 0.997.

This paper is organized as the follows. In Sect. 2, it is introduced the MRO-TRNG structure. In Sect. 3, we describe the stochastic models for oscillator-based TRNG. Also, the stochastic model for MRO-TRNG is proposed, which can be employed to calculate the lower bound of entropy and minimum entropy. In Sect. 4, we simulate the MRO-TRNG and compare the theoretical entropy with the statistical entropy. In Sect. 5, we implement the structure in FPGA. In Sect. 6, we conclude the paper.

2   Related Work

The traditional oscillator based sampling structure (i.e., oscillator-ed TRNG) is designed based on a single RO. In this paper, this type of TRNG is called SRO-TRNG for short. In SRO-TRNG, the sampling signal is generated by a slow clock, while the sampled signal is generated by a fast oscillator. If the sampling point is in the high level position of the oscillating signal, the output bit is '1'. If in the low level position, the output bit is '0'. The randomness of the SRO-TRNG comes from the jitter caused by the circuit noise. The jitter of the oscillating signal makes the position of the sampling point undetermined, thus generating a random sequence. However, as the scale of the jitter generated by the circuit noise is relatively small, the sufficient-entropy output cannot achieve a high generation rate.

The probability of sampling the jitter can be increased by increasing the number of the ROs. Inspired by the observation, Sunar et al. [13] presented a TRNG design which consisted of a large number of ROs. The Fig. 1(a) shows the MRO-TRNG proposed by Sunar, in which a series of equal length (i.e., stage) ROs connect to an exclusive-OR (XOR) tree. The output signal of the XOR tree is sampled by a D flip-flop. In order to eliminate the bias of the random signal and reduce the required number of ROs, the output signal of the D flip-flop is then post-processed by a resilient function. According to experimental observation, this implementation generates a random bit stream at 2.5 Mbps with a sampling frequency of 40 MHz, using 114 ROs (13 inverters), and a resilient function. The output sequence can pass the DIEHARD and NIST SP 800-22 statistical tests.

Wold et al. [16] analyzed and presented an enhancement of MRO-TRNG. The enhancement structure adds an extra D flip-flop between each RO and the XOR tree. This enhancement structure can significantly improve the performance of MRO-TRNG, reducing the 114 ROs in the original design to 25 ROs. The output sequence can pass the NIST SP 800-22 statistical test without post-processing, and the sampling rate is up to 100 Mbps. The MRO-TRNG structure enhanced by Wold et al. is shown in Fig. 1(b). Bochard et al. [3] compared the performance of the two MRO-TRNGs. The simulation experiment found no difference between the two structures. While, the experimental results on FPGAs were quite different: the performance of the enhanced MRO-TRNG was much better.

MRO-TRNG can significantly improve the throughput rate. However, since MRO-TRNG was proposed, there have been some controversies about the structure. Through the simulation and hardware experiments, two main problems are found in MRO-TRNGs: pseudo-randomness and phase interlock.

Pseudo-randomness. Bochard et al. [3] simulated the jitter-free MRO-TRNG, and the frequencies of ROs varied from 197.5 MHz to 202 MHz, in 250 KHz steps. When the number of ROs is more than 18, the generated sequence can pass the FIPS 140-2 and NIST SP 800-22 statistical tests. But it is obvious that the structure contains no randomness. In response, Wold et al. [16] did the restart experiment to prove there were true randomness in MRO-TRNG. They repeated restarts of MRO-TRNG from the same reset state and observed the generated sequence by capturing the random output using oscilloscope. The experiment results showed that traces of captured sequence deviated from each other. The restart experiment demonstrates that there are true-randomness in the structure, but it cannot confirm whether the entropy caused by true randomness is sufficient.

Phase Interlock. Phase interlock may encounter in the hardware implementation of MRO-TRNG. Phase interlock is a circuit phenomenon between two or more ROs. They have nearly the same frequency with their phase difference fixed (i.e., locked). The phase interlock degrades the performance of the TRNG. Varchola [15] observed the phase interlock occurred when two ROs were in circular layout, that is the ROs shared routing. Markettos et al. [9] proposed the frequency injection attack on MRO-TRNG. The frequencies of the attacked ROs can be interlocked, which made the randomness of the output significantly decrease. Yoo et al. [17] studied the impact of the ROs' location, and found that phase interlock existed when two ROs were placed close and when one RO was in the diagonal of the other RO. Then, they proposed to make the propagation

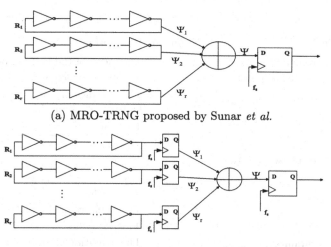

(a) MRO-TRNG proposed by Sunar *et al.*

(b) Improved MRO-TRNG proposed by Wold *et al.*

Fig. 1. The structures of MRO-TRNG

delays of oscillator output signals to the inputs of the XOR tree different. The method can eliminate the effect of phase interlock, as it reduced the number of unfilled urns.

3   Proposed Entropy Estimation Method

3.1   Notation and Definitions

Table 1 is the Parameters List. In MRO-TRNG, each RO is first sampled by the D flip-flop and then the outputs are connected by the XOR tree. Each part can be seen as an independent SRO-TRNG sampling process. For MRO-TRNG structure, we give an entropy estimation method to calculate the lower bound of entropy and analyze the security. For MRO-TRNG design, the entropy estimation method can be a guidance to ensure security of the structure from a theoretical perspective. In order to give a theoretical entropy, we provide several propositions and formulas for probability and entropy of MRO-TRNG.

3.2   Entropy Estimation for SRO-TRNG

Baudet *et al.* [2] used an approach based on phase evolution to model the jitter of the SRO-TRNG. From phase evolution of oscillating signal, they established a stochastic model for SRO-TRNG. The phase φ of SRO-TRNG is considered as one-dimensional Brownian motion. We assume that the phase evolution follows the Wiener stochastic process $(\varphi(t))_{t \in R}$ with drift $\mu > 0$ and volatility $\sigma^2 > 0$. In other words, conditioned on the values of t_0, the phase of $t_0 + \Delta t$ follows a Gaussian distribution with mean $\varphi(0) + \mu \times \Delta t$ and variance $\sigma^2 \times \Delta t$.

Table 1. Parameters List

Aspect	Parameter	Description
The parameters in the aspect of time evolution	m_x	The mean of the half-period of oscillating signal
	s_x^2	The variance of the half-period oscillating signal
	σ_t	Time jitter, $\sigma_t = s_x/m_x$
The parameters in the aspect of phase evolution	φ	The phase
	μ	The mean of the phase, $\mu = 1/2m_x$
	σ^2	The variance of the phase, $\sigma^2 = s_x^2/4m_x^3$
Other parameters	$p_{1,x}(t)$	The conditioned probability of sampling '1' at time t
	Q	Quality factor, $Q = \sigma^2 \Delta t$
	$\mathcal{Q}$	The quality factors' sum of all ROs, $\mathcal{Q} = \sum_{i=1}^{n} Q_i$
	H_{lo}	Lower bound of entropy
	H_{Lp}	Precise lower bound of entropy
	H_{La}	Approximate lower bound of entropy
	H_∞	Minimum entropy
	σ_f^2	The variance of frequency

For the sampling process, the value of the sampling bit $s(t)$ of SRO-TRNG is expressed as follows. That is to say, when the sampling point is in the high level position of the oscillating signal, the output bit is '1'. In the low level position, the output bit is '0'.

$$s(t) = \begin{cases} 1, & \varphi(t) \bmod 1 \in (0.5, 1) \\ 0, & \varphi(t) \bmod 1 \in (0, 0.5) \\ 0.5, & \varphi(t) \bmod 1 \in \{0, 0.5\} \end{cases}$$

For SRO-TRNG, the probability of sampling '1' at time $t \geq 0$ conditioned on the phase at time 0 follows [2]

$$p_{1,x}(t) = \frac{1}{2} - \frac{2}{\pi} \sum_{N=0}^{+\infty} \frac{\sin(2\pi(\mu t + x)(2N+1))}{2N+1} e^{-2\pi^2 \sigma^2 t(2N+1)^2}.$$

Min-entropy or lower bound of entropy is the most conservative measurement of entropy, and is useful in determining entropy of a TRNG in the worst case.

In the aspect of entropy calculating complexity, min-entropy or a lower bound has considerable advantages for dependent stochastic process, as only the probability in the worst case is involved. The methods for calculating a lower bound of entropy of oscillator-based TRNG are presented in [2,6].

The calculation expression of the lower bound [6], which is denoted as H_{lo}, was presented as

$$H(B_i|B_{i-1},\ldots,B_1) \geq H_{lo} = H(B_i|W_{i-1}) \approx \int_0^s H(R^{(s-u)} \bmod 2) P_W(du),$$

where B_i is the ith sampling bit and $R^{(s-u)}$ represents the number of crossing edges in the duration of $(s-u)$. The idea is inspired by the fact that the waiting time W_i tells more information about B_{i+1} than all the previous bits. Following the similar idea, [2] also provides an analytical expression for H_{lo}:

$$H_{lo} = 1 - \frac{4}{\pi^2 \ln(2)} e^{-4\pi^2 Q} + O(e^{-6\pi^2 Q}).$$

3.3 Probability Calculation for MRO-TRNG

We make the assumption that ROs in MRO-TRNG are independent. The mathematic model and simulation performance of Sunar's structure are the same as those of Wold's structure. Therefore, when modeling the stochastic behavior, we do not distinguish these two structures.

The sampling bit $s_i(t)$ of SRO-TRNG is connected to the XOR tree to generate the output bit of MRO-TRNG. Therefore, the value of the output bit $g(t)$ can be expressed as follows, where n is the number of ROs.

$$g(t) = \begin{cases} 1, \text{for } s_1(t), \ldots, s_n(t) \text{ the number of '1' is odd} \\ 0, \text{for } s_1(t), \ldots, s_n(t) \text{ the number of '1' is even} \end{cases}$$

Conditioned on the phase at time 0, we give the probability of single-bit.

Proposition 1. *For MRO-TRNG, the phase at time 0 of n ROs are $x_1, x_2, \ldots, x_n$ respectively, the probability of sampling '1' at time $t \geq 0$ conditioned on the phase at time 0 follows*

$$P[(s(t) = 1)|\varphi(0) = (x_1, x_2, \ldots, x_n)]$$
$$= \frac{1}{2} - \frac{2^{2n-1}}{\pi^n} \prod_{i=1}^n \sum_{N=0}^{+\infty} \frac{\sin(2\pi(\mu_i t + x_i)(2N+1))}{2N+1} e^{-2\pi^2 \sigma_i^2 t(2N+1)^2}.$$

Proof. We use the mathematical induction to prove the proposition. The ROs are independent, and the oscillating signal generated by each RO connect to an XOR tree. So when $n = 2$, we have

$$p_{1,(x_1,x_2)}(t) = p_{1,x_1}(t) \times p_{0,x_2}(t) + p_{0,x_1}(t) \times p_{1,x_2}(t)$$

$$= \frac{1}{2} - \frac{8}{\pi^2} \sum_{N=0}^{+\infty} \frac{\sin(2\pi(\mu_1 t + x_1)(2N+1))}{2N+1} e^{-2\pi^2 \sigma_1^2 t(2N+1)^2}$$

$$\sum_{N=0}^{+\infty} \frac{\sin(2\pi(\mu_2 t + x_2)(2N+1))}{2N+1} e^{-2\pi^2 \sigma_2^2 t(2N+1)^2}.$$

Assuming that the proposition holds for parameter $n-1$, for parameter n,

$$p_{1,(x_1,x_2,...,x_n)}(t) = p_{1,(x_1,x_2,...,x_{n-1})}(t) \times p_{0,x_n}(t) + p_{0,(x_1,x_2,...,x_{n-1})}(t) \times p_{1,x_n}(t)$$

$$= \frac{1}{2} - \frac{2^{2n-1}}{\pi^n} \prod_{i=1}^{n} \sum_{N=0}^{+\infty} \frac{\sin(2\pi(\mu_i t + x_i)(2N+1))}{2N+1} e^{-2\pi^2 \sigma_i^2 t(2N+1)^2}.$$

3.4   Lower Bound of Minimum Entropy for MRO-TRNG

Proposition 2. *For MRO-TRNG, the phase at time 0 of n ROs are $x_1, x_2, ..., x_n$ respectively, the maximum probability of single-bit at time $t \geq 0$ is*

$$f(x_1, x_2, ..., x_n) = P_{max}[(s(t) = 1)|\varphi(0) = (x_1, x_2, ..., x_n)]$$

$$= \max\{p_{1,(x_1,x_2,...,x_n)}(t), p_{0,(x_1,x_2,...,x_n)}(t)\}$$

$$= \frac{1}{2} + \frac{2^{2n-1}}{\pi^n} |(\prod_{i=1}^{n} \sum_{N=0}^{+\infty} \frac{\sin(2\pi(\mu_i t + x_i)(2N+1))}{2N+1} e^{-2\pi^2 \sigma_i^2 t(2N+1)^2})|.$$

Based on the maximum probability of single-bit obtained in Proposition 2, we calculate the conditional minimum entropy. As we show in the Appendix, the minimum entropy of the sequence is greater than or equal to the conditional minimum entropy. Then we can get the lower bound of the minimum entropy.

Proposition 3. *Let $H_\infty(s(t)|\varphi(0)) = \int_0^1 ... \int_0^1 H_\infty(s(t)|\varphi(0) = (x_1, x_2, ..., x_n)) dx_1...dx_n$ denote the average conditional minimum entropy of $s(t)$ with respect to $\varphi(0)$, it is well known the definition of minimum entropy is $H_\infty = -log_2(P_{max})$ [14] P_{max} is the maximum probability of single-bit, then by definition,*

$$H_\infty(s(\Delta t)|\varphi(0) = (x_1, x_2, ..., x_n)) = -\log_2 P_{max}[(s(t) = 1)|\varphi(0) = (x_1, x_2, ..., x_n)].$$

We can get the lower bound of minimum entropy for MRO-TRNG

$$H_\infty(s(\Delta t)) \geq H_\infty(s(\Delta t)|\varphi(0))$$

$$= \int_0^1 ... \int_0^1 (1 - \frac{1}{ln2}\varepsilon + \frac{1}{2ln2}\varepsilon^2 - -\frac{1}{3ln2}\varepsilon^3 + ...)dx_1 dx_2...dx_n,$$

where

$$\varepsilon = \frac{2^{2n}}{\pi^n} |(\prod_{i=1}^{n} \sum_{N=0}^{+\infty} \frac{\sin(2\pi(\mu_i t + x_i)(2N+1))}{2N+1} e^{-2\pi^2 \sigma_i^2 t(2N+1)^2})|.$$

3.5   Lower Bound of Entropy for MRO-TRNG

Based on the probability of single-bit obtained in Proposition 1, we give a conditional entropy and calculate a lower bound of entropy.

Proposition 4. *Let* $H(s(\Delta t)|\varphi(0)) = \int_0^1 \cdots \int_0^1 H(s(\Delta t)|\varphi(0) = (x_1, x_2, ..., x_n))$ $dx_1...dx_n$ *denote the average conditional entropy of* $s(\Delta t)$ *with respect to* $\varphi(0)$. *We can get a lower bound of entropy for MRO-TRNG based on the entropy of* $s(\Delta t)$ *conditioned on* $\varphi(0)$,

$$H > H((s(\Delta t) = 1)|\varphi(0)) = 1 - \frac{2^{3n-1}}{\pi^{2n}\ln 2}e^{-4\pi^2\mathcal{Q}} - \frac{2^{5n-2}3^{n-1}}{\ln 2\pi^{4n}}e^{-8\pi^2\mathcal{Q}} + O(e^{-12\pi^2\mathcal{Q}}),$$

(1)

where $\mathcal{Q} = \sum_{i=1}^n Q_i$ *denotes the quality factors' sum of all ROs.*

Proof. According to the definition, the conditional entropy is

$$H((s(\Delta t) = 1)|\varphi(0) = x_1, x_2, ..., x_n) = -p\log_2(p) - (1-p)\log_2(1-p),$$

where $p = P[(s(\Delta t) = 1)|\varphi(0) = x_1, x_2, ..., x_n]$.
Let

$$\varepsilon = 2P[s(\Delta t) = 1|\varphi(0) = (x_1, x_2, ...)] - 1,$$

then, we have

$$H((s(\Delta t) = 1)|\varphi(0) = x_1, x_2, ..., x_n) = 1 - \frac{1+\varepsilon}{2}\log_2(1+\varepsilon) - \frac{1-\varepsilon}{2}\log_2(1-\varepsilon)$$

$$= 1 - \frac{\varepsilon^2}{2\ln(2)} - \frac{\varepsilon^4}{12\ln(2)} - \frac{\varepsilon^6}{30\ln(2)} - \cdots$$

For arbitrarily $\mu_i t$,

$$\int_0^1 \sin^2(2\pi(\mu_i t + x_i)dx_i = \frac{1}{2}$$

$$\int_0^1 \sin^4(2\pi(\mu_i t + x_i)dx_i = \frac{3}{8}$$

So, the first item of $H(s(\Delta t)|\varphi(0))$ is

$$\int_0^1 \cdots \int_0^1 \frac{\varepsilon^2}{2\ln(2)}dx_1...dx_n$$

$$= \frac{2^{4n-1}}{\pi^{2n}\ln 2}\int_0^1 \cdots \int_0^1 \prod_{i=1}^n \sum_{N=0}^{+\infty} \frac{\sin(2\pi(\mu_i t + x_i)(2N+1))}{2N+1}e^{-2\pi^2(2N+1)^2 Q_i}dx_1...dx_n$$

$$= \frac{2^{4n-1}}{\pi^{2n}\ln 2}\prod_{i=1}^n \int_0^1 \cdots \int_0^1 (\sin^2(2\pi(\mu_i t + x_i))e^{-4\pi^2 Q_i} + O(e^{-18\pi^2 Q_i}))dx_1...dx_n$$

$$= \frac{2^{4n-1}}{\pi^{2n}\ln 2}(\frac{1}{2})^n e^{-4\pi^2\mathcal{Q}} + O(e^{-18\pi^2 Q_i})$$

$$= \frac{2^{3n-1}}{\pi^{2n}\ln 2}e^{-4\pi^2\mathcal{Q}} + O(e^{-18\pi^2 Q_i}).$$

Second item of H is

$$
\int_0^1 \cdots \int_0^1 \frac{\varepsilon^4}{12\ln(2)} dx_1...dx_n
$$

$$
= \frac{2^{8n-2}}{3\ln 2\pi^{4n}} \int_0^1 \cdots \int_0^1 \prod_{i=1}^n \frac{\sin^4(2\pi(\mu_i t + x_i)(2N+1))}{2N+1} e^{-8\pi^2(2N+1)^2 Q_i} dx_1...dx_n
$$

$$
= \frac{2^{8n-2}}{3\ln 2\pi^{4n}} \int_0^1 \cdots \int_0^1 (\sin^4(2\pi(\mu_i t + x_i)) e^{-8\pi^2 Q_i} + O(e^{-36\pi^2 Q_i})) dx_1...dx_n
$$

$$
= \frac{2^{8n-2}}{3\ln 2\pi^{4n}} (\frac{3}{8})^n e^{-8\pi^2 Q} + O(e^{-36\pi^2 Q_i})
$$

$$
= \frac{2^{5n-2} 3^{n-1}}{\ln 2\pi^{4n}} e^{-8\pi^2 Q} + O(e^{-36\pi^2 Q_i}).
$$

The entropy of the sequence is greater than or equal to the conditional entropy [2]. A lower bound of entropy can be stated based on the entropy of $s(\Delta t)$ conditioned on $\varphi(0)$.

$$
H > H((s(\Delta t) = 1)|\varphi(0)) = 1 - \frac{2^{3n-1}}{\pi^{2n} \ln 2} e^{-4\pi^2 Q} - \frac{2^{5n-2} 3^{n-1}}{\pi^{4n} \ln 2} e^{-8\pi^2 Q} + O(e^{-12\pi^2 Q}).
$$

3.6   Approximate Lower Bound of Entropy

We state the approximate lower bound of entropy as

$$
H_{La} = 1 - \frac{2^{3n-1}}{\pi^{2n} \ln 2} e^{-4\pi^2 Q} - \frac{2^{5n-2} 3^{n-1}}{\pi^{4n} \ln 2} e^{-8\pi^2 Q}. \tag{2}
$$

We give the comparison of approximate lower bound of entropy H_{La} and precise lower bound of entropy H_{Lp}, when number of ROs n varies from 25 to 50. The sum of quality factors Q varies from 0.02 to 0.1. The quality factor of every SRO-TRNG is the same. H_{Lp} is calculated based on Eq. (1) in Sect. 3.5, and H_{La} is calculated by Eq. (2). Figure 2 shows the comparison.

In Fig. 2, with Q increasing, the difference value decreases to zero. For 25-ROs and 30-ROs, when $Q \geq 0.03$. the deviation is lower than 10^{-4}. That is, when $n \leq 30$ and $Q \geq 0.03$, in calculation, the H_{La} can replace the H_{Lp}.

When $n \geq 30$ and $Q > 0.035$, the deviation is lower than 10^{-3}, the H_{La} can be a replacement of the H_{Lp} in practice.

So when the number of ROs is less than 60, and Q is less than 0.035, H_{La} can be used to replace the H_{Lp} in order to simplify the calculation.

3.7   Security Design Parameters

Based on the lower bound of entropy calculated in Proposition 4, we can get the security design parameters (e.g., sampling frequency or quality factor) for MRO-TRNG.

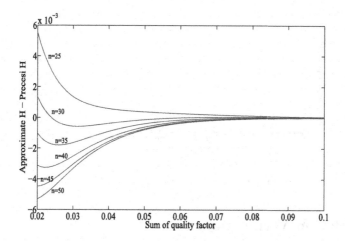

Fig. 2. The difference values between approximate entropy and precise entropy

Corollary 1. *This is a corollary of Proposition 4. The expression of quality factor Q based on the number of ROs n and entropy H as follows*

$$\mathcal{Q} = \frac{-1}{4\pi^2}\ln\Big(\frac{\pi^{4n}\ln 2}{2^{5n-1}3^{n-1}}\Big(-\frac{2^{3n-1}}{\pi^{2n}\ln 2} + \sqrt{\Big(\frac{2^{3n-1}}{\pi^{2n}\ln 2}\Big)^2 - 4\frac{2^{5n-2}3^{n-1}}{\pi^{4n}\ln 2}(H-1)}\Big)\Big).$$

The proof is omitted.

When the frequencies of ROs are around 200 MHz and standard deviation of time jitter is 1% of the half-period, we set $H > 0.997^1$, and get the security sampling frequency fs and quality factor $\mathcal{Q}$. Table 2 shows some security sampling parameters (quality factor and sampling frequency). Figure 3 shows the result with different RO numbers.

Table 2. Security sampling parameters

Number of ROs	Security quality factor	Security sampling frequency
10	0.0866	1.1543
20	0.0513	3.9023
30	0.0423	7.0921
40	0.0395	10.1249
50	0.0375	13.3207

---

[1] AIS 31 [5] gives the rule that entropy per bit greater than 0.997 can be seen as sufficient-entropy.

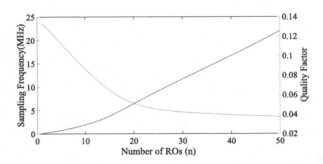

Fig. 3. Security sampling parameters

4   Simulation Verification

In this section, we carry out several Matlab simulations of MRO-TRNG to verify the entropy estimation method. In Propositions 3 and 4, we calculate a lower bound of entropy and minimum entropy. In practice, when the sampled frequency is the integral multiples of sampling frequency (that is the fractional part of $\Delta t/m_x$ is zero), the output quality of TRNG is worst [1,2,8]. We simulate the worst case situation and compare the simulation results with the theoretical entropy. Moreover, we simulate a jitter-free situation to discuss pseudorandomness in MRO-TRNG.

We simulate random sequences generation with the varied parameters (i.e., number of ROs, sampling frequency). We use the entropy estimators included in NIST SP 800-90B which is published on January 2018 [14], to estimate the min-entropy of the generated sequence. The estimation process is mainly divided into three steps as follows. The first step is to determine the track for estimation, and there are two different tracks to estimate the entropy, an IID track and a non-IID track. The second step is to estimate entropy by IID track or non-IID track. The final step is to apply restart tests and give the entropy estimate. Besides, for the random sequences generated by Matlab simulations, we calculate the approximate entropy. The approximate entropy is calculated by the approximate entropy randomness test in the NIST SP 800-22 statistical test suite [12].

The output of each sample simulation is 1Mb data, and for every parameter, experiment is repeated ten times. For the ten output sequences, we use SP 800-90B to get the sequences' minimum entropy respectively and calculate the average of the ten obtained minimum entropy as the final simulation minimum entropy. Besides, we use approximate entropy randomness test in the NIST SP 800-22 statistical test suite to get the approximate entropy.

4.1   Verification of the Worst Case

In Sect. 3, we give a entropy estimation method. In this section, we simulate the case when the sampled frequency is the integral multiples of sampling frequency, which is the worst case. The minimum entropy of generated sequences is compared with the theoretical lower bound of minimum entropy. The approximate entropy is compared with the theoretical lower bound of entropy.

The theoretical entropy estimation method is based on phase jitter, which is true randomness. However, besides jitter, same factors may make the generated sequences look like randomness which is pseudo-randomness. We set the frequencies of the ROs in MRO-TRNG the same. For the impact of different frequencies, we research in Sect. 4.2.

Parameter Setting. The frequencies of the ROs are set as 200 MHz, the size of the time jitter is 1%, so $\sigma^2 = \frac{s_x^2}{4m_x^3} = 0.01$. The number of ROs is from 5 to 30, and the sampling frequencies fs are in the interval $[2\,\text{MHz}, 20\,\text{MHz}]$. The simulation sequences generated by MRO-TRNG are calculated using SP 800-90B mentioned above to get the simulation minimum entropy and using approximate entropy randomness test to get approximate entropy.

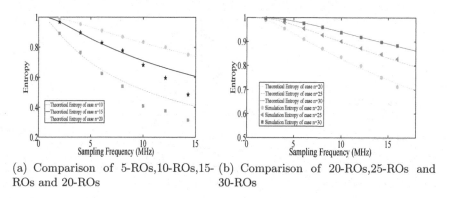

(a) Comparison of 5-ROs,10-ROs,15-ROs and 20-ROs

(b) Comparison of 20-ROs,25-ROs and 30-ROs

Fig. 4. Comparison of the theoretical minimum entropy and the simulation minimum entropy with the sampling frequency and the number of ROs varied, line denotes the theoretical lower bound of minimum entropy and point denotes simulation minimum entropy.

Results and Analysis. Figures 4 and 5 show the comparison of theoretical and simulation entropy. Figure 5 is the entropy, while Fig. 4 is the minimum entropy.

The formula obtained by Proposition 3 is used to calculate the theoretical lower bound of minimum entropy. We compare the theoretical lower bound of minimum entropy with the simulation minimum entropy obtained by SP 800-90B. When the number of ROs varies from 5 to 30, the trend of the entropy is similar. In Fig. 4, we show the comparison of theoretical entropy and simulation minimum entropy. Line denotes the theoretical lower bound of minimum entropy and point denotes simulation minimum entropy.

In Fig. 4(a), when the minimum entropy is less than 0.4, there is a distance between simulation minimum entropy and theoretical minimum entropy. When minimum entropy is less than 0.4, the result of SP 800-90B may not accurate. Except these points, the simulation minimum entropy and the theoretical minimum entropy are basically correspondence. The comparison verifies the model obtained in Proposition 3 and the probability in Proposition 1. We give the definition of the frequency ratio as the ratio of the sampled frequency and the sampling frequency, that is f/fs. We can see from Fig. 4 that the greater the frequency ratio, the greater the minimum entropy, when the number of ROs is constant. With the same sampling frequency, the greater the number of ROs, the greater the minimum entropy.

In Fig. 5, we show the comparison of theoretical entropy and simulation approximate entropy. Line denotes the theoretical lower bound of entropy and point denotes simulation approximate entropy. They have the same trend and the theoretical value is lower than simulation entropy. This is because the theoretical value is a lower bound of entropy.

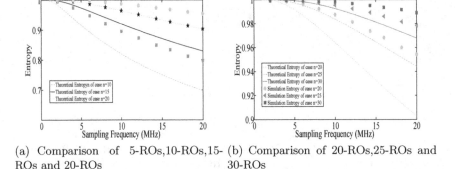

(a) Comparison of 5-ROs, 10-ROs, 15-ROs and 20-ROs

(b) Comparison of 20-ROs, 25-ROs and 30-ROs

Fig. 5. Comparison of the theoretical entropy and the simulation entropy with the sampling frequency and the number of ROs varied, line denotes the theoretical lower bound of entropy and point denotes simulation approximate entropy.

4.2   MRO-TRNG with Jitter-Free

In Proposition 4, we calculate a theoretical lower bound of entropy using the size of the jitter. However, some other factors may cause the generated sequence to look like randomness. This part, we simulate MRO-TRNG to research the impact generated by different frequencies. We carried out the experiment without involving the jitter when the frequencies of MRO-TRNG are slightly different.

Parameter Setting. The frequencies of MRO-TRNG are setted to follow a Gaussian distribution, with drift $\mu = 200$ MHz and volatility $\sigma_f^2 = 10$. The sampling

Table 3. The simulation minimum entropy of MRO-TRNG with jitter-free

Sampling frequency fs	$n = 20, H_\infty$	$n = 25, H_\infty$	$n = 30, H_\infty$
2 MHz	0.994846	0.994577	0.995309
6 MHz	0.994291	0.995198	0.995249
10 MHz	0.994815	0.99415	0.994905
14 MHz	0.994704	0.99487	0.995194
18 MHz	0.99483	0.994737	0.994716

frequencies fs are setted from 2 MHz to 20 MHz. The number of ROs is varied from 5 to 30. The generated sequences are estimated by SP 800-90B.

Results and Analysis. For the generated sequences, we calculate the simulation minimum entropy using the method mentioned above. For 20-ROs, 25-ROs and 30-ROs, the results are shown in Table 3. As the Table 3 shows, though the size of the jitter is zero, the simulation minimum entropy which is supposed to be zero reach up to 0.99. Compared with the simulation minimum entropy obtained in Sect. 4.1, the simulation minimum entropy in Table 3 is much greater than the corresponding value in Sect. 4.1.

For the number of ROs from 5 to 14, Fig. 6 shows the result. In Fig. 6(a), when the number of ROs is constant, the minimum entropy has little change with the variation of sampling frequency. With the number of ROs increasing, the minimum entropy increases. The pseudo-randomness is brought by the different frequencies. Figure 6(b) shows when the number of ROs is 14, the simulation minimum entropy of MRO-TRNG can reach up to 0.99. When the number of ROs is more than 19, the output sequences can pass FIPS 140-2 and NIST SP 800-22 statistical tests.

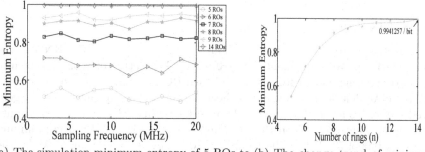

(a) The simulation minimum entropy of 5-ROs to 14-ROs

(b) The change trend of minimum entropy with the number of ROs varied

Fig. 6. The simulation minimum entropy of MRO-TRNG without jitter

5 Hardware Verification on FPGA

In this part, we propose advices on MRO-TRNG design and implement MRO-TRNG on Xilinx Spartan-6 FPGA to verify the entropy estimation model. In order to guarantee the true-randomness of the generated sequences, we propose advices from the aspect of entropy. In Sect. 3.5, Proposition 4 gives the formula of a lower bound of entropy. The combination of theoretical formula and sufficient-entropy condition can be a guidance of MRO-TRNG design. We implement the MRO-TRNG design and verify the stochastic model. Besides, in the design, we take measures to avoid phase interlock phenomenon.

5.1 Phase Interlock

As mentioned above, the phase interlock can cause a sharply decrease in entropy and affect the performance of TRNG. Interlock phenomenon shall be considered in the design. We can avoid interlock from two aspects, RO layout and frequency. Some scholars have studied the reasons from the aspect of RO layout. The phase interlock occurs, when sharing routing brings mutual interference (e.g., circular layout [15]). When two ROs place close and when one RO is in the diagonal of the other RO [17], phase interlock may occur.

In hardware implementation, we avoid the above RO layout. Besides, we make the inverters placement different to disperse the frequencies.

We tap out the signal from each RO to I/O-pins on the FPGA. We measure the signal with oscilloscope to observe the waveforms of two ROs to judge whether there is phase interlock. We observe each two of all the ROs. The waveforms are approximately the same tendency. The Fig. 7 shows one situation. In Fig. 7, the oscilloscope only captures the waveform of one RO. Thus the frequency of the other RO is different from the captured RO. The two ROs are uninterlocked. We observe the waveforms of each two ROs, and we find there are no interlocked ROs in our design.

5.2 Verification

Based on the entropy estimation method, we implement a MRO-TRNG in the FPGA platform. We implement the MRO-TRNG structure of Wold's (shown in Fig. 1(b)). The number of ROs is 30 and each RO is connected by 5 inverters.

We use Aglilent logic analyzer to collect the generated sequences, and the generated sequences are tested by statistical tests. We use SP 800-90B to estimate the minimum entropy. When the sampling frequency is 10 MHz, the minimum entropy is 0.995073. When the sampling frequency is lower than 10 MHz, the generated sequence can pass NIST SP 800-22.

We observe the standard deviation of half-period is 21.6 ps. Then we can calculate the time jitter $\sigma_t = 3.8‰$. Thus, based on the formula obtained in Proposition 4, we can get the security parameter for design. The security sampling frequency is 5.1429 MHz, that is when we set the sampling frequency as 5 MHz, the generated sequences are sufficient-entropy.

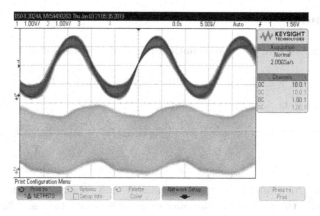

Fig. 7. Oscilloscope screenshot of two ROs waveforms, the two ROs are not interlocked.

In experimental observation, when the sampling frequency is lower than 10 MHz, the generated sequence can always pass NIST SP 800-22. However, in theory, when the sampling frequency is lower than 5 MHz, we can prove the generated sequence is sufficient-entropy. In MRO-TRNG design, we advice using the parameters based on theory model rather than the parameters based on statistical tests.

6 Conclusion

In this paper, we study the security of MRO-TRNG from the perspective of entropy and establish stochastic model. We give an entropy estimation method, which calculates a lower bound of entropy. We verify the correctness of the theory by performing experiments on the worst case. We simulate jitter-free MRO-TRNG to analyze the pseudo-randomness. MRO-TRNG without jitter can pass statistical tests, when the number of ROs is more than 19. The entropy estimation results can be used as the guidance for MRO-TRNG design to ensure the entropy is sufficient even if there exists pseudo-randomness. In FPGA hardware platform, we implement a MRO-TRNG design. At a high sampling frequency (nearly 10 MHz), the output sequence can always pass the NIST SP 800-22 statistical test. However, according to the entropy estimation method, only when the sampling frequency is no higher than 5 MHz, the entropy of the output can be guaranteed no lower than 0.997.

Acknowledgments. This work was partially supported by National Natural Science Foundation of China (No. 61602476, No. 61772518, No. 61872357 and No. 61802396), Cryptography Development Foundation of China (No. MMJJ20170205, MMJJ20180113), and Special Foundation for Industrial Transformation and Upgrading (Departmental Budget, No. 0714-EMTC-02-00577).

A Appendix

In this section, we give the mathematical proof of Proposition 3.

Let

$$\varepsilon = 2P_{\max}[s(t) = 1|\varphi(0) = (x_1, x_2, ...)] - 1,$$

then we can get

$$H_\infty(s(\Delta t)|\varphi(0) = (x_1, x_2, ...)) = -\log_2 P_{\max}[s(t) = 1|\varphi(0) = (x_1, x_2, ...)]$$

$$= -\log_2(\frac{\varepsilon + 1}{2}) = 1 - \frac{1}{ln2}\varepsilon + \frac{1}{2ln2}\varepsilon^2 - -\frac{1}{3ln2}\varepsilon^3 + ...$$

We give the relationship between the maximum probability value of the joint distribution and the product of the maximum probability values of the marginal and conditional.

$$P(AB) = P(A|B) \times P(B),$$

$$P_{\max}(AB) = \max\{P((AB)_1), P((AB)_2), ...\} \geq P((AB)_i),$$

$$P((AB)_i) = P((A|B)_i) \times P(B_i),$$

$$P_{\max}(A|B) = \max\{P((A|B)_1), P((A|B)_2), ...\} \geq P((A|B)_i),$$

$$P_{\max}(B) = \max\{P(B_1), P(B_2), ...\} \geq P(B_i),$$

$$P_{\max}(AB) = P((A|B)_i) \times P(B_i) \leq P_{\max}(B) \times P_{\max}(A|B).$$

Hence,

$$P_{\max}(s(\Delta t), \varphi(0) = (x_1, x_2, ...)) \leq P_{\max}(s(\Delta t)|\varphi(0) = (x_1, x_2, ...))$$

$$\times P_{\max}(\varphi(0) = (x_1, x_2, ...)).$$

$H_\infty = -log_2(P_{\max})$, then we can get

$$H_\infty(s(\Delta t), \varphi(0) = (x_1, x_2, ...)) \geq H_\infty(s(\Delta t)|\varphi(0) = (x_1, x_2, ...))$$

$$+ H_\infty(\varphi(0) = (x_1, x_2, ...)),$$

where

$$H_\infty(\varphi(0) = (x_1, x_2, ...)) = -\log_2(P_{\max}(\varphi(0) = (x_1, x_2, ...))) \geq 0.$$

Thus, we have

$$H_\infty(s(\Delta t), \varphi(0) = (x_1, x_2, ...)) \geq H_\infty(s(\Delta t)|\varphi(0) = (x_1, x_2, ...)),$$

$$H_\infty(s(\Delta t)) \geq H_\infty(s(\Delta t)|\varphi(0)).$$

References

1. Amaki, T., Hashimoto, M., Mitsuyama, Y., Onoye, T.: A worst-case-aware design methodology for noise-tolerant oscillator-based true random number generator with stochastic behavior modeling. IEEE Trans. Inf. Forensics Secur. **8**(8), 1331–1342 (2013)

2. Baudet, M., Lubicz, D., Micolod, J., Tassiaux, A.: On the security of oscillator-based random number generators. J. Cryptol. **24**(2), 398–425 (2011)

3. Bochard, N., Bernard, F., Fischer, V., Valtchanov, B.: True-randomness and pseudo-randomness in ring oscillator-based true random number generators. Int. J. Reconfig. Comput. **2010**, 879281:1–879281:13 (2010)

4. ISO/IEC JTC 1/SC 27, Berlin, Germany: Information Technology - Security Techniques - Random Bit Generation (2011)

5. Killmann, W., Schindler, W.: AIS 31: Functionality Classes and Evaluation Methodology for True (Physical) Random Number Generators. Version 3.1. T-Systems GEI GmbH and Bundesamt für Sicherheit in der Informationstechnik (BSI), Bonn, Germany (2001)

6. Killmann, W., Schindler, W.: A design for a physical RNG with robust entropy estimators. In: Oswald, E., Rohatgi, P. (eds.) CHES 2008. LNCS, vol. 5154, pp. 146–163. Springer, Heidelberg (2008). https://doi.org/10.1007/978-3-540-85053-3_10

7. L'Ecuyer, P., Simard, R.: TestU01: AC library for empirical testing of random number generators. ACM Trans. Math. Softw. (TOMS) **33**(4), 22 (2007)

8. Ma, Y., Lin, J., Chen, T., Xu, C., Liu, Z., Jing, J.: Entropy evaluation for oscillator-based true random number generators. In: Batina, L., Robshaw, M. (eds.) CHES 2014. LNCS, vol. 8731, pp. 544–561. Springer, Heidelberg (2014). https://doi.org/10.1007/978-3-662-44709-3_30

9. Markettos, A.T., Moore, S.W.: The frequency injection attack on ring-oscillator-based true random number generators. In: Clavier, C., Gaj, K. (eds.) CHES 2009. LNCS, vol. 5747, pp. 317–331. Springer, Heidelberg (2009). https://doi.org/10.1007/978-3-642-04138-9_23

10. Marsaglia, G.: Diehard battery of tests of randomness (1995). http://www.stat.fsu.edu/pub/diehard

11. PUB, NIST FIPS: 140-2: Security Requirements for Cryptographic Modules. Washington, DC, USA (2001)

12. Rukhin, A., Soto, J., Nechvatal, J., et al.: A Statistical Suite for Random and Pseudorandom Number Generators for Cryptographic Applications, April 2010. http://nvlpubs.nist.gov/nistpubs/Legacy/SP/nistspecialpublication800-22r1a.pdf

13. Sunar, B., Martin, W.J., Stinson, D.R.: A provably secure true random number generator with built-in tolerance to active attacks. IEEE Trans. Comput. **56**(1), 109–119 (2007)

14. Turan, M.S., Barker, E., Kelsey, J., McKay, K., Baish, M., Boyle, M.: NIST special publication 800-90B: Recommendation for the entropy sources used for random bit generation, January 2018. http://nvlpubs.nist.gov/nistpubs/SpecialPublications/NIST.SP.800-90B.pdf

15. Varchola, M.: FPGA based true random number generators for embedded cryptographic applications (2008)

16. Wold, K., Tan, C.H.: Analysis and enhancement of random number generator in FPGA based on oscillator rings. Int. J. Reconfig. Comput. **2009**, 501672:1–501672:8 (2009)

17. Yoo, S., Karakoyunlu, D., Birand, B., Sunar, B.: Improving the robustness of ring oscillator TRNGs. TRETS **3**(2), 9:1–9:30 (2010)

Secrecy on a Gaussian Relay-Eavesdropper Channel with a Trusted Relay

Keke Hu[1,2]([✉]), Xiaohui Zhang[1,2], and Yongming Wang[1,2]

[1] Institute of Information Engineering, Chinese Academy of Sciences,
Beijing 100093, China
{hukeke,zhangxiaohui,wangyongming}@iie.ac.cn
[2] School of Cyber Security, University of Chinese Academy of Sciences,
Beijing 100049, China

Abstract. Security is a crucial aspect in nowadays wireless communication systems. The open nature of wireless makes the communications more vulnerable to eavesdropping, which leads to that the physical layer security (information theoretic secrecy) is becoming attractive due to its relying on the characteristics of the transmission medium. In this paper, we study the secrecy on a gaussian relay-eavesdropper channel with a trusted relay, which is assumed to be able to decode and encode wiretap codes. We discuss several cooperative strategies to guarantee the information secrecy in some cases and bound the corresponding secrecy rate. Also, we derive a cut-set-like upper bound on the secrecy capacity for our scenario. The relative proofs are also presented in this paper.

Keywords: Physical layer security · Information theoretic secrecy · Shannon's cipher system · Cooperation · Relay

1 Introduction

Due to the ease of accessibility, nowadays wireless communication is inherent vulnerable to eavesdropping. Accordingly, relevant security approaches are proposed to guarantee the information secrecy during the wireless transmission. Recently, physical layer security, known as *information theoretic secrecy*, is becoming attractive due to its independence of any computational assumptions on eavesdroppers. Information theoretic secrecy is first introduced by Shannon in his seminal work [14], where he demonstrates that the perfect secrecy can be achieved via ciphering if the entropy of the key shared between the sender and the receiver is greater than or equal to the entropy of the desired message. In [15], Wyner introduces a degraded wiretap channel and proves that information secrecy can be guaranteed via using wiretap codes instead of secret keys.

This work was supported by the Research of Key Technologies of Global Multimedia Constellation System under Grant No. 17DZ1100700.

S. Chen et al. (Eds.): SecureComm 2019, LNICST 305, pp. 108–125, 2019.
https://doi.org/10.1007/978-3-030-37231-6_6

In [11], it extends the studies on wiretap channel to a gaussian scenario. In [6], the authors combine the Shannon's and the Wyner's results and present the secrecy capacity via using the technique combining the wiretap coding and the Shannon's ciphering schemes.

Recent studies extend the information theoretic secrecy from point-to-point systems to relay or cooperative communications. In the previous studies on relay transmission [2,7], it has been proved that the cooperative strategies between the source and the relay can indeed increase the transmission rate. Therefore, the researchers tend to investigate the impact on the information secrecy brought by the relay. In [13] it considers the relay as both an eavesdropper and a helper, and in [5] it illustrates that even an untrusted relay can also be beneficial. In [4], the relay works as a cooperative jammer and can in fact be beneficial to increase the secrecy rate in a gaussian relay channel with an eavesdropper in some cases. Further studies propose several practical cooperative schemes to enhance the secrecy via the assistance of the relay [4,8,17]. In [9,10,16], it studies a four-terminal relay-eavesdropper channel, where the relay is trusted, and presents relative bounds on secrecy rate.

In this paper, a four-terminal gaussian relay-eavesdropper channel is studied. Differentiating from the earlier relevant works [9,10,16], we assume that the trusted relay is able to decode and encode wiretap codes. Motivated by the cut-set bounds on the secrecy capacity for wiretap networks of type II discussed in [1], we derive a cut-set-like upper bound for the gaussian relay-eavesdropper channel in our scenario. Since the capacity of a general relay channel is unknown, we discuss the secrecy in the following schemes:

1. Direct transmission: the relay is not actively used in the communication, and it broadcasts a structured jamming message which has little influence on the main channel.
2. Multi-hop transmission: the relay decodes the wiretap codewords sent from the source and then encodes it into another independent wiretap codewords before forwarding. Here, the destination gains nothing directly from the source.
3. Decode-forward: the source divides the desired confidential message into two different messages and then sends them to the relay and the destination respectively, where the message of the destination is used as a secret key for the relay. The relay decodes its own confidential message via the technique combining the wiretap coding and the Shannon's ciphering schemes [12], and then encodes it into another wiretap codewords before forwarding. The destination first decodes the transmitted codewords from the relay while considering the source as part of the noise, and then decodes the transmitted codewords from the source after the message from the relay has been subtracted out.

In our assumption, the relay can encode wiretap codes, which means the relay is able to introduce its local randomness into the forwarding transmission. Then if viewing the randomness introduced by the source and the relay as common messages sent to both the destination and the eavesdropper (like in [3]), we can see that our work cannot be simply viewed as a study on a relay channel with an eavesdropper but a special four-terminal wiretap network, where two different common messages are sent to both the destination and the eavesdropper besides the confidential message sent from the source to the destination. Therefore, our work is definitely different from the aforementioned works.

Throughout this paper, we define the notations as follow: X^n denotes vector $(X(1), \ldots, X(n))$; boldface capital letter $\mathbf{X}$ denotes matrix; $\mathbf{I}$ denotes identity matrix; $\{\bullet\}^T$ denotes transpose; $[x]^+$ denotes $\max\{0, x\}$; $\mathrm{diag}(a_1, \ldots, a_n)$ denotes a diagonal matrix; $\mathcal{N}(0, P)$ denotes normal distribution with 0 mean and P variance; $\mathcal{U}[1 : N]$ denotes uniform distribution among $[1 : N]$.

The rest of the paper is organized as follow: in Sect. 2 we introduce the system model; in Sect. 3 we discuss the achievable secrecy rate for the three aforementioned schemes; in Sect. 4 we discuss the cut-set upper bound on the secrecy capacity; and the conclusion is given in Sect. 5.

2   Preliminaries

In this paper, a four-terminal discrete memoryless relay-eavesdropper channel is considered, consisting of a source, a relay, a destination and an eavesdropper. The discrete channel has two input alphabets $\mathcal{X}$ and $\mathcal{X}_r$ and three output alphabets $\mathcal{Y}$, $\mathcal{Y}_r$ and $\mathcal{Z}$.

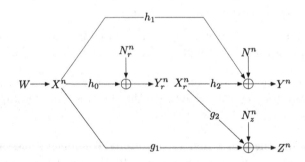

Fig. 1. The gaussian relay-eavesdropper channel.

Consider a gaussian relay-eavesdropper channel depicted in Fig. 1, which is a point-to-point gaussian wiretap channel with an extra node having relay function. The channel outputs corresponding to the inputs X and X_r are

$$Y_r = h_0 X + N_r \tag{1}$$
$$Y = h_1 X + h_2 X_r + N \tag{2}$$
$$Z = g_1 X + g_2 X_r + N_z, \tag{3}$$

where $h_0, h_1, h_2, g_1, g_2 \geq 0$ are the channel gains, and N_r, N, N_z are independent noise components with i.i.d $\sim \mathcal{N}(0,1)$. It is assumed that average power constraint P on each of X and X_r. The relay can both send X_r and receive Y_r at the same time.

The message W is the desired confidential message that uniformly distributed among the message set $\mathcal{W}_s = [1 : 2^{nR_s}]$ and $m_\mathcal{R} \in \mathcal{W}_\mathcal{R}$ is a realization of the local randomness at the source encoder. The encoder at the source maps a message $w \in \mathcal{W}_s$ and a realization of the local randomness $m_\mathcal{R}$ to a codeword X^n, $f : \mathcal{W}_s \times \mathcal{W}_\mathcal{R} \to \mathcal{X}^n$. Given the observation sequence Y_r^n and a realization of local randomness $m_{\mathcal{R}0} \in \mathcal{W}_{\mathcal{R}0}$, the relay encoder maps the signals Y_r^{i-1} and $m_{\mathcal{R}0}$ to the channel input $X_r(i)$ at time i, $f_r(i) : Y_r^{i-1} \times m_{\mathcal{R}0} \to X_r(i)$. The decoder at the destination finds a unique $\hat{w} \in \mathcal{W}_s$ according to its observation Y^n, $g : \mathcal{Y}^n \to \mathcal{W}_s$.

The average error probability is given by

$$P_e = \frac{1}{|\mathcal{W}_s|} \sum_{w \in \mathcal{W}_s} \Pr\{\hat{w} \neq w\}. \tag{4}$$

The secrecy rate R_s is said to be achievable, if there exists a sequence of codes $(2^{nR_s}, n)$ and ϵ, η where $\lim_{n \to \infty} \epsilon, \eta = 0$ such that, for n is large enough, the following holds

$$P_e \leq \epsilon$$

$$\frac{1}{n} H(W|Z^n) \geq R_s - \eta.$$

Note that if Z^n is negligible, the channel can be viewed as a special four-terminal wiretap network where W is the confidential message sent from the source to the destination, $m_\mathcal{R}$ is a common message broadcast by the source and $m_{\mathcal{R}0}$ is another common message broadcast by the relay. In such scenario, the maximum R_s equals to the maximum rate of the classical relay channel without security constraints.

3   Lower Bounds on the Secrecy Capacity of the Gaussian Relay-Eavesdropper Channel

3.1   Direct-Transmission Lower Bound

It has been proved that the secrecy can be improved via using cooperative jamming scheme [4,8,17]. However, if $h_2 \geq g_2$, the cooperative jamming may not achieve its goal. In this part, we propose another scheme, where the source sends message directly using optical point-to-point secure coding scheme while the relay transmitting structured jamming information which reduces the eavesdropper rate while has little influence on the destination. Then we obtain the relative lower bound on the secrecy capacity of the gaussian relay-eavesdropper channel (GREC) which describes the secrecy improvement as below:

Theorem 1. *The lower bound on the secrecy capacity of GREC with direct-transmission scheme is given by*

$$
C_S \geq \min \left\{ \begin{array}{l} \left[C\left(h_1^2 P\right) - C\left(\dfrac{g_1^2 P}{1 + g_2^2 P}\right) \right]^+ , \\[3mm] \left[C\left(h_1^2 P + h_2^2 P\right) - C\left(g_1^2 P + g_2^2 P\right) \right]^+ \end{array} \right\}. \tag{5}
$$

Proof. Before designing the coding scheme for direct-transmission scheme in GREC, it should be declared first that the relay works as a special jammer and cannot relay any confidential message in this scheme.

Coding scheme:

Codebook generation $\mathcal{C}$: Let $M_s = 2^{n(R_s - \epsilon)}$, $M_\mathcal{R} = 2^{n(R_\mathcal{R} - \epsilon)}$ and $M_{\mathcal{R}0} = 2^{n(R_{\mathcal{R}0} - \epsilon)}$ be integers. We generate M_s i.i.d. gaussian codewords $X_s^n(w_s)$ with average power $\lambda_s P - \varepsilon$ for $w_s \in \mathcal{W}_s = [1 : 2^{nR_s}]$, $M_\mathcal{R}$ i.i.d. gaussian codewords $X_\mathcal{R}^n(m_\mathcal{R})$ with average power $\lambda_\mathcal{R} P - \varepsilon$ for $m_\mathcal{R} \in \mathcal{W}_R = [1 : 2^{nR_\mathcal{R}}]$ and $M_{\mathcal{R}0}$ i.i.d. gaussian codewords $X_{\mathcal{R}0}^n(m_{\mathcal{R}0})$ with average power $P - \varepsilon$ for $m_{\mathcal{R}0} \in \mathcal{W}_R = [1 : 2^{nR_{\mathcal{R}0}}]$. Here, an arbitrary number ε is introduced for the power constraints, and $\lambda_s + \lambda_\mathcal{R} = 1$. The codebook is revealed to all parties.

Encoding: It is supposed that w_s is the message to be sent. The source first randomly and uniformly selects a message $m_\mathcal{R}$ from $\mathcal{W}_R$. After picking the corresponding codewords, the source constructs the codeword $X^n = X_s^n(w_s) + X_\mathcal{R}^n(m_\mathcal{R})$ and then transmits it.

Relay encoding: The relay randomly and uniformly selects $m_{\mathcal{R}0}$ from $\mathcal{W}_{R0}$ and then picks corresponding codeword $X_{\mathcal{R}0}^n(m_{\mathcal{R}0})$ as the transmitted codeword X_r^n.

Decoding: The destination utilize the sequential decoding (onion-peeling): firstly, it finds unique $\hat{m}_{\mathcal{R}0}$ while viewing the source codewords as part of the noise; secondly, it subtracts $\hat{m}_{\mathcal{R}0}$ from its observation and then finds unique $\hat{m}_\mathcal{R}$; finally, it subtracts $\hat{m}_{\mathcal{R}0}$ and $\hat{m}_\mathcal{R}$ from its observation and then finds unique $\hat{w}_s$. Then the decoder output $\hat{w}_s$.

We define the average error probability of this scheme

$$
\tilde{P}_e \triangleq \Pr\{(\hat{w}_s, \hat{m}_\mathcal{R}, \hat{m}_{\mathcal{R}0}) \neq (w_s, m_\mathcal{R}, m_{\mathcal{R}0})\} \tag{6}
$$

It can be observed that $\tilde{P}_e \geq P_e$. According to coding theorem, it can be proved that $\lim_{n \to \infty} \tilde{P}_e = 0$ if

$$
R_s + R_\mathcal{R} \leq C(h_1^2 P) \tag{7}
$$

$$
R_{\mathcal{R}0} \leq C\left(\frac{h_2^2 P}{1 + h_1^2 P}\right). \tag{8}
$$

Then we discuss the equivocation on the desired message w_s of the eavesdropper, $H(w_s|Z^n)$.

1. If the eavesdropper views X_r^n as side information, it can be acquired that

$$H(w_s|Z^n) = H(w_s) - I(w_s; Z^n)$$
$$\overset{(a)}{=} H(w_s) - I(w_s; Z^n) + I(w_s; Z^n|X^n, X_r^n)$$
$$= H(w_s) - I(X^n, X_r^n; Z^n) + I(X^n, X_r^n; Z^n|w_s),$$

where (a) is established because $I(w_s; Z^n|X^n, X_r^n) = 0$. Then we can see that the eavesdropper gains nothing on w_s if $I(X^n, X_r^n; Z^n) - I(X^n, X_r^n; Z^n|w_s)$ is small enough. First, the sum-rate of the eavesdropper is given by

$$I(X^n, X_r^n; Z^n) \leq nC(g_1^2 P + g_2^2 P). \tag{9}$$

Then, we have $I(X^n, X_r^n; Z^n|w_s) = H(X^n, X_r^n|w_s) - H(X^n, X_r^n|w_s, Z^n)$, where for the first term

$$H(X^n, X_r^n|w_s) = H(X_s^n, X_{\mathcal{R}}^n, X_{\mathcal{R}0}^n|w_s) = H(X_{\mathcal{R}}^n, X_{\mathcal{R}0}^n)$$
$$= n(R_{\mathcal{R}} + R_{\mathcal{R}0}), \tag{10}$$

and the second term

$$H(X^n, X_r^n|w_s, Z^n) \leq n\eta' \tag{11}$$

according to the Fano's inequality where $\eta' \to 0$ if $n \to \infty$.
It can be seen that if $R_{\mathcal{R}} + R_{\mathcal{R}0} = C(g_1^2 P + g_2^2 P)$, the information leakage rate is given

$$\frac{1}{n}I(w_s; Z^n) = \frac{1}{n}(H(w_s) - H(w_s|Z^n)) \leq \eta'. \tag{12}$$

and there exists a wiretap coding scheme forcing eavesdropper only decode $X_{\mathcal{R}0}^n$ and $X_{\mathcal{R}}^n$ with high probability and gain no information on w_s. Recalling the constraints (7) and (8), we then bound the secrecy rate

$$R_s \leq \left[C\left(h_1^2 P + h_2^2 P\right) - C\left(g_1^2 P + g_2^2 P\right) \right]^+. \tag{13}$$

2. However, if the eavesdropper views X_r^n as part of noise, then the equivocation of the eavesdropper can be written as

$$H(w_s|Z^n) = H(w_s) - I(X^n; Z^n) + I(X^n; Z^n|w_s).$$

Similarly, we have

$$I(X^n; Z^n) \leq nC\left(\frac{g_1^2 P}{1 + g_2^2 P}\right),$$

and

$$I(X^n; Z^n|w_s) \geq nR_{\mathcal{R}} - n\eta'. \tag{14}$$

Then if $R_0 = C\left(\frac{g_1^2 P}{1+g_2^2 P}\right)$, the information leakage rate $\frac{1}{n}I(w_s; Z^n)$ tends to 0 for n is sufficiently large. Recalling the constraint (7), the secrecy rate is bounded as

$$R_s \le \left[C\left(h_1^2 P\right) - C\left(\frac{g_1^2 P}{1+g_2^2 P}\right)\right]^+. \tag{15}$$

Combining (13) and (15), we can prove the achievability of (5) as $n \to \infty$.

In this scheme the relay broadcasts structured jamming information which has little influence on the destination. It can be seen that if $R_{\mathcal{R}0} \ge C(g_2^2 P)$, it is impossible for eavesdropper to decode $m_{\mathcal{R}0}$, which leads to (15). However, it should be noticed that the secrecy rate of the proposed scheme is lower than $C(h_1^2 P) - C(g_1^2 P)$ when $h_2 \le g_2$, which is opposite to the results of the cooperative jamming. Therefore, our scheme is applied for the situation when the channel from the relay to the destination is better than that to the eavesdropper, which can be a complement for the cooperative jamming scheme.

3.2 Multi-hop Lower Bound

The other extreme transmission scheme is to deliver the desired messages through the relay via using decode-and-forward scheme while ignoring the path between source and destination. In this scenario, we propose that the relay is able to decode and encode wiretap codes, which leading to the following theorem:

Theorem 2. *If the relay is able to encode and decode wiretap codes, the lower bound on the secrecy capacity of GREC with multi-hop scheme is given by*

$$C_S \ge \min \left\{ \begin{array}{l} \left[C\left(h_0^2 P\right) - C\left(g_1^2 P\right)\right]^+, \\ \left[C\left(\frac{h_2^2 P}{1+h_1^2 P}\right) - C\left(\frac{g_2^2 P}{1+g_1^2 P}\right)\right]^+ \end{array} \right\}, \tag{16}$$

and the bound is tight if h_1 is negligible.

Proof. We use the b transmission blocks to prove the achievability of the lower bound, while each block contains n transmissions, as depicted in Fig. 2. A sequence of $b - 1$ confidential messages $w_j, j \in [1 : b - 1]$, each being i.i.d. $\sim \mathcal{U}[1 : 2^{nR_s}]$, is transmitted through the b blocks with $w_b = 1$. It can be seen that the average rate of confidential message is $R_s(b - 1)/b$, which implies that R_s can be achieved over the b blocks if $b \to \infty$.

Coding scheme:

Codebook generation $\mathcal{C}_j$: Let $M_s = 2^{n(R_s-\epsilon)}$, $M_{\mathcal{R}} = 2^{n(R_{\mathcal{R}}-\epsilon)}$ and $M_{\mathcal{R}0} = 2^{n(R_{\mathcal{R}0}-\epsilon)}$ be integers. In j-th block, we independently generate M_s gaussian codewords $X_s^n(w_j)$ for $w_j \in \mathcal{W}_s = [1 : 2^{nR_s}]$, $M_{\mathcal{R}}$ gaussian codewords $X_{\mathcal{R}}^n(m_{\mathcal{R}})$ for $m_{\mathcal{R}} \in \mathcal{W}_{\mathcal{R}} = [1 : 2^{nR_{\mathcal{R}}}]$, M_s gaussian codewords $X_{rs}^n(\tilde{w}_{j-1})$ for

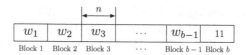

Fig. 2. Multiple transmission blocks used in the multi-hop scheme.

$\tilde{w}_{j-1} \in \mathcal{W}_s$ and $M_{\mathcal{R}0}$ gaussian codewords $X_{r0}^n(m_{\mathcal{R}0})$ for $m_{\mathcal{R}0} \in \mathcal{W}_{\mathcal{R}0} = [1 : 2^{nR_{\mathcal{R}0}}]$. It is assumed that the components of each codewords, $X_s(i)$, $X_{\mathcal{R}}(i)$, $X_{rs}(i)$, $X_{\mathcal{R}0}(i)$, have a multivariate normal distribution with zero mean and covariance matrix $\begin{bmatrix} \mathbf{\Lambda}_1 & \mathbf{\Sigma} \\ \mathbf{\Sigma}^T & \mathbf{\Lambda}_2 \end{bmatrix} \in \mathbb{R}^{4\times 4}$, where (1) $\mathbf{\Lambda}_1 = \text{diag}(\lambda_s, \lambda_{\mathcal{R}})P - \varepsilon\mathbf{I}$, (2) $\mathbf{\Lambda}_1 = \text{diag}(\lambda_{rs}, \lambda_{\mathcal{R}0})P - \varepsilon\mathbf{I}$, (3) $\mathbf{\Sigma} = (\rho_{ab}) \in \mathbb{R}^{2\times 2}$, (4) $\lambda_s + \lambda_{\mathcal{R}} = \lambda_{rs} + \lambda_{\mathcal{R}0} = 1$ and $\sum_a \sum_b \rho_{ab} = \rho$.

Encoding: It is supposed that w_j is the new message to be sent from the source to the relay in j-th block. The source first randomly and uniformly selects a message $m_{\mathcal{R}}$ from set $\mathcal{W}_{\mathcal{R}}$. After picking the corresponding codewords from codebook $\mathcal{C}_j$, the source constructs the codewords $X^n(w_j) = X_s^n(w_j) + X_{\mathcal{R}}^n(m_{\mathcal{R}})$ and then transmits it.

Relay encoding: At the end of j-th block, the relay finds $\tilde{w}_j$ from its observation Y_r^n given $\tilde{w}_{j-1}$. After randomly and uniformly picking $m_{\mathcal{R}0}$ up from set $\mathcal{W}_{\mathcal{R}0}$, the relay transmits $X_r^n(\tilde{w}_j) = X_{rs}^n(\tilde{w}_j) + X_{\mathcal{R}0}^n(m_{\mathcal{R}0})$ from the codebook $\mathcal{C}_{j+1}$ in $j + 1$-th block. By convention, we assume $\tilde{w}_0 = 1$.

Decoding: The destination cannot decode the transmission from the source and views it as part of the noise. Then it finds the unique message $\hat{w}_{j-1}$ via joint typical decoding.

The average error probability for $\mathcal{C}_j$ is defined as

$$\tilde{P}_e(\mathcal{C}_j) \triangleq \Pr\left\{(\tilde{w}_j, \hat{w}_{j-1}) \neq (w_j, \tilde{w}_{j-1})\right\}. \tag{17}$$

Since P_e of j-th block is $\Pr\left\{\hat{w}_{j-1} \neq w_{j-1}\right\}$, we can observe that $\tilde{P}_e(\mathcal{C}_j) \geq P_e$. According to the coding theorem, it can be proved that $\lim_{n\to\infty} \tilde{P}_e(\mathcal{C}_j) = 0$ if

$$R_s + R_{\mathcal{R}} \leq C\left((1 - \rho^2)h_0^2 P\right) \tag{18}$$

$$R_s + R_{\mathcal{R}0} \leq C\left(\frac{(\rho h_1 + h_2)^2 P}{1 + (1 - \rho^2)h_1^2 P}\right) \tag{19}$$

where $\rho = \dfrac{E(XX_r)}{\sqrt{E(X^2)E(X_r^2)}}$.

In our assumption, each codebook $\mathcal{C}_j$ is generated independently for each block, therefore secrecy analysis of an arbitrary block is sufficient. The information leakage rate associated with $\mathcal{C}_j$ in j-th block is given by

$$R_L(\mathcal{C}_j) \triangleq \frac{1}{n} I(w_j, \tilde{w}_{j-1}; Z^n).$$

Since the confidential messages are sent chronologically, we should ensure that the j-th block leakage has little impact on the secrecy of $j+1$-th block. Therefore, we consider $I(w_j, \tilde{w}_{j-1}; Z^n) = I(\tilde{w}_{j-1}; Z^n) + I(w_j; Z^n | \tilde{w}_{j-1})$ and then analyze the two terms in the following:

1. The equivocation on $\tilde{w}_{j-1}$ is given by

$$
\begin{aligned}
H(\tilde{w}_{j-1} | Z^n) &= H(\tilde{w}_{j-1}) - I(\tilde{w}_{j-1}; Z^n) \\
&= H(\tilde{w}_{j-1}) - I(\tilde{w}_{j-1}; Z^n) + I(\tilde{w}_{j-1}; Z^n | X_r^n) \\
&= H(\tilde{w}_{j-1}) - I(X_r^n; Z^n) + I(X_r^n; Z^n | \tilde{w}_{j-1}) \\
&\geq H(\tilde{w}_{j-1}) - nC\left(\frac{(\rho g_1 + g_2)^2 P}{1 + (1 - \rho^2)g_1^2 P}\right) + nR_{\mathcal{R}0} - n\eta'.
\end{aligned}
$$

Accordingly, we find that $\frac{1}{n}I(\tilde{w}_{j-1}; Z^n) \leq \eta'$ if the following condition is satisfied

$$
R_{\mathcal{R}0} = C\left(\frac{(\rho g_1 + g_2)^2 P}{1 + (1 - \rho^2)g_1^2 P}\right). \tag{20}
$$

Substituting (20) into (19), it can be derived

$$
R_s \leq C\left(\frac{h_2^2 P}{1 + h_1^2 P}\right) - C\left(\frac{(\rho g_1 + g_2)^2 P}{1 + (1 - \rho^2)g_1^2 P}\right). \tag{21}
$$

2. Given $\tilde{w}_{j-1}$, the equivocation of eavesdropper on w_j is written as

$$
\begin{aligned}
H(w_j | Z^n, \tilde{w}_{j-1}) &= H(w_j | \tilde{w}_{j-1}) - I(w_j; Z^n | \tilde{w}_{j-1}) \\
&\overset{(a)}{\geq} H(w_j | \tilde{w}_{j-1}) - I(w_j; Z^n | X_r^n) \\
&\overset{(b)}{=} H(w_j) - I(X^n; Z^n | X_r^n) + I(X^n; Z^n | w_j, X_r^n) \\
&\geq H(w_j) - nC\left((1 - \rho^2)g_1^2 P\right) + nR_{\mathcal{R}} - n\eta',
\end{aligned}
$$

where (a) is established since the fact that $I(w_j; Z^n | \tilde{w}_{j-1}) \leq H(w_j | \tilde{w}_{j-1}) = H(w_j | \tilde{w}_{j-1} m_{\mathcal{R}0}) = H(w_j | X_{rs}^n, X_{\mathcal{R}0}^n) \leq I(w_j; Z^n | X_{rs}^n, X_{\mathcal{R}0}^n) + n\upsilon_n$ where $\lim_{n \to \infty} \upsilon_n = 0$; (b) follows because w_j and $\tilde{w}_{j-1}$ are independent. Thus, we observe that $\frac{1}{n}I(w_j; Z^n | w_{j-1}) \leq \eta'$ if the following condition is satisfied

$$
R_{\mathcal{R}} = C\left((1 - \rho^2)g_1^2 P\right). \tag{22}
$$

Substituting (22) into (18), we then obtain

$$
R_s \leq C\left((1 - \rho^2)h_0^2 P\right) - C\left((1 - \rho^2)g_1^2 P\right). \tag{23}
$$

Here, we find that $\lim_{n \to \infty} R_L(\mathcal{C}_j) = 0$ if the conditions in (20) and (22) is satisfied. Therefore, the achievable secrecy rate should be the small one of (21) and (23). Then the maximum achievable secrecy rate can be derived if $\rho = 0$, which means there is no coherently cooperation during the transmission, and (16) is achieved.

The proof of tightness is given in Sect. 4.

3.3   Decode-Forward Lower Bound

In the multi-hop scheme, the destination views the source sequences as part of the noise and ignores the information it contains. Therefore, in the design of coding scheme, the source only consider secure transmission to the relay and the model is equivalent to a two-hop communication. However, if the destination tries to decode both the messages sent from the source and the relay simultaneously, it leads the following with proper coding scheme.

Theorem 3. *If the relay is able to encode and decode wiretap codes, the lower bound on the secrecy capacity of GREC with decode-and-forward scheme is given by*

$$C_S \geq \max_{\substack{\rho,\alpha \in [0,1] \\ \bar{\alpha}=1-\alpha}} \min \left\{ \begin{array}{l} \left[C\left(\dfrac{(\alpha + \bar{\alpha}\rho^2)h_1^2 P + h_2^2 P + 2\rho h_1 h_2 P}{1 + \bar{\alpha}(1-\rho^2)h_1^2 P} \right) \right. \\ \qquad \left. - C\left(\dfrac{(\alpha + \bar{\alpha}\rho^2)g_1^2 P + g_2^2 P + 2\rho g_1 g_2 P}{1 + \bar{\alpha}(1-\rho^2)g_1^2 P} \right) \right]^+, \\[4mm] \left[C\left(\bar{\alpha}(1-\rho^2)h_0^2 P \right) + 2C\left(\dfrac{\alpha(1-\rho^2)h_1^2 P}{1 + \bar{\alpha}(1-\rho^2)h_1^2 P} \right) \right. \\ \qquad \left. - C\left(\bar{\alpha}(1-\rho^2)g_1^2 P \right) - 2C\left(\dfrac{\alpha(1-\rho^2)g_1^2 P}{1 + \bar{\alpha}(1-\rho^2)g_1^2 P} \right) \right]^+, \\[4mm] \left[C\left(\bar{\alpha}(1-\rho^2)h_0^2 P \right) + C\left(\dfrac{\alpha(1-\rho^2)h_1^2 P}{1 + \bar{\alpha}(1-\rho^2)h_1^2 P} \right) \right]^+ \end{array} \right\}.$$

$$(24)$$

Proof. Again, we consider using b blocks to transmit a sequence of $b-1$ confidential messages w^{b-1}, where $w_j \sim$ i.i.d. $\mathcal{U}[1 : M_s]$. In this proof, we use the binning scheme, where the source and the relay cooperatively send the bin index l_j of w_j in $j+1$-th block to help the destination recover the w_j. As depicted in Fig. 3, the confidential message set $[1 : M_s]$ is partitioned into M_l equal bins $\mathcal{B}(l) = [(l-1)M_u + 1 : lM_u], l \in \mathcal{W}_l = [1 : M_l]$, where $M_s = 2^{n(R_s - \epsilon)}$, $M_l = 2^{n(R_l - \epsilon)}$ and $M_u = 2^{n(R_u - \epsilon)}$ are integers and $M_s = M_l M_u$. We introduce $u_j \in \mathcal{W}_u = [1 : M_u]$ to denote the position of w_j in the bin $\mathcal{B}(l_j)$. The indexes l_j and u_j can be viewed as two independently and uniformly distributed variables. In j-th block, the source broadcasts u_{j-1} and l_j to the destination and the relay

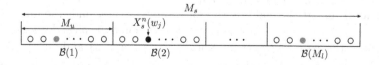

Fig. 3. Binning scheme: each w_j can be represented by u_j and l_j. The gray is the u_j in each bin and the black is w_j.

respectively; simultaneously, the relay sends $\tilde{l}_{j-1}$ to the destination, where $\tilde{l}_{j-1}$ is the estimate result relay derived in $j-1$-th block.

Coding scheme:

Message sets. We divide the sets $\mathcal{W}_u$ and $\mathcal{W}_l$ into three independent parts $\mathcal{W}_{ui} = [1 : 2^{nR_{ui}}]$ and $\mathcal{W}_{li} = [1 : 2^{nR_{li}}]$ respectively, for $i = 1, 2, 3$. In this division, we force $R_{u1} = R_{l1}$ and then use the sets $\mathcal{W}_{u1}$ and $\mathcal{W}_{l1}$ to construct $\mathcal{W}_{\otimes 1} = [1 : 2^{nR_{\otimes 1}}]$ by Xoring their corresponding elements. Similar, we force $R_{u2} = R_{l2}$ and then construct $\mathcal{W}_{\otimes 2} = [1 : 2^{nR_{\otimes 2}}]$. Therefore, we have

$$R_{u1} = R_{l1} = R_{\otimes 1} \quad \text{and} \quad R_{u2} = R_{l2} = R_{\otimes 2},$$
$$R_{\otimes 1} + R_{\otimes 2} \le R_u. \tag{25}$$

Codebook generation. $\mathcal{C}_j$ In j-th block, we randomly and independently generate M_u gaussian codewords $X_u^n(u_{j-1})$ for $u_{j-1} \in \mathcal{W}_u$, $M_{\otimes 1}$ gaussian codewords $X_{\otimes 1}^n(m_{j,\otimes 1})$ for $m_{j,\otimes 1} \in \mathcal{W}_{\otimes 1}$, M_{r1} gaussian codewords $X_{r1}^n(m_{r1})$ for $m_{r1} \in \mathcal{W}_{r1} = [1 : 2^{nR_{r1}}]$, M_{l3} gaussian codewords $X_{l3}^n(l_{j,3})$ for $l_{j,3} \in \mathcal{W}_{l3}$, $M_{\otimes 2}$ gaussian codewords $X_{\otimes 2}^n(m_{j,\otimes 2})$ for $m_{j,\otimes 2} \in \mathcal{W}_{\otimes 2}$, M_{r2} gaussian codewords $X_{r2}^n(m_{r2})$ for $m_{r2} \in \mathcal{W}_{r2} = [1 : 2^{nR_{r2}}]$, M_l gaussian codewords $X_{rl}^n(\tilde{l}_{j-1})$ for $\tilde{l}_{j-1} \in \mathcal{W}_l$, and M_{r0} gaussian codewords $X_{r0}^n(m_{r0})$ for $m_{r0} \in \mathcal{W}_{r0} = [1 : 2^{nR_{r0}}]$, respectively. Let the components of each codeword, $X_u(i), X_{l3}(i), X_{r1}(i), X_{r2}(i), X_{\otimes 1}(i), X_{\otimes 2}(i), X_{rl}(i), X_{r0}(i)$, have a multivariate normal distribution with zero mean and covariance matrix $\begin{bmatrix} \mathbf{\Lambda}_1 & \mathbf{\Sigma} \\ \mathbf{\Sigma}^T & \mathbf{\Lambda}_2 \end{bmatrix} \in \mathbb{R}^{8 \times 8}$, where (1) $\mathbf{\Lambda}_1 = \text{diag}(\alpha\lambda_u, \alpha\lambda_{\otimes 1}, \alpha\lambda_{r1}, \bar{\alpha}\lambda_{l3}, \bar{\alpha}\lambda_{\otimes 2}, \bar{\alpha}\lambda_{r2})P - \varepsilon\mathbf{I}$, (2) $\mathbf{\Lambda}_2 = \text{diag}(\lambda_{rl}, \lambda_{r0})P - \varepsilon\mathbf{I}$, (3) $\mathbf{\Sigma} = (\rho_{ab}) \in \mathbb{R}^{6 \times 2}$, (4) $\alpha + \bar{\alpha} = \lambda_u + \lambda_{\otimes 1} + \lambda_{r1} = \lambda_{l3} + \lambda_{\otimes 2} + \lambda_{r2} = \lambda_{rl} + \lambda_{r0} = 1$ and (5) $\sum_a \sum_b \rho_{ab} = \rho$.

Encoding. In j-th block, the source is able to calculate the triple $(l_{j,3}, m_{j,\otimes 1}, m_{j,\otimes 2})$ according to its randomly given message pair (u_{j-1}, l_j). Then it uniformly chooses a random message pair (m_{r1}, m_{r2}) from the sets $\mathcal{W}_{r1}$ and $\mathcal{W}_{r2}$. After picking the corresponding codewords, the source constructs the codewords

$$U^n(u_{j-1}) = X_u^n(u_{j-1}) + X_{\otimes 1}^n(m_{j,\otimes 1}) + X_{r1}^n(m_{r1}),$$
$$V^n(l_{j,3}) = X_{l3}^n(l_{j,3}) + X_{\otimes 2}^n(m_{j,\otimes 2}) + X_{r2}^n(m_{r2}),$$

and then simply transmits

$$X^n(u_{j-1}, l_j) = U^n(u_{j-1}) + V^n(l_{j,3}).$$

Note that $u_0 = l_b = 1$ by convention.

Relay encoding. At the end of j-th block, the relay first finds the unique messages $\tilde{u}_{j-1}, \tilde{m}_{j,\otimes 1}, \tilde{m}_{r1}, \tilde{l}_{j,3}, \tilde{m}_{j,\otimes 2}$ and $\tilde{m}_{r2}$ via jointly typical decoding. Then it derives the pair $(\tilde{l}_{j,1}, \tilde{l}_{j,2})$ by Xoring $(\tilde{u}_{j-1,1}, \tilde{u}_{j-1,2})$ and $(\tilde{m}_{j,\otimes 1}, \tilde{m}_{j,\otimes 2})$, respectively. At last the relay derives $\tilde{l}_j$ from Y_r^n, where $\tilde{l}_j$ is the concatenation of $\tilde{l}_{j1}, \tilde{l}_{j2}$ and $\tilde{l}_{j3}$. In $j+1$-th block, the relay will randomly and uniformly choose m_{r0} from $\mathcal{W}_{r0}$ and then transmit the codeword $X_r^n(\tilde{l}_j) = X_{rl}^n(\tilde{l}_j) + X_{r0}^n(m_{r0})$ from codebook $\mathcal{C}_{j+1}$. Note that $\tilde{l}_0 = 1$ by convention.

Decoding. The decoding at the destination is considered as two-stage process: **(1)** the destination first decodes the information sent by the relay while considering that sent by the source as part of the noise; **(2)** then the destination decodes the information sent by the source after that sent by relay has been subtracted out. At the end of j-th block, the decoder outputs $\hat{w}_{j-1}$, where $\hat{w}_{j-1}$ is the concatenation of $\hat{u}_{j-1}$ and $\hat{l}_{j-1}$.

Source	$X^n(1, l_1)$	$X^n(u_1, l_2)$	$\cdots$	$X^n(u_{b-2}, l_{b-1})$	$X^n(u_{b-1}, 1)$
Relay	$X_r^n(1)$	$X_r^n(\tilde{l}_1)$	$\cdots$	$X_r^n(\tilde{l}_{b-2})$	$X_r^n(\tilde{l}_{b-1})$
	Block 1	Block 2	$\cdots$	Block $b-1$	Block b

Fig. 4. The encoding scheme used in Theorem 3.

The encoding scheme is depicted in Fig. 4. In this coding scheme, it should be noted that **(1)** $\rho = \frac{E\{XX_r\}}{\sqrt{E\{X^2\}E\{X_r^2\}}}$; **(2)** the rates of l_j and $\tilde{l}_{j-1}$ both are R_l. We define the average error probability for $\mathcal{C}_j$

$$\tilde{P}_e(\mathcal{C}_j) \triangleq \Pr\{(\hat{u}_{j-1}, \tilde{l}_j, \hat{l}_{j-1}) \neq (u_{j-1}, l_j, \tilde{l}_{j-1})\}. \tag{26}$$

Then it can be seen that $\tilde{P}_e(\mathcal{C}_j)$ is larger than P_e in j-th block. According to the coding theorem, it can be proved that $\tilde{P}_e(\mathcal{C}_j)$ is negligible for a sufficiently large n if

$$R_u + R_{\otimes 1} + R_{r1} \leq C\left(\frac{\alpha(1-\rho^2)h_1^2 P}{1 + \bar{\alpha}(1-\rho^2)h_1^2 P}\right) \tag{27}$$

$$R_{l3} + R_{\otimes 2} + R_{r2} \leq C\left(\bar{\alpha}(1-\rho^2)h_0^2 P\right) \tag{28}$$

$$R_l + R_{r0} \leq C\left(\frac{(\rho h_1 + h_2)^2 P}{1 + (1-\rho^2)h_1^2 P}\right) \tag{29}$$

$$R_u + R_{\otimes 1} + R_{r1} + R_l + R_{r0} \leq C\left(h_1^2 P + h_2^2 P + 2\rho h_1 h_2 P\right), \tag{30}$$

where $\alpha \in [0,1]$ and $\bar{\alpha} = 1 - \alpha$.

Since in our assumption the channel is memoryless and each codebook $\mathcal{C}_j$ is independent of each other, we only need to analyze the secrecy in one block. In j-th block, the information leakage rate associated with $\mathcal{C}_j$ is defined as

$$R_L(\mathcal{C}_j) \triangleq \frac{1}{n}I(u_{j-1}, l_j, \tilde{l}_{j-1}; Z^n)$$

$$= \underbrace{\frac{1}{n}I(\tilde{l}_{j-1}; Z^n)}_{R_{L1}(\mathcal{C}_j)} + \underbrace{\frac{1}{n}I(u_{j-1}, l_j; Z^n|\tilde{l}_{j-1})}_{R_{L2}(\mathcal{C}_j)}$$

In the following, we discuss $R_{L1}(\mathcal{C}_j)$ and $R_{L2}(\mathcal{C}_j)$ respectively.

1. The equivocation on $\tilde{l}_{j-1}$ at eavesdropper in j-th block is given by

$$
\begin{aligned}
H(\tilde{l}_{j-1}|Z^n) &= H(\tilde{l}_{j-1}) - I(\tilde{l}_{j-1}; Z^n) \\
&= H(\tilde{l}_{j-1}) - I(\tilde{l}_{j-1}; Z^n) + I(\tilde{l}_{j-1}; Z^n|X_r^n) \\
&= H(\tilde{l}_{j-1}) - I(X_r^n; Z^n) + I(X_r^n; Z^n|\tilde{l}_{j-1}) \\
&\geq H(\tilde{l}_{j-1}) - nC\left(\frac{(\rho g_1 + g_2)^2 P}{1 + (1-\rho^2)g_1^2 P}\right) + nR_{r0} - n\eta'.
\end{aligned}
$$

It can be seen that $R_{L1}(C_j) \leq \eta'$ if the following condition is satisfied

$$
R_{r0} = C\left(\frac{(\rho g_1 + g_2)^2 P}{1 + (1-\rho^2)g_1^2 P}\right). \tag{31}
$$

Substituting (31) into (29), we then can derive the rate of the confidential message $\tilde{l}_{j-1}$ as

$$
R_l \leq C\left(\frac{(\rho h_1 + h_2)^2 P}{1 + (1-\rho^2)h_1^2 P}\right) - C\left(\frac{(\rho g_1 + g_2)^2 P}{1 + (1-\rho^2)g_1^2 P}\right). \tag{32}
$$

2. It is obvious that

$$
I(u_{j-1}, l_j; Z^n|\tilde{l}_{j-1}) \leq I(u_{j-1}; Z^n|\tilde{l}_{j-1}) + I(l_j; Z^n|\tilde{l}_{j-1}). \tag{33}
$$

Then we analyze the first term of (33). Given $\tilde{l}_{j-1}$, the equivocation on u_{j-1} is given by

$$
\begin{aligned}
H(u_{j-1}|Z^n\tilde{l}_{j-1}) &= H(u_{j-1}|\tilde{l}_{j-1}) - I(u_{j-1}; Z^n|\tilde{l}_{j-1}) \\
&\overset{(a)}{\geq} H(u_{j-1}) - I(u_{j-1}; Z^n|\tilde{l}_{j-1}X_r^n) + I(u_{j-1}; Z^n|\tilde{l}_{j-1}X_r^nU^n) \\
&\overset{(b)}{=} H(u_{j-1}) - I(u_{j-1}; Z^n|X_r^n) + I(u_{j-1}; Z^n|X_r^nU^n) \\
&= H(u_{j-1}) - I(U^n; Z^n|X_r^n) + I(U^n; Z^n|X_r^nu_{j-1}) \\
&\geq H(u_{j-1}) - nC\left(\frac{\alpha(1-\rho^2)g_1^2 P}{1 + \bar{\alpha}(1-\rho^2)g_1^2 P}\right) + n(R_{\otimes 1} + R_{r1}) - n\eta_1',
\end{aligned}
$$

where (a) follows since u_{j-1} and $\tilde{l}_{j-1}$ are independent, $I(u_{j-1}; Z^n|\tilde{l}_{j-1}X_r^nU^n) = 0$ and $I(u_{j-1}; Z^n|\tilde{l}_{j-1}) \leq I(u_{j-1}; Z^n|\tilde{l}_{j-1}X_r^n)$; (b) follows because $\tilde{l}_{j-1}$ is mapped into X_r^n. Accordingly, we find $\frac{1}{n}I(u_{j-1}; Z^n|\tilde{l}_{j-1}) \leq \eta_1'$ if

$$
R_{\otimes 1} + R_{r1} = C\left(\frac{\alpha(1-\rho^2)g_1^2 P}{1 + \bar{\alpha}(1-\rho^2)g_1^2 P}\right). \tag{34}
$$

Substituting (34) into (27), it can be derived

$$
R_u \leq C\left(\frac{\alpha(1-\rho^2)h_1^2 P}{1 + \bar{\alpha}(1-\rho^2)h_1^2 P}\right) - C\left(\frac{\alpha(1-\rho^2)g_1^2 P}{1 + \bar{\alpha}(1-\rho^2)g_1^2 P}\right). \tag{35}
$$

Due to the structure of $\mathcal{W}_l$, l_j can be viewed as a combination of three independent variables $l_{j,1}$, $l_{j,2}$ and $l_{j,3}$. Therefore, the second term of (33) can be rewritten as

$$
\begin{aligned}
I(l_j; Z^n|\tilde{l}_{j-1}) = {}& I(l_{j,3}; Z^n|\tilde{l}_{j-1}) + I(l_{j,2}; Z^n|\tilde{l}_{j-1}l_{j,3}) \\
& + I(l_{j,1}; Z^n|\tilde{l}_{j-1}l_{j,3}l_{j,2}).
\end{aligned}
\tag{36}
$$

Based on the Shannon's cipher system, the second term of (36) can be eliminated as follow:

$$
\begin{aligned}
I(l_{j,2}; Z^n|\tilde{l}_{j-1}l_{j,3}) = {}& H(l_{j,2}|\tilde{l}_{j-1}l_{j,3}) - H(l_{j,2}|Z^n\tilde{l}_{j-1}l_{j,3}) \\
\overset{(a)}{=} {}& H(l_{j,2}) - H(l_{j,2}|Z^n\tilde{l}_{j-1}l_{j,3}) \\
\overset{(b)}{\leq} {}& H(l_{j,2}) - H(l_{j,2}|\tilde{l}_{j-1}l_{j,3}m_{j,\otimes 1}m_{j,\otimes 2}m_{r1}m_{r2}m_{r0}) \\
\overset{(c)}{=} {}& H(l_{j,2}) - H(l_{j,2}|m_{j,\otimes 2}) \overset{d}{=} 0,
\end{aligned}
$$

where (a) follows since $l_{j,2}$, $l_{j,3}$ and $\tilde{l}_{j-1}$ are independent of each other; (b) follows since the eavesdropper cannot extract u_{j-1} from Z^n if the condition in (33) is satisfied; (c) follows since $m_{j,\otimes 2}$ is the only message related to $l_{j,2}$; (d) follows since the entropy of the secret key equals to the entropy of the transmitted message in Shannon's cipher system [14]. Similarly, $I(l_{j,1}; Z^n|\tilde{l}_{j-1}l_{j,3}l_{j,2}) = 0$. Then, it can be seen

$$
I(l_j; Z^n|\tilde{l}_{j-1}) = I(l_{j,3}; Z^n|\tilde{l}_{j-1}).
$$

Given $\tilde{l}_{j-1}$, the equivocation on $l_{j,3}$ is given by

$$
\begin{aligned}
H(l_{j,3}|Z^n\tilde{l}_{j-1}) \geq {}& H(l_{j,3}) - I(l_{j,3}; Z^n|X_r^n) \\
= {}& H(l_{j,3}) - I(l_{j,3}; Z^n|X_r^n) + I(l_{j,3}; Z^n|X_r^n V^n) \\
= {}& H(l_{j,3}) - I(V^n; Z^n|X_r^n) + I(V^n; Z^n|X_r^n l_{j,3}) \\
\geq {}& H(l_{j,3}) - nC((1-\rho^2)\bar{\alpha}g_1^2 P) + n(R_{\otimes 2} + R_{r2}) - n\eta_2'.
\end{aligned}
$$

Similarly, we find that $\frac{1}{n}I(l_j; Z^n|\tilde{l}_{j-1}) = \frac{1}{n}I(l_{j,3}; Z^n|\tilde{l}_{j-1}) \leq \eta_2'$ if the following condition is satisfied

$$
R_{\otimes 2} + R_{r2} = C\left(\bar{\alpha}(1-\rho^2)g_1^2 P\right).
\tag{37}
$$

Substituting (37) into (28), we derive

$$
R_{l3} \leq C\left(\bar{\alpha}(1-\rho^2)h_0^2 P\right) - C\left(\bar{\alpha}(1-\rho^2)g_1^2 P\right).
\tag{38}
$$

Note that the rate of the confidential message l_j is the summation of R_{l1}, R_{l2} and R_{l3}. Recalling (25), we can bound the rate of l_j as

$$
\begin{aligned}
R_l = {}& R_{l1} + R_{l2} + R_{l3} \leq R_{l3} + R_u \\
\leq {}& C\left(\bar{\alpha}(1-\rho^2)h_0^2 P\right) + C\left(\frac{\alpha(1-\rho^2)h_1^2 P}{1+\bar{\alpha}(1-\rho^2)h_1^2 P}\right) - C\left((1-\rho^2)g_1^2 P\right).
\end{aligned}
\tag{39}
$$

Meanwhile, we should consider (34) and (37) while bounding R_l since $R_{l1} + R_{l2} = R_{\otimes 1} + R_{\otimes 2}$, and then derive

$$R_l = R_{\otimes 1} + R_{\otimes 2} + R_{l3}$$
$$\leq C\left(\bar{\alpha}(1-\rho^2)h_0^2 P\right) + C\left(\frac{\alpha(1-\rho^2)g_1^2 P}{1+\bar{\alpha}(1-\rho^2)g_1^2 P}\right). \tag{40}$$

Noting that R_s is the summation of R_u and R_l, we bound the confidential message rate R_s as following: **(1)** the first term of (24) is derived by combining the results of (35) and (32); **(2)** the second term of (24) is acquired by combing the results of (35) and (39); **(3)** the third term of (24) is obtained by combing the results of (35) and (40). If we take the limit as $n \to \infty$ such that $R_L(\mathcal{C}_j) \to 0$, we prove the achievability of (24).

In our study, it should be noted that the proposed scheme is based under the assumption that $h_0 \geq h_1$ and it is obvious that the result converges to (5) in Theorem 1 if $h_0 \leq h_1$. For $h_0 \geq h_1$, it can be seen that the proposed scheme provides better performance than the direct-transmission scheme, e.g., taking $\alpha = 1$. Also, we can see that if $\alpha = 0$ the result converge to (16) in Theorem 2 which indicates that the multi-hop scheme is a special part of the proposed decode-forwarding scheme.

4   The Cut-Set Bound on the Secrecy Capacity

The following upper bound is motivated by the cut-set bounds on the secrecy capacity for wiretap networks of type II discussed in [1]:

Theorem 4. *If the relay is assumed to decode and encode wiretap code, the secrecy capacity of GREC is upper bounded as*

$$C_S \leq \max_{\rho \in [0,1]} \min \left\{ \begin{array}{l} \left[C\left((1-\rho^2)(h_0^2 P + h_1^2 P)\right) - C\left((1-\rho^2)g_1^2 P\right)\right]^+, \\ \left[C\left(h_1^2 P + h_2^2 P + 2\rho h_1 h_2 P\right) - C\left(g_1^2 P + g_2^2 P + 2\rho g_1 g_2 P\right)\right]^+ \end{array} \right\}. \tag{41}$$

Proof. According to Fano's inequality, the equivocation on W of the eavesdropper is given by

$$H(W|Z^n) = H(W|Z^n) - H(W|Y^n, Z^n) + H(W|Y^n, Z^n) \tag{42}$$
$$\leq I(W; Y^n|Z^n) + n\epsilon', \tag{43}$$

where $\lim_{n \to \infty} \epsilon' = 0$. Defining $Y^i = (Y_1, \ldots, Y_i)$ as i-length sequence, we consider to establish the second term of (41)

$$I(W; Y^n | Z^n) = \sum_{i=1}^{n} I(W; Y_i | Y^{i-1} Z^n) \tag{44}$$

$$= \sum_{i=1}^{n} \left[H(Y_i | Y^{i-1} Z^n) - H(Y_i | W Y^{i-1} Z^n) \right] \tag{45}$$

$$\overset{(a)}{\leq} \sum_{i=1}^{n} \left[H(Y_i | Y^{i-1} Z^n) - H(Y_i | W Y^{i-1} Z^n X_i X_{r,i}) \right] \tag{46}$$

$$\overset{(b)}{\leq} \sum_{i=1}^{n} \left[H(Y_i | Y^{i-1} Z_i) - H(Y_i | W Y^{i-1} Z_i X_i X_{r,i}) \right] \tag{47}$$

$$= \sum_{i=1}^{n} I(X_i X_{r,i} W; Y_i | Z_i Y^{i-1}), \tag{48}$$

where (a) follows because $H(Y_i | W Y^{i-1} Z^n X_i X_{r,i}) \leq H(Y_i | W Y^{i-1} Z^n)$; (b) follows because $H(Y_i | Y^{i-1} Z_i) \geq H(Y_i | Y^{i-1} Z^n)$ and $H(Y_i | W Y^{i-1} Z_i X_i X_{r,i}) = H(Y_i | W Y^{i-1} Z^n X_i X_{r,i})$ due to the memoryless assumption. We now introduce a random variable Q which is i.i.d $\sim \mathcal{U}[1:n]$. Then rewrite the (48) as

$$I(W; Y^n | Z^n) \leq \sum_{i=1}^{n} I(X_i X_{r,i} W; Y_i | Z_i Y^{i-1}) = n I(X_Q X_{r,Q} W; Y_Q | Z_Q Y^{Q-1} Q). \tag{49}$$

Then we define $X \triangleq X_Q$, $X_r \triangleq X_{r,Q}$, $Y \triangleq Y_Q$, $Z \triangleq Z_Q$ and $U \triangleq QY^{Q-1}$. In our case we assume that $\min(h_0, h_1) \geq g_1$ and $h_2 \geq g_2$, we can form the Markov chain $U \to (X, X_r) \to Y \to Z$. Combining the equations (43), (48) and (49), we derive

$$R_s \leq \frac{1}{n} H(W | Z^n) + \eta \leq \frac{1}{n} I(W; Y^n | Z^n) + \epsilon' + \eta$$
$$= I(XX_r; Y | ZU) + \epsilon' + \eta \leq I(XX_r; Y | Z) + \epsilon' + \eta$$
$$\leq I(XX_r; Y) - I(XX_r; Z) + \epsilon' + \eta$$
$$\leq \left[C \left(h_1^2 P + h_2^2 P + 2\rho h_1 h_2 P \right) - C \left(g_1^2 P + g_2^2 P + 2\rho g_1 g_2 P \right) \right]^+ + \epsilon' + \eta. \tag{50}$$

Next we establish the first term of (41) in a similar way

$$R_s \leq \frac{1}{n} I(W; Y^n | Z^n) + \epsilon' + \eta \leq \frac{1}{n} I(W; Y^n Y_r^n | Z^n) + \epsilon' + \eta$$

$$\leq \frac{1}{n} \sum_{i=1}^{n} I(X_i; Y_i Y_{r,i} | Z_i Y^{i+1} Y_r^{i+1} X_{r,i}) + \epsilon' + \eta \tag{51}$$

$$= I(X_Q; Y_Q Y_{r,Q} | Z_Q Y^{Q+1} Y_r^{Q+1} X_{r,Q} Q) + \epsilon' + \eta$$

Defining $X \triangleq X_Q$, $X_r \triangleq X_{r,Q}$, $Y \triangleq Y_Q$, $Z \triangleq Z_Q$ and $U \triangleq QY^{Q-1}Y_r^{Q-1}$, we have

$$R_s \leq I(X; YY_r|ZX_rU) + \epsilon' + \eta \leq I(X; YY_r|X_r) - I(X; Z|X_r) + \epsilon' + \eta$$

$$= \left[C\left((1-\rho^2)(h_0^2 P + h_1^2 P)\right) - C\left((1-\rho^2)g_1^2 P\right) \right]^+ + \epsilon' + \eta \tag{52}$$

Taking $n \to \infty$ completes the proof of the upper bound in (41).

Then we can see that if the h_1 is negligible, the cut-set-like upper bound is

$$C_S \leq \min\left\{ C\left(h_0^2 P\right) - C\left(g_1^2 P\right), C\left(h_2^2 P\right) - C\left(g_2^2 P\right) \right\},$$

which indicates that the bound in Theorem 2 is tight when $h_1 \to 0$.

5   Conclusion

In this paper, we discuss the secrecy on a gaussian relay-eavesdropper channel, where the relay is assumed to be able to decode and encode wiretap codes. Differentiating from the previous work, the relay here is able to introduce randomness to protect its forwarding message to the destination. We discuss several secure cooperative strategies for three special cases. First, we study the structured jamming scheme which can be considered as an alternative for the cooperative jamming schemes when $h_2 \geq g_2$; then, we study the multi-hop transmission scheme and indicate that the secrecy rate can be increased if the relay is able to decode and encode wiretap codes; finally, we propose a secure technique that combining the wiretap coding and the Shannon's ciphering schemes for decode-forwarding strategy, where the secret message directly transmitted to the destination is utilized as a secret key for the relay. At last, we present a cut-set-like upper bound on secrecy capacity for the gaussian wiretap channel with a trusted relay. Our work gives another way to view the relay-eavesdropper channel, if the relay works as not only a helper but also a special source that broadcasts random codes to confuse the eavesdropper. Our next work is to figure out a proper compressed-forward scheme for a relay channel with an eavesdropper.

References

1. Cheng, F., Yeung, R.W.: Performance bounds on a wiretap network with arbitrary wiretap sets. IEEE Trans. Inf. Theory **60**(6), 3345–3358 (2014)
2. Cover, T., Gamal, A.E.: Capacity theorems for the relay channel. IEEE Trans. Inf. Theory **25**(5), 572–584 (1979)
3. Csiszár, I., Korner, J.: Broadcast channels with confidential messages. IEEE Trans. Inf. Theory **24**(3), 339–348 (1978)
4. Dong, L., Han, Z., Petropulu, A.P., Poor, H.V.: Improving wireless physical-layer security via cooperating relays. IEEE Trans. Signal Process. **58**(3), 1875–1888 (2010)

5. He, X., Yener, A.: Cooperation with an untrusted relay: a secrecy perspective. IEEE Trans. Inf. Theory **56**(8), 3807–3827 (2010)

6. Kang, W., Liu, N.: Wiretap channel with shared key. In: 2010 IEEE Information Theory Workshop, pp. 1–5, August 2010

7. Kramer, G., Gastpar, M., Gupta, P.: Cooperative strategies and capacity theorems for relay networks. IEEE Trans. Inf. Theory **51**(9), 3037–3063 (2005)

8. Krikidis, I., Thompson, J.S., McLaughlin, S.: Relay selection for secure cooperative networks with jamming. IEEE Trans. Wireless Commun. **8**(10), 5003–5011 (2009)

9. Lai, L., El Gamal, H.: Cooperative secrecy: the relay-eavesdropper channel. In: 2007 IEEE International Symposium on Information Theory, pp. 931–935, June 2007

10. Lai, L., El Gamal, H.: The relay-eavesdropper channel: cooperation for secrecy. IEEE Trans. Inf. Theory **54**(9), 4005–4019 (2008)

11. Leung-Yan-Cheong, S., Hellman, M.: The Gaussian wire-tap channel. IEEE Trans. Inf. Theory **24**(4), 451–456 (1978)

12. Mansour, A.S., Schaefer, R.F., Boche, H.: On the individual secrecy capacity regions of the general, degraded, and Gaussian multi-receiver wiretap broadcast channel. IEEE Trans. Inf. Forensics Secur. **11**(9), 2107–2122 (2016)

13. Oohama, Y.: Capacity theorems for relay channels with confidential messages. In: 2007 IEEE International Symposium on Information Theory, pp. 926–930, June 2007

14. Shannon, C.E.: Communication theory of secrecy systems. Bell Syst. Tech. J. **28**(4), 656–715 (1949)

15. Wyner, A.D.: The wire-tap channel. Bell Syst. Tech. J. **54**(8), 1355–1387 (1975)

16. Yuksel, M., Erkip, E.: The relay channel with a wire-tapper. In: 2007 41st Annual Conference on Information Sciences and Systems, pp. 13–18, March 2007

17. Zhang, J., Gursoy, M.C.: Collaborative relay beamforming for secrecy. In: 2010 IEEE International Conference on Communications, pp. 1–5, May 2010

Target Information Trading - An Economic Perspective of Security

Jing Hou[1], Li Sun[1], Tao Shu[1(✉)], and Husheng Li[2]

[1] Department of Computer Science and Software Engineering,
Auburn University, Auburn, AL 36849, USA
{jzh0141,lzs0070,tshu}@auburn.edu
[2] Department of Electrical Engineering and Computer Science,
The University of Tennessee Knoxville, Knoxville, TN 37996, USA
hli31@utk.edu

Abstract. Ample evidence has confirmed the importance of information in security. While much research on security game has assumed the attackers' limited observation capabilities to obtain target information, few work considers the possibility that the information can be acquired from a data broker, not to mention exploring the profit-seeking behaviors of such an information service in the shrouded underground society. This paper studies the role of information in security problem when the target information is sold by a data broker to multiple competitive attackers. We formulate a novel multi-stage game model to characterize both the cooperative and competitive interactions of the data broker and attackers. Specifically, the attacker competition with correlated purchasing and attacking decisions is modeled as a two-stage stochastic model; and the bargaining process between the data broker and the attackers is analyzed in a Stackelberg game. Both the attackers' competitive equilibrium solutions and data broker's optimal pricing strategy are obtained. Our results show that with information trading, the target suffers from larger risks even when the information price is too high to benefit the attackers; and the information accuracy is more valuable when the target value is higher. Furthermore, the competition may weaken the information value to the attackers but benefit the data broker. The study contributes to the literature by characterizing the co-opetitive behaviors of the attackers with labor specialization, providing quantitative measures of information value from an economic perspective, and thus promoting a better understanding of the profit-seeking underground community.

Keywords: Security · Information market · Game theory · Economics

1 Introduction

Target information is undoubtedly a crucial factor of security problems in various applications for protecting critical infrastructure like transportation and computer networks. Attackers conduct surveillance to gain awareness of targets' vulnerabilities and security operations, based on which to make a selection of

© ICST Institute for Computer Sciences, Social Informatics and Telecommunications Engineering 2019
Published by Springer Nature Switzerland AG 2019. All Rights Reserved
S. Chen et al. (Eds.): SecureComm 2019, LNICST 305, pp. 126–145, 2019.
https://doi.org/10.1007/978-3-030-37231-6_7

where to attack and how much effort to take in attacking [1,2]. In reality, most often attackers have limited observation capabilities such that they may only have few or partial information about the target's vulnerability [3]. However, in some situations the attackers do not necessarily need to observe by themselves to gain the information. The widespread use of and thus an immerse demand for potential target information in hacker communities has spawned a *data brokers* industry [4]. The data brokers in crime society are specialized in collecting target information (e.g., software vulnerabilities, snippets of code, credit card numbers and compromised accounts) and sell them in black markets in exchange for financial gain [5]. For example, users of the underground forums regularly engage in the buying, selling and trading of illegally obtained information to support criminal activities [6]. As a report [7] published by TrendMicro states: "Underground hackers are monetizing every piece of data they can steal or buy and are continually adding services so other scammers can successfully carry out online and in-person fraud." The Shadow Brokers, which trades in compromised network data and exploits, is a representative of such a data broker as a hacker group. In June 2017, the computer virus NotPetya was able to spread by leveraging a vulnerability leaked by the Shadow Brokers [8]. More recently, Facebook, accused of privacy violations that could provide "material support" for terrorism potentially, was reported to face multibillion-dollar FTC fine [9]. Indeed, data brokers, as a boon to the cybercrime economy [10], have become an indispensable member of the illegally evolved supply chain called "cybercrime-as-a-service" [11].

While we do not have a clear picture of the information trading behaviors in the underground society, security researchers are taking more interest in exploring hacker communities. Initial studies of security experts have reached a consensus that one major motivation of hackers is profit-related (others include fame and skill improvement etc.) [12]. Our aim in this paper is to study the profit-driven attacking behaviors in a hacker community, with a particular emphasis on the role of target information provided by a data broker in security using economic analysis. More precisely, we would like to understand the value of traded target information—both for the sellers of this information and for the attackers that buy it. Through an economic analysis of the attacking behaviors with information trading, we would be able to provide a simple glimpse of complex society structure, and to better understand the phenomenon of hacking. These knowledge provide at least tentative insights for arriving at effective solutions to security problems with information leakage.

We consider one or multiple attackers that have limited observation capabilities of the potential target. They can approach a data broker that holds the vulnerability of the target. The target vulnerability determines how much effort the attackers need to take in order to launch a successful attack. Without the information, the attacker may choose not to act, fail or exert more effort than needed. The attackers could benefit from purchasing the information by launching a more targeted attack with less effort. Here we care about the value of the information for the attackers and how the data broker should price the information if they can obtain it, but how the data broker could obtain the information is beyond our focus. Besides, we talk about the scenario of multiple attackers when the target value can be shared among them if they all deliver successful attacks. The assumption of competition among attackers through dividing up the value of a single asset is appropriate when they share the benefits of private goods as illegal resource access (like spectrum or other network resource utilization) and monopoly privileges (like stealing electronically stored information about consumers' personal data for market exploration). Similar assumptions can be found in [13], which adopts a rent-seeking model of security games where the asset value is divided among the attackers and the defender. We are interested in whether there is a positive or negative network externality in the information market due to the competition among the attackers, that is, would the existence of more potential buyers increases the value of the data broker's information or decreases it.

With the observation of the hierarchical and competitive structure in attacker behaviors, we present and study a multi-stage model of information market. In Stage I, the data broker determines the information price to the attackers. In Stage II, the attackers decide whether to buy or not. In Stage III, after obtaining the target information, the attackers decide whether to attack the target or not. The composed game provides an integrated view of security problem with competitive attackers and target information trading. The research questions we aim to answer include: (a) How would the attacker change its attacking decision once it has bought some detailed information of the target's vulnerability from the data broker? (b) How does the competition between the attackers affect their information purchasing decision and attacking decisions? (c) Is it beneficial for the data broker to set a low price such that all attackers would buy the information? Or should the data broker enhance the price when there is more potential buyers rather than one? (d) How are the decisions affected when the data has lower quality (only partial information is available for trading)?

The problems are challenging due to the following two reasons. First, there is lack of a systematic or quantitative framework to evaluate the information in a competitive crime community. Although it is intuitive that the more information, the better for the attackers, questions are still unexplored as what is the highest price that the attacker can accept? Does an attacker always benefit from buying the information if other attackers also buy it? Or is the information more valuable if other attackers do not buy? To the best of our knowledge, this is the first paper that tries to provide a unified framework of information market in security. We will provide insights regarding the impacts of target information trading on various parties: the increased attacking probability of the target, the expected utility increase for the attackers and the profit through selling the information for the data broker.

Second, the hierarchy attacker behaviors are interdependent across multiple stages. On one hand, the attacking decisions, including whether or not to attack, and with how much effort, are affected by the attackers' knowledge of the target. On the other hand, whether or not to buy the information is determined by how much utility gain can be expected from attacking. The competition among multiple attackers makes these decisions even more complex. This is different from most competition analysis when the product can be sold to only one buyer and the game ends after the purchasing is done. Therefore, the structure of the game varies across the stages. We will model the game among the attackers as Bayesian games, to capture their limited observability, and model their purchasing-attacking decision process as a stochastic game. Besides, from the data broker's perspective, the purchasing probability of the buyers is not only determined by the competition game equilibrium among the attackers, but also affected by the target value and the price. We will use a Stackelberg game to model the pricing and purchasing decisions of the players.

Our main contributions can be summarized as follows.

- While most traditional security game model assume that target information is obtained through attackers' self-observation and learning, we consider an information market in hacker communities and propose a game-theoretic framework, which captures the multi-stage correlated behaviors of attackers. This information market model better fits the practice of a profit-seeking hacker communities with labor specialization. Our results show that in this information channel, information accuracy is more valuable for a more attractive target.
- Much previous work focus on interactions between a defender and single or multiple independent attackers, without consideration of the competitions among the attackers or the role of other players that assist in attacking. We incorporate the strategic interactions between multiple competitive attackers as in a Bayesian and stochastic game, and between the attackers and the data broker as in a Stackelberg game. Our analysis indicates that the value of information for the attackers could be weakened by their competition. Besides, with the assistance of a data broker, even if the information does not benefit the attackers under high price, the target may suffer from larger attacking risk. And the risk will be increased in a certain range confined by both the price and the target value.
- We provide the equilibrium solutions and characterize the conditions for the existence and uniqueness of the equilibrium under different target values. We show that if the target is not attractive enough, there may be multiple pure-strategy equilibria in the attackers' competition game. And whether there will be a strictly dominant pure-strategy is determined by the target value, the target vulnerability and the information price. Furthermore, in the Stackelberg game equilibria, it is not wise for the data broker to set a price low enough to attract all the buyers if the target is attractive enough to the attackers.

The remainder of this paper is organized as follows. Section 2 reviews the related literature. Section 3 introduces the model setups. In Sects. 4 and 5, we study the single attack model and the competition model, respectively. In Sect. 6, we provide an extension model with low information accuracy, and this paper is concluded in Sect. 7.

2   Related Work

Much of the research in security game has assumed that the attacker has perfect observation of the defense policy over potential targets and therefore been able to explore the value of commitment for the defender in a Stackelberg game framework [14]. Realizing that this assumption rarely hold in real-world domains, existing studies are turning their interests into the scenario of incomplete, inaccurate or uncertain information. Some work has proposed the version of the security game with bounded memory [15] or imperfect observations [16]. Others have assumed that the target information gained by the attackers can be learned more accurately by conducting a period of surveillance [17,18]. A more recent study which has pointed out the possibility that the defender is allowed to strategically disclose the number of resources to the attacker, further shows the importance of target information [19]. However, none of the above studies consider the possibility of intermediary information acquisition from a market. The value and the impacts of such a information service have hardly been addressed. Although there is already study evaluating the value of customer information for the retailers' pricing strategies in consumer market [4]. Their results cannot be applied to the security problem because the target in security problem may be not exclusive to the attackers as the merchandise is to consumers.

Our paper focuses on the information market in the context of hacker community. Hacker community is both devastating and prevalent because it facilities cooperation and allows for specialization among attackers, leading to more advanced and more economically efficient attacks. We can discern a growing interest among researchers in the enigmatic hacker community. Some studies have focused on the organization of the community, like identifying the key actors [5], discovering the types of collaborative attack patterns [20] or evaluating its sustainability [9]. Others provide a window into the society by microscopically analyzing the behaviors of the attackers, mostly addressing their cooperation in the form of coalition. Current studies assume that the attackers are heterogeneous in their non-task-specific efficiency, resource allocation or skill sets, and thus coalition is formed for more attacks or to gain higher total utility [21–23]. But the format of collusion with labor specialization, especially the information service, which is universal in hacker community, has not been fully explored. More specifically, the questions are not studied yet about how the attackers would benefit from information assistance, and what is the bargaining process that decides their reward allocations. The answers to these questions are crucial to investigate why and how information service is provided in hacker community, as well as when such cooperation is formed among profit-driven attackers. Besides, the competition among attackers for the limited resource pool is another factor that impacts the attacking decisions and rewards, while it is usually ignored in the existing research, except in [13]. In an attempt to fill the gap in the current literature on the incentives of complex behaviors in hacker society, this research take into consideration both the cooperation among attackers specialized in different tasks and competition among similar attackers. Specifically, we analyze the interactions between a data broker and two competing attackers through a multi-stage game approach. The value of information is derived and the impacts of such information service are evaluated.

3   System Model and Problem Formulation

Consider two attackers trying to attack one potential target. The attackers have limited ability to obtain the vulnerabilities (or the protection level of the defender) about the target. But they can purchase the information from a data supplier, who has full or partial knowledge about the target's vulnerabilities. The data supplier needs to set a price for the information. And given the price, the attackers determine whether or not to make a purchase. Afterwards (when the information has been revealed to the attackers if purchase is made), they will decide whether to attack the target. All the players in our model are profit-motivated.

If a attacker successfully attacks the target, it receives utility $v > 0$, otherwise it receives zero utility. The value of v (also called the target value), reflecting the target attractiveness to the attackers, is a common knowledge to all the players. We restrict our model to the target resource that consumption by one agent would reduce consumption by others. That is, when multiple attackers successfully attack the target, they equally split the target value. In a two-attacker case, either would get a utility of $\frac{1}{2}v$. This assumption relies on the fact that the target pool in reality is finite and attackers compete for a common asset pool.

We define the success of a attacker as follows: if the attacker's effort e in attacking is not smaller than the target's protection level by its defender (or owner), we say the attacker succeeds in the attack. The problem is, the attacker itself is not aware of the exact value of the target protection level, which determines the minimum level of effort for attackers to successfully attack the target. In the following analysis, we will slight abuse the terms of target protection level or vulnerability and the minimum attacking effort needed, and use one symbol to denote it: θ. A smaller value of θ indicates a lower surveillance and thus less effort to launch a successful attack. Let us suppose the attackers only know the distribution of θ, which is normalized to be uniformly distributed on $[0, 1]$, with the largest value 1 implying the defender capacity. If an attacker tries to attack the target with an effort less than the actual value of θ, then it will fail.

Measured in both the success probability of an attack and the expected gain, the attacker's total utility function with an attacking effort e is written as

$$f = \mathbf{1}_{e \geq \theta}(e) * v - C(e). \tag{1}$$

Here $C(e)$ is the attacking cost which increases with the effort e. We will assume $C(e) = e$ for simplicity. Although this assumption represents a simple linear function between the effort and the cost, it is reasonable and would not affect the major insights obtained from our analysis.

The data supplier is a broker who collects and sells data about the target vulnerability or the target owner's protection level. This information tells how much effort needed to launch a successful attack for the attackers, i.e. the actual value of θ. An attacker who buys the information could launch a targeted attack with exactly the minimum level of efforts needed. In Sect. 6, we all also study the situation when the data broker only has partial information about the target, which means that the information could only tell a more accurate range of θ than the attacker has. We are interested in how the data broker chooses to sell the data and what is the information value for all the players, and ignore the details of how the broker acquires the data.

We provide a framework for analyzing how the attacker's optimal information purchasing and attacking decisions could be made in the face of the competition and uncertainty about the target vulnerabilities. To better analyzing the impacts of competition, we assume the attackers are homogeneous. The attacker's objective is to maximize the expected benefit from an attack (taking into account the attacker's target valuation, the success probability of an attack and the cost involved in purchasing and attacking); the data broker sets the information price to maximize the expected profit (taking into account the purchasing probability of the attackers).

The model's timing proceeds as follows:

*Step*1. The data broker determines and broadcasts the information price p.

*Step*2. The attackers decide whether to buy the information or not. After the payments are made, the data broker delivers the target information to the buyer(s).

*Step*3. With the information available, the attackers decide how much effort will be taken in attacking (zero effort means not to attack).

*Step*4. After the attack, the corresponding utilities are gained by the attackers.

4 Single Attacker Model

As a benchmark, we consider the case where a monopolist attacker (*he*) will fully exploit this situation and extract all surplus from successfully attacking the target. He needs to make a decision of whether to buy the target information from a data broker (*she*), by comparing the two expected utilities as follows.

4.1 Not Buy Information

If the attacker does not buy information from the data broker, his expected utility function with effort level e is

$$f_0(e) = \int_0^e v d\theta - e = ve - e. \tag{2}$$

So the optimal solution is $e = 1$ with $f_0 = v - 1$ if $v > 1$ and $e = 0$ with $f_0 = 0$ if $v \leq 1$ (the 1st number in subscript of f denotes the number of attackers that buy the information).

4.2 Buy Information

If the attacker decides to buy the information θ from the data broker at price p and to attack the target, he would attack with exactly the effort θ.

Case 1: $v > 1$. The attacker would always attack since $\theta \leq v$, and his expected utility function is

$$f_{1,v \geq 1} = \int_0^1 (v - \theta)d\theta - p = v - \frac{1}{2} - p. \tag{3}$$

Compared with (2), if $v - \frac{1}{2} - p > v - 1$, or $p < \frac{1}{2}$, then the attacker would buy the information, else he prefers not to buy the information.

Case 2: $v \leq 1$. Only when $\theta < v$ would he attacks. Then his expected utility function is

$$f_{1,v<1} = \int_0^v (v - \theta)d\theta - p = \frac{1}{2}v^2 - p. \tag{4}$$

Similarly, compared with (2), if $\frac{1}{2}v^2 - p > 0$, or $p < \frac{1}{2}v^2$, then the attacker would buy the information, else he prefers not to buy the information.

Figure 1 plots the regions of the attacker's optimal decisions with different values of information price and target value. The attacker buys the target information only in regions I and III. On the other hand, in region II, the attacker would attack with the greatest effort $e = 1$; while in region IV, the attacker would neither buy nor attack. Specifically, the value of information for the attacker lies in region I where it helps to deduce the effort taken, or region III where attack is profitable when $\theta < v$. In other words, the value of the information for the attacker is an expected utility gain of $v - 0.5 - p - (v - 1) = \frac{1}{2} - p$ if $v > 1$ and $p \leq \frac{1}{2}$ or $\frac{1}{2}v^2 - p$ if $v \leq 1$ and $p \leq \frac{1}{2}v^2$.

Besides, what the defender (or target owner) cares about is whether or not the attacker would choose to attack the target and with how much effort (i.e. successful or not). When no information is available to the attacker, he would not attack the target as long as $v \leq 1$. But when a data broker sells the information with a price low enough, the target would be successfully attacked even if $v \leq 1$. Therefore, the target is affected by the information trading only in region III.

4.3 Optimal Pricing Decisions of the Data Broker

We assume that when the attackers are indifferent between to buy and not to buy, they always choose to buy in favor of less uncertainty. If $v \leq 1$, the information price cannot be set to be larger than $p = \frac{1}{2}v^2$, otherwise no profit can be gained by the data broker. That is, the information should be sold at $p^* = \frac{1}{2}v^2$ if $v \leq 1$. Similarly, $p^* = \frac{1}{2}$ if $v > 1$. The corresponding expected profit for the data broker in single-attacker case is $\frac{1}{2}v^2$ when $v \leq 1$ and $\frac{1}{2}$ when $v > 1$. Therefore, we could say the information value for the data broker increases with the target value until the target becomes attractive enough to the attacker that he would attack anyway even without the information.

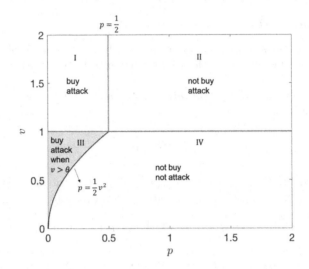

Fig. 1. The optimal decisions of single attacker

5   Competition Model

In this section we consider the scenario when there are two attackers (A and B) that could buy the same data for a target from the data broker (the sequence of the games is indicated in Fig. 2). The attackers make decisions independently. Following the work of [4], we restrict our attention to the case when the data set is sold only in one time block at Step 2 and this trade information is common knowledge (i.e., the data broker is willing to publicize its total sales quantity). Using backward induction in Stackelberg game, we first derive the attackers' optimal attacking decisions and their expected utilities assuming they have or have not bought the information, and then analyze their optimal purchasing decisions. Finally, we obtain the optimal pricing decisions for the data broker. Since the exact target information is not available to the attacker(s) before purchase, we can use a Bayesian game framework to model the scenario (with θ uniformly distributed on $[0,1]$). Besides, as the attacking game depends on the purchasing decisions made by both attackers in the previous game, the whole decision process of the attackers is modeled as a stochastic game.

5.1   Games of Attacking

In the game of attacking, the outcome depends on the informational structure—that is, on which attackers acquire information.

Both Do Not Buy Information. We first consider the situation when both attackers decide not to buy the information from the data broker. Whether or not the attackers would attack is determined by the value of the target. Therefore, we analyze the results of the attacking games with different values of v.

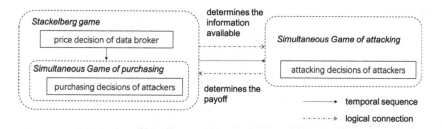

Fig. 2. Hierarchical game structure

Case 1: $v > 2$. If both attackers decide to attack, with effort e_A and e_B respectively, we suppose $e_A \leq e_B$ without loss of generality. Then attacker A's expected utility is $f_A(e_A) = \frac{1}{2}v \int_0^{e_A} d\theta - c_A = (\frac{1}{2}v - 1)e_A$, and attacker B's expected utility is $f_B(e_B) = \frac{1}{2}v \int_0^{e_A} d\theta + v \int_{e_A}^{e_B} d\theta - e_B$. To maximize $f_A(e_A)$, we have $e_A = e_B = 1$. If only one attacker attacks, his optimal decision is $e = 1$ with $f = v - 1$; and the other attacker has zero utility. The attackers' payoffs for game of attacking when both of them have no information about the target are listed in Table 1 (with attacker A's strategies listed in rows and attacker B's strategies listed in columns). The only strictly dominant pure-strategy equilibrium can be analyzed as (attack, attack) with utility $f_{0,v>2} = \frac{1}{2}v - 1$ for both attackers.

Table 1. Payoff table for game of attacking when both attackers have no information

	Attack	Not attack
Attack	$\frac{1}{2}v - 1, \frac{1}{2}v - 1$	$v - 1, 0$
Not attack	$0, v - 1$	$0, 0$

Case 2: $1 < v \leq 2$. There are two pure-strategy Nash equilibria: (attack, not attack) and (not attack, attack). In such situations we will focus on the mixed-strategy Nash equilibrium solution. We suppose attacker A chooses to attack with probability q_A^{attack} and attacker B attacks with probability q_B^{attack}. Then $f_B(attack) = q_A^{attack}(\frac{1}{2}v - 1) + (1 - q_A^{attack})(v - 1) = f_B(not\ attack) = 0$, and similar equation holds for attacker A. Therefore, in mixed-strategy Nash equilibrium, $q_A^{attack} = q_B^{attack} = 2\frac{v-1}{v}$, and the expected utility for both attackers is $f_{0,1<v\leq2} = (2\frac{v-1}{v})(2\frac{v-1}{v})(\frac{1}{2}v - 1) + 2\frac{v-1}{v}(1 - 2\frac{v-1}{v})(v - 1) = 0$.

Case 3: $v \leq 1$. Similar to the analysis above, the only strictly dominant pure strategy is (not attack, not attack) with utility $f_{0,v\leq1} = 0$ for both attackers.

Both Buy Information. When both attackers buy information from the data broker, they will make the attacking decision after they obtain the information. Therefore, the attacking game is influenced by two factors: the target value and the minimum effort needs for a successful attack.

Table 2. Payoff table for game of attacking when both attackers buy the information

	Attack	Not attack
Attack	$\frac{1}{2}v - \theta - p, \frac{1}{2}v - \theta - p$	$v - \theta - p, -p$
Not attack	$-p, v - \theta - p$	$-p, -p$

Case 1: $v > 2$. The attackers would always benefit from attacking even if they split the value v since $\frac{1}{2}v > \theta$. Therefore, it is easy to derive that the only strictly dominant pure strategy is (attack, attack), and their expected utility is

$$f_{2,v>2} = \int_0^1 (\frac{1}{2}v - \theta)d\theta - p = \frac{1}{2}v - \frac{1}{2} - p. \tag{5}$$

Case 2: $1 < v \leq 2$. If both attackers decide to attack after they get the information θ, they both get a utility of $\frac{1}{2}v - \theta - p$. If only one attackers attack, then he would get a utility of $v - \theta - p$, while the other one gets $-p$. Their payoffs for this game are listed in Table 2. Therefore, when $\frac{1}{2}v - \theta > 0$, the only pure-strategy Nash equilibrium is (attack, attack). And when $\frac{1}{2}v - \theta \leq 0$, in mixed-strategy Nash equilibrium, each attacker would attack with probability $q_A^{attack} = q_B^{attack} = 2(1 - \frac{\theta}{v})$, and the expected utility for both attackers is $-p$. Therefore, the expected utility of each attacker is

$$f_{2,1<v\leq 2} = \int_0^{\frac{1}{2}v} (\frac{1}{2}v - \theta)d\theta + \int_{\frac{1}{2}v}^1 0 d\theta - p = \frac{1}{8}v^2 - p. \tag{6}$$

Case 3: $v \leq 1$. If $\theta \geq v$, both attackers would not attack. And if $\theta < v$, the attacker gets a utility of $\frac{1}{2}v - \theta - p$ when both of them attack; when only one attacker chooses to attack, he would get a utility of $v - \theta - p$. Therefore, the only pure-strategy Nash equilibrium is (attack, attack) for the situation of $\frac{1}{2}v - \theta > 0$; and in mixed-strategy Nash equilibrium for $\frac{1}{2}v - \theta \leq 0$, each attacker would attack with probability $q_A^{attack} = q_B^{attack} = 2(1 - \frac{\theta}{v})$ and expected utility of $-p$. To sum up, the expected utility of each attacker is also $f_{2,v\leq 1} = \frac{1}{8}v^2 - p$.

Only One Attacker Buys Information. Without loss of generality, we consider the case when only attacker A buys the information. Then for attacker A, he would make the decision of attacking after he obtains the value of θ from the data broker, while attacker B has to make the attacking decision based on the distribution of θ. The payoffs for this game are listed in Table 3.

Table 3. Payoff table for game of attacking when only attacker A buys the information

	Attack	Not attack
Attack	$\frac{1}{2}v - \theta - p, \frac{1}{2}v - 1$	$v - p - \theta, 0$
Not attack	$-p, v - 1$	$-p, 0$

Case 1: $v > 2$. If both attackers decide to attack, then attacker B's utility function is $f_B(e_B) = \int_0^{e_B} \frac{1}{2} v d\theta - e_B = (\frac{1}{2}v - 1)e_B$, with $e_B = 1$ when $v > 2$. Attacker A's utility is therefore $\frac{1}{2}v - \theta - p$. If only attacker A attacks, then $f_A = v - p - \theta$, and $f_B = 0$. Else if only attacker B attacks, then $f_A = -p$, and $f_B = v - 1$. Therefore, the only pure-strategy Nash equilibrium is (attack, attack) with $f_{1,v>2,A} = \int_0^1 (\frac{1}{2}v - \theta)d\theta - p = \frac{1}{2}v - p - \frac{1}{2}$ and $f_{1,v>2,B} = \frac{1}{2}v - 1$.

Case 2: $1 < v \leq 2$. In this case, attacker B knows that if $\frac{1}{2}v - \theta \geq 0$, attacker A will certainly attack; that is, the probability of attacker A attacking is not smaller than the probability of $\frac{1}{2}v - \theta \geq 0$: $q_A^{attack} \geq \int_0^{\frac{1}{2}v} d\theta = \frac{1}{2}v$. If we assume attacker B should attack with probability q_B^{attack}, then its expected utility is $q_A^{attack} * q_B^{attack} * (\frac{1}{2}v - 1) + q_B^{attack} * (1 - q_A^{attack}) * (v - 1) = q_B^{attack} * (v - 1 - \frac{1}{2}vq_A^{attack})$. Since $q_A^{attack} \geq \frac{1}{2}v$, we have $v - 1 - \frac{1}{2}vq_A^{attack} \leq 0$. Therefore, to maximize attacker B's expected utility, $q_B^{attack} = 0$. And because attacker B would always choose not to attack, attacker A would attack when $1 < v \leq 2$. To sum up, the expected utilities are: $f_{1,1<v\leq2,A} = \int_0^1 (v - p - \theta)d\theta = v - p - \frac{1}{2}$, and $f_{1,1<v\leq2,B} = 0$.

Case 3: $v \leq 1$. Attacker B would not choose to attack even when attacker A does not attack. In this case, attacker A chooses to attack only when $\theta > v$. Therefore, $f_{1,v\leq1,A} = \int_0^v (v - p - \theta)d\theta + \int_v^1 (-p)d\theta = \frac{1}{2}v^2 - p$, and $f_{1,v\leq1,B} = 0$.

5.2 Games of Purchasing

Based on the equilibrium of the attacking games, the two attackers know their expected utilities when they choose to buy or not to buy the information. This situation forms a game of purchasing between two buyers. According to the results above under different values of v, we will analyze the game in three cases, with three payoff tables below.

Table 4. Payoff table for game of purchasing when $v \leq 1$

	Buy	Not buy
Buy	$\frac{1}{8}v^2 - p, \frac{1}{8}v^2 - p$	$\frac{1}{2}v^2 - p, 0$
Not buy	$0, \frac{1}{2}v^2 - p$	$0, 0$

Case 1: $v \leq 1$. According to the payoffs in Table 4, if $p < \frac{1}{8}v^2$, the only pure-strategy Nash equilibrium is (buy, buy). And if $\frac{1}{8}v^2 \leq p < \frac{1}{2}v^2$, there will be two pure-strategy Nash equilibria: (buy, not buy) or (not buy, buy). In the mixed strategy equilibrium, assume attacker A chooses to buy the information with probability q_A^{buy} and attacker B attacks with probability q_B^{buy}. We have $f_B(buy) = q_A^{buy}(\frac{1}{8}v^2 - 1) + (1 - q_A^{buy})(\frac{1}{2}v^2 - 1) = f_B(not\ buy) = 0$, and similar equation holds for attacker A. Therefore, in mixed-strategy Nash equilibrium, $q_A^{buy} = q_B^{buy} = \frac{\frac{1}{2}v^2 - p}{\frac{3}{8}v^2}$, and the expected utility for both attackers is 0. If $p \geq \frac{1}{2}v^2$, the only pure-strategy Nash equilibrium is (not buy, not buy).

Table 5. Payoff table for game of purchasing when $1 < v \leq 2$

	Buy	Not buy
Buy	$\frac{1}{8}v^2 - p, \frac{1}{8}v^2 - p$	$v - \frac{1}{2} - p, 0$
Not buy	$0, v - \frac{1}{2} - p$	$0, 0$

Case 2: $1 < v \leq 2$. According to the payoffs in Table 5, if $p < \frac{1}{8}v^2$, the only pure-strategy Nash equilibrium is (buy, buy). If $\frac{1}{8}v^2 \leq p < v - \frac{1}{2}$, there will be two pure-strategy Nash equilibria (buy, not buy) or (not buy, buy). In the mixed strategy equilibrium, either attacker would choose to buy with a probability of $q_A^{buy} = q_B^{buy} = \frac{v - \frac{1}{2} - p}{v - \frac{1}{2} - \frac{1}{8}v^2}$ and expected zero utility. And if $p \geq v - \frac{1}{2}$, the only pure-strategy Nash equilibrium is (not buy, not buy).

Table 6. Payoff table for game of purchasing when $v > 2$

	Buy	Not buy
Buy	$\frac{1}{2}v - \frac{1}{2} - p, \frac{1}{2}v - \frac{1}{2} - p$	$\frac{1}{2}v - \frac{1}{2} - p, \frac{1}{2}v - 1$
Not buy	$\frac{1}{2}v - 1, \frac{1}{2}v - \frac{1}{2} - p$	$\frac{1}{2}v - 1, \frac{1}{2}v - 1$

Case 3: $v > 2$. According to the payoffs in Table 6, if $p \geq \frac{1}{2}$, we have $\frac{1}{2}v - \frac{1}{2} - p < \frac{1}{2}v - 1$, and in this case, the only pure-strategy Nash equilibrium is (not buy, not buy). If $p < \frac{1}{2}$, we have $\frac{1}{2}v - \frac{1}{2} - p \geq \frac{1}{2}v - 1$, and the only pure-strategy Nash equilibrium is (buy, buy).

Figure 3 shows the equilibrium purchasing decisions under different values of price p and target value v.

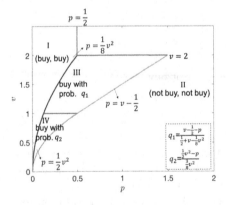

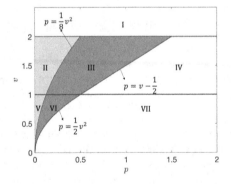

Fig. 3. The optimal purchasing decisions of two attackers

Fig. 4. Regions where attacking probability of the target is increased

By integrating the results in the game of purchasing with those in the game of attacking, We can now analyze the impacts of information trading for the target. We already know that if no information is available, when $v > 2$, both attackers attack; when $1 < v \leq 2$, each attacker attacks with a probability $2\frac{v-1}{v}$; and when $v \leq 1$, no one attacks. While if information is leaked and can be bought by the attackers at price p from a data broker, Fig. 4 summarizes the seven regions in parameter space with the shaded areas are where more possible attacks are resulted from the information trading. The light grey region is where there is 100% possibility that the attacking probability will be increased. And the dark grey region is where the increase in attacking probability is determined by the attackers' purchasing behaviors.

The detailed impacts of the information leakage and trading on the attackers' attacking probability can be shown in Table 7. In regions I, IV and VII, the attackers make the same attacking decisions as in the situation of no information trading, because the price is so high that the attackers will not buy the information from the data broker. In regions II, III, V and VI however, the attacking probabilities are clearly increased.

Table 7. Attacking probability of the attackers w/o information trading

Region	No information	With information trading
I	1	1
II	$2(1-\frac{1}{v})$	1 if $\theta \leq \frac{1}{2}v$; $2(1-\frac{\theta}{v})$ if $\theta > \frac{1}{2}v$
III	$2(1-\frac{1}{v})$	$2(1-\frac{\theta}{v})$ if both buy info.; 1 if only one buys info.; $2(1-\frac{1}{v})$ if both do not buy info.
IV	$2(1-\frac{1}{v})$	$2(1-\frac{1}{v})$
V	0	1 if $\theta \leq \frac{1}{2}v$; $2(1-\frac{\theta}{v})$ if $\theta > \frac{1}{2}v$
VI	0	$2(1-\frac{\theta}{v})$ if both buy info.; 1 when $v > \theta$ if only one buys info.; 0 if both do not buy info.
VII	0	0

One can also obtain the value of information for the attackers. If no information is available, when $v > 2$, both attackers obtain an expected utility of $\frac{1}{2}v - 1$; otherwise, both attackers get zero expected utility. If the target information can be bought, we could represent the value of information for the attackers as the amount of increase in the attacker's expected utility. If $v > 2$ and $p \leq \frac{1}{2}$, there is a expected utility increase of $\frac{1}{2} - p$; if $v \leq 2$ and $p \leq \frac{1}{8}v^2$, the attackers are expected to have a utility gain of $\frac{1}{8}v^2 - p$. The results indicate that, in the mixed equilibrium of the competition game between the attackers, they are expected to benefit from the information only when the price is less than $\frac{1}{8}v^2$ for $v \leq 2$ or $\frac{1}{2}$ for $v > 2$. However, even if the information does not benefit the attackers as the price increases, the target is expected to be attacked more likely with information leakage (in regions III and VI of Fig. 4). Besides, if we compare the results above with those when no competitor exists for the attacker in Sect. 4, we could conclude that the value of information for the attackers is indeed weakened by their competition if the target value if not large enough ($v \leq 2$).

5.3   Optimal Pricing Decisions of the Data Broker

Now we further analyze the data broker's selling strategy to maximize her profit. She could set either a low price such that both attackers buy or a high price that attackers buy with certain probability.

Case 1: $v > 2$. The data broker would not set a price larger than $\frac{1}{2}$, otherwise both attackers would not be willing to make a purchase. In this case, the data broker's expected profit is $\pi^*_{v>2} = 2 * \frac{1}{2} = 1$ with optimal price $p^* = \frac{1}{2}$.

Case 2: $1 < v \le 2$. If the data broker sets a price not larger than $\frac{1}{8}v^2$, both attackers would buy the information, which brings a profit of at most $\pi_{1<v\le2,p\le\frac{1}{8}v^2} = \frac{1}{4}v^2$ for the data broker with $p_1 = \frac{1}{8}v^2$. If the data broker sets a price that satisfies $\frac{1}{8}v^2 < p \le v - \frac{1}{2}$, the two attackers would make a purchase at the probability of $q_1 = \frac{v-\frac{1}{2}-p}{v-\frac{1}{2}-\frac{1}{8}v^2}$. In this case, an expected profit

of $\pi_{1<v\le2,\frac{1}{8}v^2<p\le v-\frac{1}{2}}(p) = q_1^2 * 2 * p + 2 * q_1 * (1 - q_1) * p = 2p\frac{v-\frac{1}{2}-p}{v-\frac{1}{2}-\frac{1}{8}v^2}$

will be gained. Because $\dfrac{\partial^2 \pi_{1<v\le2,\frac{1}{8}v^2<p\le v-\frac{1}{2}}(p)}{\partial p^2} < 0$, the optimal price p_2 sat-

isfies $\dfrac{\partial \pi_{1<v\le2,\frac{1}{8}v^2<p\le v-\frac{1}{2}}(p)}{\partial p} = 0$, i.e., $p_2 = \frac{2v-1}{4}$. Now we can easily prove that $\pi_{1<v\le2,p\le\frac{1}{8}v^2} = \frac{1}{4}v^2 < \pi_{1<v\le2,\frac{1}{8}v^2<p\le v-\frac{1}{2}} = \frac{(v-\frac{1}{2})^2}{2v-1-\frac{1}{4}v^2}$ for $1 < v \le 2$. Therefore, when $1 < v \le 2$, the data broker's maximum expected profit is $\pi^*_{1<v\le2} = \frac{(v-\frac{1}{2})^2}{2v-1-\frac{1}{4}v^2}$ with optimal price $p^* = \frac{2v-1}{4}$.

Case 3: $v \le 1$. Similarly, for both attackers buying the information, the data broker would set a price equal to $\frac{1}{8}v^2$, which brings a profit of $\pi_{v\le1,p\le\frac{1}{8}v^2} = \frac{1}{4}v^2$. If the data broker sets a price that satisfies $\frac{1}{8}v^2 < p \le \frac{1}{2}v^2$, the two attackers would make a purchase at the probability of $q_2 = \frac{\frac{1}{2}v^2-p}{\frac{3}{8}v^2}$. In this case, an expected

profit of $\pi_{v\le1,\frac{1}{8}v^2<p\le\frac{1}{2}v^2}(p) = q_2^2 * 2 * p + 2 * q_2 * (1 - q_2) * p = 2p\frac{\frac{1}{2}v^2-p}{\frac{3}{8}v^2}$ will be gained, which is maximized at $p = \frac{1}{4}v^2$, and we have $\pi_{v\le1,\frac{1}{8}v^2<p\le\frac{1}{2}v^2} = \frac{1}{3}v^2$. In this case, since $\pi_{v\le1,\frac{1}{8}v^2<p\le\frac{1}{2}v^2} > \pi_{v\le1,p\le\frac{1}{8}v^2}$, it is optimal for the data broker to set a price of $p^* = \frac{1}{4}v^2$, and $\pi^*_{v\le1} = \frac{1}{3}v^2$.

Proposition 1 summarizes this section's main results. And Fig. 5 shows the optimal pricing strategy and corresponding expected profit of the data broker. It indicates that, the information value for the broker increases with the target value when the target value is not large enough ($v \le 2$), but as the target is becoming attractive enough for the attackers ($v > 2$), the information value decreases to a certain value and remains unchanged.

Proposition 1. *The data broker's optimal price of the target information is determined by the target value for the attackers. When the target is not attractive enough, it is not wise to set a price low enough to attract two buyers. Specifically,*

(a) *if $v \le 1$, information is sold to the attackers at a price of $p^* = \frac{1}{4}v^2$, resulting each attacker making the purchase with a probability of 2/3;*

(b) if $1 < v \leq 2$, information is sold at $p^* = \frac{2v-1}{4}$, with a purchase probability of $\frac{v - \frac{1}{2}}{2v - 1 - \frac{1}{4}v^2}$ from each attacker;

(c) else if $v > 2$, information is sold to both attackers at $p^* = \frac{1}{2}$.

Proof. See the text.

If we compare the data broker's expected profit in the single-attacker scenario with that in the multi-attacker scenario, we could find that, the impacts of competition among attackers on the information value for the data broker is determined by the target value: if the target value is small ($v \leq 1.24$), the data broker benefits from more potential buyers; while if the target value is large ($v > 1.24$), the information value is larger when there is only one attacker.

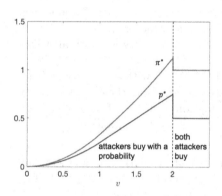

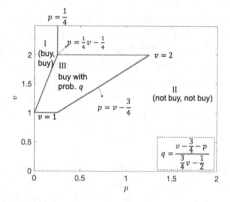

Fig. 5. The optimal pricing strategy and expected profit of the data broker

Fig. 6. The optimal purchasing decisions of two attackers under partial information

6   Extension-Partial Information Model

We consider now the possibility that the data supplier can only obtain partial information about the target, i.e., whether θ belongs to $[0, 0.5]$ or $[0.5, 1]$, but he cannot provide the exact value of θ. We analyze how this new informational structure affect attackers' purchasing and attacking decision games and model the price of information with low data quality.

6.1   Games of Attacking

We also start with the competition game of attacking given different purchasing decisions.

Both Do Not Buy Information. When nobody buys the information, the equilibrium results are the same as in Sect. 5.1.

Both Buy Information. When both attackers buy the information, two cases are considered:

Case 1: $\theta \in [0, 0.5]$. Both attackers know that θ is uniformly distributed within $[0, 0.5]$. If both of them attack, each obtains an expected utility of $f = \int_0^{0.5} \frac{1}{2}v * 2d\theta - 0.5 - p = \frac{1}{2}(v-1) - p$; else if only one attacks, then he obtains an expected utility of $f = \int_0^{0.5} v * 2d\theta - 0.5 - p = v - \frac{1}{2} - p$. Therefore, if $v > 1$, both of them would attack; if $\frac{1}{2} < v \leq 1$, each attacker would attack with probability $q_A^{attack} = q_B^{attack} = \frac{2v-1}{v}$, and the expected utility for both attackers is $-p$; otherwise, both would not attack.

Case 2: $\theta \in [0.5, 1]$. If both of them attack, each obtains an expected utility of $f = \int_{0.5}^1 \frac{1}{2}v * 2d\theta - 1 - p = \frac{1}{2}v - 1 - p$; else if only one attacks, then he obtains an expected utility of $f = \int_{0.5}^1 v * 2d\theta - 1 - p = v - 1 - p$. Therefore, if $v > 2$, both of them would attack; if $1 < v \leq 2$, each attacker would attack with probability $q_A^{attack} = q_B^{attack} = 2\frac{v-1}{v}$, and the expected utility for both attackers is $-p$; otherwise, both would not attack.

Considering the two cases $\theta \in [0, 0.5]$ and $\theta \in [0.5, 1]$ with equal probabilities for the attackers before they buy and obtain the information, the expected utility for the attacker when both of them buy information would be: $f_{2,v>2} = \frac{1}{2}(\frac{1}{2}(v-1) - p) + \frac{1}{2}(\frac{1}{2}v - 1 - p) = \frac{1}{2}v - \frac{3}{4} - p$, $f_{2,1<v\leq2} = \frac{1}{4}(v-1) - p$, and $f_{2,v\leq1} = -p$.

Only One Attacker Buys Information. For attacker B who does not buy the information, if both attackers attack, he is expecting a utility of $\frac{1}{2}v - 1$; if he attacks but attacker A does not attack, his expected utility is $v - 1$. Therefore: if $v > 2$, both attackers would attack, with $f_{1,v>2,A} = \frac{1}{2}(\frac{1}{2}v - \frac{1}{2} - p) + \frac{1}{2}(\frac{1}{2}v - 1 - p) = \frac{1}{2}v - \frac{3}{4} - p$ and $f_{1,v>2,B} = \frac{1}{2}v - 1$. If $1 < v \leq 2$, the optimal decision is (attack, not attack), with $f_{1,1.5<v\leq2,A} = \frac{1}{2}(v - \frac{1}{2} - p) + \frac{1}{2}(v - 1 - p) = v - \frac{3}{4} - p$ and $f_{1,1.5<v\leq2,B} = 0$. And if $v \leq 1$, attacker B would certainly not attack. In this case, if attacker A gets that $\theta \in [0, 0.5]$, he would only attack when $v > \frac{1}{2}$; and if A gets that $\theta \in [0.5, 1]$, he would not attack. Therefore, we have $f_{1,\frac{1}{2}<v\leq1,A} = \frac{1}{4}v - \frac{1}{4} - p$, $f_{1,v\leq\frac{1}{2},A} = 0$ and $f_{1,v\leq1,B} = 0$.

6.2   Games of Purchasing

From the equilibrium analysis above, we know that if $v < \frac{1}{2}$, both attackers would not attack, and therefore have no incentive to buy information. Figure 6 plots the attackers' optimal purchasing decisions of partial information in different ranges of v and p. Due to the page limitation, the analysis process is omitted.

The impact of partial information trading for the target is less than that of full information trading: the attacking probability increases only in the following two situations: (1) $1 < v \leq 2$, $p \leq \frac{1}{4}v - \frac{1}{4}$ and $\theta < 0.5$: both attackers would attack the target; and (2) $1 < v \leq 2$ and $\frac{1}{4}v - \frac{1}{4} < p \leq v - \frac{3}{4}$: both attackers would attack if they buy the information and find that $\theta < 0.5$, or the only one attacker who buys the information would certainly attack. But in these situations without the information, they would attack with probability $2\frac{v-1}{v}$.

As for the value of partial information to the attackers, we know that if no information is available, when $v > 2$, both attackers obtain an expected utility of $\frac{1}{2}v - 1$; when $v \leq 2$, both attackers get zero expected utility. If partial information can be traded, when $v > 2$ and $p < \frac{1}{4}$, there is a expected utility increase of $\frac{1}{4} - p$; when $1 < v \leq 2$ and $p \leq \frac{1}{4}v - \frac{1}{4}$, the attackers are expected to have a utility gain of $\frac{1}{4}v - \frac{1}{4} - p$; and when $1 < v \leq 2$ and $\frac{1}{4}v - \frac{1}{4} < p \leq v - \frac{3}{4}$, the expected utility gain is $v - \frac{3}{4} - p$.

6.3 Optimal Pricing Decisions of the Data Broker

Due to lower data quality, we are expecting a lower price compared to the scenario when full information is traded. Specifically, the following proposition summarizes our main results:

Proposition 2. *Under partial information, if $v \leq 1$, the information is of no value to both the attackers and the data broker; if $1 < v \leq 2$, information is sold at $p^* = \frac{1}{2}v - \frac{3}{8}$, with a purchase probability of $\frac{2v - \frac{3}{2}}{3v - 2}$ for each attacker; else if $v > 2$, information is sold to both attackers at $p^* = \frac{1}{4}$.*

Proof. The proof is similar to that of Proposition 1, and thus omitted here.

One can now compare the results under partial information with those under full information. The price for partial information is $\frac{1}{8}$ lower when $1 < v \leq 2$ and $\frac{1}{4}$ lower when $v > 2$. That is, information accuracy is more valuable for the data broker or the attackers for a more attractive target. Moreover, by comparing Figs. 3 and 6, we can derive that, for a target with lower value ($v < 1$), if the defender takes some effort to ensure that only partial information could be leaked, the attacking probability may decrease to zero.

7 Conclusion

We have studied a security problem with target information trading from an economic perspective. The interaction between a data broker and two attackers is formulated as a Stackelberg game where the data broker acts as the leader setting the price with the consideration of possible responses from the attackers. And the competition between two attackers is modeled as a type of stochastic game. We have evaluated the value of the information from the perspectives of different players respectively, which is related to: the acceptable price and the expected utility increase for the attackers, the changes in the attacking probabilities for the target, as well as the data broker's optimal selling strategy. We discover several interesting insights of the information market in the hacker community. For example, if the target is not so attractive, the information value for the attackers will be weakened by their competition, but the data broker would benefit from their competition; and the data broker prefers high profit margin over volume sales. Besides, information accuracy is more valuable of a more attractive target. Our results also provide some insights to the defense strategy:

to protect the information from leakage would avoid attacks if the target value is low enough, but when the target is highly attractive, more effort should be taken into the protection of the target itself than the protection of the information. Several directions for future research can stem from our paper. First, it will be worthwhile to investigate a specific type of attack. Second, the situation where the data broker does not reveal her total sales quantity is a problem that the attackers may encounter. Finally, the consideration of multiple attackers with different target evaluations would be an important future research direction.

Acknowledgments. The work of T. Shu is supported in part by NSF under grants CNS-1837034, CNS-1745254, CNS-1659965, and CNS-1460897. The work of H. Li is supported in part by NSF under grant CNS-1525226. Any opinions, findings, conclusions, or recommendations expressed in this paper are those of the author(s) and do not necessarily reflect the views of NSF.

References

1. An, B., Brown, M., Vorobeychik, Y., Tambe, M.: Security games with surveillance cost and optimal timing of attack execution. In: 12th International Conference on Autonomous Agent and Multi-agent System, St. Paul, MN, USA, pp. 223–230 (2013)
2. Southers, E.G., Tambe, M.: LAX-terror target: the history, the reason, the countermeasure. In: Security and Game Theory: Algorithms, Deployed Systems, Lessons Learned, pp. 27–50. Cambridge University Press (2011)
3. Pita, J., Jain, M., Tambe, M., Ordóñez, F., Kraus, S.: Robust solutions to Stackelberg games: addressing bounded rationality and limited observations in human cognition. Artif. Intell. **174**(15), 1142–1171 (2010)
4. Montes, R., Sand-Zantman, W., Valletti, T.: The value of personal information in online markets with endogenous privacy. Manag. Sci. **65**(3), 1–21 (2018)
5. Benjamin, V., Chen, H.: Securing cyberspace: identifying key actors in hacker communities. In: IEEE International Conference on Intelligence and Security Informatics, pp. 24–29. IEEE, Arlington (2012)
6. Motoyama, M., McCoy, D., Levchenko, K., Savage, S., Voelker, G.M.: An analysis of underground forums. In: ACM SIGCOMM Conference on Internet Measurement Conference, pp. 71–80. ACM, Berlin (2011)
7. Hacking communities in the Deep Web. https://resources.infosecinstitute.com/hacking-communities-in-the-deep-web/#gref. Accessed 5 Apr 2019
8. The hacks that left us exposed in 2017. https://money.cnn.com/2017/12/18/technology/biggest-cyberattacks-of-the-year/index.html. Accessed 5 Apr 2019
9. Facebook could reportedly face multibillion-dollar FTC fine over privacy violations. https://www.theverge.com/2019/2/14/18225440/facebook-multibillion-dollar-ftc-fine-privacy-violations. Accessed 5 Apr 2019
10. USA Information Resources Management Association: Cyber Crime: Concepts, Methodologies, Tools and Applications. IGI Global, Hershey (2011)
11. Zhu, Q., Rass, S.: On multi-phase and multi-stage game-theoretic modeling of advanced persistent threats. IEEE Access **6**, 13958–13971 (2018)
12. Leeson, P., Coyne, C.J.: The economics of computer hacking. J. Law. Econ. Policy **1**(2), 511–532 (2006)

13. Hausken, K., Bier, V.M.: Defending against multiple different attackers. Eur. J. Oper. Res. **211**(2), 370–384 (2011)
14. Yin, Z., Korzhyk, D., Kiekintveld, C., Conitzer, V., Tambe, M.: Stackelberg vs. Nash in security games: interchangeability, equivalence, and uniqueness. In: 9th International Conference on Autonomous Agents and Multi-agent Systems, Toronto, Canada, pp. 1139–1146 (2010)
15. Fang, F., Stone, P., Tambe, M.: When security games go green: designing defender strategies to prevent poaching and illegal fishing. In: 24th International Joint Conference on Artificial Intelligence, pp. 2589–2595. AAAI Press, Buenos Aires (2015)
16. Damme, E., Hurkens, S.: Games with imperfectly observable commitment. Games Econ. Behav. **21**(1–2), 282–308 (1997)
17. An, B., et al.: Security games with limited surveillance. In: 26th AAAI Conference on Artificial Intelligence, pp. 1241–1248. AAAI Press, Toronto (2012)
18. Zhuang, J., Bier, V.M., Alagoz, O.: Modeling secrecy and deception in a multiple-period attacker-defender signaling game. Eur. J. Oper. Res. **203**(2), 409–418 (2010)
19. Guo, Q., An, B., Bošanský, B., Kiekintveld, C.: Comparing strategic secrecy and Stackelberg commitment in security games. In: 26th International Joint Conference on Artificial Intelligence, Melbourne, Australia, pp. 3691–3699 (2017)
20. Du, H., Yang, S.J.: Discovering collaborative cyber attack patterns using social network analysis. In: Salerno, J., Yang, S.J., Nau, D., Chai, S.-K. (eds.) SBP 2011. LNCS, vol. 6589, pp. 129–136. Springer, Heidelberg (2011). https://doi.org/10.1007/978-3-642-19656-0_20
21. Guo, Q., An, B., Vorobeychik, Y., Tran-Thanh, L., Gan, J., Miao, C.: Coalitional security games. In: International Conference on Autonomous Agents and Multi-agent Systems, Singapore, Singapore, pp. 159–167 (2016)
22. Gholami, S., Wilder, B., Brown, M., Thomas, D., Sintov, N., Tambe, M.: Divide to defend: collusive security games. In: Zhu, Q., Alpcan, T., Panaousis, E., Tambe, M., Casey, W. (eds.) GameSec 2016. LNCS, vol. 9996, pp. 272–293. Springer, Cham (2016). https://doi.org/10.1007/978-3-319-47413-7_16
23. Roy, A., Mohapatra, P., Kamhoua, C.: Game theoretic characterization of collusive behavior among attackers. In: IEEE International Conference on Computer Communications (INFOCOM), pp. 2078–2086. IEEE, Honolulu (2018)

Cyber Threat Analysis Based on Characterizing Adversarial Behavior for Energy Delivery System

Sharif Ullah[1(✉)], Sachin Shetty[1,2], Anup Nayak[3], Amin Hassanzadeh[3], and Kamrul Hasan[1]

[1] Old Dominion University, Norfolk, VA, USA
{mulla001,sshetty,khasa001}@odu.edu
[2] Virginia Modeling, Analysis and Simulation Center, Suffolk, VA, USA
[3] Accenture Cyber Lab, Cyber Fusion Center, Arlington, VA, USA
{anup.nayak,amin.hassanzadeh}@accenture.com

Abstract. Recently, Energy Delivery Systems (EDS) has been the target of several sophisticated attacks with potentials for catastrophic damages. These attacks are diverse in techniques, attack progression, and impacts. System administrators require comprehensive analytics to assess their defense against these diverse adversarial strategies. To address this challenge, this paper proposes a methodology to assess cyber threats proactively by characterizing adversary behavior. First, we describe the different level of threat indicators and their effectiveness to understand the adversary activity. Next, we integrate static network information with dynamic attack strategy by mapping attack graphs into attacker's techniques and tactics. This contextual integration provides insights into attacker's stealthy behavior. Following the enumeration of complexity and effort for attack progression, we devise a metric to quantify the likelihood of an adversary taking an attack path for compromising an asset in EDS. We empirically evaluated our approach within an ICS test-bed. The results show the significance of our approach for characterizing adversarial behavior and gaining valuable insights on cyber risk management.

Keywords: Energy Delivery System · Attack graph · Proactive threat analysis · Adversary behavior · Attack technique and tactic

1 Introduction

Today's computer networks are mostly segregated and usually deployed with diverse cyber defense mechanisms which makes it challenging for the attacker to gain direct access to the target. This pattern is commonly seen in Industrial Control System (ICS) where a layered architecture ensures that the targets are not in close proximity to the perimeter [13]. Despite the presence of a layered architecture, the spate of attacks is increasing rapidly spanning from large enterprises to

© ICST Institute for Computer Sciences, Social Informatics and Telecommunications Engineering 2019
Published by Springer Nature Switzerland AG 2019. All Rights Reserved
S. Chen et al. (Eds.): SecureComm 2019, LNICST 305, pp. 146–160, 2019.
https://doi.org/10.1007/978-3-030-37231-6_8

the critical infrastructure (CI) network. Due to the potential severe damage and cost experienced by a victim nation, CI has been targeted intentionally and has suffered from significant losses during successful exploitation. Multiple attacks have occurred in Energy Delivery System (EDS) in the past couple of years such as Stuxnet attack in nuclear systems [11], Shamoon attack in Oil and Gas systems [8] and most recently Triton [9], the first attack on safety instrumented system.

Similar to the aforementioned cyber incidents, most of the attacks on CI occur in multiple stages. Detecting a single intrusion doesn't necessarily indicate the end of the attack as the attack could have progressed far deeper into the network. Hence, individual attack footprint seems insignificant in an isolated manner since it is usually part of a more complex multi-step attack. It takes a sequence of steps to form an attack path towards a target in the network [19]. Researchers have investigated several attack path analysis methods for identifying attacker's required effort, e.g., number of paths to a target and the cost and time required to compromise each path, to diligently estimate the level of risk in EDS. Authors in [20] evaluate the reliability of EDS by using Bayesian network for modeling the potential attack steps in the network. Katherine et al. [10] have proposed a framework to assess cyber-induced disruption to power grids by formulating attack trees created based on cyber-physical dependency model. Authors in [15] compare three Attack Graph (AG) based security metrics such as shortest path, number of paths, etc. and propose a new metric for efficient attack surface evaluation.

The aforementioned path centric metrics and threat analysis methods do not consider attack complexity in an interconnected cyber infrastructure with a variety of attack paths which makes it impractical for real attack scenarios. More specifically, most of the analysis methods only consider the topological connection between stepping stones to measure the difficulty of reaching to a target. In addition, they only assume some predefined attacker's skill set to estimate the path complexity. In reality, attacker's capabilities and knowledge evolve throughout attack paths to the target. Thus, it is of paramount importance to perform additional inspections in order to identify adversary's new opportunities obtained through an attack path. In this paper, we propose a cyber threat analysis framework based on characterizing adversarial behavior in a multi-stage cyber attack process. First, we investigate how a threat proceeds within the network by constructing adversarial Attack Graph (AG) and identifying all possible attack stages. Then we discuss how each stage can be associated with network attributes. Using a holistic view of threat's exposure provided by attack graphs, our model incorporates attacker's techniques and tactics into the stepping stones found in the AG.

We propose to add more context to each attack stage using real-world knowledge base of adversary tactics and techniques, when characterizing the adversary's progression in the attack path. Our attack path analysis model identifies the level of difficulty in taking a path by considering the complexity of path, attacker's skill set, etc. The *path hardness* is measured in terms of attacker's capability and challenges. The insight into the level of difficulty of an attack

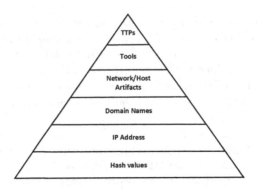

Fig. 1. Pyramid of plain model [7]

path in the network helps security administrators to pinpoint critical paths and prioritize path hardening actions.

Our contributions in this paper is threefold:

– We characterize adversarial behavior in cyber attack campaigns by integrating attacker's techniques and tactics into attack graphs and consequently uncovering attack strategy for each potential campaign in the network.
– We propose a novel set of path analysis metrics i.e. *path hardness* by taking into account attacker's evolving skills along the attack paths.
– We perform a comprehensive evaluation of the proposed framework in a real ICS testbed.

The details of the aforementioned details will be discussed in details in the following sections.

2   Overview of Threat Indicators

In order to investigate the attacker's behavior, security administrators typically track low-level threat artifacts such as hash values, IP address and domain names. These are often termed technical threat intelligence shown in the first three levels of the Pyramid of plain model [7]. Although it is relatively easy to integrate these artifacts within a defense system, a low-level indicator of compromise (IoC) is not much fruitful for defending against sophisticated adversaries. These indicators are susceptible to change over time as attackers use botnets, random domain names or dynamically change hash values with low costs. In contrary, attacker's action follows some particular sequence which is being reused with little modification. Attributes related to actions is shown in the upper three layers of the pyramid often termed as behavioral attack signatures of threats. These indicators are very hard to change for a particular group of attackers such as script kiddies, hacktivists, cybercriminals, or state-sponsored attackers. Thus, defense systems that take into account the top three threat artifacts, will present tougher obstacle to the adversary.

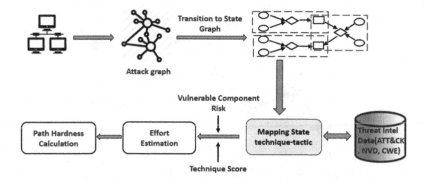

Fig. 2. Proposed cyber threat assessment framework

Network/host artifacts can be described from the perspective of the defense mechanism. For reactive defense, it represents the adversary traces in the network and host. For proactive defense, the artifacts represent the conditions that allow the attacker to propagate. Tools refer the software or utilities attackers use to accomplish their objectives. Naive attackers rely on public exploits or open source tools where skilled and stealthy attackers use obfuscation as well as utilities that are part of the operating system.

Attackers can take different strategies and paths to achieve their objectives. TTPs can capture this kind of latent behavior of the attacker. It describes attacker's approach at different levels of granularity within a cyber attack campaign. Tactic refers to how an adversary can operate part of the cyber attack campaign: what step to take next? A particular tactic might have different ramifications depending on the adversary type. Technique provides detailed description within the context of tactic: how to take the next step? In other words, the techniques are meant to facilitate the execution of different tactics. While technique consists of actions without specific direction, the procedure provides more low-level details correspond to a technique. It includes all the necessary steps to complete an action. A well-tailored procedure increases the success rate of a technique.

3 Framework

The behavioral attributes discussed in the previous section do not contain the level of information to understand attacker's behavior comprehensively. For an attacker, learning a new technique or adapting to a new method is much difficult than learning tools as well as learning tools is harder than learning network/host artifacts. We intend to identify these features and integrate them in a model for efficient threat analysis. Our proposed framework addresses the tasks illustrated in Fig. 1. We will explain each component of this framework in the following subsections.

3.1 Attack Graph and Action State Model

We use MulVal [18] to generate AG consisting of different node types to show how a set of network and system configurations result in unauthorized actions to

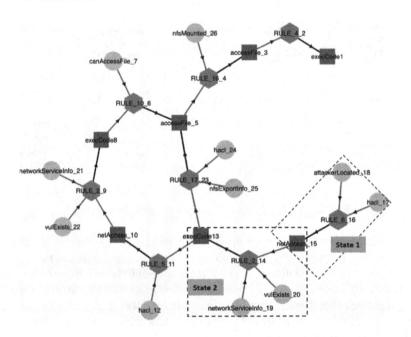

Fig. 3. A sample attack graph represented in Neo4j graph format

specific targets. Figure 3 shows a small portion of an AG generated by MulVal and converted to Neo4j graph database structure. Nodes in an AG are of three different types as also depicted in Fig. 3. The circular nodes denote system or network *configurations*, are the conditions that provide possibilities for actions by the adversary. The hexagonal nodes in the network represent the reasoning *rules* which usually represents the attack methodology leveraged by an adversary to achieve a particular goal. The *impact* nodes indicate the sub-goal for a certain action attacker could take which is shown as rectangular nodes in the figure. There are two types of edges in an attack graph: (1) configuration-to-rule edges that represent logical AND meaning all configuration conditions has to be true to cause the impact, and (2) rule-to-impact edges that represent logical OR meaning that the impact happens if at least one rule satisfies holds.

AG allows us to inspect all possible sequences of exploits an attacker can take to infiltrate a network and reach its goals. We use monotonicity assumption [17] to translate it to a *condition dependency graph* which is very beneficial for analyzing large AGs by removing cycles. states that attacker's capability doesn't decrease by launching attacks and attacker doesn't need to go back to the privileges already gained. This phenomenon allows us to decompose the AG into a state graph where each state is called *action state*. The primary objective of this transitioned model is to represent the progression of the attacker in the network over distinct actions. An *action state* (as_i) is comprised of pre-condition(s), rule and associated exploit or impact. In Fig. 3 two states have been designated for a better understanding of the model. Each action starts with enabling some pre-conditions for that action state. An enabled pre-condition gives the attacker an opportunity to cause the impact; e.g., execute an exploit. More formally, $P(e|\exists c_{pr} = F, (e, c_{pr}) \in as_i) = 0$: that is an exploit can't be executed until all it's pre-conditions are satisfied. Post-conditions OR conditions direct from *rule* to *impact*. This action state model can efficiently track the attacker's movement throughout the network. From now on we use state and action state alternately in the rest of the paper.

3.2   Mapping to Technique-Tactics

We need to map each attack state to a certain technique in order to unfold the current phase of attack strategy deployed by the attacker. MITRE proposes a model called Adversarial Tactics, Techniques, and Common Knowledge (ATT&CK) [4] characterizing malicious behaviors for each step in a cyber attack campaign. Tactics provide the high-level objective why an attacker follows a particular behavior in a system and techniques provide more fine-grained information showing how an attack is performed. Our goal is to map each attack state to the distinct high-level category defined in the ATT&CK model. By incorporating this, each attack path eventually exposes a sequence of tactics and techniques. Our evaluation finds that this sequence could form a Techniques, Tactic, and Procedures (TTPs) of the cyber Kill Chain [12,14].

ATT&CK model categorizes adversarial techniques into different tactics where each technique might fall in multiple tactics. We define a tactic l as $tc_l = \{ta_1, ...ta_t\}$ enclosing a set of techniques belonging to it. We intend to map each action state with distinct Technique-Tactic (TT) pair. In our action state model, each rule represents a threat action associated with some primitives which are ascribed as configuration nodes in our state graph. The configuration nodes are shared by multiple states in our model. Similarly, different network and system features are shared by multiple techniques. We use this phenomenon for our mapping methodology. For technique mapping, we use *rule* and *configuration* information which could map one state to several techniques. On the other hand, the tactic describes the sub-goal of a threat action which is analogous to the *impact* node in our state graph. Thus, using domain expert's knowledge, we map each state to a TT pair. From a real attack history, it is evident that each technique often requires a pre-requisite technique to accomplish its goal [5]. For instance, in APT33 the technique T1078 (*Valid accounts*) cannot be performed without *User Execution* (T1204) before. Likewise, in APT1, technique T10005 (*Data from Local System*) and T1114 (*Email Collection*) are two pre-conditions for exfiltration of compressed data (T1002). We can use this finding to improve our mapping accuracy. This will be discussed in details in our evaluation section.

4   Path Complexity and Effort Estimation

The complexity of an attack path is essential to understanding an attacker's behavior during attack progression. National Vulnerability Database (NVD) databases only provide insights into the exploitability of vulnerabilities. But

Table 1. Vulnerable component risk

Exploitability level	Likelihood level		
	Unproven	Proof-of-concept	Exploit in the wild
Easy	3	4	7
Medium	2	3	5
Hard	1	2	4

determining the presence of exploitable vulnerabilities is not sufficient for computing complexity of an attack path. Moreover, attacker's evolving skill should be considered for accurate path complexity calculation. Our framework illustrated in Fig. 2 incorporates contextual information in order to characterize the level of difficulty in taking an attack path.

4.1 Vulnerable Component Risk

Existing work focuses only on the vulnerability exploitability score to estimate the effort required to attack a host. Although there exist several vulnerabilities in a cyber infrastructure, in reality, only a fraction of them are exploited widely e.g., only 15% of known vulnerabilities are exploited in the wild [16]. Exploitability of vulnerabilities are typically computed using the Common Vulnerability Scoring System (CVSS) [3] scores that range from 0 to 10. We categorize these scores into easy (0–3), medium (4–7) and hard (8–10).

While default scoring of vulnerability only describe it's technical aspect, we also focus on attempted vulnerabilities through real attack scenarios in the field. This will lead us to derive a unique vulnerability score for our network. In order to do that we distinguish the state of an exploit into three categories:

Unproven: It refers to the unavailability of exploit code for exploiting the vulnerability. The vulnerability is identified but no potential full-fledged or general purpose exploit has been revealed. Vulnerabilities that fall in this category have a very low probability to get exploited.

Proof of Concept: The development of proof-of-concept exploit happens to be part of penetration testing and vulnerability disclosure process. Most relevant and updated information of this category can be acquired from exploit database [1]. This is a Common Vulnerabilities and Exposures (CVE) [3] compliant archive for public exploit with associating vulnerable software.

Exploited in the Wild: It refers to the vulnerabilities extensively practiced in real attacks. Marked by different reasons some vulnerabilities attract much attention and quickly get exploited. The information of this group is documented in different security reports and databases like Symantec's AttackSignature dataset [6].

Table 1 shows the risk of a vulnerable component by combining these two factors. Each entry has been assigned with some numbers considering the relative risk of the component. We can see in Table 1 that the upper right index i.e. *Easy-Exploited in the wild* pair has a higher risk for the vulnerability fallen on that class. We note that the index score can be easily modified based on security personnel's preference.

4.2 Technique Priority Score

Along with vulnerability, we like to prioritize techniques employed by the attacker in the kill chain. Two factors have been considered to determine the priority of each technique independently: *adaptability* and *exploitation*. The adaptability of a technique depends on the environment and conditions that allow it to be exercised in addition to different goals the technique can attain. A technique usable for multiple OS allows attackers to carry their attacks on various service and applications. Thus, platform-independent technique presents additional risks. Adversaries action also require a particular privilege for successful exploitation. A normal user privilege can be easily achievable than a superuser, but the later could cause catastrophic damage. We have added both aspects by analyzing *permission requirement* of a technique. Technique's effectiveness is also defined as the number of distinct goals it obtains. Expertise on a particular technique resulting in more tactics gives the attacker more opportunities to proceed in the kill chain. Therefore, the adaptability score (*ASc*) of a technique t is:

$$ASc(ta_t) = pl_t \times \sum_{i=1}^{p} pr_i^t \times \tau_t \tag{1}$$

Where pl_t and τ_t are the fraction of OS platforms and achievable tactics respectively. In addition, pr_i^t denotes the permission level i for technique t. This score is proportional to the privilege acquired by the permission. For instance, the *SYSTEM* permission has the highest rank in this context and *User* has the lowest one.

Technique's priority also depends on how it has been manifested in the real world. MITRE ATT&CK database maps each technique with their associated softwares which has been leveraged by threat actor/groups for their adversarial activities. Software is broken down into three categories such as tool, utility and malware mostly referring to open source-commercial code, operating system utilities, custom or open source software for malicious purposes, etc. Groups use techniques in part of their attack campaign or intrusion activity over time. Hence, we measure how extensively a technique has been exploited by its exploitation score.

$$ExSc(ta_t) = sf_t \times gr_t \tag{2}$$

Where sf_t and gr_t are the fraction of software and groups respectively, that utilized technique t in real-world attacks. Next, we combine these two parameters discussed above to find the priority score of a technique. This technique priority score depicts how beneficial a technique is for attackers and how likely they would use it regardless of network structure. Each technique's score TSc is calculated independently using Eqs. 1 and 2:

$$TSc(ta_t) = \beta ASc(ta_t) + (1 - \beta)ExSc(ta_t) \tag{3}$$

The tuning parameter β is specified by security administrator. This parameter refers to the relative importance of whether a technique gives more benefits to the attacker or easy to learn from real attack.

4.3   Correlation Coefficient Calculation

The attacker needs to follow a chain of actions to reach to a target in the network. It resembles a compromising chain of states in our proposed model. Each state is integrated with different database such as ATT&CK [4], NVD [3] and Common Weakness Enumeration (CWE) [2]. This knowledge base gives us the corresponding factors that influence attacker to take a particular action. Multiple techniques from different or the same tactics might have overlapped factors which help attackers in their future actions. We track these attackers evolving skills from state to state by constructing a state correlation matrix in order to quantify how each state is correlated to others. The correlation matrix between state x and y is formulated as follows: $CC_{x,y} = AMCC_{x,y} + ENCC_{x,y}$; where $AMCC$ and $ENCC$ are the attack method correlation and environmental correlation, respectively. We determine $AMCC$ by examining whether an attack follows the same technique or emerged from the same weakness. $ENCC$ refers to the environmental and system features relevant to the attacks performed in the network. These features include platform, application or service, configuration, etc.

4.4   Hardness of a Path

We define the state hardness H_{as_i} as a function of two parameters, intrinsic state hardness $H_{as_i}(intr)$ and correlated hardness $H_{as_i}(corr)$. The intrinsic state hardness refers to the difficulty of state irrespective to the attack path it belongs to. The later one is computed by correlating with the former states the attacker traversed in a particular path. The hardness of path k from host j to j' is formulated as:

$$H_{P_{j,j'}^k} = \sum_{i \in \mathcal{AS}_{P_{j,j'}^k}} H_{as_i}(intr) * H_{as_i}(corr) \tag{4}$$

The correlation between state i and q is denoted with correlation coefficient (CC_{iq}). For similar states, we introduce a decay factor (λ) representing the effort reduction in similar actions; the larger the λ is, the easier the same action will be at the next time. Thus, Eq. 4 yields as:

$$H_{P_{j,j'}^k} = \sum_{i \in \mathcal{AS}_{P_{j,j'}^k}} (\alpha_i^{-1} + TSc(ta_t)^{-1})e^{-\sum_{q=\mathcal{AS}_{P_{j,j'}^k}(0)}^{i} \frac{CC_{iq}}{\lambda}} \tag{5}$$

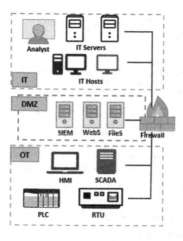

Fig. 4. ICS test-bed

Here, $(\alpha_i^{-1} + TSc(ta_t)^{-1})$ is the criticality of the state where $TSc(ta_t)$ is the technique priority score assuming state i is mapped with technique t and α_i is the vulnerable component risk for this state. The priority score reflects the defenders' priority alternatively means less hard for the attacker. In our transformed state graph each path from a source to target can be represented with a set of states. Thus we denote $\mathcal{AS}_{P_{j,j'}^k} = \{as_1, as_2, \ldots\ldots as_n\}$ as the set comprised of n action states for the path from j to j'.

5   Implementation and Results

We utilize Accenture ICS test-bed (Fig. 4) to evaluate our proposed framework. The test-bed has been designed based on the ISA-62443 architecture comprises of three zones, i.e., IT, OT and DMZ that simulate a power utility network. In the IT and OT zones, multiple workstations, servers and security devices are embedded. On the other hand in the OT zone, I/O panels are controlled by PLC and RTUs where these are subsequently interacting with SCADA server and monitored by human-machine interface (HMI) for active operation. We intentionally injected vulnerabilities in IT hosts, HMI and SCADA server. Vulnerable firmware is used in end devices like PLC and RTUs resembling real attack prone ICS network. Our analysis starts with scanning the whole network in different stages. Active and passive scanning tools like Nessus, Grassmarlin, ClarOty has been used in IT and OT zones respectively. This information is used to generate logical AG, further translated to state graph employing our methodology. For our analysis, we extracted attack paths terminating at multiple targets. Each path is comprised of a set of states from source points to different target hosts.

Then the states are being mapped to TT category. A sample state extracted from our attack path is shown below.

```
execCode('192.168.15.124',someUser):-
    vulExists('192.168.15.124','CVE-2015-2808',
    safari,remoteExploit,privEscalation)
    networkServiceInfo('192.168.15.124',safari,tcp,
    '1433',someUser)
    netAccess('192.168.15.124',tcp,'1433')
rule_desc('remote exploit of a server program')
```

By taking into account the sample state's configurations and the rule, our methodology primarily maps this state into two techniques: *exploitation for client execution (T1203)* and *exploitation of remote services (T1210)*. These techniques are associated with two different tactics such as *execution* and *lateral movement* respectively. Our domain knowledge considers *execution* as the most appropriate tactic for this sample.

Moreover, we can acquire more confidence by introducing another characteristic phenomenon in our model. The cyber kill chain (CKC) describes different phases in the adversary life cycle in an attack campaign. In our model, we can treat each attack path as a part of the superset of a CKC. Thus it follows a particular pattern for attack progression. We introduce this property for tactic identification as the pre-state and post-state analysis. Referring to our example, one of the pre-conditions *netaccess('192.168.15.124'..)* can be represented as a prior state as shown below:

```
netAccess('192.168.15.124',tcp,'1433'):-
    attackerLocated(internet)
    hacl(internet,'192.168.15.124',tcp,'1433')
rule_desc('direct network access')
```

Our initial analysis mapped this state to *initial access* tactic. Furthermore, the following state marked as *netaccess('192.168.15.123'..)* that takes our sample state (i.e. *execCode('192.168.15.124'...*) as a pre-condition represented as follow:

```
netAccess('192.168.15.123',tcp,'1433'):-
    execCode('192.168.15.124',someUser)
    hacl('192.168.15.124','192.168.15.123',tcp,'1433')
rule_desc('multi-hop access')
```

The state shown above is mapped to the *lateral movement* tactic. Thus the sequence formed as: *initial access → execution → lateral movement*, is a perfect example of a kill chain phase. Consequently, it affirms our analysis and emphasizes the effectiveness of our method for TT mapping. After mapping to TT we assign a score for each selected technique by using Eqs. 1, 2 and 3. Then we measure the vulnerable component score from 1 prior to discovering its appropriate category. This is an optional parameter, means each and every state doesn't have to hold a vulnerability. In contrary, TT is an inevitable feature of a state. Thus, TT embedded AG gives the defense planners more advantage to deploy their defensive techniques.

As we mentioned before, we generate attack paths for multiple heterogeneous targets e.g., HMI from OT, file server (FileS) and web server (WebS) from

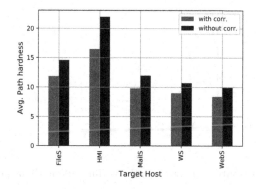

Fig. 5. Deviation of path hardness by effort correlation

DMZ and mail server (MailS) and workstation (WS) from IT zone. The decay factor can be calculated from post-compromise real attack analysis. It can be estimated by matching our correlation method to the time-to-compromise of a state. The parameter could be improved gradually by feedback method. For our convenience, we set the value 2 for decay factor means around 40% effort reduced if both states correlate perfectly.

After plugging all information into Eq. 5 we calculate the path hardness of all attack paths for each target host. Figure 5 depicts the effect of effort correlation in hardness measurement. The X-axis represents different target host we selected for our analysis and Y-axis represents average path hardness considering all attack paths direct to each host. For each host, the hardness value is computed with and without correlation. Assuming the attacker goal is the target host, each case shows the lower effort needed to traverse the path by taking account correlation than without it. Indeed, this correlation reflects attack's knowledge propagation in an attack path. It can be observed from the figure that the scale of deviation is not same for all hosts. For instance, around 25% effort reduced for attack paths towards HMI regarding correlation while it is 15% for WS. Because HMI is located in OT zone, very low level in the network contrary to WS which resides in the IT zone, very close to the perimeter. Hence, attack paths in the direction to HMI have more state to pass allowing attackers to learn more and help them to decide in the following route.

Our method we can also be used to determine the diversity of an attack path. A path having low hardness difference between correlation and non-correlation case has high diversity. Prior to an attack, the administrator can harden the most impactful path by assessing the consequence (C) of path along with it's diversity (D). Attack paths having high consequence and low diversity should be treated with high priority for this defense mechanism. This establishes a hierarchy among paths; the most critical paths of the network are those with the highest $\frac{C}{D}$ value.

Our path metric can also capture the total security posture of the network. Figure 6 shows the distribution of attack path within different hardness level

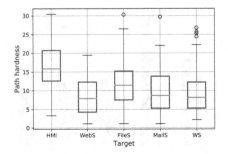

Fig. 6. Distribution of attack paths within different hardness level

for our selected target hosts. From the figure, it is determined that the concentration of distribution varies from host to host in the network. In our analysis, HMI has large path distribution between hardness range 13–21 which is relatively higher than other hosts. Although it is not the only decision factor but the host's architectural level is one of the reasons behind this scenario. EDS follows the defense-in-depth architecture where the control center is isolated with several security controls make the majority of the route very tough for the attacker. In addition, hosts remained in the same zone doesn't need to follow the same hardness level. For instance, WebS and FileS both reside in the DMZ zone exhibits a noticeable difference in path hardness distribution. Previously discussed path diversity can be utilized to interpret this situation. Depending on the configuration of a certain network, the paths towards both hosts might have variable path length along with the different scale of correlation in each path.

The aforementioned path characteristics need to be examined thoroughly for proper defense deployment. The security administrator can assign a threshold as a particular path hardness level for critical assets in the network. As the attack graph is dynamically changing over time by zero-day vulnerabilities being discovered, regular security policy variation and countermeasure enforcement, the defender must investigate the hardness of critical node in order to keep the risk of the network in an acceptable level.

6 Conclusion and Future Work

In this paper, we presented a proactive cyber threat assessment framework for EDS. We identified the behavioral signature of an action state by incorporating the techniques and tactics within an attack graph. We developed a scoring metric to quantify the likelihood of a state to be compromised. The system security planner can use the path metric to apply the remediation policies on the most critical attack paths. It will also provide insights into balancing cyber risk and operation resilience. Additionally, the evaluation results have provided insights into mapping the tactics taken in an attack path to adversarial/threat characteristics. Some adversary groups would never change the tactic while others would adapt given the situation. For future work, we like to conduct in-depth profiling of attacker behavior for diverse real-world threat actors.

Acknowledgment. This material is based upon work supported by the Department of Energy under award number DE-OE0000780 and Department of Homeland Security Grant 2015-ST-061-CIRC01. The views and opinions of authors expressed herein do not necessarily state or reflect those of the United States Government or any agency thereof.

References

1. Public exploit database. http://www.exploit-db.com
2. Common weakness enumeration, January 2017. http://cwe.mitre.org
3. National vulnerability database, January 2017. https://nvd.nist.gov
4. Mitre adversarial tactics, techniues, and common knowledge, August 2018. https://attack.mitre.org/techniques/enterprise
5. Al-Shaer, R., Ahmed, M., Al-Shaer, E.: Statistical learning of APT TTP chains from mitre ATT&CK
6. Allodi, L., Massacci, F.: Comparing vulnerability severity and exploits using case-control studies. ACM Trans. Inf. Syst. Secur. **17**(1), 1–20 (2014). https://doi.org/10.1145/2630069
7. Bianco, D.: The pyramid of plain (2014). http://detect-respond.blogspot.com/2013/03/the-pyramid-of-pain.htmldossier.pdf
8. Bronk, C., Tikk-Ringas, E.: The cyber attack on saudi aramco. Survival **55**(2), 81–96 (2013)
9. Carcano, A.: Understanding triton, the first sis cyber attack, August 2018. http://www.nozominetworks.com/blog/black-hat-understanding-triton-the-first-sis-cyber-attack
10. Davis, K.R., et al.: A cyber-physical modeling and assessment framework for power grid infrastructures. IEEE Trans. Smart Grid **6**(5), 2464–2475 (2015)
11. Falliere, N., Murchu, L.O., Chien, E.: W32.stuxnet dossier version 1.3, November 2010. http://www.symantec.com/content/en/us/enterprise/media/security_response/whitepapers/w32_stuxnet_dossier.pdf
12. Hassanzadeh, A., Burkett, R.: SAMIIT: spiral attack model in iiot mapping security alerts to attack life cycle phases. ics & scada cyber security research. In: 5th International Symposium for ICS & SCADA Cyber Security Research 2018, vol. 5, pp. 11–20. Hamburg, Germany (2018)
13. Hassanzadeh, A., Modi, S., Mulchandani, S.: Towards effective security control assignment in the industrial Internet of Things. In: 2015 IEEE 2nd World Forum on Internet of Things (WF-IoT), pp. 795–800. IEEE (2015)
14. Hutchins, E.M., Cloppert, M.J., Amin, R.M.: Intelligence-driven computer network defense informed by analysis of adversary campaigns and intrusion kill chains. Lead. Issues Inf. Warfare Secur. Res. **1**(1), 80 (2011)
15. Idika, N., Bhargava, B.: Extending attack graph-based security metrics and aggregating their application. IEEE Trans. Dependable Secure Comput. **9**(1), 75–85 (2012)
16. Nayak, K., Marino, D., Efstathopoulos, P., Dumitraş, T.: Some vulnerabilities are different than others. In: Stavrou, A., Bos, H., Portokalidis, G. (eds.) RAID 2014. LNCS, vol. 8688, pp. 426–446. Springer, Cham (2014). https://doi.org/10.1007/978-3-319-11379-1_21

17. Ou, X., Boyer, W.F., McQueen, M.A.: A scalable approach to attack graph generation. In: The 13th ACM conference on Computer and Communications Security (CCS), Alexandria, Virginia, USA, October-November 2006
18. Ou, X., Govindavajhala, S., Appel, A.W.: Mulval: a logic-based network security analyzer. In: The 14th Conference on USENIX Security Symposium (SSYM), Baltimore, MD, USA, July-August 2005
19. Ullah, S., Shetty, S., Hassanzadeh, A.: Towards modeling attacker's opportunity for improving cyber resilience in energy delivery systems. In: 2018 Resilience Week (RWS). IEEE, August 2018
20. Zhang, Y., Lingfeng, W., Xiang, Y., Ten, C.: Power system reliability evaluation with scada cybersecurity considerations. IEEE Trans. Smart Grid **6**, 1707–1721 (2015)

Bulletproof Defenses

The Disbanding Attack: Exploiting Human-in-the-Loop Control in Vehicular Platooning

Ali Al-Hashimi[1]([⊠]), Pratham Oza[2], Ryan Gerdes[2], and Thidapat Chantem[2]

[1] Utah State University, Logan, UT 84321, USA
ali.2014@aggiemail.usu.edu
[2] Virginia Tech, Arlington, VA 22203, USA
{prathamo,rgerdes,tchantem}@vt.edu

Abstract. Due to advances in automated vehicle technology and inter-vehicle communication, vehicular platoons have attracted a growing interest by academia and industry alike, as they can produce safe driving, regularize traffic flow, and increase throughput. Research has demonstrated, however, that when platoons are placed in an adversarial environment, they are vulnerable to a variety of attacks that could negatively impact traffic flow and produce collisions and/or injuries. In this work, we consider an attack that seeks to exploit human-in-the-loop control of compromised vehicles that are part of a platoon. Specifically, we demonstrate that should a human operator need to suddenly take control of a platooned vehicle, significant upstream effects, which threaten the safety of passengers in other vehicles, may be induced. To counter this so-called disbanding attack, we present an optimal centralized mitigation approach. Due to scalability, security, and privacy concerns, such an approach may not be practical in reality. Hence, we also propose a decentralized mitigation algorithm that reduces excessive speed changes and coordinates inter-platoon behaviors to minimize the attack impacts. Our algorithm is compared to the aforementioned optimal approach and is shown to produce nearly equivalent results while requiring fewer resources. Experimental results on a hardware testbed show that our countermeasure permits graceful speed reductions and can provide safety, i.e., no collisions.

Keywords: Vehicular platoons · Attacks on vehicular platoons · Mitigation of attacks

1 Introduction

Vehicular platooning is an automation technology wherein a number of vehicles are grouped together to follow each other closely and safely. This technology has been shown to provide a safe and comfortable experience that will ultimately allow passengers to focus on tasks other than driving [11]. It also enables vehicles

This grant was supported in part by NSF under grant number CPS-1658225.

© ICST Institute for Computer Sciences, Social Informatics and Telecommunications Engineering 2019
Published by Springer Nature Switzerland AG 2019. All Rights Reserved
S. Chen et al. (Eds.): SecureComm 2019, LNICST 305, pp. 163–183, 2019.
https://doi.org/10.1007/978-3-030-37231-6_9

to safely navigate at a closer distance, compared to human-driven vehicles, which improves traffic throughput and reduces congestion [29], and can help to improve fuel consumption [21]. Vehicle platooning is an example of a cyber-physical system (CPS) since it requires an integration of computation, communication, and monitoring capabilities to control a physical process. Adaptive Cruise Control (ACC) and Cooperative Adaptive Cruise Control (CACC) are the most well-known control strategies used to form and maintain platoons. ACC operation consists of using locally available information to generate appropriate acceleration commands to maintain a preset inter-vehicle separation and speed (longitudinal control). CACC, on the other hand, is an extension of ACC that employs vehicle-to-vehicle (V2V) communication, so that vehicles may exchange state information, and is able to achieve smaller inter-vehicle separations [27].

The Society of Automotive Engineers (SAE) and the National Highway Traffic Safety Administration (NHTSA) have defined levels of vehicular automation. Based on their criteria, vehicle manufacturers have been able to produce vehicles with level 2, e.g., BMW, and Ford, or level 3, e.g., Tesla, capabilities [32]. In level 2, automated vehicles can generate both longitudinal (accelerating/decelerating) and lateral (steering) control commands. This level also requires humans to monitor the road and readiness to assume control if needed. Level 3 provides more automated functionalities in terms of generating control commands and monitoring the driving environment, though it also requires human driver readiness to assume control [7]. Platooning without human oversight, a level 4 technology, is not yet a reality due to the lack of robustness in V2V communications, the cost and number of sensors required to monitor the environment, and unresolved questions regarding unexpected maneuvers on the part of other vehicles on the road [2]. Therefore, current platooning automation technology falls into the category of level 2 or level 3, and human attention is still required in the platooned vehicles in case they need to take control of the vehicles.

Transition of control is defined as the process of switching control, of an automated vehicle, to a human driver when the automated system cannot handle certain situations; e.g., a vehicle emerging from a side road abruptly and merging onto a highway without notice, oncoming traffic turning left to enter a side road and crossing an automated vehicle's path, a car parking on the road and partially blocking the roadway [23,32], or a technical failure in one or more components of the vehicle's automation system [36]. Such failures could stem from the deliberate manipulation of the automated system components such as sensors, actuators, or inter-vehicle communication [4]. A number of previous studies analyzed human driver behaviors post transition of control and their results have shown that some drivers apply maximum deceleration to handle certain situations, e.g., avoid colliding with preceding vehicles [17,22]. These studies also determined the time required to ensure a safe transition [15,23].

A platooning CPS (typically) employs a distributed controller that uses information from both local sensors and those obtained through inter-vehicle communications or connections to external networks [24]. As a result, a platooning CPS has a large attack surface by which an attacker could induce disruptive and/or fatal behaviors [12–14,16,31]. Attacks mounted against a platooning CPS can lead to the disruption of the steady-state operation (i.e., desired inter-vehicle separation and relative speed) and produce harmful effects, such as collisions or uncomfortable acceleration/deceleration, which could lead to, for example, chronic traffic jams. Also, attacks on platooned vehicles could induce a transition of control which, in turn, will disband (dissolve) the platoon since the latter is no longer automated nor complies with platooning control laws. While the security of platooning CPS has been studied from many perspectives, so far the exploitation of the human element has been left unexplored.

In the current work we examine, from an adversarial perspective, the aftereffects of automated vehicles transitioning their control to humans. Particularly, we are interested in analyzing the upstream effects of all vehicles in a platoon transitioning control to human operators (a process we refer to as the platoon disbanding) due to a system failure resulting from an attack. Although disbanding may seem a sensible fail-safe solution to prevent attackers from achieving their objective of influencing automated vehicles, we will show that transition of control can be leveraged to undermine the operation of surrounding vehicles, cause collisions, and/or induce massive congestion. The main contributions are:

- We study the effect of a "disbanding attack" that involves transition of control of multiple vehicles in a platoon. We show the harmful impacts such an attack can induce, especially how it can cause upstream (non-attacked) platoons to experience slowdowns and collisions.
- We define the disbanding attack by formulating it as an optimization problem where the objective is to maximize the deviation in vehicles' speeds, as a proxy for slowdowns and increased chances of colliding, by selecting platoon(s) to be disbanded and time(s) of disbanding.
- To mitigate the aftermath of such an attack, we formulate an optimal solution using a Model Predictive Control (MPC) technique. However, since the optimal approach is not scalable in practice, as it is centralized and information and communication intensive, we also propose a heuristic algorithm to be used locally by vehicles of intact (non-attacked) platoons. Our findings indicate that our algorithm produces nearly equivalent results in terms of reducing speed changes and avoiding accidents.
- We also demonstrate the validity of the above attack and the suggested heuristic countermeasure using experiments on a hardware testbed consisting of a motion capture system and small mobile robots acting as vehicles.

1.1   A Motivating Example

Let us consider a scenario where multiple vehicular platoons are traveling in the same direction on a highway. Although they may not be heading to the same destination, platoons drive and follow one another in order to reap platooning benefits of optimizing traffic flow and reducing congestions. While the platoons are operating at a steady-state, a malicious party utilizes one of the existing external attack techniques [19,31] in order to cause accidents. For example,

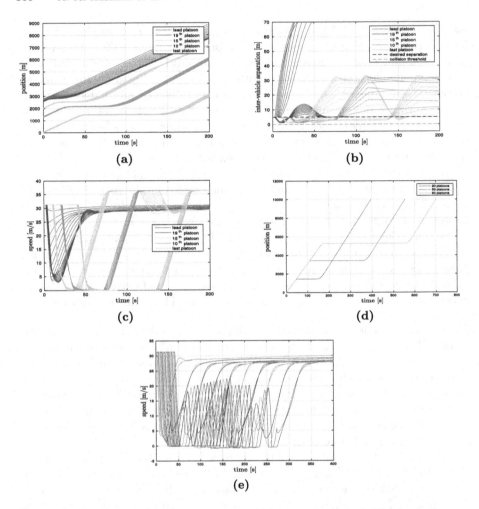

Fig. 1. (a) Position profiles of the platoons shown in the legend. The lead platoon started disbanding at t = 2 s. (b) Inter-vehicle separation profiles of the platoons shown in the legend. The lead platoon started disbanding at t = 2 s. (c) Speed profiles of the platoons shown in the legend. The lead platoon started disbanding at t = 2 s. (d) Position profile of the rear vehicle in the platoons formation, whose size is shown in the legend. (e) Speed profiles of the rear vehicles belonging to a twenty-platoon formation when multiple platoons start disbanding at different time instances. (Color figure online)

the attacker could install units on the roadside that are able to jam the sensors of multiple vehicles or modify the sensor measurements so that the targeted vehicles start behaving irregularly [25]. At this point, either the automation system will suffer a failure and, as a result, informs the driver, by sounding an auditory alarm for example [22], or the attack is detected by a mechanism, already designed for such purpose, or by a passenger, who observes an erratic behavior in the vehicle's motion. In any case, the driver must assume control of the vehicle and apply the brakes [36]. As a result, the attacked platoon is effectively disbanded as the vehicles no longer comply with platooning laws and the mounted attack fails to achieve its goals. However, intact upstream platoons, which were not the goal of the mounted external attack, will also exhibit unexpected behavior as a result of disbanding such as slowing down and coming to a complete stop, which creates discomfort for passengers, or even colliding.

Figure 1a shows the position profiles of a selected platoon, out of 20, whose indices are shown in the legend. Each platoon has ten vehicles. The lead (20th) platoon (red), which constitutes 5% of the total number of vehicles, transitions its control after being attacked at t = 2 s. We can see how the lead platoon begins disbanding when the inter-vehicle separations, shown in Fig. 1b, are no longer 5 m (the desired separation) and the platoon manages to avoid accidents. Also, Fig. 1c indicates that the vehicles of the disbanded platoon initially slow down and then begin to speed up. In response to the lead platoon being disbanded, we can see in Fig. 1c that the following (still automated) 19th intact platoon (blue) also begins to slow down. In addition, Fig. 1b shows that the inter-vehicle separation of the 19th platoon is also affected as it decreases when slowing down happens, but not below 0 m, starts increasing to above 10 m when speeding up happens, and eventually reaches to 5 m after almost one minute.

The same effect that was induced in the 19th platoon will propagate through the rest of the following platoons. For example, the 15th platoon (yellow) started decelerating until all vehicles completely stopped, as shown in Fig. 1c, for almost 30 s and then the platoon's lead vehicle started accelerating, reaching maximum speed of 36 m/s, in order to decrease the gap with respect to the preceding 16th platoon (not shown in plots) and eventually slowed down, as it is approaching the preceding platoon, after almost two minutes (These action of accelerating/decelerating result from the adopted automation control laws responding to the behavior of the preceding platoon). We can also see the same behavior in Fig. 1b where the inter-vehicle separation of the 15th platoon decreased, increased, and then settled at 5 m. The same pattern also shows on the 10th (green) and last (cyan) platoons but longer times were needed to regain the inter-vehicle separations and speeds. For this specific case of disbanding attack, 10 min were needed such that all of the affected platoons were able to re-establish (recover) the desired separations and speeds. Furthermore, Fig. 1d shows the absolute position of the last vehicle in the traffic stream, for different number of platoons, when the lead platoon was disbanded. We can see that as the number of platoons increases, the vehicle stops for a longer time and then resumes moving. Furthermore, the string of 20, 50, and 80 platoons, needed 10, 25, and 43 min, respectively, to recover. In summary, we can see in these plots that disbanding one platoon could make the following platoons respond irregularly such that they stop-and-go which in turn creates discomfort for passengers, traffic jams, inefficient use of the road, and fuel waste.

Alternatively, being aware of such effects, the attacker can target more than one platoon systematically and produce worse impacts such as multiple stop-and-go behaviors. For example, the attacker can induce disbanding by targeting every other platoon, out of twenty, at regular intervals, with 30 s increments (Fig. 1e). For the speed profiles shown in Fig. 1e, 65%, 45%, and 37.5% of the intact platoons were forced to stop-and-go once, twice, and three times, respectively. Also, 55% of the vehicles, in the intact platoons, suffered collisions.

1.2 Related Work

The objective of vehicular platooning is to combine multiple vehicles and design the proper controllers to maintain a desired separation and speed [6]. A large amount of work can be found in literature addressing how to achieve that objective. Also, different spacing policies are proposed to implement control laws that regulate the relative spacing either in front of vehicle (unidirectional control) or on both front and rear of vehicle (bidirectional control) [27]. This is achieved using either only locally sensed information or with the addition of (V2V) communication [34]. Communication schemes are proposed in [3] to transmit messages between adjacent vehicles. Also, it is possible to exchange vehicles' information by establishing vehicle-to-infrastructure (V2I) communication with road units designed for that purpose [10]. In this work, we adopt a proportional-derivative controller from [34] to form our platoons with the presence of a forward-looking V2V communication in order to implement our suggested attack mitigation (Sect. 4).

Vehicular platoons security has been the focus of extensive research in literature. For example, [13] presents a number of insider attacks that target the vehicles' CACC controllers and suggests detection schemes for those attacks. Another insider attack work is [12] where the attacker's controlled vehicle is able to modify its controller's gains such that generated commands induce instability in the entire platoon. [16] shows that it is possible for a malicious vehicle in the platoon to increase the energy consumption unnecessarily in the neighboring vehicles by misbehaving. In [14], it is shown that multiple attacker vehicles can operate within the platoon and coordinate their behavior in order to produce instability that could lead to accidents. Alternately, other work investigate external attacks where local range and range-rate sensors are targeted, to misinform the vehicle of the surrounding vehicles' information to negatively impact road efficiency and passengers' comfort and safety [19,31]. Similar to the security related works above, we also present a possible vulnerability in vehicular platoons and analyze its impacts on platoon safety. However, ours is the first work that considers the effect the presence of human control in the platoon can produce. Specifically, we try to answer: "what happens if control of multiple vehicles transition to human because to disruption of their automated systems?" or "what happens if a passenger decides to assume command of a vehicle after observing irregular behavior, owing to an already mounted attack, in its motion?". Naturally, once a human driver starts controlling the vehicle, brakes will be applied in an attempt to slow down the vehicle [36]. While such an action is helpful in avoiding accidents, it will also generate instability in the following non-attacked platoons that could lead to collisions.

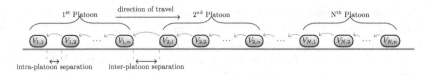

Fig. 2. A stream of n-vehicle N platoons. Green arrows represent the flow of transmitted information. (Color figure online)

1.3 Organization

Section 2 explains the vehicular platooning control laws and describes the threat model. Section 3 discusses different optimal attack scenarios and analyze their impacts. Section 4 presents effective attack countermeasures. Experimental results are presented in Sect. 5. Conclusions are given in Sect. 6.

2 System Model

The modeling of platoon dynamics and control as well as the attack mechanism are discussed in this section.

2.1 Vehicle and Platoon Models

We consider N homogeneous platoons, where every vehicle uses the same control law, with n vehicles in each (lead vehicle is indexed as n while the last vehicle is indexed as 1) as shown in Fig. 2. Each vehicle is equipped with front and rear range and range-rate sensors, to measure corresponding relative distances and speeds of surrounding vehicles, and implements an upper-level controller, responsible for determining the commanded (desired) acceleration, and a lower-level controller, which uses the desired acceleration to determine throttle and brake commands. The lower-level controller is expected to achieve the desired acceleration with some delay due to its finite bandwidth [24,27]. We will focus on the upper-level controller since the attacker can easily affect it (e.g., through attacks on sensors). The following model is used to simulate the dynamics of each jth vehicle in the ith platoon

$$\begin{bmatrix} \dot{x}_{i,j}(t) \\ \dot{v}_{i,j}(t) \\ \dot{a}_{i,j}(t) \end{bmatrix} = \begin{bmatrix} 0 & 1 & 0 \\ 0 & 0 & 1 \\ 0 & 0 & \frac{-1}{\tau} \end{bmatrix} \begin{bmatrix} x_{i,j}(t) \\ v_{i,j}(t) \\ a_{i,j}(t) \end{bmatrix} + \begin{bmatrix} 0 \\ 0 \\ \frac{1}{\tau} \end{bmatrix} u_{i,j}(t), \tag{1}$$

where x, v a, and u refer to the vehicle's absolute position, velocity, acceleration, and commanded acceleration, respectively, and τ is a time constant used to model the actuator's delay.

In this work, vehicles in a platoon use a bidirectional control technique [34] with two major benefits. First, it is able to guarantee platoon string stability to maintain desirable traffic flow [27,34]. Second, it does require vehicle-to-vehicle

(V2V) transmitted information to generate periodic control commands. We do, however, assume intermittent wireless communication is possible between vehicles for attack detection and to transmit data for the mitigation process (Sect. 4). These require a data rate far lower than that required to maintain V2V-enabled platoons. For the last vehicle in the ith platoon, we have

$$u_{i,1}(t) = k_p(x_{i,2}(t) - x_{i,1}(t) - x_d) + k_d(v_{i,2}(t) - v_{i,1}(t)), \tag{2}$$

where k_p and k_d are the controller's proportional and derivative gains, respectively, and x_d is a constant denoting inter-vehicle desired separation. For the other vehicles in the ith platoon, except the leader, we have

$$u_{i,j}(t) = k_p\{(x_{i,j+1}(t) - x_{i,j}(t) - x_d) - (x_{i,j}(t) - x_{i,j-1}(t) - x_d)\} \\ + k_d\{(v_{i,j+1}(t) - v_{i,j}(t)) - (v_{i,j}(t) - v_{i,j-1}(t))\}, \tag{3}$$

A different control structure is adopted for the platoons' lead vehicles since we expect that the platoon may encounter other platoons as they travel on the road. Lead vehicles attempt to maintain a desired separation and speed, with respect to a preceding vehicle, by using a control law given by [27]

$$u_{i,n}(t) = k_p(x_{i+1,1}(t) - x_{i,n}(t) - h.v_{i,n}(t)) + k_d(v_{i+1,1}(t) - v_{i,n}(t)), \tag{4}$$

where h is a time headway constant. Also, each lead vehicle is equipped with a transitional controller which is engaged in cases it encounters a slowly moving vehicle or a slowly driving platoon on the road. Interested readers are referred to [27] for more details on transitional controllers.

We are interested in studying the effect of control transition. Therefore, we will adopt the Intelligent Driver Model (IDM) [20], which can be used to approximate human driving behavior, to simulate the dynamics of control transitioned vehicle(s). The commanded acceleration of the disbanded platoon vehicles is calculated using

$$u_{i,j}(t) = u_{max}\{1 - (v_{i,j}(t)/v_d)^4 - (s^*(t)/(x_{i,j+1}(t) - x_{i,j}(t)))^2\}, \\ s^*(t) = r_0 + v_{i,j}(t)\{h + (v_{i,j}(t) - v_{i,j+1}(t)/(2\sqrt{u_{min}u_{max}})\}, \tag{5}$$

where v_d is the desired velocity, u_{min}, u_{max} are minimum and maximum acceleration, respectively, and r_0 is the minimum inter-vehicle separation (a vehicle cannot move if the separation is smaller than r_0).

Finally, we assume that all vehicles are equipped with a collision-avoidance technique where u_{min} will be applied when the following condition is true [3,27]

$$x_{i,j+1}(t) - x_{i,j}(t) \leq r_0 + (v_{i,j}^2(t) - v_{i,j+1}^2(t))/2u_{min}. \tag{6}$$

2.2   Threat Model

The aim of the disbanding attack in a multi-platoon scenario is to induce collisions in some platoons, by targeting one or more vehicle(s) in a different platoon, and disrupting traffic flow. This type of attack relies on compromising some aspect of a vehicle's automation system so as to force the vehicle to abandon automated operation, i.e., transition of control, and hence cause the platoon to which it belongs to disband. The action of disbanding, in turn, will impact upstream platoons. As stated earlier, the level of automation provided by the currently available automation technology is still not highly autonomous. Therefore, it is still expected that human drivers will need to take control of the automated vehicles during certain situations.

One possible attack vector that could be leveraged to compromise a vehicle's automation, and force a transition of control, is to target the vehicle's front and/or rear facing sensors that are relied upon to perceive the relative distance and speed of neighboring vehicles. Existing work has demonstrated that LIDAR, RADAR, camera, and ultra-sonic sensors, which are the most often used sensors in automated vehicles for these purposes, can be jammed or spoofed. In addition, such attacks can be targeted, easy to carryout, accomplished at a distance, and mounted against multiple vehicles at once [9,25,33,35].

To demonstrate the impacts of the disbanding attack in our study, we assume that the attacker has the capability to target the sensors of either one or multiple automated vehicles belonging to one or more platoons. Also, we assume that the mounted attack succeeds in degrading the sensing functionality of the automation system(s) employing the targeted sensor(s). We consider two possible scenarios resulting from the attack. In the case where a sensor of a single vehicle in a platoon is targeted and its automation compromised, the vehicle will utilize V2V communications and alert the other vehicles in that platoon so that they begin to transition their control[1]. In the case of targeting the sensor(s) of all vehicles in a platoon, the automation systems of those vehicles will suffer the disruption of the sensors operation, become unable to handle the current situation, and also begin the process of transition of control. In either case, the automated vehicles are forced to transition their control in an attempt to mitigate the attack and avoid accidents, effectively disbanding the platoon.

Although the process of disbanding a platoon can help with avoiding accidents, the resulting action of braking will cause upstream effects on intact (non-attacked) platoons. Those effects pose a threat to the safety of these platoons, as they cause sudden and excessive velocity changes that could lead to collisions. Disbanding attacks are extremely effective since attack-resilient platooning controllers tend to ignore human intervention in the design process.

3   Human-in-the-Loop Attacks

In this section, the disbanding attack is formulated as an optimization problem in order to find optimal attacks. Then, the simulation setup to carry out such an attack is explained.

---

[1] Disbanding (dissolving) a platoon when one vehicle reverts to manual control has been recommended in actual platooning systems [30].

3.1   Finding Optimal Disbanding Attack

Given the attacker's capabilities and platoon dynamics as described in Sect. 2, the goal of the attacker is to find which platoon(s) and at what time(s) vehicles' sensors should be attacked to induce disbanding, such that the velocity deviation of all intact vehicles is maximized, which is a fair indication of throughput and probability of collisions. To assess the impacts of disbanding attacks on platoons, we use the following metrics

- Average velocity error (deviation) describes the non-attacked platoons' slowing down as a result of disbanding another platoon(s). For the jth vehicle in the ith platoon, the average velocity error is defined as

$$E_v = \frac{1}{|T_s|} \sum_{k=1}^{|T_s|} \frac{|v_{i,j}(t_k) - v_d|}{v_d} \cdot 100, \tag{7}$$

where T_s is the attack window (in seconds), and v_d is desired speed. Since we are considering platoons, Eq. (7) is modified as follows

$$E_v = \frac{1}{N \cdot n \cdot |T_s|} \sum_{i=1}^{N} \sum_{j=1}^{n} \sum_{k=1}^{|T_s|} \frac{|v_{i,j}(t_k) - v_d|}{v_d} \cdot 100, \tag{8}$$

by which E_v is calculated for all vehicles ($N \cdot n$) throughout T_s.
- Collisions: although each vehicle is assumed to be equipped with a collision-avoidance algorithm, crashes between some of the intact vehicles can still occur. Therefore, we will indicate whether the considered attack scenario involves collisions or not.

Table 1. Parameters used in the simulations.

Parameter	Value	Description
N	[2:10]	Number of platoons
n	10	Number of vehicles per platoon
k_p	1	Controller's proportional gain
k_d	5	Controller's derivative gain
x_d	$\{5, 4\}$ m	Desired inter-vehicle separation
v_d	31 m/s	Nominal velocity
h	1.5 s	Time headway
τ	$\{0.1, 0.3, 0.5\}$ s	Time-lag constant
$v_{\max}$	36 m/s	Maximum velocity
$v_{\min}$	0 m/s	Minimum velocity
$u_{\max}$	1 m/s^2	Maximum acceleration
$u_{\min}$	-5 m/s^2	Minimum acceleration
r_0	1 m	Minimum inter-vehicle separation
T_s	180 s	Simulation time

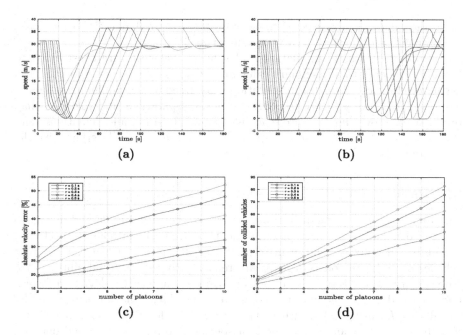

Fig. 3. (a) Speed profiles of platoons' rear vehicles (N = 10) when the lead platoon started disbanding at t = 2 s. (b) Speed profiles of platoons' rear vehicles (N = 10) when the 9th and 10th platoons started disbanding at t = 2 s and 100 s, respectively. (c) Average velocity error for optimal single-platoon disbanding cases. (d) Number of collided vehicles for optimal single-platoon disbanding cases.

Let p_d be a vector of indices of platoons to be disbanded, and t_d a vector of times of disbanding. The attacker will solve the following optimization problem

$$
\begin{aligned}
\underset{p_d, t_d}{\text{maximize}} \quad & E_v = f(p_d, t_d) \\
\text{subject to} \quad & 1 \leq p_d \leq N \\
& 1 \leq t_d \leq T_s \\
& p_d(i_1) \neq p_d(i_2) \text{ for } i_1, i_2 = 1, \ldots, \text{ no. of targeted platoons}
\end{aligned}
\tag{9}
$$

Equation (9) should be interpreted as follows: given a number of targeted platoon(s), the attacker seeks the best values for p_d and t_d such that the highest value for the cost function, E_v, will result. The constraints of the problem ensure that values of p_d and t_d are within bounds and the same platoon cannot be disbanded twice (in case of multi-platoon disbanding). We used the Genetic Algorithm (GA) Toolbox in MATLAB to solve Eq. (9).

3.2 Simulation Setup

For the theoretical results presented in this work, we used MATLAB to simulate a string of platoons, using the control algorithms and dynamics from Sect. 2.1. Table 1 indicates the setup used in all subsequent simulations. Following previous work, the value of τ was selected to be either 0.1 s [18] or 0.5 s [27]. To generalize the problem, we also simulated values in-between.

To produce realistic simulations, all vehicles' velocities are constrained to be below or equal to a maximum value and all vehicles move only forward (no negative velocities). Also, the acceleration is bounded within minimum and maximum values. Since vehicles' responses to initial separations and velocities may result in some overshoot before reaching the steady-state, all simulations were started at the steady-state so that transient response will not interfere with the attack impacts.

3.3 Results

Two different cases of the disbanding attack are shown in Fig. 3a and in Fig. 3b (for the disbanding the lead platoon and two foremost platoons, respectively, out of 10). Results are shown in terms of the absolute speed of the last/rear vehicles of intact platoons (legends are removed to reduce visual clutter). We see that disbanding results in not only slowdowns, and hence deviation form a desired speed of 31 m/s, but even complete stops. This behavior is captured by calculating E_v using (8), which is equal to 29.57% for Fig. 3a and 43.69% for Fig. 3b. For Figs. 3c and d, the total number of platoons (N) is varied between two and ten (shown on the x-axis), an actuator delay, τ, varied between 0.1–0.5 s, with an increment of 0.1 s, and a time headway (h) equal to 1.5 s.

For each value of N, the solution of (9) indicated that the optimal attack occurred by disbanding the lead platoon at one second (beginning of attack window). Figure 3c shows the optimal (maximum) average velocity error (E_v) for disbanding the lead platoon and for different values of τ. We can see clearly that more severe attack impacts are induced as the total number of platoons increases. Although all vehicle are equipped with an appropriate collision-avoidance algorithm, simulation results indicate that disbanding attacks can also cause accidents between some of the vehicles in the intact platoons, which were not the target of the attack. Figure 3d shows the number of colliding vehicles for each one of the optimal disbanding attack cases displayed in Fig. 3c. We can see that collisions occur when actuator delay is greater than 0.1 s, regardless of N, and that the total number of accidents increases as the total number of platoons increases as well.

4 Attack Mitigation

We propose two approaches, each of which proactively adjusts the commanded acceleration profiles of intact platoons' vehicles, in an attempt to mitigate attack impacts by lessening the velocity deviations and reducing the number of collisions, if possible. By using the proposed approaches, the automation of intact platoons is maintained and no transition of control will be initiated.

4.1 Optimal Mitigation

The mitigation of the disbanding attack is formulated as an optimization problem. Model-Predictive Control (MPC) is used to find an on-line solution using receding horizon [28]. The MPC based formulation is an optimal control technique that has been used successfully in several different applications [5]. It is based on minimizing a cost function (e.g., velocity deviation) in order to achieve a certain goal (e.g., mitigating disbanding attack impacts), while considering performance and physical constraints (e.g., collision-avoidance and speed and acceleration bounds). As such, this optimal approach will be used to compare and evaluate the performance of the heuristic approach suggested in Sect. 4.2, as this approach requires more computational power and connected infrastructure to perform the calculations required to carryout the mitigation.

Our objective is to compute a control sequence that will command each vehicle behind the disbanded platoon to reduce the deviation in velocity and avoid accidents. More specifically, the controller of an intact vehicle will use current measurements of velocity and acceleration in order to solve

$$\min_{\mathbf{U}} \quad 2\mathbf{M_1U} + \mathbf{U}^T\mathbf{M_2U} \tag{10}$$

$$\text{s.t.} \quad \mathbf{M_3U} \leq \mathbf{M_4}, \tag{11}$$

where U is the resulting control sequence and M_1, M_2, M_3, and M_4 are matrices formulated to consider acceleration and physical speed limits, and collision avoidance. The complete formulation is omitted due to space limit.

While this approach would yield an optimal solution for every time instance, it requires global knowledge of the platoon dynamics. Namely, to perform the calculations needed to produce U (control input to command intact vehicles), speed and acceleration measurements of all related vehicles should be available to a centralized controller; i.e., V2I and I2V capabilities are needed to receive current measurements, perform the required calculations, and transmit the resulting acceleration commands back to the corresponding vehicles. It has been shown that such communication structure is feasible [10], but not likely to be deployed in the near term and presents a single-point of failure. For that reason, in the next section we suggest an efficient, decentralized heuristic mitigation approach which requires a less sophisticated communication model and produces nearly equivalent results to the optimal approach.

4.2 Efficient Heuristic Mitigation

The goal of this approach is to modify the commanded acceleration of a vehicle by comparing the distance it will cover with the distance that will be covered by the preceding vehicle during a predefined time horizon (t_s). Initially, the acceleration commands of both vehicles are calculated according to the platooning control structures given in Sect. 2.1.

Algorithm 1: Heuristic mitigation

Input: $v_m(t_s(1)), u_m(t_s(1))$, for $m \in \{current, preceding\}$ // velocity and
        commanded acceleration values of current and preceding vehicles.

Output: $u_{current}^{new}$, // new commanded acceleration value for current vehicle.

$u_{current}^{new} \leftarrow u_{current}(t_s(1))$;

compute d_m for the interval of t_s using input data;

if $d_{preceding} < d_{current}$ **then**

$\quad u_{current}^{new} \leftarrow \dfrac{d_{preceding} - v_{preceding}\big(t_s(end) - t_s(1)\big)}{0.5\big(t_s^2(end) - t_s^1(1)\big)}$;

$\quad$ **if** *current vehicle and preceding one will collide during* t_s **then**

$\quad\quad$ search for $u_{current}^{new}$ within $[a_{min}, u_{preceding})$;

Let us consider a vehicle in an intact platoon $V_{current}$ and a preceding vehicle $V_{preceding}$, where subscripts *current* and *preceding* refer to two adjacent vehicles belonging either to the same platoon or to two different adjacent platoons. Each vehicle's dynamics are described by

$$\begin{aligned}
\dot{x}_m(t) &= v_m(t), \\
\dot{v}_m(t) &= u_m(t),
\end{aligned} \tag{12}$$

where $m \in \{current, preceding\}$, $t \in [t_s(1) : \Delta t_s : t_s(end)]$, $t_s(1)$ and $t_s(end)$ are the first and last time samples of the time horizon t_s, and Δt_s is the time increment. Under the assumption that u_m is constant for the duration of t_s and using the forward difference approximation [8], the absolute position and velocity can be calculated as follows

$$\begin{aligned}
x_m\big(t_s(k+1)\big) &= x_m\big(t_s(k)\big) + \Delta t_s v_m\big(t_s(k)\big), \\
v_m\big(t_s(k+1)\big) &= v_m\big(t_s(k)\big) + \Delta t_s u_m,
\end{aligned} \tag{13}$$

where $k = 1, \ldots, |t_s|$.

Once the vector $x_m(.)$ is obtained, the distance traveled by vehicle V_m during t_s can be calculated as $d_m = x_m\big(t_s(end)\big) - x_m\big(t_s(1)\big)$. Based on the calculated distance traveled by the current vehicle $d_{current}$ and that by the preceding one $d_{preceding}$, we proceed as follows

- If $d_{preceding} < d_{current}$, then $V_{current}$ is covering more distance and it may collide with a preceding vehicle and therefore it has to slow down by modifying its commanded acceleration $u_{current}$. To produce the same traveled distance for $V_{current}$, $u_{current}$ is selected equal to u_{new} which is calculated as

$$u_{new} = \frac{d_{preceding} - v_{current}\big(t_s(end) - t_s(1)\big)}{0.5\big(t_s^2(end) - t_s^2(1)\big)}, \tag{14}$$

Using the new acceleration command, another important consideration is to ensure that the predicted position vectors of $V_{current}$ and $V_{preceding}$, calculated using (13), will not overlap (collide) during the interval of t_s.

If that is the case, then the acceleration needs to be selected from the interval $[a_{\min} : \Delta a : u_{new})$ where Δa is a suitable acceleration increment. Namely, $u_{current}$ is set equal to the first value smaller than u_{new} within that interval. If the new value produces no collisions then it is applied. Otherwise, the next value is selected and so on.

– If $d_{preceding} \geq d_{current}$, then the commanded acceleration $u_{current}$, calculated according to the platooning control laws from Sect. 2.1, is maintained.

The steps of this approach are shown in Algorithm 1. Once the disbanding attack is detected for a single platoon, as explained in Sect. 2.2, the last vehicle of the disbanded platoon will inform the following lead intact vehicle, using the established inter-vehicle communication. The latter vehicle will calculate its acceleration command and modify it, if needed, using this mitigation approach. Furthermore, it will also inform the following vehicle to implement similar steps.

Practically, to implement the suggested approach requires that the following information should be available: commanded acceleration of the current vehicle (measured locally) and the preceding one (transmitted via the already established communication), and the velocity of the current vehicle (measured locally) and that of the preceding one (estimated form the measurements of velocity and relative velocity). The process described above will be repeated at the next time instant using the newly obtained measurements. $V_{current}$ will reuse the adopted platooning control law once the inter-vehicle distance, with respect to $V_{preceding}$, begins to increase.

Finally, it should be noted that our approach requires a far less sophisticated communication model to connect any two neighboring vehicles, performs a decentralized mitigation, and produces nearly equivalent results to the MPC-based mitigation. Hence, it is not only cheaper to implement the heuristic approach compared to the MPC-based one, the former is also more resilient.

4.3   Results and Discussion

Table 2 displays the average velocity error, E_v, collected under different scenarios for the optimal single platoon disbanding attack. Baseline, mit.1, and mit.2 refer to platoons using the control structure from Sect. 2.1, the heuristic mitigation, and MPC based mitigation, respectively. For all the cases given, the total number of platoons is equal to ten and the inter-vehicle separation, x_d, and actuator delay, τ, are varied, in order to examine various likely scenarios.

We can see (Table 2) that the baseline control does not perform well against the disbanding attack, since all cases involve accidents (except for $x_d = 5\,\mathrm{m}$ and $\tau = 0.1\,\mathrm{s}$) and an increase in E_v. On the other hand, it is clear that our approach improves the values of E_v for all attack cases.

In addition, collisions are avoided in most attack cases except when τ equals to 0.5 s. Also, the heuristic approach reduces the number of colliding vehicles. For example, the attack case with $x_d = 4\,\mathrm{m}$ resulted in accidents involving 58% and 29% of the total number of vehicles, which is 100, for the baseline and mit.1, respectively. Furthermore, for the attack case with $x_d = 5\,\mathrm{m}$ and $\tau = 0.1\,\mathrm{s}$, 80%

Table 2. Results for optimal one-platoon disbanding attack

x_d [m]	τ [s]	E_v [%]			Crash		
		Baseline	mit.1	mit.2	Baseline	mit.1	mit.2
5	0.1	29.570	24.283	23.025	No	No	No
	0.3	41.268	25.556	25.182	Yes	No	No
	0.5	52.235	28.482	28.709	Yes	Yes	Yes
4	0.1	27.995	25.063	22.798	Yes	No	No
	0.3	40.115	26.864	24.823	Yes	No	No
	0.5	52.706	29.079	29.742	Yes	Yes	Yes

Table 3. Results for optimal two-platoon disbanding attack

x_d [m]	τ [s]	E_v [%]			Crash		
		Baseline	mit.1	mit.2	Baseline	mit.1	mit.2
5	0.1	38.347	27.056	26.221	Yes	No	No
	0.3	39.839	28.548	29.129	Yes	No	Yes
	0.5	45.004	35.724	38.690	Yes	Yes	Yes
4	0.1	37.069	30.731	29.811	Yes	No	No
	0.3	40.233	33.183	34.868	Yes	Yes	No
	0.5	45.823	38.349	38.914	Yes	Yes	Yes

of the intact vehicles experienced stop-and-go behavior at least once because of the use of a collision-avoidance algorithm applying maximum deceleration. However, in our approach, and for all attack cases, all intact vehicles slowed down gradually and did not have to come to a complete stop.

Using mit.2 also helps with improving the values of E_v and avoiding collisions. By comparison, we can see that the values of E_v for both mit.1 and mit.2 are comparable. In fact, it is clear that our approach improves the results, in terms of lowering E_v and no collisions, in some attack cases. Overall, these numbers demonstrate that our heuristic approach produces nearly equivalent results to the optimal MPC approach.

Table 3 shows data for E_v collisions for different cases involving two platoons disbanding, where the total number of platoons is equal to ten. The optimal attack is found to occur by targeting the 10th (lead) and 9th platoons in the formation at times equal to 2 s and 100 s, respectively, within T_s. We can see that the baseline control produces collisions for all attacks cases. However, with either mit.1 or mit.2, the reduction in velocity is minimized and crashes are avoided completely in some cases. Also, the results for both mitigation approaches are nearly equivalent. Furthermore, by comparison with Table 2, and even with mitigation, the two-platoon disbanding attack results in more crashes, which indicates that it is a more severe attack compared to disbanding a single platoon.

Fig. 4. Experimental environment with small robots and motion capture system

5   Experimental Validation

Our proposed mitigation algorithm was evaluated on a testbed and compared with the baseline algorithm (i.e., a platoon control law with collision avoidance).

5.1   Hardware Setup

Our experimental setup consisted of small robots that represent vehicles in a stream of platoons and a motion capture system for tracking (Fig. 4). We implemented the attack and the mitigation algorithm on three 3-vehicle platoons, denoted as per the convention shown in Fig. 2. The 3rd (leading) platoon was disbanded and the response of other two platoons was captured.

To each robot is affixed multiple IR markers for tracking by the Optitrack motion capture system. 24 IR cameras, and the Motive software, enable us to capture robot positions. Position data is streamed to a command computer where an interface application utilizing the Robot Operating System (ROS) [26] framework makes the gathered position data for each robot available to our controller application. This application processes the position data and sends appropriate control commands to each robot. The controller application implemented on ROS works in the following manner:

- The raw position data is processed using an Extended Kalman Filter to reduce camera sensor noise and estimate the measured position and velocity.
- The *Pure Pursuit Controller* uses the estimated positions and circular path coordinates from the experimental environment to calculate the angular velocity command for each vehicle.
- The estimated data of all vehicles is used to calculate the relative distance and velocity. This is then fed to the upper-level controller (Sect. 2.1) and provides desired acceleration values for the robots.
- The mitigation and baseline algorithm then modify the acceleration values from the upper-level controller in case a disbanding attack is detected.
- As the vehicles only act upon instantaneous velocity commands, these acceleration values along with current measured velocities are used to calculate the desired velocities for each vehicle. The desired linear velocities for the vehicles are effected using a PI controller which acts as the lower-level controller (Sect. 2.1).

Each robot consists of a 32-bit ARM-based mbedNXP LPC1768 microcontroller on the Pololu m3pi platform to which Digi Xbee receivers are interfaced. An Xbee transmitter is also connected to the command computer. These Xbee modules allow us to establish a wireless communication channel over which the angular and linear velocity commands, calculated for each robot using the controller application, are broadcast. The robots receive the broadcast messages and calculate the left and right wheel speeds from the received angular and linear velocities as per the differential drive model.

5.2   Experimental Results

Figure 5 shows individual velocity profiles for the vehicles under consideration (three platoons with three robots in each). Figure 5a indicates the affect on velocities due to disbanding for the baseline control algorithm, given in Sect. 2.1, where we can see vehicles in the last platoon slow down suddenly (one of them stops) in response to the disbanding of the lead platoon. Figures 5b and c give the velocity profiles when the intact robots use the traveled distance mitigation approach, wherein it can be seen that the speed of vehicles in second and third platoon slow down gradually and then begin to accelerate. This mitigation approach was tested with $t_s = 0.5$ s and 1 s, respectively. The point labeled as A in Figs. 5a, b, and c indicate that the platoons are in a steady state. Point B marks the time when the attack on the lead platoon is emulated, causing all of its vehicles to disband and suddenly decelerate. Deceleration patterns of the vehicles after point B for the baseline controller clearly indicates a sudden drop in velocities for the following platoons, causing some vehicles to come to a complete stop as indicated by point C.

While there are no collisions with the baseline control, sudden deceleration/acceleration is observed. Such abrupt changes in velocities are not observed when our proposed heuristic mitigation is in place (Figs. 5b and c, where point C shows that none of the vehicles need to come to a halt). With the mitigation

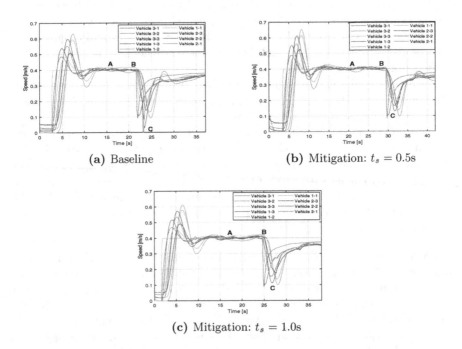

(a) Baseline

(b) Mitigation: $t_s = 0.5$s

(c) Mitigation: $t_s = 1.0$s

Fig. 5. Vehicles' velocities upon disbanding of platoon 3 for baseline control structure and proposed heuristic mitigation algorithm with $t_s = 0.5$ s and 1 s.

approach, vehicles gradually decelerate and accelerate to recover and maintain desired spacing and velocities, without collisions. Furthermore, the calculated E_v for the three experiments were 30.02%, 21.82% and 19.73% for Figs. 5a, b and c, respectively. These numbers indicate that with increasing t_s, the change in velocity is smoother and more gradual, yet collisions do not occur. However, with $t_s = 1$ s, the vehicles come to closer proximity, compared the results with $t_s = 0.5$ s. For reference, we have also uploaded short videos of our experiments [1].

6   Conclusion

We presented and studied an attack which targets vehicular platoons and can cause severe deviations in speed, including stop-and-go traffic, and collisions. The attack exploits human-in-the-loop control, whereby a vehicle switches from automated control to human driving at the onset of an attack against the sensing system of a vehicle, causing the platoon to dissolve (or disband). Calculations of key attack factors, such as identifying the platoon to disband and time to disband them, in optimal disbanding scenarios were carried out. Additionally, we proposed mitigation algorithms that reduce sudden velocity changes and also decrease the number of accidents, hence ensuring resilient performance for platoons. Simulations and experimental results corroborate theory, which indicate decreased velocity deviations and thus improved traffic flow. Finally, the proposed heuristic approach was implemented on a hardware testbed, with a motion capture system and mobile robots representing platoons, and it showed an improved performance, compared to using a baseline control algorithm.

References

1. Mitigation and baseline algorithm experiments. http://m.youtube.com/channel/UCI-UGJKT7C5E_8bs391LCpA
2. Truck platooning vision 2025 (2016). www.eutruckplatooning.com
3. Amoozadeh, M., Deng, H., Chuah, C.N., Zhang, H.M., Ghosal, D.: Platoon management with cooperative adaptive cruise control enabled by VANET. Veh. Commun. **2**(2), 110–123 (2015)
4. Axelsson, J.: Safety in vehicle platooning: a systematic literature review. IEEE Trans. Intell. Transp. Syst. **18**(5), 1033–1045 (2017)
5. Bemporad, A., Morari, M.: Robust model predictive control: a survey. In: Garulli, A., Tesi, A. (eds.) Robustness in identification and control. LNCIS, vol. 245, pp. 207–226. Springer, London (1999). https://doi.org/10.1007/BFb0109870
6. Bergenhem, C., Shladover, S., Coelingh, E., Englund, C., Tsugawa, S.: Overview of platooning systems. In: Proceedings of the 19th ITS World Congress, Austria, 22–26 October 2012
7. Blanco, M., et al.: Human factors evaluation of level 2 and level 3 automated driving concepts, August 2015
8. Borrelli, F.: Constrained Optimal Control of Linear and Hybrid Systems. LNCIS, vol. 290. Springer, Heidelberg (2003). https://doi.org/10.1007/3-540-36225-8
9. Chauhan, R., Gerdes, R.M., Heaslip, K.: Attack against an FMCW radar. In: Proceedings of Embedded Security in Cars Conference (2014)

10. Chou, C., Li, C., Chien, W., Lan, K.: A feasibility study on vehicle-to-infrastructure communication: WiFi vs. WiMAX. In: 2009 Tenth International Conference on Mobile Data Management: Systems, Services and Middleware, pp. 397–398 (2009)
11. Coelingh, E., Solyom, S.: All aboard the robotic road train. IEEE Spectr. **49**, 34–49 (2012)
12. Dadras, S., Gerdes, R.M., Sharma, R.: Vehicular platooning in an adversarial environment. In: Proceedings of the 10th ACM Symposium on Information, Computer and Communications Security, ASIA CCS 2015, pp. 167–178. ACM, New York (2015)
13. DeBruhl, B., Weerakkody, S., Sinopoli, B., Tague, P.: Is your commute driving you crazy?: A study of misbehavior in vehicular platoons. In: WISEC (2015)
14. Dunn, D.D., Mitchell, S.A., Sajjad, I., Gerdes, R.M., Sharma, R., Li, M.: Regular: attacker-induced traffic flow instability in a stream of semi-automated vehicles. In: 2017 47th Annual IEEE/IFIP International Conference on Dependable Systems and Networks (DSN), pp. 499–510 (2017)
15. Eriksson, A., Stanton, N.A.: Takeover time in highly automated vehicles: noncritical transitions to and from manual control. Hum. Factors **59**(4), 689–705 (2017)
16. Gerdes, R.M., Winstead, C., Heaslip, K.: CPS: an efficiency-motivated attack against autonomous vehicular transportation. In: Proceedings of the 29th Annual Computer Security Applications Conference, pp. 99–108. ACM (2013)
17. Gold, C., Damböck, D., Lorenz, L., Bengler, K.: "Take over!" How long does it take to get the driver back into the loop? Proc. Hum. Factors Ergon. Soc. Annu. Meet. **57**(1), 1938–1942 (2013)
18. Ploeg, J., Scheepers, B., Van Nunen, E., Van de Wouw, N., Nijmeijer, H.: Design and experimental evaluation of cooperative adaptive cruise control. In: International IEEE Conference on Intelligent Transportation Systems, pp. 260–265 (2011)
19. Jagielski, M., Jones, N., Lin, C.W., Nita-Rotaru, C., Shiraishi, S.: Threat detection for collaborative adaptive cruise control in connected cars. In: Proceedings of the 11th ACM Conference on Security & Privacy in Wireless and Mobile Networks, WiSec 2018, pp. 184–189. ACM, New York (2018)
20. Kesting, A., Treiber, M., Helbing, D.: Enhanced intelligent driver model to access the impact of driving strategies on traffic capacity. Philos. Trans. R. Soc. Lond. A Math. Phys. Eng. Sci. **368**(1928), 4585–4605 (2010)
21. Liang, K.Y., Mårtensson, J., Johansson, K.H.: Fuel-saving potentials of platooning evaluated through sparse heavy-duty vehicle position data. In: 2014 IEEE Intelligent Vehicles Symposium Proceedings, pp. 1061–1068 (2014)
22. Merat, N., Jamson, A.: How do drivers behave in a highly automated car?, pp. 514–521, October 2017. https://doi.org/10.17077/drivingassessment.1365
23. Merat, N., Jamson, A.H., Lai, F.C., Daly, M., Carsten, O.M.: Transition to manual: driver behaviour when resuming control from a highly automated vehicle. Transp. Res. Part F Traffic Psychol. Behav. **27**, 274–282 (2014)
24. Oncu, S., Ploeg, J., van de Wouw, N., Nijmeijer, H.: Cooperative adaptive cruise control: network-aware analysis of string stability. IEEE Trans. Intell. Transp. Syst. **15**(4), 1527–1537 (2014)
25. Petit, J., Stottelaar, B., Feiri, M., Kargl, F.: Remote attacks on automated vehicles sensors: experiments on camera and LiDar. Black Hat Europe **11** (2015)
26. Quigley, M., et al.: ROS: an open-source robot operating system. In: ICRA Workshop on Open Source Software, Kobe, Japan, vol. 3, p. 5 (2009)
27. Rajamani, R.: Vehicle Dynamics and Control. Mechanical Engineering Series. Springer, New York (2012). https://doi.org/10.1007/978-1-4614-1433-9

28. Rawlings, J.B.: Tutorial overview of model predictive control. IEEE Control Syst. Mag. **20**(3), 38–52 (2000)
29. Ren, W., Green, D.: Continuous platooning: a new evolutionary operating concept for automated highway systems. In: Proceedings of American Control Conference (ACC), vol. 1, pp. 21–25 (1994)
30. Robinson, T., Chan, E., Coelingh, E.: Operating platoons on public motorways: an introduction to the SARTRE Platooning Programme. In: 17th World Congress on Intelligent Transport Systems, vol. 1, p. 12 (2010)
31. van der Heijden, R., Lukaseder, T., Kargl, F.: Analyzing attacks on cooperative adaptive cruise control (CACC). In: 2017 IEEE Vehicular Networking Conference (VNC), pp. 45–52 (2017)
32. Vlakveld, W., Verkeersveiligheid, S.W.O., Rijkswaterstaat Water, Verkeer en Leefomgeving: Transition of control in highly automated vehicles: a literature review. SWOV Institute for Road Safety Research (2015)
33. Yan, C., Xu, W., Liu, J.: Can you trust autonomous vehicles: contactless attacks against sensors of self-driving vehicle. DEF CON **24** (2016)
34. Yanakiev, D., Kanellakopoulos, I.: A simplified framework for string stability analysis in AHS. In: Proceedings of the 13th IFAC World Congress, pp. 177–182 (1996)
35. Yeh, E., Choi, J., Prelcic, N., Bhat, C., Heath Jr., R.: Security in automotive radar and vehicular networks. Microw. J. **60**, 148–164 (2017)
36. Zheng, R., Nakano, K., Yamabe, S., Aki, M., Nakamura, H., Suda, Y.: Study on emergency-avoidance braking for the automatic platooning of trucks. IEEE Trans. Intell. Transp. Syst. **15**(4), 1748–1757 (2014)

Generic Construction of ElGamal-Type Attribute-Based Encryption Schemes with Revocability and Dual-Policy

Shengmin Xu[1], Yinghui Zhang[1,2]([✉]), Yingjiu Li[2], Ximeng Liu[3,4],
and Guomin Yang[5]

[1] National Engineering Laboratory for Wireless Security,
Xi'an University of Posts and Telecommunications, Xi'an 710121, China
yhzhaang@163.com
[2] School of Information Systems, Singapore Management University,
Singapore, Singapore
[3] College of Mathematics and Computer Science, Fuzhou University, Fuzhou, China
[4] Key Lab of Information Security of Network Systems, Fuzhou University,
Fuzhou, Fujian, China
[5] School of Computing and Information Technology, University of Wollongong,
Wollongong, Australia

Abstract. Cloud is a computing paradigm for allowing data owners to outsource their data to enjoy on-demand services and mitigate the burden of local data storage. However, secure sharing of data via cloud remains an essential issue since the cloud service provider is untrusted. Fortunately, asymmetric-key encryption, such as identity-based encryption (IBE) and attribute-based encryption (ABE), provides a promising tool to offer data confidentiality and has been widely applied in cloud-based applications. In this paper, we summarize the common properties of most of IBE and ABE and introduce a cryptographic primitive called ElGamal type cryptosystem. This primitive can be used to derive a variety of ABE schemes. To illustrate the feasibility, we present generic constructions of revocable attribute-based encryption and dual-policy attribute-based encryption with formal definitions and security proofs. By applying our proposed generic constructions, we also present instantiations of these schemes. Furthermore, we demonstrate the high performance of the proposed schemes via experiments.

Keywords: ElGamal-type cryptosystem · Attribute-based encryption

1 Introduction

Public-key encryption is the fundamental primitive of public-key cryptography, which removes the key-agreement process in traditional symmetric-key encryption to facilitate data sharing via the certificate list. However, conventional public-key infrastructure is vulnerable to certificate management. To address this issue, identity-based encryption (IBE) [10] was proposed to provide a new

© ICST Institute for Computer Sciences, Social Informatics and Telecommunications Engineering 2019
Published by Springer Nature Switzerland AG 2019. All Rights Reserved
S. Chen et al. (Eds.): SecureComm 2019, LNICST 305, pp. 184–204, 2019.
https://doi.org/10.1007/978-3-030-37231-6_10

paradigm by utilizing the user identity rather than searching the certificate of the receiver. Unfortunately, IBE only provides coarse-level data sharing. To overcome this drawback, attribute-based encryption (ABE) [26] was introduced. There are mainly two types of standard ABE systems: key-policy ABE (KP-ABE) and ciphertext-based ABE (CP-ABE) and they are useful in different applications. KP-ABE provides the content-based access control by specifying the receiver's policy over ciphertext's attributes for managing the accessing of sensitive information. CP-ABE offers the role-based access control by specifying the ciphertext's policy over the receiver's policy for controlling the data receiver.

IBE. Boneh and Franklin [10] proposed the first practical IBE by transforming ElGamal encryption [12] in finite fields to bilinear groups. To improve the performance, Boneh and Boyen [8,9] proposed the selectively secure IBE without random oracles and Waters [28] introduced an adaptively secure IBE in the standard model. Gentry [13] proposed an adaptive security IBE with the constant-size parameter based on the interactive assumption. Abdalla et al. [1] then proposed IBE with wildcard operation. Lewko and Waters [18] design the first adaptive security IBE with the standard assumption by applying dual system encryption [29], which also used to design the adaptive security ABE [17].

KP-ABE. In KP-ABE, the key generation center (KGC) generates the users' secret keys based on corresponding access trees, and ciphertexts are encrypted over a set of attributes. The encryptor has no control over who has access to the data except by choosing descriptive attributes for the data. The initial work was introduced by Sahai and Waters [26]. To enrich the expression, Goyal et al. [14] provided KP-ABE with monotonic span programs and Ostrovsky et al. [22] proposed KP-ABE supporting non-monotonic access structures. Attrapadung et al. [3] then proposed KP-ABE with constant-size ciphertexts.

CP-ABE. In CP-ABE, access trees are used to encrypt data and users' secret keys associate a set of attributes. The encryptor has to manage the access tree to specify the users' access right. The seminal work was introduced by Bethencourt et al. [6] with two-level random masking methodology. Waters [30] introduced the first selectively secure CP-ABE under the non-standard assumption, and Rouselakis and Waters [24] provided CP-ABE with the large universe.

Generic ABE Constructions. Generic constructions of ABE have been well studied before. Sahai et al. [25] proposed the generic ABE with piecewise key generation to derive RABE. Chow [11] provided generic ABE with the properties of key partition and ciphertext partition to build RABE with the multi-authority setting. Not surprisingly, self-updatable ABE [16] also applied a similar strategy. The core technique of them are based on the secret-splitting trick, and we also apply this concept to build generic schemes.

Many cloud-based data sharing applications are built based on IBE and ABE since they facilitate data sharing securely. However, consider usability and functionality, directly applying these scheme in cloud-based applications is insufficient. To address this problem, many cryptosystems with practical properties have been proposed, such as public-key cryptosystems with revocation (e.g., revocable IBE and ABE, RIBE/RABE for short) and dual-policy ABE (DP-ABE) with content-based and role-based access control simultaneously.

RIBE/RABE. RIBE/RABE (as shown in Fig. 1) is an extension of IBE/ABE by providing an efficient revocation mechanism. The issues of revocation have been pointed out in the corresponding seminal works [10,23] and they suggested extending each attribute with an expiration date, e.g., private keys periodically update by representing an attribute as $att\|t$, where att is the real attribute and t is the current date. However, such an approach incurs the heavy workload and unscalable because a secure channel between KGC and each user needs to be established each time. Boldyreva et al. [7] solved this issue by introducing indirect revocation, which divides the (short-term) decryption key into the long-term secret key and the public key-updating material. With this method, KGC only publishes public key-updating material in each revocation epoch. By applying tree-based structure [21], the size of the key-updating material is logarithmic in the number of system users. However, this work suffers decryption key exposure attacks. The frequently used decryption key could be compromised due to a variety of reasons, such as side-channel and key-leakage attacks. The long-term secret key will be compromised if the short-term decryption key is leaked. Seo and Emura [27] provided a strong model with perfect forward secrecy in the identity-based setting and proposed a secure RIBE under this model.

DP-ABE. To make the most advantages of both KP-ABE and CP-ABE, DP-ABE (as shown in Fig. 2) [2,4] was introduced. It is a conjunctively combined between two types of ABE. Ciphertexts are specified access trees and a set of attributes simultaneously, and the secret keys are also required to specified a set of attributes and access trees. We further category DP-ABE into two types: sequential DP-ABE and parallel DP-ABE. In sequential DP-ABE, receivers will be able to decrypt if who pass both restrictions. Interestingly, the sequential DP-ABE is similar to RABE with indirect revocation. In RABE, two restrictions are long-term secret key and public key-updating material, where long-term secret keys are related to the key-policy or the ciphertext-policy depending on the access policy of RABE, and the public key-updating as the restriction based on the revocation mechanism. In parallel DP-ABE (sometimes called one-policy DP-ABE), receivers only need to satisfy one of two limitations to review messages. It is worth to notice that Attrapadung and Yamada [4] provided the generic construction based on ABE and pairing encodings, our generic constructions are based on the different building block ElGamal type cryptosystem, which also can be used to build RABE schemes.

1.1   Contribution

In this paper, we revisit ElGamal-like schemes [12] in both identity-based [1,5,8–10,18,28] and attribute-based [3,6,14,17,20,22,24,26,30] settings and introduce a new primitive called ElGamal type cryptosystem with formal definition and security model by summarizing their common properties. By applying this primitive, we can easily derive a variety of cryptosystems. To illustrate the feasibility

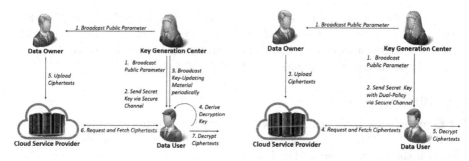

Fig. 1. System model of RABE/RIBE   **Fig. 2.** System model of DP-ABE

of our proposed ElGamal type cryptosystem, we present the generic construction of RABE with decryption exposure resistance and DP-ABE with parallel and sequential settings.

We first investigate RIBE/RABE and present the generic construction of RABE with decryption key exposure resistance. We should note that our ElGamal type cryptosystem allows the key re-randomization without the master secret key. This re-randomizable property is to remove the relationships among the long-term secret key, the public key-updating material, and the short-term decryption key. Hence, the long-term secret key is secure even both the key-updating material and the decryption key are compromised.

We then investigate DP-ABE schemes and present the concrete schemes of DP-ABE with parallel and sequential settings in the prime-order group. These schemes are the provable security under the proposed models. We then give detailed comparisons and experiment results to demonstrate the usability and high performance of our proposed schemes.

1.2   Outline

In Sect. 2, we introduce some preliminaries including the proposed ElGamal type cryptosystem and its semi-generic construction. In Sect. 3, we present definitions of DP-ABE and RABE. In Sect. 4, we give generic constructions of RABE and DP-ABE and the corresponding formal proofs. The instantiations of these schemes are presented in Sect. 5. In Sect. 6, we provide the analysis of functionality and efficiency. We summarize this paper in Sect. 6.

2   Preliminaries

2.1   Notations

Let $\mathbb{N}$ denote the set of all natural numbers, and for $n \in \mathbb{N}$, we define $[n] := 1, ..., n$. Let $\vec{u} := (u_1, u_2, ..., u_\ell)$ denote a vector of dimension ℓ in $\mathbb{Z}_p$. To simplicity, $X \in \mathcal{X}$ denotes the attributes of key and $Y \in \mathcal{Y}$ represents the attributes of ciphertexts. Depending on the policy in the underlying ABE scheme, X and

Y denote either an attribute set $\mathcal{S}$ or an access policy $\mathbb{A}$, and $\mathcal{X}$ and $\mathcal{Y}$ represent either the attribute universe Ω or the policies $\mathcal{P}$. Let $R : (\mathbb{X}, \mathbb{Y}) \rightarrow \{0, 1\}$ denote the result of sufficient condition by inputting key attributes $X \in \mathbb{X}$ and ciphertext attributes $Y \in \mathbb{Y}$, and outputting a bit 0 or 1.

2.2 Bilinear Map

Let $\mathbb{G}$ and $\mathbb{G}_T$ be two cyclic multiplicative groups of prime order p and g be a generator of $\mathbb{G}$. The map $e : \mathbb{G} \times \mathbb{G} \rightarrow \mathbb{G}_T$ is said to be an admissible bilinear pairing if the following properties hold true.

- *Bilinearity*: for all $u, v \in \mathbb{G}$ and $a, b \in \mathbb{Z}_p$, $e(u^a, v^b) = e(u, v)^{ab}$.
- *Non-degeneration*: $e(g, g) \neq 1$.
- *Computability*: it is efficient to compute $e(u, v)$ for any $u, v \in \mathbb{G}$.

2.3 Access Structure and Monotone Span Program

Definition 1 (Access Structure [14]). *Let $\{P_1, ..., P_n\}$ be a set of parties. A collection $\mathbb{A} \subseteq 2^{\{P_1, ..., P_n\}}$ is monotone if $\forall B, C : $ if $B \in \mathbb{A}$ and $B \subseteq C$, then $C \subseteq \mathbb{A}$. A monotone access structure is a monotone collection $\mathbb{A}$ of non-empty subsets of $\{P_1, ..., P_n\}$, i.e., $\mathbb{A} \subseteq 2^{\{P_1, ..., P_n\}} \setminus \{\emptyset\}$. The sets in $\mathbb{A}$ are called authorized sets, and the sets not in $\mathbb{A}$ are called unauthorized sets.*

Definition 2 (Monotone Span Program (MSP) [14]). *Let $\mathcal{K}$ be a field and $\{x_1, ..., x_n\}$ be a set of variables. A MSP over $\mathcal{K}$ is labeled matrix $\tilde{M}(\mathbb{M}, \rho)$ where $\mathbb{M}$ is a matrix over $\mathcal{K}$, and ρ is a labeling of the rows of $\mathbb{M}$ by literals from $\{x_1, ..., x_n\}$ (every row is labeled by one literal). A MSP accepts or rejects an input by the following criterion. For every input set $\mathcal{S}$ if literals, define the submatrix $\mathbb{M}_{\mathcal{S}}$ of $\mathbb{M}$ consisting of those rows whose labels are in S, i.e., rows labeled by some i such that $i \in S$. The MSP $\tilde{M}$ accepts $\mathcal{S}$ if and only if $\vec{1} \in$ span$(\mathbb{M}_{\mathcal{S}})$, i.e., some linear combination of the rows of $\mathbb{M}_{\mathcal{S}}$ given the all-one vector $\vec{1}$. The MSP $\tilde{M}$ computes a boolean function f_M if it accepts exactly those input $\mathcal{S}$ where $f_{\mathbb{M}}(\mathcal{S}) = 1$. The size of $\tilde{M}$ is the number of rows in $\mathbb{M}$.*

2.4 Definition of ElGamal Type Cryptosystem

Definition 3 (ElGamal Type Cryptosystem). *ElGamal type cryptosystem $\mathcal{ETC}$ with the key attribute universe $\mathcal{X}$ that supports the ciphertext attribute universe $\mathcal{Y}$ and the message space $\mathcal{M}$ consists of the following five algorithms:*

- *$\mathcal{ETC}.\mathsf{Init}(\lambda) \rightarrow pp$: The probabilistic initialization algorithm takes the security parameter $\lambda \in \mathbb{N}$ as input, and outputs the public parameter pp, such as the description of the bilinear group from the bilinear group generator $(g, p, \mathbb{G}, \mathbb{G}_T) \leftarrow \mathcal{G}(\lambda)$.*
- *$\mathcal{ETC}.\mathsf{Setup}(pp) \rightarrow (pk, msk)$: The probabilistic setup algorithm takes the parameter pp as input, and outputs the public key pk and the master secret key msk. It is required that the master secret key and the public key are in the form of*

$$msk = (\alpha, ...), \quad pk = (e(g, g)^{\alpha}, ...),$$

where $\alpha \in \mathbb{Z}_p$.

- $\mathcal{ETC}.\mathsf{KeyGen}(msk, X) \rightarrow sk_X$: *The probabilistic key generation algorithm takes the master secret key msk and the attributes of the secret key $X \in \mathcal{X}$ as input, and outputs the secret key sk_X. It is required that the secret key is in the form of $sk_X = (sk_1, sk_2, sk_3)$ as:*

$$sk_1 = g^{h(\alpha)} \cdot f(pk, X)^r, \quad sk_2 = g^r,$$

  where $r \in \mathbb{Z}_p$, $h(x) \in \mathbb{Z}_p$ and $f(x, y) \in \mathbb{G}$. Note that sk_3 is for recording some extra information related attributes of the secret key.
- $\mathcal{ETC}.\mathsf{Enc}(pk, Y, m) \rightarrow c_Y$: *The probabilistic encryption algorithm takes the public key pk, the attributes of the ciphertext $Y \in \mathcal{Y}$ and the message $m \in \mathcal{M}$ as input, and outputs the ciphertext c_Y. It is required that the ciphertext is in the form of $c_Y = (c_0, c_1, c_2)$ as:*

$$c_0 = m \cdot e(g, g)^{\alpha s}, \quad c_1 = g^s,$$

  where $s \in \mathbb{Z}_p$ and c_2 is some extra information related to attributes of the ciphertext.
- $\mathcal{ETC}.\mathsf{Dec}(pk, sk_X, c_Y) \rightarrow m$: *The deterministic decryption algorithm takes the public key pk, the secret key sk_X and the ciphertext c_Y as input, and outputs the message $m \in \mathcal{M}$. The decryption process is required to be two steps. The first step is to run the sub-decryption algorithm $\mathcal{D}$ to get the message hiding component $e(g, g)^{\alpha s} \leftarrow \mathcal{D}(sk_X, c_1, c_2)$. The second step is to extract the plaintext by eliminating the message hiding component as $m = c_0 / e(g, g)^{\alpha s}$.*

The consistency condition requires for all $\lambda \in \mathbb{N}$, all pp output by the initialization algorithm, pk and msk output by setup algorithm, $m \in \mathcal{M}$ and $R(X, Y) = 1$, we then have

$$\mathcal{ETC}.\mathsf{Dec}(pk, sk_X, \mathcal{ETC}.\mathsf{Enc}(pk, Y, m)) = m.$$

Next, we describe the security model called selectively indistinguishable against chosen plaintext attack (sIND-CPA) for ElGamal type cryptosystem.

Definition 4 (sIND-CPA in ElGamal type cryptosystem). *An ElGamal type cryptosystem consists of five algorithms above. For an adversary $\mathcal{A}$, we define the following experiment:*

$$\mathbf{Exp}_{\mathcal{A}, \mathcal{ETC}}^{\mathsf{sIND\text{-}CPA}}(\lambda)$$

$$Y^* \leftarrow \mathcal{A}(\lambda);$$
$$pp \leftarrow \mathcal{ETC}.\mathsf{Init}(\lambda);$$
$$(pk, msk) \leftarrow \mathcal{ETC}.\mathsf{Setup}(pp);$$
$$(m_0, m_1) \leftarrow \mathcal{A}^{\mathcal{O}_{\mathsf{KeyGen}}}(pp, pk);$$
$$b \leftarrow \{0, 1\};$$
$$c^* \leftarrow \mathsf{Enc}(pk, Y^*, m_b);$$
$$b' \leftarrow \mathcal{A}^{\mathcal{O}_{\mathsf{KeyGen}}(\cdot)}(c^*);$$
$$\text{If } b = b' \text{ return 1 else return 0.}$$

$\mathcal{O}_{\text{KeyGen}}(\cdot)$ *represents the key generation oracle which allows* $\mathcal{A}$ *to query on attributes of keys* $X \in \mathcal{X}$ *except* $R(X, Y^*) = 1$ *to return the secret key* sk_X *by running* $\mathcal{ETC}.\text{KeyGen}(msk, X)$.

An ElGamal type cryptosystem is said to be sIND-CPA *secure if for any probabilistic polynomial time adversary* $\mathcal{A}$, *the following advantage is negligible:*

$$\mathbf{Adv}_{\mathcal{A},\mathcal{ETC}}^{\text{sIND-CPA}}(\lambda) = \left| \Pr[\mathbf{Exp}_{\mathcal{A},\mathcal{ETC}}^{\text{sIND-CPA}}(\lambda) = 1] - 1/2 \right|$$

2.5   Candidates of ElGamal Type Cryptosystem

The IBE [1,5,8–10,18,28] and ABE [3,6,14,20,22,24,26,30] schemes are the instantiations of ElGamal type cryptosystems. We demonstrate three candidates of them to illustrate the feasibility of our proposed ElGamal type cryptosystem.

IBE. Let r, s denote random numbers over $\mathbb{Z}_p$, $\mathcal{I}$ be the identity space and $\ell = \log_2 \mathcal{I}$ be the length of message space. Waters' IBE [28] is given below.

$$pk = \left(e(g,g)^\alpha, u_0, u_1, ..., u_\ell \right), \quad msk := (\underline{\alpha}),$$

$$sk_{id} = \left(g^\alpha \left(u_0 \textstyle\prod_{i\in\mathcal{V}} u_i \right)^r, \underline{g^r} \right),$$

$$c_{id} = \left(m \cdot e(g,g)^{\alpha s}, \underline{g^s}, \left(u_0 \textstyle\prod_{i\in\mathcal{V}} u_i \right)^s \right),$$

where $\mathcal{V} \in [\ell]$ be the set of all i for which $id[i] = 1$.

KP-ABE. Let $\Delta_{i,\mathsf{J}} = \prod_{j\in\mathsf{J},j\neq i} \left(\frac{x-j}{i-j} \right)$ denote the Lagrange coefficient for $x, i \in \mathbb{Z}_p$ and $\mathsf{J} \subset \mathbb{Z}$, n denote the maximum size of attributes used in encryption, $\mathbb{M}$ is a matrix over $\mathbb{Z}_p$ with d rows and l columns, ρ is a mapping function that maps any number in the domain $[d]$ to the attribute universe Ω, $\mathcal{S} = (A_1, A_2, ..., A_k)$ is the attribute set and $(\{r_i\}_{i\in[d]}, s)$ represent random numbers in $\mathbb{Z}_p$. Goyal et al's KP-ABE [14] is described as follows.

$$pk = \left(e(g,g)^\alpha, \{t_i\}_{i\in[n+1]} \right), \quad msk = (\underline{\alpha}),$$

$$sk_{\mathbb{A}} = \left(\{ g^{\mathbb{M}_i \vec{u}_i} T(i)^{r_i}, g^{r_i} \}_{i\in[d]} \right),$$

$$c_{\mathcal{S}} = \left(m \cdot e(g,g)^{\alpha s}, \underline{g^s}, \{ T(i)^s \}_{\rho(i)\in\mathcal{S}} \right),$$

where the vector $\vec{u}$ is a random l dimensional vector over $\mathbb{Z}_p$ s.t. $\vec{1} \cdot \vec{u} = \alpha$ and $T(x) = g^{x^n} \prod_{i=1}^{n+1} t_i^{\Delta_{i,[n+1]}(x)}$ be a function to map any index $x \in \mathbb{Z}_p$ to the element in $\mathbb{G}$.

CP-ABE. Let $\{\phi_i\}_{i\in[n]} \in \mathbb{Z}_p$ denote a set of random numbers, Rouselakis and Waters' CP-ABE [24] is given below.

$$pk = \left(e(g,g)^\alpha, u, h, w, v \right), \quad msk = (\underline{\alpha}),$$

$$sk_{\mathcal{S}} = \left(g^\alpha w^r, g^r, \{ g^{r_i}, (u^{A_i}h)^{r_i} v^{-r} \}_{\rho(i)\in\mathcal{S}} \right),$$

$$c_{\mathbb{A}} = \left(m \cdot e(g,g)^{\alpha s}, \underline{g^s}, \{ w^{\mathbb{M}_i \vec{u}_i} v^{\phi_i}, (u^{\rho(i)}h)^{\phi_i}, g^{\phi_i} \}_{i\in[d]} \right),$$

where $\vec{u}$ is a l dimensional vector in the domain $\mathbb{Z}_p$ s.t. $\vec{u} = (s, u_2, ..., u_l) \in \mathbb{Z}_p^l$ and $r, \{r_i\}_{\rho(i) \in \mathcal{S}}, \{\phi_i\}_{i \in [d]}$ are random numbers over $\mathbb{Z}_p$. Note that referring to Definition 3, we set $h(\alpha) = \alpha$ and $f(pk, X)^r = w^r$ for above CP-ABE setting.

2.6   Tree-Based Revocation Mechanism

Naor et al. [21] introduced a tree-based revocation architecture to reduce the cost of generating and transmitting key updates from linear to logarithmic. Let st be the state representing the tree-based data structure, rl denote the revocation list recording identities of revoked users and the timestamp of revocation and t be the timestamp representing the current revocation epoch. By running subset-cover algorithm $\mathsf{KUNode}(st, rl, t)$, the KGC can derive get the key updates for all non-revoked users with the logarithmic size. When a user wants to join the system, who will be assigned a random identifier $id \in \mathcal{I}$ and an undefined leaf node in st will be labeled this identifier id. The revocation method only requires the user id to store the keys in $\mathsf{Path}(id)$, where $\mathsf{Path}(id)$ denotes nodes from the root to the leaf node id. The details of algorithm $\mathsf{KUNode}(st, rl, t)$ are given in Algorithm 1.

Algorithm 1: Node Selection Algorithm

Input: BT, rl, t

Output: Y

1 $\mathsf{X}, \mathsf{Y} \leftarrow \emptyset$;

2 **for** $(v_i, t_i) \in rl$ **do**

  if $t_i \leq t$ **then**

    $\mathsf{X} \leftarrow \mathsf{X} \cup \mathsf{Path}(v_i)$

3 **for** $x \in \mathsf{X}$ **do**

  if $x_l \notin \mathsf{X}$ **then**

    $\mathsf{Y} \leftarrow \mathsf{Y} \cup x_l$

  if $x_r \notin \mathsf{X}$ **then**

    $\mathsf{Y} \leftarrow \mathsf{Y} \cup x_r$

4 **if** $\mathsf{Y} = \emptyset$ **then**

  $\mathsf{Y} \leftarrow$ root

5 **return** Y.

---

3   Definition of Revocable ABE and Dual-Policy ABE

In this section, we introduce definitions of RABE and DP-ABE. Specifically, we first introduce the syntax and security model of RABE. Next, we introduce syntaxes of DP-ABE for both parallel and sequential settings and their corresponding security models. We should note that ElGamal type cryptosystem supports IBE which could be used to manage the timestamp in RABE to efficient revocation rather than ABE to manage the timestamp [25] causing high computation and communication costs. Note that our proposed scheme is easy to apply outsourced ABE [15] since the elegant construction of ElGamal-like encryption to reduce the cost of ciphertext decryption.

3.1 Revocable ABE

Definition 5 (RABE). *An RABE $\mathcal{RABE}$ with key attributes $X, \bar{X}_t \in \mathcal{X} \times \bar{\mathcal{X}}_t$ that support ciphertext $Y, \bar{Y}_t \in \mathcal{Y} \times \bar{\mathcal{Y}}_t$[1], the bounded system lifetime $\mathcal{T}$, an identifier space $\mathcal{I}$, the number of system users $\mathcal{N}$ and the message space $\mathcal{M}$ consists of nine algorithms given below.*

- $\mathcal{RABE}$.Setup$(\lambda) \to (pk, msk, rl, st)$*: The probabilistic setup algorithm takes parameter $\lambda \in \mathbb{N}$ as input, and outputs a public key pk, a master secret key msk, a revocation list rl and a state st.*
- $\mathcal{RABE}$.KeyGen$(msk, st, X, id) \to (sk_{id}, st)$*: The probabilistic key generation algorithm takes the master secret key msk, the state st, the key attributes $X \in \mathcal{X}$ and an identifier $id \in \mathcal{I}$ as input, and outputs the secret key sk_{id} and the state st.*
- $\mathcal{RABE}$.KeyUpdate$(msk, st, \bar{X}_t, rl) \to ku_t$*: The probabilistic key update algorithm takes the master secret key msk, the state st, the key attributes $\bar{X}_t \in \bar{\mathcal{X}}$ associated the timestamp t, the time t and the revocation list rl as input, and outputs the key-updating material ku_t.*
- $\mathcal{RABE}$.DKGen$(pk, sk_{id}, ku_t) \to dk_{id,t}$*: The probabilistic decryption key generation algorithm takes the public key pk, the secret key sk_{id} and key-updating material ku_t as input, and outputs the decryption key $dk_{id,t}$.*
- $\mathcal{RABE}$.Enc$(pk, Y, \bar{Y}_t, m) \to c_{Y,\bar{Y}_t}$*: The probabilistic encryption algorithm takes the public key pk, the ciphertext attribute $Y \in \mathcal{Y}$, the ciphertext attribute $\bar{Y}_t \in \bar{\mathcal{Y}}$ associated with the timestamp $t \in \mathcal{T}$ and a message $m \in \mathcal{M}$ as input, and outputs a ciphertext c.*
- $\mathcal{RABE}$.Dec$(pk, dk_{id,t}, c_{Y,\bar{Y}}) \to m$*: The deterministic decryption algorithm takes the public key pk, the decryption key $dk_{id,t}$ and a ciphertext $c_{Y,\bar{Y}}$ as input, and outputs a message $m \in \mathcal{M}$.*
- $\mathcal{RABE}$.Rev$(rl, id, t) \to rl$*: The deterministic revocation algorithm takes the revocation list rl, an identifier $id \in \mathcal{I}$ and the timestamp $t \in \mathcal{T}$ as input, and outputs the revocation list rl.*

---

[1] $\bar{X}_t$ and $\bar{Y}_t$ is based on the timestamp t (e.g., the bit representation of the timestamp or the policies derived from its bit representation) which is used to manage user revocation.

3.2   Security Model of RABE

Definition 6 (sIND-CPA in RABE). *An RABE consist of seven algorithms in above. For an adversary* $\mathcal{A}$, *we define the following experiment:*

$$\mathbf{Exp}^{\mathsf{sIND\text{-}CPA}}_{\mathcal{A},\mathcal{R}\mathcal{ABE}}(\lambda)$$

$$(Y^*, \bar{Y}_{t^*}) \leftarrow \mathcal{A}(\lambda);$$

$$(pk, msk, rl, st) \leftarrow \mathcal{R}\mathcal{ABE}.\mathsf{Setup}(pp);$$

$$(m_0, m_1) \leftarrow \mathcal{A}^{\mathcal{O}}(pp, pk);$$

$$b \leftarrow \{0, 1\};$$

$$c^* \leftarrow \mathsf{Enc}(pk, Y^*, \bar{Y}_{t^*}, m_b);$$

$$b' \leftarrow \mathcal{A}^{\mathcal{O}}(c^*);$$

$$\textit{If } b = b' \textit{ return } 1 \textit{ else return } 0.$$

$\mathcal{O}$ *is a set of oracles,* $\{\mathcal{O}_{\mathsf{KeyGen}}(\cdot,\cdot), \mathcal{O}_{\mathsf{KeyUpdate}}(\cdot,\cdot), \mathcal{O}_{\mathsf{Rev}}(\cdot,\cdot), \mathcal{O}_{\mathsf{DKGen}}(\cdot,\cdot)\}$ *and the details are given below:*

- $\mathcal{O}_{\mathsf{KeyGen}}(\cdot,\cdot)$ *is the key generation oracle that allows* $\mathcal{A}$ *to query key attribute* $X \in \mathcal{X}$ *and an identifier* $id \in \mathcal{I}$, *and it runs* $\mathcal{R}\mathcal{ABE}.\mathsf{KeyGen}(msk, st, X, id)$ *to return the secret key* sk_{id}.
- $\mathcal{O}_{\mathsf{KeyUpdate}}(\cdot,\cdot)$ *is the key update oracle that allows* $\mathcal{A}$ *to query key attributes* $\bar{X}_t$ *associated with the time* $t \in \mathcal{T}$, *and it runs* $\mathcal{R}\mathcal{ABE}.\mathsf{KeyUpdate}(msk, st, \bar{X}_t, rl)$ *to return the key update* ku_t.
- $\mathcal{O}_{\mathsf{Rev}}(\cdot,\cdot)$ *is the revocation oracle that allows* $\mathcal{A}$ *to query an identifier* $id \in \mathcal{I}$ *and the time* $t \in \mathcal{T}$, *and it runs* $\mathcal{R}\mathcal{ABE}.\mathsf{Rev}(rl, id, t)$ *to update the revocation list* rl.
- $\mathcal{O}_{\mathsf{DKGen}}(\cdot,\cdot,\cdot)$ *is the decryption key generation oracle that allows* $\mathcal{A}$ *to query key attributes* $(X, \bar{X}) \in \mathcal{X} \times \bar{\mathcal{X}}$, *the timestamp* $t \in \mathcal{T}$ *and an identifier* $id \in \mathcal{I}$, *and it runs* $\mathcal{R}\mathcal{ABE}.\mathsf{DKGen}(pk, sk_{id}, ku_t)$ *to return the decryption key* $dk_{id,t}$ *if the secret key* sk_{id} *and the key update* ku_t *are available. Otherwise, it first runs the key generation oracle and key update oracle to obtain the secret key* sk_{id} *and the key update* ku_t.

$\mathcal{A}$ *is allowed to issue above oracles with the following restrictions:*

1. $\mathcal{O}_{\mathsf{KeyUpdate}}(\cdot,\cdot)$ *and* $\mathcal{O}_{\mathsf{Rev}}(\cdot,\cdot)$ *can be queried at the time* t *which is greater than or equal to that of all previous queries.*
2. $\mathcal{O}_{\mathsf{Rev}}(\cdot,\cdot)$ *cannot be queried at the time* t *if* $\mathcal{O}_{\mathsf{KeyUpdate}}(\cdot)$ *was queried at the time* t.
3. *If* $\mathcal{O}_{\mathsf{KeyGen}}(\cdot,\cdot)$ *was queried on an identifier* $id \in \mathcal{I}$ *with key attributes* $X \in \mathcal{X}$ *s.t.* $R(X, Y^*) = 1$, *then* $\mathcal{O}_{\mathsf{Rev}}(\cdot,\cdot)$ *must be queried on this identifier* id *at the time* $t \leq t^*$.
4. $\mathcal{O}_{\mathsf{DKGen}}(\cdot,\cdot)$ *cannot be queried on any identifier* $id \in \mathcal{I}$ *with the key attributes* $X \in \mathcal{X}$ *s.t.* $R(X, Y^*) = 1$ *at the challenge time* t^* *or any identifier* $id \in \mathcal{I}$ *has been revoked.*

An *RABE scheme is said to be* sIND-CPA *secure if for any probabilistic polynomial time adversary* $\mathcal{A}$, *the following advantage is negligible:*

$$\mathbf{Adv}_{\mathcal{A},\mathcal{RABE}}^{\text{sIND-CPA}}(\lambda) = \big| \Pr[\mathbf{Exp}_{\mathcal{A},\mathcal{RABE}}^{\text{sIND-CPA}}(\lambda) = 1] - 1/2 \big|.$$

3.3   Definition of DP-ABE

Definition 7 (DP-ABE). *Dual-Policy Attribute-Based Encryption* $\mathcal{DP}$ *with key attributes* $(X, \bar{X}) \in \mathcal{X} \times \bar{\mathcal{X}}$ *that support ciphertext attributes* $(Y, \bar{Y}) \in \mathcal{Y} \times \bar{\mathcal{Y}}$ *and the message space* $\mathcal{M}$ *consists of following four algorithms:*

- $\mathcal{DP}.\text{Setup}(\lambda) \rightarrow (pk, msk)$: *The probabilistic setup algorithm takes as input the security parameter* $\lambda \in \mathbb{N}$, *and outputs the public key* pk *and the master secret key* msk.
- $\mathcal{DP}.\text{KeyGen}(msk, X, \bar{X}) \rightarrow sk_{X,\bar{X}}$: *The key generation algorithm takes as input the master secret key* msk, *the key attributes* $(X, \bar{X}) \in \mathcal{X} \times \bar{\mathcal{X}}$, *and outputs the secret key* $sk_{X,\bar{X}}$.
- $\mathcal{DP}.\text{Enc}(pk, Y, \bar{Y}, m) \rightarrow c_{Y,\bar{Y}}$: *The encryption algorithm takes as input the public key* pk, *the ciphertext attributes* $(Y, \bar{Y}) \in \mathcal{Y} \times \bar{\mathcal{Y}}$ *and the message* $m \in \mathcal{M}$, *and outputs the ciphertext* $c_{Y,\bar{Y}}$.
- $\mathcal{DP}.\text{Dec}(sk_{X,\bar{X}}, c_{Y,\bar{Y}}) \rightarrow m$: *The decryption algorithm takes as input the secret key* $sk_{X,\bar{X}}$ *and the ciphertext* $c_{Y,\bar{Y}}$, *and outputs the message* $m \in \mathcal{M}$.

Definition 8 (Correctness of Parallel DP-ABE). *Let* $\mathcal{PDP}$ *denote a parallel DP-ABE scheme. The consistency condition requires for all* $\lambda \in \mathbb{N}$, *the public key* pk *and the master secret key* msk *output by setup algorithm,* $m \in \mathcal{M}$ *and* $\big(R(X,Y) \vee \bar{R}(\bar{X}, \bar{Y})\big) = 1$, *we then have*

$$\mathcal{PDP}.\text{Dec}\big(sk_{X,\bar{X}}, \mathcal{PDP}.\text{Enc}(pk, Y, \bar{Y}, m)\big) = m.$$

Definition 9 (Correctness of Sequential DP-ABE). *Let* $\mathcal{SDP}$ *denote a sequential DP-ABE scheme. The consistency condition requires for all* $\lambda \in \mathbb{N}$, *the public key* pk *and the master secret key* msk *output by setup algorithm,* $m \in \mathcal{M}$, *and* $R(X,Y) = \bar{R}(\bar{X}, \bar{Y}) = 1$, *we then have*

$$\mathcal{SDP}.\text{Dec}\big(sk_{X,\bar{X}}, \mathcal{SDP}.\text{Enc}(pk, Y, \bar{Y}, m)\big) = m.$$

3.4   Security Model of DP-ABE

Definition 10 (sIND-CPA in Parallel DP-ABE). *A parallel DP-ABE* $\mathcal{PDP}$ *consists of four algorithms in above. For an adversary* $\mathcal{A}$, *we define the following experiment:*

$$\mathbf{Exp}_{\mathcal{A},\mathcal{PDP}}^{\text{sIND-CPA}}(\lambda)$$
$$(Y^*, \bar{Y}^*) \leftarrow \mathcal{A}(\lambda);$$
$$(pk, msk) \leftarrow \mathcal{PDP}.\text{Setup}(\lambda);$$
$$(m_0, m_1) \leftarrow \mathcal{A}^{\mathcal{O}_{\text{KeyGen}}}(pk);$$
$$b \leftarrow \{0, 1\};$$
$$c^* \leftarrow \mathcal{PDP}.\text{Enc}(pk, Y^*, \bar{Y}^*, m_b);$$
$$b' \leftarrow \mathcal{A}^{\mathcal{O}_{\text{KeyGen}}}(c^*);$$
$$\textit{If } b = b' \textit{ return } 1 \textit{ else return } 0.$$

$\mathcal{O}_{\text{KeyGen}}(\cdot, \cdot)$ *is the key generation oracle that allows $\mathcal{A}$ to query on any key attributes $X, \bar{X} \in \mathcal{X} \times \bar{\mathcal{X}}$ s.t. $R(X, Y^*) = \bar{R}(\bar{X}, \bar{Y}^*) = 0$, and returns the secret key $sk_{X,\bar{X}}$ by running $\mathcal{PDP}.\text{KeyGen}(msk, X, \bar{X})$.*
A parallel DP-ABE is said to be sIND-CPA secure if for any probabilistic polynomial time adversary $\mathcal{A}$, the following advantage is negligible:

$$\mathbf{Adv}_{\mathcal{A},\mathcal{PDP}}^{\text{sIND-CPA}}(\lambda) = \big| \Pr[\mathbf{Exp}_{\mathcal{A},\mathcal{PDP}}^{\text{sIND-CPA}}(\lambda) = 1] - 1/2 \big|.$$

Definition 11 (sIND-CPA in Sequential DP-ABE). *A sequential DP-ABE $\mathcal{SDP}$ consists of four algorithms in above. For an adversary $\mathcal{A}$, we define the following experiment:*

$$\mathbf{Exp}_{\mathcal{A},\mathcal{SDP}}^{\text{sIND-CPA}}(\lambda)$$
$$(Y^*, \bar{Y}^*) \leftarrow \mathcal{A}(\lambda);$$
$$(pk, msk) \leftarrow \mathcal{SDP}.\text{Setup}(\lambda);$$
$$(m_0, m_1) \leftarrow \mathcal{A}^{\mathcal{O}_{\text{KeyGen}}}(pk);$$
$$b \leftarrow \{0, 1\};$$
$$c^* \leftarrow \mathcal{SDP}.\text{Enc}(pk, Y^*, \bar{Y}^*, m_b);$$
$$b' \leftarrow \mathcal{A}^{\mathcal{O}_{\text{KeyGen}}}(c^*);$$
$$\textit{If } b = b' \textit{ return } 1 \textit{ else return } 0.$$

$\mathcal{O}_{\text{KeyGen}}(\cdot, \cdot)$ *is the key generation oracle that allows $\mathcal{A}$ to query on any key attributes $X, \bar{X} \in \mathcal{X} \times \bar{\mathcal{X}}$ except $R(X, Y^*) = \bar{R}(\bar{X}, \bar{Y}^*) = 1$, and returns the secret key $sk_{X,\bar{X}}$ by running $\mathcal{SDP}.\text{KeyGen}(msk, X, \bar{X})$.*
A sequential DP-ABE is said to be sIND-CPA secure if for any probabilistic polynomial time adversary $\mathcal{A}$, the following advantage is negligible:

$$\mathbf{Adv}_{\mathcal{A},\mathcal{SDP}}^{\text{sIND-CPA}}(\lambda) = \big| \Pr[\mathbf{Exp}_{\mathcal{A},\mathcal{SDP}}^{\text{sIND-CPA}}(\lambda) = 1] - 1/2 \big|.$$

4 Proposed Schemes

4.1 Generic Construction of Revocable ABE

Let $\mathcal{ETC}$ and $\mathcal{ETC}_t$ are ElGamal type cryptosystems. The generic construction of RABE $\mathcal{RABE}$ are described as follows.

- $\mathcal{RABE}$.Setup(λ): The setup algorithm initializes an empty revocation list $rl \leftarrow \emptyset$ and a state based on the binary tree BT with $\mathcal{N}$ leaf nodes, where $\mathcal{N}$ is the number of system users. The algorithm follows $\mathcal{SDP}$.Setup(λ) to generate the public key pk and the master secret key msk.
- $\mathcal{RABE}$.KeyGen(msk, st, X, id): The key generation algorithm chooses an unassigned leaf node from the binary tree BT and stores id in this node. For each node $\theta \in \mathsf{Path}(id)$:
  - Fetch α_θ from the node θ. If α_θ is not available, it randomly chooses $\alpha_\theta \in \mathbb{Z}_p$, and updates the state $st \leftarrow st \cup (\theta, \alpha_\theta)$.
  - Run $\mathcal{ETC}$.KeyGen(α_θ, X) $\rightarrow sk_\theta$.
  The key generation algorithm returns the secret key $sk_{id} = \{sk_\theta\}_{\theta \in \mathsf{Path}(id)}$ and the updated state st.
- $\mathcal{RABE}$.KeyUpdate($msk, st, \bar{X}_t, rl$) $\rightarrow ku_t$: Pases $\bar{X}_t$ is the key attributes based on the timestamp $t \in \mathcal{T}$. For each node $\theta \in \mathsf{KUNodes}(st, rl, t)$:
  - Fetch α_θ (α_θ always predefined in the key generation algorithm).
  - Run $\mathcal{ETC}_t$.KeyGen($\alpha - \alpha_\theta, \bar{X}_t$) $\rightarrow sk_{t,\theta}$, where α is the master secret key.
  The key update algorithm returns $ku_t = \{sk_{t,\theta}\}_{\theta \in \mathsf{KUNodes}(st, rl, t)}$.
- $\mathcal{RABE}$.DKGen(pk, sk_{id}, ku_t) $\rightarrow dk_{id,t}$: Let I and J denote sets $\mathsf{Path}(id)$ and $\mathsf{KUNodes}(st, rl, t)$, respectively. For $\theta \in \mathsf{I} \cap \mathsf{J}$, the algorithm chooses a serial of random values to re-randomize the keys $(sk_\theta, sk_{t,\theta})$ and returns the decryption key $dk_{id} = (sk_\theta, sk_{t,\theta})$.
- $\mathcal{RABE}$.Enc($pk, Y, \bar{Y}_t, m$) $\rightarrow c_{Y,\bar{Y}_t}$: Same as $\mathcal{SDP}$.Enc($pk, Y, \bar{Y}, m$).
- $\mathcal{RABE}$.Dec($pk, dk_{id,t}, c_{Y,\bar{Y}_t}$) $\rightarrow m$: Same as $\mathcal{SDP}$.Dec($dk_{id,t}, c_{Y,\bar{Y}_t}$).
- $\mathcal{RABE}$.Rev(rl, id, t) $\rightarrow rl$: The revocation algorithm returns the revocation list rl as $rl \leftarrow rl \cup (id, t)$.

Theorem 1. *If the underlying ElGamal type cryptosystems $\mathcal{ETS}_1$ and $\mathcal{ETS}_2$ are secure, the proposed generic construction is secure[2].*

4.2   Generic Construction of Parallel DP-ABE

Let $\mathcal{ETC}_{\mathsf{kp}}$ and $\mathcal{ETC}_{\mathsf{cp}}$ are ElGamal type cryptosystems based on KP-ABE and CP-ABE, respectively. The generic construction of parallel DP-ABE $\mathcal{PDP}$ are described as follows.

- $\mathcal{PDP}$.Setup(λ): The setup algorithm runs

$$\begin{cases} \mathcal{ETC}_{\mathsf{kp}}.\mathsf{Init}(\lambda) \rightarrow pp_{\mathsf{kp}}, or \\ \mathcal{ETC}_{\mathsf{cp}}.\mathsf{Init}(\lambda) \rightarrow pp_{\mathsf{cp}}. \end{cases}$$

to obtain the description of bilinear group as the public parameter pp, where $pp_{\mathsf{kp}} = pp_{\mathsf{cp}} = \mathcal{G}(\lambda)$ by the definition of ElGamal type cryptosystem. The algorithm also runs

$$\begin{cases} \mathcal{ETC}_{\mathsf{kp}}.\mathsf{Setup}(pp) \rightarrow (pk_{\mathsf{kp}}, msk_{\mathsf{kp}}), and \\ \mathcal{ETC}_{\mathsf{cp}}.\mathsf{Setup}(pp) \rightarrow (pk_{\mathsf{cp}}, msk_{\mathsf{cp}}). \end{cases}$$

---

[2] Please contact the authors for the formal security proofs of Theorem 1 to 3.

to obtain the master secret key α, where $msk_{kp} = msk_{cp} = \alpha$ by the definition of ElGamal type cryptosystem. The setup algorithm outputs

$$pk = (pp, pk_{kp}, pk_{cp}), \quad msk = (\alpha).$$

- $\mathcal{PDP}$.KeyGen$(msk, X, \bar{X})$: Parse X is the access structure in KP-ABE and $\bar{X}$ is attribute set in CP-ABE. The key generation algorithm runs

$$\begin{cases} \mathcal{ETC}_{kp}.\text{KeyGen}(\alpha, X) \to sk_X, and \\ \mathcal{ETC}_{cp}.\text{KeyGen}(\alpha, \bar{X}) \to sk_{\bar{X}}. \end{cases}$$

The key generation algorithm outputs the secret key $sk_{X,\bar{X}} = (sk_X, sk_{\bar{X}})$.
- $\mathcal{PDP}$.Enc$(pk, Y, \bar{Y}, m)$: Parse Y is the attribute set in KP-ABE and $\bar{Y}$ is the access structure in CP-ABE. The encryption algorithm runs

$$\begin{cases} \mathcal{ETC}_{kp}.\text{Enc}(pk_{kp}, Y, m) \to c_Y, and \\ \mathcal{ETC}_{cp}.\text{Enc}(pk_{cp}, \bar{Y}, m) \to c_{\bar{Y}}. \end{cases}$$

By the definition of ElGamal type cryptosystem, we have

$$c_Y = (c_Y^{(0)}, c_Y^{(1)}, c_Y^{(2)}) \ and \ c_{\bar{Y}} = (c_{\bar{Y}}^{(0)}, c_{\bar{Y}}^{(1)}, c_{\bar{Y}}^{(2)}),$$

where $c_Y^{(0)} = c_{\bar{Y}}^{(0)} = m \cdot e(g,g)^{\alpha s}$ and $c_Y^{(1)} = c_{\bar{Y}}^{(1)} = g^s$. The encryption algorithm outputs the ciphertext $c_{Y,\bar{Y}} = (m \cdot e(g,g)^{\alpha s}, g^s, c_Y^{(2)}, c_{\bar{Y}}^{(2)})$.
- $\mathcal{PDP}$.Dec$(sk_{X,\bar{X}}, c_{Y,\bar{Y}})$: The decryption algorithm runs

$$\begin{cases} \mathcal{ETC}_{kp}.\text{Dec}(pk_{kp}, sk_X, c_Y) \to m \text{ if } R(X, Y) = 1, \\ \mathcal{ETC}_{cp}.\text{Dec}(pk_{cp}, sk_{\bar{X}}, c_{\bar{Y}}) \to m \text{ if } \bar{R}(\bar{X}, \bar{Y}) = 1. \end{cases}$$

The decryption algorithm returns the message m.

Theorem 2. *If the underlying ElGamal type cryptosystems $\mathcal{ETC}_{kp}$ and $\mathcal{ETC}_{cp}$ are secure, the proposed generic construction of parallel DP-ABE is secure.*

4.3 Generic Construction of Sequential DP-ABE

Let $\mathcal{ETC}_{kp}$ and $\mathcal{ETC}_{cp}$ are ElGamal type cryptosystems based on KP-ABE and CP-ABE, respectively. The generic construction of parallel DP-ABE $\mathcal{SDP}$ are described as follows.

- $\mathcal{SDP}$.Setup(λ): Same as $\mathcal{PDP}$.Setup(λ).
- $\mathcal{SDP}$.KeyGen$(msk, X, \bar{X})$: Parse X is the access structure in KP-ABE and $\bar{X}$ is attribute set in CP-ABE. The key generation algorithm randomly picks $\alpha' \in \mathbb{Z}_p$ and runs

$$\begin{cases} \mathcal{ETC}_{kp}.\text{KeyGen}(\alpha', X) \to sk_X, and \\ \mathcal{ETC}_{cp}.\text{KeyGen}(\alpha - \alpha', \bar{X}) \to sk_{\bar{X}}. \end{cases}$$

The key generation algorithm outputs the secret key $sk_{X,\bar{X}} = (sk_X, sk_{\bar{X}})$.

- $\mathcal{SDP}$.Enc($pk, Y, \bar{Y}, m$): Same as $\mathcal{PDP}$.Enc($pk, Y, \bar{Y}, m$).
- $\mathcal{SDP}$.Dec($sk_{X,\bar{X}}, c_{Y,\bar{Y}}$): The decryption algorithm runs the sub-decryption algorithms

$$\begin{cases} \mathcal{D}_{\mathsf{kp}}(sk_X, g^s, c_Y^{(2)}) \to e(g,g)^{\alpha's}, \\ \mathcal{D}_{\mathsf{cp}}(sk_{\bar{X}}, g^s, c_{\bar{Y}}^{(2)}) \to e(g,g)^{(\alpha-\alpha')s}. \end{cases}$$

The decryption algorithm outputs the message $m = m \cdot e(g,g)^{\alpha s}/e(g,g)^{\alpha s}$.

Theorem 3. *If the underlying ElGamal type cryptosystems $\mathcal{ETC}_{\mathsf{kp}}$ and $\mathcal{ETC}_{\mathsf{cp}}$ are secure, the proposed generic construction of parallel DP-ABE is secure.*

5   Instantiations Based on ElGamal Type Cryptosystem

5.1   Instantiations of RABE

By applying the generic construction in Sect. 4.1, we can build the concrete instantiation of key-policy RABE and ciphertext RABE, and even revocable DP-ABE by dividing the master secret key into three pieces for $(X, \bar{X}, t)$, where $(X, \bar{X})$ are key attributes in DP-ABE and t is for managing user revocation. There are many concrete RABE schemes based on ElGamal type schemes. For example, the RABE with decryption key exposure resistance [31] are based on [14], and [24], the KP-ABE with efficient revocation mechanism and decryption key exposure resistance [32] are based on [14] and [28], and the CP-ABE with efficient revocation mechanism and decryption key exposure resistance [33] are based on [24] and [28]. We omit the detailed construction here since our paper focus on argue that any ElGamal type scheme as in Definition 3 can be used to build secure RABE schemes and dual-policy ABE, respectively.

5.2   An Instantiation of Parallel DP-ABE

By applying the generic construction in Sect. 4.2, we give an instantiation of parallel DP-ABE based on [14] and [24] as follows.

- $\mathcal{PDP}$.Setup(λ): Run $\mathcal{G}(\lambda)$ to obtain $(p, g, \mathbb{G}, \mathbb{G}_T)$. Pick $u, h, w, v, \{t_i\}_{i \in [n+1]} \in \mathbb{G}$ and $\alpha \in \mathbb{Z}_p$. Output

$$pk = (p, g, \mathbb{G}, \mathbb{G}_T, e(g,g)^\alpha, u, h, w, v, \{t_i\}_{i \in [n+1]}), \quad msk = (\alpha).$$

- $\mathcal{PDP}$.KeyGen($msk, X, \bar{X}$): Parse $X = (\mathbb{M}_{\mathsf{kp}}, \rho_{\mathsf{kp}})$ and $\bar{X} = (A_{\mathsf{cp}}^{(1)}, ..., A_{\mathsf{cp}}^{(k_{\mathsf{cp}})})$. Compute $sk_X = (\{g^{\mathbb{M}_{\mathsf{kp},i}\vec{u}_i} T(i)^{r_i}, g^{r_i}\}_{i \in [d_{\mathsf{kp}}]})$, where $\mathbb{M}_{\mathsf{kp}}$ has d_{kp} rows and l_{kp} columns, and $\vec{1} \cdot \vec{u} = \alpha$. Compute $sk_{\bar{X}} = (g^\alpha w^r, g^r, \{g^{r_j}, (u^{A_{\mathsf{cp}}^{(j)}} h)^{r_j} v^{-r}\}_{j \in [k_{\mathsf{cp}}]})$, where $r, \{r_j\}_{j \in [k_{\mathsf{cp}}]} \in \mathbb{Z}_p$. Output $sk_{X,\bar{X}} = (sk_X, sk_{\bar{X}})$.
- $\mathcal{PDP}$.Enc($pk, Y, \bar{Y}, m$): Parse $Y = (A_{\mathsf{kp}}^{(1)}, A_{\mathsf{kp}}^{(2)}, ..., A_{\mathsf{kp}}^{(k_{\mathsf{kp}})})$ and $\bar{Y} = (\mathbb{M}_{\mathsf{cp}}, \rho_{\mathsf{cp}})$. Pick $\vec{u} = (s, \vec{u}_2, ..., \vec{u}_l) \in \mathbb{Z}_p^l$ and compute

$$c_Y^{(3)} = (\{T(i)^s\}_{i \in [k_{\mathsf{kp}}]}), \quad c_{\bar{Y}}^{(3)} = (\{w^{\mathbb{M}_{\mathsf{cp},j}\vec{u}_j} v^{\phi_j}, (u^{\rho(i)} h)^{\phi_i}, g^{\phi_j}\}_{j \in [d_{\mathsf{cp}}]}),$$

where $\mathbb{M}_{cp}$ has d_{cp} rows and l_{cp} columns, $\{\phi_j\}_{j \in [d_{cp}]} \in \mathbb{Z}_p$. Output

$$c_{Y,\bar{Y}} = (m \cdot e(g,g)^{\alpha s}, g^s, c_Y^{(3)}, c_{\bar{Y}}^{(3)}).$$

- $\mathcal{PDP}.\text{Dec}(sk_{X,\bar{X}}, c_{Y,\bar{Y}})$: If $R(X,Y) = 1$, there exist $I : \{i : \rho_{kp}(i) \in \mathcal{S}_{kp}\}$ and take $\vec{u}$ s.t. $\sum_{i \in I} \mathbb{M}_{kp,i} \vec{u}_i = \vec{1}$. Compute

$$\prod_{i \in I} \left(\frac{e(g^{\mathbb{M}_{kp,i} \vec{u}_i} T(i)^{r_i}, g^s)}{e(T(i)^s, g^{r_i})} \right)^{\vec{u}_i} = e(g,g)^{\alpha s}.$$

If $\bar{R}(\bar{X}, \bar{Y}) = 1$, there exist $J = \{j : \rho_{cp}(j) \in \mathcal{S}_{cp}\}$ and take $\vec{u}$ s.t. $\sum_{j \in J} \mathbb{M}_{cp,j} \vec{u}_j = \vec{1}$. Also, compute

$$\prod_{j \in J} \frac{e(g^s, g^\alpha w^r)}{\left(e(w^{\mathbb{M}_{cp,j} \vec{u}_j} v^{\phi_j}, g^r) e((u^{\rho(i)} h)^{\phi_i}, g^{r_j}) e(g^{\phi_j}, (u^{A_{cp}^{(j)}} h)^{r_j} v^{-r}) \right)^{\vec{u}_j}} = e(g,g)^{\alpha s}.$$

Output $m = m \cdot e(g,g)^{\alpha s}/e(g,g)^{\alpha s}$.

5.3 An Instantiation of Sequential DP-ABE

By applying the generic construction in Sect. 4.3, we give an instantiation of sequential DP-ABE based on [14] and [24] as follows.

- $\mathcal{SDP}.\text{Setup}(\lambda)$: Same as $\mathcal{PDP}.\text{Setup}(\lambda)$.
- $\mathcal{SDP}.\text{KeyGen}(msk, X, \bar{X})$: Parse $X = (\mathbb{M}_{kp}, \rho_{kp})$ and $\bar{X} = (A_{cp}^{(1)}, ..., A_{cp}^{(k_{cp})})$. Compute $sk_X = (\{g^{\mathbb{M}_{kp,i} \vec{u}_i} T(i)^{r_i}, g^{r_i}\}_{i \in [d_{kp}]})$, where $\mathbb{M}_{kp}$ has d_{kp} rows and l_{kp} columns, $\alpha', \{r_i\}_{i \in [d_{kp}]} \in \mathbb{Z}_p$ and $\vec{1} \cdot \vec{u} = \alpha'$. Also, compute $sk_{\bar{X}} = (g^{\alpha - \alpha'} w^r, g^r, \{g^{r_j}, (u^{A_{cp}^{(j)}} h)^{r_j} v^{-r}\}_{j \in [k_{cp}]})$, where $r, \{r_j\}_{j \in [k_{cp}]} \in \mathbb{Z}_p$. Output $sk_{X,\bar{X}} = (sk_X, sk_{\bar{X}})$.
- $\mathcal{SDP}.\text{Enc}(pk, Y, \bar{Y}, m)$: Same as $\mathcal{PDP}.\text{Enc}(pk, Y, \bar{Y}, m)$.
- $\mathcal{SDP}.\text{Dec}(sk_{X,\bar{X}}, c_{Y,\bar{Y}})$: If $R(X,Y) = 1$, there exist $I : \{i : \rho_{kp}(i) \in \mathcal{S}_{kp}\}$ and take $\vec{u}$ s.t. $\sum_{i \in I} \mathbb{M}_{kp,i} \vec{u}_i = \vec{1}$. Compute

$$\prod_{i \in I} \left(\frac{e(g^{\mathbb{M}_{kp,i} \vec{u}_i} T(i)^{r_i}, g^s)}{e(T(i)^s, g^{r_i})} \right)^{\vec{u}_i} = e(g,g)^{\alpha' s}.$$

If $R(\bar{X}, \bar{Y}) = 1$, there exist $J = \{j : \rho_{cp}(j) \in \mathcal{S}_{cp}\}$ and take $\vec{u}$ s.t. $\sum_{j \in J} \mathbb{M}_{cp,j} \vec{u}_j = \vec{1}$. Also, compute

$$\prod_{j \in J} \frac{e(g^s, g^{\alpha - \alpha'} w^r)}{\left(e(w^{\mathbb{M}_{cp,j} \vec{u}_j} v^{\phi_j}, g^r) e((u^{\rho(i)} h)^{\phi_i}, g^{r_j}) e(g^{\phi_j}, (u^{A_{cp}^{(j)}} h)^{r_j} v^{-r}) \right)^{\vec{u}_j}} = e(g,g)^{(\alpha - \alpha') s}.$$

Output $m = m \cdot e(g,g)^{\alpha s}/(e(g,g)^{\alpha' s} \cdot e(g,g)^{(\alpha - \alpha') s})$.

6   Efficiency Analysis

To our knowledge, only few literature investigate DP-ABE [2,4]. Compared with our proposed scheme, as shown in Table 1, our schemes have better performances than AI09 [2] and less efficient then AY15 [4]. However, to achieve adaptive security, AY15 is in the composite-order group which is less efficient[3] since it will incur heavy workload to process data, even transmission bandwidth. Our proposed scheme applies prime-order group and has the same complexity to the existing DP-ABE schemes except for the space complexity of system parameter. In our scheme, the component of KP-ABE is based on [14] and the part of CP-ABE is based [24], where [14] has the linear space complexity on the public parameter and [24] has the constant-size public parameter. Hence, our scheme only has better space complexity on the system parameter than AI09. Although AY15 has the constant-size public parameter, the composite-order group will lead to a heavy workload.

Table 1. Theoretical analysis of DP-ABE scheme

	Space complexity			Computational complexity	
	Parameter	Secret key	Ciphertext	Encryption	Decryption
AI09 [2]	$\mathcal{O}(m+n)$	$\mathcal{O}(\mathcal{X}+\bar{\mathcal{X}})$	$\mathcal{O}(\mathcal{Y}+\bar{\mathcal{Y}})$	$\mathcal{O}(\mathcal{Y}+\bar{\mathcal{Y}})$	$\mathcal{O}(\mathcal{X}+\bar{\mathcal{X}})$
AY15 [4]	$\mathcal{O}(1)$	$\mathcal{O}(\mathcal{X}+\bar{\mathcal{X}})$	$\mathcal{O}(\mathcal{Y}+\bar{\mathcal{Y}})$	$\mathcal{O}(\mathcal{Y}+\bar{\mathcal{Y}})$	$\mathcal{O}(\mathcal{X}+\bar{\mathcal{X}})$
SDP-ABE	$\mathcal{O}(m)$	$\mathcal{O}(\mathcal{X}+\bar{\mathcal{X}})$	$\mathcal{O}(\mathcal{Y}+\bar{\mathcal{Y}})$	$\mathcal{O}(\mathcal{Y}+\bar{\mathcal{Y}})$	$\mathcal{O}(\mathcal{X}+\bar{\mathcal{X}})$
PDP-ABE	$\mathcal{O}(m)$	$\mathcal{O}(\mathcal{X}+\bar{\mathcal{X}})$	$\mathcal{O}(\mathcal{Y}+\bar{\mathcal{Y}})$	$\mathcal{O}(\mathcal{Y}+\bar{\mathcal{Y}})$	$\mathcal{O}(\mathcal{X}+\bar{\mathcal{X}})$

m denotes the maximum size of attribute set allowed to be assigned to a key;
n is the maximum size of attribute set to be associated with a ciphertext;
$\mathcal{X}$ and $\bar{\mathcal{X}}$ represent the size of attributes and policies assigned to a key;
$\mathcal{Y}$ and $\bar{\mathcal{Y}}$ represent the size of policies and attributes assigned to a ciphertext.

For experimental analysis, we focus on evaluating AI09 and our schemes since the AY15 based on the inefficient composite-order group. Our experimental simulation was performed on a PC running 64-bit Windows 10 with 3.60 GHz Intel(R) Core(TM) i7-4790 CPU and 24 GB memory. We have implemented AI09 and our schemes in Java using JPBE library [19] with Type A elliptic curve and symmetric pairing setting from "a properties" provided by JPBE library. Hence, our scheme, p is a 160-bit prime number, and elements in $\mathbb{G}$ and $\mathbb{G}_T$ have 512-bit and 1024-bit, respectively. The experimental results are presented in Fig. 3.

Figure 3a presents the experimental performances of the system initialization by increasing the maximum number of attribute set allowed to be assigned to a key and a ciphertext. Our proposed schemes are much more efficient than AI09, which only take half of the computational time in AI09. Figure 3b performs the

---

[3] Composite-order group has a much bigger size than the prime-order group. Specifically, the composite-order group needs 1024 bits if the prime-order group requires 160 bits (discrete log vs. factoring).

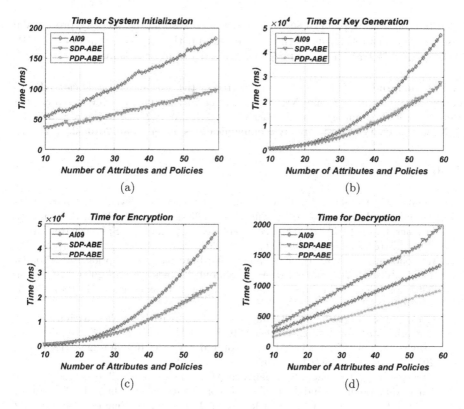

Fig. 3. Experimental performance

ms key generation, the tendency is continually increasing based on the improvement of the maximum number of attribute set and policies allowed to be assigned to keys, and our proposed schemes have the lower growth rate. Figure 3c demonstrates the performances of encryption, the tendency of encryption is similar to the experimental result in the key generation. Figure 3d presents the results of decryption. Our PDP-ABE has a better performance than others since it only requires one of key-policy and ciphertext-policy to process the decryption algorithm, which takes half of the computational cost in SDP-ABE.

Overall, the results are similar to what we expected performances in Table 1. Therefore, our scheme has better performance than the existing DP-ABE based on the prime-order group.

7 Conclusion

We resisted IBE and ABE schemes and presented a new cryptographic primitive called ElGamal type cryptosystem. ElGamal type cryptosystem is a useful primitive for designing a variety of ABE schemes. In this paper, we present generic constructions of RABE with decryption key exposure resistance and DP-ABE with parallel and sequential settings and the corresponding security proofs. We also provide instantiations of these schemes and the experimental data of DP-ABE to demonstrate high performances of our proposed schemes.

Acknowledgment. This research is supported by the National Natural Science Foundation of China under Grant Nos. U1804263 and 61702105, the Key Research and Development Program of Shaanxi under Grant 2019KW-053, and the New Star Team of Xi'an University of Posts and Telecommunications under Grant 2016-02.

References

1. Abdalla, M., Catalano, D., Dent, A.W., Malone-Lee, J., Neven, G., Smart, N.P.: Identity-based encryption gone wild. In: Bugliesi, M., Preneel, B., Sassone, V., Wegener, I. (eds.) ICALP 2006. LNCS, vol. 4052, pp. 300–311. Springer, Heidelberg (2006). https://doi.org/10.1007/11787006_26

2. Attrapadung, N., Imai, H.: Dual-policy attribute based encryption. In: Abdalla, M., Pointcheval, D., Fouque, P.-A., Vergnaud, D. (eds.) ACNS 2009. LNCS, vol. 5536, pp. 168–185. Springer, Heidelberg (2009). https://doi.org/10.1007/978-3-642-01957-9_11

3. Attrapadung, N., Libert, B., de Panafieu, E.: Expressive key-policy attribute-based encryption with constant-size ciphertexts. In: Catalano, D., Fazio, N., Gennaro, R., Nicolosi, A. (eds.) PKC 2011. LNCS, vol. 6571, pp. 90–108. Springer, Heidelberg (2011). https://doi.org/10.1007/978-3-642-19379-8_6

4. Attrapadung, N., Yamada, S.: Duality in ABE: converting attribute based encryption for dual predicate and dual policy via computational encodings. In: Nyberg, K. (ed.) CT-RSA 2015. LNCS, vol. 9048, pp. 87–105. Springer, Cham (2015). https://doi.org/10.1007/978-3-319-16715-2_5

5. Baek, J., Zheng, Y.: Identity-based threshold decryption. In: Bao, F., Deng, R., Zhou, J. (eds.) PKC 2004. LNCS, vol. 2947, pp. 262–276. Springer, Heidelberg (2004). https://doi.org/10.1007/978-3-540-24632-9_19

6. Bethencourt, J., Sahai, A., Waters, B.: Ciphertext-policy attribute-based encryption. In: IEEE S&P, pp. 321–334 (2007)

7. Boldyreva, A., Goyal, V., Kumar, V.: Identity-based encryption with efficient revocation. In: CCS, pp. 417–426 (2008)

8. Boneh, D., Boyen, X.: Efficient selective-ID secure identity-based encryption without random oracles. In: Cachin, C., Camenisch, J.L. (eds.) EUROCRYPT 2004. LNCS, vol. 3027, pp. 223–238. Springer, Heidelberg (2004). https://doi.org/10.1007/978-3-540-24676-3_14

9. Boneh, D., Boyen, X.: Secure identity based encryption without random oracles. In: Franklin, M. (ed.) CRYPTO 2004. LNCS, vol. 3152, pp. 443–459. Springer, Heidelberg (2004). https://doi.org/10.1007/978-3-540-28628-8_27

10. Boneh, D., Franklin, M.: Identity-based encryption from the weil pairing. In: Kilian, J. (ed.) CRYPTO 2001. LNCS, vol. 2139, pp. 213–229. Springer, Heidelberg (2001). https://doi.org/10.1007/3-540-44647-8_13

11. Chow, S.S.M.: A framework of multi-authority attribute-based encryption with outsourcing and revocation. In: SACMAT, pp. 215–226 (2016)

12. ElGamal, T.: A public key cryptosystem and a signature scheme based on discrete logarithms. In: Blakley, G.R., Chaum, D. (eds.) CRYPTO 1984. LNCS, vol. 196, pp. 10–18. Springer, Heidelberg (1985). https://doi.org/10.1007/3-540-39568-7_2

13. Gentry, C.: Practical identity-based encryption without random oracles. In: Vaudenay, S. (ed.) EUROCRYPT 2006. LNCS, vol. 4004, pp. 445–464. Springer, Heidelberg (2006). https://doi.org/10.1007/11761679_27
14. Goyal, V., Pandey, O., Sahai, A., Waters, B.: Attribute-based encryption for finegrained access control of encrypted data. In: CCS, pp. 89–98 (2006)
15. Green, M., Hohenberger, S., Waters, B.: Outsourcing the decryption of ABE ciphertexts. In: USENIX (2011)
16. Lee, K., Choi, S.G., Lee, D.H., Park, J.H., Yung, M.: Self-updatable encryption: time constrained access control with hidden attributes and better efficiency. In: Sako, K., Sarkar, P. (eds.) ASIACRYPT 2013. LNCS, vol. 8269, pp. 235–254. Springer, Heidelberg (2013). https://doi.org/10.1007/978-3-642-42033-7_13
17. Lewko, A., Okamoto, T., Sahai, A., Takashima, K., Waters, B.: Fully secure functional encryption: attribute-based encryption and (hierarchical) inner product encryption. In: Gilbert, H. (ed.) EUROCRYPT 2010. LNCS, vol. 6110, pp. 62–91. Springer, Heidelberg (2010). https://doi.org/10.1007/978-3-642-13190-5_4
18. Lewko, A., Waters, B.: New techniques for dual system encryption and fully secure HIBE with short ciphertexts. In: Micciancio, D. (ed.) TCC 2010. LNCS, vol. 5978, pp. 455–479. Springer, Heidelberg (2010). https://doi.org/10.1007/978-3-642-11799-2_27
19. Lynn, B.: PBC library manual (2006)
20. Malluhi, Q.M., Shikfa, A., Trinh, V.C.: A ciphertext-policy attribute-based encryption scheme with optimized ciphertext size and fast decryption. In: AsiaCCS, pp. 230–240 (2017)
21. Naor, D., Naor, M., Lotspiech, J.: Revocation and tracing schemes for stateless receivers. In: Kilian, J. (ed.) CRYPTO 2001. LNCS, vol. 2139, pp. 41–62. Springer, Heidelberg (2001). https://doi.org/10.1007/3-540-44647-8_3
22. Ostrovsky, R., Sahai, A., Waters, B.: Attribute-based encryption with nonmonotonic access structures. In: CCS pp. 195–203 (2007)
23. Pirretti, M., Traynor, P., McDaniel, P., Waters, B.: Secure attribute-based systems. In: CCS, pp. 99–112 (2006)
24. Rouselakis, Y., Waters, B.: Practical constructions and new proof methods for large universe attribute-based encryption. In: CCS, pp. 463–474 (2013)
25. Sahai, A., Seyalioglu, H., Waters, B.: Dynamic credentials and ciphertext delegation for attribute-based encryption. In: Safavi-Naini, R., Canetti, R. (eds.) CRYPTO 2012. LNCS, vol. 7417, pp. 199–217. Springer, Heidelberg (2012). https://doi.org/10.1007/978-3-642-32009-5_13
26. Sahai, A., Waters, B.: Fuzzy identity-based encryption. In: Cramer, R. (ed.) EUROCRYPT 2005. LNCS, vol. 3494, pp. 457–473. Springer, Heidelberg (2005). https://doi.org/10.1007/11426639_27
27. Seo, J.H., Emura, K.: Revocable identity-based encryption revisited: security model and construction. In: Kurosawa, K., Hanaoka, G. (eds.) PKC 2013. LNCS, vol. 7778, pp. 216–234. Springer, Heidelberg (2013). https://doi.org/10.1007/978-3-642-36362-7_14
28. Waters, B.: Efficient identity-based encryption without random oracles. In: Cramer, R. (ed.) EUROCRYPT 2005. LNCS, vol. 3494, pp. 114–127. Springer, Heidelberg (2005). https://doi.org/10.1007/11426639_7
29. Waters, B.: Dual system encryption: realizing fully secure IBE and HIBE under simple assumptions. In: Halevi, S. (ed.) CRYPTO 2009. LNCS, vol. 5677, pp. 619–636. Springer, Heidelberg (2009). https://doi.org/10.1007/978-3-642-03356-8_36

30. Waters, B.: Ciphertext-policy attribute-based encryption: an expressive, efficient, and provably secure realization. In: Catalano, D., Fazio, N., Gennaro, R., Nicolosi, A. (eds.) PKC 2011. LNCS, vol. 6571, pp. 53–70. Springer, Heidelberg (2011). https://doi.org/10.1007/978-3-642-19379-8_4

31. Shengmin, X., Yang, G., Yi, M.: Revocable attribute-based encryption with decryption key exposure resistance and ciphertext delegation. Inf. Sci. **479**, 116–134 (2019)

32. Shengmin, X., Yang, G., Yi, M., Deng, R.H.: Secure fine-grained access control and data sharing for dynamic groups in the cloud. IEEE Trans. Inf. Forensics Secur. **13**(8), 2101–2113 (2018)

33. Shengmin, X., Yang, G., Yi, M., Liu, X.: A secure IoT cloud storage system with fine-grained access control and decryption key exposure resistance. Futur. Gener. Comput. Syst. **97**, 284–294 (2019)

Online Cyber Deception System Using Partially Observable Monte-Carlo Planning Framework

Md Ali Reza Al Amin[1]($\boxtimes$), Sachin Shetty[1], Laurent Njilla[2], Deepak K. Tosh[3], and Charles Kamhoua[4]

[1] Old Dominion University, Norfolk, VA 23517, USA
{malam002,sshetty}@odu.edu
[2] Air Force Research Lab, Rome, NY, USA
laurent.njilla@us.af.mil
[3] University of Texas at El Paso, El Paso, TX, USA
dktosh@utep.edu
[4] Army Research Lab, Adelphi, MD, USA
charles.a.kamhoua.civ@mail.mil

Abstract. Cyber deception is an approach where the network administrators can deploy a network of decoy assets with the aim to expend adversaries' resources and time and gather information about the adversaries' strategies, tactics, capabilities, and intent. The key challenge in this cyber deception approach is the design and placement of network decoys to ensure maximal information uncertainty for the attackers. State-of-the-art approaches to address this design and placement problem assume a static environment and *apriori* strategies taken by the attacker. In this paper, we propose the design and placement of network decoys considering scenarios where defender's action influence an attacker to change its strategies and tactics dynamically while maintaining the trade-off between availability and security. The defender maintains a belief consisting of security state and the resultant actions are modeled as Partially Observable Markov Decision Process (POMDP). Our simulation results illustrate the defender's increasing ability to influence the attacker's attack path to comprise of fake nodes and networks.

Keywords: Cyber deception · Security · POMDP · Exploit dependency graph · POMCP

1 Introduction

The static nature of any organization's IT system leading to adversaries perform reconnaissance activity and identify potential threats. The aim of the reconnaissance phase is collecting as much as critical information about the network including network topology, open ports and services running and unpatched vulnerabilities. Having that critical information maximizes the intruder's probability to penetrate a system and gaining a foothold successfully. Patching a

S. Chen et al. (Eds.): SecureComm 2019, LNICST 305, pp. 205–223, 2019.
https://doi.org/10.1007/978-3-030-37231-6_11

vulnerability at the right time will reduce the possibility of being attacked where vulnerability patching depends upon its discovery and developing a patch for that specific weakness. Unfortunately, sometimes this period (a.k.a vulnerability exposure window) often lasts long, approximately 5 to 6 months. This extended period puts the cyber network at higher risk. To address this, one needs an active form of a defense system to thwart cyber attacks while considering attack information and providing with appropriate defense actions. But there is some issue with the development of such a system as an attacker considers a series of exploit to deep dive into the network. A few targeted cyber attacks consist of only a single vulnerability. It is always beneficial for the defender to know how the intruder can infiltrate the network and capture the attacker's progression throughout the network. With the help of cyber deception technologies (by introducing fake networks) we can alter the view of a system with a mix of real and fake information and make the network more resilient when unpatched vulnerabilities are present in the cyber network.

Cyber-deception has drawn attention from security researchers and practitioners as an approach for designing secure cyber infrastructure. It can provide two advantages: (a) Reduce likelihood of adversarial success and cost of cyber defense, (b) Provide insights into attacker's strategies, tactics, capabilities and intent. Typically, an attacker have *apriori* knowledge of the infrastructure they are targeting. In a cyber-deception approach, the defender can exploit this *apriori* knowledge to mislead the adversary in expending their resources and time by deploying network of decoy targets which thereby leads to attack paths that do not reach to a successful goal. The success of a cyber-deception strategy hinges on adversaries taking on more fake attack paths than actual attack paths that would increase the adversaries resources in distinguishing between real and fake assets.

Researchers have proposed cyber deception approaches that introduce fake networks by varying system characteristics [16], manipulating attacker's probes [2,18] and introducing virtual network interface controllers and route mutation [6]. These approaches are focused on introducing fake nodes from an attacker's point of view and assume a static environment and attacker and defender strategies. In [14], authors present a scalable defense system to limit the attacker's progression while minimizing the negative impact on the availability. Again their approach is built on a static environment leads to increase defender's effort and time to brawl with adversary. They also claim about network availability to the legitimate users while defender's taking defense actions but there is an impact whenever defender blocks any vulnerability. Sometimes to block any vulnerability defender needs to take aggressive decision which has greater impact on network availability. We overcome the above stated issue by placing network of decoys and show that up to 76% of the time attacker start with the fake initial nodes and carry out a series of exploits to achieve the fake goal state.

In this paper, we propose an approach to design and place network decoys while capturing attacker's progression. The attacker's progression is captured using exploit dependency graph [3,14] where nodes in the graph represent possible security conditions and directed hyperedge represent exploits. The defender modifies the design and placement based on the history of security alerts and prior deployments of network decoys. The defender's decision to deploy network decoys balances the trade-off between security cost and availability cost. This decision is made by solving a modified version of **Partially Observable Monte-Carlo Planning** (POMCP) algorithm [17] which provides the optimal action corresponding to current belief vector comprising of security state and prior actions. The key contributions of this paper are summarized below:

1. Embedding state space on the exploit dependency graph allows us to accurately quantify the attacker progression and provides critical information for selecting appropriate deceptive actions to mitigate the attacker progression and influence the attacker to take the path towards the fake network and keep him in the fake network.
2. Online deception algorithm that allows the defender to select actions based on the attacker behavior and achieved scalability, although for some instances the number of security states can be very large for our model. The online deception algorithm that allows one not to construct the entire state space instead of samples regions of state-space.
3. In comparison to existing network deception systems, we show that up to 76% of the time attacker start with the fake initial nodes and carry out the series of exploits to achieve the fake goal state. Whenever an attacker is in the fake network, legitimate users can take the service seamlessly from the real network.

The remainder of the paper is organized as follows. Section 2 discusses related work. Section 3 discusses the deception model. In Sect. 4, we present the defender's optimal action. Finally, Sect. 5 reports the simulation results, and we conclude in Sect. 6.

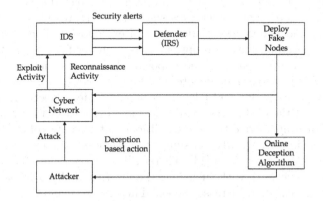

Fig. 1. Security model

2   Security Model

The proposed security model provides a way how a defender can deceive an attacker with the fake network to prevent the real network infiltration. Throughout the paper Fig. 1 will serve as the reference to describe the cyber deception approach. In this section, we demonstrate the characterization of attacker's progression using exploit dependency graph and our model framework.

2.1   Exploit Dependency Graph

Exploit dependency graph have been used to model multi-stage attack scenarios that an attacker can launch to compromise services or applications. The exploit dependency graph characterizes exploits in terms of a set of preconditions and postconditions. For a given network, exploit dependency graph can be generated using TVA (Topological Vulnerability Analysis) [9]. In an exploit dependency graph, nodes represent the security pre/post conditions and edges represent exploits.

2.2   Deploy Fake Nodes

We deploy fake nodes/networks along with the real nodes/networks whenever a reconnaissance alert is received from IDS. Attacker can certainly differentiate real nodes from fake nodes by analyzing round trip times or measured bandwidth on the link. We follow delay and bandwidth handler methods to ensure consistency of the network measurements collected during reconnaissance mission [1].

2.3   POMDP Model

State Space– An exploit dependency graph [14], a directed acyclic hypergraph (H), consists of nodes and hyperedges where nodes represent a set of security conditions (c) and hyperedges render a set of exploits (e). The security condition of the hypergraph have two options either true or false where true means attacker have certain capability and opposite. The node which defender wants to protect termed as goal node denoted by $N_r^g \subseteq N$, $N_f^g \subseteq N$ where N_r^g and N_f^g are real network goal node and fake network goal node respectively. Defender's goal is to protect the goal nodes (real nodes) and drive the attacker towards the fake nodes. Each hyperedge has two conditions in terms of exploits (e_i) termed as pre (N_i^-) and post (N_i^+). It is assumed that attacker can exploit e_i if all preconditions $j \in N_i^-$ are enabled [14]. There will be entry points for the attacker to penetrate the network without having the prior capabilities termed as initial exploits. An attacker can increase the capability set by exploiting more vulnerabilities. Whenever an exploit's attempt is successful all the postconditions of the exploit become successful.

A security state, $s \subseteq N$, is called a feasible security state if for every condition $c_j \in s$, there exists at least one exploit $e_i = (N_i^-, N_i^+) \in E$ such that $c_j \in N_i^+$ and N_i^-, $N_i^+ \subseteq s$ [14] and set $S = \{s_1, \ldots, s_n\}$ represents the state space for this model.

Action– Defender's action influence an attacker to choose a network path. So, we assume that the defender can change its network configuration on the fly based on attacker's action to prevent vertical movement. A simple mean of network configuration can be blocking a port from further communication, which will inhibit the attacker to progress. Another way to prevent attacker's progression is to apply countermeasure of any discovered exploit.

The space of defender's available action set is represented by $U = \{u^0, u^1, \dots, u^n\}$. Here, u^0 represents defender's null action which eventually means defender will not block any exploit. The remaining actions from the set U, signifies the network changes which will induce a set of blocked exploits. Each action associated with the set of blocked exploit influence the attacker to seek the available paths. Again, defender can not block any individual vulnerability rather it must select a defense action which will induces a set of blocked exploits.

Threat Model– We construct the model based on a single attacker who is attempting to penetrate the network. An attacker can only increase its capability by exploiting more vulnerabilities, on the other hand, it also increases the chance of being detected. Defender's goal is to prevent the exploitation of a vulnerability on the real network by allowing the exploitation on the fake network. The set of available exploits for real and fake network at a given state s can be defined as [14]:

$$E(s_t = s) = \{er_i = (N_i^-, N_i^+) \in |N_i^- \subset s, N_i^+ \not\subseteq s\} \tag{1}$$

$$E(s_t = s) = \{ef_i = (N_i^-, N_i^+) \in |N_i^- \subset s, N_i^+ \not\subseteq s\} \tag{2}$$

There are two important requirements that must be satisfied for an exploit $e_i = (N_i^-, N_i^+)$ to be available: (1) $N_i^- \subset s$, i.e. all of the exploit's preconditions must be satisfied: (2) $N_i^+ \not\subseteq s$, i.e. the exploit's postconditions must not all be satisfied [14].

The attack probability which defines attacker will attempt each real network exploits while security state s_t and defense action u_t for a given exploit $er_k \in E$ is given by,

$$P_{er_k}(s_t, u_t) = \begin{cases} \overline{P}_{er_k} & \text{when } er_k \in E(s_t) \backslash B(u_t) \\ \underline{P}_{er_k} & \text{when } er_k \in E(s_t) \cap B(u_t) \\ 0 & \text{when } er_k \notin E(s_t) \end{cases} \tag{3}$$

similarly for fake network,

$$P_{ef_k}(s_t, u_t) = \begin{cases} \overline{P}_{ef_k} & \text{when } ef_k \in E(s_t) \backslash B(u_t) \\ \underline{P}_{ef_k} & \text{when } ef_k \in E(s_t) \cap B(u_t) \\ 0 & \text{when } ef_k \notin E(s_t) \end{cases} \tag{4}$$

In above equations, $\overline{P}_{er_k}$ & $\overline{P}_{ef_k}$ represents the probability of attack when there is no action and $\underline{P}_{er_k}$ & $\underline{P}_{ef_k}$ defines the attack probability when defender's action block exploits.

To block any vulnerability defender will choose the action, $u \in U$, from the set of accessible defense actions represented by U for any given iteration. Attacker always tries to create a set of available initial exploits from reconnaissance state to penetrate the network. There will be a conditional probability of success for each the exploit attacker attempted So, for given exploits, er_k & ef_k, the probability of success is given by,

$$\alpha_{er_k}(s_t, u_t) = \begin{cases} \overline{\alpha}_{er_k} \ when \ er_k \notin B(u_t) \\ 0 \quad\quad when \ er_k \in B(u_t) \end{cases} \tag{5}$$

similarly for the fake network,

$$\alpha_{ef_k}(s_t, u_t) = \begin{cases} \overline{\alpha}_{ef_k} \ when \ ef_k \notin B(u_t) \\ \underline{\alpha}_{ef_k} \ when \ ef_k \in B(u_t) \end{cases} \tag{6}$$

As soon as, the exploit attempts are successful it enables all the postconditions which eventually form the updated security state as shown in Fig. 2.

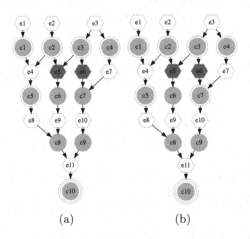

(a)   (b)

Fig. 2. Sample evolution (real network) of the security state for a given state-action pair $\alpha_{er_k}(s_t, u_t)$. (a) Consider the security state $s_t = \{c_1, c_2, c_3, c_4, c_5\}$ and defense action $u_t = u$ where $B(u) = \{e_5, e_6\}$ (here blocked exploits are shown with red shaped hyperedge). So that, the available set of exploits using Eq. (1) is $E(s_t) = \{e_5, e_6, e_7, e_8\}$ and (b) attacker attempt each exploit, which does not lie within set of blocked exploit, with a probability of attack and succeed with a probability defined by Eqs. (5, 6). In this example, only exploit e_7 is succeed and the updated security state is $s_t \in \{c_7\}$. In above figure, doubled circle shaded shape represents the security state. (Color figure online)

Defender's lack of information regarding the current security state and attacker true strategy which can be learned from noisy security alerts. In the next section, we describe how defender uses those information to construct the belief by getting security alerts from Intrusion Detection System (IDS). These security alerts are mixed of false positive and false negative alerts. For defender, it is important to differentiate those mixed alerts for better defense actions.

Defender's Observation– Defender's efficiency in terms of choosing actions to limit the attacker progression can be improved by correlating the alert with exploit activity. On the other hand, defender's efficiency can be degraded in the presence of a high rate of false alarm. To get rid of false alarm and precisely quantify attacker progression from the dependency graph we used state-based approach. From the security state, defender can create an available set of exploits to the attacker using Eq. (1) where defender can update the belief state with new security information by weighing the likelihood of individual security state. If we consider an example, for the belief matrices $b, b' \epsilon \Delta S$, some security state, $s_t \epsilon S$ and assumed attacker type let one single exploit is available $E(s_t) = \{e\}$ and assumed that if the attacker attempt to exploit e it will create a unique security alert z where no other alert will match with alert z. So, if the defender posses belief b and see the alert z, then the belief update allows for the possibility of generated alert is coming from exploit e. Otherwise, if the defender's belief reflects b' and get the alert z it will immediately discard the alert as a false alarm.

Let $Z = \{z_1, z_2, \ldots, z_n\}$ and $Z' = \{z'_1, z'_2, \ldots, z'_n\}$ represent the finite set of security alerts, real and fake network respectively, generated by the IDS which is eventually the observation set for the defender. Each of the alert from real nodes set and fake nodes set can be generated by the IDS, given by the set $Z(e_{ri}) = \{z_{A_i(1)}, z_{A_i(2)}, \ldots, z_{A_i(ai)}\} \in P(Z)$ and $Z(e_{fi}) = \{z_{D_i(1)}, z_{D_i(2)}, \ldots, z_{D_i(di)}\} \in P'(Z)$ where $P(Z)$ and $P'(Z')$ are the power set of Z and Z'. Using this security alerts defender constructs a belief, $b_t \in \Delta S$, where ΔS is the space of probability distribution over security state. The belief state specifies the probability of being in each state given the history of action and observation experienced so far, starting from an initial belief b_0 and belief update procedure is given in the next section.

Defender's Belief Update– For any defense action $u_t = u$ and observation $y_{t+1} = y_k$, the belief update is defined as $b_{t+1} = [T_j(b_t, y_k, u)]_{s_j \in S}$ where (j)'th is the update function, $T_j(b_t, y_k, u) = P(S_{t+1} = s_j \mid U_t = u, Y_{t+1} = y_k, B_t = b_t)$ is given by [14],

$$b_{t+1}^j = T_j(b_t, y_k, u) = \frac{p_j^u(b_t) r_{jk}^u(b_t)}{\rho(b_t, y_k, u)} \tag{7}$$

The above terms are defined below,

$$p_j^u(b_t) = P(S_{t+1} = s_j \mid U_t, B_t) = \sum_{s_i \in S} b_t^i \, p_{ij}^u \tag{8}$$

$$r_{jk}^u(b_t) = P(Y_{t+1} \mid S_{t+1} = s_t, U_t, B_t) = \sum_{s_i \in S} b_t^i \, r_{ijk}^u \tag{9}$$

$$\rho(b_t, y_k, u) = P(Y_{t+1} \mid U_t, B_t) = \sum_{s_j \in S} r_{jk}^u(b_t) \, p_j^u(b_t) \tag{10}$$

where p_{ij}^u is the transition probability from state s_i to s_j under defense action u, and $r_{jk}^u(b_t) = P(Y_{t+1} \mid S_{t+1} = s_t, U_t = u, B_t = b_t)$ is the probability that IDS will generate observation vector y_k when transitioning from state s_i to state s_j under a defense action u. Equation (8) defines the trajectory of beliefs based on security alerts termed as observations and series of actions. Under a defense action u, transition probability s_i to s_j is controlled by a set of exploit events. For the available set of exploits from Eq. (1), each event in the set of exploit is in binary form (successful and unsuccessful).

The belief update procedure is a controlled Markov Chain where control is defender's action [14]. The majority of POMDP planning methods operate under Bayes theorem [15]. For a large scale cyber network, a single Bayes update procedure could be computationally infeasible. To plan efficiently for large-scale POMDP, we adopted the model described in [17] for the approximation of the belief state.

3   Defender's Actions

As soon as the attacker progress through the network defender will take action to limit the attacker's progression. Selection of action step can be improved if defender have some domain knowledge beforehand. To aid with the domain knowledge, we introduce the utility function. Before taking any defensive action it is also necessary to measure the impact on availability and security cost.

3.1   Utility Function

Attacker build an array of node utility function based on the base score metrics for exploiting vulnerabilities [13]. For every exploit, the attacker uses the metrics to justify the attack success probability which is illustrated in Eq. (13) and serves as the attacker's initial knowledge about the network and vulnerability. Defender also create the same utility array. From [13], we borrow the impact (I), and exploitability (V) metrics to define the defender's utility.

$$I = 10.41 * (1 - (1 - CI) * (1 - II) * (1 - AI)) \tag{11}$$

$$V_i = 20 * AC * AI * AV \tag{12}$$

The above terms are defined as CI = ConfImpact, II = IntegImpact, AI = AvailImpact, I = Impact, V_i = Exploitability, AC = AccessComplexity, AI = Authentication and AV = Accessvector. The utility array function is defined below

$$U_{a(r,f)} = I * V_i \tag{13}$$

Example 1: Consider a scenario where there are five nodes and attacker sends scan queries to the neighbors of node 1. Defender needs to respond the scan queries deceptively by mixing of true/false information at random. Here, 2, 3 are real nodes and 4, 5 are fake nodes having following vulnerabilities $vul(n_2)$, $vul(n_3)$, $vul(n_4)$ and $vul(n_5)$. Defender wants to drive the attacker towards node 4 and 5. We are assuming that using above utility array equation defender come up with following values $U_a(n_2) = 15$, $U_a(n_3) = 5$, $U_a(n_4) = 30$, and $U_a(n_5) = 50$. A true rational attacker will go after node 5.

3.2   Cost Function

In cyber-deception, there is a possibility where you can leverage the availability cost over the security cost. There are two benefits of using vyber-deception when the attacker is in the fake network: (1) defender can collect as much as intelligence information on the adversary which helps to derive the attacker's capability, intentions, and targets etc., (2) defender can maximize the network availability to the trusted user during a cyber attack. An availability cost c_a for each action defender could take to drive the adversary towards the fake network. For some defense actions there will be no impact on the availability, and sometimes there will be a greater impact. To formalize this notion, we represent the availability cost $c_a : U \rightarrow \mathbb{R}$ for each defense action taken by the defender similarly for the security cost $c_s : S \times U \rightarrow \mathbb{R}$ to depict the cost while the system is in various security state under defense action u. Here, we are considering the availability of a node regarding end-to-end packet delay (considering IT system). If the delay exceeds the limit, the node will still available but legitimate users could not able take services. For instance, the delay in practice can be the time it takes a user to begin to interacting with the page, or the time it takes to completely load the whole content of the page, which defines the availability factor.

End-to-End Packet Delay. Packet starts journey from a host (source), passes through a series of routers and ends it journey in another host (destination) [12]. Lets assume that, d_E and N represents total delay and number devices between a source and destination. The end-to-end delay defined in [8] as

$$d_E = N(d_{proc} + d_{trans} + d_{prop} + d_{queue}) + d_{proco} \tag{14}$$

The above equation's terms are defined as following d_{proc} = processing delay, d_{trans} = transmission delay, d_{prop} = propagation delay, d_{queue} = queuing delay and d_{proco} = processing overhead because of authentication, integrity and confidentiality. For an uncongested enterprise network, $d_{queue} \simeq 0$ and the distance between source and destination node is very small so that $d_{prop} \simeq 0$. The processing delay, d_{proc}, is often negligible; however, it strongly influences a router's maximum throughput, which is the maximum rate at which a router can forward packets [12]. So that, Eq. (14) can be reduced to

$$d_E = N \times d_{trans} \tag{15}$$

where $d_{trans} = L/R$, L = packet size and R = transmission rate.

For every defense action defender will measure the total end-to-end packet delay. So, the availability cost in terms of delay is defined as following $c_u = d_E$. We assign more cost to the goal conditions (attacker's target node) as defender's goal is to keep away the attacker from achieving the goal. The total cost in terms of a security state and defense action is given below

$$c(s_t, u_t) = (1 - f)c_s(s_t, u_t) + f * d_E(u_t) \qquad (16)$$

Here, f (weighted factor) determines which cost focused more where f = 0 represents defender is concerned only with security cost, $f = 1$ means defender is only concerned with availability cost. The proposed online deception algorithm, based on an existing online solver [17], computes the optimal action from deception standpoint to deceive the attacker with fake network while balancing availability and security cost.

Algorithm 1. Defender's Belief Update Algorithm

Initialize: n_k, $\mathfrak{B}_{t+1} = U_{a(r,f)}$, numAdded = 0

1: **procedure** BELIEFUPDATE($\mathfrak{B}_t, u_r, y_r$)
2:     **while** $numAdded < n_k$ **do**
3:         $(s) \sim \mathfrak{B}_t$
4:         $(s'y, -) \sim G(s, u_r)$
5:         **if** $y^{Z(s)} = y_r^{Z(s)}$ **then** [If alerts Z(s) match]
6:             $\mathfrak{B}_{t+1} \leftarrow \mathfrak{B}_{t+1} \cup \{s'\}$
7:             $numAdded \leftarrow numAdded + 1$

---

4 Online Deception Algorithm

Although embedding state space on the dependency graph allows us to accurately quantify the level of progression of the attacker but still computing the optimal deceptive action is a challenge where high diemsionality [19] of deception actions are present while interacting with the attacker. Offline POMDP solver is a way to compute the optimal action for each belief state before runtime. Although such solvers have improved their efficiency, capturing the optimal action can be intractable for large networks. To resolve this issue, Silver and Veness [17] developed an online algorithm termed as Partially Observable Monte-Carlo Planning (POMCP) to handle large-scale network while computing optimal action. Online methods interleave the computation and execution (runtime) phases of a policy [14], yielding a much more scalable approach than offline methods.

POMCP algorithm is based on and makes use of POMDP [11]. There are two types of nodes in POMCP: belief nodes and action nodes where belief nodes represent a belief state and action nodes are the children nodes of belief nodes that can be reached by doing an action. In this work, action selection procedure

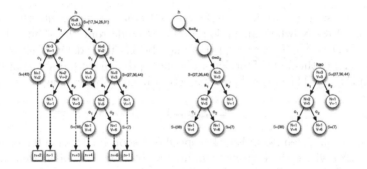

Fig. 3. An illustration of POMCP in an environment with 2 actions, 2 observations, 50 states, and no intermediate rewards. The agent constructs a search tree from multiple simulations, and evaluates each history by its mean return (left). The agent uses the search tree to select a real action a, and observes a real observation o (middle) [17].

is as same as POMCP algorithm described in [17] and belief update procedure is modified based on [14] where it solves the large observation space problem. Modified belief update procedure is given in Algorithm 1, where $\mathfrak{B}_t$ is a state-action pair named particles. The action selection step involves Monte-Carlo simulation from the current belief state to assess the quality of various deception action. An agent begins the simulation by calling a generative model provides a sample successor state, observation and cost given a state and action, $(s',y,c) \sim G(s,u)$. Calling generative model and successive sampling from the current belief creates histories of search tree Fig. 3 **Monte-Carlo Tree Search (MCTS)** uses Monte-Carlo simulation for assessing search tree nodes [5]. In the search tree nodes represent histories and branches from the node in forwarding direction represents the possible future histories because of having partial observability of the fundamental process. A simpler version of MCTS uses greedy tree policy in the very beginning of the simulation, where it selects the action with the highest value. To improve the greedy action selection, UCT algorithm [10] is used. In the search tree, each action selection is done using UCB1 [4] and state is being viewed as multi-armed bandit rule to balance the exploration and exploitation. In the UCT algorithm, there is an option to use the domain knowledge [10] to initialize the new nodes. We use the utility array function U_{ar} as our initial domain knowledge which is improved during more simulation runs. The optimum action for the defender while interacting with the attacker turns into a POMDP. Casting optimum action is defined as below,

$$V^{\pi}(b_0) = \sum_{t=0}^{\infty} \gamma^t c(b_t, u_t)$$

$$= \sum_{t=0}^{\infty} \gamma^t E\big[c(s_t, u_t)\big|\, b_0, \pi\big]$$

(17)

where $0 < \gamma < 1$ is the discount factor and $c(b_t, u_t)$ represents the cost for each belief state b_t when an action u_t is selected from the space of action where $c(b_t, u_t) = \sum_{s_i \in S} b_t^i c(s_t, u_t)$. For each belief state, defense action generates according to the policy function and belief update must follow the procedure defined in Eq. (7). The optimal policy π^* is obtained by optimizing the long-term cost.

$$\pi^* = \arg\min_{\pi} V^{\pi}(b_0) \tag{18}$$

The optimal policy defined in Eq. (18) specifies the optimal action for each belief state $b_t \in \Delta S$ where the expected minimum expected cost calculated over the infinite time horizon. The defender will chose the action where the cost makes trade-off between availability and security cost.

In POMCP, a belief state updates when a sample observation matches with real-world observation, but for large observation space, it barely matches with real-world observation. In the modified belief update procedure presented in Algorithm 1, check a statement whether each incoming alert $z_i \in Z$ match with over a security state, $Z(s) = Z(e)$. The alerts are generated whenever an attacker attempts an exploit. Alerts not in $Z(s)$ cannot be generated by exploit activity for that security state. We refer those alerts are false alarms for the defender.

To evaluate the scalability of our approach, we experimented our online deception algorithm on a graph consisting 160 conditions (nodes), 150 exploits (hyperedges), 60 defense actions, 35 security alerts resulting more than 10^9 observation vectors. The resulting security states from this example exceed 100 million.

5   Experimental Results and Discussion

To evaluate the scalability of our approach, we experimented our online deception algorithm on a graph consisting 160 conditions (nodes), 150 exploits (hyperedges), 60 defense actions, 35 security alerts resulting more than 10^9 observation vectors. The resulting security states from this example exceed 100 million. In this simulation, we assume that attacker is a true rational type where his aggression, knowledge, and stealthiness are moderate, high and high respectively. Using the state-based alert correlation we creates a probability table for alert detection with assumed attacker type where column represents exploit activity and rows are triggered alert. The probability of detection table is not presented here due to high volume of dataset.

Under null defender's action, the probability of attacking real nodes and fake nodes are same. For this simulation, we assume that the exploit dependency graph is already generated using TVA (Topological Vulnerability Analysis) [14]. We use the [7] software package to use the POMCP solver in our simulation and use python and MatLAB to implement our model. Attacker's progression depends on the defender's action and we assume that defender moves first with null action and wait for the attacker to proceed. In this simulation, we use the sample exploit dependency graph presented in Fig. 4 to evaluate our approach

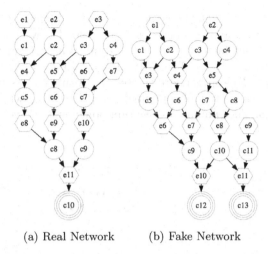

(a) Real Network   (b) Fake Network

Fig. 4. A sample Exploit Dependency graph with real network (left) and fake network (right). The above dependency graph for real network $H = (N, E)$ consists of $n_{c_r} = 10$ security conditins and $n_{e_r} = 11$ exploits (in the form of hyperedges). Triple-encirled nodes are represent as goal conditions $N_r^g = \{c_{10}\}$ and $N_f^g = \{c_{12}, c_{13}\}$.

and present our simulation results. Attack probabilities for each of the exploit under assumed true rational attacker type,

$$(\overline{P}_{er_k}, \underline{P}_{er_k} = (0.8, 0.3) \quad for \quad er_k \in E_0$$
$$(\overline{P}_{ef_k}, \underline{P}_{ef_k} = (0.8, 0.3) \quad for \quad ef_k \in E_0$$
$$(\overline{P}_{er_k}, \underline{P}_{er_k} = (0.7, 0.3) \quad for \quad er_k \in \{e_4, e_5, e_6, e_8, e_9\}$$
$$(\overline{P}_{ef_k}, \underline{P}_{ef_k} = (0.9, 0.7) \quad for \quad ef_k \in \{e_5, e_7\}$$
$$(\overline{P}_{er_k}, \underline{P}_{er_k} = (0.6, 0.4) \quad for \quad er_k \in \{e_7, e_{10}, e_{11}\}$$
$$(\overline{P}_{ef_k}, \underline{P}_{ef_k} = (0.9, 0.8) \quad for \quad ef_k \in \{e_7, e_8\}$$

similarly, probability of success are,

$$\alpha_{er_k} = \begin{Bmatrix} 0.7 \; when \; er_k \in E_0 \\ 0.5 \; when \; er_k \in E \backslash E_0 \end{Bmatrix}$$

$$\alpha_{ef_k} = \begin{Bmatrix} 0.85 \; when \; ef_k \in E_0 \\ 0.7 \;\; when \; ef_k \in E \backslash E_0 \end{Bmatrix}$$

As we defined earlier, the space of actions is the power set of each defense action. In this simulation, we consider three actions for real network which induce a set of block exploits defined as, $B(u^1) = \{e_1, e_2, e_3\}$, $B(u^2) = \{e_4, e_5, e_6, e_7, e_8\}$,

$B(u^3) = \{e_9, e_{10}, e_{11}\}$. Similarly for fake network two actions, $B(u^1) = \{e_5, e_7\}$, $B(u^2) = \{e_7, e_8\}$ where the cost of each action is 0.30. The weight cost in Eq. (16) is 0.5 and the discount factor $\gamma = 0.95$. In total (real & fake) there are $n_s = 356$ security states and $n_z = 12$ security alerts leading to $2^{12} = 4096$ distinct observation vectors. To approximate the belief, all simulations use particles $n_k = 1500$. The sample evolution of computed deception policy when $N_{Sim} = 5000$ is given in Fig. 5, 6. The computed deception policy is intuitive.

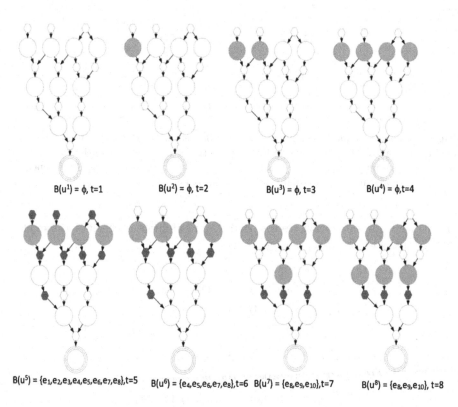

Fig. 5. Sample evolution of deception policy when attacker is in real network. Security state is represented by shaded node and blocked exploits are represented by red shaped hyperedge. (Color figure online)

It is assumed that the security state starts from the empty state defined as, $s_0 = \phi$. The defender uses utility array function to construct the initial belief which is defined in Eq. (13). We run the simulation for 5000 times. The defender initially (from t = 1 to t = 4) does not take any action to save the availability cost. As the attacker progress and enable more conditions, defender's belief gradually updates based on the received security alerts. Then defender begins to deploy actions (t = 5) to block exploits. As we know from monotonicity assumption, once a security condition is enabled it remains enabled all the time.

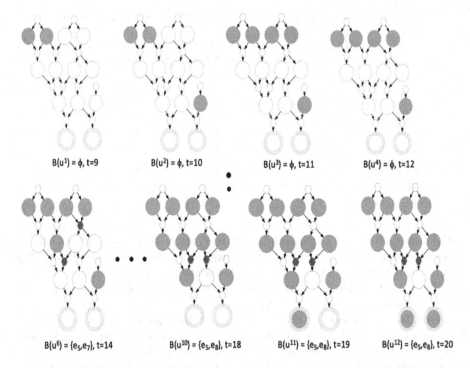

$B(u^1) = \phi, t=9$ $B(u^2) = \phi, t=10$ $B(u^3) = \phi, t=11$ $B(u^4) = \phi, t=12$

$B(u^6) = \{e_5, e_7\}, t=14$ $B(u^{10}) = \{e_5, e_8\}, t=18$ $B(u^{11}) = \{e_5, e_8\}, t=19$ $B(u^{12}) = \{e_5, e_8\}, t=20$

Fig. 6. Sample evolution of deception policy when attacker is in fake network. Security state is represented by shaded node and blocked exploits are represented by red shaped hyperedge. (Color figure online)

Whenever defender's belief reflects that attacker is close to goal conditions, it will block the exploits to prevent the attacker from reaching the goal. As we can see from Fig. 5 at time step t = 8, defender blocks exploits $\{e_8, e_9, e_{10}\}$ which prevents attacker to move forward. From this point, the attacker will try to progress from another point as he received the response from the defender in the reconnaissance stage with a mix of true and false information. Then he moves toward the fake network, Fig. 6, based on his available set of exploits dictated by Eq. (1). At this stage defender let the attacker move forward. From time step t = 9 to 13, defender action is null. As it (fake) is same as the real network from the attacker perspective, the defender will take action only when attacker have an alternative way to reach the next security state (see time steps t = 14–20 in Fig. 6). This way attacker will have more confidence that he is in the right track and ultimately he gains nothing. On the other hand, the defender can save more availability cost and learn the attacker which will increase defender's certainty about attacker.

In Table 1, we present our performance evaluation data while attacker start to exploit real initial nodes vulnerability and ended up with real to real network end state and real to fake end state. The numerical numbers in the 2nd column represent how many times out of 25 sample runs attacker start with real network

Table 1. Performance evaluation table for real to real and real to fake

Simulation runs	Attacker starts with real node	Attacker ends on real node	Attacker ends on fake node
500	15	13	2
1000	13	10	3
1500	11	7	4
2000	10	6	4
3000	8	3	5
4000	7	1	6
5000	6	0	6

initial nodes and 3rd column represents how many times attacker ended up with real network end state without transition to the fake network and 4th column represents how many times attacker make transition from real network to fake network and end up with fake goal state. In Table 2, we presents the same statistics for the fake network.

From Table 2, we can see that up to 76% of the time attacker start with the fake initial nodes and carry out the series of exploit to achieve the fake goal state. When the $N_{Sim} = 500$, out of 25 sample runs 15 times attacker start with the real network (Table 1) and 13 times ended up with real network goal state because of poor quality of possible future histories estimation. When the number of simulation increases and more possible future histories are taken into account, the action estimation quality increased as well as policy function (e.g. $N_{sim} = 5000$, 19 times out of 25 times attacker start and ended up with fake goal state).

Table 2. Performance evaluation table for fake to fake and fake to real

Simulation runs	Attacker starts with fake node	Attacker ends on fake node	Attacker ends on real node
500	10	10	0
1000	12	12	0
1500	14	14	0
2000	15	15	0
3000	17	17	0
4000	18	18	0
5000	19	19	0

In Fig. 7, we plot the discounted cost against each time step for 25 sample runs while attacker in real network state. When $N_{sim} = 500$, 15 times attacker starts with the real network where out of 15 times attacker reached the real goal state (node) 13 times. Trajectories which ended up with red circle represents the path where attacker reached the goal. Initially, for low simulation counts e.g., $N_{sim} = 500$ defender does not have much information about attacker's strategy, capability. Because of this, defender aggressively blocks exploit from the very beginning ($t = 0$) which eventually produces low quality of estimation and ended up with less availability. For poor estimation, attacker also reaches into the goal node several times as shown in Fig. 7 upper left corner. As soon as, simulation count increases more possible future histories are included which results high quality of estimation (which set of exploits to be blocked). As it is evident from Fig. 7 bottom right corner, though attacker starts with real network for 5000 trials but could not reach any goal state.

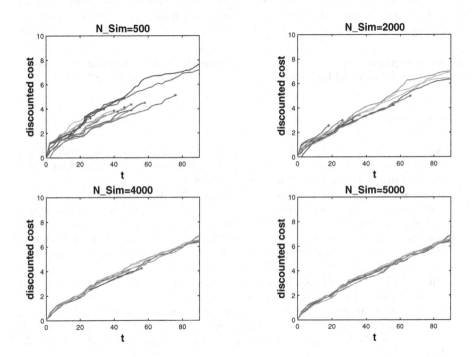

Fig. 7. Discounted cost

6   Conclusion

In this paper, we develop a technique to alter the view of the system with a mix of real and fake information and a cyber deception approach where defender's action influence an attacker to take different attack path while maintaining availability cost and security cost. To do so, we use an exploit dependency graph which describes attacker progression throughout the network. For every cyber defense system, there is a goal to maintain the availability to the trusted user while security is at a satisfactory level. Scalability is achieved via online deception algorithm where it samples from large-scale cyber domain instead of creating the entire state space. Using our approach, a defender not only saves availability cost but also learns the attacker movement in the fake networks. This knowledge will help the defender to make better security planning for the future. One future research direction could be modeling the attacker type so that defender can precisely identify the attacker type based on an attacker knowledge, stealthiness and aggression level. Having the capability of identifying an attacker type will improve the efficiency of a defender to choose the deception algorithm. For example, if the attacker's (knowledge, stealthiness, aggression level) is (low, low and low), and the defender is deploying a deception algorithm for (high, high, moderate) attacker, then the defender is wasting the available resources which is not an efficient way to deal with the attacker. In a resource constraint environment it is very critical to know the attacker type before deploying any deception algorithm.

Acknowledgment. This work is supported by the Office of the Assistant Secretary of Defense for Research and Engineering (OASD (R & E)) agreement FA8750-15-2-0120.

References

1. Achleitner, S., La Porta, T.F., McDaniel, P., Sugrim, S., Krishnamurthy, S.V., Chadha, R.: Deceiving network reconnaissance using sdn-based virtual topologies. IEEE Trans. Network Serv. Manag. **14**(4), 1098–1112 (2017)
2. Albanese, M., Battista, E., Jajodia, S., Casola, V.: Manipulating the attacker's view of a system's attack surface. In: 2014 IEEE Conference on Communications and Network Security (CNS), pp. 472–480. IEEE (2014)
3. Ammann, P., Wijesekera, D., Kaushik, S.: Scalable, graph-based network vulnerability analysis. In: Proceedings of the 9th ACM Conference on Computer and Communications Security, pp. 217–224. ACM (2002)
4. Auer, P., Cesa-Bianchi, N., Fischer, P.: Finite-time analysis of the multiarmed bandit problem. Mach. Learn. **47**(2–3), 235–256 (2002)
5. Coulom, R.: Efficient selectivity and backup operators in Monte-Carlo tree search. In: van den Herik, H.J., Ciancarini, P., Donkers, H.H.L.M.J. (eds.) CG 2006. LNCS, vol. 4630, pp. 72–83. Springer, Heidelberg (2007). https://doi.org/10.1007/978-3-540-75538-8_7
6. Duan, Q., Al-Shaer, E., Jafarian, H.: Efficient random route mutation considering flow and network constraints. In: 2013 IEEE Conference on Communications and Network Security (CNS), pp. 260–268. IEEE (2013)
7. Emami, P., Hamlet, A.J., Crane, C.: Pomdpy: an extensible framework for implementing pomdps in python (2015)
8. Hasan, K., Shetty, S., Hassanzadeh, A., Salem, M.B., Chen, J.: Modeling cost of countermeasures in software defined networking-enabled energy delivery systems. In: 2018 IEEE Conference on Communications and Network Security (CNS), pp. 1–9. IEEE (2018)
9. Jajodia, S., Noel, S.: Topological vulnerability analysis. In: Jajodia, S., Liu, P., Swarup, V., Wang, C. (eds.) Cyber Situational Awareness. ADIS, pp. 139–154. Springer, Boston (2010). https://doi.org/10.1007/978-1-4419-0140-8_7

10. Kocsis, L., Szepesvári, C.: Bandit based Monte-Carlo planning. In: Fürnkranz, J., Scheffer, T., Spiliopoulou, M. (eds.) ECML 2006. LNCS (LNAI), vol. 4212, pp. 282–293. Springer, Heidelberg (2006). https://doi.org/10.1007/11871842_29

11. Kurniawati, H., Hsu, D., Lee, W.S.: Sarsop: efficient point-based pomdp planning by approximating optimally reachable belief spaces. In: Robotics: Science and systems, Zurich, Switzerland, vol. 2008 (2008)

12. Kurose, J., Ross, W.K.: computer Networking: A Top Down Approach. Addison Wesley, Boston (2007)

13. Mell, P., Scarfone, K., Romanosky, S.: A complete guide to the common vulnerability scoring system version 2.0. In: Published by FIRST-Forum of Incident Response and Security Teams, vol. 1, p. 23 (2007)

14. Miehling, E., Rasouli, M., Teneketzis, D.: A pomdp approach to the dynamic defense of large-scale cyber networks. IEEE Trans. Inf. Forensics Secur. 13(10), 2490–2505 (2018)

15. Ross, S., Pineau, J., Paquet, S., Chaib-Draa, B.: Online planning algorithms for pomdps. J. Artif. Intell. Res. 32, 663–704 (2008)

16. Schlenker, A., et al.: Deceiving cyber adversaries: a game theoretic approach. In: Proceedings of the 17th International Conference on Autonomous Agents and MultiAgent Systems, pp. 892–900. International Foundation for Autonomous Agents and Multiagent Systems (2018)

17. Silver, D., Veness, J.: Monte-carlo planning in large pomdps. In: Advances in Neural Information Processing systems, pp. 2164–2172 (2010)

18. Trassare, S.T., Beverly, R., Alderson, D.: A technique for network topology deception. In: Military Communications Conference, MILCOM 2013–2013 IEEE, pp. 1795–1800. IEEE (2013)

19. Ullah, S., Shetty, S., Hassanzadeh, A.: Towards modeling attacker's opportunity for improving cyber resilience in energy delivery systems. In: 2018 Resilience Week (RWS), pp. 100–107, August 2018. https://doi.org/10.1109/RWEEK.2018.8473511

SEVGuard: Protecting User Mode Applications Using Secure Encrypted Virtualization

Ralph Palutke$^{(\boxtimes)}$, Andreas Neubaum, and Johannes Götzfried

Department of Computer Science, Friedrich-Alexander Universität
Erlangen-Nürnberg (FAU), Erlangen, Germany
{ralph.palutke,andreas.neubaum,johannes.goetzfried}@fau.de

Abstract. We present *SEVGuard*, a minimal virtual execution environment that protects the confidentiality of applications based on AMD's *Secure Encrypted Virtualization* (SEV). Although SEV was primarily designed for the protection of VMs, we found a way to overcome this limitation and exclusively protect user mode applications. Therefore, we migrate the application into a hardware-accelerated VM and encrypt both its memory and register state. To avoid the overhead of a typical hypervisor, we built our solution on top of the plain Linux *Kernel Virtual Machine* (KVM) API. With the help of an advanced trapping mechanism, we fully support system and library calls from within the encrypted guest. Furthermore, we allow unmodified code to be transparently virtualized and encrypted by appropriate memory mappings. The memory needed for our minimal VM can be directly allocated within SEVGuard's address space. We evaluated our execution environment regarding correctness and performance, confirming that SEVGuard can be practically used to protect existing legacy applications.

Keywords: AMD SEV · Virtual machine encryption · Confidentiality

1 Introduction

Traditional software protection solutions typically rely on obfuscation to increase the time an attacker needs to reverse engineer the functionality of a software product. Obfuscation, however, only raises the bar for attackers but can eventually be broken. To overcome the limitations of obfuscation, and to provide verifiable security under certain assumptions, emerging technologies such as Intel *Software Guard Extensions* (SGX) [5] and AMD SEV [11] provide *Trusted Execution Environments* (TEEs) on commodity hardware [14].

Although with the *Trusted Platform Module* (TPM) a hardware trust anchor has been available for quite some time, the TPM could never really be practically used for software protection. The reason is that the TPM design only provides a *Static Root of Trust* (SRoT), enabling the verification of a PC's boot process but

© ICST Institute for Computer Sciences, Social Informatics and Telecommunications Engineering 2019
Published by Springer Nature Switzerland AG 2019. All Rights Reserved
S. Chen et al. (Eds.): SecureComm 2019, LNICST 305, pp. 224–242, 2019.
https://doi.org/10.1007/978-3-030-37231-6_12

not of its processes or VM instances. SGX and SEV for the first time provide support for *dynamically* placing software inside so-called *enclaves*, relying on a *Dynamic Root of Trust* (DRoT).

Intel and AMD proposed different approaches for their DRoTs in the recent past that cannot be used interchangeably. While SGX focuses on a per-process RoT, aiming at *Digital Rights Management* (DRM), SEV focuses on the protection of entire VMs, aiming at cloud computing. Although there are projects which provide a unified solution across different TEEs [12,13], none of them provides DRM on top of real SEV hardware. Protecting selected code with SEV is a challenging task as user mode applications need to be transparently virtualized and encrypted.

1.1 Contribution

Our solution was motivated by the question of how to protect existing user mode applications using SEV which is not primarily designed for software protection but for cloud computing. With SEVGuard, we provide an execution environment built on top of AMD SEV that is able to protect existing user mode applications.

In detail, our contributions are:

- while up to now only Intel CPUs through SGX could be used to protect applications from higher privileged attackers, we design a minimal virtual execution environment on top of AMD SEV which also enables AMD CPUs to protect user mode applications.
- to avoid the performance and resource overhead of a typical hypervisor or even an entire guest OS, we rely on the plain KVM API of the Linux kernel. Consequently, we also reduce the *Trusted Computing Base* (TCB) to the minimally required amount of code and data.
- we fully support system calls as well as calls to untrusted shared libraries with the help of an advanced trapping mechanism.
- we set up guest page tables with appropriate mappings to allow unmodified applications to be transparently virtualized. Memory for our minimal VM can be directly allocated within the address space of the SEVGuard process.
- we evaluate our execution environment regarding correctness and performance, confirming that SEVGuard can be used to protect existing legacy code bases.

1.2 Related Work

Prior to the release of SEV, there already existed theoretical approaches for full memory encryption [7] as well as practical software-based implementations for swap space [19], and the encryption of user mode processes based on the Linux kernel [9,17]. Beyond that, *HyperCrypt* provides a hypervisor-based memory encryption of a target system's memory [8].

TEEs have been mentioned in publications about cloud computing [22] and in the context of software protection multiple times. *Haven* [3] was designed to securely run unmodified legacy applications, while *VC3* [20] offers distributed *Map-Reduce* computations that keep the data being processed hidden from cloud providers. *Scone* [2] introduced entirely isolated Linux systems by augmenting Docker containers and *Graphene-SGX* [21] provided a library operating system for unmodified applications. *Opaque* [23] offers confidentiality for database queries by placing parts of a database within a TEE. However, all those solutions build on Intel SGX and do not consider AMD's SEV.

There are solutions which protect software on top of abstracted TEEs [12,13] and can in theory support SGX as well as SEV. Current concrete implementations, however, either rely on simulation or do not implement the SEV back end at all. There is a lot of research regarding SEV's security [6,10,16]. Despite the discovered vulnerabilities, we rely on the security assumptions of SEV and provide an execution environment for the protection of existing user mode applications.

1.3 Outline

The remainder of this paper is structured as follows. First, we give background information which are necessary for the understanding of our approach (Sect. 2). We then present the design (Sect. 3) and implementation (Sect. 4) of SEVGuard and evaluate it regarding correctness and performance (Sect. 5). Finally, we summarize our work and point out future research directions (Sect. 6).

2 Background

We now present necessary background information for the design and implementation of SEVGuard. Readers that are familiar with AMD's SEV (Sect. 2.1) or KVM's ioctl API (Sect. 2.2) may safely skip this section.

2.1 Secure Encrypted Virtualization

SEV provides a mechanism to transparently encrypt the memory of a hardware-based VM. It relies on a cryptographic co-processor, the *Platform Security Processor* (PSP), which is responsible for executing the SEV firmware code. With the help of a hierarchic system of cryptographic keys, a secure channel is established, which is used to transfer further information between the guest owner and the trusted firmware. During the guest's launch, the SEV firmware attests the integrity of the initial VM state by measuring a hash over owner-specified data. The hash is then transferred to the guest owner, who can verify the integrity of the guest. That way, an attacker cannot tamper the guest image prior to its launch. Furthermore, the channel provides the guest owner with the possibility to inject further secret data into the VM without the host being able to interfere. To this end, the SEV firmware decrypts the data, making it accessible to the guest.

The memory encryption itself relies on a processor feature called *Secure Memory Encryption* (SME). SME has been designed to protect a system's memory from a wide variety of physical attacks with the help of an AES hardware engine inside the memory controller. Software can enable the protection on a page granularity by setting the *C-bit* in the corresponding *Page Table Entrys* (PTEs). Upon a software access, the respective memory pages are transparently decrypted by the hardware. For PTEs that have not set the C-bit, the engine does not take any action, so that the general access time for unencrypted memory remains unchanged. The encryption key, generated during each boot process, is managed and isolated solely by the SME firmware. Hence, an attacker trying to physically acquire the protected memory would only read the encrypted data, as the key never leaves the memory controller.

SEV enhances SME's security concept by providing additional protection against software-based attacks that target a hardware-accelerated VM. This allows a guest to be securely isolated even against untrusted hosts or hypervisors. For each VM, the trusted hardware generates a different AES key which can neither be tampered by the host nor any other VM. Like with SME, the memory protection is enabled by setting the C-bit in the guest's private page tables. Independently of the C-bit's state, SEV requires code pages and page tables to be permanently encrypted. This is because any instruction fetch is transparently decrypted. That way, no code can be injected nor manipulated without knowing the VM-specific encryption key. Similarly, the guest page tables must remain encrypted as an attacker could otherwise subvert the memory encryption by disabling selected C-bits. Moreover, *Direct Memory Access* (DMA) to protected guest memory is strictly forbidden, as it would inherently undermine SEV's page table-based protection concept. To launch an SEV-protected VM, software can utilize the SEV firmware via dedicated instructions. Typically, hypervisors provide an ioctl-based interface to allow user mode applications (e.g. QEMU) to execute and manage SEV guests. Due to several attacks against SEV, AMD introduced an extension called *Secure Encrypted Virtualization - Encrypted State* (SEV-ES). In contrast to plain SEV, its successor also encrypts a guest's CPU register state as well as parts of its *Virtual Machine Control Block* (VMCB) (the central control structure to manage a VM) during a context switch to the hypervisor. That way, an attacker has no chance to read or modify guest content. Further details can be found in AMD's processor manuals [1].

2.2   The KVM API

KVM, the build-in hypervisor of modern Linux systems, offers a convenient way of hardware-accelerated virtualization. For AMD CPUs, KVM heavily relies on the usage of its processor extension AMD-V, which provides guest execution at a nearly native performance. Centered around the ioctl mechanism, KVM provides an extensive API for creating, managing and controlling hardware-based VMs without depending on any existing VM implementation. The API serves as an abstraction layer over the architecture-specific virtualization features of a particular processor architecture. User mode tools like *QEMU* and *kvmtool* are typically built on top of KVM's API to manage their guests.

The KVM API can be subdivided into three different classes. Initially, a user mode process requests a handle to the KVM subsystem by opening KVM's device file. The handle is subsequently used to issue *System IOCTLs* to query and modify the whole subsystem. This includes the setup of new VMs that serve guests as execution environments. The creation of a new VM in turn results in a VM-specific descriptor which can then be used to issue *VM IOCTLs*. They are further used to configure attributes that affect a particular VM, e.g. its memory layout. Additionally, they can be used to create and assign *virtual CPUs* (vCPUs) to a respective VM which, yet again, are specified by a resulting vCPU descriptor. These descriptors are used when issuing *vCPU IOCTLs* which control the operation of a specific vCPU and thus the execution of the actual guest code. Due to the hardware acceleration, the guest directly runs on the processor and is only interrupted after the occurrence of certain (configured) events. In this case, a *VMEXIT* is generated and the KVM hypervisor withdraws the processor from the respective VM. Afterwards, control is transferred to a predefined handler routine which is part of the respective host process. To obtain the necessary information about the exit event, KVM provides a vCPU-specific central control structure that is shared between both the host process and the hypervisor. The host then has the chance to query the exit reason and handle the event before resuming the guest's operation. Meanwhile, KVM provides support for SEV-protected VMs via the ioctl interface. KVM forwards these ioctl commands to the SEV firmware through both the DRAM command buffer and the respective MMIO registers. To isolate address spaces of both the host and its VMs, the processor provides *Nested Page Tables* (NPT), a second-level address translation that converts a guest's physical memory into real physical memory. Like with conventional paging, NPT allow a fine-grained configuration of memory access rights that are under control of the hypervisor respectively the host. Any violation results in a trap to the hypervisor which in turn is able to handle the fault.

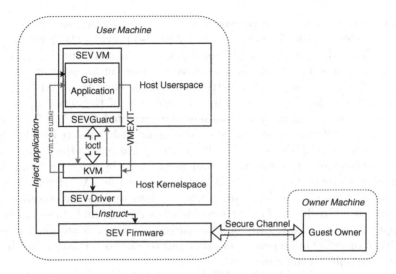

Fig. 1. SEVGuard architecture. The red path shows a context switch from the guest to the host due to the generation of a VMEXIT. The blue path outlines the process of SEVGuard resuming its guest after handling the respective exit event. During the VM's setup, the guest owner has the chance to inject further secrets over a secure communication channel. (Color figure online)

3 Design of SEVGuard

In this section, we present the design of SEVGuard. We first provide an architectural overview and describe the mechanism behind migrating an user-specified application into an SEV-protected VM (Sect. 3.1). We then present the initial memory layout of the lightweight VM (Sect. 3.2). Finally, we illustrate the concept of our host call interface (Sect. 3.3).

3.1 Architectural Overview

The architecture of SEVGuard is based on a lightweight, SEV-protected execution environment that relies on KVM's ioctl API (Fig. 1). We set up a user machine which enables an SEV protected VM to run on top of KVM. To minimize the TCB, we solely rely on KVM's ioctl API in order to set up the virtual execution environment. Subsequently, the SEVGuard process is able to instruct the hypervisor to manage and control the VM. Furthermore, the API can be used to communicate with the SEV driver to make use of the SEV hardware. In addition, we connect an owner machine that is used to deploy an encrypted version of the confidential guest application through an SEV-secured channel.

After copying the confidential application into the minimal VM, SEVGuard subsequently encrypts the guest's initial memory with the help of SEV. Furthermore, several gate functions allow the guest to securely request host functionality, e.g., libraries and system calls. Thus, neither untrusted host libraries nor a kernel need to be mapped or copied into the VM, preventing an attacker from injecting malicious code. The host call interface also provides the guest with the possibility to exchange information despite both its memory and CPU registers are encrypted. In contrast, the host is prevented from invoking arbitrary guest functionality due to the guest's instruction pointer encryption. Although the gates and their related data structures are not part of the actual application (and thus not confidential), they still must be protected from being tampered by an attacker. Otherwise, an attacker could maliciously subvert the gate functions and turn off SEV's protection from within the guest. Hence, the guest owner has the chance to verify the initial guest image by attesting its integrity during SEV's provisioning process before launching the VM. Hereinafter, the encrypted application can be securely injected into the VM by consulting the SEV firmware. Finally, the host process launches the VM and starts to execute the application as a guest. Although our current design does not guarantee the integrity of the SEVGuard process or other parts of the host, this does not breach the confidentiality of the guest.

With the occurrence of a VMEXIT (red path in Fig. 1), KVM withdraws the executing processor from the guest and passes control to the SEVGuard process. After handling the corresponding event, SEVGuard instructs KVM to resume the guest (blue path in Fig. 1).

In summary, SEVGuard fulfills the following design goals:

1. An encrypted application is moved into an SEV-protected VM.
2. The execution environment of the guest is kept as lightweight as possible.
3. The framework provides a mechanism that allows the guest to remotely request untrusted host functionality, e.g., shared libraries or system calls.
4. Direct calls from the untrusted host into the guest are prevented.
5. The integrity of the guest's initial memory layout is verified before its launch.

3.2   Virtual Machine Layout

SEV was originally designed to protect an entire VM including an OS kernel as well as its user mode applications. This requires the emulation of both virtual hardware devices and firmware functionality, as well as the setup of a fairly complex initial guest state. For the purpose of isolating a single user mode application, this would imply a high overhead. Hence, we propose a minimal VM design that only provides the most essential features to enable the trusted execution of confidential applications. Therefore, SEVGuard relies on the use of KVM's ioctl API (Sect. 2.2) which offers the possibility to execute even small code pieces in a sandboxed environment.

After acquiring access to the KVM subsystem, SEVGuard is able to instruct the hypervisor to create a new virtual execution environment. To adapt the VM for our specific use case, SEVGuard specifies a particular memory layout and initial state. To assign some physical memory, the host process allocates several pages and instructs KVM to map them into the VM. The guest memory is initialized with code and data that is required by SEVGuard's host call interface

(Sect. 3.3). Since the mechanism does not contain any confidential secrets, its respective parts can simply be copied into the guest's memory. Nevertheless, the integrity of the entire initial guest memory must be protected prior to enabling SEV's encryption. During the course of the attestation process, this is achieved by generating a hash value and sending it over a secure channel to the guest owner. Therefore, an attacker cannot tamper with the guest code prior to the VM's launch. After verifying the hash measurement, the guest owner deploys the application over the same communication channel, encrypted with its transport key. That way, all confidential secrets are forwarded to the trusted co-processor which decrypts the packet, encrypts its content with the VM's key and securely injects it into the VM. Without the host being able to intervene, the PSP transparently decrypts the secret data every time the guest accesses the underlying memory. To make the guest memory accessible to the user mode code, we set up a four-level paging hierarchy that translates guest virtual addresses into their physical counterparts. Besides memory, we assign multiple vCPUs to the guest VM. The remaining host memory is mapped as non-present, in order to prevent the guest from accidentally accessing untrusted code. To have the possibility to handle certain exit events, we map each vCPU's control structure kvm_run into the address space of the host process. The structure enables SEVGuard to retrieve information about the cause of a VMEXIT. Thus, certain events, e.g. the invocation of host functionality, can be handled by the SEVGuard process. Furthermore, the VM's control registers are configured to enter the guest in long mode with paging enabled. Although x64 processors make little use of segmentation nowadays, it is still necessary to set up a *Global Descriptor Table* (GDT) and appropriately initialize the segment registers on each processor. To make it possible to invoke system calls from within the guest, both an *Interrupt Descriptor Table* (IDT) as well as certain *Model Specific Registers* (MSRs) need to be initialized appropriately (Sects. 3.3 and 4.2). Finally, each vCPU requires its own stack to enable a proper execution of the guest code.

To enable SEV's protection features, the host must properly configure its respective MSRs. Despite our development machine only supporting plain SEV, we implemented SEVGuard as it would already be SEV-ES ready. Its additional security features provide even more protection against secret data leaks (Sect. 2.1). To inform the processor which memory pages need to be decrypted during a guest access, we enable the C-bit in each corresponding PTE. Before launching the guest, our framework instructs the SEV firmware to encrypt most of the guest memory. An exception are some data structures required by the gate functions, as these need to be shared between the host and the guest (Sect. 4.3). Nevertheless, encrypting both the guest's page tables and its code pages were mandatory for its successful execution, as these pages are always decrypted upon access (Sect. 2.1). This is to prevent an attacker from subverting the guest encryption by disabling certain C-bits.

3.3   Host Call Interface

With the VM's initial state set up, SEVGuard can finally instruct KVM to launch the VM via the vmrun instruction. The guest then executes the confidential application until it reaches certain (predefined) events that trigger a VMEXIT. Consequently, KVM passes control to a specified exit handler that is mapped into the SEVGuard process. After retrieving information about the cause of the exit, the host process is able to handle the event and resume the guest. We implemented a method that allows the guest to invoke non-confidential functionality, e.g., system or host library calls. During the invocation of this untrusted functionality, the guest forces a context switch to the host, which executes the desired code and returns the result back to its caller. Due to the guest's memory and register encryption, the host cannot directly access information like a function's target address or its arguments. For the same reason, the host cannot simply write back the result of a function to the respective return register. To exchange information between the host and the guest, we designed a protocol that transfers data through controlled gates using shared memory. These gates serve as a secure way to enter or exit the guest. In the following, we provide further details on either calling untrusted functionality provided by shared libraries (blue path in Fig. 2) or requesting system calls (red path in Fig. 2). On terminating the application, a final VMEXIT is triggered and SEVGuard tears down the VM.

Library Calls. To provide the guest with the possibility to invoke functions of dynamically linked libraries, the framework redirects corresponding calls to a *special Guest Libcall Gate* (GLG). This requires either support from the compiler or rewriting the source/binary of the application. In addition, the guest copies information like a library function's target address and its arguments to a dedicated *Shared Libcall Area* (SLA) which is shared with the host. Special care needs to be taken regarding pointer arguments to guest virtual memory, because these need to be accessible from the host. Therefore, the GLG allocates further unencrypted memory where it copies the referenced data into. As both the host and the guest share the same process space, the host library can simply access the newly allocated memory. After propagating the SLA with the required data, the gate triggers a VMEXIT. The hypervisor subsequently transfers control to a *Host Libcall Gate* (HLG) which is mapped into the SEVGuard process. The HLG further on extracts the guest data from the SLA and natively executes the desired functionality. As the SLA was not encrypted during the initial setup of the VM, it can be directly accessed by the host process. Afterwards, it writes back the result to the same entry of the SLA and instructs KVM to resume the guest. The GLG then copies the result from the SLA to the particular return register and reverts to its caller continuing its initial execution flow.

Alternatively, an application can benefit from a performance increase by statically linking its libraries. As these libraries would also be migrated in the protected VM, calling its functions would not require any context switches to the host anymore. To prevent the guest from being subverted, its owner must strictly ensure the integrity of these libraries, however.

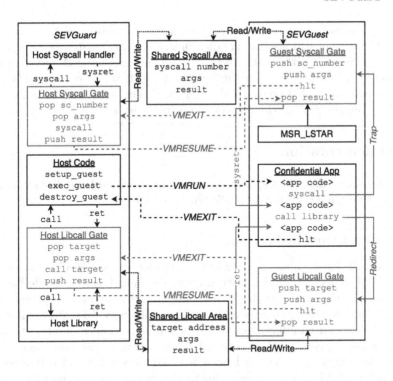

Fig. 2. SEVGuard's host call interface which enables the guest to request untrusted host functionality. The red path visualizes the system call mechanism from inside the guest, while the blue path illustrates the redirection of shared library calls. (Color figure online)

System Calls. Since we assume the entire host to be untrusted, we cannot allow the execution of its kernel inside the guest VM. Furthermore, copying a trusted kernel into the address space of every protected guest application would consume a high amount of memory. Like with library calls, the guest must execute system calls through the host. In contrast to the invocation of a library function, a system call does not require to be rewritten to a wrapper similar to the GLG. The register encryption which takes place with SEV-ES prevents the host from accessing guest registers that contain the actual system call number or its arguments. Therefore, we set up one custom handler for each system call mechanism provided by modern AMD64 processors (Sect. 4.2). Similar to the GLG, these *Guest Syscall Gates* (GSGs) forward a system call's arguments to another shared memory region called the *Shared Syscall Area* (SSA). To prevent the guest from leaking any additional register content, the gates parse the respective system call tables and only pass the relevant registers to the host. The GSG then forces a VMEXIT to transfer control to a *Host Syscall Gate* (HSG). After the context switch, the HSG reads the system call number and the arguments from the SSA, and sets up the appropriate host registers prior to executing the actual system call. This traps to the host kernel's system call handler which invokes the system call specific handler function. After returning from kernel space, the HSG writes the result to the corresponding field of the SSA. It then resumes the guest which continues its execution inside the respective GSG, right after the instruction that triggered the VMEXIT. There, the system call's result is copied from the SSA to the respective return register.

4   Implementation

In this section, we describe the implementation of SEVGuard and discuss selected problems that were particularly challenging to solve.

4.1   Control Flow Redirections

Each time the guest causes a VMEXIT, the processor forces a context switch to the KVM hypervisor, which in turn transfers control to a host-side handler. To limit the performance overhead, we configured KVM to intercept only such events that are necessary to achieve our design goals (Sect. 3.1). Most exit events require a particular handling, before the guest has the chance to retry the faulting operation. Therefore, the processor cannot advance the guest instruction pointer. Nevertheless, SEVGuard must not retry every kind of exit event. In particular, VMEXITs that emerged due to the guest requesting host functionality, must be resumed at the instruction following the trap. Otherwise, the guest would be stuck in an infinite loop. As the guest instruction pointer is encrypted in case of SEV-ES, it cannot manually be modified from outside the VM, however. Therefore, we choose to intercept the `hlt` instruction which automatically advances the instruction pointer, allowing the guest to be resumed accordingly. To enable the guest to call untrusted host functionality, it executes the `hlt` instruction within its gate functions after setting up the appropriate argument registers. This transfers control to the host-side gates, which handle the event and then resume the guest with the `vmresume` instruction.

4.2   System Call Trapping

Modern 64-bit AMD architectures, provide two distinctive ways to invoke a system call. While the first relies on the newer `syscall/sysret` fast call mechanism, the legacy way of issuing software interrupt 0x80 is still available for compatibility reasons. Although directly executing a system call is barely used, some programs might still rely on this possibility, as the system call interface on Linux is built for compatibility. Most applications, however, use the respective system call wrappers provided by shared libraries such as the *Libc*. Nowadays, 64-bit applications typically use the fast call mechanism to avoid the additional costs of a software interrupt. To support both the legacy and the modern way of directly issuing a system call, we had to set up the appropriate system call handlers.

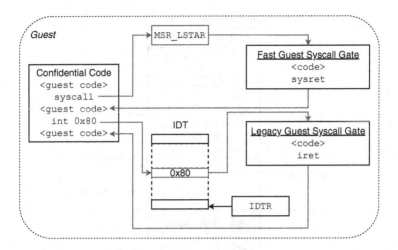

Fig. 3. Guest system call trapping mechanism. The red path shows the modern way to issue a fast system call with the help of `syscall/sysret` and the **LSTAR** MSR. The blue path illustrates the legacy way of issuing software interrupt 0x80 which relies on a properly configured IDT. (Color figure online)

For legacy system calls, we set up a guest-private IDT and assign the address of a custom legacy system call handler to interrupt vector 0x80 (red path in Fig. 3). This handler is denoted as the legacy GSG. In contrast, to enable the guest to support fast system calls, a different setup is required. To save the additional overhead of parsing the IDT, issuing a system call via `syscall` relies on the use of dedicated MSRs (blue path in Fig. 3). Hence, we assign the address of the fast GSG to the **LSTAR** MSR, which specifies the location of the respective system call handler (Sect. 3.3). Moreover, the **STAR** MSR is initialized to declare the appropriate code and stack segment selectors of both the invoked GSG and its caller.

As both mechanisms define their own ABIs for argument passing, the guest needs to parse the appropriate system call table in order to determine which registers to forward to the host. This prevents the guest from leaking any additional register state. After the context switch, the respective HSG sets up the necessary register state and issues the system call with the same mechanism previously used by the guest.

4.3 Reserved Guest Area

To securely transfer information between the SEVGuard process and its protected guest, we designed a precise communication protocol that is based on shared memory (Sect. 3.3). During the launch of the VM, the host prepares a fixed size *Reserved Guest Area* (RGA) within guest memory (see Fig. 4). The area contains non-confidential guest code, e.g., the gate functions, as well as data structures that are used to communicate with the host.

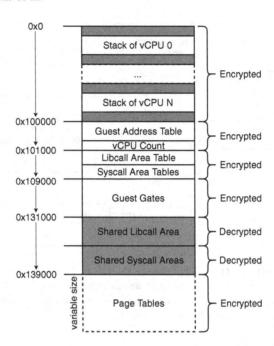

Fig. 4. Layout of the RGA. The grey areas between the guest stacks represent guard pages that serve as a stack overflow protection. The green areas are memory which is shared between the host and its guest. Apart from the shared memory ranges, all remaining guest memory is encrypted with SEV-ES. (Color figure online)

The RGA reserves its first 100 pages for the guest stacks, which are bidirectionally isolated by non-presently mapped guard-pages that mitigate overflows. The actual number and size of these stacks depend on the user's configuration and are dynamically adapted to the number of active vCPUs.

Following the stack area, is the so called *Guest Address Table* (GAT) that is used to reference important code and data like the guest's gate functions. Similar to the *Global Offset Table* (GOT) of an ELF binary, the table serves as a redirection layer to keep certain symbols position independent.

Depending on the guest requesting either a library or system call, necessary data are located in the SLA or the SSA. That way, information like the host function's target address (respectively system call number), a pointer to its arguments (which must also be placed in shared memory), the argument count as well as its return value, is made accessible to the host. As SEVGuard provides its guest with the possibility to issue both fast and legacy system calls (Sect. 4.2), the RGA offers one separate SSA for each mechanism. For each vCPU, both the SLA and the SSAs supply only one entry, because a vCPU is fully suspended upon a VMEXIT. This ensures multiple vCPUs do not interfere with each other. To access the correct entry, the guest must first determine the ID of the currently running vCPU. Since the guest cannot consult the host to find out about the ID, we introduced further data structures within the RGA. These are called the *Libcall Area Table* (LAT) respectively the *Syscall Area Tables* (SATs). Each entry of these tables represents an index into one of the shared areas and provides the address range of a particular guest stack. The actual code and data of the guest gates are placed in the RGA's *Guest Gates* section. The guest's page tables directly follow the RGA. Since they have a variable size which depends on the number of maximum supported page tables, they cannot be included into the RGA.

To facilitate the host to access the relevant data during a host call, the shared areas must stay unencrypted. The remaining RGA is encrypted with the VM's AES key during its setup. To locate the appropriate shared area entry, a guest gate compares the stack pointer register of the current vCPU with the stack ranges provided by the respective area table entries. As each stack is exclusively assigned to a specific vCPU, a match determines its ID and thus the index into the respective shared area. On the host-side, a gate determines the relevant shared area entry by simply querying KVM for the ID of the vCPU that caused the trap. Like before, the ID serves the host as an index into one of the shared areas. Having access to the entry, the host checks the presence of a host call by verifying its target address or system call number. In case of a valid value, the host assumes an HLT event induced by the guest, and thus a host call. Otherwise, the `hlt` instruction was legitimately executed by the application. After returning from the host, the guest clears the whole entry to mark the call as resolved.

5   Evaluation

In this section, SEVGuard is evaluated regarding correctness and performance. To this end, we protect small example applications using SEVGuard. Our experiments were performed on a standard server machine with an AMD EPYC CPU (AMD EPYC 7301) and 128 GB of RAM. As a host operating system, we used an unmodified installation of Ubuntu 18.04.1 LTS 64-bit with an SEV-patched Linux kernel (version 4.16.0-sev).

5.1   Correctness

To show SEVGuard's ability to correctly protect the confidentiality of an application, we deployed pseudo-confidential test data to the guest's physical memory. More precisely, we launched guest code that generates successive strings with a length of 100 bytes on its heap. We then acquired the system's physical memory with the *Linux Memory Extractor* (LiME) (version 4.13.0-32-generic). As LiME currently does not support the acquisition of selected address ranges, we were forced to dump the entire physical memory of the host. By loading LiME's kernel module with the format specifier `padded`, a memory dump, which pads all non-System RAM ranges, is created. This has the advantage, that all RAM ranges match their exact location in the physical memory. For verification purposes, the guest provides the base addresses of the strings to the host. Based on these addresses, we calculate the corresponding offsets within the memory dump and analyze their respective values.

Our results revealed that none of the target strings appeared within any of our memory dumps. To ensure the presence of the test data, we subsequently decrypted the relevant parts of the dumps via SEV's debug mode. Eventually, we verified that the test data were indeed correctly located in the memory images. We therefore conclude, that our implementation correctly encrypts guest physical memory using SEV's protection features.

5.2   Performance

Due to the hardware-accelerated virtualization, guest code almost executes with native performance. However, we expect SEVGuard to introduce a small performance overhead that should mainly originate from its redirection mechanism as well as the additional time to bootstrap a VM. To evaluate the exact overhead, we compared the performance of different applications regarding both their native and virtualized execution. In this context, we evaluated the overhead factor of SEVGuard in comparison to the application's native performance. For a preferably realistic measurement, we evaluated both computationally and I/O intensive programs. All test applications were executed with a `nice` value of -20 which constitutes the highest possible process priority on Linux systems. Each application was executed single-threaded, pinned to a single CPU core during the entire measurement. For maximum precision, we used the *high resolution clock* introduced with the *chrono* namespace of the C++ standard. Although we kept the system mostly idle during the measurements, we chose a clock that delivers the *wall* time, as this method provides the most realistic results. As the TCB and the memory consumption of a full-featured guest operating system would violate our design goals, we forego to include this scenario into our performance evaluation. However, we expect the boot phase of a full guest to be more time consuming. On the contrary, the execution of the confidential application itself should finish faster due to the lack of context switches between the guest and the host during system and library calls.

Compared to the launch time of a natively executed application, SEVGuard requires the setup of a minimal virtualized execution environment. Our experiments revealed that the startup of an application running on top of SEVGuard, only requires 6.1 s. This includes the guest's initial memory encryption and attestation measurements using debugging keys. Especially for long living processes, e.g. server applications, this additional startup overhead appears neglectable.

Besides the guest's general startup time, we measured the round trip time of a set of context switches from the guest to the host and back to the guest. For this, we considered a host gate that instantly resumes the guest. We found out, that the round trip time equals 0.24 ms which amounts to at most *4,176 host calls per second*.

To measure the performance of a CPU intensive application, we wrote a small program that adds the first 10 billion numbers within a loop. For the evaluation of an I/O intensive task, we developed a benchmark application that prints out

Table 1. Performance evaluation for both CPU and I/O intensive tasks that were executed natively and on top of SEVGuard.

Task	Measurement	Native	SEVGuard	Overhead factor
CPU intensive	Total run time	30.6 s	34.9 s	0.14
	Plain run time	29.7 s	30.3 s	0.02
	Add operations	336/μs	330/μs	0.02
I/O intensive	Total run time	27.5 s	285.8 s	9.39
	Plain run time	23.0 s	279.4 s	11.15
	Library calls	434,782/s	3,584/s	120.31

the numbers instead of adding them up. This time, however, we limited the range to the first million numbers due to the long run time of the benchmark. Observing the CPU load, we could verify that the processes claim their core 100% during execution. We evaluated the applications' performance regarding both total execution time and the plain duration of their run times (from executing vmrun to the last VMEXIT). Furthermore, we measured the number of add operations respectively library calls in a given time frame. Table 1 lists the results of our measurements averaged over ten runs.

With native execution, the CPU intensive task performs up to *336 additions per microsecond*. Running the application on top of SEVGuard, *330 additions per microsecond* could be achieved. This leads to a reduction of add operations of about *2%* which basically results from library calls that originate from the use of the timer or the final output to the console. Excluding the overhead of a particular launch, the application natively runs for 29.7 s. Using SEVGuard's protection, the process runs 30.3 s. Consequently, this results in an overhead of only *2%* compared to the native performance. Taking the launch of both the native and the virtualized environments into account, the native environment has a total run time of 30.6 s, while the usage of SEVGuard requires 34.9 s, resulting in an overhead of *14%*. The results confirm our initial expectations, namely that the main overhead occurs from SEVGuard's redirection mechanism. The arithmetic task does not require a lot of host calls.

The evaluation of the I/O benchmark revealed a native run time (excluding its launch) of 23.0 s. However, the execution on top of SEVGuard required 279.4 s. This means an overhead factor of *11.15*. In terms of the number of required function calls per second, the native environment facilitates the execution of *434,782* calls, while SEVGuard only achieved *3,584* calls (call reduction of factor *120.31*). As expected, this number is only marginally lower than the upper bound of 4,176 transitions per second. Finally, the total run time requires 27.5 s under native execution and 285.8 s using SEVGuard. Therefore, the results of the I/O evaluation reveal an overhead factor of *9.39*. This comes from the guest's heavy use of the printf function together with the fact that each of these calls requires a context switch to the host and back to the guest. Note that this test case provides a worst case scenario, since typical applications request host functionality way less frequently.

6   Conclusion and Future Work

To conclude, we give an outlook over future research directions (Sect. 6.1) and summarize our work (Sect. 6.2).

6.1   Future Work

We restricted our research to virtualize single-threaded applications. While SEV-Guard theoretically supports multi-threaded executables, the guest does currently not provide any sort of synchronization mechanism. Furthermore, our implementation does not support applications that make use of object-oriented features like polymorphism based on the concept of virtual address tables. This is because polymorphism would require the guest to dynamically resolve the actual target address. Similarly, an application cannot use library callbacks as these need the host to directly invoke guest functionality, which is strictly forbidden by our current design. Also, the use of dynamically loaded libraries via dlopen(3) is not supported at the moment.

The current SEVGuard implementation restricts its use to the protection of entire applications. However, typically not all parts of an application are considered confidential. Thus, isolating individual parts might sometimes be preferred and would further diminish the TCB. Similar to Intel SGX, the guest owner would have to specify the confidential parts and make sure that solely those parts are shifted into the VM. As SEV-ES encrypts the guest instruction pointer, a protected VM can either be launched or resumed. Thus, the guest can only be entered at the same address it previously exited. To support library callbacks or enable the host to call functions within the encrypted VM, the guest must implement a secure dispatching mechanism. Using shared memory, the host could provide the guest with the requested target address and prompt the dispatcher to call the corresponding function. The implementation of such a dispatcher is part of future work.

In addition to the current standalone solution, SEVGuard could be combined with platform independent TEE frameworks like Google Asylo [18] or Microsoft Open Enclave [15]. Those frameworks currently support Intel's SGX and aim to support ARM TrustZone in the near future. Thus, SEVGuard could be implemented as an SEV back end for both Asylo and Open Enclave.

To get a better understanding of the usability and effectiveness of our prototype, further evaluations regarding performance and security need to be conducted. In this respect, a direct comparison between both SEVGuard and similar projects that build upon Intel SGX seems of particular interest. While our current performance evaluation gives a first insight about best and worst case scenarios, considering everyday applications would provide a more realistic picture. Eventually, the resilience of SEVGuard's host call interface should be verified against malicious hosts which falsify responses to the guest (e.g. Iago attacks [4]).

6.2   Conclusion

In this paper, we presented SEVGuard, a novel approach to protect the confidentiality of selected user mode applications. Based on AMD's hardware virtualization extensions, we leverage KVM's ioctl API to manage and control lightweight VMs that serve the confidential applications as virtual execution environments. The implementation relies on the encryption features of AMD SEV to shield the guest from higher privileged software layers and guarantee code and data confidentiality. To provide the guest with the possibility to invoke both library and system calls, we introduce a host call interface that redirects the execution flow to the host. To give a better understanding of the internals of our prototype, we provided insight into the most important implementation specifics. We demonstrated that SEVGuard can be practically deployed to correctly protect an application's confidentiality, while keeping its performance overhead and resource consumption reasonably low. Finally, we listed several improvements to enhance the functionality of SEVGuard.

Acknowledgments. We would like to thank Felix Freiling for his helpful comments and productive suggestions. This work was supported by the German Research Foundation (DFG) as part of the Transregional Collaborative Research Centre "Invasive Computing" (SFB/TR 89).

References

1. AMD: Amd64 architecture programmer's manual volume 2: system programming. AMD Developer Zone (2018). https://support.amd.com/TechDocs/24593.pdf
2. Arnautov, S., et al.: SCONE: secure Linux containers with Intel SGX. In: 12th USENIX Symposium on Operating Systems Design and Implementation, OSDI (2016)
3. Baumann, A., Peinado, M., Hunt, G.C.: Shielding applications from an untrusted cloud with haven. In: 11th USENIX Symposium on Operating Systems Design and Implementation, OSDI (2014)
4. Checkoway, S., Shacham, H.: Iago attacks: why the system call API is a bad untrusted RPC interface. In: ASPLOS, vol. 13, pp. 253–264 (2013)
5. Costan, V., Devadas, S.: Intel SGX explained. IACR Cryptology ePrint Archive (2016). http://eprint.iacr.org/2016/086
6. Du, Z., et al.: Secure encrypted virtualization is unsecure. CoRR (2017). http://arxiv.org/abs/1712.05090
7. Duc, G., Keryell, R.: CryptoPage: an efficient secure architecture with memory encryption, integrity and information leakage protection. In: 22nd Annual Computer Security Applications Conference (ACSAC 2006), 11–15 December 2006, Miami Beach, Florida, USA, pp. 483–492 (2006)
8. Götzfried, J., Dörr, N., Palutke, R., Müller, T.: Hypercrypt: hypervisor-based encryption of kernel and user space. In: 11th International Conference on Availability, Reliability and Security, ARES 2016, Salzburg, Austria, 31 August–2 September 2016, pp. 79–87. IEEE Computer Society (2016)

9. Götzfried, J., Müller, T., Drescher, G., Nürnberger, S., Backes, M.: RamCrypt: kernel-based address space encryption for user-mode processes. In: Proceedings of the 11th ACM on Asia Conference on Computer and Communications Security, ASIACCS 2016, pp. 919–924. ACM, New York (2016)
10. Hetzelt, F., Buhren, R.: Security analysis of encrypted virtual machines. In: Proceedings of the 13th ACM SIGPLAN/SIGOPS International Conference on Virtual Execution Environments, VEE 2017, Xi'an, China, 8–9 April 2017, pp. 129–142. ACM (2017). https://doi.org/10.1145/3050748.3050763
11. Kaplan, D., Powell, J., Woller, T.: AMD memory encryption. Technical report, AMD, April 2016. http://developer.amd.com/wordpress/media/2013/12/AMD_Memory_Encryption_Whitepaper_v7-Public.pdf
12. Lazard, T., Götzfried, J., Müller, T., Santinelli, G., Lefebvre, V.: TEEshift: protecting code confidentiality by selectively shifting functions into tees. In: Proceedings of the 3rd Workshop on System Software for Trusted Execution, SysTEX 2018, pp. 14–19. ACM (2018). https://doi.org/10.1145/3268935.3268938. http://doi.acm.org/10.1145/3268935.3268938
13. Lefebvre, V., Santinelli, G., Müller, T., Götzfried, J.: Universal trusted execution environments for securing SDN/NFV operations. In: Doerr, S., Fischer, M., Schrittwieser, S., Herrmann, D. (eds.) Proceedings of the 13th International Conference on Availability, Reliability and Security, ARES 2018, Hamburg, Germany, 27–30 August 2018, pp. 44:1–44:9. ACM (2018). https://doi.org/10.1145/3230833.3233256
14. Maene, P., Götzfried, J., de Clercq, R., Müller, T., Freiling, F., Verbauwhede, I.: Hardware-based trusted computing architectures for isolation and attestation. IEEE Trans. Comput. **67**, 361–374 (2017)
15. Microsoft: Open enclave SDK (2019). https://openenclave.io/sdk
16. Morbitzer, M., Huber, M., Horsch, J., Wessel, S.: SEVered: subverting AMD's virtual machine encryption. In: Stavrou, A., Rieck, K. (eds.) Proceedings of the 11th European Workshop on Systems Security, EuroSec@EuroSys 2018, Porto, Portugal, 23 April 2018, pp. 1:1–1:6. ACM (2018). https://doi.org/10.1145/3193111.3193112
17. Peterson, P.: Cryptkeeper: improving security with encrypted RAM. In: 2010 IEEE International Conference on Technologies for Homeland Security (HST), pp. 120–126, November 2010
18. Porter, N.: Asylo: an open-source framework for confidential computing (2018). https://cloudplatform.googleblog.com/2018/05/Introducing-Asylo-an-open-source-framework-for-confidential-computing.html
19. Provos, N.: Encrypting virtual memory. In: 9th USENIX Security Symposium, Denver, Colorado, USA, 14–17 August 2000
20. Schuster, F., et al.: VC3: trustworthy data analytics in the cloud using SGX. In: IEEE Symposium on Security and Privacy, SP 2015, San Jose, CA, USA, pp. 38–54. IEEE Computer Society (2015). https://doi.org/10.1109/SP.2015.10
21. Tsai, C., Porter, D.E., Vij, M.: Graphene-SGX: a practical library OS for unmodified applications on SGX. In: USENIX Annual Technical Conference (2017)
22. Übler, D., Götzfried, J., Müller, T.: Secure remote computation using Intel SGX. In: Sicherheit, Schutz und Zuverlässigkeit (SICHERHEIT 2018), Bonn. Gesellschaft für Informatik (GI) (2017)
23. Zheng, W., Dave, A., Beekman, J.G., Popa, R.A., Gonzalez, J.E., Stoica, I.: Opaque: an oblivious and encrypted distributed analytics platform. In: 14th USENIX Symposium on Networked Systems Design and Implementation, NSDI (2017)

Blockchains and IoT

A Behavior-Aware Profiling of Smart Contracts

Xuetao Wei[1](✉), Can Lu[1], Fatma Rana Ozcan[1], Ting Chen[2], Boyang Wang[1], Di Wu[3], and Qiang Tang[4]

[1] University of Cincinnati, Cincinnati, USA
weix2@ucmail.uc.edu
[2] University of Electronic Science and Technology of China, Qingdao, China
[3] Hunan Univeristy, Changsha, China
[4] New Jersey Institute of Technology, Newark, USA

Abstract. The inception of blockchain techniques has been revolutionizing various domains, e.g., Internet of Things, supply chain and healthcare. Ethereum smart contracts emerge as the promising blockchain application, which could enable distrustful parties to participate in the automatic and trustful transactions. Given the increasing importance of Ethereum smart contracts, understanding them becomes imperative. However, prior work only studied smart contracts with general high-level patterns, and one critical question has not been answered yet: *how do smart contracts behave individually?* In this paper, we present a behavior-aware profiling of individual smart contract from a multi-party perspective, which improves the visibility of the smart contract ecosystem. We conduct a detailed study of the behavior of individual smart contract on two real-world datasets, and our profiling reveals interesting and surprising observations. For example, a few contract completion chains have more than 50 contracts and all of them belong to the **Finance** category. We also discuss the implications that lead to recommendations to improve the security and performance of the smart contract ecosystem. Overall, our work effectively complements previous work towards generating a comprehensive understanding of smart contracts.

Keywords: Smart contracts · Profiling · Behavior

1 Introduction

The blockchain is a disruptive technology that attracts significant attention from both academia and industry. It could serve as the infrastructure of various domains, including Internet of Things, supply chain, and healthcare [16]. Such popularity can attribute to its decentralized and immutable nature.

In the seminal paper [13], Nakamoto advocated the Bitcoin network, which truthfully transfers the cryptocurrency among distrustful participants. The consensus among distrustful participants is reached through the Proof of Work protocol [13]. Since then, the advances of blockchain technologies ignite the passion

© ICST Institute for Computer Sciences, Social Informatics and Telecommunications Engineering 2019
Published by Springer Nature Switzerland AG 2019. All Rights Reserved
S. Chen et al. (Eds.): SecureComm 2019, LNICST 305, pp. 245–258, 2019.
https://doi.org/10.1007/978-3-030-37231-6_13

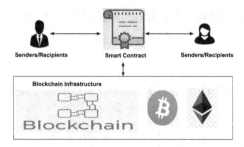

Fig. 1. A smart contract includes three parties: senders, recipients and the blockchain infrastructure

for creating various types of cryptocurrencies [12]. However, the potential of blockchain technologies is far beyond cryptocurrencies. In order to extend its broader impact and enable new applications, smart contracts were invented to implement contractual activities into computer programming codes running on top of the blockchain [15]. The execution of smart contracts totally depends on the programmable codes, which cannot be altered once they are deployed onto the blockchain. Participants of smart contracts from multiple parties strictly follow contractual rules regardless of whether they trust each other. The invention of smart contracts enables people to take advantage of the blockchain infrastructure to facilitate societal activities, which unleash many benefits without the centralized settings.

Given the increasing importance of smart contracts, it is imperative to understand them first before we can assess, reason and manage them. Several efforts have focused on analyzing the blockchain and smart contracts in general, e.g., reporting general high-level trends and patterns [1,2,8]. Others have studied security issues [9,10,19]. However, none of them focused on the behavior of *individual* smart contract, which hinders our deeper understanding of smart contracts in practice. The question we address here is: *how do smart contracts behave individually?*

In this paper, we present a behavior-aware profiling of smart contracts. Our work profiles the behavior of individual smart contract from a multi-party perspective, which includes senders, recipients and the blockchain infrastructure, as shown in Fig. 1. The goal is to develop a profile that is intuitive and useful so that users and developers can assess, manage and reason about smart contracts. We envision that our work effectively complements previous work towards generating a comprehensive understanding of smart contracts. Our contribution can be summarized as follows:

– We present a behavior-aware profiling of individual smart contract from a multi-party perspective, which is simple, yet effective to improve the visibility of the smart contract ecosystem.

- We characterize the behavior of individual smart contract based on two real-world datasets, and present interesting and surprising observations, some of which are listed below:
  - 96% of smart contracts have less than 10 senders, but some have more than 50 senders. Similarly, 98% of smart contracts have less than 10 recipients, but there also exist some contracts that have even more than 50 recipients.
  - 74% of smart contracts have never made an internal transaction since the time they were deployed.
  - The `Wallet` contracts probably are the most active contracts.
  - 75% of contract invocation chains consist of three smart contracts. The longest contract invocation chain has five smart contracts, which is a member of the `Game` category.
  - 96% smart contracts invoke only one contract during the time of their complete execution. A few contract completion chains have more than 50 contracts and all of them belong to the group of `Finance` contracts.
  - Gas need of a clear majority of `Library` contracts (95%) is very low. `Library` contracts do not require much gas because they generally serve for basic and specific purposes such as math and string transformations.
- We demonstrate that our profiling could reveal the complexity of the behavior of smart contracts. We also discuss the implications and propose several recommendations to better improve the security and performance of the smart contract ecosystem, including (a) documenting best practices of developing smart contracts, (b) developing certified `Library` contracts that can be trustingly used by others, and (c) building an official and trustworthy store to manage smart contracts.

2   Datasets

In this paper, we focus on smart contracts on the Ethereum. We collect two datasets, Dataset1 and Dataset2. Due to the Etherscan [6] only has the partial information of smart contracts, we instrument the Ethereum platform to obtain large-scale smart contracts with the complete information, which is referred to Dataset1. Dataset2 from [2] has 656 smart contracts that are classified into five categories. As shown in [2], manual inspection was used to categorize smart contracts, which is not suitable for Dataset1 that is large-scale. Thus, Dataset1 has no category information.

Dataset1: We log all the trades on the Ethereum as DATA1. Since smart contracts can only be created by create trades, we extract all create trades in DATA1 to generate the list of all smart contracts as LIST1, which includes ~600K smart contracts. By calling "eth.getCode()" method, we use this API to get runtime bytecodes by contract addresses. We obtain all runtime bytecodes for all contracts, and then through deduplicating smart contract addresses that have the same bytecode, we get all unique contract address list named as LIST2, which includes ~160K smart contracts. Finally, we iterate over DATA1 to find the transactions related to these unique smart contracts, which is named as DATA2.

Dataset2: We obtain the data of smart contracts with categories from [2] and extract their corresponding transactions from DATA2 above. There are five categories in this data. Finance contracts are used to manage, gather, or distribute money. Notary contracts are used to exploit the immutability of the blockchain to store some data persistently, which could certify their ownership and provenance. Game contracts include contracts that implement games of chance, games of skill as well as the mix of chance and skill. Wallet contracts handle keys, send transactions, manage money, deploy and watch contracts. Library contracts implement general-purpose operations to be used by other contracts.

Fig. 2. The distribution of who the senders are

Fig. 3. CDF vs. #senders per smart contract

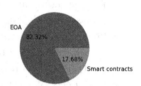

Fig. 4. The distribution of who the recipients are

3   Profiling Without the Consideration of Categories

In this section, we will present the profiling results based on the following questions and discuss their implications. The results are based on the Dataset1.

Who are senders of smart contracts?: *Senders are not only EOAs (Externally Owned Accounts), but also smart contracts.* A smart contract carries its own mission when it is created. It can be used by other users rather than its creator, which serves to the public by its service. In Fig. 2, we could observe that a great portion of senders of smart contract transactions are EOAs. This is reasonable if we consider that smart contracts are supposed to be used by the participating EOAs. However, we could also observe that some of the senders of smart contract transactions are smart contracts as well. This observation implies that smart contracts can be involved as collaborative components of the whole transaction path rooted from one smart contract. This flexibility can better support other smart contracts' functions in their tasks. It can be regarded as similar to the modular function concept used in the object-oriented programming language, so that it could help smart contract developers to facilitate the deployment process and improve the resource utilization of smart contracts on the blockchain platform. To examine the distribution of the number of senders for each smart contract, we apply cumulative distribution function (CDF) to the senders (Fig. 3). Regarding Fig. 3, we could observe that *around 96% of smart contracts have less than 10 senders.* This implies most of the smart contracts on Ethereum might be not popular at all. On the other hand, remaining smart contracts can be considered as being actively used, even *some of them have more than 50 senders*, which points to the potential popularity of a smart contract.

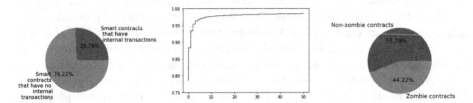

Fig. 5. The distribution of smart contracts that have at least one internal transaction and have no internal transactions

Fig. 6. CDF vs. # recipients per smart contract

Fig. 7. The distribution of the zombie contracts and non-zombie contracts

Who are recipients of smart contracts?: *Though most of the recipients of smart contract transactions are EOAs, around 18% of recipients are smart contracts, which is much enough to be non-negligible.* Figure 4 illustrates that the majority of the recipients of transactions are externally owned accounts. It indicates that EOA users are still much more active than smart contracts on Ethereum blockchain. Once such a smart contract is executed, it finishes all tasks on its own and makes the necessary transactions with particular EOAs. On the other hand, when a smart contract transaction is sent to another smart contract, it means that the caller contract cannot finish a task by only itself, and it can use other smart contracts to complete the task in a more efficient way. As shown in Fig. 4, a non-negligible amount of recipients (18%) are smart contracts that are used to complete other contracts' tasks. Additionally, we can consider the number of recipients that each individual smart contract has to profile recipients. Figure 6 shows the cumulative distribution of the number of recipients each smart contract has. *98% of smart contracts have less than 10 recipients*, which shows the smart contracts usually have their own special transaction receivers. On the other hand, *there also exist some contracts that have even more than 50 recipients*. Such contracts are usually used for transferring particular assets to many recipients, e.g., `Finance`.

Did all smart contracts make internal transactions?: As mentioned earlier, there are two types of transactions in Ethereum. One is an external transaction, which should be sent from an externally owned account. External transactions are stored in the blockchain and open to the public. The other type of transactions, namely internal transactions, are produced by the execution of a smart contract. Internal transactions cannot occur by themselves, they should be triggered by an external transaction. Also, they are not written to the blockchain.

From the mechanism of Ethereum, the outermost layer of a complete transaction must be an external transaction. If the destination address is a contract and the transaction will be generated downward, then the subsequent transactions should be internal transactions. Different smart contracts can include different kinds of operations, so their internal transactions can be completely different.

Figure 10 shows the cumulative distribution of the number of internal transactions each smart contract has. We could observe that more than 90% of smart contracts have less than 20 internal transactions. So that again, it points out the majority of Ethereum smart contracts are not such actively used. From the same graph, we could also find that *a great number of smart contracts (74%) have never made an internal transaction since the time they were deployed* as shown in Fig. 5. There are two reasons for this. One is that there is no function that triggers an internal transaction in the contract's source code. The other one is the smart contract has never been executed which should be triggered by an external transaction. Although there are many kinds of smart contracts available in Ethereum platform, their activeness percentage is quite low so that *a considerable proportion of smart contracts (44%) have never interacted with other accounts even once.* Such never-used contracts are named as *zombie contracts* as shown in Fig. 7.

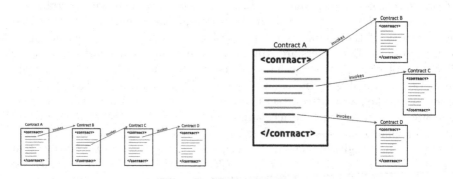

Fig. 8. The contract invocation chain   **Fig. 9.** The contract completion chain

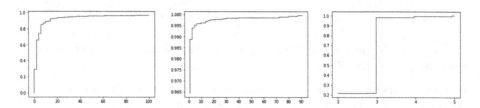

Fig. 10. CDF vs. # of internal transactions per smart contract has

Fig. 11. CDF vs. contract completion chain lengths of all smart contracts

Fig. 12. CDF vs. contract invocation chain lengths of all smart contracts

How does a smart contract invoke another smart contract?: Typically, one contract could complete one task by itself. However, as we observe, some smart contracts will leverage other smart contracts to complete a task. We refer this feature as the *chain of smart contracts* and explain the chains in two different ways. First, each time a contract invokes another contract, there will be a connection established between them. Once invocation series reach to a final contract, they will make a chain. We named such chains as *contract invocation chain*, as shown in Fig. 8. Additionally, Fig. 12 illustrates the cumulative distribution of lengths of such chains. Currently, *the longest contract invocation chain has 5 smart contracts. Most of (around 75%) contract invocation chains include three contracts.* Moreover, 22% of them consist of two smart contracts, which can be arguably denoted as "chains", and only 2% of contract invocation chains have four or five smart contracts.

The second type of contract chains is constructed as the result of the caller contract execution. When such a contract is executed, it may invoke one or more other contracts until it stops the execution. We define a group of contracts invoked by one contract throughout one execution as *contract completion chain*, as shown in Fig. 9. In Fig. 11, we observe that nearly *96% smart contracts invoke only one contract during the time of their complete execution.* Furthermore, *3% of them invokes two other contracts until their execution stops.* Finally, only around *1% of contracts involve more than two contract invocations in their source code.*

How do smart contracts use the gas?: As illustrated in the cumulative distribution of gas usage of all contract transactions in Ethereum (Fig. 13), gas usage can be quite changeable. This implies that the complexity of smart contract operations and their gas usage depend on the smart contract's goals and a wide variety of contract operations exist among Ethereum's smart contracts. Even so, we could say that most of smart contract transactions (60%) have used less than 10,000 units of gas to achieve the contract's task. Since a transaction of simple ETH transfer from one address to another uses 21,000 units of gas, we could see that 10,000 units of gas are not high and *most of the smart contract transactions probably achieve simpler tasks than the ETH transfer.*

4   Profiling with the Consideration of Categories

In this section, we will present the profiling results based on Dataset2 that has the categories.

Which categories of smart contracts act as senders more?: Senders of smart contracts correspond to the sender field in a transaction that has also a smart contract as the recipient. Figure 14 shows that the cumulative distribution of the number of times when a contract has the role of the sender in its contract-to-contract transactions for each category of smart contracts. Notably, sending transactions is the most popular among the `Wallet` contracts as 60% of them are in sender role of its transactions for at least one time. This is because `Wallet` contracts are mainly used for sending assets. `Library` contracts as the senders

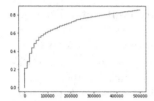 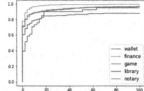 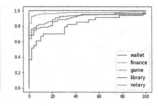

Fig. 13. CDF of contracts vs. gas usage of all smart contract txns

Fig. 14. CDF of contracts vs. #txns in which contracts as senders in each category

Fig. 15. CDF of contracts vs. #txns in which contracts as recipients in each category

can also be counted as relatively popular since 40% of them has made at least one transaction. Moreover, around 18% of Library contracts invoke other contracts more than 20 times. *Distribution patterns of other categories are quite similar to each other and sending transactions to other smart contracts is not as popular as in Wallet or Library contracts.*

Among all recipients of contract transactions, including both EOAs and smart contracts, recipient distribution of the transactions which are sent by the five categories of contracts are quite changeable (Fig. 16). For the transactions that have been carried out by Finance, Game, and Library contracts, EOAs are mostly in the recipient role. Especially, the number of smart contracts as the recipients of Library and Finance categories are near to 0 as observed in Fig. 15. It is a fact that the Library contracts do not invoke other smart contracts since their main job is to be used as a help in achieving other smart contracts' tasks. Thus, the Library contracts are always in the recipient role in contract-to-contract transactions. Also, since the Finance contracts are mostly used for managing and distributing money to EOAs, they usually do not need to invoke other smart contracts to finish their tasks. Another interesting fact is that unlike the other categories, smart contracts have received far more transactions from the Wallet contracts than EOAs have received. This is because EOAs actively use Wallet contracts and send their transactions to the Wallet

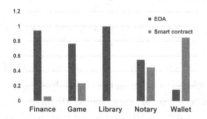 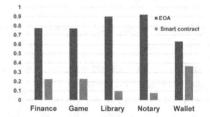

Fig. 16. The distribution of each category's recipients

Fig. 17. The distribution of each category's senders

contracts so that these contracts can send transactions to other smart contracts or deploy and watch other smart contracts on behalf of EOAs.

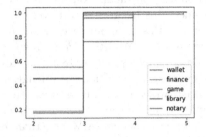

Fig. 18. CDF vs. contract invocation chain lengths in each category

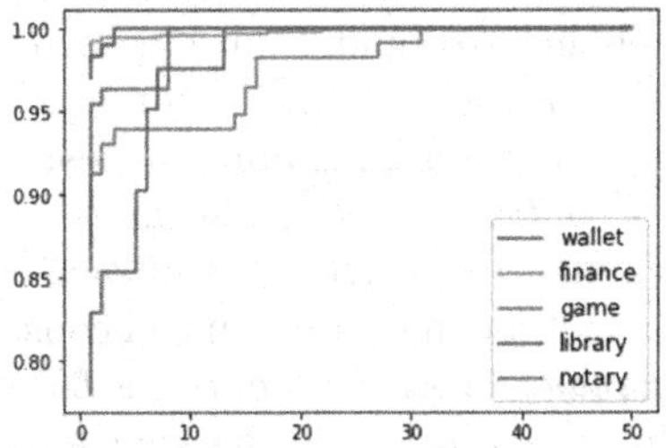

Fig. 19. CDF vs. contract completion chain lengths in each category

Which categories of smart contracts act as recipients more?: Figure 15 illustrates the category-based distribution of how many times each contract being the recipient of a transaction. Note that, these transactions are limited with only the ones between smart contracts. For example, around 70% of Wallet contracts are in the recipient role in less than 15 transactions. Surprisingly, a great portion of Library contracts (more than 95%) have not received any transactions, that means, they are not invoked by other smart contracts even once. This is quite lower than the expectations since the main purpose of Library contracts is being used by other contracts. This implies that *the power and usefulness of Library contracts have not been much discovered yet.* Among all categories, Wallet contracts are more uniformly distributed than the others based on the number of times being a transaction's recipient. Around 30% of Wallet contracts received transactions from other contracts more than 20 times. This indicates that *Wallet contracts probably are the most active contracts on Ethereum blockchain.* They are frequently invoked by EOAs as well as other smart contracts. It is also worth mentioning Notary and Game contracts have a considerable amount of received transactions and we can say that it shows their potential popularity in the future.

In order to observe the big picture of transaction senders, we additionally processed the transactions that include not only smart contracts but also externally owned accounts (Fig. 17). For each category of transactions, while the smart contract which belongs to the category in question is in the recipient role, the sender can be any smart contract or EOA. For each category, the number of sender EOAs is higher than that of smart contracts. This can be caused by two factors. First, the group of EOA accounts in Ethereum is still quite bigger than the smart contracts. Second, smart contracts do not invoke other smart contracts as much as EOAs invoke. However, this is not completely true for the Wallet contracts since they are already controlling their users' transactions by themselves.

How does a smart contact invoke another smart contract in different categories?: In order to gather the length of the chain of smart contracts, two types of chains are observed, namely contract invocation chains and contract completion chains for each category of smart contracts. Contract invocation chains are built from the invocation connections between smart contracts until the invocation series stop at a final contract. Based on our category-based contract invocation chain analysis, overall, *the longest invocation chain has five smart contracts and it is a member of the Game category*. Figure 18 illustrates the cumulative distribution of each category's contract invocation chain lengths. Note that, a contract chain can consist of at least two contracts. It indicates that *the Finance contracts and the Library contracts are mostly involved in such contract invocation chains that have at least three contracts* (81% of Finance and 82% of Library categories), and also, the Notary contracts have almost equal numbers of chains for 3-contract (30%) and 4-contract (24%) invocation chain groups. Multi-contract invocation chains do not seem much popular in the remaining categories since they mostly have 2-contract invocation chains. It might be concluded from these results that especially in Finance and Library categories, *using someone's contract probably provides convenience for smart contract developers to do their jobs in a more efficient way*. This indicates in these categories, a great number of contracts are open to the development.

Contract completion chains are constructed as the result of one contract invoking other contracts until it stops running. Figure 19 shows the cumulative distribution of contract completion chain lengths of each smart contract category. There are *only a few completion chains have more than 50 contracts and all of them belong to the group of Finance contracts*. Therefore, they are ignored for the sake of the graph's clearness since one of them consists of 359 contracts. However, it is also worth to mention that one contract in Finance category has been interestingly successful to use other contracts in its source code. *For each category, category-based contract completion chains mostly consist of between 2 and 20 contracts*. Especially for the Wallet category, completion chain lengths can quite vary. Moreover, for the Game category, the percentage of longer chains are higher than the others. It is obvious that the contract developers of these categories are relatively aware of the usefulness of invoking other contracts instead of writing a contract from zero by themselves, which could probably provide them efficiency and help saving considerable time during the development process.

How do different categories of smart contracts use the gas?: Figure 20 displays the cumulative distribution of gas needs for contract completion of each contract category. As seen on the figure, *gas need of a clear majority of Library contracts (95%) is very low. Library contracts do not require much gas because they generally serve for basic and specific purposes such as math and string transformations, so they are mostly formed as short contracts*. Among the other four categories, gas requirement of Notary contracts is relatively stable in comparison with others since nearly 70% of Notary contracts require between 150,000 and 200,000 unit of gas to finish their tasks. This could imply that the Notary contracts usually achieve the similar amount and type of tasks so that they need a similar amount of gas units. On the other side, gas requirement distribution of **Finance** and **Game** contracts show a diversified behavior, which indicates that there could be many different functions of smart contracts belong to these categories.

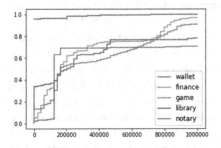   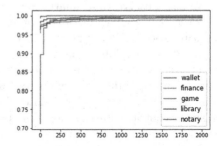

Fig. 20. CDF vs. the transaction gas in each category

Fig. 21. CDF vs. the contract value in each category

Are all the transactions money-based?: Smart contracts can send money to other accounts or receive money from other accounts on Ethereum blockchain. It does not happen as usual as between EOAs because smart contract usage is not still as popular as transferring money between EOAs. Figure 21 shows the cumulative distribution of transaction values occurred only between the smart contracts. *Most of the contracts make 0-valued transactions since these transactions are not usually money-based.* They could be produced only by executing the functions in the contract that do not require any money transfer. Interestingly, *while only around 5% of the other four categories have more than 0 value, this percentage increases to 10% in case of the Game contracts.* This could be explained as the **Game** accounts are transferring more money since some types of **Game** contracts such as lotteries are purely based on the money transfer and it is normal to frequently transfer money from such contracts to other contracts.

5   Implications and Discussion

Smart contracts go beyond the cryptocurrency. We could observe that EOAs still dominate the role of senders to invoke smart contracts, but the number of smart contracts as senders is increasing, which indicates that **smart contracts are extending their roles participating in the smart contract ecosystem, not just limited as callees.** Furthermore, most smart contracts have less than 10 senders and 10 recipients, which may indicate **the scale and popularity of each smart contract is still far from the expectation.**

Though the increasing number of smart contracts have been deployed, there are a non-trivial amount of smart contracts that never made any internal transaction and interacted with others. This may attribute to the immature nature of the smart contract ecosystem. First, the poor practice of developing smart contracts is prevalent in the smart contract community. Second, there is no clear regulation from the blockchain platform. Thus, **documentation of best practices of developing smart contracts and rules of deploying them is strongly needed for this uprising community.** For example, the blockchain platform should urge developers to self-destruct these "zombie contracts".

We also observe that smart contracts invoke many contracts, which forms either the invocation chain or the completion chain. However, **it is better to be cautious about the practice of invoking many other contracts**, especially for the Finance related contracts. This is because the security risk increases when the invocation chain or the completion chain of a smart contract grows. For example, the input data of a smart contract could be polluted [19]. Such pollution from any contract along the chain could significantly impact the correctness of the smart contract. Furthermore, the buggy contracts make this situation even worse.

From the performance perspective, it is also **necessary to revisit the development of such smart contracts by minimizing the number of invoked smart contracts.** For example, we observe that a few completion chains have more than 50 contracts in the Finance contracts. Due to the blockchain scalability and the increasing length of the blockchain, it is taking more time to finish one transaction. The increasing complexity of contract dependency makes this situation even worse, which is not good for the time-sensitive smart contracts, e.g., Finance and Game contracts.

Considering all smart contract chain observations together, we could say that the high potential of both smart contract chains has not been discovered enough by the contract developers yet. However, smart contract development is still quite new for the developers and it is improving day by day. When the power of chains is realized, it will make all contract developers' jobs easier and probably enable us to see more powerful, secure, and efficient contract solutions in the future.

This also raises the importance of **developing certified Library contracts that can be trustingly used by other smart contracts** to improve both security and performance concerns. This finally reaches to the proposition of **building an official and trustworthy store for smart contracts**, like Google Play Store for Android Apps. First, developing such a store could let developers place their smart contracts without directly deploying them into the blockchain and easily revise the smart contracts by fixing the bugs or vulnerabilities. Second, the store could certify each smart contract and filter the risky smart contracts before reaching to users. Third, the store could facilitate the ecosystem of smart contracts by involving more developers and users to sell and buy smart contracts.

Overall, **the smart contract ecosystem is still immature, which needs more efforts on understanding and improving it.**

6   Related Work

None of previous work characterized the behavior of *individual* smart contract.

Smart Contracts Characterization and Performance: Current characterization of smart contracts focused on design patterns, the programming code, and execution traces. Bartoletti et al. [2] studied generally the design patterns of smart contracts and how they were implemented on different blockchains. Chen et al. [1] discovered the money flow patterns in Ethereum contracts via the graph analysis [17]. Dickerson et al. [5] enabled smart contracts to be executed in parallel in order to improve their efficiency. Nikolic et al. [14] presented a characterization on the trace vulnerabilities from one million smart contracts, and a practical tool to test trace properties. Ontologies were presented in order to reduce the conceptual ambiguity of smart contracts for the public [4]. Kiffer et al. [8] studied the contract equality and similarity and found most contracts are direct- or near-copies of other contracts. Our work complements the previous work towards generating a comprehensive understanding of smart contracts.

Smart Contracts Security and Privacy: Luu et al. [10] investigated the security of smart contracts and discovered the vulnerabilities that can be used to manipulate the smart contracts to gain profit. A formal verification framework was proposed to analyze and verify both the runtime safety and functional correctness of smart contracts [3]. When smart contracts interact with the external data sources, the trust of data feeds becomes the critical issue to ensure the operation of smart contracts correctly. Town Crier [19] was proposed to provide an authenticated data feed for smart contracts, which is a high-trust bridge between data websites and the blockchain. Juels et al. [7] demonstrated that smart contracts could be abused for criminal purposes, which highlights the urgency of promoting effective policies to realize the great beneficial promise of smart contracts. A finite state machine-based approach was proposed to design secure smart contracts and a set of design patterns were also introduced to enhance security and functionality [11]. Due to the public blockchain exposing the transaction history, Hawk [9] was proposed to preserve the privacy of smart contracts. It enables people to write the private smart contract without the burden to implement the cryptography. Velner et al. [18] demonstrated that using the smart contract can withhold the blocks, which would undermine the entire pooled mining model.

7   Conclusion

In this paper, we have presented a behavior-aware profiling of individual smart contract from a multi-party perspective, which improves the visibility of the smart contract ecosystem. We have conducted a detailed study of the behavior of individual smart contract on two real-world datasets, and revealed interesting and surprising results. The implications of such study and the proposed recommendations could better help us improve the security and performance of the smart contract ecosystem.

Acknowledgement. This research was, in part, supported by the funds from the Ohio Cyber Range and Hyperconnect Lab Inc. Any opinions, findings, and conclusions or recommendations expressed in this material are those of the authors and do not necessarily reflect the views of our sponsors.

References

1. Chen, T., et al.: Understanding ethereum via graph analysis. In: IEEE INFOCOM (2018)
2. Bartoletti, M., Pompianu, L.: An empirical analysis of smart contracts: platforms, applications, and design patterns. In: Brenner, M., et al. (eds.) FC 2017. LNCS, vol. 10323, pp. 494–509. Springer, Cham (2017). https://doi.org/10.1007/978-3-319-70278-0_31
3. Bhargavan, K., et al.: Formal verification of smart contracts: short paper. In: ACM PLAS (2016)
4. de Kruijff, J., Weigand, H.: Ontologies for commitment-based smart contracts. In: Panetto, H., et al. (eds.) OTM 2017. LNCS, vol. 10574, pp. 383–398. Springer, Cham (2017). https://doi.org/10.1007/978-3-319-69459-7_26
5. Dickerson, T., Gazzillo, P., Herlihy, M., Koskinen, E.: Adding concurrency to smart contracts. In: Proceedings of ACM PODC (2017)
6. Etherscan, June 2019. https://etherscan.io/
7. Juels, A., Kosba, A., Shi, E.: The ring of gyges: investigating the future of criminal smart contracts. In: ACM CCS (2016)
8. Kiffer, L., Levin, D., Mislove, A.: Analyzing ethereum's contract topology. In: ACM IMC (2018)
9. Kosba, A., Miller, A., Shi, E., Wen, Z., Papamanthou, C.: Hawk: the blockchain model of cryptography and privacy-preserving smart contracts. In: IEEE S&P (2016)
10. Luu, L., Chu, D.-H., Olickel, H., Saxena, P., Hobor, A.: Making smart contracts smarter. In: ACM CCS (2016)
11. Mavridou, A., Laszka, A.: Designing secure ethereum smart contracts: a finite state machine based approach. In: Meiklejohn, S., Sako, K. (eds.) FC 2018. LNCS, vol. 10957, pp. 523–540. Springer, Heidelberg (2018). https://doi.org/10.1007/978-3-662-58387-6_28
12. Mukhopadhyay, U., Skjellum, A., Hambolu, O., Oakley, J., Yu, L., Brooks, R.: A brief survey of cryptocurrency systems. In: IEEE PST (2016)
13. Nakamoto, S.: Bitcoin: a peer-to-peer electronic cash system (2008)
14. Nikolic, I., Kolluri, A., Sergey, I., Saxena, P., Hobor, A.: Finding the greedy, prodigal, and suicidal contracts at scale. In: ACSAC (2018)
15. O'Shields, R.: Smart contracts: legal agreements for the blockchain. NC Banking Inst. **21**, 177 (2017)
16. Pilkington, M.: 11 blockchain technology: principles and applications. In: Research Handbook on Digital Transformations, p. 225 (2016)
17. Sergey, I., Hobor, A.: A concurrent perspective on smart contracts. In: Brenner, M., et al. (eds.) FC 2017. LNCS, vol. 10323, pp. 478–493. Springer, Cham (2017). https://doi.org/10.1007/978-3-319-70278-0_30
18. Velner, Y., Teutsch, J., Luu, L.: Smart contracts make bitcoin mining pools vulnerable. In: Brenner, M., et al. (eds.) FC 2017. LNCS, vol. 10323, pp. 298–316. Springer, Cham (2017). https://doi.org/10.1007/978-3-319-70278-0_19
19. Zhang, F., Cecchetti, E., Croman, K., Juels, A., Shi, E.: Town crier: an authenticated data feed for smart contracts. In: ACM CCS (2016)

A Performance-Optimization Method for Reusable Fuzzy Extractor Based on Block Error Distribution of Iris Trait

Feng Zhu[1,2], Peisong Shen[1(✉)], and Chi Chen[1,2]

[1] State Key Laboratory of Information Security,
Institute of Information Engineering, Chinese Academy of Science, Beijing, China
{zhufeng,shenpeisong,chenchi}@iie.ac.cn
[2] School of Cyber Security, University of Chinese Academy of Sciences,
Beijing, China

Abstract. Fuzzy extractors convert repeated noise readings of a source into same uniformly distributed key. To eliminate noise, non-secret helper data is extracted from the initial enrolment in the registration phase and acts as the "error correct" tool in the verification phase. However, error correct code based fuzzy extractors have cross-matching problems. Reusable fuzzy extractors are proposed to realize multiple registrations of the same biometrics and provide privacy-enhancing features such as revocability and protection against cross-matching. Nonetheless, Canetti's reusable fuzzy extractors named sample-then-lock suffer from heavy storage and computing resources burdens.

In this paper, after conducting a thorough correlation analysis between performance and error tolerance in Canetti's reusable fuzzy extractors, we find that decreasing error tolerance threshold can improve storage and computation performance of reusable fuzzy extractors. Based on statistical analysis of the block error distribution of iris trait, we propose an iris-code preprocessing method which uses Hadamard code to lower error tolerance. We conduct an experiment on a public iris dataset and experimental result shows that our method can improve the performance and security of the reusable fuzzy extractor schemes.

Keywords: Biometrics protection · Reusable fuzzy extractors · Iris-code

1 Introduction

With the popularity of mobile devices, biometrics are widely used in user authentication systems. Compared to traditional authentication methods, biometric-based authentication schemes have three advantages: identity binding, no memory and "carry-over". However, biometrics authentication has two major weaknesses: fuzzy and non-renewable property. Fuzziness means that the repeated reading values of the same biometric are similar but not identical. The classical

S. Chen et al. (Eds.): SecureComm 2019, LNICST 305, pp. 259–272, 2019.
https://doi.org/10.1007/978-3-030-37231-6_14

cryptography can't tolerate the deviation between acquisitions of the same biometric trait. Non-renewability means that once raw biometrics are compromised, they cannot be revoked, cancelled, or reissued. At the same time, intrinsic traits of a human are in limited number. Therefore, it is necessary to protect the raw biometrics.

Although the system stores biometric templates instead of original trait data, an experienced adversary can recover the initial biometrics from templates such as minutiae points [9,15]. Therefore, it is necessary to secure biometric templates. Feature transformation [2,3,12] and key-based protection [4–6,8,11] are effective solutions to protect templates.

The conception of non-invertible feature transformation has been first presented in [14]. The main idea is that biometric templates are transformed by a non-invertible and similarity-preserving function before they are stored. However, the security of these approaches depends on the secure storage of the transform parameters and it is difficult to construct the transformations satisfying necessary requirements [16].

In order to solve these problems, key based protection is proposed. The main idea of key based protection is to establish a link between biometrics and cryptographic keys, such as key-binding and key-extracting. Juels and Wattenberg [11] proposed the first key based protection scheme, fuzzy commitment. In their scheme, error correct code (ECC) is used to overcome fuzziness of biometrics for the first time. Specifically, differences between multiple acquisitions of the biometric are considered as "noise" and ECC is used to eliminate "noise".

On the basis of previous work, Dodis et al. [8] systematically summarized the concept of error correct code based fuzzy extractors and proposed a key-extractor method, which showed how to extract a random certainty secret from a noise input (such as biometrics) in Hamming, set difference and edit metrics. In a fuzzy extractor scheme, it usually consists of two main algorithms, a generating algorithm (Gen) and a reproducing algorithm (Rep). In Gen module, a random secret is generated and a public helper data is extracted from enrolled biometric. In Rep module, the secret will be recovered by the public helper data and certificated biometric, if the distance between certificated and registered biometrics is less than the given threshold value.

However, error correcting code based fuzzy extractors have a problem of being vulnerable to cross-matching attack [13]. Helper data is stored in plaintext in the database and is sent to the user for each verification, so it is not difficult for attackers to achieve helper data. When a biometric is enrolled multiple times and several instances of helper data from same biometric are generated, an adversary can select out helper data which belong to the same biometric according to the similarity of helper data.

Reusable fuzzy extractors can solve the problems mentioned above. Boyen et al.[4] introduced the conception of reusability and the definition of reusable fuzzy extractors. In a reusable fuzzy extractor scheme, a trait can be securely enrolled multiple times and the generated data are irrelevant. Based on the concept of reusable fuzzy extractors, Canetti et al. [5] proposed a feasible construction named sample-then-lock. The approach applies cryptographic digital lockers to achieve reusability. The construction is robust and reusable, but it suffers from heavy computing and storage resources burdens. On the basis of Canetti's construction, Cheon et al. [6] designed a threshold scheme to achieve the decline of storage consumption. However, due to applying the threshold scheme, their solution consumes much computing consumption.

1.1 Our Contribution

In this paper, we point out that the performance of Canetti's construction [5] still has the promotion space. The main idea of our scheme is to decrease storage and computing consumption by reducing the error tolerance threshold without affecting recognition accuracy. We find that resource requirements are highly related to the error tolerance of the biometrics. When the error tolerance is higher, it requires more lockers which results in more storage space and computing cost. In order to fix this problem, we propose a performance-optimization method which uses Hadamard code to preprocess iris-codes. We summarize our contribution as follows:

- We analyse the relationship between performance and error tolerance in the reusable fuzzy extractors and give a mathematical formalization of the relationship.
- We measure the intra-class and inter-class block error distribution in a public iris database. Combining the analysis of the intra-class and inter-class block error distribution, we propose a performance-optimization method based on Hadamard code that can effectively reduce error tolerance without increasing false acceptance rate (FAR) and false rejection rate (FRR).
- We conduct an experiment to demonstrate the performance of our method on grayscale iris dataset. Meanwhile, we analyse the security and performance of our approach to show that it is secure and effective.

1.2 Road Map

In Sect. 2, we provide some preliminaries for our work. In Sect. 3, we analyse the relationship between performance and error tolerance in the reusable fuzzy extractors. In Sect. 4, we give our performance-optimization method which is based on error distribution. In Sect. 5, we analyse the security and performance of our construction. Finally, we conclude our work in Sect. 6.

2 Preliminaries

In this section, we introduce reusable fuzzy extractors, block error distribution and Hadamard code.

2.1   Entropy

Let X_i be a random variable over some alphabet Z for $i = 1, \ldots, n$. We denote by a random variable $X = X_1, \ldots, X_n$ the tuple $(X_1, \ldots, X_n)$. The *minentropy* $H_\infty(X)$ of X is defined as

$$H_\infty(X) = -\log[\max_x Pr(X = x)].$$

The *average (conditional) minentropy* $\tilde{H}_\infty(X|Y)$ of X given Y defined as

$$\tilde{H}_\infty(X|Y) = -\log[\mathbb{E}_y \max_x Pr(X = x|Y = y)].$$

For a given distinguisher D, the *computational distance* between variables X and Y is defined by $\delta^D(X, Y) = |\mathbb{E}[D(X)] - \mathbb{E}[D(Y)]|$. For a class of distinguishers $\mathcal{D}$, we define $\delta^{\mathcal{D}}(X, Y) = \max_{D \in \mathcal{D}} \delta^D(X, Y)$. We will consider the class $\mathcal{D}_s$ of distinguishers (circuit) of size at most s which output a single bit.

2.2   Reusable Fuzzy Extractors

Fuzzy extractors consist of two parts: Gen algorithm and Rep algorithm. Gen algorithm extracts a string r from an enrolled biometric data w and generates a helper data $p \in \{0, 1\}^*$. Rep algorithm inputs verified biometric data w' and p generated in the Gen algorithm. The previous r can be recovered if w' is enough similar to w. In this subsection, we give the formal definition of computational fuzzy extractors and reusable fuzzy extractors.

Definition 1 (computational fuzzy extractors [8]). *Let $\mathcal{W}$ be a family of probability distributions over $\mathcal{M}$. A pair of randomized procedures "generate" (Gen) and "reproduce" (Rep) is an $(\mathcal{M}, \mathcal{W}, \kappa, t)$ - computational fuzzy extractor that is $(\varepsilon_{sec}, s_{sec})$-hard with error δ if Gen and Rep satisfy the following properties:*

- *The generate procedure Gen on input $w \in \mathcal{M}$ outputs an extracted string $r \in \{0, 1\}^\kappa$ and a helper string $p \in \{0, 1\}^*$.*
- *The reproduction procedure Rep takes an element $w' \in \mathcal{M}$ and a bit string $p \in \{0, 1\}^*$ as inputs. The correctness property guarantees that if $dis(w, w') \leq t$ and $(r, p) \leftarrow$ Gen(w), then $\Pr[\mathsf{Rep}(w', p) = r] \geq 1 - \delta$, where the probability is over the randomness of (Gen, Rep).*
- *The security property guarantees that for any distribution $W \in \mathcal{W}$, the string r is pseudorandom conditioned on p, that is $\delta^{D_{s_{sec}}}((R, P), (U_\kappa, P)) \leq \varepsilon_{sec}$.*

Definition 2 (reusable fuzzy extractors [5]). *Let $\mathcal{W}$ be a family of probability distributions over $\mathcal{M}$. Let (Gen, Rep) be a $(\mathcal{M}, \mathcal{W}, \kappa, t)$-computational fuzzy extractor that is $(\varepsilon_{sec}, s_{sec})$-hard with error δ. Let $(W^1, W^2, \ldots, W^\rho)$ be ρ-correlated random variables such that each $W^j \in \mathcal{W}$. Let D be an adversary. Define the following game for all $j = 1, \ldots, \rho$:*

- **Sampling** The challenger samples $w^j \leftarrow W^j$ and $u \leftarrow \{0,1\}^\kappa$.
- **Generation** The challenger computes $(r^j, p^j) \leftarrow Gen(w^j)$.
- **Distinguishing** The advantage of D is

$$Adv(D) := Pr[D(r^1, \dots, r^{j-1}, r^j, r^{j+1}, \dots, r^\rho, p^1, \dots, p^\rho) = 1]$$
$$- Pr[D(r^1, \dots, r^{j-1}, u, r^{j+1}, \dots, r^\rho, p^1, \dots, p^\rho) = 1].$$

(Gen, Rep) is $(\rho, \varepsilon_{sec}, s_{sec})$-reusable if for all $D \in D_{s_{sec}}$ and for all $j = 1, \dots, \rho$, the advantage is at most ε_{sec}.

2.3   Block Error Distribution

In this subsection, we introduce the definition of block error and block error distribution in Hamming metric.

Definition 3. Let $b = b_1 \dots b_8 \in \mathcal{B}$ be a block, where $b_i \in \{0,1\}$ and $\mathcal{B} = \{0,1\}^8$ is an input space. Let $b' \in \mathcal{B}$ be a block and E_{block} be the value of block error. $E_{block}(b, b')$ is Hamming distance between b and b'. Therefore, $E_{block}(b, b') \in \{0, 1, \dots, 8\}$.

In Definition 3, we give the concept of block error. In short, the block error is Hamming distance between two block. We can divide the value of block error into three levels: low block error ($E_{block} = 0, 1, 2$), medium block error ($E_{block} = 3, 4, 5$) and high block error ($E_{block} = 6, 7, 8$).

Based on the definition above, we can infer the definition of block error distribution.

Definition 4. Let $\mathcal{M} = \{0,1\}^{8n}$ be an input space and $w = w_1 \dots w_{8n} \in \mathcal{M}$, where $w_i \in \{0,1\}$ and n is a positive integer. Let $b_i = w_{8i-7} \dots w_{8i}$ be a block, where $i = 1, 2, \dots, n$. Therefore, w can denote $b_1 \dots b_n$. Let $w' = w'_1 \dots w'_{8n} \in \mathcal{M}$ and w' can denote $b'_1 \dots b'_n$. Let $D_{E_{block}}$ denote the block error distribution and thus the block error distribution of w and w' is $D_{E_{block}}(w, w') = \{E_{block}(b_1, b'_1), \dots, E_{block}(b_n, b'_n)\}$, where $E_{block}(b_i, b'_i) \in \{0, 1, \dots, 8\}$. Therefore, $D_{E_{block}}(w, w') = \{N_{E_{block}=i} \mid 0 \le i \le 8\}$, where $N_{E_{block}=i}$ denotes the number of blocks whose block error equals i.

Definition 4 is used to analyse the difference of inter-class and inter-class block error distributions.

2.4   Hadamard Code

In this subsection, we introduce the basic concept of Hadamard code and show the encoding and decoding process.

The Hadamard code is a kind of linear code over a binary alphabet. It maps k length messages to 2^k length codewords. The Hadamard code has a precise Hamming weight 2^{k-1}. The Hamming weight implies that the distance of the code is also 2^{k-1}.

Punctured Hadamard code is used to achieve noise reduction in our scheme. In standard coding theory notation for block codes, the punctured Hadamard code is a $[2^k, k+1, 2^{k-1}]_2$-code, which means 2^k block length, $k+1$ message length (or dimension) and 2^{k-1} minimum distance. $[2^k, k+1, 2^{k-1}]_2$-Hadamard code can be generated by a Hadamard matrix H_k of dimension $k \times k$. Further details about Hadamard code can be found in [1].

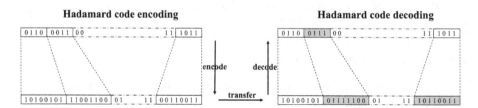

Fig. 1. The encoding and decoding of Hadamard code (faulty bit blocks are marked gray).

Figure 1 illustrates the encoding and decoding flow of Hadamard error correction. Obviously, Hadamard code is a bit-level ECC and able to correct small error. Therefore, Hadamard code can be used to eliminate small "noise" of iris-code since the "noise" affects individual bits in iris-code.

3   Analysis of Fuzzy Extractor Scheme

In this section, we analyse the relationship between performance and error tolerance in the reusable fuzzy extractors.

3.1   Description

In this subsection, we describe Canetti's construction [5] in detail. In Gen, a random string $r \in \{0,1\}^\kappa$ is chosen to act as the locked key. The key is locked respectively by some substrings $v_1, ..., v_\ell$ which are selected from an input string w. In Rep, verifier must extract substrings $v'_1, ..., v'_\ell$ corresponding to $v_1, ..., v_\ell$. The same r will be reproduced by unlock function if there exists i satisfied $v_i = v'_i$ for $1 \le i \le \ell$.

Construction (Sample-then-Lock) [5]. Let $\mathcal{M} = \{0,1\}^n$ be an input space and $w = w_1 \dots w_n \in \mathcal{M}$, where $w_i \in \{0,1\}$. Let ℓ be a positive integer and let (lock, unlock) be an ℓ-composable secure digital locker with error γ. To recover the random value r in Rep, information on how the substrings are generated should be stored. Thus a helper value p containing the indices of the bits of $w = w_1 \dots w_n$ which are used for each substring is generated along with r in Gen. The algorithms are described in Table 1.

Table 1. Sample-then-Lock [5]

Gen	Rep
Input: $w = w_1 \ldots w_n$.	Input: $w' = w'_1 \ldots w'_n$, $p = p_1 \ldots p_n$.
1. Sample $r \xleftarrow{\$} \{0,1\}^\kappa$.	
2. For $i = 1, \ldots, \ell$:	1. For $i = 1, \ldots, \ell$:
(i) Choose uniformly random	(i) parse p_i as $c_i, (j_{i,1}, \ldots, j_{i,k})$.
$1 \le j_{i,1}, \ldots, j_{i,k} \le n$.	
(ii) Set $v_i = w_{j_{i,1}}, \ldots, w_{j_{i,k}}$.	(ii) Set $v'_i = w'_{j_{i,1}}, \ldots, w'_{j_{i,k}}$.
(iii) Set $c_i = \text{lock}(v_i, r)$.	(iii) Set $r_i = \text{unlock}(v'_i, r)$.
(iv) Set $p_i = c_i, (j_{i,1}, \ldots, j_{i,k})$.	If $r_i \ne \bot$, output r_i.
Output: (r, p), where $p = p_1 \ldots p_\ell$.	Output: $\bot$.

3.2 Security

To instantiate Canetti's construction, k is chosen as security parameter. To make the false rejection rate (FRR) less than δ, it will require the following condition:

$$(1 - (1 - \frac{t}{n})^k)^\ell + \ell \cdot \gamma \le \delta. \tag{1}$$

The value $\ell \cdot \gamma$ denotes the maximum probability of the condition that Rep may be incorrect due to an error in one of the lockers. Using the approximation $e^x \approx 1 + x$, we can get

$$(1 - (1 - \frac{t}{n})^k)^\ell \approx (1 - e^{-\frac{tk}{n}})^\ell \approx \exp(-\ell e^{-\frac{tk}{n}}). \tag{2}$$

In fact, the value γ in Eq. 1 can be made very small in known locker constructions. Therefore, if γ is small enough so that $\ell \cdot \gamma \le \delta/2$, we can get

$$\ell \approx \log \frac{2}{\delta} \cdot e^{\frac{tk}{n}}. \tag{3}$$

Iteration number ℓ is exponentially related with error tolerance $\frac{t}{n}$ and security parameter k, where error tolerance $\frac{t}{n}$ hinges on threshold Hamming distance. Therefore, the value of iteration number ℓ depends on security parameter k and error tolerance.

3.3 Formal Analysis of Performance

In this subsection, we quantitatively analyse the performance of reusable fuzzy extractors. Performance includes two measurement index: storage space and computing cost. At the same time, they both have a linear relationship with iteration number ℓ.

Storage Space. Let parameter S denote storage overhead and L_{hash} denote the output length of hash function. In a reusable fuzzy extractor scheme, storage space is used to store helper data. The length of each helper data is value a, so storage overhead is $a \cdot \ell$. The value a depends on output size of hash function L_{hash} and the length of substring v_i, where L_{hash} is a fixed value and the length of v_i is $k \log n$. Therefore, storage space mainly relies on iteration number ℓ and the security parameter k:

$$S = a \cdot \ell \approx (k \log n + L_{hash}) \cdot \log \frac{2}{\delta} \cdot e^{\frac{tk}{n}}. \tag{4}$$

Computing Cost. Let parameter T_{total} denote computing cost and T_{unlock} denote the computation requirement of each unlocking. Computing cost is the maximum required time of Rep, which is $\ell \cdot T_{unlock}$. The parameter T_{unlock} approximates a fixed value λ. Therefore, computing cost mainly relies on iteration number ℓ:

$$T_{total} = T_{unlock} \cdot \ell \approx \lambda \cdot \log \frac{2}{\delta} \cdot e^{\frac{tk}{n}}. \tag{5}$$

As Eqs. 4 and 5 shown above, storage space S and computing cost T_{total} are associated with security parameter k and iteration number ℓ, where iteration number ℓ depends on security parameter k and error tolerance $\frac{t}{n}$. In order to ensure security, k must be large enough. Therefore, reducing error tolerance $\frac{t}{n}$ can effectively decrease storage space S and computing cost T_{total}.

4   Block Error Distribution and Our Scheme

The iris trait can be easily represented by binary sequence, so iris is a suitable example to research how to reduce the error rate of the trait. It benefits our analysis of the performance improvement.

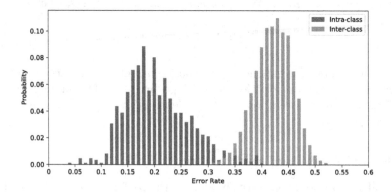

Fig. 2. The intra-eyes and inter-eyes distributions.

In this paper, we use the Infrared iris images of UTIRIS.v1 [10] as testing dataset and Daugman's method [7] as iris feature extraction algorithm.

The length of iris-code generated by [7] is 2048 bits. According to the experiment and statistical analysis, we can get intra-eyes and inter-eyes distributions, as shown in Fig. 2.

Through our experiment on the Infrared iris images of UTIRIS.v1 [10], the intra-eyes and inter-eyes distributions approximate normal distribution. At the same time, the average Hamming distance of intra-eyes and inter-eyes is 0.18 and 0.43, respectively. The cross region of intra-eyes and inter-eyes is small. Therefore, the inter-eyes and intra-eyes can be distinguished in Hamming metric by setting appropriate error tolerance. To balance security and matching accuracy, the value of error tolerance is in the cross region which is between the maximum Hamming distance of intra-eyes and the minimum Hamming distance of inter-eyes.

4.1   Analysis of Block Error Distribution

In this subsection, we provide the intra-class and inter-class block error distribution of iris-code, which is a rationale of our scheme. The difference of the intra-class and inter-class error distribution is used to seek for solution how to decrease the intra-class distance without shortening the inter-class distance.

Through the experiment and statistical analysis on the Infrared iris images of UTIRIS.v1 [10] by Daugman's method [7], we get the intra-class and inter-class block error distribution of iris-code. Figure 3 shows the experimental result.

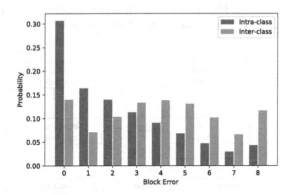

Fig. 3. The intra-class and inter-class block error distribution

It can be concluded from Fig. 3 that the block error distribution has three features:

- **Intra-class block error distribution.** The distribution of intra-class block error approximates inverse proportional distribution except block error equals 8. As the block error increases, the proportion of block error presents a decreasing trend. This trend illustrates that intra-class block error distribution is concentrated in low block error area.

- **Inter-class block error distribution.** The distribution of inter-class block error approximates secondary distribution, the peak value is 4 except block error equals 0 and 8. Based on our statistical analysis, inter-class error block is mainly distributed in medium block error area.
- **Difference.** The number of the intra-class low block error is more than that of the inter-class. Meanwhile, the numbers of intra-class medium and high block error are less than that of the inter-class.

Through the analysis of the data above, we summarize two points. Firstly, with respect to the inter-class block error, the intra-class block error concentrates the low block error. Meanwhile, the number of intra-class low block error is more than that of the inter-class low block error. Secondly, in the cross region, the intra-class and inter-class iris-code still satisfy three features above. Therefore, reducing the low block error can decrease the intra-class distance of iris-code without lowering the inter-class distance, FAR and FRR.

In summary, our target is to design a method which can only correct low block error without decreasing medium and high block error.

4.2   Our Construction

Our construction consists of three modules: feature extractor, noise reduction and reusable fuzzy extractors. Feature extractor module extracts biometric template for raw trait. Noise reduction module generates correction data which is able to optimize the input biometric data. Reusable fuzzy extractors extract key from the optimized biometric data. Figure 4 shows the overall process.

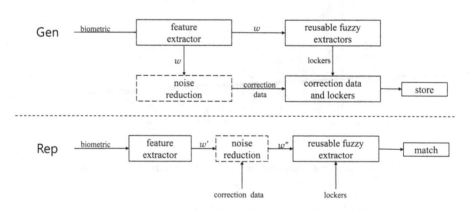

Fig. 4. Gen and Rep of our construction

On the basis of Canetti's reusable fuzzy extractors, our construction adds noise reduction module to lower error tolerance threshold. $[8, 4, 4]_2$-Hadamard code is used to achieve this function. More precisely, the block length is 8 bit, message length is (or dimension) 4 bit and minimum distance is 4 bit. According to coding theory, the error correct capability of $[8, 4, 4]_2$-Hadamard code is 0.25. Combined with the analysis of block error distribution, $[8, 4, 4]_2$-Hadamard code can correct low block error without decreasing medium and high block error. Therefore, $[8, 4, 4]_2$-Hadamard code is an appropriate method to achieve noise reduction.

Let $\mathcal{M} = \{0, 1\}^{8n}$ be an input space and $w, w' \in \mathcal{M}$. Let s be the random number and $s = s_1 \ldots s_n$, where $s_i \in \{0, 1\}$. Let h be the correction data. The function Enc and Dec denote Hadamard encoding and decoding, respectively. The parameter w'' is optimized iris-code. Let ℓ be a positive integer and let (lock, unlock) be an ℓ-composable secure digital locker with error γ. To recover the random value r in Rep, information on how the substrings are generated should be stored. Thus a helper value p containing the indices of the bits of $w = w_1 \ldots w_{8n}$ which are used for each substring is generated along with r in Gen. The algorithms are described in Table 2.

Table 2. Gen and Rep of our scheme

Gen	Rep
Input: $w = w_1 \ldots w_{8n}$.	Input: $w' = w'_1 \ldots w'_{8n}$, (h, r, p).
1. Sample $s \xleftarrow{\$} \{0, 1\}^{4n}$.	1. $s'_{decode} = h \oplus w'$.
2. $s_{encode} = Enc(s)$.	2. $s' = Dec(s'_{decode})$.
3. $h = s_{encode} \oplus w$.	3. $s'_{encode} = Enc(s')$.
4. Sample $r \xleftarrow{\$} \{0, 1\}^{\kappa}$.	4. $w'' = s'_{encode} \oplus h$.
5. For $i = 1, \ldots, \ell$:	5. For $i = 1, \ldots, \ell$:
(i) Choose uniformly random	(i) parse p_i as $c_i, (j_{i,1}, \ldots, j_{i,k})$.
$1 \leq j_{i,1}, \ldots, j_{i,k} \leq n$.	
(ii) Set $v_i = w_{j_{i,1}}, \ldots, w_{j_{i,k}}$.	(ii) Set $v'_i = w''_{j_{i,1}}, \ldots, w''_{j_{i,k}}$.
(iii) Set $c_i = \text{lock}(v_i, r)$.	(iii) Set $r_i = \text{unlock}(v'_i, r)$.
(iv) Set $p_i = c_i, (j_{i,1}, \ldots, j_{i,k})$.	If $r_i \neq \bot$, output r_i.
Output: (h, r, p), where $p = p_1 \ldots p_\ell$.	Output: $\bot$.

In Gen, the feature extractor module generates an iris-code w, which is the input of reusable fuzzy extractors and our scheme. Then reusable fuzzy extractors output digital lockers and our scheme outputs correction data. Finally, the digital lockers and the correction data are stored.

In Rep, the feature extractor module generates a verification iris-code w'. Then our scheme corrects low block error of iris-code w' by the correction data and generates an optimized iris-code w''. Finally, the reusable fuzzy extractor uses the digital lockers and the optimized iris-code w'' to extract the key.

5 Experimental Results

We compile our C++ source codes under the GNU C++ standard and run them on ubuntu 18.04 machine that has a Intel(R) Core(TM) i7-4790 3.60 GHz CPU with a 4 GB RAM. Our experimental results consist of the feature performance evaluation and scheme overall evaluation. The feature performance evaluation measures the FAR and FRR of our construction. The scheme overall evaluation measures the performance and security of our schemes.

In the feature performance evaluation, our construction can reduce FAR and FRR compared with Canetti's [5]. In the cross region (the area [0.3, 0.4]-error rate in Fig. 2), the Hamming distance of intra-eyes and inter-eyes drop by 0.065 and 0.051, respectively. The decline of intra-class Hamming distance is more than that of the inter-class. It causes the reduction of cross region, which means smaller FAR and FRR. Figure 5 shows ROC curves about FAR and FRR.

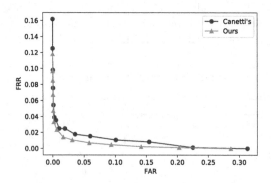

Fig. 5. ROC curves of Canetti's [5] and our scheme using UTIRIS.v1 [10] for best EER performance.

In the scheme overall evaluation, we measure the average time for 1 unlock under various sets of parameters, and obtain results as displayed in Table 3. We find that the extra computing and storage cost of our construction can be neglected. The extra storage of Hadamard correction data is 256 bytes, which is far less than the storage of digital lockers. Meanwhile, the extra computing cost of Hadamard code is 0.11 ms, which is far less than the computing cost of unlocking digital lockers.

Table 3 shows that error tolerance of our scheme will reduce by 5% compared with Canetti's [5]. The lower error tolerance means that our scheme needs less number of lockers. It results in improving the performance and security of reusable fuzzy extractors.

On one hand, our scheme can improve the performance under the same security. To prove it, we fix security parameter $k = 80$. The storage space and computing cost of our scheme decrease by 85% compared with Canetti's.

On the other hand, our scheme can improve the security under similar performance. When the performance of our scheme is similar to that of Canetti's (security parameter $k = 80$), the security parameter k of our scheme is increased by $\frac{100-80}{80} = 25\%$.

Table 3. The performance and security of our scheme and Canetti's [5] with security parameter $k = 80$ and 500 iris-code

Scheme	Error tolerance	Storage space	Computing cost
Canetti's [5]	0.20	2.71 GB	$15.5 \times 1.77 \times 10^1$ s
Our ($k = 80$)	0.15	50.9 MB	$15.5 \times 3.26 \times 10^{-1}$ s
Our ($k = 100$)	0.15	2.94 GB	$15.7 \times 1.61 \times 10^1$ s
Canetti's [5]	0.22	13.4 GB	$15.5 \times 8.78 \times 10^1$ s
Our ($k = 80$)	0.17	252 MB	$15.5 \times 1.61 \times 10^0$ s
Our ($k = 100$)	0.17	13.1 GB	$15.7 \times 8.22 \times 10^1$ s
Canetti's [5]	0.24	66.6 GB	$15.5 \times 4.35 \times 10^2$ s
Our ($k = 80$)	0.19	1.22 GB	$15.5 \times 7.99 \times 10^0$ s
Our ($k = 100$)	0.19	67.3 GB	$15.7 \times 4.14 \times 10^2$ s
Canetti's [5]	0.26	330 GB	$15.5 \times 2.15 \times 10^3$ s
Our ($k = 80$)	0.21	6.04 GB	$15.5 \times 3.96 \times 10^1$ s
Our ($k = 100$)	0.21	333 GB	$15.7 \times 2.01 \times 10^3$ s

6   Conclusion

We analyse the relationship between the performance of reusable fuzzy extractors and the error tolerance. We find out that the requirement of storage space and computing cost is too large to be used in realistic scenario. To solve this problem, we propose a performance-optimization scheme which is based on relationship between error tolerance and performance in the reusable fuzzy extractor scheme. In order to lower the error tolerance, our construction uses Hadamard code to correct low block error. Our scheme reduces the requirement of storage space and computing cost. The experiment proves that our scheme can greatly improve the performance of fuzzy extractors which are based on the Canetti's construction.

Acknowledgement. This work has been supported by National Key R&D Program of China (No. 2017YFC0820700), National Science and Technology Major Project (No. 2016ZX05047003), Biometrics Cryptography Project (No. NJHXCO1710021) and Cyberspace Security Defense Theory and Key Technology Project (No. Z181100002718001).

References

1. Agaian, S.S.: Hadamard Matrices and Their Applications. Springer, Heidelberg (1985). https://doi.org/10.1007/BFb0101073
2. Ang, R., Safavi-Naini, R., McAven, L.: Cancelable key-based fingerprint templates. In: Boyd, C., González Nieto, J.M. (eds.) ACISP 2005. LNCS, vol. 3574, pp. 242–252. Springer, Heidelberg (2005). https://doi.org/10.1007/11506157_21
3. Boult, T.E., Scheirer, W.J., Woodworth, R.: Revocable fingerprint biotokens: accuracy and security analysis. In: IEEE Conference on Computer Vision and Pattern Recognition, CVPR 2007, pp. 1–8 (2007)

4. Boyen, X.: Reusable cryptographic fuzzy extractors. In: ACM Conference on Computer and Communications Security, pp. 82–91 (2004)
5. Canetti, R., Fuller, B., Paneth, O., Reyzin, L., Smith, A.: Reusable fuzzy extractors for low-entropy distributions. In: Fischlin, M., Coron, J.-S. (eds.) EUROCRYPT 2016. LNCS, vol. 9665, pp. 117–146. Springer, Heidelberg (2016). https://doi.org/10.1007/978-3-662-49890-3_5
6. Cheon, J.H., Jeong, J., Kim, D., Lee, J.: A reusable fuzzy extractor with practical storage size: modifying Canetti *et al.*'s construction. In: Susilo, W., Yang, G. (eds.) ACISP 2018. LNCS, vol. 10946, pp. 28–44. Springer, Cham (2018). https://doi.org/10.1007/978-3-319-93638-3_3
7. Daugman, J.: How iris recognition works. IEEE Trans. Circ. Syst. Video Technol. **14**(1), 21–30 (2004). https://doi.org/10.1109/TCSVT.2003.818350
8. Dodis, Y., Reyzin, L., Smith, A.: Fuzzy extractors: how to generate strong keys from biometrics and other noisy data. In: Cachin, C., Camenisch, J.L. (eds.) EUROCRYPT 2004. LNCS, vol. 3027, pp. 523–540. Springer, Heidelberg (2004). https://doi.org/10.1007/978-3-540-24676-3_31
9. Galbally, J., et al.: An evaluation of direct attacks using fake fingers generated from ISO templates. Pattern Recogn. Lett. **31**(8), 725–732 (2010). https://doi.org/10.1016/j.patrec.2009.09.032. http://www.sciencedirect.com/science/article/pii/S0167865509002669, Award Winning Papers from the 19th International Conference on Pattern Recognition (ICPR)
10. Hosseini, M., Araabi, B., Soltanian-Zadeh, H.: Pigment melanin: pattern for iris recognition. IEEE Trans. Instrum. Measur. **59**(4), 792–804 (2010). https://doi.org/10.1109/TIM.2009.2037996
11. Juels, A., Wattenberg, M.: A fuzzy commitment scheme. In: Proceedings of the 6th ACM Conference on Computer and Communications Security, pp. 28–36. ACM (1999)
12. Maiorana, E., Campisi, P., Ortega-Garcia, J., Neri, A.: Cancelable biometrics for hmm-based signature recognition. In: IEEE International Conference on Biometrics: Theory, Applications and Systems, pp. 1–6 (2008)
13. Nandakumar, K., Nagar, A., Jain, A.K.: Hardening fingerprint fuzzy vault using password. In: Lee, S.-W., Li, S.Z. (eds.) ICB 2007. LNCS, vol. 4642, pp. 927–937. Springer, Heidelberg (2007). https://doi.org/10.1007/978-3-540-74549-5_97. http://dl.acm.org/citation.cfm?id=2391659.2391765
14. Ratha, N.K., Connell, J.H., Bolle, R.M.: Enhancing security and privacy in biometrics-based authentication systems. IBM Syst. J. **40**(3), 614–634 (2001). https://doi.org/10.1147/sj.403.0614
15. Ross, A., Shah, J., Jain, A.K.: From template to image: reconstructing fingerprints from minutiae points. IEEE Trans. Pattern Anal. Mach. Intell. **29**(4), 544–560 (2007). https://doi.org/10.1109/TPAMI.2007.1018
16. Sutcu, Y., Li, Q., Memon, N.: Secure sketches for protecting biometric templates. In: Campisi, P. (ed.) Security and Privacy in Biometrics, pp. 69–104. Springer, London (2013). https://doi.org/10.1007/978-1-4471-5230-9_4

Detecting Root-Level Endpoint Sensor Compromises with Correlated Activity

Yunsen Lei and Craig A. Shue[(✉)]

Worcester Polytechnic Institute, 100 Institute Road, Worcester, MA, USA
{ylei3,cshue}@wpi.edu

Abstract. Endpoint sensors play an important role in an organization's network defense. However, endpoint sensors may be disabled or sabotaged if an adversary gains root-level access to the endpoint running the sensor. While traditional sensors cannot reliably defend against such compromises, this work explores an approach to detect these compromises in applications where multiple sensors can be correlated. We focus on the OpenFlow protocol and show that endpoint sensor data can be corroborated using a remote endpoint's sensor data or that of in-network sensors, like an OpenFlow switch. The approach allows end-to-end round trips of less than 20ms for around 90% of flows, which includes all flow elevation and processing overheads. In addition, the approach can detect flows from compromised nodes if there is a single uncompromised sensor on the network path. This approach allows defenders to quickly identify and quarantine nodes with compromised endpoint sensors.

Keywords: Endpoint security · Compromise detection · Software-defined networking

1 Introduction

To protect their organizations, defenders typically deploy a mixture of perimeter and defense-in-depth techniques, such as endpoint tools and sensors. Perimeter and endpoint defenses have varying strength: perimeter defenses can be centrally administered and have a global view while endpoint sensors often have detailed context about the associated endhost and can detect intra-subnet traffic. End-user activity on the endpoint represents a common vector for threats to enter an organization [8]. The value of context around these user actions has caused even leaders of perimeter-based defenses to begin creating endpoint sensors [2].

While endpoint sensors can play an important role, they come with a significant risk: an adversary could compromise the sensor to silence its reporting or to provide false information. Many endpoint solutions, such as firewalls, host-based

---

Shue holds stock in ContexSure Networks, Inc., an arrangement that has been reviewed and approved by WPI's Conflict Management Committee.

S. Chen et al. (Eds.): SecureComm 2019, LNICST 305, pp. 273–286, 2019.
https://doi.org/10.1007/978-3-030-37231-6_15

intrusion detection systems, and anti-virus, rely upon a least-privilege assumption in which the end-user operates in a regular user account. Those solutions further assume that processes running as an administrator user and all kernel space functionality will remain uncompromised. In the event of a root-level compromise, these tools may use anti-circumvention techniques to hinder their removal or sabotage, but they ultimately cannot offer any security guarantees. In some cases, the data provided by endpoint sensors can be corroborated with data from other sensors in the network. A sensor's reports about network flows, for example, can be easily corroborated by examining the data flows reported by sensors on other machines.

In this paper, we examine how an endpoint sensor providing data via the OpenFlow protocol can be evaluated using data from other OpenFlow nodes. In the OpenFlow protocol, an OpenFlow agent seeks guidance from a logically-centralized controller whenever the agent encounters a packet for which it lacks a matching flow rule in its cache. When these caches are empty or when fine-grained (i.e., connection-specific) flow rules are used, each OpenFlow agent along the new flow's path will "elevate" a request to the controller. Accordingly, a controller can receive multiple reports about each new connection and determine if the OpenFlow agent requests are consistent. If it detects any inconsistency, the controller may be able to pinpoint a compromised or faulty node.

In this paper, we make the following contributions:

- **Implement an Endpoint Flow Verification System:** In our Correlated Host-based OpenFlow Sensor Enforcement (CHOSE) system, an endpoint sensor reports flow and contextual data (e.g., originating user and application) for each new network connection. We correlate these reports across endpoint and in-network devices to detect potentially compromised endpoints.
- **Evaluate the System's Security and Performance:** Our system can detect and block flows with inaccuracies that indicate a compromised sensor even before a flow is fully established. We further find that legitimate flows can corroborated by remote sensors and complete their first round trip in less than 20 ms for about 90% of flows. We find that a controller can easily detect a faulty OpenFlow agent when a single non-compromised sensor is on the flow's path.

2   Background and Related Work

In this section, we provide a brief overview of the OpenFlow protocol and its use. We then describe prior work related to host-based software-defined networking (SDN) and the detection of endpoint compromises.

2.1   OpenFlow and Software-Defined Networking (SDN)

The OpenFlow protocol [5] provides an API for a logically-centralized controller to interact with a set of packet forwarding devices, which are often network switches. In OpenFlow, a switch will send a `PacketIn` packet to an OpenFlow controller whenever the switch encounters a packet whose fields are not a match for any of the switch's cached rules. When issuing the `PacketIn` request, the switch includes a copy of the associated packet. The controller consults its policy to determine the appropriate action. The controller may optionally create a `FlowMod` packet to order the switch to store a new rule with match criteria corresponding to the flow along with an action the switch should take on future matching packets. Finally, the controller issues a `PacketOut` message that indicates what the controller should do with the packet contained in the `PacketIn` message.

The OpenFlow protocol allows a controller to essentially treat each OpenFlow switch as a configurable rule cache. A controller could reactively push fine-grained rules, which typically specify a fixed flow tuple (i.e., IP_{source}, IP_{dest}, transport protocol, $port_{source}$, $port_{dest}$.) that will only match a single connection. The use of these fine-grained rules can be attractive for security purposes because the resulting packet elevations give the OpenFlow controller detailed visibility into the communication occurring on the network. This empowers the controller to act as a network-wide flow-based access controller.

2.2 Host-Based SDN

While OpenFlow was originally designed for use with physical hardware in network switches, one of the more popular OpenFlow implementations is in software. Open vSwitch (OVS) [9] is often used on virtual machine (VM) hypervisors to provide SDN functionality between VMs. In the Scotch approach, Wang et al. [12] proposed using OVS to enhance the scalability of fine-grained flows by using OVS on VM hypervisors.

Taylor et al. [10] proposed a host-based SDN that provides information about the end host in addition to the network flow information. Najd and Shue [7] transformed Taylor's host-based SDN into an OpenFlow compatible implementation that could complete a flow elevation to a controller in less than 9 ms. These latter two host-based SDNs fall into the class of endpoint sensors that we focus on in this paper.

2.3 Detecting Compromises on Endpoints

Once a host is compromised, an attacker may attempt to conceal the compromise in order to remain persistent or to spread laterally across the network. When trust assumptions, such as a trustworthy OS or kernel space, are violated, attackers can deactivate a host's defenses. As an example, malware has been found to deactivate anti-virus [6] to evade detection. Attackers may also disguise their traffic, using mimicry techniques [11], to appear legitimate.

To relax assumptions about a trustworthy OS, trusted hardware, such as trusted platform modules (TPMs) or secure co-processors, can be used to provide attestations. These approaches tend to suffer from fragility to minor changes (when a static root of trust is used) [4] or from classic time-of-check-time-of-use (TOCTOU) issues [3] (when a dynamic root of trust is used).

In this work, we proceed in a different direction: we try to detect sensors that provide inaccurate data, or omit data, by comparing their outputs with other sensors on the network. This distributed monitoring approach can highlight attacks even without special trusted hardware.

3   Correlated Host-Based OpenFlow Sensor Enforcement

In this section, we provide example attacks, their consequences, and how correlated sensing could help. We then describe the system and threat model we are considering. We then describe the Correlated Host-Based OpenFlow Sensor Enforcement (CHOSE) system and scenarios in which it is effective.

3.1   Example Endpoint Sensor Compromises

An organization may use endpoint firewalls or host-based intrusion detection systems (HIDS) in order to provide defense-in-depth protections.

The organization may configure each endpoint with a set of firewall and HIDS rules that must be enforced to detect and prevent the spread of attacks or data ex-filtration. If a host is somehow compromised, the compromise may occur at the administrator or root level due to the end-user running with administrator privileges or due to a privilege escalation attack. The attacker could simply disable the endpoint firewall or IDS to engage in arbitrary network communication and to prevent event reporting. With correlated sensing, other network sensors could detect the disallowed communication. For example, a host on the network receiving an illicit flow from another compromised machine on the network could report the issue. In some cases, sensors may be redundant (e.g., at both endpoints) while in other cases, they may have correlated behavior (e.g., IDSes and netflow records). Both types of data can help a defender detect inconsistencies that belie a host compromise.

3.2   System Overview and Threat Model

In Fig. 1, we provide an example local area network for an organization.

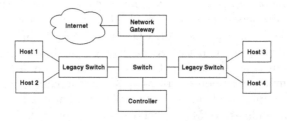

Fig. 1. An example enterprise network with OpenFlow agents on each end-point.

In this example, the trusted computing base (TCB) includes the Open-Flow controller and the network switches. The physical connections between the switches, hosts, and controllers are considered uncompromised and reliable. The hosts on the network are not part of the TCB; the sensor data obtained from these hosts could be erroneous or absent due to a root-level compromise on a host. In some cases, a set of compromised hosts may collude with a goal of evading detection. In other cases, a compromised host may communicate with an uncompromised host. In that case, the uncompromised host will report the communication. If any switch is an OpenFlow switch, it is in the TCB and it is managed by the controller, so it can be configured so that any communication through the OpenFlow switch will be reported to the controller.

We consider an adversary who focuses on maintaining persistence, the ability to move laterally within an organization, and to maintain communication with a command and control system. That adversary requires covert communication channels. Such an adversary would forgo resource exhaustion DoS attacks since they are easily detected and can be trivially mitigated by prior work [1]. Accordingly, we omit any further analysis of DoS attacks.

The defender's goal is to receive a full reporting of all communication flows that occur in the network in a logically-centralized controller. The defender wants to block any flow requests from sensors that are inconsistent with other sensors. With full accounting of flows, the defender can construct arbitrary access control policies. Since the development of effective network access control policy is its own active research area, we consider it beyond the scope of this work.

3.3   Corroborated Sensing Deployment Scenarios

Some organizations deploy specialized security middleboxes, such as firewalls or IDSes, that can vet communication. Often, these middleboxes are deployed at network perimeters and they do not inspect internal traffic, such as intra-subnet flows. These organizations may deploy endpoint sensors to gain insight into intra-subnet traffic. But, with root-level compromises on the endpoints, these sensors may fail to produce complete or accurate data. With sensors at both endpoints, a network operator is more likely to detect a compromised sensor.

Using the network in Fig. 2 left as an example, consider a TCP SYN packet sent by Host 1 to Host 2. If both Host 1 and Host 2 provide OpenFlow sensor data, the controller will receive independent reports of this SYN packet within PacketIn elevations from these hosts (shown by lines 1 and 2 for Host 1 and lines 5 and 6 for Host 2). In this case, if either Host 1 or Host 2 provided inaccurate information about the SYN packet, or neglected to engage in a PacketIn elevation entirely, the controller will easily be able to detect the mismatch.

This detection mechanism goes to the heart of the attacker's goals. To establish communication for command and control or to propagate the attack to other machines, the adversary must establish new connections. However, an OpenFlow endpoint sensor will reveal this flow when the adversary makes the connection attempt, causing the adversary to be detected. The attacker must alter a sensor to avoid this reporting, but any alteration will result in a mismatch on the remote host's sensor.

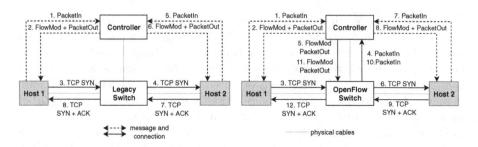

Fig. 2. When both endpoints run an OpenFlow agent, if either is uncompromised, that uncompromised sensor will alert the central coordinator of inconsistencies via its `PacketIn` data. When an OpenFlow switch is on the network path, the controller receives `PacketIn` data that allows it to identify which endpoint, if any, is faulty.

In the Fig. 2 left example, the controller will receive conflicting information and know one of the two hosts is compromised, but will not know which has the error. However, if the switch is an OpenFlow switch, as shown in Fig. 2 right, the controller can determine which host is deceptive. The OpenFlow switch would provide information about the `SYN` packet (shown by lines 4 and 5). Further, since the OpenFlow switch is in the network's TCB, its reports can be used as ground-truth data. Without a ground-truth, network operators would need to check both hosts for a potential compromise.

When using corroborated sensing, particularly when only the endpoints have sensors (e.g., Fig. 2), the controller must be careful in how it manages the rules it stores at each endpoint. By pushing uni-directional flow rules in its initial `FlowMod` messages, the controller can detect if the destination fails to properly elevate traffic. In the `FlowMod` messages in Message 2 in Fig. 2 left and Messages 2 and 5 in Fig. 2 right, the controller only pushes an approval for the flow in the direction from Host 1 to Host 2. When responding to the destination, and on agents elevating the `SYN+ACK` packets, the controller orders the agents to store a bi-directional `FlowMod` approving both directions of the flow.

In Fig. 3, we show the process that would occur if either Host 1 or Host 2 was compromised in this example scenario. In the event Host 1 is compromised, it could fail to send a `PacketIn` in Step 1 or send an inaccurate `PacketIn` (e.g., a `PacketIn` with inaccurate payload or header information) and receive the controller's approval. However, Host 2 would then send a `PacketIn` in Step 5 and the controller would notice the discrepancy between the two `PacketIn` messages, deny the flow in Step 6 and drop all the packets in the flow, preventing the application at Host 2 from receiving them.

If Host 2 were compromised (the right side of Fig. 3), a similar process would occur, but the detection would be slightly delayed. In this case, the first 4 steps would proceed and Host 2 would either neglect to provide a `PacketIn` in Step 5 or provide inaccurate information. Since the `SYN` packet would already have reached Host 2 in Step 4, Host 2 could process the message and respond in Step 7. However, if the controller only pushes a unidirectional `FlowMod` rule in Step 2,

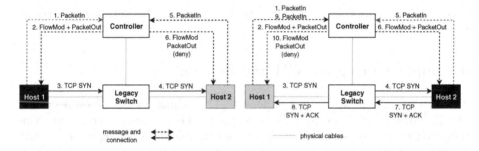

Fig. 3. When one of the hosts is compromised (shaded in black), the controller will notice a discrepancy when receiving a `PacketIn` from the non-compromised host (shaded in gray).

Host 1 would again elevate the packet to the controller in Step 9. At that point, the controller would note that Host 2 failed to send a proper `PacketIn` (Step 5) and would insert a denial `FlowMod` into Host 1 in Step 10, preventing the application at Host 1 from communicating with the compromised host.

When both hosts are malicious and only legacy switches connect the hosts, it is possible for the hosts to collude and choose not to elevate packets to the controller. Without a middlebox or an OpenFlow switch that connects the devices, this situation cannot be avoided.

3.4   Uncorroborated Data in Endpoint Sensors

In the OpenFlow data, all sensor data can be corroborated since the only information, the elevated packet, is included it its entirety and is independently witnessed by multiple vantage points. However, other sensors may include data that is only available at a single vantage point.

The host-based SDNs created by Taylor et al. [10] and Najd et al. [7] provide additional information about the network flows. Some of that information includes the user account and originating application on a sending endpoint and the destination server and its user on a receiving endpoint. Since this context is only available on the respective endpoints, neither the other endpoint nor a middlebox can corroborate that contextual data. Accordingly, a compromised host could arbitrarily forge this contextual data.

A controller may be able to detect obvious signs of forgery, such as a connection on port 22, commonly associated with the SSH protocol, purportedly originating from an email client. However, a sophisticated adversary would likely be able to craft contextual data that would plausibly be associated with the verifiable network headers and packet payload.

Some endpoint sensors, such as a reporting engine for an anti-virus tool, may engage in communication that is completely unverifiable by other sensors. These sensors would not be able to effectively use correlated sensing on its own.

To gain trust in information that cannot be corroborated, trusted hardware or VM introspection techniques may play a role. However, in situations where corroboration is possible, correlated sensing can provide benefits without requiring special hardware.

4   Implementing the CHOSE System

The CHOSE system has three components: (1) a standard OpenFlow agent for physical switches, (2) an OpenFlow-compatible host agent for Microsoft Windows machines, and (3) a custom OpenFlow controller that manages connections for both switches and end-hosts. For the OpenFlow agent, we use the built-in OpenFlow agent on an enterprise-grade switch. In the remainder of this section, we focus on the host agent and the functionality in the OpenFlow controller.

4.1   Host Agent for Microsoft Windows

We created a host-based SDN agent for Microsoft Windows using a kernel-mode Windows driver. The driver uses the Windows Filtering Platform (WFP) to monitor all socket operations. The Application Layer Enforcement (ALE) filtering approach provided by WFP allows us to monitor traffic at a per-connection or per-socket level rather than having to process packets individually, enabling us to replicate the OpenFlow process natively in Windows.

The SDN agent communicates to an SDN controller using a modification to the OpenFlow protocol. As with standard OpenFlow, the agent elevates a packet by including an OpenFlow header and encapsulating a copy of the original packet. However, the SDN agent also includes contextual information about the application in a custom structure that follows the encapsulated packet. This contextual information includes the application path of the sending application, the user running the software, and the process identifier among other fields. The OpenFlow communication is then encrypted and authenticated using AES encryption and a SHA-256 message authentication code (MAC). Upon receiving a response from the SDN controller, the host-based agent either drops the packet (for discard decisions) or updates the flow status in the WFP framework and re-injects the packet into the network kernel queue for delivery.

4.2   OpenFlow Controller Customization

The SDN controller must support both the Windows OpenFlow agent and traditional OpenFlow agents running on switches. When receiving a `PacketIn`, this controller distinguishes the OpenFlow agent type based on the destination transport layer port and handles the communication in separate threads of execution. When the first `PacketIn` on the path arrives, the controller consults its normal policy rules to determine whether the flow should be allowed. If not, it sends `FlowMod` and `PacketOut` messages to the agent that order the packet and all other packets in the flow to be dropped. If the controller policy dictates the flow should be allowed, the controller stores a record of the flow in a local list of active flows and then sends `FlowMod` and `PacketOut` messages to the requesting OpenFlow agent to approve the source to destination direction of the flow.

Since the controller sent a `FlowMod` only to the originating OpenFlow agent during its approval, subsequent OpenFlow agents on the path will again elevate the packet to the controller. If the controller receives a `PacketIn` from an Open-Flow agent, and that agent is not the first agent that should have appeared on the flow, the controller will check to see if it already has an entry for the flow in its active flows list. If it does not, the controller will send `FlowMod` and `PacketOut` messages to the agent that order the packet and all other packets in the flow to be dropped. It will also make note of the OpenFlow agent that failed to elevate the flow. Alternatively, if the controller sees that the flow is in its active list and was previously approved, it will order the OpenFlow agent to approve the flow.

In this approach, the controller makes only unidirectional forwarding approvals in its `FlowMod` messages. This is essential to detecting compromised or malfunctioning agents that are at or near the destination. When a reply is issued, such as the `SYN+ACK` packet in a TCP connection, each agent on the reverse path will again elevate the packet to the controller. At that point, the controller can confirm it has received all the expected requests from agents in the original direction. It can then send a `FlowMod` message that updates the original uni-directional flow approval to instead allow bi-directional communication on each agent on the path.

With this approach, the controller receives corroboration on packets elevated from each OpenFlow agent any time there are multiple OpenFlow agents on the path. Further, if at least one OpenFlow agent on the path is not compromised, the controller will be able to detect the existence of any compromised agent on the path that omitted or modified the flow information.

5   Evaluating the Security and Performance of CHOSE

In this section, we describe our experimental setup, our performance evaluation process and results, and the security evaluation methodology and results. In our evaluation, we aim to answer two questions: (1) What overhead does correlated sensing introduce to an existing SDN deployment? (2) What security guarantees does correlated sensing offer to such a system?

5.1   Experiment Setup

In both our performance and security evaluation, we configure our network to match Fig. 2. We use an HP 2920-24G enterprise switch with OpenFlow enabled to connect our hosts and controller. Our controller runs on a laptop that runs VirtualBox to host an Ubuntu 16.04 VM. We configure the controller with 2 IP address and place one of the IP addresses under the control of OpenFlow so that the communication between sensors and controller will also be subject to the OpenFlow's elevation model. We then connect two end-hosts to the switch.

The first host is a Mac mini that runs VirtualBox to host a Windows 10 VM. The second host is a Macbook Pro that runs VirtualBox to host a Windows 10 VM.

5.2   Performance Evaluation

To determine the overhead associated with correlated sensing, we compare it with regular OpenFlow behavior in both switch-based and host-based SDN configurations. We create an HTTP client program to connect to an HTTP server. Our client creates connections in a serial fashion. We ensure that the tested OpenFlow agents will perform a flow elevation for each new connection. Since the system uses `FlowMod` rules to avoid elevating subsequent packets in a flow, the overheads associated with packet elevations will only affect the first round trip in a flow. Accordingly, we use the round-trip time (RTT) on the first set of packets in the flow as our performance metric.

By comparing the time required under varying deployment scenarios, we can determine the latency associated with elevation requests from switch and end-host agents along with the time required for the controller to correlate flow requests. We use the following four scenarios in our testing:

– **Scenario 1: Switch-Based OpenFlow Only:** In this scenario, neither of the hosts run an OpenFlow agent. The physical OpenFlow switch elevates each new connection it sees to the OpenFlow controller. The controller is configured to approves all new flow requests it receives from the switch. Since this controller engages in minimal computation, this scenario provides a baseline for a physical switch's performance.
– **Scenario 2: Host-Based Sensors Only:** In this scenario, both of the hosts run our Windows OpenFlow agents which gather contextual and flow data and include this information in elevation requests for each new connection. In this case, OpenFlow is disabled on the physical switch and the controller only needs to processes the modified OpenFlow messages for the host sensors.
– **Scenario 3: Both Switch and Host Sensors:** This scenario uses OpenFlow agents at both hosts and the physical switch. The controller processes packet elevations from both types of agents. However, the controller statelessly approves the flows independently and does not perform any correlation or analysis of the requests across OpenFlow agents.
– **Scenario 4: Full Sensing and Flow Correlation:** In this scenario, the OpenFlow agents run at the hosts and the physical switch. The controller examines the elevations across OpenFlow agents and correlates the requests to identify discrepancies or missing elevation requests.

Round Trip Timings. For each of these scenarios, we conduct 500 trials, with each trial consisting of a new connection in which the RTT for the initial packets are measured. Once the connection is established, it is immediately terminated and the next trial begins. We present the results of these trials in Fig. 4.

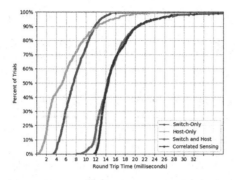

Fig. 4. Round-trip time of serial connections across 500 trials.

The overhead of the correlated sensing is the timing difference between the third scenario and the fourth scenario. In Fig. 4, the distribution curve of the round-trip times associated with these two scenarios largely overlap, indicating that the performance costs of correlated sensing are not significant.

From these experiments, we see that most flows complete in less than 15 ms, even with correlated sensing, and that around 90% of flows complete in less than 20 ms. This overhead only affects the first 2 packet within a TCP connection which is significantly less than a comparable DNS look-up time. The performance of the host-based only sensor is faster in most cases than the switch-only sensor. This appears to be due to the physical switch using its relatively-slow integrated processor for performing flow elevations in software whereas it can use a hardware table for subsequent packet forwarding once a `FlowMod` is installed. As one might expect, the RTTs in the third scenario, which requires elevations from the hosts and the switch, are roughly the sum of the times in scenarios 1 and 2.

Parallel Connections. We next examine the performance of the SDN approaches in a more real-world setting, we use end-to-end timing of a short HTTP connection. Using parallel threads, we generate HTTP requests on Host 1 to an HTTP server running on Host 2. The client application on Host 1 is designed to use a separate TCP connection for each HTTP request. It issues an HTTP `GET` request for a short HTML document. After the server provides the HTML document, the client closes the connection. Using a varying thread count on the client, we measure how many new connections can be created by the client in a five minute (300 s) period.

In Table 1, we show the results of the parallel connection experiments. We see that in the host-only scenario, the hosts and controller can handle an average of roughly 74 new flows per second. We create a fifth scenario that uses correlation only at the endpoints sensors, called Scenario 5, and see that it largely keeps pace with Scenario 2 up to 50 concurrent threads, but starts to slow down at 100 concurrent threads. That likely indicates that controller bottlenecks begin to form at that higher thread count.

Table 1. Number of flows created in five minute period.

Number of threads	Scenario 1: Switch-Only	Scenario 2: Host-Only	Scenario 3: Switch and Host	Scenario 4: Full Correlation	Scenario 5: Host Correlation
10	2,919	2,965	2,813	2,365	2,830
20	5,431	5,520	4,525	4,519	5,221
50	13,440	13,782	10,052	9,214	13,054
100	23,841	23,298	16,389	16,194	19,926

Additionally, when looking at Scenarios 3 and 4 in Table 1, we note a marked decrease in the number of new flows during the testing period compared to the other cases. In essence, it appears that these scenarios were latency bound: each thread had to spend more time in elevations because there were serial elevations for each thread from the hosts and the switch. As we see from Fig. 2 that the number of OpenFlow messages required (namely `PacketIn` messages and the associated `PacketOut+FlowMod` responses) are increased by a factor of three in Scenarios 3 and 4 because the hosts and the switch are each performing the elevations and the switch is also elevating the end-hosts' own `PacketIn` messages. As a result, each thread simply spends more time waiting for the initial round-trip.

5.3   Security Evaluation

We examine the effectiveness of the correlated sensing approach using the configuration described by Scenario 4 in the performance evaluation. We create four cases in which we vary the proper operation status of the client and the server. Across the four possible combinations, we vary whether the host elevates packets normally or whether it evades proper operation by not elevating the packet appropriately.

Table 2. Number of connections allowed and denied by scenario.

Case number	Client status	Server status	Client flows approved	Server flows approved	Client flows rejected	Server flows rejected
1	Normal	Normal	500	500	0	0
2	Normal	Evades	500	0	0	500
3	Evades	Normal	0	N/A	500	N/A
4	Evades	Evades	0	N/A	500	N/A

In Table 2, we show the results of testing these four cases across 500 trials each. As expected, when both the client and server are operating normally, all the flows are approved. In the second case, where the client acts properly but the server agent does not, the initial packets are approved and reach the server, but the server's responses are dropped because the server failed to elevate both the client's original packet and the server's response packet to the controller. Scenarios 3 and 4 proceed identically since the controller denies the packets when the OpenFlow switch elevates them because the client failed to originally elevate the packets. In that case, the packets are discarded before the server can receive them, so the server never knows to create a response.

As we discussed in Sect. 3.3, if the switch between the hosts is legacy, the uncompromised host triggers the controller's detection rather than the Open-Flow switch. Further, if both hosts are compromised with a legacy switch, the communication goes undetected. We omit these cases for brevity.

In these experiments, we simply disable the sensor rather than having it create forged data. Since the flow decisions use the network tuple (IP addresses, ports, and transport protocol), any alteration of these fields would constitute a new flow and thus the forgery in an elevation request would cause the actual packets to not match a flow rule when an uncompromised agent elevates the packet, resulting in a drop rule by the controller. Alterations of other fields in the packet headers could be detected simply by including those fields in the controller's local active flows table.

6 Conclusion

In this work, we examine how network operators can detect even root-level compromises that affect the accuracy of data reported by host-based sensors by correlating that data with other sensors in the network. We focus on the Open-Flow protocol and show that if a single non-compromised sensor exists on the network path a flow takes, a centralized network controller can detect discrepancies in the information reported by any compromised sensors on that same path with perfect accuracy. Our performance results show that this correlated sensing comes with little extra cost over a standard OpenFlow deployment. In around 90% of cases, the round trip time of the first packet exchange in a connection takes less than 20 ms, which includes all of the required flow elevation. Since this flow elevation occurs only during the first round-trip of a new flow, these overheads are unlikely to affect the user experience while offering tangible security benefits.

Acknowledgement. This material is based upon work supported by the National Science Foundation under Grant No. 1422180.

References

1. Bawany, N.Z., Shamsi, J.A., Salah, K.: DDoS attack detection andmitigation using SDN: methods, practices, and solutions. Arab. J. Sci. Eng. **42**, 425–441 (2017). https://doi.org/10.1007/s13369-017-2414-5

2. Bhattarai, R., Valle, E., Dhanraj, M., Kelly, R.: Advanced endpoint protection test report. Technical report, Palo Alto Networks (2018). https://www.paloaltonetworks.com/resources/whitepapers/2018-nss-labs-advanced-endpoint-protection-report
3. Bratus, S., D'Cunha, N., Sparks, E., Smith, S.W.: TOCTOU, traps, and trusted computing. In: Lipp, P., Sadeghi, A.-R., Koch, K.-M. (eds.) Trust 2008. LNCS, vol. 4968, pp. 14–32. Springer, Heidelberg (2008). https://doi.org/10.1007/978-3-540-68979-9_2
4. Butterworth, J., Kallenberg, C., Kovah, X., Herzog, A.: Problems with the Static Root of Trust for Measurement. Black Hat USA (2013)
5. McKeown, N., Anderson, T., Balakrishnan, H., Parulkar, G., Peterson, L., Rexford, J., Shenker, S., Turner, J.: Openflow: enabling innovation in campus networks. SIGCOMM Comput. Commun. Rev. **38**, 69–74 (2008)
6. Min, B., Varadharajan, V.: A novel malware for subversion of self-protection in anti-virus. Softw. Pract. Exper. 361–379 (2016). https://doi.org/10.1002/spe.2317
7. Najd, M.E., Shue, C.A.: DeepContext: an openflow-compatible, host-based SDN for enterprise networks. In: IEEE Conference on Local Computer Networks (LCN), pp. 112–119 (2017). https://doi.org/10.1109/LCN.2017.12
8. Neely, L.: Exploits at the Endpoint: SANS 2016 Threat Landscape Survey. SANS Institute InfoSec Reading Room, September (2016). https://www.sans.org/reading-room/whitepapers/firewalls/paper/37157
9. Pfaff, B., et al.: The design and implementation of open vSwitch. In: 1 USENIX Symposium on Networked Systems Design and Implementation (NSDI 2015), pp. 117–130 (2015). https://www.usenix.org/conference/nsdi15/technical-sessions/presentation/pfaff
10. Taylor, C.R., MacFarland, D.C., Smestad, D.R., Shue, C.A.: Contextual, flow-based access control with scalable host-based SDN techniques. In: IEEE International Conference on Computer Communications, pp. 1–9 (2016)
11. Wagner, D., Soto, P.: Mimicry attacks on host-based intrusion detection systems. In: ACM Conference on Computer and Communications Security, pp. 255–264 (2002). https://doi.org/10.1145/586110.586145
12. Wang, A., Guo, Y., Hao, F., Lakshman, T., Chen, S.: Scotch: elastically scaling up SDN control-plane using vSwitch based overlay. In: ACM International on Conference on Emerging Networking Experiments and Technologies, pp. 403–414 (2014). https://doi.org/10.1145/2674005.2675002

Footprints: Ensuring Trusted Service Function Chaining in the World of SDN and NFV

Montida Pattaranantakul[1,3,4(✉)], Qipeng Song[1], Yanmei Tian[2], Licheng Wang[2], Zonghua Zhang[1,3], and Ahmed Meddahi[1]

[1] IMT Lille Douai, Institute Mine-Télécom, Lille, France
{montida.pattaranantakul,qipeng.song,zonghua.zhang,
ahmed.meddahi}@imt-lille-douai.fr
[2] Beijing University of Posts and Telecommunications, Beijing, China
tianym0213@163.com, wanglc2012@126.com
[3] CNRS UMR 5157 SAMOVAR Lab, Télécom SudParis, Évry, France
[4] National Electronics and Computer Technology Center, Pathumthani, Thailand

Abstract. Network Function Virtualization (NFV) and Software Defined Networking (SDN) empower Service Function Chaining (SFC), which integrates an ordered list of Virtualized Network Functions (VNFs) together for implementing a particular service. However, the high-level SFC policy specification cannot guarantee that the VNFs are always chained in an expected manner (or the packet flows of the service are forwarded to the VNFs of concern in a predefined order). An attacker can manage to bypass or evade the security VNFs (*e.g.*, firewall, virus scanner, DPI) and deviate the packets flows from the pre-specified path. It is thus a significant need to have an efficient self-checking mechanism in place, ensuring the SFC to be implemented in a secure and correct way. We develop such a scheme based on an improved crypto primitive, *Lite identity-based ordered multisignature*, which enforces all the VNFs in the same service chain to sequentially sign the packets received. Then the last hop of the chain will verify the aggregate signature, so as to validate the authenticity of the VNFs, as well as their orders in the chain. We leverage the IETF Network Service Header (NSH) to implement our scheme and run the experiments in a real-world environment to evaluate its performance in terms of computational overhead and latency.

Keywords: NFV · SDN · SFC · Aggregate signature · Pairings

1 Introduction

Service Function Chaining (SFC) [7,12], also known as VNF forwarding graph, refers to the capability of defining a set of service functions (*e.g.*, firewall, NAT, DPI) which are then stitched together in the network to create a service chain. Thanks to this capability, network operators can arbitrary set up different service

© ICST Institute for Computer Sciences, Social Informatics and Telecommunications Engineering 2019
Published by Springer Nature Switzerland AG 2019. All Rights Reserved
S. Chen et al. (Eds.): SecureComm 2019, LNICST 305, pp. 287–301, 2019.
https://doi.org/10.1007/978-3-030-37231-6_16

chains from the instantiated VNFs to meet their application-specific requirements. For example, in data center use case, a service chain can be specified as SFC_i : firewall → virus scan → DPI → NAT. Recently, we have seen some research efforts paid to SFC, with focus on optimizing the resources used for creating a service chain. One significant issue that has been overlooked is the gap between high-level SFC specification and its enforcement at data plane. It lacks efficient mechanisms that can ensure the SFC specification is correctly and securely enforced. In other words, we cannot make sure that a service chain specification is correctly translated into the network flow classification with accurate packet forwarding rules. Also, we cannot guarantee that the packet flows associated with a particular service chain are traversed correctly to appropriate and legitimate VNFs according to the predefined policy. Anomalous flow redirection and path deviation [20,23] are interesting threat model examples that can be used by the attackers to manipulate the original service function path. Their objective is to bypass or evade from security functions in the service chain, ultimately leading to the violation of SFC policy. To achieve the objective, attackers can either launch rule modification attack [3,10,23] against victim switches at SDN data plane or topology tampering attack [4,8,21] at SDN control plane. For the former case, a successful rule modification attack can subvert the original rules installed on the victim switch, and redirect the packets. In the later case, attackers can poison the controller's global view of the network topology, and deceive the controller to trust a spoofed topology. Despite various security countermeasures have been proposed, few of them can protect service chain as a whole, and it is extremely difficult to detect and trace back the anomalies in the dynamic NFV and SDN environments.

To tackle the challenges, we propose a new security primitive, called *Lite identity-based ordered multisignature*, which provides efficient self-verification mechanism for examining the behavior of packet traversal and verifying the correct sequence of service function in the service chain. The idea is straightforward indeed: we expect the packets to leave footprints in each VNF so that they can be validated and tracked. We leverage NFV orchestrator and SDN controller, as well as IETF Network Service Header (NSH), to implement the signature scheme for achieving five properties simultaneously, *i.e.*, unforgeability, authenticity, re-order protection, constraint-size of keys and aggregate signatures, and fast signature and verification. We provide sound theoretical proof and show that the proposed scheme can prevent many attacks like anomalous flow redirection and path deviation. The implementation details and prototype development are also presented to demonstrate the feasibility and effectiveness of our scheme.

2   Related Work

Although the concept of *Service Function Chain* has been proposed long time ago, it has not been really implemented due to the limitations of traditional networks. Thanks to the promising benefits of NFV and SDN [17], SFC finds its interesting use case and becomes an active research direction. Nowadays, there are several ongoing research works attempting to address the different challenges raised by SFC. Unfortunately, few studies are devoted to security and dependability issues, the most related work falls into two general categories.

Static Verification. ChainGuard [6] makes use of SFC-related rules stored within the flow tables of virtual switches to gather the actual SFC Overlay and Traffic Steering (SOTS) snapshot and model it as property-based graphs. These graphs are then used to examine whether the actual SOTS is conformed to the required SFC specification. SFC-Checker [22] contains a Stateful Forwarding Graph (SFG) representing how packets are forwarded, how the states of service function are changed, and how the state changes affect the forwarding path. A Quantitative Forwarding Graph (QFG) [24] was built on top of the exiting work on SFG [22] to extend the capability of SLA verification. After a careful study on their approaches, we observed that they introduce two major drawbacks. First, it is a static verification. The verification has been examined based on the forwarding graph that is indeed generated according to the network information such as topology, flow tables, service states, *etc.* This may incur much overhead, as a verifier must periodically pull the underlying information from the data plane elements (*e.g.*, the flow tables from virtual switches), and regularly regenerate the forwarding graph. Second, it is non-trivial to extract the right information from a large number of flow tables entries which are relevant for SFC verification.

Active Verification. SFC Path Tracer [5] is a tool for troubleshooting SFC. The controller artificially injects probe packet in the chain input to generate the trace. Once the probe packet traverses the network elements in the target chain, it is mirrored by the trace tool to discover which forwarder handled the packet. SDNsec [20] and REV [23] are implemented based on Message Authentication Code (MAC). Each switch along the forwarding path computes MAC and attaches as a tag to each packet. To compute MAC, they use a symmetric key with the shared key sharing between controller and the corresponding switches on the path. The controller can instruct any switches to provide report and thus inspects the path that was taken through analyzing the tag. In addition to SDNsec, REV leverages a public/private key pair to enforce a destination switch to generate signature, and attaches it together with a verification report. One problem of REV is that it comes at the cost of complicated key management and has a high packet overhead, because it is implemented with RSA primitive. Although SDNsec attempted to reduce the key management cost by using only symmetric key for MAC computation (*i.e.*, 128-bits AES), it still incurs engineering complexity to modify and eventually add specific forwarding information (*e.g.*, flow ID, forwarding entry and path validation fields) into the packet header. The same complexity issue also occurs in SFC Path Tracer, as it requires to set specific bits in the IP header to trigger OpenFlow rules and installed the related trace rules in switch tables, so as to instruct the switches to copy those mirrored packets to the trace tool. As a result, heavy traffic overhead could be generated between the controller and switches.

3   Background and Challenges

This Section firstly explains SFC background, its relationships with SDN and NFV Management and Orchestration (NFV MANO) in ETSI NFV framework, and then highlight the potential challenges.

3.1   SFC Working Principles

The implementation of SFC involves several steps, ranging from the specification of high-level network service, resource allocation, VNF instantiation and placement, to VNF selection, SFC composition, traffic steering and forwarding. For better understanding SFC architecture and its relationship with SDN and NFV, we start with explaining the architecture model from high-level business description to low-level service deployment. As presented in Fig. 1, the network operators specify high-level description about network service, such as application topology, network policy, and SFC policy which instruct the traffic flows of a particular user to go through an appropriate set of ordered service functions from a given source to destination. In particular, NFV orchestrator parses the information w.r.t VNF descriptions to VNF Manager (VNFM) for instantiating specific VNFs (*e.g.*, virus scan, firewall, DPI), and the corresponding information to Virtualized Infrastructure Manager (VIM) for allocating NFVI resources. The SDN controller is used to receive all the necessary instructions from VIM, managed data-plane elements (*e.g.*, classifier, Service Function Forwarders (SFFs), VNFs, and proxy devices), provided SFC data path programmability, and configured the flow rules.

Specifically, classifier acts as entry and exit points for SFC-based traffic steering. It performs packet classification, provides SFC encapsulation, and directs the matched traffic to appropriate service function paths. To encapsulate the packets, it adds NSH-header [15], also known as service chaining encapsulation protocol for SFC, which contains Service Path Identifier (SPI) and Service Index

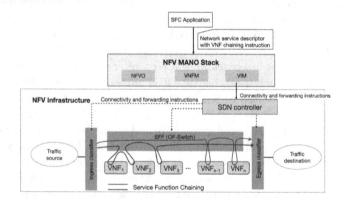

Fig. 1. Intra-domain orchestrated architecture with the corresponding SFC workflow

(SI) to each packet. The SPI represents the service path for a particular SFC and identifies the ordering (position) of VNFs that must be performed. The SI is used to determine the next VNF to be traversed. Once the packet reaches SFF, it removes the outer encapsulation and trigger a lookup based on SPI and SI to identify the outgoing encapsulation. For example, the packets are either forwarded to SFFs or VNFs. Meanwhile, VNF is responsible for specific treatment of the received packets. It can be either NSH-aware or NSH-unaware VNFs. In the case of NSH-unaware VNF, an additional proxy function need to be added.

3.2 Challenges

As SFC is currently still a concept-level technology, many challenges need to be tackled. Below we intend to articulate some SFC security challenges.

- **VNF authenticity:** Verifying the authenticity of service functions has not yet been addressed in much detail so far, especially in the context of SFC. One of the grand challenges is that the network operators may not even notice and have the right to examine whether a set of VNFs involved in a service chain is compromised, or whether there exists any malicious VNF instances. An example attack scenario is that an adversary may launch topology tampering attack [4,8] or DDoS attack [21] to make the legitimate VNFs unavailable and manage to impersonate these victim nodes, receiving and responding the packets on their behalf. This situation misleads the network nodes, including controller and other VNF instances, to communicate and synchronize with the adversary instead of the legitimate ones.
- **Reliable and consistent VNF chaining:** The ability to build a complex or a specific service chain by composing several types of VNFs is one of the key features provided by SFC. However, a newly proposed NFV/SDN-enabled SFC can be vulnerable to new pitfalls which can be exploited by the attackers. For example, they may target individual SFF by using rule modification attacks to tamper the flow rules [3,10,23]. As a result, the packets can be deviated from their original path, ultimately violating original SFC policies. Considering the gap by design between NFV orchestrator, SDN controller and virtualized functions at data plane, it is challenging to examine the actual SFC deployment and make sure it is truly conformed to the predefined SFC policy.
- **Ordering property preservation:** In particular, end-to-end application traffic flows are often required to traverse various VNFs in a sequence manner as specified in SFC policy. One of the key observations is that these VNF instances involved in a particular service chain have been deployed independently. Each VNF is responsible for specific treatment of the received packets, and totally unrelated to others [19]. Although many service functions in a service chain are clearly defined in a strict order, it is almost impossible for network operators to verify the ordering property of VNFs in their actual SFC deployment. Out-of-order traversal attack [9,23] is an attack example that can substantially disrupt the ordering (position) of VNFs in the service

chain. Our careful survey indicates that an efficient self-verification mechanism for examining the correct sequence of service functions (or correct packet
traversal) in a service chain has not been extensively studied.

4 Problem Statement

4.1 System Model

Typically, in each intra-domain orchestrated architecture, there is a centralized controller which manages and controls a set of data-plane elements (*e.g.*,
classifier, SFFS). Network operators can either specify high-level SFC policies
using Network Service Descriptor (NSD) or directly interact with SDN controller through the provided SFC API. The controller translates SFC policies
into a specific service function path, adjusts the path based on VNF status and
overlay links, and installs a set of forwarding rules on the data-plane elements
accordingly. To steer the traffic flows, SFF uses the flow rules installed in its
flow tables to determine the forwarding path and decide which action needs to
be performed. Specifically, the flow rules consist of two parts: (1) *match fields*
which filters packet headers; and (2) *instructions* indicate what actions need to
be taken when the matched packets are found, *e.g.*, drop packet, forwarding to
the port. Upon the arrival of new packet, SFF checks if the packet matches any
existing flow rules. If so, it processes the packet based on the matching rule with
the highest priority. Otherwise, it sends a Packet-In message to controller to ask
for proper actions. The controller decides on the route of packet and sends the
corresponding rules to SFF through a standard control channel like OpenFlow
[14]. This event is known as Flow-Mod messages. Figure 2 illustrates an example

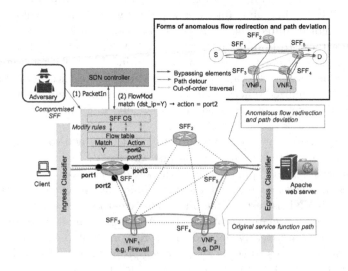

Fig. 2. Rule installation in SFF and the relevant attack models

where a routing action is taken once a matched packet with destination Y (*e.g.*, Apache web server) and source X (*e.g.*, client) arrived at SFF1.

4.2   Threat Model

This Section presents several important threat models that potentially lead to anomalous flow redirection or path deviation. Specifically, those attack models aim to not only compromise authenticity and integrity of VNFs, but also the ordering property of service chains. We generally consider two families of attacks.

Rule modification attacks [3,10,23], which target at the victim SFFs for changing the original service function path. Once such attack succeeds, an attacker can manipulate the SFF's flow rules to redirect anomalous packets. Specifically, it can be further classified into three different forms (as shown in the right corner of Fig. 2): (1) *Bypass elements*, in which one or more VNFs on the intended service chain are bypassed; (2) *Path detour*, the packets are redirected back to the original path after being forwarded to certain anomalous VNFs; and (3) *Out-of-order traversal*, the purpose of this attack is to use brute force to compromise the ordering property of the service chain specified in the SFC policy. To achieve these goals, attackers can compromise the SFF by exploiting the vulnerabilities of its hosting OS and install backdoor program that allows them to arbitrarily perform malicious operations, *e.g.*, install, delete, or modify the flow tables. As shown in Fig. 2, attacker can modify the output port of forwarding rule installed at the flow table of the compromised $SFF1$ in order to evade from security functions (*e.g.*, firewall and DPI) involved in a service chain.

Topology tampering attacks [4,8,21], in which attackers intend to spoof the controller's view of the network topology, and deceive it to believe in a spurious topology. This finally causes the false flow rule installation in the SFFs, making it possible to redirect the traffic flow from victim VNF to the one under attacker's control. As a matter of fact, SDN controller maintains a global view of network topology, including hosts, virtual machines, VNFs, SFFs, and their link connections, by the Host Tracking Service (HTS) and the Link Discovery Service (LDS). In particular, the controller keeps listening to the Packet-In messages coming from SFFs in order to maintain the Host Profile. An attacker can launch host location hijacking to corrupt HTS module by spoofing the victim's address information (*e.g.*, VNF's IP address), which leads to the inconsistent location information between the existing Host Profile and the information received from incoming Packet-In messages. As a result, the HTS believes that the host has been migrated and moved to a new location (which is not true), and then updates the new location information in the Host Profile. One of the major reasons leading to this attack is the lack of host authenticity checking.

5   Proposed Solution

To tackle the aforementioned challenges and solve the identified problem, we intend to develop an efficient self-checking scheme that can preserve the authenticity of VNFs, as well as the integrity and ordering property of the particular

Table 1. Notations used in Lite identity-based ordered multisignature formulation

Notations	Description
$e(.,.)$	A symmetric bilinear form. For example, $e(g^a, g^b) = e(g,g)^{ab} = e(g^b, g^a)$
$\mathbb{Z}, \mathbb{Z}_p, \mathbb{Z}_p^*$	A set of integers, the integers modulo $p \geq 2$, and the multiplicative group modulo p
$\mathbb{G}, \mathbb{G}_T$	Groups of the same prime-order p on rational points of an elliptic curve over a finite field
$1_{\mathbb{G}}, 1_{\mathbb{G}_T}$	The identity elements of $\mathbb{G}, \mathbb{G}_T$ respectively
$\mathbb{G}^*$	A set of generators of $\mathbb{G}$, $i.e.$, $\mathbb{G}^* = \mathbb{G} - 1_{\mathbb{G}}$
$\{0,1\}^*$	A set of all binary strings of finite length
$|x|$	If x is a string then $|x|$ is its length in bits
$x\|y$	If x, y are strings then $x\|y$ denotes an encoding from which x and y are uniquely recoverable

service chains. Also, such a scheme needs to be fully distributed, lightweight and scalable, in order to be implemented in the extremely dynamic NFV and SDN environments. We seek the design foundation from digital signature scheme, especially the ones meeting our design requirements, $e.g.$, ordered multisignatures and identity-based sequential aggregate signatures [2]. The motivation is straightforward, $i.e.$, generating footprints for packet flows at each VNFs. Specifically, each VNF involved in a service chain needs to attest its signature on the packet received, while a verifier can later verify the signature and determine whether the security properties of concern for a particular service chain is well preserved.

5.1   Design Properties

The new security primitive we propose is called *Lite identity-based ordered multisignature*, and its main objective is to achieve the following properties.

- **Unforgeability:** it should be computationally infeasible for any adversary to produce a forged aggregate signature implicating an honest identity.
- **Authenticity:** signer's authenticity should be preserved. Given a message, the corresponding aggregate signature does not only provide the knowledge indicating that some specific group of signers ($e.g.$, VNF appliances) signed it, but also to the order in which they signed.
- **Re-order protection:** it must enforce an additional unforgeability with respect to the ordering of signers. In other words, it should not be possible to re-order the positions of honest signers, even if all other signers are malicious.
- **Constant size:** the sizes of aggregate signature at any stage should be constant regardless the number of signers and messages.

- **Signature and verification accelerations:** an alternative solution to minimize overall computational overhead is to ignore verification call at intermediate nodes and accelerate the construction time using three pairing computations. As our objective aims to verify the dependability and consistency for the entire SFC, so that there is no need to perform intensive verification before signing. While three pairing computations in the terms of (X, Y, Z) can help to accelerate the construction times in both signature and verification. Such each term is executed in parallel, resulting in a much faster computation time when compared to a typical model-based one-time processing. See Sect. 5.2 for more construction details.

5.2   Construction Methodology

To construct the proposed scheme, there are four steps involved. All the notations used in our formulation are summarized in Table 1.

Setup: the algorithm first run $\mathcal{G}$ as a bilinear-group generation algorithm to obtain outputs $(p, \mathbb{G}, \mathbb{G}_T, e)$. It then chooses a random generator $g \in \mathbb{G}^*$, a random number $\alpha \in \mathbb{Z}_p$, and two cryptographic hash functions $H_1 : \{0,1\}^* \to \mathbb{G}$ and $H_2 : \{0,1\}^* \to \mathbb{Z}_p^*$. It returns $(p, \mathbb{G}, \mathbb{G}_T, e, g, g^\alpha, H_1, H_2)$ as the public parameters; where α and g^α indicate the master secret key (msk) and the master public key (mpk) respectively.

Key derivation: on inputs msk and user's identity $id \in \{0,1\}^*$ (say IP address, etc.), the algorithm computes and returns the user's secret key sk_{id}.

$$sk_{id} = H_1(id)^\alpha \tag{1}$$

Signing: on inputs his/her own secret key sk_{id_i}, a message m, and the corresponding signature σ from an intended path $L = (id_1, ..., id_{i-1})$, the algorithm first parses σ as a three pairing computations $(X, Y, Z)^1$. Then, the signer with identity id_i continues to performs the following steps:

- Pre-computation[2]: $s^{(i)} = s_1 s_2 \cdots s_i$; where $s_j = H_2(id_1 || id_2 || \cdots || id_j)$ for $j = 1, 2, \cdots, i$.
- Choosing random number by the ith signer: $r^{(i)} \in \mathbb{Z}_p^*$.
- Computation:

$$X' \leftarrow H_1(m)^{r^{(i)} \cdot s^{(i)}} \cdot sk_{id_i} \tag{2}$$

$$Y' \leftarrow H_1(H_1(m))^{r^{(i)}} \cdot sk_{id_i} \tag{3}$$

---

[1] For the first signer ($i = 1$), σ is defined as $(1_\mathbb{G}, 1_\mathbb{G}, 1_\mathbb{G})$.
[2] If the intended signing order fixed, then s needs be computed only once. Whenever the intended signing sequence change, this step needs to be re-executed.

- Finally, the algorithm returns $(X \cdot X', \ Y^{1/s_i} \cdot Y', Z^{1/s_i} \cdot g^{r^{(i)}})$; where $1/s_i$ means $s_i^{-1} \bmod p$.

Verification: on inputs mpk, a message m, and the corresponding signature σ from the intended path $L = (id_1, .., id_n)$, the algorithm first returns 0 if all of $id_1, ..., id_n$ are not distinct. This check is needed to ensure that there are no signers repetition occurred during signature construction. If the above condition is met, it parses σ as (X, Y, Z) and a verifier performs the following steps:

- Pre-computation[3]: $s = s^{(n)} = s_1 s_2 \cdots s_n$; where $s_j = H_2(id_1 || id_2 || \cdots || id_j)$,

$$S = \prod_{i=1}^{n} H_1(id_i)^{\frac{1}{\prod_{j=i+1}^{n} s_j}} \tag{4}$$

$$T = \prod_{i=1}^{n} H_1(id_i) \tag{5}$$

- Verification: the algorithm checks whether the following two equations hold true simultaneously. If not, the algorithm returns 0. Otherwise, it returns 1 indicating that the signature σ is valid with respect to the intended path, authenticated signers and their ordering properties $id_1, \cdots, id_n$.

$$e(Y, g) \overset{?}{=} e(H_1(H_1(m)), Z) \cdot e(S, g^\alpha) \tag{6}$$

$$e(X, g) \overset{?}{=} e(H_1(m), Z^s) \cdot e(T, g^\alpha) \tag{7}$$

To summarize, the proposed scheme aims at examining the behavior of packet traversal. That says whether the packets associated with a particular service chain are indeed traversed through all intended VNFs in sequence manner as specified in SFC policy. Thanks to the verifiability properties of signing order and ordinary signature given by the proposed scheme, that provide a verifier the ability to examine the consistency of service chain and to ensure that only the *honest* participants are able to produce a valid aggregate signature on that message. Since the verifier knows a certain number of signer's identity (say a set of IP addresses of VNFs involved in a service chain) and their sequences, so that it can straightforwardly verify its consistency from the bilinearity condition of a pairing. As a result, any missing, detouring, bypassing one or more VNFs along the intended path, out-of-order traversal, or the occurrence of impersonating the target VNFs, can lead to unsatisfied condition under bilinear maps.

6 Implementation and Evaluation

In this Section, we present the proof of concept (PoC) implementation of our proposal over NFV/SDN environment, and evaluate its performance in terms of computational overhead and end-to end latency.

---

[3] If the intended signing order fixed, then s, S, T needs be computed only once. Otherwise, this step needs to be re-executed.

6.1 Implementation Details

The correctness of our digital signature scheme can be theoretically proved, but its implementation in real environment is non-trivial, and we need to solve the following technical challenges: (1) generate and distribute the cryptographic parameters to each involved VNF node; (2) add signature generation into VNF nodes; and (3) transmit packets with signature. To address these challenges, we propose the following solutions.

A Trusted Private Key Generator (PKG). The first challenge requires a PKG to generate its master public key mpk, the master secret key msk, and the public parameters such as elliptic curve type, key size, user's secret key sk_{id}, *etc.*, (as discussed in the *Setup* step of Sect. 5.2). Such a PKG server is developed and run alongside the ODL SFC controller. To create a service chain, a SFC description file including information identities of each service function, the SPI associated with a particular service chain and SI which is used to determine the next VNF to be traversed, is simultaneously sent to PKG and ODL controller. With this information, PKG generates public parameters and distribute them to each involved VNF through REST API. The implementation of PKG is built on top of PBC (Pairing-Based Cryptography) library [16], PyPBC (Python binding for PCB) [18] and Python Flask web framework.

NSH and OMS Aware VNF. In our implementation, the first VNF on a given service chain is in charge of generating and inserting the aggregate signature. Then the next hop downstream VNFs should be able to retrieve the signature from the received packet and update it with the new value generated based on the *Signing* method described in Sect. 5.2. To achieve the goal, we developed NSH and OMS (Ordered Multisignature) aware VNF, to be able to parse the NSH header and perform the appropriate operations (*e.g.*, generating, inserting or updating the aggregate signature). Meanwhile, the signature verification is done at the last classifier on a service chain, namely just before leaving SFC domain. We developed a verification service as an extended function and deployed alongside of the egress classifier to take charge of signature validation. In addition, a message m which is used as input in signing process can be any given value if it is known by all VNF nodes on a particular service chain. However, the NSH payload is not suggested to be used as m, because the content of payload may be modified by some VNFs (*e.g.*, NAT) along the service path. This leads to the failure of signature verification.

Extended NSH Metadata Type-1. To use our proposed scheme, the signature should be inserted into the packets. In the current implementation, we leverage the metadata field of NSH header, which has two types according to the specification of RFC8300: (1) NSH MD type-1, which has fixed 16 bytes length; (2) NSH MD type-2, which has a variable length. However, Type-1 has no sufficient room to occupy the signature, while Type-2 has not been implemented so far. Therefore, we extend NSH MD Type-1 with an extra variable signature field. Also, we use one non-reserved bit in the NSH base header as *signature bit* to indicate that the packet are carried with signature (value 1), and 0 otherwise. If a packet with signature has been received by a VNF, the signature will be extracted from the NSH header and updated with the newly generated value using its VNF's secret key sk_{id} shared by the PKG at the SFC setup step.

6.2   Performance Evaluation

Our prototype implementation is developed using VirtualBox virtualization and the Vagrant tool. The hardware specification of the host system that runs the testbed is based on Linux desktop with 2.5 GHz Intel Core i7 CPU and 16G RAM. All the deployed network nodes including controller, VNFs, classifiers and SFFs are implemented as docker containers running inside Vagrant VM with Ubuntu/xenial 64, each node has been customized with 2 CPU cores and 4G RAM. Our motivation to use OpenDaylight (version Fluorine) [13] as an ODL SFC controller, which is developed with fully NSH encapsulation support, while allowing us to use it for developing a prototype that carries aggregate signature generated from our proposed approach.

Computational Overhead. To evaluate the performance of our proposed scheme, we ran a set of experiments and examined the relationship between the processing capacity of our proposed scheme and the number of VNFs involved in a service chain. In practice, we used PBC library with Type A pairings to create a group of $\mathbb{G}$ and $\mathbb{G}_{\mathbb{T}}$ on the rational points of a elliptic curve $y^2 = x^3 + x$ over a finite filed. Using embedding degree (the degree of certain extension of the ground filed), which is $k = 2$, the elements in $\mathbb{G}$ can be respectively represented using 512, 256, and 160 bits for achieving the equivalent standard security level, 256, 180, and 80 bits [1]. It is clear that less bit-length of elements in $\mathbb{G}$ incur less complexity, and less security level. However, to achieve the lowest security level, at least 80 bits security are required, leading to 160 bits elliptic curve key.

We ran the experiment 50 epochs with different key sizes and calculate the 95% confidence interval. As shown in Fig. 3, we observed that the lower bound latency goes linearly. It strongly depends on three major factors: (1) the employed cryptographic parameter settings which include the type of pairing operations over the specified elliptic curve, the length of elements in $\mathbb{G}$ and keys, as well as signing and verification algorithms; (2) the total number of VNFs in a service chain; and (3) the processing delays caused by signing operations conducted by each VNF and the verification operation at the last egress classifier. For example, if we only consider the processing delay w.r.t signature and verification constructions, without taking into account other parameters such as the parameter settings, times for packet transmission and manipulation (*e.g.*, inserting, parsing or updating the signature into NSH's header), the overall processing delays for a particular service chain $\mathcal{D}_{SFC_i}$ can be obtained in the form: $\mathcal{D}_{SFC_i} = \sum_{i=1}^{N} d_{s_i} + d_v$; where d_{s_i} is the delay time takes by each VNF to complete signing, and d_v is the delay time to verify and validate the signature. In

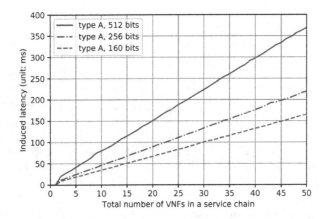

Fig. 3. The relationships between number of VNFs in a service chain and latency

practice, the number of VNFs involved in a service chain is normally less than 10 (the exemplified SFC use cases are given in [11]). For example, to achieve the lowest bound of security level (80 bits), it takes around 34.76 ms to successfully validate signature when 10 VNF nodes were involved in the service chain. This latency is minimal and acceptable for most of network services.

Latency. To evaluate the end-to-end packet transmission latency brought by the proposed scheme. We run 6 groups of experiments, in which the number of VNF nodes involved in a service chain is varied from 2 to 7. Not that these numbers of VNFs are reasonable value when considering several typical SFC deployment use cases discussed in [11]. Within each group experiment, the case without signature scheme is used as comparison reference. We consider two OMS enabled cases with different elliptic curve key sizes (*i.e.*, 160 bits and 256 bits). Also, we apply a probabilistic method into our scheme to reduce as much as possible the end-to-end latency related to the service chain. At the initialization stage, the first VNF is configured to sign a received packet based on a given probability. That says, in our experiment, we consider the cases of signing probability 100%, 50% and 10% respectively[4].

To evaluate the performance, we continuously sent 100 ping messages from client to server and measured the end-to-end latency. The results are illustrated in Fig. 4. To achieve the lowest security level (160 bits elliptic key), if signing probability is set as 100%, 50%, and 10%, on average the latency respectively increased around 5.80, 3.25, and 1.52 times when compared to a conventional packet transmission without signature. The experimental results showed that the overall latency is significantly reduced, especially with 10% signing probability, the resulting latency can be almost ignored.

---

[4] When signing probability is set as 100%, every packets have to be signed. While 10% and 50% mean on average only 10 and 50 out of every 100 packets will be signed.

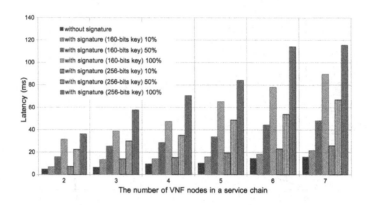

Fig. 4. Transmission of ping packets with and without signature construction

7 Conclusion

SFC plays a key role in integrating various VNFs together for achieving a particular service in NFV and SDN. But a gap between SFC policy specification (*e.g.*, forward graph in NFV orchestrator, high-level policies in SDN controller) and enforcement remains, leaving attackers to possibly manipulate the SFC. For example, evading from the security functions or launch blackhole attacks. This paper presented an efficient self-checking scheme for ensuring trust service functions chaining (SFC) in NFV and SDN. More specifically, the scheme aims at preserving authenticity of VNFs and their order in SFC by using an identity-based ordered multisignature scheme. Each VNF involved in a service chain must sign the packets it receives, and the last hop of the chain verifies the signature. As the aggregate signature has compact and constant size, it can be easily inserted into NSH header with minimal computational overhead. We theoretically proved the security and effectiveness of the scheme, and experimentally demonstrated its feasibility (w.r.t latency) in real-world environment. Our future work will be focused on the implementation, deployment, and evaluation of our scheme in several different use cases, *e.g.*, web service, email, video service. We also expect to leverage NSH MD Type-2 and improve our proposal with an efficient probabilistic model to find the optimal tradeoff between the transmission overhead and detection performance.

References

1. Barker, E.B., Barker, W.C., Burr, W.E., Polk, W.T., Smid, M.E.: SP 800-57. Recommendation for key management, Part 1: General (revised). Technical report (2007)
2. Boldyreva, A., Gentry, C., O'Neill, A., Yum, D.H.: Ordered multisignatures and identity-based sequential aggregate signatures with applications to secure routing. In: CCS 2007, pp. 276–285 (2007)

3. Chi, P.W., Kuo, C.T., Guo, J.W., Lei, C.L.: How to detect a compromised SDN switch. In: NetSoft 2015, pp. 1–6, April 2015
4. Dhawan, J., Poddar, R., Mahajan, K., Mann, V.: SPHINX: detecting security attacks in software-defined networks. In: NDSS 2015, pp. 1–15, February 2015
5. Eichelberger, R.A., Ferreto, T., Tandel, S., Duarte, P.A.P.R.: SFC path tracer: a troubleshooting tool for service function chaining. In: IM 2017, pp. 568–571 (2017)
6. Flittner, M., et al.: ChainGuard: controller-independent verification of service function chaining in cloud computing. In: NFV-SDN 2017, pp. 1–7 (2017)
7. Halpern, J., Pignataro, C.: Service function chainning (SFC) architecture, October 2015. https://tools.ietf.org/html/rfc7665
8. Hong, S., Xu, L., Wang, H., Gu, G.: Poisoning network visibility in software-defined networks: new attacks and countermeasures. In: NDSS 2015, pp. 1–15 (2015)
9. Kim, T.H.J., Basescu, C., Jia, L., Lee, S.B., Hu, Y.C., Perrig, A.: Lightweight source authentication and path validation. In: SIGCOMM 2014 (2014)
10. Li, Q., Zou, X., Huang, Q., Zheng, J., Lee, P.P.C.: Dynamic packet forwarding verification in SDN. IEEE Trans. Dependable Sec. Comput. 16, 1–16 (2018)
11. Liu, W., Li, H., Huang, O., et al.: Service function chaining (SFC) general use cases, September 2014. https://tools.ietf.org/html/draft-liu-sfc-use-cases-08
12. Medhat, A.M., et al.: Service function chaining in next generation networks: state of the art and research challenges. Commun. Mag. 55(2), 216–223 (2017)
13. OpenDaylight fluorine release, August 2018. https://www.opendaylight.org/what-we-do/current-release/fluorine
14. OpenFlow switch specification, June 2012. https://www.opennetworking.org/wp-content/uploads/2014/10/openflow-spec-v1.3.0.pdf
15. Quinn, P., Elzur, U., Pignataro, C.: Network service hearder (NSH), January 2018. https://www.rfc-editor.org/rfc/pdfrfc/rfc8300.txt.pdf
16. Pairing-based cryptography library (2006). https://crypto.stanford.edu/pbc/
17. Pattaranantakul, M., He, R., Song, Q., Zhang, Z., Meddahi, A.: NFV security survey: from use case driven threat analysis to state-of-the-art countermeasures. IEEE Commun. Surv. Tutor. 20(4), 3330–3368 (2018)
18. Python binding for PBC, November 2017. https://github.com/debatem1/pypbc
19. Quinn, P., Nadeau, T.: Problem statement for service function chaining, April 2015. https://tools.ietf.org/html/rfc7498#page-6
20. Sasaki, T., Pappas, C., Lee, T., Hoefler, T., Perrig, A.: SDNsec: forwarding accountability for the SDN Data plane. In: ICCCN 2016, pp. 1–10 (2016)
21. Sim, Y., Lee, H.Y.: Poster: denial-of-service attack using host location hijacking in software-defined network. In: Euro S&P 2016, pp. 1–2 (2016)
22. Tschaen, B., Zhang, Y., et al.: SFC-checker: checking the correct forwarding behavior of Service Function Chaining. In: NFV-SDN 2016, pp. 134–140 (2016)
23. Zhang, P.: Towards rule enforcement verification for software defined networks. In: IEEE INFOCOM 2017, pp. 1–9 (2017)
24. Zhang, Y., Wu, W., Banerjee, S., Kang, J., et al.: SLA-verifier: stateful and quantitative verification for service chaining. In: IEEE INFOCOM 2017, pp. 1–9 (2017)

Security and Analytics

Hecate: Automated Customization of Program and Communication Features to Reduce Attack Surfaces

Hongfa Xue[✉], Yurong Chen, Guru Venkataramani, and Tian Lan

The George Washington University, Washington, D.C., USA
{hongfaxue,gabrielchen,guruv,tlan}@gwu.edu

Abstract. Customizing program and communication features is a commonly adopted strategy to counter security threats that arise from rapid inflation of software features. In this paper, we propose **Hecate**, a novel framework that leverages dynamic execution and trace to create customized, self-contained programs, in order to minimize potential attack surface. It automatically identifies program features (i.e., independent, well-contained operations, utilities, or capabilities) relating to application binaries and their communication functions, tailors and eliminates the features to create customized program binaries in accordance with user needs, in a fully unsupervised fashion. **Hecate** makes novel use of deep learning to identify program features and their constituent functions by mapping dynamic instruction trace to functions in the binaries. It enables us to modularize program features and efficiently create customized program binaries at large scale. We implement a prototype of **Hecate** using a number of open source tools such as DynInst and TensorFlow. Evaluation using real-world executables including OpenSSL and LibreOffice demonstrates that **Hecate** can create a wide range of customized binaries for diverse feature requirements, with the highest accuracy up to 96.28% for feature/function identification and up to 67% reduction of program attack surface.

Keywords: Program customization · Deep learning · Binary analysis

1 Introduction

Feature creep, referring to the ongoing expansion and addition of new features (e.g., excessive capabilities and utilities) in communication protocols and programs [8], leads to not only software system bloat, but also an increased attack surface with higher possibility of vulnerabilities and exploitation. A number of proposals have been made to identify redundant features and to enable customization through static code analysis techniques such as [15,26,32].

In this paper, we propose **Hecate**, a framework that leverages dynamic execution and trace to create customized, self-contained programs to minimize the

© ICST Institute for Computer Sciences, Social Informatics and Telecommunications Engineering 2019
Published by Springer Nature Switzerland AG 2019. All Rights Reserved
S. Chen et al. (Eds.): SecureComm 2019, LNICST 305, pp. 305–319, 2019.
https://doi.org/10.1007/978-3-030-37231-6_17

corresponding attack surface. A key feature of **Hecate** is that it makes novel use of deep learning to identify program and communication-related features in binary in an automated fashion. It employs the test-cases to invoke different program features, applies trace splicing to extract dynamic execution paths (of invoked features) from the complete instruction trace, maps the paths to owner functions in the binary code, finally identifies program features (as targets for customization) through their constituent functions. We note that this is a challenging problem, since full symbol or debug information is often not available in optimized and obfuscated binaries, while static analysis techniques such as execution path alignment [14] cannot easily achieve scalability and accuracy. **Hecate** addresses the challenge by leveraging deep learning. In particular, we consider this mapping from execution path trace to their onwer funcsions as a multi-class classification problem, where each function is considered as a class label, the function's binary code as samples of the class, and an execution path extracted from dynamic instruction trace as the testing sample. Thus, we employ Recursive Neural Network (RNN) to obtain binary code vector embeddings at lexical level and train a multi-class Convolutional Neural Network (CNN) classifier to identify the feature-constituent functions. Instead of extracting the instructions of a limited code fragment, our approach automatically identify various features in large-scale program binaries with accuracy up to 96.28%, in a fully unsupervised fashion.

Identifying the feature-constituent functions enables us to modularize and tailor program features, in accordance with user needs. We propose program customization techniques to tailor program binaries using union, intersection, and subtraction operations if a target feature combination is not readily available in the test-cases. The customized program can be viewed as a sub-graph of the original CFG.

We implement a prototype of **Hecate** using two major modules: feature identification and feature tailoring. It leverages several open-source tools and deep learning algorithms to identify function boundaries and bodies from binary executable. Evaluation using real-world applications, e.g., OpenSSL [22] and LibreOffice [17], shows that **Hecate** achieves an average 92.76% accuracy for function mapping and feature identification. It is able to create a wide range of customized executables and significantly reduces the program size and attack surface up to 85% and 67.6% respectively.

The main contributions of our work are as follows:

- We propose **Hecate**, an automated framework for software mass customization using only binaries. Provided with test-cases for different features, **Hecate** automatically identifies program features and customizes them in accordance with user needs.
- **Hecate** leverages deep learning to identify program features in an unsupervised fashion. In particular, it maps dynamic execution paths from the instruction trace to feature-constituent functions in the executable using a multi-class CNN classifier, achieving an average 92.76% accuracy.

– We implement a prototype of **Hecate** using open-source tools, including ByteWeight [3], RNNLM Toolkit [13], and Tensor-Flow [2]. Evaluation using real-world applications, such as OpenSSL, shows that **Hecate** can efficiently customize large-scale software, and significantly reduce the attack surface by up to 67%.

2 Hecate Design Overview

Software customization comprises two tasks: (i) identifying program features from a binary executable by analyzing and mapping dynamic instruction trace that invokes different features, and (ii) tailoring and rewriting the binary, in accordance with user needs, to create customized, self-contained programs.

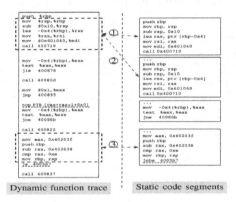

Fig. 1. An illustrative example of feature identification by mapping dynamic instruction trace to functions in static code from OpenSSL.

2.1 Challenges

The goal of **Hecate**'s feature identification is to map dynamic instruction trace (relating to different features) to feature-constituent functions in binary. Ideally, it is possible to log the virtual addresses of each executed instruction. Then we can get the memory layout of each binary module (e.g., through /proc/pid/ma ps on Linux). With these two pieces of information, we could uniquely map a dynamic trace back to static code. However, there are some scenarios in practice where the address is not available. For example, commercial software and operating system are usually slightly obfuscated to deter reverse engineering and unlicensed use. Further, system and kernel libraries are often optimized to reduce disk space requirements [6]. It may be difficult to even locate function entry points (FEPs) since the full symbol or debug information is usually not available in optimized binaries [3]. Thus, we have to utilize code patterns to match dynamic traces. This is a challenging problem because dynamic trace and static code often have different patterns and cannot be accurately matched through techniques such as execution path alignment [14]. Consider the example shown in Fig. 1 with dynamic instruction trace and binary code snippet from OpenSSL. First, as Arrows 1 and 2 indicate, the same basic block from dynamic instruction trace could have multiple matches in the binary, and cannot be uniquely mapped to a single function. Second, the same binary instruction can be interpreted into different verbal presentations, in which case different disassemblers will give different outputs. As Arrow 3 indicates, the binary value 77H can be translated to the opcode either "ja" (jump above) or "jnbe" (jump not below), causing direct pattern matching to fail. Further, when loops and recursive function calls exist in the binary, it is difficult to correctly identify these structures in dynamic instruction trace. We conducted an experiment using a substring matching approach to map the opcode pattern between instruction traces and binary code. Examining two applications, bzip2 and OpenSSL, function mapping techniques only achieves an average accuracy of 76.31% and 73.02%, respectively.

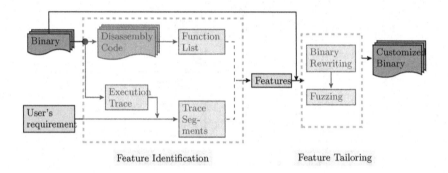

Fig. 2. Hecate system diagram

2.2   Problem Statement

To introduce our problem of software customization, we first need a definition of what a feature is in binary code.

Definition 1. *Function.* *The term* function *in this paper particularly refers to the function identified in static binary code, which is a collection of basic blocks with one entry point (i.e., the next instruction after a call instruction) and possibly multiple exit points (i.e., a return or interrupt instruction). All code reachable from the entry point before reaching any exit point constitutes the body of the assembly function. For a given program, we use $\mathcal{F} = \{f_k, \forall k\}$ to denote the set of all functions existing in the static binary code.*

Definition 2. *Feature.* *A program feature is defined as a set of constituent functions – denoted by $F_i = \{f_i^1, f_i^2, ..., f_i^n\} \subseteq \mathcal{F}$ – which uniquely represent an independent, well-contained operation, utility, or capability of the program.*

A feature at the binary level may not always correspond to a software module at the source level. We use $T = \{F_i, \forall i\}$ to denote the set of all available features in the program.

The goal of **Hecate** is that, given a program binary, test cases invoking program features, and user's customization requirement (i.e., a set of desire features $\hat{T} \subseteq T$), it will produce a modified binary that contains the minimum set of functions to satisfy the user's requirement and to support all desired features in $\hat{T}$. We perform the customization after abstracting the program into Control Flow Graph (CFG). From the perspective of CFG, the customized binary is composed of a CFG that is a subgraph of the original program CFG.

2.3 Approach and System Architecture

Hecate consists of two major modules: feature identification and feature tailoring. Its system architecture is illustrated in Fig. 2. Users provide their requirements (i.e., a list of features that are needed) as well as test-cases to reach different features. **Hecate** takes the program binary and customization requirement as inputs and generate a customized binary consisting of only the desired features. For feature identification, **Hecate** first builds a function library based on static analysis of program binary, including dynamically linked libraries. Byteweight, a learning-based binary analysis tool, is employed to identify function body directly from static program binaries. Next, execute the program using the test-cases provided, analyze the dynamic instruction trace, extract execution paths relating to different features (or feature combinations), and maps them to constituent-functions in the program binary.

The feature tailoring module is explained in Sect. 4. It modularizes program features through their constituent functions and modifies the program binary in accordance with user's customization requirements. The CFG of the customized program can be viewed as a sub-graph of that of the original program, which is able to retain the behavior of only the desired features. At last, a fuzzing engine can be employed to generate inputs and further test the customized binary.

3 Feature Identification

Feature Identification uses trace splicing to extract dynamic execution paths and maps them to owner functions in the binary code, enabling us to identify program features through their constituent functions. In this paper, we define an *execution path* as a sequence of instructions that are executed from a function entry point to an exit point. The function containing the execution path is known as the *owner function*. Our approach leverages deep learning and works in a fully unsupervised, autonomous fashion.

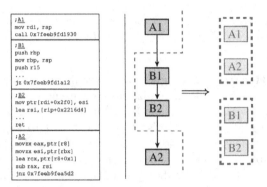

Fig. 3. Extracting dynamic execution paths of each individual function through trace splicing. Boxes stand for basic blocks. A_1 and A_2 belong to function A while B_1 and B_2 belong to function B.

3.1 Function Recognition

We first construct the pre-image and image of our function mapping, using trace splicing and deep-learning tools, respectively. The pre-image is defined as the set of execution paths obtained from dynamic instruction trace, while the image is defined as the set of functions recognized in static program binaries.

We run the target executable with provided test cases to invoke different (combinations of) program features, and collect instruction trace to capture the dynamic execution of the program. The trace is then spliced to extract execution paths belonging to different functions, which serves as the pre-image of our function mapping. Consider the illustrative example shown in Fig. 3, where a sequence of 4 basic blocks, A_1, B_1, B_2, A_2, are captured in dynamic trace, when function f_B is called inside function f_A. Clearly, we cannot directly map the entire sequence to functions in binary code, because it contains two separate execution path, belonging to functions f_A and f_B, respectively. We employ two different methods to splice dynamic trace and extract different execution paths: (1) We track call stack changes together with instruction trace. By recognizing *push* and *pop* operations on the call stack, we can infer function call events, and slice and associate basic blocks that belong to the same function. (2) From the instruction trace, instructions that perform function calls and returns will be recognized and put embedded function calls into different layers.

We remove duplicate basic blocks in execution traces to improve the accuracy of function mapping. Furthermore, every time a function is invoked, a different execution path may be traversed inside the function. These execution paths will be separated and mapped to their owner functions independently, minimizing the probability of false negative in function mapping. In this paper, we unitize ByteWeight [3], a learning-based tool that identifies function bodies from binary.

3.2 Function Mapping

In this paper, we leverage deep learning to propose a solution to enable automated function mapping. model binary instruction sequences using Recursive Neural Network (RNN). The framework is constructed with two key components. First, to obtain vector embedding for a given execution path (that consists of an instruction sequence), we use RNN to map each term in the binary instructions (e.g., opcodes and operands) to a vector embedding at the lexical level, resulting in a signature vector for the entire execution path. Second, we consider the mapping problem as a multi-class classification problem, where each function is considered as a class label, different execution paths obtained from the function's binary code as samples of that class, and an execution path extracted from dynamic instruction trace as the testing sample. We employ a multi-class Convolutional Neural Network (CNN) classifier to identify the owner functions of an arbitrary dynamic instruction trace. Our deep learning approach is inspired by the related work on source code analysis [24, 25, 30].

Embedding Binary Code at the Lexical Level. Consider a disassembly code corpus from a target program, with m distinct terms (e.g., different opcodes and operands) across the whole corpus. We use an RNN with n hidden nodes to convert each term in the code corpus into an embedding vector $U \in \mathbb{R}^{n \times m}$. RNN is known as an effective approach for modeling sequential information, such as sentences in texts or program code. Figure 4 presents the training process of our RNN model for binary code. The input $x_t \in \mathbb{R}^{m+n}$ at time step t is a one-hot vector representation corresponding to the current term, e.g., 'eax'. The hidden layer state vector, $s_t \in \mathbb{R}^n$, stores the current state of the network at step t and captures the information that has already been calculated. Specifically, it can be obtained using the previous hidden state s_{t-1} at time step $t-1$ and the current input x_t at time step t:

$$s_t = f(Ux_t + Ws_{t-1}) \tag{1}$$

Function f is a nonlinear function, e.g., $tanh$ [12]. $U \in \mathbb{R}^{n \times m}$ and $W \in \mathbb{R}^{n \times n}$ are the shared parameters in all time steps.

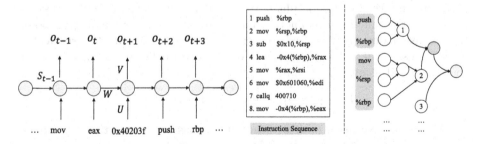

Fig. 4. An illustration of RNN.   **Fig. 5.** An illustration of RAE.

The output, $O_t \in \mathbb{R}^m$, is a vector of probabilities predicting the distribution of the next term in the code corpus. It is calculated based on current state vector along with another shared parameter $V \in \mathbb{R}^{m \times n}$, i.e.:

$$O_t = softmax(V s_t) \tag{2}$$

The parameters $\{U, V, W\}$ are trained using backpropagation through time (BPTT) method in our RNN network (We skip the technical details here and refer readers to [4]). Once RNN training is complete, each term in the code corpus will have a unique embeddings U from Eq. (1), which comprises its semantic representation cross the corpus. We compute such embeddings U to represent the terms of binary instructions at lexical level.

Generating Signature at the Syntax Level. We use Autoencoder to combine embeddings $U \in \mathbb{R}^{nm}$ of the terms from multiple instructions and to obtain a signature vector for a given execution path. Autoencoder is widely used to generate vector space representations for a pairwise composed term with two phases: encode phase and decode phase. It is a simple neural network with one input layer, one hidden layer, and one output layer. As shown in Fig. 5, we apply Autoencoder recursively to a sequence of terms, which is known as the Recursive Autoencoder (RAE). Let $x_1, x_2 \in \mathbb{R}^{nm}$ be the vector embeddings of two different terms, computed using RNN. During encode phase, the composed vector embeddings $Z(x_1, x_2)$ is calculated by:

$$Z(x_1, x_2) = f(W_1[x_1; x_2] + b_1), \tag{3}$$

where $[x_1; x_2] \in \mathbb{R}^{2nm}$ is the concatenation of x_1 and x_2, $W_1 \in \mathbb{R}^{nm \times 2nm}$ is the parameter matrix in encode phase, and $b \in \mathbb{R}^{nm}$ is the offset. Similar to RNN, f again is a nonlinear function, e.g., $tanh$. In decode phase, we need to assess if $Z(x_1, x_2)$ is well learned by the network to represent the composed terms. Thus, we reconstruct the term embeddings by:

$$O[x_1; x_2] = g(W_2[x_1; x_2] + b_2), \tag{4}$$

where $O[x_1; x_2]$ is the reconstructed term embeddings , $W_2 \in \mathbb{R}^{nm \times 2nm}$ is the parameter matrix for decode phase, and $b_2 \in \mathbb{R}^{nm \times 1}$ is the offset for decode phase and the function g is another nonlinear function. For training purpose, the reconstruction error is used to measure how well we learned term vector embeddings. Let $\theta = \{W_1; W_2; b_1; b_2\}$. We use the Euclidean distance between the inputs and reconstructed inputs to measure reconstruction error, i.e.,

$$E([x_1; x_2]; \theta) = ||[x_1; x_2] - O[x_1; x_2]||_2^2 \tag{5}$$

For a given execution path with multiple terms and instructions, we adopt a greedy method [23] to train our RAE and recursively combine pairwise vector embeddings. The greedy method uses a hierarchical approach – it first combines vector embeddings of adjacent terms in each instruction, and then combines the results from a sequence of instructions in an execution path. Figure 5 shows an example of how to combine the vector embeddings to generate a signature vector. It shows a (binary) execution path with a sequence of 8 instructions. The greedy method is illustrated as a binary tree. Node 1 gives the vector embedding for the first instruction $Inst_1 = (push\ \%rbp)$ encoded from terms $[push; \%rbp]$. Then, we continue to process the remaining instructions, e.g., Nodes 2 and 3, until we derive the final vector embedding (i.e., the signature vector) for the instruction sequences of the given execution path.

Multi-class Classification for Function Mapping. Function mapping aims to recognize the owner function (in static binary) of a given execution path obtained from the dynamic trace. We consider each function as a class label, different execution paths obtained from the function binary code as samples of that class, and an execution path extracted from dynamic instruction trace as the testing sample. Then, the mapping becomes a multi-class classification problem, which is solved using Convolutional Neural Networks (CNN) in this paper. We adopt the sentence classification model proposed in [9,33] for natural language processing and train a multi-class classifier using CNN for function mapping. Note that another line of work, such as tainting [19,31], can be used for feature identification. We consider this as future work.

To obtain training samples for each class, we use CFG analysis to construct different execution paths for each function identified in the binary code. More precisely, once the function boundaries and bodies are recognized, we use a Depth First Search (DFS) to traverse the static CFG of each function and construct related execution path using a *random walk*.

4   Feature Tailoring

Feature tailoring creates customized software that consists of the desired features and their constituent functions in accordance with user needs. It has to address a number of challenges. First, a single execution trace may not reach all desired features, requiring us to merge multiple outputs from feature identification. Second, different features often share some common constituent functions. If the goal of tailoring is to remove certain features, we need to identify and retain the shared functions in the customized binary.

4.1   Feature Tailoring

Let $\hat{\mathcal{F}}$ be a set of target program features for tailoring. If the constituent functions of each feature $F_i \in \hat{\mathcal{F}}$ can be successfully identified, we can simply create a superset of their constituent functions, i.e., $\hat{F} = \cup F_i$. Two techniques are developed next to (i) create a customized program by retaining only the features in $\hat{F}$ (e.g., if user only needs these features) and (ii) remove the features in $\hat{F}$ from the binary (e.g., if they are deemed as unnecessary or vulnerable). When $\hat{F}$ cannot be directly identified, we leverage set operations, including union, intersection, and subtraction, to construct $\hat{F}$ from available feature combinations, in order to fulfill feature tailoring.

Tailoring via Set Operations. When the target features' constituent functions $\hat{F}$ are not directly identifiable, **Hecate** employs set operations including union, intersection, and subtraction to compute $\hat{F}$ from known feature combinations. **Union:** A feature may contain multiple execution paths that cannot be dumped and identified in a single execution. **Hecate** will collect traces from different program executions to identify and compute the union of the related feature-constituent functions. **Intersection:** A program may contain concurrent features that cannot be identified separately from the available execution trace. For instance, OpenSSL's *choosing cipher suite* feature is always coupled with the execution of encryption/hash functions in dynamic trace. To identify the constituent functions of *choosing cipher suite* feature, we can take the intersection of multiple executions with different choices of encryption/hash functions. **Subtraction:** This operation allows us to identify the unique constituent functions of given features. So, we can safely remove them without affecting the soundness of other features due to shared functions.

4.2   Binary Rewriting

We use feature tailoring to derive a set of functions to eliminate in program binary. Simply replacing these function bodies with "NOP"s would not generate a valid executable, because (i) some code segments in the eliminated function body may be shared with other functions, and (ii) there may exist data segments that are inserted into the eliminated functions and must be preserved.

To address these issues, **Hecate** utilizes a static binary rewriter, DynInst, to modify the program binary by rewriting the binaries in basic blocks level in the CFG. As DynInst is capable to abstract the program basic blocks in the form of CFG. To remove the features in the programs, there are two steps in **Hecate**. First, **Hecate** removes the functions that should not be called. The call site of the eliminated functions will be replaced to redirect the program to

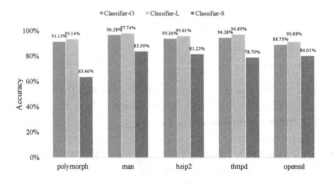

Fig. 6. Accuracy of function mapping during feature identification

exit point. Second, for those functions cannot be removed from the first step (e.g., For indirect function calls, the address of the callee function cannot be decided beforehand and can potentially lead to any other addresses), we replace the rest of the function body with "NOP". Furthermore, a verification process is performed using program fuzzing approaches [32] by **Hecate** to validate the effectiveness and correctness of feature tailoring.

5   Evaluation

5.1   Experiment Setup

Our experiments are conducted on a 2.80 GHz Intel Xeon(R) CPU E5-2680 20-core server with 16 GByte of main memory. The operating system is Ubuntu 14.04 LTS.

Benchmarks. In our evaluation, we select three sets of real-world applications: (i) Non-interactive applications including two applications from SPEC 2006 Benchmark suite [1], bzip2 and hmmer; two applications from a bug benchmark suite *bugbench* [11], polymorph and man and (ii) Interactive applications including a light-weight web server thttpd, version beta 2.23, an open source office suite LibreOffice and a web browser links. (iii) An implementation of Transport Layer Security (TLS) & Secure Sockets Layer (SSL) protocol, OpenSSL.

Dataset and Training. In our function mapping module, we collect static execution paths as training dataset and dynamic execution paths as testing dataset for evaluating the accuracy of the pre-trained models. We selected the highest quality model and extracted the matrix of embeddings. We have observed that a well trained function mapping model is with the hidden node size as 500 in RNN and 200 maximum iterations for RAE, which is chosen as the parameters of deep neural network in function mapping module.

5.2   Accuracy of Function Mapping

In this section, we evaluate the accuracy of the pre-trained function mapping module in **Hecate** and presents the accuracy of five representative applications. We construct the testing dataset as follows: We collect the dynamic instruction traces for each identified function in the binary and perform the same *random walk* process to generate execution paths as mentioned in Sect. 3.2. The testing dataset size is controlled to be 30% as big as the training dataset We also observed that due to the different amount of training data we can obtain from different functions, the mapping accuracy will be higher if we split functions into large and small categories, by using the median number of training data sample size. We trained three CNN classifiers for each application, one is trained cross all the functions as an overall classifier (Classifier-O), and the other two are trained for large functions (Classifier-L) and small functions (Classifier-S) respectively.

The function mapping accuracy is plotted in Fig. 6. We achieve an overall average accuracy of 92.76%, with the highest up to 96.28% in *man* from *bugbench*. In general, the mapping accuracy of larger programs, such as bzip2 and thttpd, is higher than smaller programs like polymorph. Because the number of execution traces used for training our CNN classifiers in those programs is much larger than that in polymorph, there are 189,855 training execution paths in bzip2 comparing to 10,806 in polymorph). For the applications with more functions, such as OpenSSL that has 4,023 functions, the overall accuracy can be as low as 88.75% since there are more classes for classification. We also note that all of the Classifier-Ls outperforms the Classifier-Os. For instance, in *polymorph*, the accuracy of Classifier-L is 93.14% whereas the accuracy of Classifier-O is 91.13%. However, we observe that the accuracy for Classifier-S is lower than Classifier-L. The reason is that functions trained in Classifier-Ss are relatively small, with limited training data samples for classification. In particular, the accuracy of Classifier-S is 63.46% for polymorph, which is the worst among all the applications. We further analyzed and found that the median number of training data size is 7 for polymorph, which means almost half of the functions have only less than 7 training data samples. The lack of training data leads to a bad performance for classification.

5.3   Impact on Program Security

We evaluate the impact of feature customization on program security here. As shown previously, the reduction of code size also shrink the attack surface and eliminate possible vulnerabilities in programs. We survey the known CVEs of different programs that can be removed by feature customization. For instance, in OpenSSL, (i) the *CVE-2014-0160*, known as *Heartbleed* bug, can be eliminated by removing the *heartbeat* extension; (ii) the *CVE-2016-7054*, which can lead to DoS attack can be neutralized by removing **-CHACHA20-POLY1305* ciphersuites; (iii) the *CVE-2016-0701*, which can cause information leakage, can be negated by avoiding using DH ciphersuites; The *CVE-2015-5212* in LibreOffice (an integer underflow bug) can be removed by disabling the printer functionality when users don't need it.

In total, we found 101 CVEs in OpenSSL distributions during 2014–2017, 34 CVEs in LibreOffice, 13 CVEs in Thttpd and 9 CVEs in Bzip2. Not all vulnerabilities can be disabled by our feature customization. Some vulnerabilities are in the functions that are necessary for program execution. *CVE-2010-0405* in Bzip2 is an integer overflow bug in function *BZ2_decompress*. In most of the cases, decompression is a feature that users will not remove. The number and ratio of program features that can be removed are shown in Table 1. We evaluate the security impact of **Hecate** using the ratio of CVEs that can be removed by feature customization.

Table 1. Impact on Application and Communication security

Program	# Removed CVEs	% Features removed
OpenSSL (2014–2017)	45	44.6
LibreOffice	23	67.6
Thttpd	5	38.5
Bzip2	2	22.2

6 Related Work

Code Analysis and De-bloating: Several prior works have proposed program customization frameworks only based one methods like de-bloating [7], cross-host tainting [5] and so on. In terms of binary reuse, it has been studied by several works [27,28]. The main challenge of reusing binary code is it only focuses on reusing partial code in the program high-level assembly code. Some existing works try to find memory-related vulnerabilities in source code or IR by direct static analysis [20,21,29]. As such, the two approaches are quite complementary and when combined together, can present an improved framework for eliminating attack surfaces in programs.

Learning-Based Approach for Vulnerability Removal: Prior work has studied bug/vulnerabilities removal using learning-based approaches. StatSym [30] and SARRE [10] propose frameworks combining statistical and formal analysis for vulnerable path discovery. SIMBER [25] proposes a statistical inference framework to eliminate redundant bound checks and improve the performance of applications without sacrificing security.

7 Conclusion, Future Work and Opportunities

In this paper, we design and evaluate a binary customization framework **Hecate**, that aims to generate customized program binaries with *just-enough* features and can satisfy a broad array of customization demands. Feature identification and feature tailoring are two major modules in **Hecate**, with the former one discovering the target features using both static code and execution traces, and the latter one modifying the features to reconstruct a customized program. Our experiment results demonstrate that **Hecate** is able to identify features with the highest accuracy up to 96.28% and reduce the attack surface by up to 67%.

Generating test cases to cover all corner cases of a feature is a challenging problem in general. To deal with this problem, we note that some approaches, such as fuzzing techniques [18], can be useful. As reported in Sect. 5, our deep learning-based function mapping model achieves an average accuracy of 92.7%. However, we could increase the training data size by collecting the dynamic execution paths and use related machine learning optimization like cross-validation to split small data set [16] for further performance improvements.

Moreover, more complex deep learning algorithms can be further tested, such as bi-directional RNN and long-short-term memory (LSTM), which have been proven a better performance for modeling longer sequential information. We will consider the above concerns as our future work.

Acknowledgments. This work was supported by the US Office of Naval Research (ONR) under Awards N00014-15-1-2210 and N00014-17-1-2786. Any opinions, findings, conclusions, or recommendations expressed in this article are those of the authors, and do not necessarily reflect those of ONR.

References

1. SPEC CPU (2006). https://www.spec.org/cpu2006/
2. Abadi, M., et al.: TensorFlow: a system for large-scale machine learning. In: OSDI (2016)
3. Bao, T., Burket, J., Woo, M., Turner, R., Brumley, D.: BYTEWEIGHT: learning to recognize functions in binary code. In: USENIX (2014)
4. Bishop, C.M.: Machine Learning and Pattern Recognition. Information Science and Statistics. Springer, Heidelberg (2006)
5. Chen, Y., Sun, S., Lan, T., Venkataramani, G.: TOSS: tailoring online server systems through binary feature customization. In: FEAST Workshop (2018)
6. Harris, L.C., Miller, B.P.: Practical analysis of stripped binary code. ACM SIGARCH Comput. Archit. News **33**, 63–68 (2005)
7. Jiang, Y., Wu, D., Liu, P.: JRed: program customization and bloatware mitigation based on static analysis. In: IEEE Computer Software and Applications Conference (2016)
8. Jiang, Y., Zhang, C., Wu, D., Liu, P.: Feature-based software customization: preliminary analysis, formalization, and methods. In: High Assurance Systems Engineering (2016)
9. Kim, Y.: Convolutional neural networks for sentence classification (2014). arXiv preprint arXiv:1408.5882
10. Li, Y., Yao, F., Lan, T., Venkataramani, G.: SARRE: semantics-aware rule recommendation and enforcement for event paths on android. IEEE Trans. Inf. Forensics Secur. **11**(12), 2748–2762 (2016)
11. Lu, S., Li, Z., Qin, F., Tan, L., Zhou, P., Zhou, Y.: Bugbench: benchmarks for evaluating bug detection tools. In: Workshop on the Evaluation of Software Defect Detection Tools (2005)
12. Mikolov, T., Karafiát, M., Burget, L., Černocký, J., Khudanpur, S.: Recurrent neural network based language model. In: Annual Conference of the International Speech Communication Association (2010)
13. Mikolov, T., Kombrink, S., Deoras, A., Burget, L., Cernocky, J.: RNNLM-recurrent neural network language modeling toolkit. In: ASRU Workshop (2011)
14. Ming, J., Xu, D., Jiang, Y., Wu, D.: BinSim: trace-based semantic binary diffing via system call sliced segment equivalence checking. In: USENIX Security (2017)
15. Oh, J., Hughes, C.J., Venkataramani, G., Prvulovic, M.: LIME: a framework for debugging load imbalance in multi-threaded execution. In: Proceedings of the 33rd International Conference on Software Engineering. ACM (2011)
16. Smith, G.C., Seaman, S.R., Wood, A.M., Royston, P., White, I.R.: Correcting for optimistic prediction in small data sets. Am. J. Epidemiol. **180**(3), 318–324 (2014)

17. Open-Source: LibreOffice
18. Stephens, N., et al.: Driller: augmenting fuzzing through selective symbolic execution. In: NDSS (2016)
19. Venkataramani, G., Doudalis, I., Solihin, Y., Prvulovic, M.: FlexiTaint: a programmable accelerator for dynamic taint propagation. In: IEEE International Symposium on High Performance Computer Architecture (2008)
20. Venkataramani, G., Doudalis, I., Solihin, Y., Prvulovic, M.: Memtracker: an accelerator for memory debugging and monitoring. ACM Trans. Archit. Code Optim. (TACO) 6(2), 5 (2009)
21. Venkataramani, G., Hughes, C.J., Kumar, S., Prvulovic, M.: DeFT: design space exploration for on-the-fly detection of coherence misses. ACM Trans. Archit. Code Optim. (TACO) 8(2), 8 (2011)
22. Viega, J., Messier, M., Chandra, P.: Network Security with OpenSSL: Cryptography for Secure Communications. O'Reilly Media Inc., Cambridge (2002)
23. White, M., Tufano, M., Vendome, C., Poshyvanyk, D.: Deep learning code fragments for code clone detection. In: IEEE/ACM International Conference on Automated Software Engineering (2016)
24. Xue, H., Chen, Y., Venkataramani, G., Lan, T., Jin, G., Li, J.: MORPH: enhancing system security through interactive customization of application and communication protocol features. In: Poster in ACM Conference on Computer and Communications Security (2018)
25. Xue, H., Chen, Y., Yao, F., Li, Y., Lan, T., Venkataramani, G.: SIMBER: eliminating redundant memory bound checks via statistical inference. In: De Capitani di Vimercati, S., Martinelli, F. (eds.) SEC 2017. IAICT, vol. 502, pp. 413–426. Springer, Cham (2017). https://doi.org/10.1007/978-3-319-58469-0_28
26. Xue, H., Sun, S., Venkataramani, G., Lan, T.: Machine learning-based analysis of program binaries: a comprehensive study. IEEE Access 7, 65889–65912 (2019)
27. Xue, H., Venkataramani, G., Lan, T.: Clone-hunter: accelerated bound checks elimination via binary code clone detection. In: ACM SIGPLAN International Workshop on Machine Learning and Programming Languages (2018)
28. Xue, H., Venkataramani, G., Lan, T.: Clone-slicer: detecting domain specific binary code clones through program slicing. In: FEAST Workshop. ACM (2018)
29. Yao, F., Chen, J., Venkataramani, G.: JOP-alarm: detecting jump-oriented programming-based anomalies in applications. In: IEEE 31st International Conference on Computer Design (ICCD). IEEE (2013)
30. Yao, F., Li, Y., Chen, Y., Xue, H., Lan, T., Venkataramani, G.: StatSym: vulnerable path discovery through statistics-guided symbolic execution. In: Dependable Systems and Networks (DSN) (2017)
31. Yao, F., Venkataramani, G., Doroslovački, M.: Covert timing channels exploiting non-uniform memory access based architectures. In: Great Lakes Symposium on VLSI. ACM (2017)
32. Zalewski, M.: American fuzzy lop (2007)
33. Zhang, K., et al.: Personal attributes extraction based on the combination of trigger words, dictionary and rules. In: Proceedings of the Third CIPS-SIGHAN Joint Conference on Chinese Language Processing, pp. 114–119 (2014)

Phish-Hook: Detecting Phishing Certificates Using Certificate Transparency Logs

Edona Fasllija[1(✉)], Hasan Ferit Enişer[2], and Bernd Prünster[3]

[1] A-SIT Secure Information Technology Center Austria, Graz, Austria
edona.fasllija@a-sit.at
[2] Computer Engineering Department, Bogazici University, Istanbul, Turkey
hasan.eniser@boun.edu.tr
[3] Institute of Applied Information Processing and Communications,
Graz University of Technology, Graz, Austria
bernd.pruenster@iaik.tugraz.at

Abstract. Certificate misissuance is a growing issue in the context of phishing attacks, as it leads inexperienced users to further trust fraudulent websites, if they are equipped with a technically valid certificate. *Certificate Transparency* (CT) aims at increasing the visibility of such malicious actions by requiring *certificate authorities* (CAs) to log every certificate they issue in public, tamper-proof, append-only logs. This work introduces *Phish-Hook*, a novel approach towards detecting phishing websites based on machine learning. Phish-Hook analyses certificates submitted to the CT system based on a conceptually simple, well-understood classification mechanism to effectively attest the phishing likelihood of newly issued certificates. Phish-Hook relies solely on CT log data and foregoes intricate analyses of websites' source code and traffic. As a consequence, we are able to provide classification results in near real-time and in a resource-efficient way. Our approach advances the state of the art by classifying websites according to five different incremental certificate risk labels, instead of assigning a binary label. Evaluation results demonstrate the effectiveness of our approach, achieving a success rate of over 90%, while requiring fewer, less complex input data, and delivering results in near real-time.

Keywords: TLS · Certificate Transparency · CA · Certificate misissuance · Machine learning · Phishing detection

1 Introduction

Transport Layer Security (TLS) [18], critically relies on *certificate authorities* (CAs) as trust anchors. A series of security incidents related to either compromised CAs or poor CA certification practices have shown that this high degree

S. Chen et al. (Eds.): SecureComm 2019, LNICST 305, pp. 320–334, 2019.
https://doi.org/10.1007/978-3-030-37231-6_18

of trust put into certificate authorities was, at times, misplaced. A prominent example is the incident related to the compromised Dutch CA *DigiNotar* [10] where attackers managed to issue TLS certificates for fake websites impersonating Gmail and Facebook. Similar incidents occurred with a Malaysian subordinate CA *DigiCert Sdn. Bhd.* and the large U.S.-based CA *TrustWave* [13]. Events like these challenge the conceptually simple trust model the current TLS *public key infrastructure* (PKI) system is based on.

Moreover, the popularity of free and automated TLS certificates by companies like *Let's Encrypt* and *Cloudflare* has led to a massive surge in the use of automatically-issued certificates on phishing sites. A recent statistical report from *PhishLab* [23] indicates that 49% of phishing sites were using HTTPS in the third quarter of 2018. This percentage has rapidly increased from 25% just one year ago, and from 35% in the second quarter of 2018. Current security mechanisms in browsers fail at detecting fraudulent websites if they are provisioned with mistakenly or maliciously issued certificates that are technically valid. Furthermore, when such a misissuance happens, it can take weeks or even months until the suspect certificates are detected and revoked. This window of vulnerability gives malicious actors plenty of time to do damage.

Google responded to the need for auditing the web's PKI system by implementing *Certificate Transparency* (CT) [13]—an open and public framework that audits and monitors TLS certificates in near real-time. CT publicly records TLS certificates in append-only logs as they are issued, in a way that enables anyone to audit a CA's activity and notice the issuance of suspect certificates for the domains they own. The instant visibility of newly issued certificates can significantly reduce the amount of time needed until a malicious site or CA misconduct can be detected.

Our main research contribution is an effective mechanism that detects phishing websites in near real-time by leveraging machine learning techniques to evaluate CT logs. We identify eight features and build a classification model that is able to utilize different algorithms to maximize fraud detection rates. This model is trained and evaluated on real data and accounts for the asymmetric distribution between legitimate websites and phishing sites for broad real-world applicability.

This paper is organized as follows: Sect. 2 summarizes the fundamental principles of the web's PKI, TLS certificates, Certificate Transparency, and covers phishing techniques. Section 3 describes previous research done on the topic. Section 4 delves into the design and the properties of *Phish-Hook*, our machine-learning-based phishing detection approach. Sect. 5 focuses on the evaluation of our approach and reports on our model's performance based on different classification models. Section 6 finally concludes this work and elaborates on possible future work directions.

2   Background

Confidentiality and integrity of web traffic are ensured using the HTTPS protocol and the supporting public key infrastructure. During the setup of a TLS channel and its underlying TCP connection, a client is required to authenticate a server by validating its certificate. A website is successfully authenticated if it uses a certificate that has not expired (and has not been revoked) and if a certificate chain can be built up to one of the certificate authorities present in the browser's trusted CA list.

The web's current PKI system allows *any* trusted CA, or intermediate CA, to issue certificates for *any* subject identity. This assumption of trustworthy CAs introduces a vulnerability to attacks based on improperly issued certificates, either as a result of CA compromise, negligence, errors, or even malicious behavior. The following section explains how this can be exploited to enable phishing, while Sect. 2.2 explains the reasoning behind utilizing Certificate Transparency as a promising building block in the fight against fraud.

2.1 Phishing Attacks

Malicious actors use several ways to trick users into visiting a website with a domain name similar to that of a legitimate website. Examples include typo-squatting [21], homoglyph (name spoofing) attacks [5], or incorporating a legitimate domain as a prefix, inner part, or suffix, as explained below.

Considering the domain `phish-hook.com`, a typo-squatting attack would try to register domains by incorrectly spelling the domain name such as `phihs-hook.com` or `phish-hok.com`. On the other hand, homoglyphic attacks rely on character substitution using look-alike glyphs from the Unicode sets to create fake domain names that are nearly indistinguishable from real ones to the naked eye. A quick look at the *confusables* file [6] published by the Unicode consortium, reveals that just for the character i in phish-hook, up to 41 look-alike glyphs exist that can be utilized by attackers to produce examples such as `phish-hook.com`, `phish-hook.com`, or `phiʃsh-hook.com`.

In addition, domains such as `www-phish-hook.com`, `login-phish-hook.com`, and `www.phish-hook.com.malicious.fakedomain.name` can be built by incorporating the legitimate domain name into a longer domain. More details on these techniques are provided in Sect. 4.2, where we explain how features were extracted from the certificates present in CT logs as part of our solution. The following section provides an overview of Certificate Transparency and the motivation behind the system's design.

2.2 Certificate Transparency

Certificate Transparency (CT) provides visibility of newly issued certificates and CA operations. This open framework monitors and audits TLS certificates by complementing the TLS ecosystem with three main components: *Certificate Logs*, *Monitors*, and *Auditors*. Certificate log servers maintain cryptographically assured, append-only logs of issued certificates. Monitor servers periodically check these logs to determine whether an illegitimate certificate has been issued for a particular domain. Auditors check whether logs are cryptographically consistent and whether a particular certificate is registered in the logs.

The strength of the framework stems from the append-only, cryptographically-assured nature of the logs. On a technical level, this is accomplished by relying on a *Merkle Tree* (a data structure made up of linked cryptographic hashes [14]). This ensures that back-dated certificates cannot be inserted into the log, and added certificates cannot be edited or deleted afterward. In the CT-augmented certificate issuance process, a CA submits a newly-issued certificate to the log, and is provided with a *Signed Certificate Timestamp* (SCT)—a proof of inclusion to the log—in return. The SCT can be added to a certificate either as an X.509v3 certificate extension, a TLS extension or during the handshake as part of OCSP stapling [13]. This enables clients to verify whether the SCT was provided by a trusted CT log by validating its signature and eventually deciding on whether to accept a certificate as valid or not according to their CT policy.

The following section elaborates on how machine learning has been used in the past to detect fraudulent websites. It summarises both work conducted prior to the introduction of CT and works already leveraging CT.

3 Related Work

One of the earliest proposals for using machine learning to detect phishing websites based on certificates was published by Mishari et al. [15]. The authors crawled certificates of both legitimate and phishing websites and used them to build a classifier based on, amongst others, features either directly extracted or computed from certain X.509 certificate fields. Their proposal was the first to showcase the potential of using certificate information beyond client-side server authentication to identify fraudulent websites that use HTTPS.

In another more recent effort, Dong et al. [8] propose to employ *Deep Neural Networks* (DNNs) to identify potentially rogue certificates (and eventually CA misconduct) in a timely manner using features extracted from standard X.509 certificates. The authors additionally address the dataset imbalance (between rogue vs. benign certificate sets) by generating artificial rogue certificates.

Similar to the work by Dong et al. [8], Torroledo et al. [22] propose to use DNNs to detect malicious use of TLS certificates. The authors perform a detailed feature engineering and identify more than thirty features to classify malicious websites. Results indicate that their system can detect malware certificates and phishing certificates with an accuracy of a 94.8% and 88.6%, respectively.

Ghafir et al. [9] investigate the problem of malicious certificate detection as means to defend against *advanced persistent threats* (APTs). They base their proposal to detect APT *command and control* (C&C) communications on a blacklist of three certificate fields, namely SHA-1 fingerprints, serial and subject. The module they propose analyses network traffic, filters secure communications and matches certificates that were used in these communications to the certificates in the blacklist.

Kumar et al. [12] construct a certificate linter that checks certificates in the wild for compliance to the *CA/Browser Forum Baseline Requirements* [3] and

RFC5280 [7]. Their findings indicate that the certificate misissuance rate has dramatically dropped since 2017 (down to 0.02%). Nonetheless, authors propose an alternative way to make CA operations auditable and showcase how their linter can be harnessed to identify poor CA practices.

It was not until very recently that CT was envisioned as a potential data source for the detection of suspicious phishing domains. In 2018, companies like Facebook[1] and SSL Mate's *Certspotter*[2] started offering notification services about suspiciously issued certificates to subscribing domain owners based on CT log monitoring. Nonetheless, their approaches to solving the phishing detection problem are not disclosed nor analysed for efficacy or accuracy.

Finally, Scheitle et al. [19] conducted a pilot experiment in order to gain insights about the viability of using CT logs as phishing detection source. The authors employ regular expression matching to find potential phishing domains by means of CT. They observe that most phishing domains are constructed by combining fully qualified domains (FQDN) of popular legitimate target domains. Their paper aims at investigating variant implications that CT has had on the Internet ecosystem and is not focused solely on phishing detection. They do not employ any automated machine-learning based detection mechanism, but rather base their phishing detection approach on regular expression matching and visual inspection. They conclude that CT being used as data source for phishing detection opens a promising new research direction.

We bring this idea forward by using CT logs as source for valuable data to train and validate a classifier that predicts the phishing likelihood of certificates submitted to the logs. We automate the phishing detection process by utilising machine learning algorithms and employing a heuristics based scoring methodology to assign five different phishing scores. In contrast to other machine-learning-based approaches summarized in this section, we do not require downloading a large set of certificates, but collect and label the data needed while streaming certificate updates from the CT logs. By applying our classifier to certificates newly submitted to the CT logs, we can detect phishing attempts in near real time and dramatically reduce the window of vulnerability for such attacks.

4   Phish-Hook

We propose the idea of using CT logs as the sole data source for phishing detection by presenting a machine-learning-based solution called *Phish-Hook*. Compared to other contributions discussed in Sect. 3, we do not require to download and parse the certificates of corresponding websites, nor do we use extra features from the websites' source code or monitor traffic. As we will show in Sect. 5, this approach delivers highly accurate results based on directly applying machine learning techniques to certificates. This phishing detection system is composed of three main components: namely the *Certificate Collector*, the *Feature Extractor*, and the *Classifier*. The CT logs feed the *Certificate Collector*, which in

---

[1] https://developers.facebook.com/tools/ct/subscriptions/.

[2] https://sslmate.com/certspotter/.

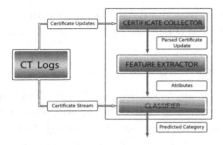

Fig. 1. Phish-Hook system components

turn passes the parsed CT logs to the *Feature Extractor* component. The set of attributes generated from the *Feature Extractor* is finally used to train our *Classifier* model. New certificates streamed from the CT logs are then fed into the trained *Classifier* to be classified into on of five incremental phishing likelihood scores. Figure 1 provides an illustration of Phish-Hook's main components.

The following section describes the data collection methodology, while Sect. 4.2 elaborates on the extraction of certificate features, and Sect. 4.4 discusses the algorithms used to train the *Classifier*'s model.

4.1 Data Collection

Given our aspiration of directly leveraging the CT logs to build the classifier model, we built our own training dataset and used the *CertStream*[3] open-source library to interact with the CT network and aggregate CT log data. The Structure of the parsed CT logs is shown in Listing 1:

Listing 1. Parsed Certificate Log Update Entry

```
1  {"message_type": "certificate_update",
2  "data": {
3      "update_type": "X509LogEntry",
4      "leaf_cert": {...
5          "subject": {
6              "aggregated": "/CN=phish-hook.com",
7              "C": null,
8              "ST": null,
9              "L": null,
10             "O": null,
11             "OU": null,
12             "CN": "phish-hook.com"
13         },
14         ...
15     "all_domains":
16     [
17      "login.phish-hook.com"
18      "phish-hook.com"]
19     },
20     "chain": [{
21         "subject": {
22             "aggregated": "/C=US/O=Let's Encrypt/CN=Let's Encrypt Authority X3",
23             "C": "US",
24             "ST": null,
25             "L": null,
26             "O": "Let's Encrypt",
27             "OU": null,
28             "CN": "Let's Encrypt Authority X3"},
29             ...],
30         "cert_index": 27910635, }}}
```

---

[3] https://medium.com/cali-dog-security/introducing-certstream-3fc13bb98067.

The following section provides details on the features used to train our classifier model extracted from certificate updates submitted to CT logs.

4.2   Feature Selection

Certificate Transparency augments raw certificate data with time as another dimension. Our contribution is rooted in the assumption that small amounts of highly characteristic data are meaningful enough to enable classification of phishing sites based on a relatively simple machine learning model. In contrast to related work on this sector, our solution thus employs only a comparatively small set of features and still delivers highly accurate results. In addition, Phish-Hook evaluates features directly from the parsed CT log entries without requiring to download the respective certificates. On a technical level, the data points were extracted from the CT log entry fields representing domain names ([data][leaf_cert][subject][aggregated] and [data][all_domains]) and the certificate issuer fields ([chain][subject][aggregated]) of each certificate update entry.

As existing data indicating which features are relevant when it comes to detecting phishing websites from CT log entries is hard to come by, we aggregated and analyzed reports on phishing in general. Based on this, we derived the following feature set:

F1 small_levenshtein_distance. Section 2 summarized some of the most common techniques utilised by attackers to generate misleading domain names for phishing attacks, such as typosquatting, homograph attacks, etc. Our first feature is based on this, and on further observations made by Scheitle et al. [19] suggesting that the majority of phishing website certificates registered in the CT logs is constructed by incorporating domain names of popular legitimate domains. The value of F1 is assigned by calculating the Levenshtein Distance—a measure of similarity between two strings—of sub-words of the domain registered with the certificate to suspicious popular keywords (for example: phish-hook vs phish_hook). Table 1 summarizes the popular keywords that were used in order to calculate F1. In case the computed distance to the keywords is below a certain threshold, we consider this an indicator of suspiciousness.

F2 deeply_nested_subdomains. We consider domain names with unusually long subdomains such as www.phish-hook.com.security.account-update.gq to be an indicator of suspiciousness. Similar domains have been widely used by attackers to impersonate legitimate websites by hiding the primary domain in deeply nested subdomains. These attacks particularly target small devices such as tablets or mobile phones that can not display the full (long) domain at once.

F3 issued_from_free_CA. Section 1 already pointed out that HTTPS phishing has been increasing significantly in the past couple of years and is about to become prevalent. The ubiquity of automated, fast, and free certificates has given both good and bad actors the advantage of easily obtaining a SSL/TLS certificate for their websites. The problem actually does not lie on the free and automated certificate issuance itself, but on the ongoing debate on which actors of the Internet ecosystem have the responsibility of policing the content of nature of websites. In one of their position papers [1], Let's Encrypt disagrees that it is a CA's responsibility to check for malicious or phishing content at the level of domain validated certificates. They instead prefer to delegate this responsibility to services such as Google Safe Browsing or Microsoft SmartScreen. Additional reports [16] ranking such free CAs in top positions with respect to the number of phishing certificates blocked led us to consider certificates obtained from free CAs as a potential indicator of suspiciousness.

F4 suspicious_tld. Unlike the other lower level domains that can be generally reserved by domain owners, top-level domains are generally prominent domains such as `.com`, `.net`, `.edu` or `.org` that end users are familiar with. Malicious actors often target these top-level domains in their attempt to create malicious sites. The low cost at which a large number of newly added TLDs is available makes certain TLDs more popular amongst attackers. Based on observations made from available reports [20] on most abused TLDs, we consider top-level domains such as `.ga'`, `'.gdn'`,`'.bid''.country'`,`'.kim'`, etc. that were widely adopted for phishing purposes as suspicious. The complete list of the TLDs considered can be found in Table 1.

F5 inner_tld_in_subdomain. Attackers may include popular top-level domains (such as 'org', 'com', or 'net') in the inner domain in order to mislead users that are familiar with them into trusting a fraudulent website. The presence of such a TLD in an inner sub-domain is therefore considered suspicious.

F6 suspicious_keywords. Another well-known phishing technique is the inclusion of popular keywords from famous applications of social media, commerce, or cryptocurrency in a domain name. We therefore check whether each CT certificate update entry contains one of the keywords present in Table 1, and consider a match suspicious.

F7 high_shannon_entropy. F7 aims to detect algorithmically generated malicious domain names in particular. This feature lays its foundation on the observation that these domain names differ significantly in terms of randomness when compared to human generated domains. In order to do so, we calculate the Shannon entropy—i.e. degree of randomness—of the domain a certificate was issued for. An unusually high entropy may then serve as indicator for maliciously issued certificates from attackers.

F8 hyphens_in_subdomain. F8 is similar to F2, but instead of checking for the presence of multiple periods ('.'), we check for the presence of multiple hyphens ('-') in the sub-domain, as both of these characters can be used to attach popular keywords of legitimate domains to generate malicious ones. Hence, for F8, we consider an unusually high number of hyphens an indicator of a suspicious website.

Table 1. Suspicious keywords and TLDs [24]

Generic		Apple	Email	Cryptocurrency	Social media	Financial	E-commerce	Other	TLDs		Misc.
activity	office	appleid	outlook	poloniex	facebook	moneygram	overstock	skype	'.bank'	'.online'	.com-
alert	online	icloud	office365	coinhive	tumblr	westernunion	alibaba	github	'.business'	'.party'	-com.
purchase	recover	iforgot	microsoft	bithumb	reddit	bankofamerica	aliexpress		'.cc'	'.pw'	.net-
authentication	safe	itunes	windows	kraken	youtube	wellsfargo	leboncoin		'.center'	'.racing'	.org-
authorize	secure	apple	protonmail	localbitcoin	twitter	paypal	amazon	netflix	'.cf'	'.ren'	cgi-bin
bill	security		tutanota	bitstamp	linkedin	citigroup			'.click'	'.review'	.com-
client	service		hotmail	bittrex	instagram	santander			'.club'	'.science'	.net.
support	transaction		gmail	blockchain	flickr	morganstanley			'.country'	'.stream'	.org.
unlock	update		google	bitflyer	whatsapp	barclays			'.download'	'.study'	.com.
wallet	account		outlook	coinbase		hsbc			'.ga'	'.support'	.gov-
form	login		yahoo	hitbtc		scottrade			'.gb'	'.tech'	.gov.
log-in	password,		google	lakebtc		ameritrade			'.gdn'	'.tk'	.gouv-
live	signin		yandex	bitfinex		merilledge			'.gq'	'.top'	-gouv-
manage	sign-in			bitconnect		bank			'.info'	'.vip'	.gouv.
verification	verify			coinsbank					'.kim'	'.win'	
webscr	invoice								'.loan'	'.work'	
authenticate	confirm								'.men'	'.xin'	
credential	customer								'.ml'	'.xyz'	
									'.mom'		

4.3   Classification Workflow

In a nutshell, our system works as follows: We stream certificate updates from CT logs, while simultaneously labelling the data for each feature. We also employ a heuristic methodology to compute a total phishing likelihood score according to the presence or absence of a feature, or the computed value of a feature. We use this overall score to classify the certificate and assign the resulting feature called *phishing_likelihood_category* out of five different categories, namely **legitimate, potential, likely, suspicious,** and **highly-suspicious.**

4.4   Learning Phase

This section goes into the details of the training phase. After collecting and labelling the data from CT, we employ supervised learning algorithms to train several classifier models in order to predict a certificate's phishing likelihood.

One challenge was having *imbalanced* classes: The number of phishing websites recorded publicly in CT logs is much smaller than the number of legitimate websites. Thus, collecting the dataset from CT logs results in a very small number of datapoints labelled as *phishing* compared to the number of datapoints labelled as *legitimate*. To give an idea of the imbalance in the data: in a dataset of approximately 600000 datapoints, the number of *highly-suspicious, suspicious, likely, potential* and *legitimate* instances are 223, 230, 251, 719 and 602676, respectively. This situation is referred to as *imbalanced classes problem* [11] and is a common phenomenon in phishing detection-related learning processes.

Oversampling or undersampling techniques are potential countermeasures to overcome this challenge. We employ SMOTE (Synthetic Minority Over-sampling Technique) [4] and random *undersampling* to address the challenge presented by the imbalanced classes problem. We chose to oversample *highly-suspicious, suspicious, likely and potential* classes and undersample *legitimate* instances, resulting with a much more balanced dataset.

5   Evaluation

This section describes how Phish-Hook was evaluated and discusses the obtained results. It compares different key performance measures of our system against existing work and clearly illustrates that our work presents a significant step forward towards phishing detection. Most importantly, our system achieves its results in near real-time based on a small set of only eight features and a simple machine learning model. This not only makes it possible to react to phishing sites as soon as they emerge, but also enables debugging and presenting the decision-making process in a humanly-comprehensible manner. As our system relies on traditional machine learning approaches, training and classification outperform Deep Neural Networks in the time domain.

The following section describes the test setup and how we trained and evaluated our model based on an existing, pre-classified data set. Section 5.2 then establishes which metrics we used to measure the performance of Phish-Hook, while Sect. 5.3 pits different classifiers against each other to evaluate which one is best suited for the task at hand.

5.1 Training Dataset

To evaluate the performance of Phish-Hook, we made use of the pre-classified phishing detection dataset publicly available under the UCI Machine Learning Repository [2]. This dataset consists of 11055 data points with 30 features. Part of the features correspond directly to X.509 certificate fields, while others are derived from certificates fields and/or website source code. Each feature takes a ternary value of $[-1, 0, 1]$ representing *phishing*, *suspicious*, and *legitimate* respectively. Unlike features, result labels can take only two values: *phishing* and *legitimate*.

This data set and the classification process do not account for CT log data. However, our small set of simple features can be modelled as a subset of it and thus aligns well with the pre-classified data to provide a ground truth. This works because CT log data overlaps with the features present in the UCI Machine Learning Repository dataset. The following section briefly presents the metrics used for the evaluation process.

5.2 Metrics

In machine learning, classification is defined as the problem of assigning a new observation to one category, based on a training set of data containing observations (or instances) whose category membership is known. In our case, we basically want to predict if a website is legitimate or not.

The most basic metric used to quantify the performance of a classifier is *accuracy*, i.e. the ratio of the number of correct predictions to the total predictions made. In problems with (highly) imbalanced classes, however, accuracy can easily be boosted by always outputting the category of the largest class. Consequently, accuracy is inadequate on its own as a performance measure and additional metrics such as precision, recall and the so-called F_1 *score* (see Eq. 3) are typically used to measure the true aptitude of a classifier.

Precision and Recall are calculated according to Eqs. 1 and 2, with tp, fp, and fn denoting the number of correctly identified instances, the number of incorrectly identified instances, and the number of incorrectly rejected instances respectively:

$$Precision = \frac{tp}{tp + fp} \tag{1}$$

$$Recall = \frac{tp}{tp + fn} \tag{2}$$

$$F_1\ score = \frac{2 \times Recall \times Precision}{Recall + Precision} \tag{3}$$

Table 2. Classification results

	Parameters	Accuracy	Precision	Recall	F_1 score
DT	max_depth = 2	91.06	91.12	91.06	91.07
	max_depth = 5	91.42	91.46	91.42	91.39
	max_depth = 10	89.39	89.44	89.39	89.40
SVM	kernel = 'linear' C = 0.03	91.62	91.68	91.62	91.58
	kernel = 'linear' C = 0.3	91.29	91.37	91.29	91.25
	kernel = 'linear' C = 1	91.39	91.45	91.39	91.35
KNN	k = 1	86.41	86.40	86.41	86.37
	k = 3	86.38	86.40	86.38	86.32
	k = 10	87.23	87.23	87.23	87.19
MLP	network_size = 3 × 5	90.08	90.16	90.08	90.03
	network_size = 5 × 10	89.55	89.94	89.55	89.44
	network_size = 1 × 100	89.06	89.63	89.06	88.92

All of these scores apply to binary classification problems, which matches the UCI Machine Learning Repository dataset. Our solution, on the other hand, introduces a granular metric, classifying websites in one of five categories in the range of [**legitimate**, **potential**, **likely**, **suspicious**, **highly-suspicious**]. In order to evaluate our results against the pre-classified data, we introduced **suspicious** as the threshold for classifying a certificate to be issued for a phishing website. The following section presents the classification performance of Phish-Hook based on different classifiers.

5.3 Results

Although Deep Neural Networks are currently hailed as an almost universal solution (not only) to classification problems, we have intentionally focused our work on classical machine learning approaches for reasons of performance and comprehensibility. We thus pitched the performance of well-understood algorithms such as k-nearest neighbour (KNN), support vector machines (SVMs), decision tree classifiers (DT), and multilayer perceptrons (MLP) against each other.

We report accuracy, precision, recall, and F_1 scores regarding the classification of phishing websites for each approach in Table 2. On a technical level, our work is based on the *scikit-learn* [17] Python library.

Evaluation results are reported for various parameters tuned for each algorithm, such as maximum depth for DT, network size for MLP, and the penalty parameter C for the SVM classifier. The results demonstrate the effectiveness of our approach, with an accuracy of over 90%, while maintaining precision, recall, and F_1 scores of also over 90%. Support vector classifiers outperform others for the certificate classification task, closely followed by decision trees by a small margin. Reported results show that our approach can outperform existing solutions while requiring fewer, less complex features. Labelling happens on-the-fly without the need to download immense amounts of certificate data and results in accurately detecting phishing attempts in almost real time when applied to newly submitted CT log data.

5.4 Discussion

The first major insight from these results is that our assumption about the choice of features to extract from CT log entries to identify phishing sites actually holds true for real-world data. Most importantly, this confirms that Certificate Transparency log data is indeed a valuable source of data that can be machine-processed to mount automated alert systems. In addition, using traditional, well-understood machine learning techniques results in a system whose classification process is comprehensible by humans and thus debuggable. We therefore argue for the use of simple machine learning models such as SVMs and DTs for two reasons: Firstly, the inner workings of the models are the easiest to understand and align with human intuition and basic algorithmic though processes. Secondly, classifers such as decision trees consume the least resources both during training and classification and can therefore be operated on commodity hardware. By solely relying on CT log data, the network traffic produced by Phish-Hook is also kept to a minimum. Our system's low demand for computational resources makes it even possible to deploy it on end-user devices such that it can alert users whenever they are about to access a phishing website. In addition, we advance the current state of the art with respect to detecting fraudulent websites fitted with genuine certificates by providing more than just an absolute (binary) decision, about a website's legitimacy. This aligns with the transparent decision making process in the sense that uncertainty is reflected in the classification results, whenever it arises.

6 Conclusions

This work presented *Phish-Hook*, an effective and accurate CT-log-based phishing detection system using classical machine learning algorithms. By not relying on deep neural networks, our system cannot only be trained efficiently, but remains debuggable and humanly comprehensible while in operation. As phishing heavily relies on the human factor to be successful, we firmly believe that the same holds true for phishing detection systems. We advance the current state of the art in phishing detection not only in a purely technical manner but also by our process being transparent to the user, providing more granular classification results according to five different incremental certificate risk labels.

On a technical level, our design is based on the assumption that a small set of eight features extracted directly from CT log data is sufficient to successfully classify phishing websites. Thus, Phish-Hook foregoes the need to analyze website source codes or inspect traffic. Evaluation results show that this assumption holds true, as our system outperforms existing solutions and is able to correctly identify more than 90% of phishing websites in near real-time. Our approach thus demonstrates the utility of decision trees and support vector machines—classical machine learning algorithms—for the problem at hand. This presents a major advantage over the likes of deep learning, as not only the results, but also the process of obtaining them remains intelligible. As a consequence, Phish-Hook can be improved and extended in intuitive, straight forward ways and the results will always be comprehensible by humans. Potential future work directions thus include the incorporation of additional features extracted from other CT log fields, such as validity period, extensions, etc.

In summary, Phish-Hook is able to reliably classify phishing websites based solely on CT log data in near real-time as they appear. This can significantly reduce the time it takes to detect phishing websites and consequently mitigate their impact.

References

1. Aas, J.: The CA'S role in fighting phishing and malware. https://letsencrypt.org/2015/10/29/phishing-and-malware.html. Accessed 29 Apr 2019
2. Asuncion, A., Newman, D.: UCI machine learning repository (2007)
3. Ca/browser forum baseline requirements documents. https://cabforum.org/baseline-requirements-documents/. Accessed 13 Apr 2019
4. Chawla, N.V., Bowyer, K.W., Hall, L.O., Kegelmeyer, W.P.: Smote: synthetic minority over-sampling technique. J. Artif. Int. Res. **16**(1), 321–357 (2002). http://dl.acm.org/citation.cfm?id=1622407.1622416
5. Homoglyph advanced phishing attacks. https://www.cisco.com/c/en/us/support/docs/security/email-security-appliance/200146-Homoglyph-Advanced-Phishing-Attacks.pdf. Accessed 13 Apr 2019
6. Unicode Consortium: Recommended confusable mapping for IDN (2015). https://www.unicode.org/Public/security/8.0.0/confusables.txt. Accessed 13 Apr 2019
7. Cooper, D., Santesson, S., Farrell, S., Boeyen, S., Housley, R., Polk, W.: RFC 5280: Internet X.509 public key infrastructure certificate and certificate revocation list (CRL) profile. IETF, May 2008
8. Dong, Z., Kane, K., Camp, L.J.: Detection of rogue certificates from trusted certificate authorities using deep neural networks. ACM Trans. Priv. Secur. (TOPS) **19**(2), 5 (2016)
9. Ghafir, I., Prenosil, V., Hammoudeh, M., Han, L., Raza, U.: Gmalicious SSL certificate detection: a step towards advanced persistent threat defence. In: Proceedings of the International Conference on Future Networks and Distributed Systems, p. 27. ACM (2017)
10. Hoogstraaten, H.: Black tulip report of the investigation into the DigiNotar certificate authority breach, August 2012
11. Kotsiantis, S., Kanellopoulos, D., Pintelas, P., et al.: Handling imbalanced datasets: a review. GESTS Int. Trans. Comput. Sci. Eng. **30**(1), 25–36 (2006)
12. Kumar, D., et al.: Tracking certificate misissuance in the wild. In: 2018 IEEE Symposium on Security and Privacy (SP), pp. 785–798. IEEE (2018)

13. Laurie, B., Langley, A., Kasper, E.: Certificate transparency. Technical report (2013)
14. Merkle, R.C.: A digital signature based on a conventional encryption function. In: Pomerance, C. (ed.) CRYPTO 1987. LNCS, vol. 293, pp. 369–378. Springer, Heidelberg (1988). https://doi.org/10.1007/3-540-48184-2_32
15. Mishari, M.A., De Cristofaro, E., Defrawy, K.E., Tsudik, G.: Harvesting SSL certificate data to identify web-fraud. arXiv preprint arXiv:0909.3688 (2009)
16. Phishiest certificate authorities. https://toolbar.netcraft.com/stats/certificate_authorities. Accessed 29 Apr 2019
17. Pedregosa, F., et al.: Scikit-learn: machine learning in Python. J. Mach. Learn. Res. **12**, 2825–2830 (2011)
18. Rescorla, E., Dierks, T.: The Transport Layer Security (TLS) Protocol Version 1.2. RFC 5246, August 2008. 10.17487/RFC5246, https://rfc-editor.org/rfc/rfc5246.txt
19. Scheitle, Q., et al.: The rise of certificate transparency and its implications on the internet ecosystem. In: Proceedings of the Internet Measurement Conference 2018, pp. 343–349. ACM (2018)
20. Spamhaus: The 10 most abused top level domains. https://www.spamhaus.org/statistics/tlds/. Accessed 30 Apr 2019
21. Szurdi, J., Kocso, B., Cseh, G., Spring, J., Felegyhazi, M., Kanich, C.: The long "taile" of typosquatting domain names. In: 23rd USENIX Security Symposium (USENIX Security 2014), pp. 191–206 (2014)
22. Torroledo, I., Camacho, L.D., Bahnsen, A.C.: Hunting malicious TLS certificates with deep neural networks. In: Proceedings of the 11th ACM Workshop on Artificial Intelligence and Security, pp. 64–73. ACM (2018)
23. Volkman, E.: 49 percent of phishing sites now use https. Technical report (2018). https://info.phishlabs.com/blog/49-percent-of-phishing-sites-now-use-https
24. x0rz: Phishing catcher. https://github.com/x0rz/phishing_catcher

IIFA: Modular Inter-app Intent Information Flow Analysis of Android Applications

Abhishek Tiwari[✉], Sascha Groß, and Christian Hammer

University of Potsdam, Potsdam, Germany
{tiwari,saschagross,chrhammer}@uni-potsdam.de

Abstract. Android apps cooperate through message passing via intents. However, when apps have disparate sets of privileges inter-app communication (IAC) can accidentally or maliciously be misused, e.g., to leak sensitive information contrary to users' expectations. Recent research has considered static program analysis to detect dangerous data leaks due to inter-component communication (ICC), but suffers from shortcomings for IAC with respect to precision, soundness, and scalability.

As a remedy we propose a novel pre-analysis for static ICC/IAC analysis. Our main contribution is the first fully automatic ICC/IAC information flow analysis that is scalable for realistic apps due to modularity, avoiding combinatorial explosion: Our approach determines communicating apps using short summaries rather than inlining intent calls between components and apps, which entails simultaneously analyzing all apps installed on a device.

Using benchmarks we establish that IIFA outperforms state-of-the-art analyses in terms of precision and recall. But foremost, applied to the 90 most popular applications from the Google Playstore, IIFA demonstrated its scalability to a large corpus of real-world apps.

Keywords: Android · Inter-component communication · Intent · Static analysis

1 Introduction

To protect sensitive information on Android, various information flow control (IFC) analyses have been developed. These analyze the (potential) flow of information in apps and report a warning if a flow from a sensitive data source to an untrusted/public data sink (like sending sensitive information to the internet) is determined to be possible at runtime. Information flow is not restricted to a single component, but occurs frequently between components of the same [11,16] and even different apps [22]. Our study, using the top 90 apps from the Google play store, revealed more than 10,000 inter-component calls. Scrutinizing the flows between components therefore becomes imperative.

© ICST Institute for Computer Sciences, Social Informatics and Telecommunications Engineering 2019
Published by Springer Nature Switzerland AG 2019. All Rights Reserved
S. Chen et al. (Eds.): SecureComm 2019, LNICST 305, pp. 335–349, 2019.
https://doi.org/10.1007/978-3-030-37231-6_19

Android's inter-component communication (ICC) mainly leverages so-called *intents*. The major challenge in identifying IFC through intents is identifying which information flows from one component to another. Leveraging static analysis is non-trivial because the receiver and the intent data may be unknown at analysis time, being strings that might be composed at runtime.

Some tools consider intents during information flow analysis [4, 14, 16, 22] but suffer from multiple shortcomings: For ICC flows, they have a mediocre precision and recall, but fail significantly for IAC. To match senders and receivers these approaches merely verify that the receiver-identifying data matches but ignore other intent attributes that need to correspond, which leads to significant imprecision. Further, the majority of related works [2, 13, 16, 22] propose a merging-based approach for IAC, inlining senders and receivers into a huge singleton "app" to analyze, which does not scale up for realistic apps, and even if it did, the complexity to analyze the merged app inflates. However, as most combinations of apps do not communicate via intents the whole effort is mostly futile. Simultaneously, the merging process itself may introduce spurious data flow paths, increasing analysis imprecision. Even worse, each time an app is updated or installed on a device this merging and re-analysis process must be repeated.

Our Contributions. In this work we propose a novel information-flow analysis for IAC (and ICC) based on an intent-flow pre-analysis that evades combinatorial explosion of analyzing all potential communication partners, while excluding infeasible communication paths. Our approach can predict which combinations of apps communicate by separating information flow analysis within app components from thorough matching of communication partners. In a first step we create a database of summary information about senders of intents, their characteristics, as well as apps registered to receive implicit intents. Subsequently, we identify potential communication partners based on a novel matching algorithm which takes the potential intra-component flows into account. These flows are provided by a baseline IFC analysis for all potential intent receivers. We leverage senders' outbound intent data as input to the information flows identified in respective receivers, eliminating the need for inlining or merging apps and thus combinatorial explosion, as only summaries of actual communication partners are subsumed. In case multiple apps are involved in intent communication our approach performs a fixed point iteration through the DB information. Remember that our tool is not a stand-alone IFC analysis tool. Rather, IIFA leverages flows and slices generated by other IFC analyzers. As these tools are already heavily engineered for the intra-app case, we concentrated on the peculiarities of intent communication and evasion of inlining and combinatorial explosion.

As a noteworthy novelty, our approach is modular and thus compositional with respect to app installation. Whenever a new (version of an) app is available for analysis, the database is updated (in case of new version) or extended (new app) to include the intents broadcast or received by this app. Only the new app has to be (re-)analyzed, as well as combinations with flows identified in potential receivers. We aim to answer the following research questions:

- **RQ1:** *Does our pre-analysis approach negatively impact the precision or soundness of the results with respect to state-of-the-art analyses?*
- **RQ2:** *Does our approach scale to a realistic corpus of real-world apps?*

We implemented our approach as a tool called *IIFA* and evaluated it on DroidBench [6], the IccTA extension of DroidBench [16], ICC Bench [22], our own benchmarks (https://github.com/mig40000/ICC-Benchmark) evaluating key and type matching of intent extra data, and a large set of apps from the Google Playstore. We compared our results with multiple related analysis tools. Our tool (combined with an external baseline intra-component IFC analysis) achieves perfect precision and soundness on all benchmark sets with respect to the ground truth provided, being more than on par with related IFC tools. Additionally, we demonstrate that IIFA can improve the IAC precision of other base IFC analyses with experiments, and assess the scalability of IIFA, applying it to the 90 most downloaded Playstore apps. Our experiments demonstrate that due to its compositionality IIFA's execution time scales well even to a large corpus of real-world apps. In summary, we provide the following contributions:

- *Compositional DB-backed Analysis.* We propose a modular pre-analysis approach for intent communication, in particular for analyzing inter-app communication, based on summaries for all app components containing intent senders, receivers, and the exact intent characteristics including types and keys of data transmission.
- *Novel Matching Algorithm.* We present a novel algorithm which matches intent senders with intent receivers based on these summaries and even detects flows through more than two components via a fixed-point iteration.
- *Evaluation of IIFA.* We implemented our analysis (IIFA) and evaluated it on multiple large-scale datasets. The evaluation shows that our pre-analysis approach does not negatively impact precision and recall with respect to the most relevant previous work on benchmarks, including a novel suite assessing the correct matching of intent attributes. We demonstrate that we can effectively evade combinatorial explosion, analyzing ICC/IAC information flows of the top 90 real-world apps in approximately 2.2 h (excluding the baseline IFC analysis).

2 Background

2.1 Android Components

Android apps are written (mostly) in Java, but instead of defining a *main* method they consist of four component types: *Activities* are user interfaces to be interacted with. *Services* run in the background, intended for computationally expensive operations. *Broadcast receivers* register themselves to receive system or app events. *Content providers* provide data via storage mechanisms. Each app defines a manifest file (*AndroidManifest.xml*) providing essential information about the app, e.g., its components and their capabilities.

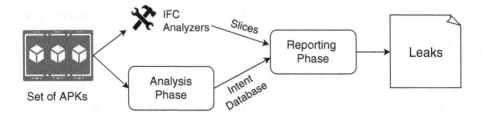

Fig. 1. Analysis framework

Apps are compiled to Dalvik bytecode [10], which is specialized for execution on Android. Together with additional metadata and resources Dalvik bytecode is compressed into an Android Package (APK) that can be published in market places, such as the Google Playstore. Oberheide and Miller [17] demonstrated that the security analysis on the Playstore can easily be circumvented. Even though Google's security mechanisms are constantly evolving, potential for malicious and vulnerable software in the Google Playstore remains.

2.2   Android Intents

Android provides a dedicated mechanism for two components to communicate. A component can send an *intent* as a message, e.g., to notify another component of an event, trigger an action of another component, or transmit information to another component. Note the universal nature of intents on Android: Intents can be sent from the system to apps (and vice versa), from one app to another (inter-app communication, IAC), or even from one component to another within the same app (intra-app-communication, ICC) [9].

Additional information can be associated with an intent: The *intent action* specifies an action supposed to be performed by the receiving component. A component declares intent actions to be received via an intent filter in the manifest file. The intent's sender is unknown on the receiver side. The *target component* mandates a specific receiver for an intent. Setting *intent extra data* adds additional information to be used as parameters by the receiving component.

Note that none of this information is mandatory. When a target component is specified an intent is called *explicit*, otherwise *implicit*. Explicit intents are delivered to the given target component only, while implicit intents can be delivered to any component with a matching intent filter. If multiple components could receive an implicit intent, the user is asked to resolve the intent manually, generally displaying a list of potential receiver apps. Li et al. [16] found that at runtime 40.1% of the intents in Google Playstore apps are explicit intents. Broadcast intents are relayed to every component registered for an intent action instead of only one of them. As intents are the universal means of inter-component communication their analysis becomes critical. In this work we propose a modular approach to precisely analyze information flow through Android intents.

3   Methodology

The fundamental problem of intent analysis for static analysis is the dynamic nature of intents. Static IFC analyses generally leverage dataflow analyses like backwards slicing to determine whether sensitive information (e.g., a device id) may flow into a sink (e.g., internet). However, if a slice contains statements where data is extracted from a received intent, it cannot determine the data's sensitivity without detailed knowledge on possible senders and their semantics.

Figure 1 presents the major building blocks of our analysis framework. In the *analysis phase* a set of APKs under inspection (e.g., all apps installed on a device) is processed and the extracted information stored into a SQL database named *IntentDB*. We collect two sets of information, app-specific information, i.e., package and class name, and registered intent filters to receive implicit intents, as well as intent sender-specific information, i.e., information required to identify potential receiver(s), key, type, and the actual data being sent.

The database is fed into the *reporting phase* together with the receiving app's information flows from a baseline (intra-component) IFC analyzer. If a flow originates at a *getXXXExtra* method[1], we consider the respective sender's outbound data as the actual data source to that flow. Remember that data can only successfully be transmitted via *put/getExtra* methods if the key parameters of both methods match and the signatures of the *put* and *get* methods correspond (e.g. the parameter type of the *put* method equals the return type of the *get* method). Thus we determine all potential senders of this intent based on matching the target component or intent action. For each of these senders we extract the *key*, *value*, and *put* signature (see Sect. 3.1) from the database. If the key and the put signature match this *getXXXExtra* method invocation[2], we determine the sensitivity of the transmitted value based on a categorization of sources. If the value is considered sensitive, we report a potential information flow violation.

Structure of *IntentDB*: Table 1 shows an example entry (from the Telegram messenger app) of the database. As apps consist of several classes, this table has potentially multiple entries for the same app. All entries belonging to one app can be identified by the unique package name. Similarly, each class can send out several intents and hence for each intent sent we will list a separate entry (package name & class name are the same). The column "Put Signature" is considered for mapping the *put* method to the corresponding *getXXXExtra* method at the time of intent resolution. Depending on the non-empty fields, an entry in the database represents an intent receiver and/or sender. If the *Intent Filter* field is set, the app may receive intents. If either the *Target Component* or the *Intent Action* field is set, it acts as an intent sender.

---

[1] *getXXXExtra* methods retrieve type-specific data from a received intent that has been added through the corresponding *putExtra* method.

[2] The *getXXXExtra*'s key is determined via backward slicing.

Table 1. Example database for a class that can receive as well as send intents

Package name	Class name	Intent filter	Target component	Intent action	Key	Value	Put signature
org.telegram. messenger	Firebase-InstanceId-Service	com.google. firebase.IN-STANCE_ ID_EVENT	null	com.google. android. gcm.intent. SEND	"google.to"	String url = "google.com/ iid"	putExtra (String, String)

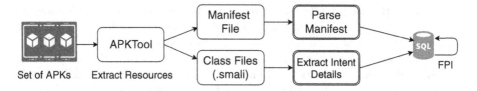

Fig. 2. Analysis Phase, FPI stands for fixed point iteration

3.1   Analysis Phase

Figure 2 depicts the workflow of the analysis phase. In the sequel, we describe the details of each component.

Apktool. A set of APKs is processed by *Apktool* [1], which extracts and decodes the resources of an APK (e.g., *manifest.xml*). It decodes the Dalvik bytecode file (*classes.dex*) of the APK to more comprehensible Smali class files [7].

Manifest Parser. Parsing the manifest file extracts various app details (first set of information), i.e., *package and class name*, as well as *supported intent filters*. This information is mapped to the first three columns of the table and identifies potential receivers of an intent. Even though intent receivers are typically registered in the manifest file, the *registerReceiver* method can register an intent receiver at runtime. In our experiment with 90 apps, we find 433 dynamically registered receivers ($\approx$5% of all intent receivers). We scan class files for dynamically registered receivers and store them in IntentDB.

Dynamic Intent Data Extraction (Extract Intent Details). In this module, we scan each class file for methods that initiate an intent (sender methods), e.g., *startActivity*. The *Android documentation* [9] defines 25 such methods including 12 variants of *startActivity*, 11 variants of *broadcast*, *startService* and *bindService*.

– **Identifying Target Component/Intent Action.** For every sender method we compute its backward slice to find the corresponding intent initialization(s). The goal is to identify its target component (for an explicit intent) or intent action (implicit intent). The intent type depends on the intent's constructor but can be altered using the *explicit-transformation* methods *make-MainActivity*, *makeRestartActivityTask*, *setClass*, *setClassName*, *setComponent*, *setPackage* or *setSelector*, which can also *change* the target component

Listing 1.1. Transit Flow

```
1 // APP A (OutFlowActivity)
2 TelephonyManager tel = (...) getSystemService(TELEPHONY_SERVICE);
3 String imei = tel.getDeviceId(); // source
4 Intent i = new Intent("action_test");
5 i.putExtra("data", imei);
6 startActivity(i); // sink
7 // APP B (Intermediate Activity) -- Capable of receiving "action_test"
8 Intent i = getIntent();
9 String imei = i.getStringExtra("data");
10 Intent newIntent = new Intent("action_test2");
11 newIntent.putExtra("secret", imei);
12 startActivity(newIntent);
13 //APP C (InFlow Activity) -- Capable of receiving "action_test2"
14 Intent i = getIntent();
15 String imei = i.getStringExtra("secret");
16 smsManager.sendTextMessage("1234567890", null, imei, null, null); // sink
```

after the fact. We analyze these cases to extract the actual target: In the case of an explicit intent, we identify the name of the target component. For an implicit intent, we extract the intent action. Any app defining this intent action as supported intent filter (dynamically or in its manifest file) is a potential receiver of this intent. Unfortunately, one cannot always statically determine intent details (e.g., intent action) as they may be influenced by runtime information, which is a general limitation of static analysis. We conservatively approximate such situations, i.e., may include several potential intent actions into the database. Future work may rule out non-matching substrings of potential target name/action strings similar to reflection analyis [12].

– **Identifying Key-Value Pairs.** There are several methods to associate extra data with an intent, generally leveraging *key-value* pair schemes. Senders register a value specifying the key, e.g., *Intent.putExtra("key", "value")* will register the string *"value"* as data for the key *"key"*, which can be extracted by a corresponding receiver using the *Intent.getExtra("key")* method. Trying to receive a key with a non-matching data type results in no value being transmitted. Therefore precise analysis mandates a correct matching of *get* and *put* methods. Unlike related work [16,22] we handle the respective *put/get* method pairs for all basic data types and store the precise signature of any *put* method in *IntentDB* to consider matching types and keys when resolving values received by *getXXXExtra* methods at intent receivers.

Fixed Point Iteration. Intent communication may involve more than two apps/components. In our experiments with 90 apps, we find 54 cases where more than two components were involved in a transitive information flow. In such a case, *IntentDB* contains a *getXXXExtra* method in the column *Value*. For example, in Listings 1.1, app A is sending the device id (secret data) to app B. App B forwards this data to app C, and finally app C leaks it via an SMS. The first 3 rows of Table 2 show the table *IntentDB* after analyzing all APKs. To resolve transitive flows through multiple components we perform a fixed point iteration through all entries of *IntentDB* for which *Value* contains a *getXXXExtra* method. The *com.appB* entry in Table 2 is such an example where data from a received intent is being sent out via another intent. In order to identify the received data, we determine all apps from which this component could receive the intent on which *getXXXExtra* is invoked. In our example *com.appB* receives from *com.appA*. Finally, we match the corresponding *key-value* pair through their *get-put* signatures and create a new entry, replacing the original source (*getXXXExtra* method) by the transmitted value. The created entry for our example is shown in gray in Table 2. To accommodate for modular analysis and thus potential new compatible senders, we retain the old database entry (row 2). The reporting phase described in the next section now matches the added row with the intent received in App C to reveal the transitive information flow of sensitive data to the SMS sink.

Table 2. *IntentDB* for Listing 1.1. Fixed point iteration adds the last row

Pckg. name	Class name	Intent filter	Target component	Intent action	Key	Value	Put signature
com.appA	OutFlow Activity	null	null	action_test	"data"	Device ID	putExtra (String, String)
com.appB	Interm. Activity	action_test	null	action_test2	"secret"	getString Extra ("data")	putExtra (String, String)
com.appC	InFlow Activity	action_test2	null	null	null	null	null
com.appB	Interm. Activity	action_test	null	action_test2	"secret"	Device ID	putExtra (String, String)

3.2 Reporting Phase

In the reporting phase, we process information flows obtained by a baseline IFC analyzer together with *IntentDB*. For ICC/IAC we are only interested in flows with sources that are potential intent receivers, i.e., a *getXXXExtra* method (together with its key and signature). For every *getXXXExtra* method in a reported information flow, we extract all potential senders to this receiver from *IntentDB*, i.e., apps that use an intent with a matching target component or a matching intent action. Finally, we match *get-put* method pairs and *keys* to determine senders that actually send data to this receiver and report it as a (potential) leak if the transmitted data stems from a sensitive source[3].

For example, data flows from the *getStringExtra* method of the intent received on line 14 (Listing 1.1) to the data sink *sendTextMessage* in App C. Our analysis thus matches any sender of the intent action *action_test2* and finds two

---

[3] We utilize the categorization of sources and sinks from R-Droid [3].

rows in IntentDB (Table 2). We check whether any of those uses the key *secret*, which both of them do. Then we match the signature of *getStringExtra* with the sender's Put Signature, where again both match. Finally, we verify if one of the potentially transmitted values (*Device ID, getStringExtra("data")*) is sensitive, thus reporting the former as an illicit information flow.

Partial Support for String and Array Access Resolution. IIFA understands the Smali signature of String methods and applies partial evaluation in order to recover strings created by concatenation, substring, and other String manipulation methods. Concretely, it extracts parameters, applies the respective functionality and returns the resulting string. More contrived examples like converting a string to an array of chars (to be manipulated) are beyond the scope of our tool as we are currently not targeting obfuscated code.

4 Evaluation

We empirically evaluated our tool, IIFA, in two steps:

- *Comparative evaluation on benchmark sets.*
- *Evaluation on real-world apps from the Google Playstore.*

All experiments were performed on a MacBook Pro with a 2,9 GHz Intel Core i7 processor and 16 GB DDR3 RAM and MacOS High Sierra 10.13.1 installed. We used a version 1.8 JVM with 4 GB maximum heap size.

Table 3. Summary of Tool Results for Micro-Benchmarks

ICC comparison							
IccTA Extension + ICC-Bench + Attribute-Mismatch-ICC-Benchmark (34 test cases)							
Precision, Recall and F1-measure	FlowDroid	AppScan	DidFail	DIALDroid	Amandroid	IccTA	Our Tool
Precision $p = \checkmark/(\checkmark + \star)$	25%	16.7%	75%	71%	62%	80%	100%
Recall $r = \checkmark/(\checkmark + \circ)$	80%	62.5%	24%	80%	60%	96%	100%
F_1-measure $2pr/(p + r)$	0.41	0.26	0.36	0.75	0.61	0.87	1
IAC comparison							
DroidBench IAC + Attribute-Mismatch-ICC-Benchmark (10 test cases)							
Precision $p = \checkmark/(\checkmark + \star)$	0%	0%	63%	73%	52%	0%	100%
Recall $r = \checkmark/(\checkmark + \circ)$	0%	0%	21%	56%	76%	0%	100%
F_1-measure $2pr/(p + r)$	0	0	0.31	0.63	0.43	0	1

4.1 RQ1: Precision and Soundness of IIFA

Benchmark Evaluation Datasets. Remember that IIFA is not a stand-alone tool. Therefore its intention cannot be to replace any of the related works that analyze intra-component information flows. Rather we are propagating ICC/IAC analysis as a pre-analysis, and our experiments in this section are to show that this design decision preserves the precision or soundness of the analysis results. In order to evaluate the precision and soundness, we use four separate benchmark sets and compare the results of IIFA (combined with a basic intra-component information flow analysis) to related approaches that aim at analyzing both intra-component and ICC/IAC information flows simultaneously.

- The intent-related cases of the DroidBench test suite [6] (**14 test cases**)
- The extension proposed by IccTA [16] (**18 test cases**)
- ICC-Bench, proposed by Wei et al. [22] (**9 test cases**)
- Our extension[4], Attribute-Mismatch-ICC-Benchmark, which evaluates correct matching of types and keys for data exchanged (**7 test cases**)

Note that the mentioned benchmark sets include several advanced usage scenarios of intents. An example of these scenarios is the usage of callback methods that are triggered after an event has been delivered to its target, which requires information tracking at both sender and receiver sides. Another challenge is string manipulation, e.g., of keys for intent extra data. Finally one case passes an intent with sensitive data through multiple components before finally leaking the stored data. The authors of each benchmark set provide a ground truth for each test case, which we use to measure precision and soundness.

Comparative Evaluation. Based on true positives (tp), false positives (fp), and false negatives (fn) we use the following metrics to compare the performance of IIFA with the related tools:

$$\textbf{Precision} \quad \textbf{Recall} \quad F_1\textbf{-measure}$$
$$p = \frac{tp}{tp+fp} \quad r = \frac{tp}{tp+fn} \quad \frac{2pr}{p+r}$$

We applied IIFA to the original DroidBench benchmark set, where 14 test cases are relevant for intent communication. On these benchmarks IIFA achieved perfect precision and recall ratios. We further applied IIFA to the IccTA extension of Droidbench [6], ICC-Bench [22], and Attribute-Mismatch-ICC-Benchmark, and compared the results to the six most prominent tools for Android intent information flow analysis: FlowDroid [2] and AppScan [13] are limited to ICC, IccTA [16] and AmanDroid [22] require an additional tool to support IAC, DidFail [14] and DIALDroid [4] come with their own inter-app analysis. Table 3 summarizes the results of the different tools on these benchmark sets.

Matching the key and/or type of intent extra data is not reported in Li et al. [16], DidFail [14], or AmanDroid [22]. They merely create a lifecycle method that connects the sender of an intent with (the respective) receiver(s), thus creating a data flow between these components. In our experiments both IccTA and Amandroid failed to detect a key and/or type mismatch during ICC (see Sect. 3.1) due to missing checks of these constraints, resulting in significant precision loss with respect to previous benchmark suites alone.

---

[4] https://github.com/mig40000/ICC-Benchmark.

Table 4. IAC analysis support vs Android API

Tool	IAC support	API 19	>API 19
AmanDroid	✗̌	✓	–
DidFail	✓	– ⚡	– ⚡
AppScan	✗	–	–
DroidSafe	✗̌	✓	– ⚡
DIALDroid	✓	✓	⚡
FlowDroid	✗	–	–
IccTA	✗̌	✓	– ⚡

✓ supported, ✗ not supported
✗̌ Not supported by default,
additional configuration required

✓ supported, – fails, ⚡ crashes

Our Approach: IIFA. We apply IIFA's pre-analysis to the same benchmarks, leveraging R-Droid [3] to generate the intra-app flows[5] as it does not interfere with our IAC/ICC model. Comparing the results with the ground truth revealed perfect precision and soundness results.

> **Answer to RQ1:** *Our design of IIFA as a pre-analysis does not negatively impact precision and soundness, but enables precise matching not only of intent actions but also of the key and/or type of intent extra data without additional constraint solving to exclude infeasible flows.*

4.2 RQ2: Evaluating the Scalability of IIFA

Evaluation on Real-World Apps. We applied IIFA to the 90 most popular apps from the Google playstore, which arguably contain some of the most challenging apps for program analysis, e.g. due to their size. IIFA successfully analyzes each of these apps. Table 4 (extended from [20,21]) lists the related works along with their IAC analysis capabilities in general and for API levels of Android. It is important to observe that none of the tools (that support IAC analysis) is able to analyze an app using API version greater than 19 (i.e. Android KitKat). As this Android version was released in 2013, it is almost impossible to find APKs amenable for analysis by these tools, rendering them obsolete for IAC analysis of realistic Android apps. While probably technically solvable with some engineering effort, we will argue in the sequel, that only pre-analysis is scalable to analyze the IAC information flows for all apps installed on a given device.

As 60% of all intents are implicit, analyzing IAC flows becomes paramount to detect hidden or accidental leaks of sensitive data contrary to user expectations. ApkCombiner was proposed to merge APKs in order to extend standard ICC analysis mechanisms (where all potential communicating components are in one APK) to IAC. As mentioned in the previous paragraph, APKCombiner fails for practically all relevant APKs. But even if merging was possible (some related

---

[5] Note that any other tool that resolves intra-component flows (in particular those of Table 3 except for DIALDroid) would also have been a possible base analysis, but may have interfered with our ICC/IAC model.

work merges directly in their tools) analyzing the resulting APK faces combinatorial explosion of potential communication paths and would require additional constraint solving technologies to prune unrealizable inter-component data flow paths due to mismatching communication partners (e.g. intent action) or keys/-types of the data exchanged via intend extra data.

In contrast IIFA propagates a divide-and-conquer approach where ICC/IAC communication partners are determined and constraints solved in a pre-analysis based on summary information extracted from each app in isolation. The base IFC analyses then only need to provide intra-component information flows (program slices), which is what most of these tools have originally been designed and leverage intricate optimizations for. To demonstrate the advantage of the pre-analysis approach we created a potential IAC flow from a widely used real-world app *Katwarn* to a synthetic app (written using target API level 19 to enable analysis by these tools). One of *Katwarn*'s activities (*GuardianAngelService*) shares the last known location via an implicit intent. An app that declares the corresponding intent filter (*kwrn:ga:location:update*) may receive this intent. Our synthetic app declares the *kwrn:ga:location:update* intent filter and illicitly intercepts this intent. Analyzing this IAC without IIFA failed as APKCombiner was incapable of merging these two apps, and tools that create their own paths, e.g., DIALDroid, crashed.

IIFA's Scalability vs Merging-Based Analysis. Every tool except Did-Fail and DIALDroid requires merging of APKs to extend their ICC capabilities to IAC. To analyze inter-app communication, *ApkCombiner* [15] was proposed in order to merge two or more apps into one. However, *ApkCombiner* supports only Android app versions published on or before 2014, and crashes with the recent apps, thus being practically unusable. But even if the merging process itself was not problematic, it would aggravate the scalability issues reported in related work [16], and confirmed in an independent recent comparative study [21]. Practically attempting to analyze a huge APK with all of the top 90 apps from the Google Playstore would lead to a combinatorial explosion of communication paths between potentially communicating components to be analyzed, precluding any precise static analysis. In particular as we found in our study with the top 90 apps from the Google Playstore that 60% of intents are implicit and thus the receiver may not be unique. Alternatively, one would have to eagerly merge all combinations of (at least) two complete apps. This is at least 8,100 combinations for our 90 apps already, most of which are not communicating. However, this approach assumes that there is no communication involving more apps than the maximum tuple size. Unfortunately there is no guarantee for this assumption unless analyzing all tuples of larger size (which does not scale anymore). In contrast, IIFA analyzes the communication compositionally based on small summaries in a database and combines only the transmitted ICC/IAC data with the intra-app flows of respective intent receivers. The average per app execution time of IIFA over 90 apps is 87.91 s. On average, the analysis phase took 46.81 s (maximum 52.20, minimum 32.40 s) and the reporting phase 41.10 s (maximum 48.60, minimum 35.10 s).

Considering that (intra-app) static IFC analyses usually require a large amount of time to analyze real world apps, IIFA's additional cost is quite feasible for a realistic usage scenario.

> **Answer to RQ2:** *IIFA's modular analysis avoids combinatorial explosion of the potential flow paths in a single merged APK (containing all potential communication partners), or of analyzing all tuples of a given size. Therefore, we were able to analyze the ICC/IAC flows of the 90 most downloaded real-world apps in approx. 2.2h (ignoring the time to compute intra-component slices).*

5   Related Work

Arzt et al. proposed Flowdroid [2], a static taint analysis tool that includes an extensive component lifecycle model. Flowdroid was originally designed for intra-component analysis and cannot analyze string manipulations. R-Droid [3] is an information flow analysis tool that resolves common string manipulations. It does not support intents but conservatively reports every flow to an intent sender function as a leak. AppScan [13] is a commercial tool to detect vulnerabilities in mobile and web apps, including information leaks in Android apps. However, it only supports intra-app ICC analysis and requires the source code of the inspected apps.

IccTA [16] leverages static taint analysis to analyze ICC flow leaks. It ignores some "rarely used ICC methods such as startActivities" [16], multi-threading and slightly involved string analysis, which may lead to missed information leaks. While the IccTA paper reports no experience with IAC, their GitHub page proposes the usage of APKCombiner [15], but as IccTA already has scalability issues, merging apps will aggravate this situation and may require eager combinations of all tuples of apps, resulting in combinatorial explosion. DIAL-Droid [4] is designed to analyze ICC and IAC flows. However, it often fails (IAC) or aborts (ICC) to analyze implicit intents. Additionally, DIALDroid is unable to detect flows involving more than two components. Wei et al. proposed Amandroid [22], which computes control and data flow graphs to resolve intents and inlines the invoked component's lifecycle. However, Amandroid ignores several sink functions as well as extra types and keys for intent data resolution. Droid-Safe [11] improves intent resolution via precise points-to analysis and string resolution. As their ICC resolution does not take extra types and keys into account their results are imprecise. Klieber et al. proposed DidFail [14] that analyzes information flow in Android applications. However, DidFail is limited to the analysis of Activities and implicit intents. Zhang et al. [23] proposed AndroidLeaker, a hybrid approach to detect intent-based privacy leaks on Android. They require instrumenting all apps under inspection, which may not be feasible due to self-integrity checks. Unlike IIFA, AndroidLeaker requires manual adaption of sources and sinks for each new Android version. Epicc [19] analyzes Android ICC precisely but focuses on ICC-related vulnerabilities. It does not fully resolve information flows [22]. ScanDroid [8] analyzes Android intents via a constraint system. However, the lack of distinction between component contexts leads to imprecise analysis results. DroidChecker [5] is a taint analysis tool for Android apps supporting intents. Due to imprecise permission handling, DroidChecker is neither sound nor complete. Further, it cannot handle dynamic features of Java, such as polymorphism. Octeau et al. [18] proposed IC3, an analysis tool for Android intents, which requires expert knowledge in the form of source code annotations.

6   Conclusion

In this work we propose a novel pre-analysis approach to analyze information flows through Android's intents. Using a database of precise intent communication summaries, IIFA avoids the combinatorial explosion of inlining all potential communication partners. We compared IIFA to six related tools on several standard and a novel benchmark sets. IIFA's precision and recall rates are on par or even better than previous tools, which demonstrates that our scalability improvements do not come at the cost of other essential analysis properties.

Acknowledgements. This work was partially supported by the German Federal Ministry of Education and Research (BMBF) through the project SmartPriv (16KIS0760) and the German Research Foundation (DFG) via the collaborative research center "Methods and Tools for Understanding and Controlling Privacy" (SFB 1223), project B02.

References

1. 2.0, A.: Apktool. GitHub, July 2017. https://ibotpeaches.github.io/Apktool/
2. Arzt, S., Rasthofer, S., Fritz, E.A.: Flowdroid: precise context, flow, field, object-sensitive and lifecycle-aware taint analysis for android apps. ACM SIGPLAN Not. **49**(6), 259–269 (2014)
3. Backes, M., Bugiel, S., Derr, E., Gerling, S., Hammer, C.: R-droid: Leveraging android app analysis with static slice optimization. In: 11th ACM on ASIACCS. pp. 129–140. ACM (2016)
4. Bosu, A., Liu, F., Yao, D.D., Wang, G.: Collusive data leak and more: large-scale threat analysis of inter-app communications. In: AsiaCCS 2017, Abu Dhabi, United Arab Emirates, April 2–6, 2017, pp. 71–85 (2017)
5. Chan, P.P., Hui, L.C., Yiu, S.M.: Droidchecker: analyzing android applications for capability leak. In: Proceedings of the Fifth ACM Conference on Security and Privacy in Wireless and Mobile Networks, pp. 125–136. ACM (2012)
6. Christian Fritz, S.A., Rasthofer, S.: Droid-benchmarks. https://github.com/secure-software-engineering/DroidBench. Accessed Dec 2017
7. Freke, J.: Baksmali. https://github.com/JesusFreke/smali
8. Fuchs, A.P., Chaudhuri, A., Foster, J.S.: Scandroid: automated security certification of android. University of Maryland, Technical report (2009)
9. Google: Android intent documentation. https://developer.android.com/reference/android/content/Intent.html. Accessed May 2017

10. Google: Dalvik byteycode documentation. https://source.android.com/devices/tech/dalvik/dalvik-bytecode. Accessed May 2017
11. Gordon, M.I., Kim, D., Perkins, J.H., Gilham, L., Nguyen, N., Rinard, M.C.: Information flow analysis of android applications in droidsafe. In: NDSS (2015)
12. Grech, N., Kastrinis, G., Smaragdakis, Y.: Efficient reflection string analysis via graph coloring. In: Millstein, T. (ed.) ECOOP. vol. 109, pp. 26:1–26:25 (2018)
13. IBM: Ibm security appscan source. https://www-03.ibm.com/software/products/en/appscan. Accessed May 2017
14. Klieber, W., Flynn, L., Bhosale, A., Jia, L., Bauer, L.: Android taint flow analysis for app sets. In: Proceedings of the 3rd ACM SIGPLAN International Workshop on the State of the Art in Java Program Analysis, pp. 1–6. ACM (2014)
15. Li, L.: Apk combiner. GitHub, December 2014. https://github.com/lilicoding/ApkCombiner
16. Li, L., Bartel, A., Bissyandé, E.A.: Iccta: detecting inter-component privacy leaks in android apps. In: Proceedings of the 37th International Conference on Software Engineering, vol. 1. pp. 280–291. IEEE Press (2015)
17. Oberheide, J., Miller, C.: Dissecting the android bouncer. SummerCon2012, New York (2012)
18. Octeau, D., Luchaup, D., Dering, M., Jha, S., McDaniel, P.: Composite constant propagation: application to android inter-component communication analysis. In: Proceedings of the 37th International Conference on Software Engineering, vol. . pp. 77–88. IEEE Press (2015)
19. Octeau, D., McDaniel, P., Jha, S., Bartel, A., Bodden, E., Klein, J., Le Traon, Y.: Effective inter-component communication mapping in android with EPICC: an essential step towards holistic security analysis. In: Proceedings of the 22nd USENIX Security Symposium,pp. 543–558 (2013)
20. Pauck, F., Bodden, E., Wehrheim, H.: Do android taint analysis tools keep their promises? In: Proceedings of the 2018 26th ACM Joint Meeting on European Software Engineering Conference and Symposium on the Foundations of Software Engineering. ESEC/FSE 2018, ACM, New York (2018)
21. Qiu, L., Wang, Y., Rubin, J.: Analyzing the analyzers: Flowdroid/ICCTA, Amandroid, and Droidsafe. In: Proceedings of the 27th ACM SIGSOFT International Symposium on Software Testing and Analysis, pp. 176–186. ACM (2018)
22. Wei, F., Roy, S., Ou, X., et al.: Amandroid: a precise and general inter-component data flow analysis framework for security vetting of android apps. In: Proceedings of the 2014 ACM SIGSAC Conference on Computer and Communications Security, pp. 1329–1341. ACM (2014)
23. Zhang, Z., Feng, X.: AndroidLeaker: a hybrid checker for collusive leak in android applications. In: Larsen, K.G., Sokolsky, O., Wang, J. (eds.) SETTA 2017. LNCS, vol. 10606, pp. 164–180. Springer, Cham (2017). https://doi.org/10.1007/978-3-319-69483-2_10

Power Analysis and Protection
on SPECK and Its Application in IoT

Jing Ge[1,2], An Wang[1,3](✉), Liehuang Zhu[1], Xin Liu[1], Ning Shang[1],
and Guoshuang Zhang[4]

[1] School of Computer Science, Beijing Institute of Technology, Beijing 100081, China
wanganl@bit.edu.cn
[2] State Key Laboratory of Cryptology, P.O. Box 5159, Beijing 100878, China
[3] State Key Laboratory of Information Security, Institute of Information
Engineering, Chinese Academy of Sciences, Beijing 100093, China
[4] Science and Technology on Information Assurance Laboratory,
Beijing 100072, China

Abstract. Emerging applications such as the Internet of Things (IoT)
promotes the development of lightweight cryptography. SPECK is a
lightweight block cipher, specially designed for limited resource devices
that was presented by National Security Agency. Nevertheless, before
using SPECK in any practical application, protection against side-
channel attacks must be paid attention to. In this paper, we take two
attack positions into account and make effort to implement correlation
power analysis on a naive software implementation of SPECK algorithm
in the IoT application scenario. Our experimental results show that the
real key fixed in the register can be successfully recovered when attack
the XOR operations, while there is always an interference item that confuses the correct key when attack the modulo addition operation. Furthermore, we proposal a countermeasure against power attacks in the
IoT application, and the protected SPECK only cost 53.01%, 6.27% and
318.18% of extra code, RAM and time, respectively.

Keywords: SPECK · Lightweight · Side-channel · Correlation power
analysis · Mask

1 Introduction

Due to the emerging era of pervasive computing and the Internet of Things
(IoT), an increasing number of portable intelligent devices such as wireless sensors, smart cards and RFID tags sprung up in daily life. With limited resources
and computing capability, these devices often deal with sensitive data and have

Supported by National Natural Science Foundation of China (Nos. 61872040,
U1836101), National Cryptography Development Fund (No. MMJJ20170201), Foundation of Science and Technology on Information Assurance Laboratory (No. KJ-17-009).

S. Chen et al. (Eds.): SecureComm 2019, LNICST 305, pp. 350–362, 2019.
https://doi.org/10.1007/978-3-030-37231-6_20

certain requirements for security. Nevertheless, traditional cryptographic algorithms are no longer suitable for resource-constrained devices because of higher requirements on hardware and software resources. Thus, lightweight cryptography which achieves both performance and security requirements is currently a very active research domain in the cryptography community [1]. We have recently seen the apparition of many lightweight block ciphers, hash functions and stream ciphers, among them, lightweight block ciphers are in the majority [2]. While an abundant of lightweight block ciphers appeared, most were designed to perform well on a single platform and were not meant to provide high performance across of devices [3]. In 2013, Ray et al. proposed two families of block ciphers, SIMON and SPECK, whose target is to satisfy the need for secure, flexible, and analyzable lightweight block ciphers [4].

Side-channel attack technology is a hot topic in international cryptography research. The threat of side-channel attacks against circuits, in which a cipher whose safety is computationally secured has been embedded, is pointed out [5]. Cryptographic algorithms are mostly implemented in embedded hardware. These devices tend to leak processed data and operations through physical channel information such as power consumption, electromagnetic emanations and time delay. Based on kinds of leakage, it can obtain the intermediate information of cryptographic operation directly and recover the long key in segments, so it is easier to attack the actual cryptosystem than traditional cryptoanalysis [6]. Particularly, power analysis attacks are identified as the most dangerous types of attacks due to using power consumption can easily analyze confidential information.

For all we know, many studies have been reported on implementing side-channel attacks on SIMON and applying their relevant countermeasures against these attacks [7–9]. As for SPECK, whose security is well documented [10,11], only Chen et al. carried out a tiny side-channel resistant SPECK for Field Programmable Gate Array (FPGA) [12], other studies on SPECK implemented in software embedded in devices have not been published up till now. In this paper, we show that naive software implementation is vulnerable to the correlation power attack and perform experiments for the correlation power attack. Furthermore, we come up with a countermeasure against this attack on SPECK algorithm.

2   Preliminaries

2.1   Specification of SPECK

The ten versions of SPECK have been optimized for outstanding performance in both hardware and software implementations. SPECK encrypts a block of $2n$ bits where n is the word size and supports the word sizes of $n = 16, 24, 32, 48$ and 64 bits. Besides, the key size is commonly notated by mn for a value m in $\{2, 3, 4\}$. According to various combinations block sizes and key sizes, the round of encryption ranges from 22 to 34.

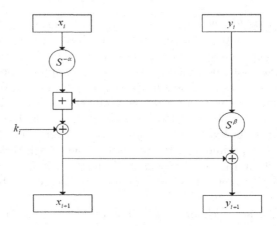

Fig. 1. SPECK round function.

Figure 1 shows the round function of SPECK family. At first, the plaintext is divided into two parts, each of size n. Afterwards three different types of operations are applied during the encryption maps: an addition modulo 2^n, bitwise XOR, and left and right circular shifts, which enable high throughput and efficient implementation on most microprocessors. We use S^j and S^{-j} to represent left and right circular shifts, respectively, by j bits. And k_i is the ith round key starting from 0. Hereby, the round function can be defined by:

$$x_{i+1} = (S^{-\alpha}(x_i) + y_i) \oplus k_i$$
$$y_{i+1} = S^{\beta}(y_i) \oplus x_{i+1} \tag{1}$$

In fact, the same round function is also employed for the key scheduling, but there is a matter needed attention while making use of this function. Comparing with the encryption round function, the key used in key scheduling can be viewed as the plaintext, and the constant representing the round number should be regarded as the key. Obviously, the above description can also be formulized. Let K be an initial key for a SPECK cipher, and K $= (l_{m-2}, \ldots, l_0, k_0)$, where $l_i, k_0 \in GF(2^n)$, for a value of m in $\{2, 3, 4\}$. k_i and l_i are given by:

$$l_{i+m-1} = (y_i + S^{-\alpha}(l_i)) \oplus i$$
$$k_{i+1} = S^{\beta}(k_i) \oplus l_{i+m-1} \tag{2}$$

2.2 Power Analysis Attacks

A lot of embedded devices tend to inevitably leak physical information such as power consumption [13], electromagnetic radiation [14] and time delay [15], which can be utilized to acquire sensitive information of users. Side-channel attacks exactly take advantage of this leakage and have become a most powerful attack aimed at cryptographic devices. Varieties of side-channel attacks include timing attacks, power analysis attacks, electromagnetic radiation attacks, fault attacks and so on. Among them, power analysis attacks are the easiest and the most effective, which consist of three types: Simple Power Analysis (SPA), Correlation Power Analysis (CPA) [16] and Differential Power Analysis (DPA).

SPA can directly analyze power traces obtained during encryption or decryption, which makes use of the dependence of the secret key. Namely, attackers attempt to gain the key directly or indirectly from only one specified power trace, which makes implementing SPA attack a challenging work. Generally, attackers are supposed to have a good command of concrete cryptographic algorithm in devices. In addition, complicated statistic approaches are used to extract the signal. In contrast, although more power traces are essential in CPA and DPA attacks, the attacker only need to know what the cryptographic algorithm is rather than how to implement specified details. In a CPA attack, the attacker uses certain plaintexts and the fixed value in internal register to perform encryption, then the same plaintexts with the guessed key experience the exact cryptographic operations. Thus, two kinds of power traces will be acquired. According to key points selected from these traces, the key in a register can be recovered by correlation analysis. In a DPA attack, the attacker makes a guess at a bit in the unknown key, partitions the power traces in accordance with some internal register values depended on this guess, and checks if the partitions show meaningful difference.

3 Correlation Power Analysis on Non-linear Layer of SPECK

3.1 Attack Method

It is vital to have a good knowledge of specific details about encryption algorithms in SPA attacks, and DPA attacks take advantage of differential approach to analyze leaked message of the key. Comparing with two types of attacks, apart from no need for implementation details, CPA improves the statistical method DPA used, in which case a more suitable correlation coefficient was considered to replace the difference score for statistical analysis [18]. Therefore, less power traces would be obtained to retrieve the fixed key and CPA is chosen to attack SPECK algorithm. In the following, we focus on the version of SPECK (SPECK32/64) processing 32-bit plaintext blocks with a 64-bit key in 22 rounds.

Owing to the correlation between power consumption of cryptographic devices and the data being processed, in the actual attack, the attacker needs to map the operand to the value of power consumption. That is, to select an effective power simulation mathematical model to model the power consumption. Commonly used power consumption models are Hamming Weight (HW) model and Hamming Distance (HD) [16] model. HW [13] model is on account of the assumption that the power consumption of the cryptographic device is proportional to the number of 1 in the data being processed. HD model not only focuses on the processed data itself, but also takes the data values before and after the processed data into account. It is intractable to employ HD model because that the attacker needs to command more information about crypto-graphic devices. Apart from little information of devices needed, HW model is suitable for software implementation of the cryptography system. Hence in our CPA attack, we select HW model to analyze the leakage of power consumption information.

For convenience and simplicity, we recover the real key in bytes. Here are our attack procedures:

(1) At first, it is essential to select the appropriate attack location, which means finding an intermediate value generated in encryption.

(2) The experimental platform was set up to collect power consumption during the encryption. For example, n groups of random plaintexts and the key fixed in the register are used to perform SPECK algorithm, then we can obtain a group of power traces, denoted as $P_1, P_2, \ldots P_n$.

(3) According to power traces and HW model, we select sample points to find the intermediate leakage point, where the hamming weight of median has the greatest correlation with power consumption. Furthermore, the power consumption of each trace at the leakage point is expressed as $T_1, T_2, \ldots T_n$.

(4) In order to calculate the assumed median, we guess the first byte of the fixed subkey represented as k in the first encryption round, and the initial value of k is 0.

  (a) n groups of plaintexts are applied to compute separately with the guessed k and then n groups of intermediate values of x are also known. After that, we calculate their corresponding Hamming weight, presented as $HW(x)$.

  (b) We use n groups of $HW(x)$ and n groups of T to calculate correlation coefficient, denote as r:

$$r = \frac{\sum\limits_{i=1}^{N}(HW_i - \overline{HW})(T_i - \overline{T})}{\sqrt{\sum\limits_{i=1}^{N}(HW_i - \overline{HW})^2}\sqrt{\sum\limits_{i=1}^{N}(T_i - \overline{T})^2}} \tag{3}$$

  (c) $k = k + 1$, repeat step (4) and not finish until $k > 255$.

(5) Finally, the key with the greatest correlation coefficient is the real key that we want to retrieve.

3.2   Experimental Results

In our experiment, we implement SPECK algorithm as MCS-51 C codes on STC89C52 processor of MathMagic side-channel analyzer, which can be viewed as an IoT application scene. With sampling rate 1GSa/s, the power consumption can be acquired accurately during the encryption. In addition, the obtained power traces are analyzed by C# program. A fixed key: key = 0x1122334455667788 in the register is used to conduct our experiment. We assume the real key is not known during the attack, and the real key is just to verify whether our experimental result is true or not.

With respect to the choice of attack location, we try to attack addition modulo 2^n operation in the second round of encryption function. In AES, the attack position of CPA is after the S-box, for that the S-box is a non-linear operation. If two guessed keys differ by only one bit, the hamming weight difference obtained after the S-box confusion is generally not 1, which is very conducive to distinguishing the correct key from the wrong key. Taking advantage of the characteristics of non-linear operations, the median value after modulo addition is selected to attack in SPECK algorithm.

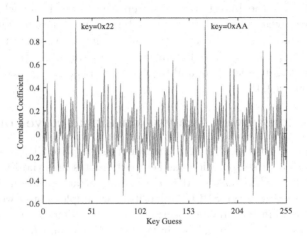

Fig. 2. The recovered subkey of the first round.

The intermediate value after addition modulo 2^n is the result that the plaintext is divided into left and right two parts and experiences a series of operations, so the four-bit leakage information here is related to the eight-bit plaintext and as well related to the eight-bit key information of the first round. Corresponding to that, the eight-bit key can be recovered by only utilizing the four-bit information leakage. However, it is necessary to emphasize that the eight bits of the key were not in order. Because before the second round of addition modulo 2^n, the median hidding the key information undergoes a circular shift operation.

Due to the carry problems in addition, the leakage analysis is required to start from the low position. Furthermore, the high-order position bit is affected by the low-order position carry and the recovery of the high-order position key is based on the completion of the low-order position key recovery. In our experiment, we concentrate on leakage of the lowest four bits, whose corresponding key information is the 6th, 7th, 8th, 9th, 13th, 14th, 15th and 16th bits of the initial key. These eight bits are regarded as the value of a byte to make key guess. Theoretically, the correct key restored in the register is the value 0x22 after taking the eight bits.

100 waveforms were collected up and 8500 sampling points were selected for CPA attack. The experimental results are shown in Fig. 2. In particular, the correlation coefficients of two guessing keys were the same, and the same correlation coefficient was the greatest among all guessing keys. We collected more waveforms and conducted a lot of experiments, each of which presented the identical result. There was always a guessing key whose correlation coefficient was the same to correlation coefficient of the correct key, which became the interference term.

By comparing the two keys, we found the problem. There was always a key confusing the correct key so that the left and right parts of the four bits of plaintext information were added to get the identical result or one existed carry problem, but the lowest four bits were the same. From what has been discussed above, when CPA is performed after the modulo addition operation, there is always an interference item to confuse the correct key. On the other hand, the key must be recovered from the low to the high. If the low key is guessed wrong, the high key is bound to go wrong. Therefore, we choose another place to implement CPA.

4   Correlation Power Analysis on Linear Layer of SPECK

In this section, we chose another attack location to complete CPA to recover fixed in the register. The first operation the key participates in is the XOR operation in the first round, which can be regarded as our attack position. Besides, the equipment we used and the SPECK algorithm we implemented were the same as the experiments in the previous section. The only difference was the location of the attack. Let K be an initial key in the used device, and $K = (l_2, l_1, l_0, k_0)$, where $k_0 = 0 \times 1122$, $l_0 = 0 \times 3344$, $l_1 = 0 \times 5566$, $l_2 = 0 \times 7788$.

We first went through the CPA for the first round, and Fig. 3 shows the result of leakage analysis. The leakage points with absolute value of the correlation coefficient more than 0.9 were recorded, and the correlation coefficients were analyzed separately. Theoretically, the same correct key could be obtained. After a lot of experimental verification, we could successfully deciphered the key.

The first round of XOR attacks can only restore 16-bit keys. To restore the complete key information, the four round function must be attacked. In these four attacks, all operations are the same except that the number of rounds is different. However, it is worth noting that the recovered key in each round except for the first round is not the initial key, but the subkey used in each round, namely k_i.

After four rounds of attack with eight CPA, the recovered key is shown in Fig. 4. As shown in the figure, $k_0 = 0 \times 1122$, $k_1 = 0 \times DD00$, $k_2 = 0 \times DDA8$, $k_3 = 0 \times 9836$. The initial key can be calculated according to the formula generated by the key.

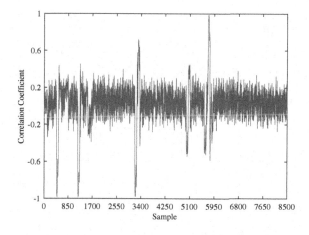

Fig. 3. The leakage analysis of CPA with attacking XOR operation.

$$l_3 = k_1 \oplus S^2(k_0) = 0 \times \text{DD00} \oplus S^2(0 \times 1122) = 0 \times 9988$$
$$l_0 = S^7((l_0 \oplus 0 \times 0000) - \text{k}_0) = S^7((0 \times 9988 \oplus 0 \times 0000) - 0 \times 1122) = 0 \times 3344$$
$$l_4 = k_2 \oplus S^2(k_1) = 0 \times \text{DDA8} \oplus S^2(0 \times \text{DD00}) = 0 \times \text{A9AB}$$
$$l_1 = S^4((l_4 \oplus 0 \times 0001) - k_1) = S^7((0 \times \text{A9AB} \oplus 0 \times 0001) - 0 \times \text{DD00}) = 0 \times 5566$$
$$l_5 = k_3 \oplus S^2(k_2) = 0 \times 9836 \oplus S^2(0 \times \text{DDA8}) = 0 \times \text{EE95}$$
$$l_2 = S^7((l_5 \oplus 0 \times 0002) - \text{k}_2) = S^7((0 \times \text{EE95} \oplus 0 \times 0002) - 0 \times \text{DDA8}) = 0 \times 7788$$
$$(4)$$

By calculation, the initial key we got was the correct key, which means it is feasible to carry out CPA after XOR operations.

5 Countermeasure Against Power Attacks

Many countermeasures targeted at power attacks such as masking and hiding [19] have been put forward, which weaken the correlation between sensitive intermediate values and energy consumption to achieve the purpose of protection. Moreover, the basic principle of masking is to add random mask data into the input of the cryptographic module to cover up the real data. At the same time, the corresponding de-mask circuit needs to be designed. For that the result of the encryption is also masked, it is necessary to eliminate the influence of masking at the end of the calculation and restore the real ciphertexts.

In our paper, we brainstorm a masking scheme to protect SPECK algorithm from correlation analysis attacks. There are both boolean operations and modulo addition operations in SPECK algorithm round function, in which case secure conversion between boolean masking and modulo addition should be considered while masking. Here is our scheme.

First and foremost, we add a random mask m_p to the plaintext during encryption. It is worth noting that m_p should be split into m_x and m_y with the plaintext

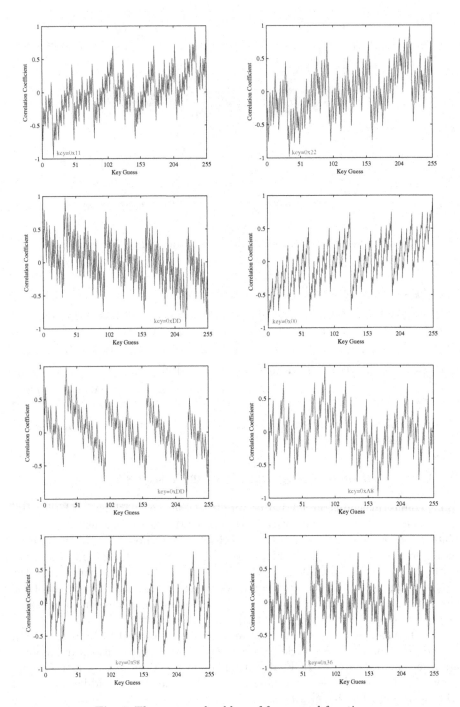

Fig. 4. The recovered subkey of four round function.

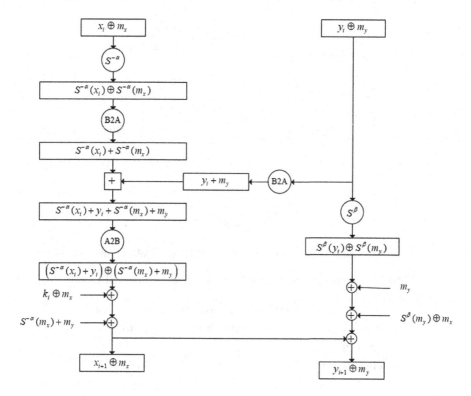

Fig. 5. Masked SPECK round function.

segmented into two parts. Besides, for the sake of reducing the frequency of random mask changes, we raise a method to take off the mask to guarantee that the masked value is the same in each round of encryption function. Figure 5 shows masked SPECK round function, and the "B2A" and "A2B" modules represent *Boolaen To Arithmetic* and *Arithmetic To Boolean* conversions respectively. By adding the masked values m_x and m_y again, original unmasked x_{i+1} and y_{i+1} will also be masked and not change the random masks of each round function. The goal of extra masked data $S^{-\alpha}(m_x) + m_y$ and $S^{\beta}(m_y) \oplus m_x$ is getting rid of the effect of other masks. In addition, we should emphasize that it will leak encryption information if switch the order of these two masking procedures.

We implement both the original and our masked round function of SPECK algorithm in software embedded in devices. Comparation of their performance is shown in Table 1, and the efficiency of CPA on masked SPECK is presented in Fig. 6. The red trace represents correlation coefficient of the right key, and other traces show the wrong guessed key. It is obvious that our masking scheme can commendably protect SPECK algorithm from CPA. In contrast, our timing overhead is four to five times larger, we cannot avoid the timing overhead because conversions between boolean and arithmetic masking are necessary in SPECK masking.

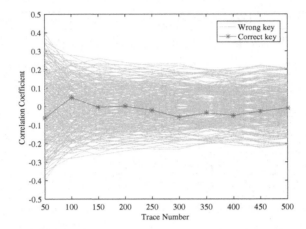

Fig. 6. The efficiency of CPA on masked SPECK. (Color figure online)

Table 1. Comparisons between unmasked and masked SPECK.

	Unmasked SPECK	Masked SPECK	Extra cost
Code	1079B	1651B	53.01%
RAM	255B	271B	6.27%
Time	0.44 ms	1.84 ms	318.18%

6   Conclusion

In this paper we have presented a security analysis of the SPECK block cipher from a side-channel point of view. In the IoT application scenario, we implemented CPA on a naive software implementation of SPECK algorithm for two different attack positions. By comparison, we find that the XOR operation of the attack can successfully recover the real key fixed in the register, while when the attack location of the modulo addition operation is selected, there is always an interference item that confuses the correct key. Moreover, we proposal a countermeasure against power attacks, which can effectively protect SPECK from power attacks.

References

1. Eisenbarth, T., Kumar, S.S., Paar, C., Poschmann, A., Uhsadel, L.: A survey of lightweight-cryptography implementations. IEEE Des. Test Comput. **24**(6), 522–533 (2007)
2. Omrani, T., Rhouma, R., Sliman, L.: Lightweight cryptography for resource-constrained devices: a comparative study and rectangle cryptanalysis. In: Bach Tobji, M.A., Jallouli, R., Koubaa, Y., Nijholt, A. (eds.) ICDEc 2018. LNBIP, vol. 325, pp. 107–118. Springer, Cham (2018). https://doi.org/10.1007/978-3-319-97749-2_8

3. Banik, S., Pandey, S.K., Peyrin, T., Sasaki, Y., Sim, S.M., Todo, Y.: GIFT: a small present – towards reaching the limit of lightweight encryption. In: Fischer, W., Homma, N. (eds.) CHES 2017. LNCS, vol. 10529, pp. 321–345. Springer, Cham (2017). https://doi.org/10.1007/978-3-319-66787-4_16
4. Beaulieu, R., Shors, D., Smith, J., Smith, T.-C., Weeks, B., Wingers, L.: The SIMON and SPECK Families of Lightweight Block Ciphers. IACR Cryptology ePrint Archive 2013, 404 (2013)
5. Heuser, A., Picek, S., Guilley, S., Mentens, N.: Side-channel analysis of lightweight ciphers: does lightweight equal easy? IACR Cryptology ePrint Archive 2017, 261 (2017)
6. Bache, F., Plump, C., Gneysu, T.: Confident leakage assessment - a side-channel evaluation framework based on confidence intervals. In: DATE 2018, pp. 1117–1122 (2018)
7. Takahashi, J., Fukunaga, T.: Fault analysis on SIMON family of lightweight block ciphers. In: Lee, J., Kim, J. (eds.) ICISC 2014. LNCS, vol. 8949, pp. 175–189. Springer, Cham (2015). https://doi.org/10.1007/978-3-319-15943-0_11
8. Bhasin, S., Graba, T., Danger, J.-L., Najm, Z.: A look into SIMON from a side-channel perspective. In: HOST 2014, pp. 56–59 (2014)
9. Shanmugam, D., Selvam, R., Annadurai, S.: Differential power analysis attack on SIMON and LED block ciphers. In: Chakraborty, R.S., Matyas, V., Schaumont, P. (eds.) SPACE 2014. LNCS, vol. 8804, pp. 110–125. Springer, Cham (2014). https://doi.org/10.1007/978-3-319-12060-7_8
10. Beaulieu, R., Shors, D., Smith, J., Treatman-Clark, S., Weeks, B., Wingers, L.: Notes on the design and analysis of SIMON and SPECK. IACR Cryptology ePrint Archive 2017, 560 (2017)
11. Song, L., Huang, Z., Yang, Q.: Automatic differential analysis of ARX block ciphers with application to SPECK and LEA. In: Liu, J.K., Steinfeld, R. (eds.) ACISP 2016. LNCS, vol. 9723, pp. 379–394. Springer, Cham (2016). https://doi.org/10.1007/978-3-319-40367-0_24
12. Chen, C., İnci, M.S., Taha, M., Eisenbarth, T.: SpecTre: a tiny side-channel resistant speck core for FPGAs. In: Lemke-Rust, K., Tunstall, M. (eds.) CARDIS 2016. LNCS, vol. 10146, pp. 73–88. Springer, Cham (2017). https://doi.org/10.1007/978-3-319-54669-8_5
13. Kocher, P., Jaffe, J., Jun, B.: Differential power analysis. In: Wiener, M. (ed.) CRYPTO 1999. LNCS, vol. 1666, pp. 388–397. Springer, Heidelberg (1999). https://doi.org/10.1007/3-540-48405-1_25
14. Gandolfi, K., Mourtel, C., Olivier, F.: Electromagnetic analysis: concrete results. In: Koç, Ç.K., Naccache, D., Paar, C. (eds.) CHES 2001. LNCS, vol. 2162, pp. 251–261. Springer, Heidelberg (2001). https://doi.org/10.1007/3-540-44709-1_21
15. Kocher, P.C.: Timing attacks on implementations of Diffie-Hellman, RSA, DSS, and other systems. In: Koblitz, N. (ed.) CRYPTO 1996. LNCS, vol. 1109, pp. 104–113. Springer, Heidelberg (1996). https://doi.org/10.1007/3-540-68697-5_9
16. Brier, E., Clavier, C., Olivier, F.: Correlation power analysis with a leakage model. In: Joye, M., Quisquater, J.-J. (eds.) CHES 2004. LNCS, vol. 3156, pp. 16–29. Springer, Heidelberg (2004). https://doi.org/10.1007/978-3-540-28632-5_2

17. Reparaz Dominguez, O.: Analysis and design of masking schemes for secure crypto-
    graphic implementations. Analyse en ontwerp van maskeringsschema's voor veilige
    cryptografische implementaties. Katholieke Universiteit Leuven, Belgium (2016)
18. Stepnek, F., Bucek, J., Novotny, M.: Differential power analysis under constrained
    budget: low cost education of hackers. In: DSD, pp. 645–648 (2013)
19. Mangard, S., Oswald, E., Popp, T.: Power Analysis Attacks. Springer, Boston
    (2007). https://doi.org/10.1007/978-0-387-38162-6. ISBN 978-0-387-30857-9, pp.
    I–XXIII, 1–37

Machine Learning, Privately

Adversarial False Data Injection Attack Against Nonlinear AC State Estimation with ANN in Smart Grid

Tian Liu and Tao Shu$^{(\boxtimes)}$

Department of Computer Science and Software Engineering, Auburn University,
Auburn, USA
{tzl0031,tshu}@auburn.edu

Abstract. Artificial neural network (ANN) provides superior accuracy for nonlinear alternating current (AC) state estimation (SE) in smart grid over traditional methods. However, research has discovered that ANN could be easily fooled by adversarial examples. In this paper, we initiate a new study of adversarial false data injection (FDI) attack against AC SE with ANN: by injecting a deliberate attack vector into measurements, the attacker can degrade the accuracy of ANN SE while remaining undetected. We propose a population-based algorithm and a gradient-based algorithm to generate attack vectors. The performance of these algorithms are evaluated through simulations on IEEE 9-bus, 14-bus and 30-bus systems under various attack scenarios. Simulation results show that DE is more effective than SLSQP on all simulation cases. The attack examples generated by DE algorithm successfully degrade the ANN SE accuracy with high probability.

Keywords: Smart grid · AC state estimation · False data injection attack · Adversarial learning

1 Introduction

With the increase of residential and industrial power demand, nowadays a regional or nationwide power outage often leads to catastrophes in the matter of public safety. After the Northeast Blackout of the US in 2003, the US and Canada have reached a consensus in transferring into smart grid system, which is cleaner, more efficient, reliable, resilient and responsive than traditional grid. While the transition provides many attractive new features such as remote and automatic grid monitoring, control, and pricing, it also raised serious security challenges by opening up traditional power system to many potential attacks in the cyber space. In the 2015 Ukraine power outage [4,12], the hacker successfully compromised the information systems of three energy distribution companies and caused power disruption to over 225,000 customers. Since then, cyber attacks in

© ICST Institute for Computer Sciences, Social Informatics and Telecommunications Engineering 2019
Published by Springer Nature Switzerland AG 2019. All Rights Reserved
S. Chen et al. (Eds.): SecureComm 2019, LNICST 305, pp. 365–379, 2019.
https://doi.org/10.1007/978-3-030-37231-6_21

smart grid have become a realistic and growing concern. Therefore, it is significant and urgent to identify possible threats, and propose countermeasures to eliminate such threats, so as to reduce the potential loss of the society.

State estimation (SE) plays an important role in system monitoring and control, as it provides current system status for control center operators to take actions in advance to avoid potential accidents. In *alternating current* (AC) power flow systems, states and measurements are non-linearly related, several efforts have been made to adopt artificial neural networks (ANNs) for AC SE to better model this non-linear relationship [1,11,15,16]. Although the training phase of these ANN models is costly, it has been shown that these ANN SE models are more accurate. However, studies have shown that SE is vulnerable to *false data injection* (FDI) attacks [13]. The adversary can corrupt state variables by injecting a well-coordinated false data to meter measurements, while evading detection. FDI attacks on *direct current* (DC) power flow model can be linearly formulated, hence it is easy to understand their impact and propose countermeasures against them. Nonetheless, FDI attacks towards AC SE are more complicated. The non-linearity between state variables and measurements diffuses the strength of false injection, and makes it hard to identify how the change of measurements would result in the errors to state variables. There are few studies tackling the FDI attacks to AC SE. Jia et al. [9] claims that the ability of malicious attack designed for DC power flow model is alleviated on AC power flow model. Several FDI attacks against AC SE are derived from DC FDI attack and predominantly based upon *weighted least square* (WLS) [7,17].

In the area of image classification, Szegedy first noticed that neural networks may be easily fooled by well-coordinated samples with small perturbations [20]. Since then, there have been many efforts in exploring the robustness of ANN by designing adversarial attacks [6,19].

In this paper, we are interested in examining whether the above vulnerability of ANN presented in image classification problem can be extended to SE problem in smart grid. Furthermore, we attempt to develop algorithms that can systematically generate polluted measurements that maximize ANN SE error while eluding from being detected by the bad data detector. By answering these questions, we intend to establish new understanding on the security vulnerabilities of the latest high-accuracy ANN AC SE models. To the best of our knowledge, our work is the first in the literature that studies FDI to ANN AC SE models.

Solving our problem faces new and significant challenges. First, our problem has an optimization nature in the sense that we seek the optimal attack vector that maximizes the attack outcomes, while the goal of the image-classification counterparts is just to find a feasible attack vector. Second, the attack model in our problem considers the attacker's access and resource constraints, by which the attacker only has access to and can only manipulate a certain numbers of meters. In contrast, the image-classification problem has no such constraint and the attacker is allowed to change any pixel of the image. Lastly, the output of ANN SE model is a continuous value, whereas that of the image-classification is discrete and covers a limited number of pre-defined cases. Due to these fundamental structural differences, the existing results from image-classification ANN are not directly applicable to our problem. The main contributions of our work include the following four-fold:

- In creating the target ANN SE models for large-scale grid systems, a novel penalty term is proposed for the loss function, which significantly improves the accuracy of the ANN on modeling voltage phase angle.
- An optimization-based FDI attack formulation is proposed for AC SE under the nonlinear ANN model, which can accommodate various practical constraints on the attacker, including its resource and meter accessibility.
- We adapt DE and SLSQP to solve the above optimization, targeting at two different attack scenarios: DE generates attack vectors for which the attacker can compromise any k meters, while DE and SLSQP target on the scenario where the attacker is restricted to compromise specific k meters.
- The effectiveness of the proposed attack models is verified based on extensive simulations on three test systems under various attack scenarios. Our results show that the DE attack succeeds for more than 80% cases even with a small number of compromised meters and low false injection level.

This paper is structured as the following. We start by providing preliminary for SE and bad data detection in Sect. 2. We construct AC SE models with ANN as targets for our attacks in Sect. 3. Subsequently, we introduce our adversary model in Sect. 4. Our two attack algorithms, DE algorithm and SLSQP algorithm would be presented in Sect. 5. Finally, the experimental analysis and the comparison of our two attacks on target models and conclusions are presented in Sects. 6 and 7.

2   Preliminaries

In AC power flow model, measurements of power flows are non-linearly dependent on state variables, as characterized by the following equations: $\mathbf{z} = h(\mathbf{x}) + \mathbf{e}$, where $\mathbf{z}$ and $\mathbf{x}$ denote a N_m-dimension measurement vector and a N_n-dimension state vector, respectively, $\mathbf{e}$ denotes a N_m-dimension vector of normally distributed measurement errors, and h is a set of nonlinear functions relating states to measurements. In an over-determined case ($N_m > N_n$), the state variables are determined from WLS optimization over a residual function $J(\mathbf{x})$ [21]:

$$\hat{\mathbf{x}} = \arg\min_x J(\mathbf{x}), \text{where } J(\mathbf{x}) = (\mathbf{z} - h(\mathbf{x}))^T \mathbf{W}(\mathbf{z} - h(\mathbf{x})) \tag{1}$$

Here, the weight matrix $\mathbf{W}$ is defined as $diag\{\sigma_1^{-2}, \sigma_2^{-2}, ..., \sigma_{N_m}^{-2}\}$, and σ_i^2 is the variance of the ith measurement ($i = 1, ..., N_m$).

Bad measurements would be introduced due to various reasons, such as measuring noise, transmission error, meter malfunction and malicious attack. The ability to detect and identify bad data is extremely critical to the stability of a smart grid. Most bad data detection schemes rely on the residuals $J(\hat{x})$ as their decision variable. In particular, given the assumption that $\mathbf{e}$ is normally distributed, it is shown that $J(x)$ follows $\chi^2(K)$ distribution, where $K = N_m - N_n$

is the degree of freedom [21]. Any residual exceeding some pre-determined threshold τ is recognized as a bad data:

$$z \text{ is identified as a bad data, if } J(\hat{\mathbf{x}}) = (\mathbf{z} - h(\hat{\mathbf{x}}))^T \mathbf{W}(\mathbf{z} - h(\hat{\mathbf{x}})) > \tau. \qquad (2)$$

The threshold τ can be determined by a significant level α in hypothesis testing, by which the false alarms would occur with probability α.

3   ANN-Based AC SE

In lack of actual state-measurement data from real power grid, the training and testing cases in our study are generated based on simulations over the IEEE test systems (9-bus, 14-bus, 30-bus). A Matlab package, MATPOWER [22], is used for data generation and power flow analysis. Note that the use of simulated data in training does not affect the validity of the proposed ANN model. Usually the model is trained off-line, and then to be retrain or improved with the accumulation of actual data following the same procedure.

State variables, including magnitudes and phase angles of bus voltages may change within a small range under different loads. To account for this dynamic behavior, we consider a series of loads of the power grid ranging from 80% to 120% to simulate actual load pattern. For each instance of the load, the states are calculated by power flow analysis using MATPOWER. According to [2], ±2% error is allowed in a power measurement reading. In line with this specification, we add an independent Gaussian noise ϵ to each measurement reading ψ, so that the simulated measurement reading becomes $(1 + \epsilon)\psi$, where $\epsilon \sim N(0, 0.67\%^2)$. For each of systems, 10,000 and 1,000 state-measurement pairs are generated for training and testing, respectively.

Three ANN SE models are trained for the three systems, respectively. Following [1,8,14,15], each ANN SE model possesses a multi-layered perceptron architecture. We use mean WLS error as loss function:

$$loss(\mathbf{z}, \mathbf{x}) = \frac{1}{N} \sum_{i=1}^{N} (\mathbf{z} - h(\mathbf{x}))^T \mathbf{W}(\mathbf{z} - h(\mathbf{x})) \qquad (3)$$

where N is number of training samples. Our experiments show this loss function works well for small-scale systems (such as 9-bus and 14-bus power grid), but fails to provide accurate estimation for voltage phase angles in larger scale systems (30-bus power grid). This is consistent with previous findings in [14]. To address this issue, we revise the loss function in Eq. (3) by adding a new penalty term of the *mean square error* (MSE) between the actual and the estimated states, leading to the new loss function in Eq. (4) specially designed for large-scale systems. In this new loss function, a small constant c is added to balance both error terms so that the gradient descent works on both terms simultaneously. Our experiments show that by adding this new penalty term, the voltage phase angle estimation error is reduced from 12% to 1.3% in 30-bus system.

$$loss(\mathbf{z}, \mathbf{x}) = \frac{1}{N} \sum_{i=1}^{N} (\mathbf{z} - h(\mathbf{x}))^T \mathbf{W}(\mathbf{z} - h(\mathbf{x})) + c\frac{1}{N} \sum_{i=1}^{N} (\mathbf{x} - \hat{\mathbf{x}})^2 \qquad (4)$$

After the ANN models are trained, the testing data is used to evaluate their performance. A good SE model should preserve two properties: (1) provide accurate SE irrespective of the noise in the measurements; (2) bad-data alarms not triggered by regular measurement noise. Accordingly, we evaluate the estimation accuracy of the ANNs by *maximum absolute relative error* (MARE) between the true and the estimated values. An estimation is considered accurate if MAREs of the voltage magnitude and the voltage phase angle do not exceed 1% and 5%, respectively. Table 1 summarizes the performance evaluation results based on a significant level $\alpha = 0.01$ for the trained ANN models. It is clear from these tables that the proposed ANN models are able to estimate AC states accurately, and have low false alarm rate for bad data under regular measurement noises.

Table 1. ANN SE model evaluation

Test system	MARE ($|V|$)	Accuracy ($|V|$)(%)	MARE (θ)	Accuracy (θ)(%)	Bad data (%)
9-bus	2.4×10^{-5}	100	1.6×10^{-2}	96	0
14-bus	5.6×10^{-5}	100	1.6×10^{-2}	99	3
30-bus	6.5×10^{-5}	100	1.3×10^{-2}	98	5

4 Adversarial Model and Attack Formulation

4.1 Adversarial Model

The goal of the attacker is to launch a FDI attack, in which the attacker aims to decide and inject a manipulated measurement vector into the measurement under given resource and meter accessibility constraints, such that the injection can maximize SE error while remaining stealthy.

The attacker is assumed to have full knowledge of the topology and configuration of the power grid, such as the nodal admittance matrix. Such information could be accessed or estimated from public database or historical records. In addition, the attacker is also assumed to know everything about the ANN SE model, including the architecture and the parameters. These information could be obtained by the attacker either through breaking into the information system of the power grid (similar to the 2015 Ukraine case) or through training a shadow ANN that mimics the real ANN SE model on a substitute data set. The attacker is also assumed to know the threshold of the bad data detector. Although these assumptions render a strong attacker that may not always represent the practical cases, it enables us to evaluate the robustness and vulnerabilities of the ANN SE models under the worst-case scenario, providing an upper bound on the impact of FDI attacks on ANN AC SE.

In addition to the bad data detection threshold, the adversary is also facing other constraints, including the set of meters she has access to, the maximum number of meters she can compromise, and the maximum amount of errors she can inject into a true measurement to avoid being detected.

Note that in this paper we only consider the FDI attacks that happen during the operational phase of the ANN SE. In other words, the adversary is only able to tamper the measurement inputs after the ANN model is trained. It is not allowed to perturb either the training data or the trained model. The investigation of training data and model pollution is out of the scope of this paper and will be studied in our future work.

4.2   Attack Formulation

Let $\mathbf{z}_a$ be the measurement vector in the presence of FDI attack, then $\mathbf{z}_a$ can be described as:

$$\mathbf{z}_a = \mathbf{z} + \mathbf{a} = h(\mathbf{x}) + \mathbf{a}, \tag{5}$$

where $\mathbf{a}$ is a N_m-dimension non-zero attack vector. Given the input of manipulated measurement $\mathbf{z_a}$, the output by the ANN SE f is as follows:

$$\hat{\mathbf{x}}_\mathbf{a} = f(\mathbf{z_a}) = f(\mathbf{z} + \mathbf{a}) \tag{6}$$

According to Eq. (2), an adversary intending to elude from bad data detection must satisfy the following condition:

$$J(\hat{\mathbf{x}}_\mathbf{a}) = (\mathbf{z_a} - h(\hat{\mathbf{x}}_\mathbf{a}))^T \mathbf{W}(\mathbf{z_a} - h(\hat{\mathbf{x}}_\mathbf{a})) \leq \tau \tag{7}$$

The error injected to SE hence can be calculated by:

$$\hat{\mathbf{x}}_\mathbf{a} - \hat{\mathbf{x}} = f(\mathbf{z_a}) - f(\mathbf{z}). \tag{8}$$

With the above notations, the problem of finding the best adversarial injection $\mathbf{a}$ for a given measurement $\mathbf{z}$ can be formulated as a constrained optimization:

$$
\begin{aligned}
\underset{\mathbf{a}}{\text{maximize}} \quad & \|\hat{\mathbf{x}}_\mathbf{a} - \hat{\mathbf{x}}\|_p \\
\text{subject to} \quad & (\mathbf{z} - h(\hat{\mathbf{x}}_\mathbf{a}))^T \mathbf{W}(\mathbf{z_a} - h(\hat{\mathbf{x}}_\mathbf{a})) < \tau, \\
& \|\mathbf{a}\|_0 \leq L, \\
& a_i^l \leq a_i \leq a_i^u, i = 1, ..., N_m, \\
& z_i^{min} \leq z_{a_i} \leq z_i^{max}, i = 1, ..., N_m,
\end{aligned}
\tag{9}
$$

where L is the maximum number of meters the attacker can compromise, $[a_i^l, a_i^u]$ provides limits of modification to each compromised meter, and $[z_i^{min}, z_i^{max}]$ denotes the valid range for each measurement, ensuring the manipulated measurement to still be within the power range permitted on that particular unit. The strength of measurement modification depends on the attacker's resource and meter accessibility constraints, which have not been considered in previous work. In our work, by limiting the measurement manipulation to a subset of meters, we are able to prevent from injecting excessive errors, which can be easily detected by univariate analysis. In addition, if the adversary can locate high precision meters, she can avoid injecting too much errors into those meters and instead allocate resource to other meters to improve the overall attack outcomes.

The objective function in the optimization Eq. (9) requires a distance metric $\| \cdot \|_p$ to quantify attack impact. This distance metric should be carefully defined to reflect the severity of physical impact on the power grid caused by the SE error. In reality, the voltage magnitudes in the state are always limited in a tight range to ensure stable electricity supply, while the voltage phase angles could vary in a relatively large range, and hence an erroneous estimation of the latter may seriously affect the consistent operation of the power grid, but cannot be easily detected. Therefore, we define the adversary's objective function as the maximum change to the voltage phase angles θ:

$$\|\hat{\mathbf{x}}_{\mathbf{a}} - \hat{\mathbf{x}}\|_\infty = \max(|\hat{\theta}_{a_1} - \hat{\theta}_1|, ..., |\hat{\theta}_{a_n} - \hat{\theta}_n|) \tag{10}$$

5   Attack Methodology

5.1   Solving the Proposed Attack with DE

As a population based stochastic optimization algorithm, DE algorithm was first proposed in 1996 by Rainer et al. [18]. The population is randomly initialized within the variable bounds. In each generation, a mutant vector is produced by adding a target vector (father) with a weighted difference of other two randomly chosen variables. Then a crossover parameter mixes father and mutant vector to form a candidate solution (child). A comparison is drawn between father and child, whichever that is better will enter the next generation.

We follow [19] to encode our measurement attack vector into an array, which contains a fixed number of perturbations, and each perturbation holds two values: the compromised meter index and the amount to inject to that meter. The use of DE and the encoding has the following three advantages: **1. Higher probability of finding global optimum** - In each generation, the diversity introduced by mutation and crossover operations ensures the solution not stuck in local optimum, and thus leads to a higher probability of finding global optimum. **2. Adaptability for multiple attacks** - DE can adapt to different attack scenarios based on our encoding method. By DE can search for both meter indices and injection amount or only search for injection amount to these specified meters, by specifying the number of meters to compromise or fixing the meter indices. **3. Parallelizibility to shorten attack time** - As the smart grid scale increases, generating one attack vector may take from seconds to minutes. An attacker must finish attack vector generation and injection before next SE takes place. As it is based on a vector population, DE is parallelization friendly, so as to significantly expedite the computation for the attack vector.

Next, we present how we adapt DE algorithm to our proposed attack. The pseudo code for the proposed attack using DE is presented in Algorithm 1:

- **Deal with duplicate meter indices** - Instead of outputting the exact meter value, we select to output the injection vector to narrow down search space. We use two approaches to ensure the uniqueness of meter indices in the solution. First, we generate meter indices without replacement in population initialization. Second, we add a filter in the crossover operation. This filter keeps the meter indices unchanged if the newly selected meter index is repetitive with previous meter indices.

- **Ensure the measurement after injection is within range** - A valid measurement reading must satisfy $z_i^{min} \leq z_i + a_i \leq z_i^{max}$ for all i, where z_i^{min} and z_i^{max} are lower and upper limit power permitted on z_i. We use an intuitive approach by replace $\mathbf{z_a} = \mathbf{z+a}$ with $\mathbf{z_a} = min(max(\mathbf{z_a}, \mathbf{z}^{min}), \mathbf{z}^{max})$, where the min and max are element-wise operations.

- **Deal with the overall constraint** - In addressing constraints with DE, using a penalty function has been the most popular approach. However, they do not always yield satisfactory solutions since the appropriate multiplier for the penalty term is difficult to choose and the objective function may be distorted by the penalty term. Therefore, we use a heuristic constraint handling method [5]. A pair-wise comparison is performed between fathers and children in order to differentiate better solutions from population. The three criteria of the pair-wise comparison are as the following: 1. If both vectors are feasible, the one with the best objective function value is preferred. 2. If one vector is feasible and the other one is not, the feasible one is preferred. 3. If both two vectors are infeasible, the one with the smaller constraint violation is preferred. The above comparisons handle constraint in two steps: first, the comparison among feasible and infeasible solutions provides a search direction towards the feasible region; then, the crossover and mutation operations keep the search near the global optimum, while maintaining the diversity among feasible solutions.

5.2 Solving the Proposed Attack with SLSQP

In some gradient based attack algorithms in image classification [3, 20], the logistic function is added to the objective function as a penalty term and the parameter for the penalty term is chosen by line search. These algorithms aim to find a feasible solution, not the optimal one. Therefore, we use a conventional optimization algorithm (SLSQP) [10]. SLSQP is a variation on the SQP algorithm for non-linearly constrained gradient-based optimization. In our SLSQP attack, we encode the solution to a N_m-dimension vector, in which the ith element denotes the injection amount to the ith meter. This encoding allows the attacker to generate attack vectors with a set of specified meters by placing upper and lower bounds to corresponding elements in the attack vector. To solve the proposed optimization problem, we first construct the Lagrangian function:

$$\mathcal{L}(\mathbf{a}, \lambda) = f(\mathbf{a}) + \lambda \cdot g(\mathbf{a}), \tag{11}$$

where

$$\begin{cases} f(\mathbf{a}) = \|\hat{\mathbf{x}}_\mathbf{a} - \hat{\mathbf{x}}\|_\infty \\ g(\mathbf{a}) = (\mathbf{z} - h(\hat{\mathbf{x}}_\mathbf{a}))^T \mathbf{W}(\mathbf{z_a} - h(\hat{\mathbf{x}}_\mathbf{a})) < \tau \end{cases} \tag{12}$$

Algorithm 1. DE attack

Input: measurement $\mathbf{z}$, GEN_{MAX} {maximum number of generations}, N {population size}, f {objective function}, g{constraint function}, CR {crossover rate}
Output: injection vector $\mathbf{a}$
 1: $g = 0$
 2: Population initialization $\mathbf{a}_{i,0}$ for $i = 1, ..., N$. Meter indices are randomly select without replacement and injection amounts are randomly select within the univariate bound.
 3: Evaluate the $f(\mathbf{a}_{i,g})$ and constraint violation $CV(\mathbf{a}_{i,g}) = max(g(\mathbf{a}_{i,g}), 0)$, for $i = 1, ..., N$
 4: **for** $g = 1 : MAX_{GEN}$ **do**
 5:   **for** $i = 1 : N$ **do**
 6:     Randomly select r_1 and r_2
 7:     $j_{rand} = randint(1, N_m)$
 8:     **for** $j = 1 : D$ **do**
 9:       **if** $(rand_j[0, 1) < CR$ **or** $j = j_{rand})$ **and** the meter index not repetitive with previous meter indices **then**
10:         $u_{i,g+1}^j = x_{best,G}^j + F(x_{r_1,g}^j - x_{r_2,g}^j)$
11:       **else**
12:         $u_{i,g+1}^j = x_{i,G}^j$
13:       **end if**
14:     **end for**
15:     Evaluate $f(\mathbf{u}_{i,g+1})$ and $CV(\mathbf{u}_{i,g+1})$
16:     Update the population if the child $\mathbf{u}_{i,g+1}$ is better than the father $\mathbf{x}_{i,g}$ by the above three criteria
17:   **end for**
18: **end for**

In each iteration k, the above problem can be solved by transferring to a linear least square sub-problem in the following form:

$$\max_{\mathbf{d}} \quad \|(\mathbf{D^k})^{1/2}(\mathbf{L^k})^T\mathbf{d} + ((\mathbf{D^k})^{-1/2}(\mathbf{L^k})^{-1}\nabla(\mathbf{a^k})\| \tag{13}$$

$$\text{subject to} \quad \nabla g(\mathbf{a}^k)\mathbf{d} + g(\mathbf{a}^k) \geq 0$$

where $L^k D^k (L^k)^T$ is a stable factorization of the chosen search direction $\nabla_{zz}^2 \mathbf{L}(\mathbf{z}, \lambda)$ and is updated by BFGS method. By solving the QP sub-problem for each iteration, we can get the value of $\mathbf{d}^k$, i.e., the update direction for $\mathbf{z}^k$:

$$\mathbf{z}^{k+1} = \mathbf{z}^k + \alpha \mathbf{d}^k \tag{14}$$

where α is the step size, which is determined by solving an additional optimization. The step size $\psi(\alpha) := \phi(\mathbf{a}^k + \alpha d^k)$ with $\mathbf{x}^k$ and d^k are fixed, can be obtained by a minimization:

$$\phi(\mathbf{a}^k; r) := f(\mathbf{a}^k) + max(r \cdot g(\mathbf{a}), 0) \tag{15}$$

with r being updated by:

$$r^{k+1} := max(\frac{1}{2}(r^k + |\lambda|, |\lambda|)) \tag{16}$$

6   Attack Evaluation

Here, both FDI attacks are evaluated on IEEE 9-bus, 14-bus, and 30-bus test systems. The simulation is done in Python, using package *TensorFlow* and *SciPy*, on a computer with a 3.5 GHz CPU and a 16 GB memory.

Depending on the attacker's capability and practical constraints, the attacker can launch attack under different scenarios. Inspired by [13], we construct two attack scenarios to facilitate the evaluation: (1) **Any k meter attacks.** The attacker can access all meters, but the number of meters to compromise is limited by k. In this scenario, the attacker can wisely allocate the limited resources, by selecting meters and injection amounts that will maximize her attack impact. (2) **Specific k meter attacks.** The attacker has the access to k specific meters. For example, the attacker may only access the a set of meters in a small region. She needs to determine injection amount to maximize attack impact.

We perform the experiment as follows. To fairly compare attack performance on different test systems, we choose the percentage of meters being compromised, R, to be 5%, 10% and 20%. For each R, we explore the attack performance under different error injection levels: 2%, 5% and 10%. Each experiment runs on 1000 measurement instances, and is repeated for 10 times to reduce randomness.

We consider four metrics throughout evaluating the effectiveness of the attacks. We measure the MAE and MARE of the error injected to voltage phase angles. We also report the success probability, where success is defined as the attack produce more than 1% or 5% MARE to voltage magnitude or phase angle, respectively. Moreover, since the smart grid is assumed to be a quasi-static system and the states change slowly over time, we want to investigate if the time allows an adversary to mount an FDI attack to smart grid.

6.1   Any k Meter Attack

Under this scenario, the attacker can access all meters and has freedom to choose any k meters to compromise. The way we encode the attack vector in DE enables the search for better meters in every generation. In contrast, SLSQP only allows us to put constraint on specific meter indices. Therefore, only DE can be used to find attack vectors in any k meter attack.

Our DE attack inject error to one of voltage phase angles while other values keep unchanged. In Fig. 1(b) and (c), for injection level 10% and 20%, the maximum injections are concentrated around 5% and seldom go beyond 10%, due to the overall constraint of bad data detection.

In general, the success probability and attack impact increase as the attacker controls more resource. The attack would succeed with larger probability (80% of simulation instances) by compromising 10% of meters with injection level 10%. Especially for 14-bus system, the attack achieves 100% success for any combination of R and injection level (Fig. 2).

Interestingly, for 30-bus system, the impact of compromising 10% of meters surpasses that of compromising 20% of meters. Moreover, the performance of 20% of meter compromised drops drastically as the injection level increases.

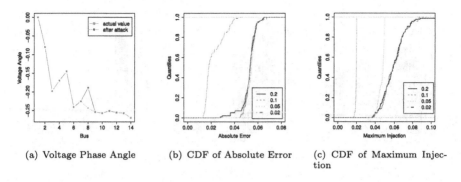

(a) Voltage Phase Angle

(b) CDF of Absolute Error

(c) CDF of Maximum Injection

Fig. 1. An example of a 5-m attack to 14-bus system

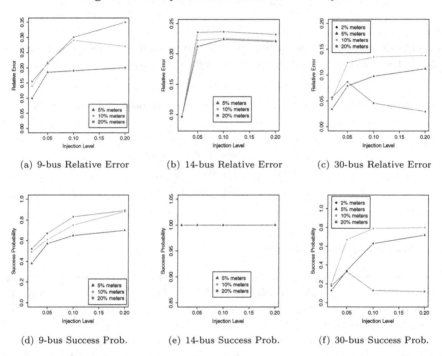

(a) 9-bus Relative Error

(b) 14-bus Relative Error

(c) 30-bus Relative Error

(d) 9-bus Success Prob.

(e) 14-bus Success Prob.

(f) 30-bus Success Prob.

Fig. 2. Relative error (first row) and success prob. (second row) of Any k meter attack with $N = 400$ and $G_{MAX} = 400$

A possible explanation for this might be that, as the expansion of search dimension and space, it would require more attempts to find a satisfactory solution.

Figure 3 shows the first seven cumulative meter indices' frequency in the attack vectors. Injection to meters with higher frequency can introduce larger errors to state variables. Our DE attacks provide a practical way for systematically identifying key meters whose readings have a higher weight on the AC

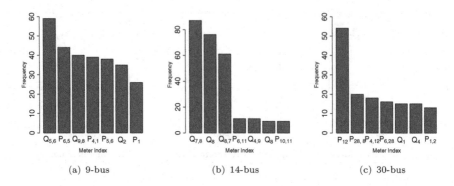

(a) 9-bus   (b) 14-bus   (c) 30-bus

Fig. 3. Cumulative frequency of meters presenting in attack vectors

SE, and thus may guide the utility company to reach a more focused protection towards these key meters under resource and budget constraints.

Table 2. Average NFEs and execution time (in second) of any k attacks

Test system	NFEs	Time (s)
9-bus	500–1500	0.25–0.45
14-bus	500–3500	0.5–1.73
30-bus	800–5600	1.5–2.7

6.2 Specific k Meter Attack

To explore the effect of population size and iteration number, we evaluate the average *number of function evaluations* (NFEs) before delivering a successful attack or there is no significant change in the solution. The NFEs and corresponding running time are shown in Table 2.

In this constrained scenario, the attacker is able to compromise specific k meters due to physical location restrictions. DE and SLSQP are implemented and compared under this attack scenario. To search the injection amounts to specific k meters, DE specifies the indices of the k meters in population initialization and disables the mutation operation, while SLSQP only allows modifications to the k meters in the attack vector. We randomly select R to be 5%, 10% and 20% from test systems and perform the same set of experiments using both DE and gradient-based algorithm and compare their performance by the same metrics.

In general, DE algorithm outperforms the gradient-based algorithm in effectiveness (Fig. 4). This is not surprising, as DE brings in more diversity in every generation while SLSQP only explores neighbors in each iteration.

Table 3 shows the execution time of DE attack with 1×10^4 NFEs and SLSQP attack with 100 iterations. Both attacks can be finished quickly within 3 s, which

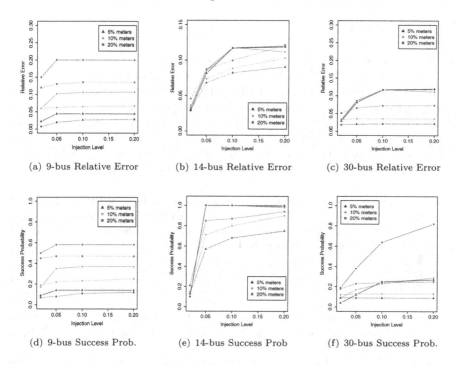

(a) 9-bus Relative Error   (b) 14-bus Relative Error   (c) 30-bus Relative Error

(d) 9-bus Success Prob.   (e) 14-bus Success Prob   (f) 30-bus Success Prob.

Fig. 4. Relative error (first row) and success prob. (second row) of specific k meter attack

is feasible for an attacker to mount on smart grid. The comparison of running time between them can be misleading, since the execution time highly relies on NFEs for DE and max iteration numbers for SLSQP. In addition, the execution time can be further shortened by implementing a early-stop criteria or parallel processing for DE, or adjusting the max iteration numbers for SLSQP. Therefore, taking no account for running time, our experiments exhibit clear pattern that DE attack is more effective than SLSQP attack.

Table 3. Execution time (in second) comparison of specific k attacks

Test system	DE (s)	SLSQP (s)
9-bus	0.12–0.4	0.036–0.6
14-bus	0.06–0.6	0.14–1.0
30-bus	0.3–3.0	0.26–2.2

7 Conclusions

In this paper, we perform the first study of adversarial FDI attacks against ANN-based AC SE. We first create target models that are sufficiently strong. Then we formulate the adversarial FDI attack into an optimization problem. We extensively evaluate the proposed attacks under two attack scenarios on three test systems, with adapted DE and SLSQP aiming to find attack vectors. In the any k meter attack, our results show that the DE attack is successful with high probability even with a small number of compromised meters and low false injection level. DE outperforms SLSQP in the specific k meter attack.

Acknowledgement. The work of T. Shu is supported in part by NSF under grants CNS-1837034, CNS-1745254, CNS-1659965, and CNS-1460897. Any opinions, findings, conclusions, or recommendations expressed in this paper are those of the author(s) and do not necessarily reflect the views of NSF.

References

1. Abdel-Nasser, M., Mahmoud, K., Kashef, H.: A novel smart grid state estimation method based on neural networks. Int. J. Interact. Multimed. Artif. Intell. **5**(1), 92–100 (2018)
2. ANSI: ANSI C12.1-2008: American National Standard for Electric Meters: Code for Electricity Metering (2008)
3. Carlini, N., Wagner, D.: Towards Evaluating the Robustness of Neural Networks. Technical report (2017). https://doi.org/10.1109/SP.2017.49. http://nicholas.carlini.com/code/nn
4. Case, D.U.: Analysis of the cyber attack on the Ukrainian power grid. Electricity Information Sharing and Analysis Center (E-ISAC) (2016)
5. Deb, K.: An efficient constraint handling method for genetic algorithms. Comput. Methods Appl. Mech. Eng. **186**(2–4), 311–338 (2000)
6. Goodfellow, I.J., Shlens, J., Szegedy, C.: Explaining and harnessing adversarial examples. arXiv preprint arXiv:1412.6572 (2014)
7. Hug, G., Giampapa, J.A.: Vulnerability assessment of AC state estimation with respect to false data injection cyber-attacks. IEEE Trans. Smart Grid **3**(3), 1362–1370 (2012)
8. Jain, A., Balasubramanian, R., Tripathy, S.: Topological observability: artificial neural network application based solution for a practical power system. In: 2008 40th North American Power Symposium, pp. 1–6. IEEE (2008)
9. Jia, L., Thomas, R.J., Tong, L.: On the nonlinearity effects on malicious data attack on power system. In: 2012 IEEE Power and Energy Society General Meeting, pp. 1–8. IEEE (2012)
10. Kraft, D.: A software package for sequential quadratic programming. Forschungsbericht Deutsche Forschungs und Versuchsanstalt für Luft und Raumfahrt **88**, 33 (1988)
11. Kumar, D.M.V., Srivastava, S.C., Shah, S., Mathur, S.: Topology processing and static state estimation using artificial neural networks. IEE Proc. Gener. Transm. Distrib. **143**, 99–105 (1996)

12. Liang, G., Weller, S.R., Zhao, J., Luo, F., Dong, Z.Y.: The 2015 Ukraine blackout: implications for false data injection attacks. IEEE Trans. Power Syst. **32**(4), 3317–3318 (2017). https://doi.org/10.1109/TPWRS.2016.2631891
13. Liu, Y., Ning, P., Reiter, M.K.: False data injection attacks against state estimation in electric power grids. ACM Trans. Inf. Syst. Secur. (TISSEC) **14**(1), 13 (2011)
14. Menke, J.H., Bornhorst, N., Braun, M.: Distribution system monitoring for smart power grids with distributed generation using artificial neural networks. arXiv preprint arXiv:1801.04705 (2018)
15. Mosbah, H., El-Hawary, M.: Multilayer artificial neural networks for real time power system state estimation. In: 2015 IEEE Electrical Power and Energy Conference (EPEC), pp. 344–351. IEEE (2015)
16. Onwuachumba, A., Musavi, M.: New reduced model approach for power system state estimation using artificial neural networks and principal component analysis. In: 2014 IEEE Electrical Power and Energy Conference, pp. 15–20. IEEE (2014)
17. Rahman, M.A., Mohsenian-Rad, H.: False data injection attacks against nonlinear state estimation in smart power grids. In: 2013 IEEE Power & Energy Society General Meeting, pp. 1–5. IEEE (2013)
18. Storn, R., Price, K.: Differential evolution-a simple and efficient heuristic for global optimization over continuous spaces. J. Glob. Optim. **11**(4), 341–359 (1997)
19. Su, J., Vargas, D.V., Sakurai, K.: One pixel attack for fooling deep neural networks. CoRR abs/1710.08864 (2017). http://arxiv.org/abs/1710.08864
20. Szegedy, C., et al.: Intriguing properties of neural networks. arXiv preprint arXiv:1312.6199 (2013)
21. Wood, A.J., Wollenberg, B.F., Sheblé, G.B.: Power Generation, Operation, and Control. Wiley, New York (2013)
22. Zimmerman, R.D., Murillo-Sánchez, C.E., Thomas, R.J.: MATPOWER: steady-state operations, planning, and analysis tools for power systems research and education. IEEE Trans. Power Syst. **26**(1), 12–19 (2011)

On Effectiveness of Adversarial Examples and Defenses for Malware Classification

Robert Podschwadt[✉] and Hassan Takabi

University of North Texas, Denton, TX 76201, USA
robertpodschwadt@my.unt.edu, takabi@unt.edu

Abstract. Artificial neural networks have been successfully used for many different classification tasks including malware detection and distinguishing between malicious and non-malicious programs. Although artificial neural networks perform very well on these tasks, they are also vulnerable to adversarial examples. An adversarial example is a sample that has minor modifications made to it so that the neural network misclassifies it. Many techniques have been proposed, both for crafting adversarial examples and for hardening neural networks against them. Most previous work was done in the image domain. Some of the attacks have been adopted to work in the malware domain which typically deals with binary feature vectors. In order to better understand the space of adversarial examples in malware classification, we study different approaches of crafting adversarial examples and defense techniques in the malware domain and compare their effectiveness on multiple data sets.

Keywords: Adversarial machine learning · Malware detection · Android

1 Introduction

Machine learning and deep neural networks in particular have been highly successful in different applications. For example, they can be used for image recognition with human accuracy or above [1,2], and they have also been employed to perform malware detection [3–5]. However, it has been shown that neural networks could be vulnerable to adversarial examples created by perturbing input data. Most adversarial machine learning research [6–9] focuses on images data since it is easy to visualize the perturbations, and all changes made to an image still produce a valid image. When perturbing malware instead of images [10,11], there are more constraints that need to be taken into consideration. This paper investigates neural networks applied to malware classification task. We focus on a range of attacks and defense mechanisms proposed in recent years, providing an overview of the algorithms and comparing their efficacy in a consistent manner. With an increasing number of attacks and defenses available, it is non-trivial to compare their effectiveness. Most publications use different datasets and different model architectures which makes it even harder to compare different approaches. Currently there is no straightforward way of telling

© ICST Institute for Computer Sciences, Social Informatics and Telecommunications Engineering 2019
Published by Springer Nature Switzerland AG 2019. All Rights Reserved
S. Chen et al. (Eds.): SecureComm 2019, LNICST 305, pp. 380–393, 2019.
https://doi.org/10.1007/978-3-030-37231-6_22

which defense is efficient against which attack and vice versa. In this paper, we compare twelve attacks, their effectiveness against undefended models, and the impact of four proposed defenses. To achieve this, we use two different datasets from the malware domain and train deep neural networks on both. We implement or use existing implementations of the attacks and defenses to gain a better understanding of which defenses are effective in the malware domain. Our results show that all defenses, except for adversarial training, perform worse on malware than they do on images.

2 Background

2.1 Threat Model

In a malware detection system, the goal is to accurately distinguish between malware and non-malware. The attacker is the author of a malicious program, and their goal is to evade detection by the system. In order to evade the detection system the attacker has two options. The first option is to "sabotage" the classifier to the point that it becomes untrustworthy; the second is to modify their software is such a way that the classifier views it as benign. It is possible that the target of an attacker is to have a benign sample classified as malicious but it is a less straightforward attack like flooding the classifier with false-positives therefore eroding the users trust in the system. While neural networks bring advantages for malware detection, their use leaves the system vulnerable to attacks that can be leveraged against neural networks in general. If an attacker can mislabel instances that are in the training data it is called a data poisoning attack [12,13]. The goal of data poisoning is to evade the classifier by having it trained on mislabeled data. In this paper, we consider a less powerful attacker who can only interact with the system after it has been trained and has no influence over the training data. All they can do is present an instance to the detection system and receive the classification result. For most methods of creating adversarial examples, the attacker needs access to the internal structure and information of the model. But even with only query access to the system, attacks are still possible. Papernot et al. [14] have shown that any black box attack can be transformed into a semi white box attack. This is due to transferability of machine learning algorithms. It has been shown that adversarial examples created on one model can also be used to attack another model as long as the models have learned a similar enough decision boundary. For this reason, attacks considered in this paper are all white box attacks.

2.2 Adversarial Examples

First described by Szedgy et al. [15] adversarial examples are instances that are very close to a legitimate instance but are classified differently. Given an instance x with the class label $C(x) = t$, one can find an instance x' such that $C(x') \neq t$. An additional constraint is that some distance metric $||x - x'||$ should be kept small, meaning changes made to the sample should be as small as possible. In images that usually means that it is impossible for a human to perceive the changes between x and x'. Different norms including L_0 [16,17], L_1 [18], L_2 [17], and L_∞ [19] have been used. Since we are working with binary feature indication vectors, feature values can either be 0 or 1. Therefore the L_∞ norm would always be 1 if at least one change was made. The $||x - x'||_0$ norm yields all the changes that have been made. This makes L_0 a good choice.

3   Experiments

3.1   Datasets

We use the Drebin dataset [20] of Android apps. It contains extracted features for both classes. Drebin relies on static features, i.e., those that can be extracted from an app without executing it. The specific features are: requested hardware, requested permissions, app components, filtered intents, restricted API calls, used permissions, suspicious API calls and network addresses. Those features come either from the manifest or decompiling the code. We also run experiments on another dataset, APDS, which consists of permissions extracted from android apps. It contains 398 instances with 330 features; 50% of the samples are malware and 50% are benign. The data is available on *kaggle* [21].

3.2   The Victim Model

To test the performance of attacks and defenses we define a victim model. Our model consist of four fully connected hidden layers with ReLU as the activation function (details in Table 1). We trained the model for 100 epochs using the Adam optimizer with a learning rate of .001, $\beta_1 = .9$, $\beta_2 = .999$ using binary cross entropy as the loss function. See Table 2 for the performance of the model. For all of our training, we use 56.25% of the data as training data, 18.75% as validation data and 25% as test data.

Table 1. Architecture of the victim model

Layer	Neurons	Activation
Fully connected	300	ReLU
Fully connected	250	ReLU
Fully connected	200	ReLU
Fully connected	128	ReLU
Fully connected	2	Softmax

Table 2. Accuracy (acc) of the *victim model* on the test set, false negatives rate (FNR), false positives rate (FPR), true positives rate (FPR) and true negatives rate (TNR)

Dataset	acc	FNR	FPR	TPR	TNR
Drebin$_{500}$	0.99	0.10	0.01	0.89	0.99
APDS	0.98	0.04	0.0	0.96	1.0

3.3   Feature Selection

The Drebin dataset is composed of features for over 120,000 instances of which roughly 5,500 are malware. Each instance has more than 550,000 features. Building a neural network graph with features that size leads to memory problems very quickly. Grosse et al. [10] find that only a small number of features are used for creating adversarial examples. In order to test more complex models we employ feature selection. We use the scikit-learn [22] implementation of SelectKBest with chi-squared as the scoring function and run feature selection for different values of K. The accuracy on the benign class does not change much with the number of features, due to the class imbalance. With 500 and 1000 features we achieve 99.6% accuracy on the benign class and 89.2% on the malware class. Throughout the paper, we indicate that we have used feature selection by giving the number features K used as follows: $Drebin_K$.

4   Attack Mechanisms

4.1   Jacobian-Based Saliency Maps Attack (JSMA)

Grosse et al. [10] adapted the approach developed for images in [23] based on Jacobian-based Saliency Maps Attack (JSMA). The Jacobian matrix is the matrix of the forwards derivatives for every feature of a sample w.r.t. the output classes. The feature with maximum positive gradient towards the desired output class is selected and perturbed. In order to guarantee a correctly functioning adversarial example, features are only added and not removed. Calculating the Jacobian and changing a feature are repeated multiple times, until a maximum number of allowed perturbations have been made or misclassification is achieved. The attack is effective against our victim models (Table 3). On APDS we achieve an evasion rate of 100%. On the $Drebin_{500}$ data we were only able to evade the classifier 33% of the time. The change column gives the average changes made to all adversarial examples.

Table 3. Attack based on JSMA [10] with a maximum of 25 perturbations.

Dataset	acc	acc adv	FNR	FNR adv	# Features changed	Evasion
$Drebin_{500}$	0.99	0.98	0.01	0.19	1.89	0.33
APDS	0.93	0.63	0.12	0.56	13.57	1.00

4.2   Feature Enabling and Disabling

Stokes et al. [24] propose different variants for creating adversarial examples, relaxing the constraints on allowed modifications. Instead of only adding features, which preserve the functionality of the malware, they also allow for the removal of features. The authors reason that attackers can find different ways to implement the same malicious behavior. We include these methods for completeness.

They propose three iterative methods which are based on the Jacobian using positive features and negative features. A positive feature is a feature that is an indicator of malware, meaning that the Jacobian for the malware class with respect to the input is positive for this feature. Similarly, a negative feature is an indicator for the benign class. From these attributes, the authors develop three different iterative methods for creating adversarial examples. For every iteration the Jacobian of the sample is calculated w.r.t. the output classes and one feature is perpetuated. This done until the maximum number of allowed perturbations is reached or the sample is misclassified. Iteratively disabling positive features is called the dec_pos attack, and enabling negative features, inc_neg. These approaches can be applied in alternating fashion to get dec_pos + inc_neg. Instead of choosing the feature with the maximum value, a random feature can be chosen. This leads to three more different techniques; randomized dec_pos, randomized inc_neg and randomized dec_pos + inc_neg. Note that inc_neg is the same strategy as the one described in [10]. We apply the attacks to our victim model trained on $Drebin_{500}$ and the results can be seen in Table 4.

Table 4. Attacks from Stokes et al. [24]. Numbers on $Drebin_{500}$

Attack	acc	acc adv	FNR	FNR adv	Change	Evasion
dec_pos	0.99	0.98	0.05	0.16	1.65	0.25
inc_neg	0.99	0.98	0.05	0.19	1.89	0.32
dec_pos inc_neg	0.99	0.98	0.05	0.16	0.08	0.27
rand. dec_pos	0.99	0.98	0.05	0.15	2.09	0.24
rand. inc_neg	0.99	0.99	0.05	0.06	0.09	0.06
rand dec_pos inc_neg	0.99	0.99	0.05	0.12	0.23	0.18

The randomized inc_neg achieves no additional evasions at all, suggesting that randomly enabling features is not a good approach. The relative effectiveness of the attacks is similar over all compared models. The notable difference is that on $Drebin_{500}$ inc_neg achieves a higher evasion with only slightly increased average change when compared to dec_pos. On the other victim model, dec_pos is able to achieve the same rate as inc_neg although at a smaller change cost.

4.3 Fast Gradient Sign Method (FGSM)

Huang et al. [25] propose four different approaches. The first two methods are based on the Fast Gradient Sign Method (FGSM). It is a one step method of moving the sample in the direction of the greatest loss. A more powerful variation of the attack is multi step $FGSM^k$ where k is the number of iterations. To apply this method to the discrete malware domain rounding is required. The authors propose two different rounding schemes: deterministic rounding $dFGSM^k$ and random rounding $rFGSM^k$. A third method is introduced which explores the possible feature space more thoroughly. This method is called multi-step Bit Gradient Ascent(BGA^k). BGA^k works by setting a bit if the feature contributes more than the average feature to the l_2 norm of the loss. Another method is multi-step Bit Coordinate Ascent BCA^k. At every step the bit corresponding to the feature with the maximum partial derivative of the loss is changed. The results on Drebin$_{500}$ can be found in Table 5.

Table 5. $FGSM^k$, $rFGSM^k$, $dFGSM^k$, BGA^k and BCA^k [25]. Results on Drebin$_{500}$

Attack	acc	acc adv	FNR	FNR adv	Change	Evasion
$dFGSM^k$	0.99	0.99	0.05	0.10	7.16	0.15
$rFGSM^k$	0.99	0.99	0.05	0.10	7.16	0.15
BGA^k	0.99	0.99	0.05	0.05	1.14	0.05
BCA^k	0.99	0.99	0.05	0.09	1.26	0.12

The iterative variants of FGSM produce the most effective adversarial examples when it comes to evasion. The rounding scheme employed has very little effect. On the APDS model both attacks achieve 100% evasion rate. BGA^k fails to achieve any significant evasion across all models, while BCA^k performs very differently depending on the model. On Drebin$_{500}$ BCA^k achieves 12% evasion rate which is almost 2.5 times the natural evasion rate of 5%. On APDS the evasion rate achieved is 14% which is barely more than the natural rate of 12%.

4.4 MalGAN

Malgan is an attack introduced by Hu et al. [26]. It uses a Generative Adversarial Network (GAN) [27] to create adversarial examples. The idea behind GAN is to create data by training neural networks. For our experiment we use the same architecture as [26]. The Generator takes a legitimate sample as input and a 10D noise vector. This gets fed into a fully connected layer with 256 units and *ReLU* activation function. This layer is fully connected to the output layer with *Sigmoid* as activation function. The size of the output layer is the size of a sample. After the last layer, the output is rounded and transformed into a proper binary feature representation and the constraint of only adding features is enforced. For the Discriminator, we use a simple network with one hidden layer, 256 neurons, and *ReLU* activation. The output layer includes one neuron with *Sigmoid* activation.

The generator and discriminator are trained for 100 epochs. Every epoch the generated adversarial examples are tested against a black box detector. At the end, the generator with highest misclassification rate on the black box is

Table 6. Hu et al. [26] approach which uses a GAN to create adversarial examples

Dataset	acc	acc adv	FNR	FNR adv	Change	Evasion
$Drebin_{500}$	0.99	0.99	0.05	0.03	227.46	0.0
APDS	0.93	0.70	0.12	0.43	163.90	0.77

used. For the black box detector a model with two hidden layers is used. The first hidden layer has 256 and the second one has 128. Both use *ReLU* as the activation and a dropout of 0.2 during training. The output layer has two neurons and uses *softmax* activation function. The black box is trained for 200 epochs using *Adam* with a learning rate of .001, $\beta_1 = .9$, $\beta_2 = .999$ (see Table 6).

Interestingly, when attacking the $Drebin_{500}$ victim model no evasion at all is achieved. In fact the opposite happens, and all adversarial examples get classified correctly, improving model performance. On APDS the attack achieves an evasion rate of 77%. The attack on the $Drebin_{500}$ model could possibly be made more effective by using a more complex Discriminator and/or Generator. Also noteworthy is the high modification count. The original approach as presented in [26] offers no way of controlling the modification count. It is possible to add a penalty to the loss of Generator that penalizes large modifications. Another potentially interesting idea to pursue is to use more stable GAN training methods such as Wasserstein GANs [28] and Improved Wasserstein GANs [29].

Table 7. Comparison of the effectiveness of the different attacks on all victim models

Attack	Evasion (in %) on: $Drebin_{500}$	APDS
natural	5.6	11.7
dfgsm_k	15.0	100.0
rfgsm_k	15.0	100.0
bga_k	5.6	11.7
bca_k	12.7	13.7
JSMA	32.8	100.0
random_inc_neg	6.0	11.7
dec_pos	25.4	100.0
inc_neg	32.8	100.0
random_dec_pos	24.7	100.0
random_dec_pos_inc_neg	18.1	96.1
dec_pos_inc_neg	27.0	100.0
malgan	0.0	77.1

4.5   Attack Effectiveness

The effectiveness of an attack can be measured by its ability to create adversarial examples that evade the classifier. The previous experiments have shown that not all attacks work equally well. The victim model also influences the effectiveness. We summarize the evasion rates in Table 7. There are a few interesting things to note. First, the evasion rate for the $Drebin_{500}$ model is lower for all attacks except BGA^k and random inc_neg. The natural evasion is still lower for the $Drebin_{500}$ model. BGA^k on $Drebin_{500}$ achieves 0.0% increase in evasion. For random inc_neg, the increase in evasion is 7.4% for $Drebin_{500}$. This makes the model trained on the $Drebin_{500}$ dataset more resistant to adversarial examples than the other models. A possible explanation is that we perform feature selection on the data before training the model. Zhang et al. [4] investigate feature selection as a possible defense against evasion attacks.

5   Defense Mechanisms

5.1   Distillation

Distillation was originally introduced as a technique to train smaller models. To achieve this, the smaller model is trained with soft class labels which is the output of the bigger model. Distillation as a defensive technique also trains a second network with soft class labels, but in this case the two networks have the same architecture. The idea is not to make the network smaller but to make it more resilient to adversarial examples. Papernot et al. [30] propose the idea for the image classification domain, and [10] and [24] have investigate distillation as a possible defense against adversarial examples in malware detection. In their experiments, it did not perform as well on malware as on images. Additionally, choosing a temperature T that is too high will actually hurt the performance of the model. We chose $T = 10$ in accordance with the result of [24]. As the table shows, distillation does not actually add any robustness to the network. The impact on accuracy is almost negligible. The undefended network achieves an accuracy of 93% while the distilled network manages an accuracy of 91.6%. When training the $Drebin_{500}$ model with distillation and $T = 10$ the model already has a 1.0 FPR, making evasion attacks superfluous. This may be due to feature selection, the class imbalance, or a combination of the two.

5.2   Adversarial Training

Szegedy et al. [15] propose a strategy called adversarial training. The idea is that adding adversarial examples to the training data acts as regularization. This improves the generalization capabilities of the model and therefore makes it more resistant against adversarial examples. The idea has been picked up by many different researchers and modified. Kurakin et al. [31] introduce a scalable adversarial training framework based on mini batches. They also find that examples created with single step methods such as FGSM offer greater benefits than iterative approaches. On the other hand, when using adversarial samples for adversarial training Mossavi et al. [8] find that using DeepFool samples increases robustness, whereas using FGSM samples could lead to decreases in robustness. Tramèr et al. [32] find that models trained with adversarial training are more resistant to white box attacks but are still vulnerable to black box attacks. Multiple authors have looked at adversarial training as a defense in the malware domain. [10] find that the amount of adversarial examples introduced during training needs to be carefully controlled. In their experiments, adding more than 100 adversarial examples during training left the network more vulnerable. Al-Dujaili et al. [25] describe adversarial learning as a saddle point problem. It relies on finding the parameters θ for a classifier that minimizes a loss function L when assigning class labels y to inputs x taken from a dataset $\mathcal{D}$. Creating an adversarial example x_{adv} is a maximization problem. Given all binary representations $\mathcal{S}(x) \subseteq \mathcal{X}$ of an example x that still preserve the functionality of x. We are looking for $\mathcal{S}^*(x) \subseteq \mathcal{S}(x)$ that maximizes the loss. To create an adversarial example we need to find $\bar{x}$ for which the loss is maximal. Combining both the learning problem and the loss gives us the equation for adversarial learning

$$\theta^* \in \arg \min_{\theta \in \mathbb{R}^P} \mathbb{E}_{(x,y)\sim\mathcal{D}} \left[\max_{\bar{x} \in \mathcal{S}(x)} L(\theta, \bar{x}, y) \right] \tag{1}$$

The outer minimization problem can be solved by various different gradient descent algorithms. The inner maximization problem can be solved by multiple methods. [25] propose four different approaches, discussed earlier in the attacks section. Theoretically, any method to create adversarial examples can be used here. We use $dFGSM_k$ to create adversarial examples. The results suggest that adversarial training is very efficient at making the network more robust against adversarial examples. A possibly beneficial strategy is using adversarial examples from different attacks during training.

5.3   Ensembles

A modification of the ensemble method is proposed by Tramèr et al. [32], a defense called *Ensemble Adversarial Training*. As in normal adversarial training, adversarial examples are included in the dataset. In Ensemble Adversarial Training, the adversarial examples come not only from the model being trained but also from another pretrained model. This training technique enhances the defense against black box attacks. [24] looked at ensemble learning to defend malware detectors as well. In our experiments we train three different models and combine them into an ensemble. For ensembles to work, it is best to have models that behave differently. For that reason we have chosen three very different architectures. The three architectures are as follows: (1) For our first model we have chosen a very wide but rather flat architecture. It consists of two fully connected hidden layers with 1000 neurons each; (2) The second model was designed to be the opposite of the first model a rather flat but deeper architecture. It consists of eight hidden layers with 64 neurons each; (3) The third model is a rather small model with 2 hidden layers consisting of 256 neurons for the first one and 128 for the second. All models use *ReLU* as activation for all layers, except the last layer which uses *softmax*. To force a greater difference between the models, we employ dropout of 0.5. We train all three models for 200 epochs using the Adam optimizer with default parameters.

Compared to the victim model, the natural evasion of the ensemble is better, but the ensemble does not add anything in terms of adversarial robustness. The ensemble performs worse, when under attack. This backs up Goodfellow et al. claims that ensemble is not a good defense. A potential idea that could improve the resistance of ensembles in a black box setting is having the different classifiers work on different features. Binary programs do not typically get fed to the classifier directly. Features are extracted first [20]. The two main ways of extracting features from an application are dynamic and static feature extraction. Dynamic feature extraction collects the features running time while static extraction does not execute the program and only performs analysis on the compiled code or other available resources. Different models in the ensemble can use different features to train on. This might improve the resilience, although Rosenberg et al. [33] have devised an attack that works with an ensemble of two classifiers where one classifier learns from static and the other learns from the dynamic features.

5.4 Random Feature Nullification

To make the gradient harder for an attacker to compute, Wang et al. [34] introduce a defense called random feature nullification. During training and classification a random set of features gets disabled. This is achieved by choosing a binary vector I_{p^i} of uniformly distributed zeros and computing the Hadamard-Product of the instance x_i and the vector I_{p^i}. Increasing the number of features that are nullified will hurt the performance, and not disabling enough will have no impact on the attacker's ability to create adversarial examples. It is simple to see that with nullifying all features the input would be a vector of all zeros, making meaningful predictions impossible. Disabling only a very small subset of features, especially on high dimensional data, decreases the chances of hitting features that are important for an attacker. The results vary a lot, which is to be expected given the random nature of the network. It is possible that averaging could make the model more robust. This raises the question, though, of whether averaging would hurt the robustness and could be exploited by an attacker. In the end averaging over different runs is analogous to having an ensemble of classifiers with averaged results. As shown earlier an ensemble offers little to no improvement in adversarial robustness.

6   Discussion

Comparing the different defense mechanisms paints a bleak picture (comparison in Table 8). Distillation has almost no positive impact on adversarial robustness and effectively hurts it against certain attacks. Random feature nullification could be potentially beneficial, as it increases the robustness significantly, but in

Table 8. Comparison of the different attacks effectiveness on all victim models. Reported is evasion (in %). Used defenses: undefended (undef.), Distillation (Dist.), Random Feature Nullification (RFN), Adversarial Training (AT) and Ensembles (Ens.)

Attack	undef.	Dist.	RFN	AT	Ens.
natural	11.7	12.0	85.6	2.7	8.7
dfgsm_k	100.0	100.0	13.7	7.8	100.0
rfgsm_k	100.0	100.0	9.8	7.8	100.0
bga_k	11.7	100.0	72.5	3.9	100.0
bca_k	13.7	31.4	68.5	3.9	17.6
JSMA	100.0	100.0	100.0	27.5	100.0
random_inc_neg	11.7	13.7	3.9	3.9	15.7
dec_pos	100.0	100.0	96.1	100.0	100.0
inc_neg	100.0	100.0	100.0	27.5	100.0
random_dec_pos	100.0	100.0	86.3	100.0	100.0
random_dec_pos_inc_neg	96.1	90.2	51.0	25.5	98.0
dec_pos_inc_neg	100.0	100.0	100.0	25.5	100.0
malgan	77.1	95.8	100.0	62.5	12.5

our experiments it also reduced the performance considerably. While the ensemble proves to be helpful in improving performance, it does not protect against adversarial evasion. It is possible that having classifiers in the ensemble, trained on different feature representations, would make the system more robust. The only defense that provided significant robustness is adversarial training. We use the saddle point formulation presented in [24]. It improves robustness against all attacks that adhere to our threat model. We suggest a possible improvement to training process that includes adversarial examples from more than one attack, possibly hardening the classifier further against more attacks. The problem with adversarial training is that it is most efficient against attacks that have been used during the training. Therefore, it does not necessarily provide robustness against new yet unknown attacks. Even if a defense does not impact the performance of the classifier significantly, it might make it more vulnerable to certain adversarial examples creation methods. This poses the question of whether the defenses we employ today in fact make models more vulnerable to future attacks.

A good defense should ideally be robust against unknown attacks. So far, none of the defenses provide any mathematical hardness guarantees in the way that encryption does in traditional security. There is no guarantee that would make it impossible or computationally infeasible for an attacker to create adversarial examples. Not only is the problem of adversarial examples unsolved as shown in [17], defense performance also varies when applied to malware data. This suggests that the defense needs to be adapted to the domain. An approach tailored more directly to binary data could improve resilience. There is currently no special adaptation for binary data in machine learning and neural networks. In image classification, convolutional layers have moved feature extraction into the network itself. In text processing, embedding layers have done the same. For binary data no such layers exist. Security could be taken into consideration in the design of such layers for malware detection, as well as in feature extraction.

7   Related Work

Yuan et al. [35] have compiled a summary of available methods for creating adversarial examples and defenses. Their work is not limited to malware but contains a section on applications to malware detection. They provide an overview of the different approaches and the underlying algorithms but do not provide any numbers which would allow for a comparison based on effectiveness. Carlini et al. [17] look closely at ten available defenses and show that none of them are unbeatable. All of them are in the image domain. Rosenberg et al. [33] use recurrent neural networks (RNN) to do malware detection on dynamic features. The authors pair the RNN with an deep neural network (DNN) to learn from the static features. Their goal is to come up with an attack which evades a system that takes advantage of different feature representations. The dynamic features that the RNN learns from are call sequences. The attack on the static classifier works similar to the attacks described in this paper. The attack on the RNN is based on an attack working on text data [36]. The paper also features a comparison of different RNN architectures and the effectiveness of the attack on a given architecture, with a simple RNN being the must vulnerable and BLSTM being the most robust. An interesting discovery the authors make is that the transferability property of adversarial examples, described in [15], also holds true for RNNs. Hu et al. [37] propose an attack to leverage against black box classifiers, training their own substitute RNN and using a generative RNN to create adversarial examples. Chen et al. [38] develop an approach to defend the classifier that relies on feature selection and ensembles. Their feature selection technique is named SecCLS and the ensemble learning technique is called SecENS. By combining both methods, the authors develop a system called SecureDroid. In [11] Chen et al. propose a secure two phased learning system. During the offline learning phase a classifier is trained and during the online detection phase suspicious false negatives are used in further training the classifier. Yang et al. [39] propose feature evolution and confusion. These techniques look at how different features evolve over different versions of malware and can be used to create new synthetic malware instances for a classifier to be trained on.

8   Conclusion

We studied the space of adversarial examples in malware classification by evaluating twelve attacks and four defenses on different datasets. Our experiments show that attacks work reliably and it is relatively easy and straightforward to create adversarial examples. The defenses, on the other hand, are not as straightforward and might not always be suitable. The right choice of defense depends on many different factors such as dataset, model architecture and more. Our results show that most defense mechanisms adapted from image classification, with the exception of adversarial training, are not efficient in the malware domain, and there is a need for approaches tailored to binary data to ensure robustness of the classifiers.

References

1. Devries, T., Taylor, G.W.: Improved regularization of convolutional neural networks with cutout. CoRR, abs/1708.04552 (2017)
2. Zagoruyko, S., Komodakis, N.: Wide residual networks. CoRR, abs/1605.07146 (2016)
3. Raff, E., Barker, J., Sylvester, J., Brandon, R., Catanzaro, B., Nicholas, C.: Malware detection by eating a whole EXE (2017)
4. Zhang, F., Chan, P.P.K., Biggio, B., Yeung, D.S., Roli, F.: Adversarial feature selection against evasion attacks. IEEE Trans. Cybern. **46**(3), 766–777 (2016)
5. Saxe, J., Berlin, K.: Deep neural network based malware detection using two dimensional binary program features. In: 2015 10th International Conference on Malicious and Unwanted Software (MALWARE), pp. 11–20, October 2015
6. Goodfellow, I.J., Shlens, J., Szegedy, C.: Explaining and harnessing adversarial examples (2014)
7. Carlini, N., Wagner, D.A.: Adversarial examples are not easily detected: bypassing ten detection methods. CoRR, abs/1705.07263 (2017)
8. Mohsen Dezfooli, S.M., Fawzi, A., Frossard, P.: DeepFool: a simple and accurate method to fool deep neural networks. CoRR, abs/1511.04599 (2015)
9. Kurakin, A., Goodfellow, I.J., Bengio, S.: Adversarial examples in the physical world. CoRR, abs/1607.02533 (2016)
10. Grosse, K., Papernot, N., Manoharan, P., Backes, M., McDaniel, P.D.: Adversarial perturbations against deep neural networks for malware classification. CoRR, abs/1606.04435 (2016)
11. Chen, S., Xue, M., Fan, L., Hao, S., Xu, L., Zhu, H.: Hardening malware detection systems against cyber maneuvers: an adversarial machine learning approach. CoRR, abs/1706.04146 (2017)
12. Biggio, B., Nelson, B., Laskov, P.: Poisoning attacks against support vector machines (2012)
13. Huang, L., Joseph, A.D., Nelson, B., Rubinstein, B.I.P., Tygar, J.D.: Adversarial machine learning. In: Proceedings of the 4th ACM Workshop on Security and Artificial Intelligence, AISec 2011, pp. 43–58 (2011)
14. Papernot, N., McDaniel, P.D., Goodfellow, I.J., Jha, S., Celik, Z.B., Swami, A.: Practical black-box attacks against deep learning systems using adversarial examples. CoRR, abs/1602.02697 (2016)
15. Szegedy, C., et al.: Intriguing properties of neural networks. CoRR, abs/1312.6199 (2013)
16. Su, J., Vargas, D.V., Kouichi, S.: One pixel attack for fooling deep neural networks. arXiv preprint arXiv:1710.08864 (2017)
17. Carlini, N., Wagner, D.A.: Towards evaluating the robustness of neural networks. CoRR, abs/1608.04644 (2016)
18. Carlini, N., Katz, G., Barrett, C., Dill, D.L.: Ground-truth adversarial examples. arXiv preprint arXiv:1709.10207 (2017)

19. Warde-Farley, D., Goodfellow, I.: 11 adversarial perturbations of deep neural networks. In: Perturbations, Optimization, and Statistics, p. 311 (2016)
20. Arp, D., Spreitzenbarth, M., Hübner, M., Gascon, H., Rieck, K.: DREBIN: effective and explainable detection of android malware in your pocket (2014)
21. Dataset malware/beningn permissions android. https://www.kaggle.com/xwolf12/datasetandroidpermissions/home
22. Pedregosa, F., et al.: Scikit-learn: machine learning in Python. J. Mach. Learn. Res. **12**, 2825–2830 (2011)
23. Papernot, N., McDaniel, P.D., Jha, S., Fredrikson, M., Celik, Z.B., Swami, A.: The limitations of deep learning in adversarial settings. CoRR, abs/1511.07528 (2015)
24. Stokes, J.W., Wang, D., Marinescu, M., Marino, M., Bussone, B.: Attack and defense of dynamic analysis-based, adversarial neural malware classification models. CoRR, abs/1712.05919 (2017)
25. Huang, A., Al-Dujaili, A., Hemberg, E., and Una-May O'Reilly: Adversarial deep learning for robust detection of binary encoded malware. CoRR, abs/1801.02950 (2018)
26. Hu, W., Tan, Y.: Generating adversarial malware examples for black-box attacks based on GAN. CoRR, abs/1702.05983 (2017)
27. Goodfellow, I.J., et al.: Generative adversarial nets. In: Advances in Neural Information Processing Systems 27: Annual Conference on Neural Information Processing Systems 2014, Montreal, Quebec, Canada, 8–13 December 2014, pp. 2672–2680 (2014)
28. Arjovsky, M., Chintala, S., Bottou, L.: Wasserstein GAN (2017)
29. Gulrajani, I., Ahmed, F., Arjovsky, M., Dumoulin, V., Courville, A.C.: Improved training of wasserstein GANs. CoRR, abs/1704.00028 (2017)
30. Papernot, N., McDaniel, P.D., Wu, X., Jha, S., Swami, A.: Distillation as a defense to adversarial perturbations against deep neural networks. CoRR, abs/1511.04508 (2015)
31. Kurakin, A., Goodfellow, I.J., Bengio, S.: Adversarial machine learning at scale. CoRR, abs/1611.01236 (2016)
32. Tramèr, F., Kurakin, A., Papernot, N., Boneh, D., McDaniel, P.: Ensemble adversarial training: attacks and defenses (2017)
33. Rosenberg, I., Shabtai, A., Rokach, L., Elovici, Y.: Generic black-box end-to-end attack against RNNs and other API calls based malware classifiers. CoRR, abs/1707.05970 (2017)
34. Wang, Q., Guo, W., Zhang, K., Xing, X., Giles, C.L., Liu, X.: Random feature nullification for adversary resistant deep architecture. CoRR, abs/1610.01239 (2016)
35. Yuan, X., He, P., Zhu, Q., Bhat, R.R., Li, X.: Adversarial examples: attacks and defenses for deep learning. CoRR, abs/1712.07107 (2017)
36. Papernot, N., McDaniel, P.D., Swami, A., Harang, R.E.: Crafting adversarial input sequences for recurrent neural networks. CoRR, abs/1604.08275 (2016)
37. Hu, W., Tan, Y.: Black-box attacks against RNN based malware detection algorithms. CoRR, abs/1705.08131 (2017)
38. Chen, L., Hou, S., Ye, Y.: Securedroid: enhancing security of machine learning-based detection against adversarial android malware attacks. In: Proceedings of the 33rd Annual Computer Security Applications Conference, ACSAC 2017, pp. 362–372. ACM, New York, NY, USA (2017)
39. Yang, W., Kong, D., Xie, T., Gunter, C.A.: Malware detection in adversarial settings: exploiting feature evolutions and confusions in android apps. In: Proceedings of the 33rd Annual Computer Security Applications Conference, ACSAC 2017, pp. 288–302. ACM, New York, NY, USA (2017)

PrivC—A Framework for Efficient Secure Two-Party Computation

Kai He, Liu Yang[✉], Jue Hong, Jinghua Jiang, Jieming Wu, Xu Dong, and Zhuxun Liang

Baidu Inc., Beijing, China
{hekai07,yangliu11,hongjue,jiangjinghua,wujieming,
dongxu01,liangzhuxun}@baidu.com

Abstract. Secure Multiparty Computation (SMC) allows mutually distrusted parties to jointly evaluate a function on their private inputs without revealing anything but the output of the function. SMC has been extensively studied for decades by the research community and significant progresses have been made, both in the directions of computing capability and performance improvement. In this work, we design and implement PrivC, an efficient framework for secure two-party computing. Our design was based on arithmetic sharing, oblivious transfer, and garbled circuits. We demonstrate the efficiency of our design and implementation using benchmark datasets and real world applications at our organization. Evaluations have shown that PrivC outperforms several other competitive two-party frameworks.

Keywords: Secure Multiparty Computing · Secret sharing · Oblivious transfer

1 Introduction

Privacy has become a major concern nowadays, as people are more and more dependent on online services provided by different organizations. Activities like map navigation, searching, online shopping, etc. often disclose users' personal information to service providers. Data collected from users are valuable to service providers. However, improper use of collected data may result in privacy compromise or even major data leakage [19], which in turn may cause property damage to individuals or even financial losses to service providers.

To protect individual privacy, strict regulations have been proposed by countries and organizations [1,2]. In addition, privacy protecting techniques have been developed during the past decades. These techniques broadly fall into three categories: statistically-based [28], information flow-based [16], and crypto-based [12]. Statistically-based approaches often introduce anonymization, perturbation, randomization, aggregation, or noise adding to the process of data analysis at the price of accuracy degradation. Representative techniques

© ICST Institute for Computer Sciences, Social Informatics and Telecommunications Engineering 2019
Published by Springer Nature Switzerland AG 2019. All Rights Reserved
S. Chen et al. (Eds.): SecureComm 2019, LNICST 305, pp. 394–407, 2019.
https://doi.org/10.1007/978-3-030-37231-6_23

include k-anonymization [28] and differential privacy [15]. Information flow-based approaches employ techniques in program analysis to trace privacy leakage in applications. Crypto-based approaches preserve privacy by hiding sensitive information, e.g., via encryption, secret sharing, tokenization, etc.

In this paper we focus on secure multi-party computing (SMC), which is a crypto-based technique. SMC allows distrusted parties to jointly evaluate a function on their private inputs without revealing anything but the output of the function. The start of SMC can be dated back to the Millionaire problem [31]. Over years, more general problems were studied and three lines of techniques have been developed: garbled circuits (GC), arithmetic circuits (AC), and boolean circuits (BC). Early SMC protocols usually had high overhead on both time and space complexity, making them less practical. Recently, research works in [9,11,13,14,24,30] have demonstrated significant performance improvement in this area, bringing back the topic to public attention again. Since then, SMC has been employed to address real problems, e.g., the sugar beets auction system of Danish government [10], the private log analysis service at Google [11], etc.

Our work was motivated by privacy challenges encountered in real production environment at Baidu. In particular, we have faced a lot of situations where one department needs to perform data analysis with inputs from different departments. However, according to regulations of data management, data exchange between different departments requires a tedious, complicated and strict workflow consisting of rounds of application and approval. Sensitive data like user ids, phone numbers, and credit card numbers are even not allowed to go through departments. Even worse, there is no way to guarantee that the exchanged sensitive data is properly handled (e.g., clearance) at the end of its lifecycle. This actually increases the risk of data leakage. To address the above issues, we first tried several open source SMC implementations [9,11,13,14,30]. However, none of them is tailored for real production environment, where large data volume, stability, and performance are major concerns. Many of them work well for small datasets, but exposed severe performance and stability (e.g., crash) issues as data size increases.

In this paper we present PrivC, a practical implementation of two-party computing framework. PrivC allows software engineers to write secure computing code without the need to understand the underlying mechanism. PrivC is built upon arithmetic circuits and garbled circuits. It supports basic operations of addition, subtraction, multiplication, division, and comparison for both integers and fixed-point data types. Vector and matrix operations are implemented to support machine learning applications as well. We also make optimization on the underlying communication protocol, and parallelize some of the computation to improve performance. We have evaluated PrivC via benchmark datasets, as well as real-world applications from Baidu, including abnormal data access detection, suspicious file downloading, and data verification. Results show that PrivC outperforms several competitive 2PC frameworks while providing qualified stability.

1.1 Our Contribution

The first contribution of this paper is that we provide a product-level design and implementation of a two-party secure computing framework, namely PrivC, to meet the demand of performance and stability at our organization. With a series of optimization, PrivC outperforms several SMC frameworks for the most commonly used operations. In particular, compared to SPDZ [13], ABY [14], and EMP [30], the addition and multiplication operations in PrivC are at least two times faster for the Int64 data type. For 64-bit fixed-point operations, the addition and multiplication of PrivC are at least an order of magnitude faster than the other three tools. For a machine learning benchmark dataset, MNIST [23] (70,000 images, each has 784 features), a multi-classification application written in PrivC completes the training and testing in 13.5 h, while code written in other three frameworks failed to complete, either running out of memory of or taking unacceptable time.

The second contribution is that we have applied PrivC to preserve privacy in cross-department data analysis in product environment, including abnormal data warehouse access behavior detection, suspicious file downloading detection, and data verification. The practice testifies the performance and stability of PrivC.

1.2 Outline

This paper is organized in the following way. We present related work in Sect. 2, followed by some preliminaries in Sect. 3. We describe the main algorithms and protocols used in our work in Sect. 4 and the design of PrivC in Sect. 5. We present the evaluation in Sect. 6, and conclude in Sect. 7.

2 Related Work

Secure multi-party computing was formally introduced by Yao in the Millionaire's problem [31]. The problem was later generalized to compute any Boolean circuit by two parties with private inputs. The basic idea of Yao's approach was to encrypt a Boolean circuit (called garbled circuit) by one party, and evaluate the encrypted circuit by the other one. The two party problem was followed up by a generalization to multi-party by Goldreich, et al [18]. Their approach was based on additive secret sharing of all inputs [18]. The BGW [8] protocol defines how to compute polynomial functions with Shamir secret sharing. Secret sharing schemes can tolerate an adversary controlling up to t out of n parties. For additive secret sharing schemes [9,18], $t < n$, and for Shamir secret sharing schemes [8,11], $t < \frac{n}{2}$.

Fairplay [24] was the first work that implements a two-party generic secure function evaluation. It defines a SDFL language that allows human to specify functions that need to be evaluated. Fairplay was later extended to FairplayMP to support multi-parity computing [7]. Garbled circuits (GCs) are capable of processing any function that can be expressed as Boolean circuits. However, the size of circuits can be very large if the problem is complex, as a circuit is encrypted bit-by-bit. Arithmetic circuits (ACs) are usually faster than GCs in arithmetic computing and are better at solving problems that can be expressed as polynomial functions. Two-party arithmetic circuit protocols need generation of triples to assist the computing [18]. Triples generation can be performed using semi-homomorphic encryption or OT [27]. Early work of OTs [6,26,27] was mainly based on public-crypto operations and was inefficient. The invention of OT-extension [20] has significantly speeded up the triples generation, which in turn significantly improves performance of two-party AC protocols.

ABY [14] was a work that leverages the performance of ACs and the expressiveness of GCs (also called Yao circuits) and Boolean circuits (BCs). It allows programmers to build AC, BC, and YC in a mixed way. Our work bears the similarity with ABY in that we also implement AC and GC. However, we differ from ABY in the fact that ABY relies on its own compiler to translate a user's code into circuits at an offline phase. In our work, code written in PrivC is compiled directly by the C++ compiler into binary executables. As we will show, our work has much better performance than ABY. EMP [30] is a GC-based two-party computing framework that support both semi-honest and malicious models. EMP is fast and friendly to programmers. Our work differs from EMP in that we rely on arithmetic circuits to implement arithmetic operations, and use GC to perform non-arithmetic operations.

SPDZ [13] is an SMC implementation based on additive secret sharing and semi-homomorphic encryption. It supports both semi-honest and malicious model. Our work only considers semi-honest model. Our benchmark evaluation shows that PrivC is faster in four out of five atomic operations than SPDZ for the Int64 data type. For 64-bits fixed-point operations, PrivC is at least five times faster than SPDZ for all atomic operations. SEPIA [11] is a multi-party framework implemented at Google to perform privacy-preserving log analysis. It was based on Shamir secret sharing [29]. SEPIA is fast, and easy to use, but does not support decimal operations. Our PrivC distinguishes from SEPIA by two aspects: the first, PrivC supports both integer and decimal operations; the second, our implementation is based on additive sharing and garbled circuits. Sharemind [9] is a three-party framework that provides rich arithmetic operations, while PrivC is two-party based.

Oblivious transfer (OT) is a technique that allows a sender transfers one of several enclosed pieces of information to a receiver, but remains unknown to which information is received by the receiver, and the receiver can disclose only one piece of information. OT is an important building block in SMC and was first introduced by Rabin [27]. Early OT protocols [6,26,27] were based on public crypto and were inefficient. Ishai et al., proposed to an approach that uses public crypto operations to generate a small number of "base" OTs, and extends the "base" OTs to massive number of OTs using symmetric crypto operations [20]. Their work is called OT-extension, and has significantly improved the performance of OT generation.

3   Preliminaries

3.1   Notation

The description in this section borrows notations from [14]. In our following discussion, we use P_0 and P_1 to denote two parties that run a secure computation. We use $x \oplus y$ for bitwise XOR and $x \wedge y$ for bitwise AND. For a list x, we denote its ith element by $x[i]$. If x is a sequence of bits, then $x[i]$ denotes the ith bit of x, and $x[0]$ denotes the least significant bit of x. We use κ to denote the symmetric security parameter.

We use $\langle x \rangle^t$ to denote a shared variable x, where the superscript $t \in \{A, Y\}$ indicates the type of sharing, A for arithmetic sharing, and Y for garbled sharing. For a shared variable $\langle x \rangle^t$, we use $\langle x \rangle_i^t$ to denote the share held by P_i ($i \in \{0, 1\}$). We define a sharing operation $\langle x \rangle^t = \mathsf{SHR}_i^t(x)$ to denote that P_i shares a varialbe x with P_{1-i}. The recovering operation is denoted by $x = \mathsf{REC}_i^t(\langle x \rangle^t)$, meaning that P_i obtains a share of x from P_{1-i} and reconstructs x from the two shares. An operation $\bullet$ on shared variables are denoted by $\langle z \rangle^t = \langle x \rangle^t \bullet \langle y \rangle^t$ for $t \in \{A, Y\}$. For example, $\langle z \rangle^A = \langle x \rangle^A + \langle y \rangle^A$ adds two arithmetic shares and returns the arithmetic shares of the sum.

3.2   Oblivious Transfer

In this work, we use 1-out-of-2 OT where the sender sends two pieces of information (m_0, m_1) and the receiver inputs a choice bit $c \in \{0, 1\}$ and obtains m_c as output. The receiver learns nothing about the other message m_{1-c}, and the sender keeps unknown which message is learned by the receiver, i.e., the sender learns nothing about c.

OTs can be generated efficiently through OT extension. We use random-OT (R-OT) and correlated-OT (C-OT) [3] to further increase OT efficiency. In R-OT, the sender obtains random (m_0, m_1) and the receiver obtains t from an OT-extension such that $t = m_0$ or m_1 according to receiver's choice bit. In C-OT, instead of having to obliviously transfer two fixed independent bit strings, the sender transfers two random bit strings with a fixed correlation function $f(\cdot)$. Namely, the sender obtains a random m_0 and a correlated $m_1 = f(m_0)$.

4   Algorithms

In this section, we present the algorithms and protocols used in our framework, which mainly follow [14] with some optimizations in the implementation. In particular, we employ two types of circuits: arithmetic circuit (Sect. 4.1) and Yao's garbled circuit (Sect. 4.2).

4.1   Arithmetic Circuit

In 2PC protocol of arithmetic circuits, an ℓ-bit value x is additively shared in the ring $\mathbb{Z}_{2^\ell}$ as the sum of two values modulo 2^ℓ. The basic protocols for arithmetic circuits are described as follows, mainly based on [14].

Sharing Semantics. For a ℓ-bit variable x, its arithmetic shares between two parties should satisfy the following property: $\langle x \rangle_0^A + \langle x \rangle_1^A \equiv x \bmod 2^\ell$ with $\langle x \rangle_0^A, \langle x \rangle_1^A \in \mathbb{Z}_{2^\ell}$.

Share Generation. $\mathsf{SHR}_i^A(x)$: P_i randomly chooses $r \in_R \mathbb{Z}_{2^\ell}$, computes $\langle x \rangle_i^A = x - r$, and sends r to P_{1-i}, who computes $\langle x \rangle_{1-i}^A = r$.

Reconstruction. $\mathsf{REC}_i^A(x)$: Both parties send its share to the other side to recover the value of a variable, i.e., P_{1-i} sends its share $\langle x \rangle_{1-i}^A$ to P_i who computes $x = \langle x \rangle_0^A + \langle x \rangle_1^A$.

Operations. Every polynomial can be expressed as an arithmetic circuit, which can be translated to a sequence of additions and multiplications.

Addition. To compute the sum of two arithmetic shared values, i.e., $\langle z \rangle^A = \langle x \rangle^A + \langle y \rangle^A$, P_i locally computes $\langle z \rangle_i^A = \langle x \rangle_i^A + \langle y \rangle_i^A$.

Multiplication. $\langle z \rangle^A = \langle x \rangle^A \cdot \langle y \rangle^A$: multiplication of two arithmetic shared values is performed via the help of a pre-computed Beaver's triple [4] a_i, b_i, c_i satisfying $\langle c \rangle_0^A + \langle c \rangle_1^A = (\langle a \rangle_0^A + \langle a \rangle_1^A) \cdot (\langle b \rangle_0^A + \langle b \rangle_1^A)$. Step 1: P_i sets $\langle e \rangle_i^A = \langle x \rangle_i^A - \langle a \rangle_i^A$ and $\langle f \rangle_i^A = \langle y \rangle_i^A - \langle b \rangle_i^A$. Step 2: both parties perform $\mathsf{REC}^A(e)$ and $\mathsf{REC}^A(f)$. Step 3: P_i computes $\langle z \rangle_i^A = i \cdot e \cdot f + f \cdot \langle a \rangle_i^A + e \cdot \langle b \rangle_i^A + \langle c \rangle_i^A$.

Triples Generation. The OT extension based triples generation protocol [17] has been proved as an efficient approach. In our framework, we employ a fast correlated OT extension based approach to generate triples as in [14]. The details are omitted due to space limit.

4.2   Yao's Garbled Circuit

In Yao's protocol, one party called garbler represents a function as a Boolean circuit and assigns each wire w two random encryption keys (also called labels) (k_0, k_1) with $k_0, k_1 \in \{0, 1\}^\kappa$. The garbler encrypts the output keys of each gate on its all combinations of the two input keys using an encryption function. She then sends the garbled circuit, together with her input keys, to another party called evaluator. The evaluator obtains the garbled values of his inputs by using one or more OTs, then evaluates the garbled circuit and obtains the output.

In the following description, we assume P_0 is a garbler and P_1 is an evaluator. The garbler generates wire keys by randomly selecting a κ-bit string R with $R[0] = 1$. For each wire w, she randomly selects $k_0 \in_R \{0, 1\}^\kappa$ and computes $k_1 = k_0 \oplus R$. The least significant bit $k_0[0]$ resp. $k_1[0] = 1 - k_0[0]$ is called permutation bit. Note that the above techniques are free-XOR [22] and point-and-permute [5].

Sharing Semantics. The intuition behind garbled sharing is that P_0 holds two keys k_0 and k_1 for each wire w, and P_1 receives only one of the two keys according to his choice bit, but P_0 remains unknown whether the received key corresponds to bit 1 or 0. This is achieved by letting P_0 and P_1 engaged in an OT protocol where P_0 acts as sender and P_1 acts as receiver.

Share Generation. For a wire with two keys k_0 and $k_1 = k_0 \oplus R$, a value x can be shared as $\langle x \rangle_0^Y = k_0$ and $\langle x \rangle_1^Y = k_0 \oplus xR$. **Case 1:** denoted by $\mathsf{SHR}_0^Y(x)$, i.e., if P_0 needs to share a value x, she randomly chooses $\langle x \rangle_0^Y = k_0 \in_R \{0,1\}^\kappa$ and sends $k_x = k_0 \oplus xR$ to P_1. **Case 2:** denoted by $\mathsf{SHR}_1^Y(x)$, i.e., if P_1 needs to share a value x, then both parties run a correlated OT where P_0 acts as sender, inputs $(k_0, k_1 = k_0 \oplus R)$ with $k_0 \in_R \{0,1\}^\kappa$ and P_1 acts as receiver with his choice bit x and obliviously obtains $\langle x \rangle_1^Y = k_x$.

Reconstruction. $\mathsf{REC}_i^Y(x)$: P_{1-i} sends his/her permutation bit $\pi = \langle x \rangle_{1-i}^Y[0]$ to P_i. P_i recovers the value of x by computing $x = \pi \oplus \langle x \rangle_i^Y[0]$.

Operations. The computing of any Boolean circuits can be performed by evaluating a sequential number of XOR and AND. In our design, we use XOR and AND to implement other bit gates such as OR, NOT, and word gates such as +, -, *, and /.

XOR. $\langle z \rangle^Y = \langle x \rangle^Y \oplus \langle y \rangle^Y$ is evaluated using the free-XOR technique in [22]: P_i locally computes $\langle z \rangle_i^Y = \langle x \rangle_i^Y \oplus \langle y \rangle_i^Y$.

AND. To compute $\langle z \rangle^Y = \langle x \rangle^Y \wedge \langle y \rangle^Y$, P_0 creates a garbled AND table $(\langle z \rangle^Y, T) \leftarrow \mathsf{GbAND}(\langle x \rangle^Y, \langle y \rangle^Y)$, where GbAND is a garbling function as defined in [32]. P_0 then sends the garbled table T, together with the keys of her inputs, to P_1, who decrypts T using keys $\langle x \rangle_1^Y$ and $\langle y \rangle_1^Y$ and obtains $\langle z \rangle_1^Y$.

More details like complexity analysis can be found in [14] and thus are omitted here.

4.3   Sharing Conversions

In our design, for some operations, e.g., division, we need to convert values from their arithmetic sharing to garbled sharing, or the other way back, in order to leverage the expressiveness of garbled circuits and the performance of arithmetic circuits on polynomial evaluation. We follows the circuit conversion approach in [14], which is briefly described below.

Arithmetic to Yao's Garbled Sharing (A2Y): The conversion of a value x from its arithmetic share $\langle x \rangle^A$ to garbled share $\langle x \rangle^Y$ can be done by securely evaluating an addition circuit. In particular, P_0 generates garbled sharing of $x_0 = \langle x \rangle_0^A$ by doing $\langle x_0 \rangle^Y = \mathsf{SHR}_0^Y(x_0)$, and P_1 generates garbled sharing of $x_1 = \langle x \rangle_1^A$ by doing $\langle x_1 \rangle^Y = \mathsf{SHR}_1^Y(x_1)$. After that, the two parties compute $\langle x \rangle^Y = \langle x_0 \rangle^Y + \langle x_1 \rangle^Y$.

Yao to Arithmetic Sharing (Y2A): An ℓ-bits word x can be shared by an array of Yao sharing $\{\langle x[i] \rangle^Y\}_{i \in \{0, \dots, \ell-1\}}$. Let $x_i = \sum_{j=0}^{\ell-1} 2^j \cdot \langle x[j] \rangle_i^Y[0]$, notice that $x = x_0 \oplus x_1$. Analogously, a technique similar to the arithmetic multiplication triples generation can be used. The general idea is to perform a C-OT for each bit where we obliviously transfer two values that are additively correlated by a power of two. The receiver can obtain one of these values and, by summing them up, the parties obtain a valid arithmetic share.

5   Design of PrivC

PrivC is implemented using C++ language. It supports both 2PC integer and decimal operations. We create two data types, named Int64 and Fix64, to represent 64-bit integer and fixed-point numbers respectively. Operations are provided over both Int64 and Fix64, mostly in the way of operator overloading in C++, which means no extra circuit compiler is required. Furthermore, PrivC carries out free circuit conversion as needed. For example, if a code block only involves operations of addition or multiplication, the underlying protocol will be arithmetic circuit. If a division operation is followed, then the operands are automatically converted from arithmetic sharing to garbled sharing without any intervention, which leverages the performance of AC and the expressiveness of GC. Below we present the detailed design of PrivC.

5.1   Operators

Addition and Subtraction are implemented by overloading the operator+- in C++. They represent the addition and subtraction operations on arithmetic sharing, i.e., $\langle z \rangle^A = \langle x \rangle^A + \langle y \rangle^A$. The operations only involves local computing and no communication is needed.

Scalar Operations represent operations between a secret shared value and a plaintext value. Note that $\langle x+a \rangle^A = \langle x \rangle_0^A + a + \langle x \rangle_1^A$. For operator+- to plaintext operand, P_0 locally adds a to $\langle x \rangle_0^A$. For an operator* to a plaintext operand, P_i times $\langle x \rangle_i^A$ by a. This holds true due to the fact that $a\langle x \rangle^A = a \cdot \langle x \rangle_0^A + a \cdot \langle x \rangle_1^A$.

Multiplication is implemented by overloading operator*. It represents $\langle z \rangle^A = \langle x \rangle^A \cdot \langle y \rangle^A$. To reduce number of communication rounds, we generate triples in batch and store them in a buffer. When running out the buffered triples, another batch will be generated. We also extend the multiplication operator * to implement the **inner product** of vectors. We further optimize the multiplication in triples generation. This is achieved by observing that both Int64 and Fix64 are 64-bit sharings while the length of OT masks generated by cryptographic hash function are long enough for two sharings (SHA1 for 160-bits). This indicates that we can generate two triples $\langle c \rangle^A = \langle a \rangle^A \cdot \langle b \rangle^A$ and $\langle c' \rangle^A = \langle a' \rangle^A \cdot \langle b \rangle^A$ for the same multiplier $\langle b \rangle^A$ in one shot. Such an optimization saves one half of C-OTs while computing two multiplications that share a same multiplier. This optimization is also employed to speed up **matrix multiplication** in PrivC.[1]

Division is implemented by overloading the operator/ in C++. Note that $\mathbb{Z}_{2^\ell}$ is not friendly with inverse operation, and thus division is implemented using garbled circuit. For a ℓ-bits division, $O(\ell^2)$ GbANDs are invoked during the evaluation.

---

[1] We learnt this trick from [25].

Comparison is implemented by overloading `operator<==>` in C++. This is achieved by converting the operands to their garbled sharing and evaluating the comparison operation in garbled circuits. At the end of the evaluation, we reconstruct the resulting garbled bit when necessary.

Conditional Statement. Unfortunately, C++ disallows the overloading of conditional operator. We implement the conditional statement via a function named `if_else`. `if_else` takes a conditional garbled bit $\langle c \rangle^{Y}$[2], possibly generated by some comparison functions, e.g., <, and two branching variables $\langle a \rangle^{A}, \langle b \rangle^{A}$, and returns $\langle a \rangle^{A}$ if $\langle c \rangle^{Y}$ is a *true* sharing; otherwise it returns $\langle b \rangle^{A}$. Still we convert all operands to garbled sharing and evaluate a garbled MUX (a gate-level `if_else`). The output of MUX is converted to arithmetic sharing. To evaluate an ℓ-bits garbled MUX, $O(\ell)$ GbANDs are invoked.

We summarize the computation and communication cost of all operations in Table 1. As we can see, division is the most expensive one among all operations we have implemented.

Table 1. The computation (number of symmetric crypto operations), communication (bits) cost, and number of messages of different operations on ℓ-bit values, where κ is the symmetric security parameter.

Operation	Computation	Communication	Round	OT
$+, -, \times$ (scalar)	0	0	0	0
$\times$	0	2ℓ	1	2ℓ
$\div$	$6\ell(\ell+2)$	$2\kappa\ell(\ell+2)$	4	3ℓ
$<, =, >$	18ℓ	$6\kappa\ell$	4	3ℓ
`if_else`	18ℓ	$6\kappa\ell$	4	3ℓ
C-OT	3	$\kappa + \ell$	1	N/A

5.2   Notes for Fix64

In PrivC, decimal operations are implemented by fixed-point arithmetic in the type of Fix64, where half of bits are used to represent the fractional part. Fixed-point numbers behave almost the same as integers $\in \mathbb{Z}_{2^{\ell}}$ except that we need to do rounding and truncation after multiplication.

When evaluating multiplication on Fix64, rather than generating triples on larger ring (say $\mathbb{Z}_{2^{96}}$), we let the addition and multiplication in the correlation function $f_i(x) = (\langle a \rangle_0^A \cdot 2^i + x) \mod 2^{\ell}$ be performed on 64-bits fixed-point numbers. Such an approach saves us 32 C-OTs. Correctness follows from the fact that fixed-point multiplication is distributive over addition.

---

[2] We provide a class `Bool` to express 1-bit Yao sharing.

Generating triples using this approach could cause some precision loss since every multiplication is rounded up in the correlation function $f_i(\cdot)$. To resolve this issue, we add a fixed compensation on estimation to the generated triples. As we will see in Sect. 6, such an optimization does not cause any precision issue for all the datasets and applications we have evaluated.

6   Evaluation

We evaluate the performance of PrivC in terms of atomic operations and real-world applications in product environment. We compare the results with ABY, EMP and SPDZ, which are most relevant to our work.

6.1   Experimental Settings

The experiments are conducted on two servers running Ubuntu 16.04.3 LTS, with 128 GB of RAM each. The CPU settings are both Intel(R) Xeon(R) CPU E5-2650 v4, 48 processors at 2.20 GHz. The two servers are located in the same IDC, with 10 Gbps NIC and the measured average network delay is 100 μs.

6.2   Workloads

We present the workloads used in our evaluation, which are used for training linear logistic regression (LR) models and performing private set intersection (PSI) operations.

MNIST Dataset. The MNIST dataset [23] contains images of handwritten digits from "0" to "9". It has 60,000 training samples, and 10,000 test samples, each with 784 features representing 28×28 pixels in the image. Each feature is a grayscale between 0-255. We split the features among two parties and train an LR model by running code written in PrivC.

Abnormal Data Warehouse Access. The dataset is an one-day access logs from two data warehouses, composing of 1471 users' access logs, among which we use 100 labeled records for training and the remaining 1371 rows for testing. Each sample has six features describing the accessing actions. Half of features are from one party, and the rest and the label are from another. We train an LR model by running code written in PrivC to predict abnormal data access behavior.

Abnormal File Download. This dataset describes the file downloading behavior of users. The size of the dataset is about one million, where 30,000 records are used for training, and the remaining 997,000 records are used for testing. The dataset has six features, where three of them are owned by one department, and the other three features and the label are owned by another department. An LR model is trained by running code written in PrivC between the two departments.

Private Set Intersection. It is a usual case at our organization that two departments want to find out the percentage of common users, e.g., to decide AD coverage, in product environment without revealing users that do not belong to the intersection. We implement a 2PC PSI application for this scenario. The datasets consist of real user groups from two departments, with the size ranging from 10,000 to 50 million.

6.3   Benchmarking of Atomic Operations

We first evaluate the performance of all the atomic operations of PrivC, and compared the results with ABY, EMP, and SPDZ. Table 2 shows the running time in microseconds of different implementations for the Int64 and Fix64 data types. Each test result is an average of 10,000 runs.

For integer operations, it can be observed that PrivC outperforms all other implementation in four out of the five atomic operations. The division operation of PrivC is slower than EMP and SPDZ, mainly due to the time spent on circuit conversion. ABY does not provide division operator for integer. For decimal operations, results show that PrivC outperforms the other three frameworks in four out of the five operations. In particular, the addition and multiplication operator of PrivC is more than an order of magnitude faster than the others. Note that ABY uses SIMD gates to process multiple data elements in a single operation. SIMD gates are faster than the regular gates in ABY. We did not evaluate SIMD gates.

Table 2. The rounded up running time (in μs, the less the better) per atomic operation in the LAN setting, averaged over 10,000 sequential operations. Note: ABY does not provide division operation for integer data type, nor comparison for decimal data.

	ADD		MUL		DIV		CMP		EQ	
	Int64	Fix64	Int64	Fix64	Int64	Fix64	Int64	Fix64	Int64	Fix64
ABY	61990	85,736	65080	95,427	NA	208,501	62,638	NA	62,634	NA
EMP	1765	4,487	2885	4,426	3025	**4,574**	1718	4,574	1749	3,132
SPDZ	887	1,638	931	35,819	**1747**	90,128	81567	77,256	31144	26,352
PrivC	**107**	**108**	**404**	**395**	9218	18,281	**1,157**	**1,116**	**674**	**650**

6.4   Application Performance

MNIST Dataset. The performance of secure LR training on MINIST by PrivC is shown in Table 3. The training completes in 48736 s (about 13.5 h) for 2 epochs, and generates a model with accurate rate of 86.36%. We also tried to implement the same task using ABY's code, but failed due to OOM with unclear reason.

Table 3. The performance of PrivC on the MNIST Dataset, the Data Warehouse Access Dataset, and the File Download Dataset.

Dataset name	Time (s)	Memory (MB)	Accuracy
MNIST dataset	48,736.0	11,750	0.8636
Data warehouse access logs	1.6	172	1.0
File download logs	261.0	468	0.999

Abnormal Data Warehouse Access. We train an LR model using 100 records for one epoch and test the accuracy using the other 1371 records. The results are shown in Table 3. The training completes in 1.6 s and consumed 172 MB of memory, resulting an overfitted model. We note that more data may be helpful to resolve the overfitting issue.

Abonomal File Download. We use 30,000 records for a 2 epochs training and the rest 997,000 records for testing. As shown in Table 3, the task completes in 261 s and consumes 468 MB memory, resulting a model with 99.90% accuracy.

Private Set Intersection. Table 4 shows that our PSI application in PrivC is able to complete in about 10 min with each party has a dataset of 50 million records. To our best knowledge, this is by far the largest PSI dataset reported in literature.

Table 4. The running time (in seconds) of our PSI implementations in PrivC. Note: the implementation was based on the protocol in [21]

Size of datasets	10,000	1000,000	10,000,000	20,000,000	50,000,000
Running time (s)	2.43	12.56	118.70	237.26	603.14

Table 5 shows the memory space, communication cost, and network bandwidth consumed by our PSI implementation written in PrivC. It can be observed that the memory consumption increases almost linearly with the size of datasets.

Table 5. The memory and communication cost of our PSI implementation (MB)

Dataset size	MEM	NET_IN	NET_OUT	NET_TOTAL
10,000	12.6	0.3	0.7	1.0
1000,000	644.7	34.7	66.8	101.5
10,000,000	4,784.8	357.4	679.4	1,054.8
20,000,000	9,290.5	1,501.5	2,720.1	4,221.6
50,000,000	22,616.2	2,020.7	3,401.4	5,422.1

For datasets with 50 million of records, our implementation consumes about 22.6 GB of memory, and the network communication cost is about 5.4 GB.

7 Conclusion

In this work, we present the design and implementation of PrivC, a product-level two party secure computing framework. Our design was based on arithmetic and garbled circuits. We have evaluated the performance of the atomic operations provided by PrivC and compared the numbers with several other competitive 2PC frameworks. Overall, PrivC outperforms the other three frameworks for the most commonly used operations. In addition, we have demonstrated the effectiveness and efficiency of PrivC using a machine learning benchmark dataset and real-world applications at our organization. In the future, we plan to apply PrivC to address more privacy challenges. We are in the process of opening the source code of PrivC.

Acknowlegements. We thank Prof. Sheng Zhong, Yuan Zhang, and Jingyu Hua at Nanjing University for their insightful discussions with us on our work. We also thank Dr. Tao Wei, Chief Security Scientist, and Dr. Yueqiang Cheng, Staff Security Scientist at Baidu for their feedbacks and suggestions on our paper.

References

1. EUGDPR - Information Portal. https://eugdpr.org/. Accessed 26 Mar 2019
2. What is HIPAA (Health Insurance Portability and Accountability Act)? https://searchhealthit.techtarget.com/definition/HIPAA. Accessed 26 Mar 2019
3. Asharov, G., Lindell, Y., Schneider, T., Zohner, M.: More efficient oblivious transfer and extensions for faster secure computation. In: ACM CCS, pp. 535–548 (2013)
4. Beaver, D.: Efficient multiparty protocols using circuit randomization. In: Feigenbaum, J. (ed.) CRYPTO 1991. LNCS, vol. 576, pp. 420–432. Springer, Heidelberg (1992). https://doi.org/10.1007/3-540-46766-1_34
5. Beaver, D., Micali, S., Rogaway, P.: The round complexity of secure protocols (extended abstract). In: STOC, pp. 503–513 (1990)
6. Bellare, M., Micali, S.: Non-interactive oblivious transfer and applications. In: Brassard, G. (ed.) CRYPTO 1989. LNCS, vol. 435, pp. 547–557. Springer, New York (1990). https://doi.org/10.1007/0-387-34805-0_48
7. Ben-David, A., Nisan, N., Pinkas, B.: FairplayMP: a system for secure multi-party computation. In: ACM CCS, pp. 257–266 (2008)
8. Ben-Or, M., Goldwasser, S., Wigderson, A.: Completeness theorems for non-cryptographic fault-tolerant distributed computation. In: STOC, pp. 1–10 (1988)
9. Bogdanov, D., Laur, S., Willemson, J.: Sharemind: a framework for fast privacy-preserving computations. In: ESORICS, pp. 192–206 (2008)
10. Bogetoft, P., et al.: Secure multiparty computation goes live. In: Dingledine, R., Golle, P. (eds.) FC 2009. LNCS, vol. 5628, pp. 325–343. Springer, Heidelberg (2009). https://doi.org/10.1007/978-3-642-03549-4_20
11. Burkhart, M., Strasser, M., Many, D., Dimitropoulos, X.A.: SEPIA: privacy-preserving aggregation of multi-domain network events and statistics. In: USENIX Security Symposium, pp. 223–240 (2010)

12. Chaum, D.L.: Untraceable electronic mail, return addresses, and digital pseudonyms. Commun. ACM **24**(2), 84–90 (1981)
13. Damgård, I., Pastro, V., Smart, N., Zakarias, S.: Multiparty computation from somewhat homomorphic encryption. In: Safavi-Naini, R., Canetti, R. (eds.) CRYPTO 2012. LNCS, vol. 7417, pp. 643–662. Springer, Heidelberg (2012). https://doi.org/10.1007/978-3-642-32009-5_38
14. Demmler, D., Schneider, T., Zohner, M.: ABY - a framework for efficient mixed-protocol secure two-party computation. In: NDSS (2015)
15. Dwork, C.: Differential privacy. In: ICALP (2), pp. 1–12 (2006)
16. Felt, A.P., Chin, E., Hanna, S., Song, D., Wagner, D.A.: Android permissions demystified. In: ACM CCS, pp. 627–638 (2011)
17. Gilboa, N.: Two party RSA key generation. In: Wiener, M. (ed.) CRYPTO 1999. LNCS, vol. 1666, pp. 116–129. Springer, Heidelberg (1999). https://doi.org/10.1007/3-540-48405-1_8
18. Goldreich, O., Micali, S., Wigderson, A.: How to play any mental game or A completeness theorem for protocols with honest majority. In: STOC, pp. 218–229 (1987)
19. Isaac, M., Frenkel, S.: Facebook security breach exposes accounts of 50 million users (2018). https://www.nytimes.com/2018/09/28/technology/facebook-hack-data-breach.html. Accessed 26 Mar 2019
20. Ishai, Y., Kilian, J., Nissim, K., Petrank, E.: Extending oblivious transfers efficiently. In: Boneh, D. (ed.) CRYPTO 2003. LNCS, vol. 2729, pp. 145–161. Springer, Heidelberg (2003). https://doi.org/10.1007/978-3-540-45146-4_9
21. Kolesnikov, V., Kumaresan, R., Rosulek, M., Trieu, N.: Efficient batched oblivious PRF with applications to private set intersection. In: ACM CCS, pp. 818–829 (2016)
22. Kolesnikov, V., Schneider, T.: Improved garbled circuit: free XOR gates and applications. In: ICALP (2), pp. 486–498 (2008)
23. LeCun, Y., Cortes, C., Burges, C.J.: MNIST handwritten digit database. http://yann.lecun.com/exdb/mnist/. Accessed 26 Mar 2019
24. Malkhi, D., Nisan, N., Pinkas, B., Sella, Y., et al.: Fairplay - secure two-party computation system. In: USENIX Security Symposium, pp. 287–302 (2004)
25. Mohassel, P., Zhang, Y.: SecureML: a system for scalable privacy-preserving machine learning. In: IEEE Symposium on Security and Privacy, pp. 19–38 (2017)
26. Naor, M., Pinkas, B.: Efficient oblivious transfer protocols. In: SODA, pp. 448–457 (2001)
27. Rabin, M.O.: How to exchange secrets with oblivious transfer. In: Technical Report. vol. TR-81. Aiken Computation Lab, Harvard University (1981)
28. Samarati, P., Sweeney, L.: Generalizing data to provide anonymity when disclosing information. In: PODS, vol. 98, p. 188 (1998)
29. Shamir, A.: How to share a secret. Commun. ACM **22**(11), 612–613 (1979)
30. Wang, X., Malozemoff, A.J., Katz, J.: EMP-toolkit: efficient MultiParty computation toolkit (2016). https://github.com/emp-toolkit
31. Yao, A.C.C.: Protocols for secure computations. In: FOCS, pp. 160–164 (1982)
32. Zahur, S., Rosulek, M., Evans, D.: Two halves make a whole. In: Oswald, E., Fischlin, M. (eds.) EUROCRYPT 2015. LNCS, vol. 9057, pp. 220–250. Springer, Heidelberg (2015). https://doi.org/10.1007/978-3-662-46803-6_8

CoRide: A Privacy-Preserving Collaborative-Ride Hailing Service Using Blockchain-Assisted Vehicular Fog Computing

Meng Li[1], Liehuang Zhu[2(✉)], and Xiaodong Lin[3]

[1] Key Laboratory of Knowledge Engineering with Big Data (Hefei University of Technology), Ministry of Education; School of Computer Science and Information Engineering, Hefei University of Technology, Hefei 230601, China
mengli@hfut.edu.cn
[2] School of Computer Science and Technology, Beijing Institute of Technology, Beijing, China
liehuangz@bit.edu.cn
[3] School of Computer Science, University of Guelph, Guelph, Canada
xlin08@uoguelph.ca

Abstract. Ride-hailing services have experienced remarkable development throughout the world, serving millions of users per day. However, service providers, such as Uber and Didi, operate independently. If they are willing to share user data and establish collaborative-rides (c-rides), more ride services and commercial interests will be produced. Meanwhile, these collaborations raise significant security and privacy concerns for both users and service providers, because users' sensitive information and service providers' business secrets could be leaked during c-rides. Moreover, data auditability and fairness must be guaranteed. In this paper, we propose CoRide: a privacy-preserving <u>Co</u>llaborative-<u>Ride</u> hailing service using blockchain-assisted vehicular fog computing. First, we anonymously authenticate users and disclose a targeted user only if all collaborative service providers are present while requiring no trusted authority. Then, we construct a consortium blockchain to record c-rides and create smart contracts to pair riders with drivers. Private proximity test and query processing are utilized to support location authentication, driver screening and destination matching. Last, we modify Zerocash to achieve anonymous payment and defend double spending attacks. Finally, we analyze the security of CoRide and demonstrate its efficiency through extensive experiments based on an Ethereum network.

Keywords: Ride hailing · Privacy · Blockchain · Fog computing

1 Introduction

Ride-hailing services (RHSs) have proliferated in the past decade, thanks to the promotion of share economy and the increased connectivity, serving millions of

© ICST Institute for Computer Sciences, Social Informatics and Telecommunications Engineering 2019
Published by Springer Nature Switzerland AG 2019. All Rights Reserved
S. Chen et al. (Eds.): SecureComm 2019, LNICST 305, pp. 408–422, 2019.
https://doi.org/10.1007/978-3-030-37231-6_24

Fig. 1. A common practice for a RHS driver to find riders

users (i.e., riders and drivers) worldwide per day [1]. RHSs allow riders and drivers to send ride requests and responses to the platforms, and set up rides conveniently through user-friendly mobile applications. Meanwhile, fog computing [2] has been introduced in vehicular networks to provide real-time services, such as surface condition monitoring. It locally collects and pre-processes users' data by fog nodes, i.e., road-side units (RSUs) to save unnecessary bandwidth for transmitting data to a remote cloud server [3].

However, service providers (SPs), like Uber, Lyft, and Didi, have their own datasets which inevitably lead to information isolated islands. For instance, an Uber rider/driver searches for a Uber driver/rider already for a long time, but there are no Uber users close by. This situation results in not only time waste but frustrating user experience. It would be nice if a driver/rider from another SP jumps in to help this Uber rider/driver which is a win-win situation. The competitions between SPs are also fierce, if one SP triumphs in the end, it will possibly incur rapacious monopoly [4] where the service quality declines and the ride fare grows. These are bad news for users. Hence, there is an urgent need to unite SPs. Nowadays, it is very common that drivers run several apps from different SPs on several smartphones to find riders shown in Fig. 1. However, this is inconvenient for drivers who have to continuously monitor these apps and smartphones which is unsafe. Also they have to register to multiple SPs, it could put drivers' personal information at greater risk which is unnecessary.

To tackle this problem, we point out that *SPs can collaborate with each other and share user data* [5]. We propose a concept of "collaborative-ride" (c-ride) which refers to a ride paired through collaborations between multiple SPs. The benefits of c-rides are multi-folds: a rider saves time in waiting a ride; a driver make more money by picking up more ride orders; collaborative SPs gain more profits and improve service quality by adopting user feedback after c-rides; c-rides also improve city mobility, alleviate traffic congestion, and reduce emission of automobile exhaust. We assume that c-ride users adopt the same data formats for matching and payment.

Unfortunately, along with the advantage of c-rides come some vital security and privacy concerns, since users' sensitive information (i.e., identity, location, transaction) and SPs' *business secrets* are included in c-rides, and SPs/RSUs are semi-honest. Firstly, the priority is to authenticate users' identities in an anonymous way. Different from existing work [6,7], we argue that the ideal way to track a targeted user has three requirements: (1) only if all SPs participate, (2) no trusted authority is required, and (3) other users still remain anonymous. Secondly, the users' locations should be authenticated to defend the location cheating attack [8], e.g., a rider in a remote area reports an urban(false) location to an RSU such that a matched driver travels a long way to pick him up. Thirdly, we need to match users' get-on locations, destinations and conditions (e.g., driving age, vehicle brand) simultaneously while they are encrypted to protect privacy. Next, a rider ought to pay a ride fare to a driver at the end of the c-ride, although Zerocash [9] can achieve anonymous payment, but it cannot resist the double spending attack [10], i.e., the rider uses a same randomness in the Pour transaction and withdraw the fare before the driver does, so the driver will be unable to receive the fare. Lastly, different from existing settings [3,7,11,12], SPs have business secrets in collaborations that they have not encountered before. For example, if the Uber's identity is not hidden, anyone could estimate the service fees or commissions based on Uber's fare estimator and commission standard (25% of all fares) in order to acquire its corporate income from c-rides; if Uber's drivers keep picking up Didi's riders in a certain area, Uber will know Didi's confidential operation situation (i.e., rider resource deficiency) and convene more drivers to occupy the market in this area.

Given that these c-rides are formed by different SPs, it is crucial to record them in a consistent and tamper-proof ledger to guarantee data auditability and fairness. A blockchain [13–16] is a feasible tool to tackle this problem. First, SPs are distrustful of other SPs for their scandals. SPs and RSUs may collude to control the matching process to maximize profits. Second, although c-rides can be anonymized to protect privacy, storing them on a public blockchain still confronts information leakage. If the ledger is owned by one SP, it may arbitrarily tamper with the blockchain. Hence, we resort to a consortium blockchain (*CB*) which is owned by collaborative SPs and constructed by distributed RSUs. A *CB* is a permissioned blockchain running among identified parties and it secures transactions between users who do not fully trust each other but share a common goal. *CB* is already applied in searchable encryption and vehicular networks. Fairness means that riders receive correct c-ride matching results, drivers redeem exact c-ride fares, and SPs charge service fees from drivers in c-rides. Efficiency is also important to the system, including how to efficiently match rides with drivers and how to efficiently maintain the *CB*.

To address the above issues, we propose CoRide: a privacy-preserving collaborative ride hailing service using consortium blockchain-assisted vehicular fog computing. To the best of our knowledge, this is first work to focus on the information isolation problem in commercial RHSs, call for a collaboration among SPs, and present a secure and effective solution. Contributions are as follows.

– We first introduce a concept of "c-ride" and it refers to a new system model for RHS where several SPs are collaborating. More importantly, we eliminate the need of an online trusted authority, which is required in traditional setting. Further, we establish a corresponding security model where users may launch the false location attack, RSUs may be compromised, and SPs may collude with RSUs to interfere with matching processes.

- We propose CoRide to preserve users' conditional privacy [7] and disclose a targeted user only if all SPs are present. We construct an immutable CB among SPs to record c-rides and create automatically enforced smart contracts on RSUs to match riders with drivers. Specifically, we leverage private proximity test [17] to authenticate users' locations and establish secret keys for user matching and negotiation, we utilize privacy-preserving query processing [18] to support driver screening and destination matching. Further, we use Proof-of-Stake (PoS) mechanism [19] to reach consensus. Last, we modify Zerocash [9] to achieve anonymous under double spending attack.
- We prove the security and privacy properties of CoRide. Most significantly, we simulate CoRide in a Ethereum network [20] with laptops, desktops and commercial cloud servers. Extensive experiments are conducted to demonstrate the practicability and efficiency of CoRide.

2   Problem Statement

2.1   System Model

Our system model consists of a certificate authority CA, n_1 SPs, n_2 RSUs, n_3 riders and n_4 drivers. Let SP_i, RS_i, R_i, D_i represent the i-th SP, RSU, rider and driver. CA generates keys used for users and SPs, and stays offline after system initialization. Each SP runs its own ride-hailing service and collaborates with other SPs to form a c-ride hailing system. SPs co-generate a set of keys for user matching and fare payment. SPs collect c-ride requests and responses from RSUs, construct a consortium blockchain CB to store c-ride records, and obtain service fees from drivers in c-rides. An RSU locally collects real-time requests and responses, authenticates users, verifies data integrity, uploads encrypted c-ride data to SPs, puts transactions as well as hash value of c-ride data on the blockchain. The network is synchronous in the sense that an upper bound can be determined during which any RSU is able to communicate with other RSUs. A rider registers to CA and his SP, deposits some money on CB to send a request to a local RSU for a c-ride, and pays a fare to a matched driver after the c-ride. A driver registers to CA and her SP, responses to a c-ride hailing message broadcasted by a local RSU, and receives a fare from a rider after the r-ride.

2.2   Security Model

External adversaries can eavesdrop on communication channels, launch attacks, such as impersonation attack, replay attack and tampering attack. SPs are interested in the privacy of users and eager to profile them and their activities by mining some private information from c-ride data [21–23], and they may collude with RSUs to interfere with the matching process toward gaining extra profits. RSUs may be compromised by adversaries or colluding with SPs, thus the matching results will be incorrect. Users are honest-but-curious and a part of them may launch location cheating attacks to mislead an RSU.

2.3 Design Goals

Security. Security contains data confidentiality, data integrity, user authentication and location authentication. The scheme should protect c-ride data from illegal entities, verify requests and responses before they are accepted, authenticate users' identities in an anonymous way, and validate users' locations.

Privacy. (1) User privacy: (anonymity) any user's identity/location is protected from other entities in a normal c-ride; (unlinkability) any two requests/responses from a same rider/driver cannot be linked together; (traceability) any company cannot know any user's real identity unless all SPs disclose it together; (transaction privacy) any transaction's payer, payee, and transferred amount are protect from other entities. (2) SP privacy: any SP cannot know which SP it shares a c-ride with, other SPs' number of users, and ride fares.

Data Auditability. All SPs are able to manage an internally shared ledger and every permissioned entity can verify all c-rides based on it.

Fairness. The rider receives correct matching results within a period of time if he pre-pays for a c-ride. The driver receives a fare after c-ride and cannot gain extra fees. The SPs get a service fee from drivers in c-rides.

3   The Proposed Scheme CoRide

3.1   System Initialization

First, given a security parameter k, CA generates three multiplicative cyclic groups G_1, G_2, G_3 of the same prime order p. Let g_1, g_2 be the generators of G_1, G_2 respectively, and $e : G_1 \times G_2 \to G_3$ be a bilinear map. CA chooses two random numbers $u, v \in \mathbb{Z}_p^*$ as group private keys for SPs, computes $U_1 = g_1^u$, $U_2 = g_2^u$, $V = g_1^v$ as group public keys, and distributes u, v among SPs such that SP_i has two secret shares ss_{i1}, ss_{i2} and u, v can only be recovered by all SPs [24]. CA selects a collision-resistant hash function $H_1 : \{0, 1\}^* \to \mathbb{Z}_p^*$ [7]. Given a security parameter λ, CA picks a signature scheme Sig $:= (\mathcal{G}^{\mathsf{Sig}}, \mathcal{K}^{\mathsf{Sig}}, \mathcal{S}^{\mathsf{Sig}}, \mathcal{V}^{\mathsf{Sig}})$, a public-key encryption scheme Enc $:= (\mathcal{G}^{\mathsf{Enc}}, \mathcal{K}^{\mathsf{Enc}}, \mathcal{E}^{\mathsf{Enc}}, \mathcal{D}^{\mathsf{Enc}})$, a private-key encryption scheme Enc$'$ $:= (\mathcal{G}^{\mathsf{Enc}'}, \mathcal{K}^{\mathsf{Enc}'}, \mathcal{E}^{\mathsf{Enc}'}, \mathcal{D}^{\mathsf{Enc}'})$, samples par^{Sig}, par^{Enc} and $par^{\mathsf{Enc}'}$, generates $\{sk_{SP_i}^{\mathsf{Enc}}, pk_{SP_i}^{\mathsf{Enc}}\}$. CA sets public parameters $par_1 := (p, G_1, G_2, G_3, g_1, g_2, e, U_1, U_2, V, H_1, par^{\mathsf{Sig}}, par^{\mathsf{Enc}}, \{pk_{SP_i}^{\mathsf{Enc}}\})$ [9].

Second, SPs divide the c-ride hailing area into a grid set $\mathcal{GR} = \{gr[1], gr[2], ..., gr[n_G]\}$ and form them into a tree such that the root index is 1 and the node index increases from top to bottom. SPs choose par_2 including an environmental signal filtering function ϕ, a Bloom filter B with length f, a hash function tuple $h := \{h_1, h_2..., h_o\}$ and $\mathcal{GR}$. Third, SPs select par_3 including a length w for prefix, an indistinguishable Bloom filter B' with f' twins, a hash function $H'(.) = H'(.)\%2$, and an authentication code HMAC [18]. Last, given a security parameter λ, SPs select a hash function H_2, three collision-resistant pseudo-random functions $\mathsf{PRF}_x^{add}(i) = \mathsf{PRF}_x(00||i), \mathsf{PRF}_x^{sn}(i) = \mathsf{PRF}_x(01||i), \mathsf{PRF}_x^{pk}(i) = \mathsf{PRF}_x(10||i)$ where x is a seed, construct C_{POUR} for NP statement POUR at λ, probabilistically sample a proving key pk_{POUR} and a verifying key vk_{POUR} [9], establish decentralized payment scheme $\Pi^{DAP} := (\mathsf{CreateAdd}, \mathsf{Deposit}, \mathsf{Pour}, \mathsf{Redeem})$, and create $SC := (\mathsf{Verify}, \mathsf{Hail}, \mathsf{Match})$. It is worth pointing out that smart contract prevents RSUs and SPs from colluding to gain their own benefits. SPs set $par_4 := (H_2, \mathsf{PRF}_x^{add}(i), \mathsf{PRF}_x^{sn}(i), \mathsf{PRF}_x^{pk}(i), pk_{\mathsf{POUR}}, vk_{\mathsf{POUR}}, SC)$.

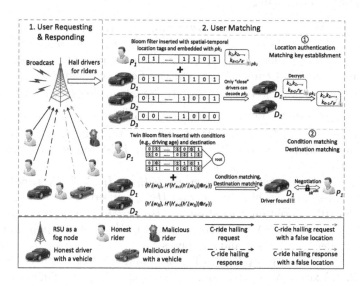

Fig. 2. C-ride requesting and responding

3.2   Entity Registration

A rider with identity R_i belonging to SP_z joins the c-ride hailing system by first registering to CA: CA chooses a secret key SK_{R_i}, computes $\{\mathcal{E}\}^{\mathsf{Enc}}(R_i||SK_{R_i})$, i.e., a multi-encryption of R_i and SK_{R_i} using $\mathcal{E}^{\mathsf{Enc}}$ and $\{pk_{SP_j}^{\mathsf{Enc}}\}_{j=1,j\neq z}^s$, chooses a random number $r_{R_i} \in \mathbb{Z}_p^*$ with $r_{R_i} + u \neq 0 \mod p$, computes $\hat{r}_{R_i} = g_1^{1/(r_{R_i}+u)}$, and returns SK_{R_i}, an authorized anonymous key $ak_i := (r_{R_i}, \hat{r}_{R_i})$, $\{\mathcal{E}\}^{\mathsf{Enc}}(R_i||SK_{R_i})$ and a signature $\sigma_{R_i}^{CA}$ on $(\hat{r}_{R_i}, \{\mathcal{E}\}^{\mathsf{Enc}}(R_i||SK_{R_i}))$ to R_i. R_i sends $(\hat{r}_{R_i}, \{\mathcal{E}\}^{\mathsf{Enc}}(R_i||SK_{R_i}), \sigma_{R_i}^{CA})$ to SP_z which stores $(\hat{r}_i^u, \{\mathcal{E}\}^{\mathsf{Enc}}(R_i||SK_{R_i})$ after checking the signature's validity. R_i chooses l_i random numbers $\{x_{ij}\}_{j=1}^{l_i}$ as private keys and computes public keys $\{Y_{ij} = g_1^{x_{ij}}\}_{j=1}^{l_i}$. Then R_i selects $K+1$

secret keys $\mathcal{SK}_{R_i} := \{sk_{R_i 1}, sk_{R_i 2}, ..., sk_{R_i K+1}\}$ and constructs a pseudo-random hash function tuple $h'_{R_i}(.) := \{h'_{R_i 1}(.), h'_{R_i 2}(), ..., h'_{R_i K}(.)\}$ where $h'_{R_i j}(.) :=$ $\mathsf{HMAC}_{sk_{R_i j}}(.)\% f'$ for $1 \leq j \leq K$ and $h'_{R_i K+1}(.) = \mathsf{HMAC}_{sk_{R_i K+1}}(.)$. Next, R_i computes $(sk^{\mathsf{Enc}}_{R_i}, pk^{\mathsf{Enc}}_{R_i}) = \mathcal{K}^{\mathsf{Enc}}(par_{\mathsf{Enc}})$, randomly samples a seed $s^{sk}_{R_i}$, computes $s^{pk}_{R_i} = \mathsf{PRF}^{add}_{s^{sk}_{R_i}}(0)$, and sets $add^{pk}_{R_i} := (s^{pk}_{R_i}, pk^{\mathsf{Enc}}_{R_i}), add^{sk}_{R_i} := (s^{sk}_{R_i}, sk^{\mathsf{Enc}}_{R_i})$. R_i also buys some intercompany tokens from SP_z as digital currency. Similarly, a driver D_j obtains $(SK_{D_j}, ak_{D_j}, \{\mathcal{E}\}^{\mathsf{Enc}}(D_j||SK_{D_j}), \sigma^{CA}_{D_j}, add^{pk}_{D_j}, add^{sk}_{D_j})$.

SPs utilize RSUs in c-rides by permitting them to join the $\mathcal{CB}$ network and executing the smart contract SC on each RSU to perform user matching and fare payment. Each RSU RS_m has $add^{sk}_{RS_m} := (s^{sk}_{RS_m}, sk^{\mathsf{Enc}}_{RS_m})$, an address public key $add^{pk}_{RS_m} := (s^{pk}_{RS_m}, pk^{\mathsf{Enc}}_{RS_m})$ and a public signing key pair $(sk^{\mathsf{Sig}}_{RS_m}, pk^{\mathsf{Sig}}_{RS_m})$.

3.3 C-Ride Requesting

A rider R_i belonging to SP_z is now hailing a c-ride through a local RSU RS_m. First, R_i deposits two coins $\mathbf{c}_1, \mathbf{c}_2$ of value v_1, v_2 at RS_m as a prepaid fare. R_i randomly samples a PRF^{sn} seed τ, two commitment trapdoors tr_1, tr_2, and computes $cm_1 := \mathsf{Com}_{tr_1}(s^{pk}_{R_i}||\tau), cm_2 := \mathsf{Com}_{tr_2}(v_1||cm_1)$ where Com is a statistically-hiding non-interactive commitment scheme [9]. R_i sets $\mathbf{c}_1 := (add^{pk}_{R_i}, v_1, \tau, tr_1, tr_2, cm_2)$ and a deposit transaction $\mathsf{tx}^{\mathsf{Dep}}_{R_i 1} := (cm_2, v_1, cm_1, tr_2, time)$. After obtaining $\mathbf{c}_2, \mathsf{tx}^{\mathsf{Dep}}_{R_i 2}, R_i$ uploads $(\mathbf{c}_1, \mathbf{c}_2)$ and $(\mathsf{tx}^{\mathsf{Dep}}_{R_i 1}, \mathsf{tx}^{\mathsf{Dep}}_{R_i 2})$ via RS_m to coin pool CP and transaction pool TP, respectively. This step is not necessary for each requesting.

Second, R_i computes a pseudo-identity $pid_{R_i} = H(R_i||RS_m||time)$, collects environmental signals within time period (t_1, t_2), inserts observations $y(t_1, t_2)$ into $B_{R_i 1} = \{0\}^f$ to obtain a location tag $B_{R_i 1} := \mathsf{Ins}(h(y_i(t_1, t_2)), B_{R_i 1})$ [17]. R_i computes a pair of RSA keys $sk_{R_i}, pk_{R_i} \in \{0, 1\}^{len}$, embeds pk_{R_i} into $B_{R_i 1}$: $En_{R_i} = \mathsf{Encode}(f, len, pk_{R_i})$, and computes $S_{R_i} = En_{R_i} - B_{R_i 1}$. R_i transforms current location loc_{R_i} into $\mathcal{GR}_{R_i}$ to be the minimal set of vicinity region, and inserts grid indexes into $B_{R_i 2} := \mathsf{Ins}(h(\mathcal{GR}_{R_i}||pk_{R_i}), B_{R_i 2})$. By doing this, R_i has embedded his public key for proximity matching and encrypted current location.

Third, R_i encrypts $\mathcal{SK}_{R_i}$ and a random number $r_{B'}$ using pk_{R_i} and obtains $E_{R_i} = \mathcal{E}^{\mathsf{Enc'}}(pk_{R_i}, \mathcal{SK}_{R_i}||r_{B'})$. For non-numeric conditions, R_i encodes it into a keyword by concatenating its corresponding attribute name and obtains a set of condition keywords $\mathcal{W}_{R_i}$ [18]. For each keyword w_j, R_i hashes it into f' twins $B'_{R_i 1} := \mathsf{Ins}(h'(w_j), B'_{R_i 1})$. For each twin $B'_{R_i 1}[h'_i(w_j)]$, R_i assigns $B'_{R_i 1}[h'_i(w_j)][H'(h'_{K+1}(h'_i(w_j)) \oplus r_{B'})] = 1$ and $B'_{R_i 1}[1 - h'_i(w_j)][H'(h'_{K+1}(h'_i(w_j)) \oplus r_{B'})] = 0$. For the numeric destination grid gr_{R_i}, R_i computes its prefix family, encodes it into a keyword by concatenating its corresponding attribute name, and computes a similar $B'_{R_i 2}$. Then, R_i constructs an IBTree T_{R_i} using two leaf nodes $B'_{R_i 1}$ and $B'_{R_i 2}$. Using this method, R_i has encrypted his matching keys, conditions, and destination. R_j generates an encrypted c-ride data packet $Pa_{R_i} = \mathcal{E}^{\mathsf{Enc'}}(SK_{R_i}, loc_{R_i}||\mathcal{W}_{R_i}||gr_{R_i}||time)$.

Last, R_i forms a c-ride request $Req_{R_i} := (t_1, t_2, S_{R_i}, B_{R_i 2}, E_{R_i}, T_{R_i}, Pa_{R_i})$, computes an anonymous certificate $C_{R_i} := \{Y \| V_1 \| V_2 \| \tilde{h} \| \tilde{s}_1 \| \tilde{s}_2 \| \tilde{s}_3\}$ and a signature σ_{R_i} on Req_{R_i} [7], and sends $(pid_{R_i}, Req_{R_i}, C_{R_i}, \sigma_{R_i})$ a local RSU RS_m. The process of c-ride requesting and responding is depicted in Fig. 2.

3.4 C-Ride Responding

After receiving Req_{R_i}, RS_m first runs SC.Verify. RS_m verifies the validity of C_{R_i}, σ_{R_i} [7] and verifies cm_2 in $\mathsf{tx}_{R_i 1}^{\mathsf{Dep}}$ is a coin commitment of a coin of value v_1. RS_m sets $cm' := \mathsf{Com}_{tr_2}(v_1 \| cm_1)$ and accepts $\mathsf{tx}_{R_i 1}^{\mathsf{Dep}}$ if $cm' := cm_2$, else reject it. Similarly, RS_m verifies $\mathsf{tx}_{R_i 2}^{\mathsf{Dep}}$. RS_m uploads $\mathbf{c}_1, \mathbf{c}_2$ to CP and $\mathsf{tx}_{R_i 1}^{\mathsf{Dep}}, \mathsf{tx}_{R_i 2}^{\mathsf{Dep}}$ to TP.

Then RS_m runs SC.Hail. RS_m broadcasts a hailing message $hail_{R_i} := \{t_1, t_2, S_{R_i}, E_{R_i}\}$ to drivers nearby. After receiving $hail_{R_i}$, each available driver D_j belonging to $SP_{z'}$ at current location loc_{D_j} computes a pseudo-identity pid_{D_j}, computes B_{j1} as the rider did, and recovers a pk'_{R_i} from S_{R_i} [17]. We note that only when D_j is in R_i's vicinity, can D_j recover pk_{R_i} correctly and D_j cannot verify whether she has retrieved a correct pk_{R_i}. D_j chooses a communication key $sk_{D_j}^{com}$, computes $eid_{D_j} = \mathcal{E}^{\mathsf{Enc}}(pk'_{R_i}, pid_{D_j} \| sk_{R_j}^{com})$ and broadcasts eid_{D_j}. D_j collects $eids$ from nearby drivers to form a location proof $\mathcal{P}_{D_j}$, and computes $h(gr_{D_j} \| pk'_{R_i})$. By doing this, D_j has encrypted her current location gr_{D_j}.

Next, D_j can decrypt E_{R_i} using correct pk'_{R_i} to obtain $(\mathcal{SK}_{R_i} \| r_{B'}) = \mathcal{D}^{\mathsf{Enc}'}(pk'_{R_i}, E_{R_i})$. Given a set of condition keywords $\mathcal{W}_{D_j}$, D_j computes $\mathcal{TR}_{D_j 1}$ containing $\{h'(w), H'(h'_{R_i K+1}(h'_{R_i}(w)) \oplus r_{B'})$ for each keyword w. D_j computes destination trapdoors $\mathcal{TR}_{D_j 2}$. Using this method, D_j has encrypted her conditions and potential destinations. D_j generates an encrypted data packet $Pa_{D_j} = \mathcal{E}^{\mathsf{Enc}'}(SK_{D_j}, loc_{D_j} \| \mathcal{W}_{D_j} \| gr_{D_i} \| time)$. D_j forms a c-ride response $Res_j := (eid_{D_j}, \mathcal{P}_{D_j}, h(gr_{D_j} \| pk'_{R_i}), \mathcal{TR}_{D_j 1}, \mathcal{TR}_{D_j 2}, Pa_{D_j})$, and sends $(pid_{D_j}, Res_{D_j}, C_{D_j}, \sigma_{D_j})$ to RS_m.

Last, RS_m runs SC.Match. RS_m queries $h(gr_{D_j} \| pk'_{R_i})$ and $\mathcal{TR}_{D_j 1}, \mathcal{TR}_{D_j 2}$ into $B_{R_i 2}$ and T_{R_i}, returns to R_i one eid_{D_j} existing in $\hat{B}_{i2}$ and T_{R_i}. R_i decrypts $pid_{D_j} \| sk_{R_j}^{com} = \mathcal{D}^{\mathsf{Enc}}(sk_{R_i}, eid_{D_j})$. R_i communicates with D_j using sk_j^{com} to determine a precise pick-up/get-off location. After receiving a confirmation from R_i and D_j, RS_m uploads Pa_{R_i}, Pa_{D_j} to SPs for backup and sends a handshake transaction $\mathsf{tx}_{R_i D_j}^{Han}$ with a signature to TP:

$$\mathsf{tx}_{R_i D_j}^{Han} = (pid_{R_i}, pid_{D_j}, RS_m, V_1^{R_i}, V_2^{R_i}, V_1^{D_j}, V_2^{D_j}, H_2(Pa_{R_i} \| Pa_{D_j}), time).$$

3.5 C-Ride Termination

After a c-ride is complete, the rider R_i pays a fare to a matched driver D_j by splitting previously deposited two old coins $\mathbf{c}_1, \mathbf{c}_2$ to two new parts: the first one is for his refund and the second one is sent for D_j. Specifically, for $a \in \{1, 2\}$, R_i computes $sn_a = \mathsf{PRF}_{add_{R_i}^{sk}}^{sn}(\tau_a)$, randomly samples a PRF^{sn} seed τ_a^{new}

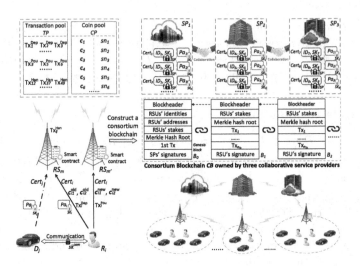

Fig. 3. Construction of the consortium blockchain

(the second one is sampled by D_j to defend double spending attacks) and two commitment trapdoors tr_{a1}^{new}, $tr_{a,2}^{new}$, computes $cm_{a1}^{new} := \mathsf{Com}_{tr_{a1}^{new}}(s_a^{pk,new}||\tau_a^{new})$ and $cm_2^{new} := \mathsf{Com}_{tr_{a2}^{new}}(v_a^{new}||cm_{a1}^{new})$, sets $\mathbf{c}_a^{new} := (add^{pk,new}, v_a^{new}, \tau_a^{new}, tr_a^{new}, tr_a^{new}, cm_2^{new})$ and sets $\mathbf{C}_a = \mathcal{E}^{\mathsf{Enc}'}(sk_{D_j}^{com}, v_a^{new}||\tau_a^{new}||tr_{a1}^{new}||tr_{a2}^{new})$. Here, $s_1^{pk,new}$ and $s_2^{pk,new}$ correspond to R_i and D_j, respectively.

Then R_i generates $(sk^{\mathsf{Sig}}, pk^{\mathsf{Sig}})$, computes $h^{\mathsf{Sig}} = H_2(pk^{\mathsf{Sig}})$, $h_1 = \mathsf{PRF}_{s_{R_i1}^{sk}}^{pk}$ (h^{Sig}), $h_2 = \mathsf{PRF}_{s_{R_i2}^{sk}}^{pk}(h^{\mathsf{Sig}})$, sets $\overrightarrow{x} := (root, sn_1, sn_2, cm_{12}^{new}, cm_{22}^{new}, 0, h^{\mathsf{Sig}}, h_1, h_2)$, $\overrightarrow{a} := (path_1, path_2, \mathbf{c}_1, \mathbf{c}_2, add_{R_i1}^{sk}, add_{R_i2}^{sk}, \mathbf{c}_1^{new}, \mathbf{c}_2^{new})$, computes a non-interactive proof π for the statement $\overrightarrow{x}$, sets $M := (\overrightarrow{x}, \pi, \mathbf{C}_1, \mathbf{C}_2)$, computes $\sigma = \mathcal{S}^{\mathsf{Sig}}(sk^{\mathsf{Sig}}, M)$, sets a pour transaction $\mathsf{tx}_{R_i}^{\mathsf{Pou}} := (root, sn_1, sn_2, cm_{1,2}^{new}, cm_{2,2}^{new}, 0, info, pk^{\mathsf{Sig}}, h_1, h_2, \pi, \mathbf{C}_1, \mathbf{C}_2, \sigma, time)$, where $path$ gives the authentication path from a coin commitment appearing in the list of all coin commitments to the root of a Merkle tree over the list. R_i sends $(\mathbf{c}_1^{new}, \mathbf{c}_2^{new}, \mathsf{tx}_{R_i}^{\mathsf{Pou}})$ to an RSU $RS_{m'}$ (Fig. 3).

Next, $RS_{m'}$ runs $SC.\mathsf{Verify}$ and verifies $\mathsf{tx}_{R_i}^{\mathsf{Pou}}$. If it passes, $RS_{m'}$ uploads $\mathbf{c}_1^{new}, \mathbf{c}_2^{new}$ to CP and sends $\mathsf{tx}_{R_i}^{\mathsf{Pou}}$ to TP.

Last, D_j redeems her fare $\mathbf{c}_2^{new}$ through her SP by computing $(v_2, \tau_2^{new}, tr_{21}^{new}, tr_{22}^{new}) = \mathcal{D}^{\mathsf{Enc}'}(sk_{D_j}^{com}, \mathbf{C}_2)$, verifies that whether $cm_{22}^{new} := \mathsf{Com}_{tr_{22}^{new}}(v_2^{new}||\mathsf{Com}_{tr_{21}^{new}}(s_{D_j}^{pk,new}||\tau_2^{new}))$ and $sn_2' = \mathsf{PRF}_{add_{D_j}^{sk}}^{sn}(\tau_2)$ is not on CP. If they pass, D_j outputs $\mathbf{c} := (add_{D_j}^{pk}, v_2^{new}, \tau_2^{new}, tr_{21}^{new}, tr_{22}^{new}, cm_{12}^{new})$ and pays a fixed service fee (e.g., \$1/c-ride) to SP.

We use PoS mechanism [19] to periodically elect a leader RSU to generate a new block and avoid forks. Rather than RSUs spending computational resources and time on the leader election process, they instead run a function that randomly selects one RSU proportionally to the stake or balance that each RSU possesses according to the current blockchain ledger. Specifically, each RSU is a stakeholder and its stake is the number of paired c-rides.

3.6 User Tracking

If a complaint has been filed against a malicious user i with a pseudo-identity pid_i and an anonymous certificate C_i, SPs recover the group secret keys u, v together from their secret shares and compute $V_2^u/V_1^v = \hat{r}_i^u \cdot V^{uro}/U_1^{vro} = \hat{r}_i^u \cdot g_1^{uvro}/g_1^{uvro} = \hat{r}_i^u$ and track the encrypted identity of i through looking up the entry $\{\hat{r}_i^u, \{\mathcal{E}\}^{\mathsf{Enc}}(i\|SK_i)\}$ in their tracking list. If a matched record is found at SP_z, SP_z first asks the other SPs to decrypt $\{\mathcal{E}\}^{\mathsf{Enc}}(i\|SK_i)$ using their secret keys to obtain $i\|SK_i = \{\mathcal{D}\}^{\mathsf{Enc}}(\{\mathcal{E}\}^{\mathsf{Enc}}(i\|SK_i))$, and then recover its c-ride data $(time\|loc_i\|\mathcal{W}_i\|gr_i) = \mathcal{D}^{\mathsf{Enc}'}(\mathcal{E}^{\mathsf{Enc}'}(SK_i, Pa_i))$. Finally, SPs append this malicious user into an intercompany blacklist. It is worth noting that even though the group secret keys are recovered, CoRide still needs all SPs to recovers the identity of a user which prevents any SP opening an identity on its own.

4 Security and Privacy Analysis

Security. First, a rider R_i's current location is inserted into a Bloom filter B_{R_i1} and his public key pk_{R_i} is embedded into a fuzzy extractor S_{R_i}. Any entity which is not physically close to R_i cannot obtain pk_{R_i}. Due to the nature of the BCH decoder, any driver D_j cannot tell whether she has extracted a correct pk_{R_i} [17]. Therefore, no one can acquire R_i's location. A driver's current location is transformed into o hash values $h(gr_{D_j}\|pk'_{R_i})$. SPs and RSUs cannot learn D_j's location without R_i's public key. Since the RSUs do not relay $h(gr_{D_j}\|pk'_{R_i})$ to R_i, R_i cannot know D_j's location either. Second, the IBtree based querying scheme is IND-CKA secure against an adaptive adversary $\mathcal{A}$ [18] because a probabilistic polynomial-time simulator can be constructed to simulate future unknown queries, and $\mathcal{A}$ is not able to distinguish the results of the real secure index from those of the simulator with a non-negligible probability. The use of secure one-way hash functions h achieves one-wayness and the use of the hash function $H'(.)$ achieves equivocation for each item in an indistinguishable Bloom filter IBF. For each twin in an IBF, the cell is randomly chosen. A random number is used in an IBF to cut off relations between IBFs. Third, the data integrity is guaranteed by users' signatures [7]. We generate a signature on a user' r-ride request and a driver's c-ride response by using anonymous authentication, and the RSU cannot recover a user i's anonymous key $\hat{r}_i$ from the anonymous certificate C_i. Fourth, a user's location is authenticated by the location tags [17], if he is not near drivers, he cannot collect corresponding environmental signals which are used to provide a location proof.

Privacy. First, a user's anonymous certificate reveals nothing about user's identity and it is randomized in each c-ride requesting and c-ride responding.

Each user computes a new pseudo-identity in each requesting and responding. Users' locations are transformed into Bloom filters as explained above. Every two requests/responses from a same rider/driver cannot be linked together because they use different pseudo-identities, randomized location Bloom filters, randomized c-ride data packets. Users' identities are encrypted by all SPs' public keys such that they can only be disclosed if all SPs agree to reveal them unanimously. Even if a SP can open a user's anonymous key, its corresponding identity and secret key are encrypted by all SPs. Therefore, the anonymity, unlinkability, and traceability are guaranteed. Second, transaction privacy is protected due to the ledger indistinguishability of Zerocash [9] meaning that the transactions disclose no information to the adversary $\mathcal{A}'$ beyond the values of deposited coins, information strings, and number of transactions, even when the adversary adaptively induces honest parties to perform transaction operations of its choice. In a ledger indistinguishability experiment L-IND, challenger $\mathcal{C}$ samples a random bit b, initializes two Π^{DAP} oracles $\mathcal{O}_0$ and $\mathcal{O}_1$ and maintains two ledgers L_0 and L_2. $\mathcal{C}$ provides $\mathcal{A}'$ with $L_{\text{left}} := L_b$ and $L_{\text{right}} := L_{1-b}$. In L-IND, $\mathcal{A}'$ issues two queries Q_0, Q_1 of the same type. If the type is CreateAdd, then a same address is created at $\mathcal{O}_0$ and $\mathcal{O}_1$; if it is to Deposit, Pour or Redeem, then Q_0 is forwarded to L_0 and Q_1 to L_1; if $\mathcal{A}'$ inserts arbitrary transactions, Q_0 is forwarded to L_{left} and Q_1 is forwarded to L_{right}. In each case, the response to $\mathcal{A}$ is computed independently of b. At the end of L-IND, $\mathcal{A}'$ outputs a bit b', and it wins if $b' = b$. Ledger indistinguishability guarantees that $\mathcal{A}'$ wins L-IND with a probability at most negligibly bigger than $1/2$, i.e., $\mathsf{Adv}_{\Pi,\mathcal{A}'}^{\text{L-IND}}(\lambda) < negl(\lambda)$. Third, during any c-ride, the information of which SP a user belongs to is not included in any interaction or anonymized, such as $Cert_i, pid_i$. Although a user's The anonymous certificate $Cert_i$ and the corresponding encrypted identity and secret key $\{\mathcal{E}\}^{\text{Enc}}(i, SK_i)$ can be used to disclose his identity and SP related information, they are only stored at his SP and revealing them requires efforts from all SPs. The fare is also protect from SPs via Zerocash. Although c-ride data are stored at all SPs, they cannot be opened unless all SPs participate.

Data Auditability. We build a consortium blackchain to keep c-ride records in a verifiable and tamper-proof manner. The stakeholders, i.e., RSUs, must be invited or permitted by SPs to join the blockchain network and create new blocks. Other entities without an invitation from SPs cannot insert any block to the blockchain. Each RSU maintains a backup of an intercompany shared and append-only ledger of c-ride records. All the transactions can be verified by entities within the blockchain network and each RSU runs a smart contract to faithfully pair users, which guarantees immutability.

Fairness. Due to the verifiability of smart contracts, the matching process is protected from malicious tampering and riders can always receive correct pairing results, even though a SP can collude with an RSU. Transaction non-malleability guarantees that no adversary can change the data stored within a pour transaction tx^{Pou} and transaction balance guarantees that no adversary can obtain extra fare than what she deposited or received via payments from riders. Moreover, the second randomness number τ_2^{new} in ride termination phase is sampled by driver and the $add_2^{pk,\text{new}}$ is the driver's public address, therefore, only the driver can redeem the new coin poured by the rider. The SP can get a service fee from drivers when they redeem their fares.

5 Performance Analysis

5.1 Implementation Details

We instantiate 100 riders and 100 drivers on a laptop with 8.00 GB of RAM, an Intel Core i7-7500 CPU @2.70 GHz, running Windows 10 Home. The smart contracts are deployed on 10 desktops with 6 GB of RAM, an Intel Core i5 CPU@3.20 GHz, running 64-bit Microsoft Windows 7 Enterprise. We instantiate 3 service providers by an Amazon cloud servers, two Alibaba cloud servers. The cryptographic toolset we used is Miracl. Table 1 lists experimental parameters.

Table 1. Experimental parameters

Parameters	Value
$p, q, n_1, n_2, n_3, n_4, n_G, n_{Tx}$	$\|p\| = 160$, $\|q\| = 512, 3, 10, 100, 100, 1023, 8$
$H_1, H'(.), H_2; h, h'$	SHA256; {SHA224, SHA384, SHA512}
$\mathsf{PRF}_x^{add}(.), \mathsf{PRF}_x^{sn}(.), \mathsf{PRF}_x^{pk}(.)$; Sig/Enc, Enc'	$SHA3 - 224; RSA, AES$
l, f, f', o, K	$10, 1000, 1000, 3, 2$

5.2 Experiments on Simulated Network

We first count the number of the cryptographic operations to analyze its computational costs. The main time consuming operation for a rider is Request which takes approximately 56 ms, each driver spends 55 ms on responding to a hailing message, and it costs an RSU less than 85 ms to verify a c-ride request and 1.86 ms to match a rider and driver. Detailed results are shown in Table 2.

Table 2. Computational costs

Rider (ms)				Driver (ms)			RSU (ms)			
Register	Deposit	Request	Pour	Register	Respond	Redeem	Verify1[a]	Verify2[b]	Matching	BICr.[c]
37.00	0.06	56.47	0.05	37.00	55.23	0.06	0.02	84.38	1.86	1.73

Rider (KB)			Driver (KB)		RSU (KB)			SP (ms)		
Deposit	Request	Pour	Respond	Redeem	BrCa[d]	Match	BICr	Dublin	Beijing	Dublin
0.61	0.90	1.02	0.92	0.21	0.15	0.72	0.26	33	263	114

[a] Verify tx^{Dep}; [b] Verify $(pid, Res/Req, C, \sigma)$; [c] Create a new block; [d] Broadcast

5.3 Comparison with Existing Work

We first compare the computational costs for riders in their Deposit, Request and Pour, because they are the main operations for a rider, even though the other three schemes do not have Deposit and Pour. Figure 4(a) shows that CoRide outperforms PPRS and ORide, and approximates AMA. The computational costs for drivers are compared in Respond and Redeem, Fig. 4(b) shows a similar result as Fig. 4(a). RSUs have two operations Verify and Match. Verify in our scheme contains verifying deposited coins and verifying users' certificates and signatures. The comparison results in Fig. 4(c) shows that CoRide has the lowest cost among all schemes in Verify and has a small cost in Match. Then we compare the communication overhead for riders. Since the riders have to deposit coins and pour coins, their communication overhead in CoRide are inevitably higher than other schemes, as depicted in Fig. 4(d). For the drivers, their communication overhead is moderate in comparison, as depicted in Fig. 4(e). Each RSU has to run Broadcast, Match, and BlockCreation, and the other schemes do not have an RSU in their designs. The result is depicted in Fig. 4(f).

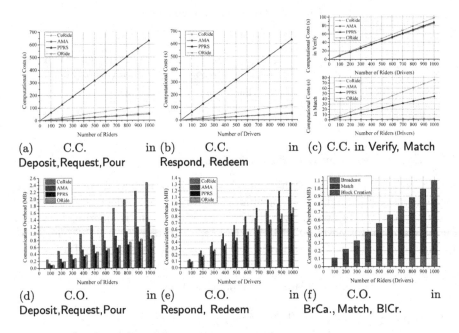

(a)   C.C.   in (b)   C.C.   in (c) C.C. in Verify, Match
Deposit, Request, Pour   Respond, Redeem

(d)   C.O.   in (e)   C.O.   in (f)   C.O.   in
Deposit, Request, Pour   Respond, Redeem   BrCa., Match, BlCr.

Fig. 4. Comparison with existing work.

6 Conclusion

Traditional privacy-preserving ride hailing schemes rely on a central service provider to complete user matching tasks and different service providers have isolated user datasets. In this study, we proposed a concept of collaborative-ride and constructed a decentralized design using fog computing and blockchain technologies to pair riders with drivers from different service providers, record c-rides on an intercompany ledger, and defend malicious adversaries. Different from existing RHS schemes, our matching results are verifiable and immutable, and anonymous payment between users is also achieved. Experimental results demonstrate the practicability and efficiency of our scheme.

Acknowledgment. This work was supported by the National Natural Science Foundation of China (NSFC) under the grant No. U1836102 and the China National Key Research and Development Program under Grant 2016YFB0800301.

References

1. 2017: The Year The Rideshare Industry Crushed The Taxi (2017). https://rideshareapps.com/2015-rideshare-infographic
2. Bonomi, F., Milito, R.A., Zhu, J., Addepalli, S.: Fog computing and its role in the internet of things. In: Proceedings Mobile Cloud Computing Workshop, pp. 13–16 (2012)
3. Zhu, L., Li, M., Zhang, Z., Zhan, Q.: ASAP: an anonymous smart-parking and payment scheme in vehicular networks. In: IEEE TDSC (2018)
4. How to keep Uber from becoming a terrifying monopoly (2017). http://theweek.com/articles/681459/how-keep-uber-from-becoming-terrifying-monopoly
5. Private mobility services need to share their data. Here's how (2017). https://www.citylab.com/transportation/2017/07/private-mobility-services-need-to-share-their-data-heres-how/532482
6. Boneh, D., Boyen, X., Shacham, H.: Short group signatures. In: Franklin, M. (ed.) CRYPTO 2004. LNCS, vol. 3152, pp. 41–55. Springer, Heidelberg (2004). https://doi.org/10.1007/978-3-540-28628-8_3
7. Lu, R., Lin, X., Luan, T.H., Liang, X., Shen, X.: Pseudonym changing at social spots: an effective strategy for location privacy in VANETs. In: IEEE TVT (2012)
8. He, W., Liu, X., Ren, M.: Location cheating: a security challenge to location-based social network services. In: Proceedings 31st ICDCS, pp. 740–749 (2011)
9. Ben-Sasson, E., et al.: Zerocash: decentralized anonymous payments from bitcoin. In: Proceedings IEEE 35th S&P, pp. 459–474 (2014)
10. Garman, C., Green, M., Miers, I.: Accountable privacy for decentralized anonymous payments. In: Grossklags, J., Preneel, B. (eds.) FC 2016. LNCS, vol. 9603, pp. 81–98. Springer, Heidelberg (2017). https://doi.org/10.1007/978-3-662-54970-4_5
11. Li, M., Zhu, L., Lin, X.: Privacy-preserving traffic monitoring with false report filtering via fog-assisted vehicular crowdsensing. In: IEEE TSC (2019)
12. Zhu, L., Li, M., Zhang, Z.: Secure fog-assisted crowdsensing with collusion resistance: from data reporting to data requesting. IEEE IoT J. **6**, 5473–5484 (2019)
13. Nakamoto, S.: Bitcoin: A peer-to-peer electronic cash system (2008)
14. Conti, M., Kumar, S., Lal, C., Ruj, S.: A survey on security and privacy issues of bitcoin. IEEE Commun. Surv. Tutorials **20**(4), 3416–3452 (2018)
15. Jaballah, W.B., Conti, M., Lal, C.: A survey on software-defined VANETs: benefits, challenges, and future directions. https://arxiv.org/abs/1904.04577

16. Baza, M., Nabil, M., Lasla, N., Fidan, K., Mahmoud, M., Abdallah, M.: Blockchain-based firmware update scheme tailored for autonomous vehicles. arXiv preprint arXiv:1811.05905 (2018)

17. Zheng, Y., Li, M., Lou, W., Hou, Y.T.: Location based handshake and private proximity test with location tags. IEEE TDCS **14**(4), 406–419 (2017)

18. Li, R., Liu, A.X.: Adaptively secure conjunctive query processing over encrypted data for cloud computing. In: Proceedings IEEE 33rd ICDE, pp. 697–708 (2017)

19. Kiayias, A., Russell, A., David, B., Oliynykov, R.: Ouroboros: a provably secure proof-of-stake blockchain protocol. In: Katz, J., Shacham, H. (eds.) CRYPTO 2017. LNCS, vol. 10401, pp. 357–388. Springer, Cham (2017). https://doi.org/10.1007/978-3-319-63688-7_12

20. Ethereum. https://github.com/ethereum/mist/releases

21. Ni, J., Zhang, K., Lin, X., Yang, H., Shen, X.: AMA: anonymous mutual authentication with traceability in carpooling systems. In: Proceedings ICC, pp. 1–6 (2016)

22. Pham, A., Dacosta, I., Endignoux, G., Troncoso-Pastoriza, J.R., Huguenin, K., Hubaux, J.-P.: ORide: a privacy-preserving yet accountable ride-hailing service. In: Proceedings 26th USENIX Security Symposium, pp. 1235–1252 (2017)

23. Sherif, A.B.T., et al.: Privacy-preserving ride sharing scheme for autonomous vehicles in big data era. IEEE IoT J. **4**(2), 611–618 (2017)

24. Pedersen, T.P.: Non-interactive and information-theoretic secure verifiable secret sharing. In: Feigenbaum, J. (ed.) CRYPTO 1991. LNCS, vol. 576, pp. 129–140. Springer, Heidelberg (1992). https://doi.org/10.1007/3-540-46766-1_9

Better Clouds

Non-Interactive MPC with Trusted Hardware Secure Against Residual Function Attacks

Ryan Karl, Timothy Burchfield, Jonathan Takeshita, and Taeho Jung[(✉)]

University of Notre Dame, Notre Dame, IN 46556, USA
{rkarl,tburchfi,jtakeshi,tjung}@nd.edu

Abstract. Secure multiparty computation (MPC) has been repeatedly optimized, and protocols with two communication rounds and strong security guarantees have been achieved. While progress has been made constructing non-interactive protocols with just one-round of online communication (*i.e.,* non-interactive MPC or NI-MPC), since correct evaluation must be guaranteed with only one round, these protocols are by their nature vulnerable to the residual function attack in the standard model. This is because a party that receives a garbled circuit may repeatedly evaluate the circuit locally, while varying their own inputs and fixing the inputs of others to learn the values entered by other participants. We present the first MPC protocol with a one-round online phase that is secure against the residual function attack. We also present rigorous proofs of correctness and security in the covert adversary model, a reduction of the malicious model that is stronger than the semi-honest model and better suited for modeling the behaviour of parties in the real world, for our protocol. Furthermore, we rigorously analyze the communication and computational complexity of current state of the art protocols which require two rounds of communication or one round during the online-phase with a reduced security requirement, and demonstrate that our protocol is comparable to or outperforms their complexity.

Keywords: Non-Interactive MPC · Communication round complexity · Trusted hardware

1 Introduction

Secure multiparty computation (MPC) is formally defined as functionality that allows a group of parties to jointly compute a function over their inputs, while keeping those inputs private. Two conditions must be satisfied: Correctness (the correct value must be computed from the given inputs) and Security (no information about the function's inputs should be gleaned after computation, other than the output). One of the primary tools for achieving this goal is the garbled circuit [35], where one party (the sender) encrypts a Boolean circuit and then assigns two randomly generated strings (labels) to each wire in the circuit: one each for 0 and 1. The sender also encrypts the output entry for each

S. Chen et al. (Eds.): SecureComm 2019, LNICST 305, pp. 425–439, 2019.
https://doi.org/10.1007/978-3-030-37231-6_25

of the circuit's gate's truth tables so that the table can only be decrypted if a receiving party has the correct two input labels. A great deal of work has been invested into extending and optimizing MPC protocols to build more secure, efficient, and scalable MPC systems [26,36]. Generally, modern MPC protocols are divided into three phases: the function-independent preprocessing phase, where parties do not need to know their inputs or the function to be computed, the function-dependent preprocessing phase, where parties know the function, but do not know their inputs, and the online phase, where parties evaluate the agreed function over their respective inputs [33].

Great progress has been made improving the computational complexity of these systems, but it is only recently that researchers have started to investigate improving these protocols' communication round complexity, or the minimum number of sets of parallel messages sent between parties in the protocol. For example, if during a protocol party A must wait to receive a message from party B before sending a followup message back to party B, we would consider this to be a two-round protocol. Note that in many cases, especially when MPC is conducted over the Internet, communication round complexity is the primary bottleneck, as network latency slows the delivery of packets necessary for continuing the protocol [5]. This problem becomes worse when parties are geographically distant, and is currently a major obstacle preventing MPC from being deployed in a global setting [34]. For several years, the total number of rounds needed has continued to decrease. To the best of our knowledge, the most efficient known protocols that satisfy security requirements in the standard model require two rounds of online communication [6,11–13,16,23,31].

In an effort to further reduce the number of rounds of communication, there has been a movement among MPC researchers to construct non-interactive MPC protocols (NI-MPC) which only require one-round of online communication [4, 19–21]. Clearly, this would have many practical benefits, since it would allow participants in the protocol to immediately terminate communication as soon as they received the needed response from other participants, and not waste energy and other resources maintaining an Internet connection while awaiting further messages. However, all NI-MPC protocols with a one-round online phase are vulnerable to the residual function attack, and thus cannot guarantee input privacy of participants under the standard security model [25]. In this attack, because correct evaluation must be guaranteed with only one round, the party that receives a garbled circuit should be able to repeatedly evaluate the circuit locally on different inputs while fixing the inputs of others until they learn the values inputted by other participants.

Existing works [4,20,22] choose to relax the security of the standard model, and define a new model of security that allows adversaries to learn nothing more than what can be discovered via this attack, which they define as the "best-possible security" for any given set of corrupted parties. Intuitively, this means that the adversary is prevented from learning more than they can via the residual function attack, as this is, practically speaking, the most meaningful security that can be achieved in the standard model given the one-round constraint. In more formal terms, they assert that if the evaluator colludes with a set of corrupted parties, denoted T, it is allowed to learn the value of the original function on the honest parties inputs combined with every possible choice of inputs from set T. As long as nothing more than that is learned, their relaxed security model defines that the protocol is secure.

This paper aims to design an NI-MPC scheme constructed with only one communication round in the online phase without sacrificing security or privacy. Achieving this goal is challenging, because any MPC protocol with only one communication round in the standard model is vulnerable to the residual function attack described above. We address this by building our protocol using secure functionality available in trusted hardware (*e.g.,* TPM and Intel SGX). The TPM is a mature cryptoprocessor technology that has existed for over a decade and has been internationally standardized by the ISO, and Intel SGX is a set of instructions that protect application code and data from being disclosed or modified. Both types are widely available in consumer and enterprise systems. For the purposes of our protocol, we use various secure functionalities including a *monotonic counter, binding, sealing, and remote attestation. Monotonic counters* enable us to only permit certain steps of our protocol to be executed a finite number of times. Combining this with *binding and sealing* will limit the users' ability to perform arbitrary evaluation for launching the aforementioned residual function attack. We also make use of *remote attestation* to verify the integrity of the protocol. All functions are available in both TPM and Intel SGX.

Although there has been some controversy over the use of a TPM, which we address in a later section, TPMs are rapidly becoming a major part of the digital security and privacy ecosystem, having been deployed in hundreds of millions of devices and on almost all commercial PCs and servers [1]. The Intel SGX is a newer development, but it is maintained and supported by Intel, making it credible and trusted hardware for practical purposes.

We have the following contributions in this paper.

1. We propose the first NI-MPC protocol that is secure under standard security models even though there is only one communication round in the online phase.
2. We provide a comprehensive analysis of existing state-of-the-art MPC schemes which require two rounds of communication or one-round during the online-phase and demonstrate that our NI-MPC protocol is comparable to or outperforms their asymptotic complexity.
3. We prove that our NI-MPC protocol is secure by showing simulation-based security under standard models.

2   Related Work

Since BMR [3], there have been many advances made in improving the round complexity of MPC using garbled circuits. [28] combines the BMR protocol with the SPDZ protocol [10] to achieve a twelve-round protocol given certain assumptions concerning the adversary, which was later improved to six rounds after modifying the protocol to use SHE instead of SPDZ [29]. Later, [19] were able to achieve a four-round MPC protocol under standard polynomial-time hardness assumptions by utilizing a black-box proof of security. This was later combined with tamper-proof hardware tokens to achieve a three-round protocol [25]. Following this work, [5] presented a four-round protocol that can be optimized to three or two rounds after performing several precomputations.

Recently, there has been much interest in constructing two-round MPC protocols, as this was shown in [23] to be necessary to securely compute certain common functionalities. [11] achieved the first two-round MPC scheme by relying on indistinguishability obfuscation, but later this assumption was reduced to witness encryption [16]. Following this work, two-round protocols were achieved in [31] based on the learning with errors assumption (LWE), in [6] based on the DDH assumption, and in [13] based on bilinear maps, after using ideas from [9]. Currently, the protocol with the best known communication round complexity which makes the least assumptions is [14], which notably achieves a two-round protocol by only relying on oblivious transfer (OT). This protocol was later made more efficient by minimizing the number of public key operations required, but it still requires two communication rounds [12].

However, there has been less work constructing protocols with a one-round online phase. "One-round" protocols for the two-party setting [27] and the mobile agents setting [8] have been constructed, but their "one round" refers to sending two messages back and forth (i.e., one round of exchange), so these protocols would be categorized as a two-round protocol with the current round definition.

Recently, there has been an interest in constructing Non-Interactive MPC (NI-MPC) protocols that have only one round of communication, but use a weaker security model that tolerates the residual function attack. [4] was the first to initiate study in this area, and notably achieved protocols for several special use cases such as group products, symmetric functions, etc. Later, [21] robustly studied the setting of NI-MPC to develop a unified framework for studying secure multi-party computation (MPC) under restricted interaction patterns, and went on to build more efficient NI-MPC protocols. These techniques were later improved [22] to concretely improve the communication and computational complexity of NI-MPC, after further developing a theory of the best-possible information theoretic security that could be achieved in this setting. This theory showed that for NI-MPC, since the communication strings for each player in a particular evaluation depend on each other, an adversary can prevent any simulator from generating views computationally indistinguishable from those in a real execution of the protocol by performing the attack. This makes proving security impossible for NI-MPC under standard security definitions using simulation proofs. Recently, [20] also proposed a protocol that notably achieved NI-MPC without the commonly assumed correlated randomness at the expense of relying on fully homomorphic encryption, which negatively impacts its overall efficiency. A summary of our comparison of different protocols is presented in Tables 1 and 2.[1]

---

[1] Note that the notation $O(1^\lambda)$ is used commonly in the literature to indicate the complexity grows linearly with respect to the security parameter [6, 12–14, 16, 31].

Table 1. Comparison of existing two-round MPC and our protocol

Paper	Computation complexity	Communication complexity	Assumptions
[16]	$O((DL)^\omega)$ where L is the circuit depth, D is the dimension parameter of the matrix, and $\omega >= 2.3727$ is the matrix multiplication exponent	$O(q^\lambda)$ where q is the size of the input, and λ is the security parameter	Honest majority, a broadcast channel, point-to-point channels, and witness encryption
[6]	$O(M/\delta)$ where M is an upper bound on the difference between inputs and δ is an upper bound on the error probability	$O(S) + poly(\lambda)$ where S is the size of the circuit and λ is the security parameter	DDH Assumption, multiple servers, and Public Key Infrastructure
[12]	$O((nS\lambda)^k)$ where n is the number of parties, S is the size of the circuit, λ is the security parameter, and k is constant	$O(1^\lambda) + \Omega(S)$ where λ is the security parameter and S is the size of the circuit	2-round OT
[14]	$O((n\lambda)^k)$ where n is the number of parties, λ is the security parameter, and k is constant	$O(1^\lambda)$ where λ is the security parameter	2-round OT
[31]	$O((DL)^\omega)$ where L is the depth of the circuit, D is the dimension parameter of the matrix, and $\omega >= 2.3727$ is the matrix multiplication exponent	$O(Sm\lambda)^k$ where k is a constant, S is the size of the input, m is the size of the output, and λ is the security parameter	CRS model, broadcast channel, LWE, and NIZKs
[13]	$O((nS\lambda)^k)$ where n is the number of parties, S is the size of the circuit, λ is the security parameter, and k is constant	$O(1^\lambda) + \Omega(S)$ where λ is the security parameter and S is the size of the circuit	Standard Bilinear Map Assumptions
[11]	$O((DL)^\omega)$ where L is the depth of the circuit, D is the dimension parameter of the matrix, and $\omega >= 2.3727$ is the matrix multiplication exponent	$O(S^\lambda)$ where S is the size of the input, and λ is the security parameter	Indistinguishability obfuscation, CCA-secure public key encryption, NIZKs, and 1 honest party
Ours	$O(n^2 S)$ where n is the number of parties and S is the size of the circuit	$O(1^\lambda)$ where λ is the security parameter	Trusted Hardware

3   Preliminaries

Both TPM and Intel SGX are equipped with the secure functionalities we need for constructing NI-MPC schemes that are secure under a standard (*i.e.,* not relaxed) security model. We chose to rely on the TPM in this paper for the implementation, because of its availability. Almost all laptops and desktops are equipped with a TPM, and it is even compatible with embedded systems. Because our scheme relies on the functionality, rather than the hardware itself, it can be implemented using Intel SGX as well.

Table 2. Comparison of Existing NI-MPC and our Protocol

Paper	Computation complexity	Communication complexity	Assumptions
[4]	Polynomial in the communication complexity	$O(n^t)$ where n is the number of parties and t is a constant $0 \le t \le n$	Correlated randomness
[22]	$O(\binom{n}{n/2}n)$ where n is the number of parties	$O(nsA)$ where n is the number of parties, s is a random vector in field F^k where k is a constant, and A is the number of AND gates	One-way functions for reusable correlated randomness and non-interactive key exchange for PKI setup
[21]	$O(2^n)$ where n is the number of parties	$O(n2^n)$ where n is the number of parties	Fully homomorphic encryption and indistinguishibility obfuscation for general circuits
[20]	$O((DL)^\omega)$ where L is the depth of the circuit, D is the dimension parameter of the matrix, and $\omega >= 2.3727$ is the matrix multiplication exponent	$O(Sm\lambda)^k$ where k is a constant, S is the size of the input, m is the size of the output, and λ is the security parameter	PKI and a common random string
Ours	$O(n^2 S)$ where n is the number of parties and S is the size of the circuit	$O(1^\lambda)$ where λ is the security parameter	Trusted Hardware

*Ours is the only scheme secure against residual function attacks under standard security models.

3.1   GNIOT for Non-interactivity and Covert Security

To achieve a protocol with a one-round online phase, our protocol relies on a special Oblivious Transfer (OT) called Generalized Non-Interactive Oblivious Transfer (GNIOT), proposed in [18], which makes use of the monotonic counter. Traditional OT allows a sender to safely transfer one of potentially many pieces of information to a recipient, but the sender cannot determine which piece was transferred. This idea was first proposed by Rabin in 1981 [32] for the two-party case, but in the years following has been extended to support multiple parties, and transferring more than one piece of information [7]. Traditional OT requires two or more communication rounds, but GNIOT requires just one round for the multiparty case.

Besides, with GNIOT, users are unable to receive more than one valid input for each input wire, making it impossible for malicious users to publish messages with fake inputs to others while locally evaluating the circuit with true inputs.

3.2 Justification of Using TPMs

TPMs have been underutilized when designing cryptographic protocols, due to impressions that they are insecure, an undesirable assumption to make, or simply too difficult to use [1]. TPMs have gained a reputation of being insecure, partially due to notable security breaches of TPM 1.2 [15]. However, a new and patched version (TMP 2.0) was released in 2015 with an updated specification that avoids the shortcomings of its predecessor. In 2017, an attack was reported against TPM 2.0, but this attack was only successful against an improperly implemented code library developed by Infineon, and did not exploit any underlying weakness in the TPM 2.0 specification itself. There are no known threats against the TPM 2.0.

While standard algorithmic assumptions (DDH, LWE, *etc.*) are preferable, since they do not impose hardware requirements, certain functionality cannot be supported in the standard model without relying on secure hardware. We argue it is worthwhile to make this assumption to support the computation of many useful functions in certain settings, *e.g.,* where a one-round online phase is desirable, if there are no known alternatives. Some of the functionality that cannot be supported without relying on secure hardware include: unconditional and non-interactive secure computation for one-time programs against malicious adversaries, interactive secure computation from stateless tokens based on one-way UC-secure functions, and program obfuscation from stateless tokens against malicious adversaries [17].

3.3 Definitions

Adversary Model. When considering weaknesses in our protocol, we consider three types of adversarial behavior: a *semi-honest* adversary, *covert* adversary, and *fully malicious* adversary. A *semi-honest* adversary will not deviate from behavior prescribed by the protocol, though they may carry out local computation to attempt to gain information about other parties' private inputs. The semi-honest attacker model provides only weak guarantees of security (though in some situations more realistic), but allows more efficient cooperation. Conversely, a *fully malicious* adversary may deviate from a protocol in any way, and may attempt to carry out a wide range of malicious behavior. This behavior may include gaining information about other parties' private inputs, giving incorrect information to other parties, or even preventing the completion of the protocol.

A protocol robust against fully malicious adversaries provides a strong security guarantee, but may be less efficient and more complex.

When discussing the security of our scheme, we use the *covert adversary* model as described in [2] to model users. Under the covert adversary model, while adversaries may behave in a fully malicious manner, they will refrain from deviating from the protocol if such an action would probably be noticed by other parties. In other words, a covert adversary will be only honest-but-curious unless they are likely to be able to behave maliciously with only a small chance of being detected.

Note that NI-MPC protocols cannot achieve active security against fully malicious adversaries as a result of the non-interactivity. Because each party sends all of their messages to the other parties in one round, if a malicious party chooses to send malformed data to other parties, the honest parties will not become aware of this until after they have sent their messages. In this way, the adversary can recover all of the data needed to complete the protocol successfully while preventing others from having access to enough valid data needed to complete the protocol. For our protocol, we thus find it most salient to consider the case where the computing parties may be covert adversaries and a trusted garbler is semi-honest. (If the trusted garbler is not semi-honest, then it becomes impossible to guarantee the security or correctness of the protocol.)

Simulation Correctness and Security. We define correctness and security as a simulation as is commonly done in the literature [6, 12–14, 16, 31] so that we can use simulation based proof techniques later in Sect. 6. Note that because this is a protocol, and not an encryption scheme, techniques such as proving IND-CCA or IND-CPA do not directly demonstrate the security of the entire protocol.

Definition 1 (Correctness). *An MPC scheme π for a class of functions F is said to correctly compute F among players if, for any $f \in F$ and for any set of inputs $X := (x_1, \cdots, x_n)$ in the domain of f where the i-th player P_i controls x_i, all players receive $f(X)$ from the scheme with a probability not less than $1 - \mathsf{negl}(\lambda)$ for some negligible function $\mathsf{negl}(\cdot)$ and the security parameter λ.*

Definition 2 (Security). *An MPC scheme π for a class of functions F is said to be secure for F against covert adversary if, for any $f \in F$ and for any probabilistic polynomial time adversary $\mathcal{A}$ controlling a subset A of all players, there exists a probabilistic polynomial-time simulator $\mathcal{S}$ such that for any set of inputs $X := (x_1, \cdots, x_n)$ in the domain of f where the i-th player P_i controls x_i,*

$$\{\mathcal{S}(f(X), A, \{x_j \mid P_j \in A\})\}_\lambda \stackrel{c}{\equiv} \{\mathsf{View}_A^\rho(X)\}_\lambda$$

where $\stackrel{c}{\equiv}$ refers to computational indistinguishability, λ is the security parameter, and $\mathsf{View}_A^\pi(X)$ represents the messages received by members of A during the execution of protocol π and any cheating by a covert adversary can be detected with significant probability.

4   High-Level Description of Our Protocol

Figure 1 in Sect. 5 presents a formal description of the proposed protocol. We provide a high level description here. Our protocol relies on the monotonic counter functionality, a secure functionality that stores a non-negative integer which can only be read from or incremented [1]. With this, along with binding and sealing, we can limit the user's access to a public/private key pair stored on the trusted hardware to a finite number of times, after which the ability of users to make use of the keys to perform an action is revoked [25]. We also make use of the remote attestation functionality implemented with the Attestation Identity Key (AIK) in TPM. AIK is a special-purpose TPM-resident cryptographic key used to provide platform authentication and verify that users have not performed unauthorized changes to the software. By querying the TPM, we can certify that the software currently running on the device is in the presence of a cryptographic key that came from an identifiable piece of hardware that will function correctly. In the event this certification fails, we can deny a malicious party's access. Note that such a functionality is available in Intel SGX as well.

We assume that the parties have access to trusted hardware which supports a monotonic counter, and have agreed on the circuit to be evaluated C (we will say the circuit has $\mathcal{N}$ input wires). We denote the number of parties as n (we sometimes refer generally to party $\mathcal{P}_i$ for $i \in [1, n)$. To participate in our protocol, each party queries the on-board trusted hardware to generate a public/private key pair $(\mathcal{K}_{\mathbf{p}_i}, \mathcal{K}_{\mathbf{s}_i})$ stored in the secure memory that can only be used $\mathcal{W}_i$ times where $\mathcal{W}_i$ will denote the number of input wires a party controls. This behaviour can be enforced using the TPM by assigning an upper bound to the cryptographic keys that depends on the monotonic counter.

Each time the keys are used, the monotonic counter is incremented, but after the counter exceeds the assigned bound, users will no longer be able to use the keys. To certify that these keys were generated correctly, each party certifies it did not tamper with the key generation process by broadcasting a certification using the TPM's AIK of the public key. A semi-honest garbler also creates a symmetric key $\mathcal{R}^{(i)}$. After generating the garbled circuit, for each party $\mathcal{P}_i$ the garbler encodes both of $\mathcal{P}_i$'s possible inputs as wire labels (we work with Boolean circuits, so these labels correspond to 0 or 1) for each wire $w \in \mathcal{W}_i$ and encrypts using the symmetric key. Note that to an adversary, the wire labels appear to be random strings whose length is proportional to the security parameter, so the adversary cannot evaluate the garbled circuits without retrieving the correct keys from the TPM. The garbler then proceeds to split the symmetric key $\mathcal{R}^{(i)}$ into $\mathcal{W}_i$ secret shares. Following this, each encoded input is paired with a secret share of $\mathcal{R}^{(i)}$ as a tuple, referred to as an intermediate ciphertext. This intermediate ciphertext is encrypted using the public key $\mathcal{K}_{\mathbf{p}_i}$. Then each respective $\mathcal{P}_i$'s encrypted intermediate ciphertexts are then broadcast to them.

Because the number of decryptions permitted using the public key is equal to the number of input wires of the garbled circuit, due to the monotonic counter, each party can only decrypt one possible input for each wire. This means that no party can decrypt both encoded inputs corresponding to 0 and 1 for a wire and perform the residual function attack described above, as this will use up a decryption that they need to recover the input to one of the remaining input wires. They can only decrypt one encoded input per wire or they will be unable to complete the protocol. After decrypting the encrypted intermediate ciphertexts, the parties can locally combine the secret shares to recover the symmetric key $\mathcal{R}^{(i)}$ that was used to encrypt the encoded inputs to the circuit and recover the wire labels. Since the wire labels reveal nothing about a party's choice of input, they can be sent to the other parties, and be used by each party to locally evaluate the circuit to receive the output.

Note that NI-MPC protocols cannot achieve active security against fully malicious adversaries as a result of their non-interactivity as described above, because all parties send all of the data the other parties need to complete the protocol in one round simultaneously. The best that can be achieved is covert security, which models the situation where malicious adversaries are willing to cheat only if they are not caught. In our protocol, if an adversary sends malformed data to another honest party, the honest party will be unable to finish evaluating the circuit, but because all data sent can be traced back to the sending party with significant probability. The honest party will know who acted maliciously, and notify the other participating parties of the bad behaviour.

5   Our Protocol

Our protocol employs the following algorithms as building blocks: gen, enc_pub, enc_sec, dec_pub, dec_sec, and garble. Any algorithms that have the described input/output can be adopted.

- **gen**$(\lambda) \rightarrow \mathcal{R}, \mathcal{K}_\mathbf{p}, \mathcal{K}_\mathbf{s}$: this is an algorithm that takes the security parameter λ as input and outputs a symmetric key $\mathcal{R}$ and a public/private key pair ($\mathcal{K}_\mathbf{p}$, $\mathcal{K}_\mathbf{s}$). For example, RSA/ECC or AES key generation algorithms.
- **enc_pub**$(\mathcal{K}_\mathbf{p}, \mathcal{X}) \rightarrow \mathcal{PK}_{\mathcal{K}_\mathbf{p}}(\mathcal{X})$: this is a public key encryption algorithm that takes public key $\mathcal{K}_\mathbf{p}$ and plaintext $\mathcal{X}$ as input and returns ciphertext $\mathcal{PK}_{\mathcal{K}_\mathbf{p}}(\mathcal{X})$. For example, RSA or ECC encryption algorithms.
- **enc_sec**$(\mathcal{R}, \mathcal{X}) \rightarrow \mathcal{SK}_{\mathcal{R}(\mathcal{X})}$: this is a symmetric key encryption algorithm that takes symmetric key $\mathcal{R}$ and plaintext $\mathcal{X}$ as input and returns ciphertext $\mathcal{SK}_{\mathcal{R}}(\mathcal{X})$. For example, the AES encryption algorithm.
- **dec_pub**$(\mathcal{K}_s, \mathcal{PK}_{\mathcal{K}_\mathbf{p}}(\mathcal{X})) \rightarrow \mathcal{X}$: this is a public key decryption algorithm that takes private key $\mathcal{K}_\mathbf{s}$ and ciphertext $\mathcal{PK}_{\mathcal{K}_\mathbf{p}}(\mathcal{X})$. For example, the RSA or ECC decryption algorithms.
- **dec_sec**$(\mathcal{R}, \mathcal{SK}_{\mathcal{R}}(\mathcal{X})) \rightarrow \mathcal{X}$: this is a decryption algorithm that takes symmetric key $\mathcal{R}$ and ciphertext $\mathcal{SK}_{\mathcal{R}}(\mathcal{X})$ as input and returns plaintext $\mathcal{X}$. For example, the AES decryption algorithm.

- **garble(C)** $\rightarrow$ **GC**: this is a circuit garbling algorithm that takes as input a circuit C and returns a garbled circuit GC. For example, a garbling algorithm or related software tools (i.e. Frigate [30]) from the survey [24] may be used.

Our protocol is described in detail in Fig. 1. Note that in the preprocessing phase, ordinarily our protocol would be vulnerable to the residual function attack, as an adversary could hypothetically decrypt more than one ciphertext pair $(\mathcal{C}_{w,0}, \mathcal{C}_{w,1})$ associated with an input wire to recover its associated symmetric key and gain access to both wire labels. This would allow them to evaluate the function repeatedly over both inputs while fixing the input of others, until they learn the values inputted by other participants. However, because the number of decryptions of the ciphertexts $\mathcal{C}_{w,0}$ or $\mathcal{C}_{w,1}$ is limited with the monotonic counter in the trusted hardware, if they attempt to perform more decryptions than specified for the circuit, they will be unable to access enough shares of the symmetric key to later recover $\mathcal{R}^{(i)}$ and complete the protocol. As a result, the residual function attack is blocked. Also, note that only steps 2 and 4 of the initialization phase and step 1 of the online phase require a communication round. However, the communication in the initialization phase only needs to occur once during setup. After this, communication only occurs during the online phase for each iteration of the protocol.

6 Proofs

6.1 Proof of Correctness and Security

Simulation Correctness. Our protocol π correctly computes Boolean circuits as defined in Definition 1.

Proof. We include this proof in the full version of the paper.

Simulation Security. Assuming $|\mathcal{C}| = O(\log \lambda)$, all parties use the TPM as the protocol describes, the public key and symmetric key encrypted ciphertexts supported by the TPM are indistinguishable, players properly perform attestation with their keys, and the semi-honest, noncolluding garbler correctly garbles circuits, our protocol π securely computes Boolean circuits as defined in Definition 2.

Proof. We include this proof in the full version of the paper.

Our Protocol π

Initialize: Given the security parameter 1^λ, this phase distributes garbled circuit GC and ciphertext pair $\mathcal{C}_{w,(0,1)}$ corresponding to each wire controlled by each player.

Preprocess: This phase can be run in advance of the online phase. All players $\mathcal{P}_i$ run this phase along with the garbler $\mathcal{G}$. Note steps 2 and 4 require one round each but this is a one time cost.

1. Each $\mathcal{P}_i$ calls **gen** and queries the TPM to generate a $\mathcal{W}_i$ time use count limited public/private key pair $(\mathcal{K}_{\mathbf{p}_i}, \mathcal{K}_{\mathbf{s}_i})$ where $\mathcal{W}_i$ is the number of input wires $\mathcal{P}_i$ controls for circuit C.
2. Each $\mathcal{P}_i$ certifies its $\mathcal{K}_{\mathbf{p}_i}$ by using an Attestation Identity Key via a Trusted Platform Module, and broadcasts $\mathcal{K}_{\mathbf{p}_i}$.
3. The semi-honest garbler $\mathcal{G}$, which is "separate" from the function evaluation, takes the previously agreed upon circuit C, calls **garble**, and computes a corresponding garbled circuit GC.
4. Using GNIOT, for every player $\mathcal{P}_i$ with $\mathcal{W}_i$ input wires and public key $\mathcal{K}_{\mathbf{p}_i}$, the semi-honest garbler $\mathcal{G}$ calculates a symmetric cipher key $\mathcal{R}^{(i)}$ and splits $\mathcal{R}^{(i)}$ into $\mathcal{W}_i$ shares $\mathcal{R}_w^{(i)}$ for $w \in [\mathcal{W}_i]$. Let the labels in the garbled circuit GC of an input wire $w \in [\mathcal{W}_i]$ be called $x_{w,0}$ and $x_{w,1}$ for the Boolean values 0 and 1 respectively. The garbler then calls **enc_sec** to encrypt the each label and **enc_pub** to encrypt each tuple of an encrypted label and a secret share, and computes and broadcasts $\mathcal{C}_{w,0} = \mathcal{PK}_{\mathcal{K}_{P_i}}(\mathcal{SK}_{\mathcal{R}^{(i)}}(x_{w,0}), \mathcal{R}_w^{(i)})$ and $\mathcal{C}_{w,1} = \mathcal{PK}_{\mathcal{K}_{P_i}}(\mathcal{SK}_{\mathcal{R}^{(i)}}(x_{w,1}), \mathcal{R}_w^{(i)})$ for all $w \in \mathcal{W}_i$.

Online: This phase communicates all parties' inputs to each individual party. All players $\mathcal{P}_i$ run this phase. Note this step requires one round.

1. Each $\mathcal{P}_i$ decrypts either $\mathcal{C}_{w,0}$ or $\mathcal{C}_{w,1}$ (for $w \in [\mathcal{W}_i]$) using their private key $\mathcal{K}_{\mathbf{s}_i}$ stored on their TPM to get intermediate ciphertexts $\mathcal{T}_{w,0} = (\ \mathcal{SK}_{\mathcal{R}^{(i)}}(x_{w,0})$, $\mathcal{R}_w^{(i)})$ or $\mathcal{T}_{w,1} = (\ \mathcal{SK}_{\mathcal{R}^{(i)}}(x_{w,1}), \mathcal{R}_w^{(i)})$, as part of the GNIOT, by calling **dec_pub**.
2. Then $\mathcal{P}_i$ extracts each $\mathcal{R}_w^{(i)}$ which are then recombined to recover the symmetric key $\mathcal{R}^{(i)}$.
3. Then $\mathcal{R}^{(i)}$ is used to decrypt either $\mathcal{SK}_{\mathcal{R}^{(i)}}(x_{w,0})$ or $\mathcal{SK}_{\mathcal{R}^{(i)}}(x_{w,1})$, by calling **dec_sec**, based on the choice of $\mathcal{P}_i$ to recover either $x_{w,0}$ or $x_{w,1}$, and complete the GNIOT.
4. The parties broadcast their chosen $x_{w,0}$ or $x_{w,1}$ to each party but the semi-honest garbler (wire labels appear as random strings to an adversary).

Evaluate (offline): This phase evaluates the garbled circuit. All players $\mathcal{P}_i$ run this phase locally.

1. Each party $\mathcal{P}_i$ inputs one of $x_{w,0}$ or $x_{w,1}$ for $w \in [\mathcal{W}_i]$ into the garbled circuit GC to reveal the output and return the plaintext circuit output.
2. Parties learn a specific input is corrupted when they input the $x_{w,0}$ or $x_{w,1}$ they receive from an adversarial party A to a wire A owns and evaluation fails for that wire. When this happens, they all abort the protocol and broadcast a notification to all other parties the $x_{w,0}$ or $x_{w,1}$ from A was corrupted.

Fig. 1. Our MPC protocol that evaluates a Boolean circuit among n players.

7 Conclusions and Future Work

This paper demonstrates the first MPC scheme constructed with one communication round in the online phase that does not sacrifice security or privacy and can be proven secure in the standard model. Previous protocols subject to this one-round constraint in the standard model were vulnerable to the residual function attack, where a party that receives a garbled circuit may repeatedly evaluate the circuit locally while varying their own inputs and fixing the input of others to learn the values entered by other participants. We overcome this problem by building our protocol using a secure hardware primitive, specifically a Trusted Platform Module (TPM), a mature cryptoprocessor technology. We rigorously analyzed the communication and computational complexity of current state of the art protocols which require two rounds of communication or one-round during the online-phase with a reduced security requirement, and demonstrated that our protocol is comparable to or outperforms their complexity. Also, we provided rigorous proofs of correctness and security in the covert adversary model for our protocol. We are actively developing an implementation of the algorithms in our NI-MPC scheme with Microsoft's TPM 2.0 Simulator, and the MPIR, OpenSSL, and TPM.CPP libraries. Our code is available at https://github.com/Ryan-Karl/one_round_mpc_with_tpm. We hope that this further improves the viability of MPC as a practical solution for facilitating private communication, especially in global environments.

References

1. Arthur, W., Challener, D.: A Practical Guide to TPM 2.0: Using the Trusted Platform Module in the New Age of Security. Apress, New York (2015)
2. Aumann, Y., Lindell, Y.: Security against covert adversaries: efficient protocols for realistic adversaries. In: Vadhan, S.P. (ed.) TCC 2007. LNCS, vol. 4392, pp. 137–156. Springer, Heidelberg (2007). https://doi.org/10.1007/978-3-540-70936-7_8
3. Beaver, D., Micali, S., Rogaway, P.: The round complexity of secure protocols. In: STOC, pp. 503–513. ACM (1990)
4. Beimel, A., Gabizon, A., Ishai, Y., Kushilevitz, E., Meldgaard, S., Paskin-Cherniavsky, A.: Non-interactive secure multiparty computation. In: Garay, J.A., Gennaro, R. (eds.) CRYPTO 2014. LNCS, vol. 8617, pp. 387–404. Springer, Heidelberg (2014). https://doi.org/10.1007/978-3-662-44381-1_22
5. Ben-Efraim, A., Lindell, Y., Omri, E.: Optimizing semi-honest secure multiparty computation for the internet. In: CCS, pp. 578–590. ACM (2016)
6. Boyle, E., Gilboa, N., Ishai, Y.: Group-based secure computation: optimizing rounds, communication, and computation. In: Coron, J.-S., Nielsen, J.B. (eds.) EUROCRYPT 2017. LNCS, vol. 10211, pp. 163–193. Springer, Cham (2017). https://doi.org/10.1007/978-3-319-56614-6_6
7. Brassard, G., Crepeau, C., Robert, J.-M.: All-or-nothing disclosure of secrets. In: Odlyzko, A.M. (ed.) CRYPTO 1986. LNCS, vol. 263, pp. 234–238. Springer, Heidelberg (1987). https://doi.org/10.1007/3-540-47721-7_17

8. Cachin, C., Camenisch, J., Kilian, J., Müller, J.: One-round secure computation and secure autonomous mobile agents. In: Montanari, U., Rolim, J.D.P., Welzl, E. (eds.) ICALP 2000. LNCS, vol. 1853, pp. 512–523. Springer, Heidelberg (2000). https://doi.org/10.1007/3-540-45022-X_43

9. Cho, C., Döttling, N., Garg, S., Gupta, D., Miao, P., Polychroniadou, A.: Laconic oblivious transfer and its applications. In: Katz, J., Shacham, H. (eds.) CRYPTO 2017. LNCS, vol. 10402, pp. 33–65. Springer, Cham (2017). https://doi.org/10.1007/978-3-319-63715-0_2

10. Damgård, I., Pastro, V., Smart, N., Zakarias, S.: Multiparty computation from somewhat homomorphic encryption. In: Safavi-Naini, R., Canetti, R. (eds.) CRYPTO 2012. LNCS, vol. 7417, pp. 643–662. Springer, Heidelberg (2012). https://doi.org/10.1007/978-3-642-32009-5_38

11. Garg, S., Gentry, C., Halevi, S., Raykova, M.: Two-round secure MPC from indistinguishability obfuscation. In: Lindell, Y. (ed.) TCC 2014. LNCS, vol. 8349, pp. 74–94. Springer, Heidelberg (2014). https://doi.org/10.1007/978-3-642-54242-8_4

12. Garg, S., Miao, P., Srinivasan, A.: Two-round multiparty secure computation minimizing public key operations. In: Shacham, H., Boldyreva, A. (eds.) CRYPTO 2018. LNCS, vol. 10993, pp. 273–301. Springer, Cham (2018). https://doi.org/10.1007/978-3-319-96878-0_10

13. Garg, S., Srinivasan, A.: Garbled protocols and two-round MPC from bilinear maps. In: FOCS, pp. 588–599. IEEE (2017)

14. Garg, S., Srinivasan, A.: Two-round multiparty secure computation from minimal assumptions. In: Nielsen, J.B., Rijmen, V. (eds.) EUROCRYPT 2018. LNCS, vol. 10821, pp. 468–499. Springer, Cham (2018). https://doi.org/10.1007/978-3-319-78375-8_16

15. Goodin: Ex-army man cracks popular security chip. The Register (2010). http://theregister.co.uk/2010/02/17/infineon_tpm_crack/

16. Dov Gordon, S., Liu, F.-H., Shi, E.: Constant-round MPC with fairness and guarantee of output delivery. In: Gennaro, R., Robshaw, M. (eds.) CRYPTO 2015. LNCS, vol. 9216, pp. 63–82. Springer, Heidelberg (2015). https://doi.org/10.1007/978-3-662-48000-7_4

17. Goyal, V., Ishai, Y., Sahai, A., Venkatesan, R., Wadia, A.: Founding cryptography on tamper-proof hardware tokens. In: Micciancio, D. (ed.) TCC 2010. LNCS, vol. 5978, pp. 308–326. Springer, Heidelberg (2010). https://doi.org/10.1007/978-3-642-11799-2_19

18. Gunupudi, V., Tate, S.R.: Generalized non-interactive oblivious transfer using count-limited objects with applications to secure mobile agents. In: Tsudik, G. (ed.) FC 2008. LNCS, vol. 5143, pp. 98–112. Springer, Heidelberg (2008). https://doi.org/10.1007/978-3-540-85230-8_8

19. Halevi, S., Hazay, C., Polychroniadou, A., Venkitasubramaniam, M.: Round-optimal secure multi-party computation. In: Shacham, H., Boldyreva, A. (eds.) CRYPTO 2018. LNCS, vol. 10992, pp. 488–520. Springer, Cham (2018). https://doi.org/10.1007/978-3-319-96881-0_17

20. Halevi, S., Ishai, Y., Jain, A., Komargodski, I., Sahai, A., Yogev, E.: Non-interactive multiparty computation without correlated randomness. In: Takagi, T., Peyrin, T. (eds.) ASIACRYPT 2017. LNCS, vol. 10626, pp. 181–211. Springer, Cham (2017). https://doi.org/10.1007/978-3-319-70700-6_7

21. Halevi, S., Ishai, Y., Jain, A., Kushilevitz, E., Rabin, T.: Secure multiparty computation with general interaction patterns. In: Proceedings ACM Conference on Innovations in Theoretical Computer Science, pp. 157–168. ACM (2016)

22. Halevi, S., Ishai, Y., Kushilevitz, E., Rabin, T.: Best possible information-theoretic MPC. In: Beimel, A., Dziembowski, S. (eds.) TCC 2018. LNCS, vol. 11240, pp. 255–281. Springer, Cham (2018). https://doi.org/10.1007/978-3-030-03810-6_10
23. Halevi, S., Lindell, Y., Pinkas, B.: Secure computation on the web: computing without simultaneous interaction. In: Rogaway, P. (ed.) CRYPTO 2011. LNCS, vol. 6841, pp. 132–150. Springer, Heidelberg (2011). https://doi.org/10.1007/978-3-642-22792-9_8
24. Hastings, M., Hemenway, B., Noble, D., Zdancewic, S.: SoK: general purpose compilers for secure multi-party computation. In: SoK: General Purpose Compilers for Secure Multi-Party Computation. IEEE (2019)
25. Hazay, C., Polychroniadou, A., Venkitasubramaniam, M.: Composable security in the tamper-proof hardware model under minimal complexity. In: Hirt, M., Smith, A. (eds.) TCC 2016. LNCS, vol. 9985, pp. 367–399. Springer, Heidelberg (2016). https://doi.org/10.1007/978-3-662-53641-4_15
26. Huang, Y., Evans, D., Katz, J., Malka, L.: Faster secure two-party computation using garbled circuits. In: USENIX Security, SEC 2011, p. 35. USENIX Association, Berkeley (2011)
27. Kolesnikov, V., Schneider, T.: Improved garbled circuit: free XOR gates and applications. In: Aceto, L., Damgård, I., Goldberg, L.A., Halldórsson, M.M., Ingólfsdóttir, A., Walukiewicz, I. (eds.) ICALP 2008. LNCS, vol. 5126, pp. 486–498. Springer, Heidelberg (2008). https://doi.org/10.1007/978-3-540-70583-3_40
28. Lindell, Y., Pinkas, B., Smart, N.P., Yanai, A.: Efficient constant round multiparty computation combining BMR and SPDZ. In: Gennaro, R., Robshaw, M. (eds.) CRYPTO 2015. LNCS, vol. 9216, pp. 319–338. Springer, Heidelberg (2015). https://doi.org/10.1007/978-3-662-48000-7_16
29. Lindell, Y., Smart, N.P., Soria-Vazquez, E.: More efficient constant-round multiparty computation from BMR and SHE. In: Hirt, M., Smith, A. (eds.) TCC 2016. LNCS, vol. 9985, pp. 554–581. Springer, Heidelberg (2016). https://doi.org/10.1007/978-3-662-53641-4_21
30. Mood, B., Gupta, D., Carter, H., Butler, K., Traynor, P.: Frigate: a validated, extensible, and efficient compiler and interpreter for secure computation. In: 2016 IEEE European Symposium on Security and Privacy (EuroS&P), pp. 112–127. IEEE (2016)
31. Mukherjee, P., Wichs, D.: Two round multiparty computation via multi-key FHE. In: Fischlin, M., Coron, J.-S. (eds.) EUROCRYPT 2016. LNCS, vol. 9666, pp. 735–763. Springer, Heidelberg (2016). https://doi.org/10.1007/978-3-662-49896-5_26
32. Rabin, M.: How to exchange secrets with oblivious transfer. Harvard University Technical report (1981)
33. Wang, X., Ranellucci, S., Katz, J.: Authenticated garbling and efficient maliciously secure two-party computation. In: CCS, pp. 21–37. ACM (2017)
34. Wang, X., Ranellucci, S., Katz, J.: Global-scale secure multiparty computation. In: CCS, pp. 39–56. ACM (2017)
35. Yao, A.C.C.: How to generate and exchange secrets. In: FOCS, pp. 162–167. IEEE (1986)
36. Zahur, S., Rosulek, M., Evans, D.: Two halves make a whole. In: Oswald, E., Fischlin, M. (eds.) EUROCRYPT 2015. LNCS, vol. 9057, pp. 220–250. Springer, Heidelberg (2015). https://doi.org/10.1007/978-3-662-46803-6_8

A Study of the Multiple Sign-in Feature in Web Applications

Marwan Albahar[1], Xing Gao[2], Gaby Dagher[1], Daiping Liu[3], Fengwei Zhang[4,5], and Jidong Xiao[1(✉)]

[1] Boise State University, Boise, USA
jidongxiao@boisestate.edu
[2] University of Memphis, Memphis, USA
[3] Palo Alto Networks, Santa Clara, USA
[4] SUSTech, Shenzhen, China
[5] Wayne State University, Detroit, USA

Abstract. Nowadays, more and more web applications start to offer the multiple sign-in feature, allowing users to sign into multiple accounts simultaneously from the same browser. This feature significantly improves user experience. Unfortunately, if such a feature is not designed and implemented properly, it could lead to security, privacy, or usability issues. In this paper, we perform the first comprehensive study of the multiple sign-in feature among various web applications, including Google, Dropbox. Our results show that the problem is quite worrisome. All analyzed products that provide the multiple sign-in feature either suffer from potential security/privacy threats or are sacrificing usability to some extent. We present all issues found in these applications, and analyze the root cause by identifying four different implementation models. Finally, based on our analysis results, we design a client-side proof-of-concept solution, called *G-Remember*, to mitigate these issues. Our experiments show that *G-Remember* can successfully provide adequate context information for web servers to recognize users' intended accounts, and thus effectively address the presented multiple sign-in threat.

Keywords: Web security · Multiple sign-in feature · Cookies

1 Introduction

Historically, most websites allowed users to access only one account at any given time using the same browser. As a result, users who needed to access multiple accounts (e.g., personal and business) at the same time from the same machine had to either use different browsers, or use some browser extensions [4]. In the past decade, the *multiple sign-in feature* was introduced as a solution to this problem, which enables users to sign in simultaneously using multiple accounts from the same browser. e.g., Google started offering this feature in 2010 [1]. Since then, many other well-known web applications have started to offer this feature, including Dropbox, Yahoo, Twitter, and Instagram.

© ICST Institute for Computer Sciences, Social Informatics and Telecommunications Engineering 2019
Published by Springer Nature Switzerland AG 2019. All Rights Reserved
S. Chen et al. (Eds.): SecureComm 2019, LNICST 305, pp. 440–453, 2019.
https://doi.org/10.1007/978-3-030-37231-6_26

However, as of now, there is no standard that defines expected behaviour for safe and secure multiple-account access, and how cookies should be shared among multiple accounts. As a result, the design and implementation of this feature varies from one web application to another. In this paper, we attempt to fill this gap by analyzing how web applications differentiate among multiple accounts connected from the same browser. To the best of our knowledge, this is the first work that studies the design and implementation details of the multiple sign-in feature in major web applications. One major finding of our study is that most products provided by Google and Dropbox lack sufficient isolation and are not able to differentiate among multiple accounts connected from the same browser, which could lead to:

1. usability issues. When the user attempts to access some web resource (R) via one account (A), which has the proper permission to access R, yet the web server mistakenly thinks the user is using another account (B), which does not have the proper permission to access R. The user's access would therefore be denied. This is a mistake, and could hurt user experience.
2. security and privacy issues. When the multiple sign-in feature is used in conjunction with capability-based access control, the problem is exacerbated. More specifically, when the capability-based access control is used, and the server fails to differentiate among the user's multiple accounts, the consequence is, one account could interfere with another account. This includes peeking into another account, gaining extra access to undisclosed information belonging to another account, or even altering the contents in files belonging to another account.

After analyzing corresponding web traffic (i.e., http requests and responses), we have identified the root cause of why the web server is not able to differentiate among the user's multiple accounts. When the user clicks a URL to access certain web resource, the web server oftentimes could not recognize the user's accounts because the context information (i.e., information about a specific account) included within the http request is inadequate. To address this problem, we have implemented a client-side proof-of-concept solution to force users to provide necessary context information such that the web server is able to identify which account it is currently dealing with. With such a solution, the aforementioned usability, security, and privacy issue would be solved.

1.1 Contribution

The contributions of this paper can be summarized as follows:

- We conduct the first systematic analysis of the design and implementation of the multiple sign-in feature among different web applications. We identify four different implementation models used by different web applications to implement the multiple sign-in feature, and we discuss why they are, or are not, able to differentiate among multiple accounts.

- For web applications that fail to differentiate among users' multiple accounts, we present what usability, security, and privacy problems could happen. We also report our major findings with respect to Google and Dropbox applications. Specifically, for the first time, we define and report a problem that we call it the **cross-account information leakage problem**.
- We implement a client side proof-of-concept solution, that includes a browser extension, to help users provide context information for the web server. Our experimental results show that our solution enables web servers to grant clients access resources using the correct account, thus avoid the aforementioned usability, security, and privacy issues.

2   Background

2.1   Multiple Accounts

When multiple accounts are involved, cookies become more complicated. Some cookies are shared among multiple accounts, while others are non-shared and bound to a specific account. Take Google's products as an example. Shared cookies usually have the domain attribute as google.com and the path attribute as "/". By contrast, the domain attribute of a non-shared cookie is more specific and typically includes more subdomain information. For instance, most cookies related to Gmail accounts have the domain attribute of mail.google.com, and their paths are longer, like /mail/u/0, /mail/u/1, /mail/u/2, etc. The numbers 0, 1, and 2 denote the login order of this account, with the first signed-in Gmail account's cookies having the path of /mail/u/0, the second one having /mail/u/1, and so forth. As we will explain in Sect. 6, it is because Gmail uses separate cookies and create separate URLs for different accounts that make it possible to differentiate among a user's multiple accounts connecting from the same browser. Unfortunately, most other Google products do not have such a separation. The consequence of this is Google fails to differentiate among users' multiple accounts. The same problem also occurs in Dropbox.

2.2   Capability-Based Access Control: Sharing a File via a Link

Online storage service products such as Google Drive, Dropbox, Microsoft Onedrive, typically support two classic access control mechanisms: access control list (ACL) and capability-based access control. Both mechanisms provide secure access controls, and to the best of our knowledge, there is no literature proving that one is more secure than the other. However, in this work, we identify that, when the multiple sign-in feature is used in conjunction with the capability-based access control, security problems could happen.

More specifically, most problems we have identified happen when the user has multiple accounts signed in and one file is shared via a link - whoever has the link can access the file. This file could be stored in a Google drive, or in a Dropbox folder. The link is the capability in the context of capability-based access control, while in other situations, the capability could be a token, ticket, or a key [12], which gives a subject an access to an object. To ensure such a capability is not extended to a untrustworthy person, on the one hand, the owner should try to keep the link privately and only share it with a trustworthy party; On the other hand, service providers typically make such a capability hard to predict. For example, a typical Google document URL includes a randomly generated string of more than 40 characters, which makes such URLs almost unguessable to a random person. As far as we know, there is no existing literature or reports showing any evidence that such long URLs, when used in the context of HTTPS (which is exactly what Google and Dropbox have adopted), can be exploited by attackers. Furthermore, to the best of our knowledge, Google or Dropbox have not, in any of their documents, told their users that such long URLs are insecure. Therefore, it is reasonable and understandable for people to share files in such a manner - whoever has the link can access the file. In the remaining part of this paper, we assume all the file sharing situations we talk about refers to this type of sharing. Also, in Google Drive, with such a sharing method, when an account accesses a file shared by another account, the shared file would be automatically saved in this destination account's Google Drive.

In summary: our observation - web applications fail to differentiate among users' multiple accounts, plus the fact - when a shared file (shared via the above method) is accessed by another account, the shared file will be automatically saved in the other account's online drive, could cause several security problems, as described in the next section.

3 Threat Model

Overall, we consider the following three multiple sign-in scenarios where security or privacy problems exhibit. All of them involves some type of information leakage. In the following, we use Google Drive as an example, and we will present our findings in Dropbox in Sect. 5. We use Alice to denote the victim, use **GP** to denote Alice's personal Google account, and use **GB** to denote Alice's business Google account.

– **Classic cross site request forgery (CSRF) attack.** Considering an attacker Bob, who knows the victim Alice's personal email address **GP**, but has no knowledge of Alice's work email address **GB**. We also assume at work, Alice shares that email address with several other co-workers - meaning they all have access to **GB**'s Google Drive storage. Now let us say Bob has some Alice's sensitive (e.g., sexual) videos or pictures, and he wants to distribute these videos or pictures to Alice's co-workers, but he doesn't know how to get their contact information. To achieve his malicious goal, Bob could send a link to Alice's A1 account and share the videos or pictures with Alice. And if Alice has both **GP** and **GB** account active running in the same browser, and then she opens the link (from within its **GP** account's inbox) - just as every other CSRF attack instance, the victim needs to have its account active and has to click on the link or access some web page which includes the link. Unfortunately, Google thinks it's **GB** attempting to open the link

- In Sect. 4, we will explain why and when Google would think this way. Thus, the moment Alice opens the videos or the pictures, the videos and/or pictures will be automatically saved in **GB**'s drive. As we just mentioned, **GB** is a shared email address for work. Therefore, on a different day, Alice's co-worker Eva, or any other co-workers, signs in to **GB** from a different computer or device, would be still able to view those videos and pictures. This describes a classic CSRF attack scenario.

  This same attack could also be performed so as to help attackers to spread malicious programs or virus, or ransomware, which might require more social engineering tricks. Note that even if Bob is not a bad actor - for example, Bob is Alice's friend, and is just sharing some private files between two friends, the fact that Alice's private information being automatically saved in her business account Google Drive, is still a problem. In the following, we call this the **cross-account information leakage problem**.

- **Information leakage from one user's account to another user's account.** Alice signs her personal Google account from a public or shared device, on which Bob already has one of his accounts signed in from the same browser. This case frequently occurs in public devices, like a desktop in a public library. It could also happen in a professional talk or conference presentation, where the speaker oftentimes has to login his/her account in other people's laptops (e.g., laptops provided by the conference organizer or the session chair) so as to get presentation materials from his/her email box or some online drive space. Note that in this scenario, Bob has no bad or malicious intentions, yet the cross-account information leakage problem could unexpectedly expose Alice's sensitive information or data to Bob. In the example of Google drive, once Alice visits her Google drive documents, Alice's documents could be automatically saved in Bob's Google drive folder without Alice's knowledge.

- **User's one account is hacked, while other accounts are NOT hacked.** User Alice signs multiple personal accounts, and one of which was hacked by the attacker Bob (e.g., the account and password are leaked). In recent years, credential leaking has been not rare: a dark web leaks 1.4 billion leaked passwords in 2017 [2]; twitter exposes the passwords of 330 million users in plain text [5]; and 272 million email username/password combinations are possessed by hackers in 2016 [3]. We assume the victim Alice sets different passwords for her different accounts, as this is a very basic security practice. Thus, except for the compromised account, Bob should not be able to directly obtain information from Alice's other accounts. Yet, once again, in the example of Google drive, once Alice accesses her data on Google drive, her data could be automatically saved in that compromised account's Google drive folder, which is under Bob's control.

4   Google Multiple Accounts

Our study shows most Google products fail to differentiate among multiple accounts, although Gmail is an exception. In this section, we specifically use Google Drive as a case study.

Google Drive. Google *Drive* provides a file synchronization and storage service which empowers users to share and synchronize files across different devices. It also allows file sharing across different users. When sharing files with others, for each file, the owner can set the permission, indicating whether other users can view or edit the file. The owner can then send a link of the file to other people, and a common sharing scenario is whoever has the link can access the file. The problem happens when the receiver has more than one account active in the same browser, and he/she intends to use one of his/her accounts to click the link and open the file. Since such link usually does not contain any context information, Google is unable to decide the intended account, and thus opens the file with some account at its choice (i.e., the Google-chosen account) - as opposed to the user's (i.e., the user-chosen account) choice.

Determine the Google-Chosen Account. To determine which account would be the Google-chosen account, we further conduct experiments to understand the implicit policy used by the Google server side. We first register three regular Google accounts with the *gmail.com* domain. We also have three *Gmail* education (formerly known as G Suite for Education) accounts with the *.edu* domain. We use one regular account (denoted as G_s) and one *.edu* account (denoted as E_s) to share the file. Other accounts are signed in on the receiving end from the same browser, denoted as G_1, G_2, E_1, and E_2, respectively. We use different accounts to share the file, and change the sign-in sequence of testing accounts, to understand the policy for the *default account* (i.e., the Google-chosen account). The results are listed in Table 1.

We first share the file using the regular account G_s. We change the log-in sequence of other two regular accounts G_1, G_2, and find that the **first** log-in account is always used to open the file (acting as the *Google-chosen account*). This is also the same case when we sign in two *.edu* accounts, E_1 and E_2: the first log-in account is the *Google-chosen account*. However, if we sign in one regular account and one *.edu* account, the regular account with *.gmail.com* domain will always be the *Google-chosen account*. Changing the log-in sequence will not affect the *Google-chosen account* here.

We then share the file using an *.edu* account E_s, and repeat the experiments. In this case, the first log-in account will always be the *Google-chosen account*, even if two different types of accounts are signed in (e.g., E_1 and G_1). The policy is implemented on the Google server side, thus obscure to users. From our experiments, we find that this policy depends on the log-in sequence and types of accounts.

Security Implications. As can be seen from our experimental results in Table 1, among the 16 sharing experiments, in 50% of the experiments, the

Table 1. Experiments on Google Drive to determining the Google-chosen accounts

File sharing		Log-in sequence		Google-chosen account
From	User-chosen account	First	Second	
G_s	G_1	G_1	G_2	G_1
G_s	G_2	G_1	G_2	G_1
G_s	G_1	G_2	G_1	G_2
G_s	G_2	G_2	G_1	G_2
G_s	E_1	E_1	E_2	E_1
G_s	E_2	E_1	E_2	E_1
G_s	E_1	E_2	E_1	E_2
G_s	E_2	E_2	E_1	E_2
G_s	G_1	G_1	E_1	G_1
G_s	E_1	G_1	E_1	G_1
G_s	G_1	E_1	G_1	G_1
G_s	E_1	E_1	G_1	G_1
E_s	G_1	G_1	E_1	G_1
E_s	E_1	G_1	E_1	G_1
E_s	G_1	E_1	G_1	E_1
E_s	E_1	E_1	G_1	E_1

Google-chosen account is not the user-chosen account. Meaning Google wrongly chose an account that is not what the user intended, and this could lead to security or privacy problems. Once the shared document is opened by the *Google-chosen account*, this document will be recorded in that account's history. Even if this *Google-chosen account* is later on signed in from another device, the file is still accessible to the account. The user with control of the *Google-chosen account* can then get the information, or even tamper the file if this file is shared with write permission. In particular, suppose Eva shares a file by sending Alice's education account with a sharable link. The file is accessible by anyone who knows the link, but the link is kept privately by Eva. In this case, without knowing the link, other users are still unable to read or write the file. However, Bob successfully signs his *Gmail* account in the Alice's machine through the third cases mentioned in the threat model (Sect. 3). As mentioned before, the regular *Gmail* account with the *gmail.com* domain will become the *Google-chosen account*. As a result, when Alice clicks the link, Bob will get the access of the target file. In other words, the multiple sign-in feature, when used in conjunction with the capability-based access control, could cause a file to be shared to an user against the recipient's will and without the recipient's knowledge.

Table 2. Experiments on Dropbox file sharing to determining the Dropbox-chosen accounts

File sharing	Log-in sequence		Sharing manner	Dropbox-chosen account
User-chosen account	First	Second		
D_B	$\mathbf{D_B}$	D_P	link, view file	$\mathbf{D_B}$
D_P	$\mathbf{D_B}$	D_P	link, view file	$\mathbf{D_B}$
D_B	$\mathbf{D_B}$	D_P	invite people, view folder	$\mathbf{D_B}$
D_P	D_B	$\mathbf{D_P}$	invite people, view folder	$\mathbf{D_P}$
D_B	$\mathbf{D_B}$	D_P	invite people, view file	$\mathbf{D_B}$
D_P	D_B	$\mathbf{D_P}$	invite people, view file	$\mathbf{D_P}$
D_B	D_P	$\mathbf{D_B}$	invite people, view folder	$\mathbf{D_B}$
D_P	$\mathbf{D_P}$	D_B	invite people, view folder	$\mathbf{D_P}$
D_B	D_P	$\mathbf{D_B}$	invite people, view file	$\mathbf{D_B}$
D_P	$\mathbf{D_P}$	D_B	invite people, view file	$\mathbf{D_P}$
D_B	D_B	$\mathbf{D_P}$	invite people, request file	$\mathbf{D_P}$
D_P	D_B	$\mathbf{D_P}$	invite people, request file	$\mathbf{D_P}$
D_B	D_B	$\mathbf{D_P}$	link, request file	$\mathbf{D_P}$
D_P	D_B	$\mathbf{D_P}$	link, request file	$\mathbf{D_P}$
D_B	$\mathbf{D_P}$	D_B	invite people, request file	$\mathbf{D_P}$
D_P	$\mathbf{D_P}$	D_B	invite people, request file	$\mathbf{D_P}$
D_B	$\mathbf{D_P}$	D_B	invite people, request file	$\mathbf{D_P}$
D_P	$\mathbf{D_P}$	D_B	invite people, request file	$\mathbf{D_P}$

5   Dropbox Multiple Accounts

5.1   How Dropbox Multiple Accounts Works

Dropbox is mainly for online storage sharing. Dropbox allows users to have a personal account and a business account; users can have both accounts active in the same browser. Users can access their person account by visiting the URL https://www.dropbox.com/personal and access their business account by visiting the URL https://www.dropbox.com/work.

Dropbox uses a cookie called "Last_active_role" to record the **last active** account, which could be the personal account, or the business account. For example, when both pages are open, if the user refreshes the personal account page, the personal account will be considered as the last active account; if the user then refreshes the business account page, the business account will become the last active account.

5.2   Main Problem

The main problem of Dropbox occurs when resource sharing is happening. At the time of this study, Dropbox supports three types of resource sharing: regular file, paper, showcase. We perform various experiments to measure each of these three services, and we find several issues. Since both Dropbox and Google Drive are storage sharing products, most problems we identify in Dropbox are similar to those problems in Google Drive. They exhibit in a similar manner: i.e., there is a mismatch between the user-chosen account and the server-chosen account. In the following, we use the term *"Dropbox-chosen* account" to represent this server-chosen account. We also define the "user-chosen account" in the Dropbox context as follows: in order to use Dropbox, users need to register an account with their email address. Thus, each Dropbox account is essentially bound with an email address. Therefore, the "user-chosen account" in the Dropbox context is similar to the Google Drive situation - the resource recipient opens the resource from within its email box. We conduct different experiments to determine the Dropbox-chosen account. In the following, we use **D1** to denote the business account, and **D2** to denote the personal account.

Dropbox File. Similar to Google drive, Dropbox allows users to share files in different ways. The owner can generate a link and send the link to the recipient over either an email or an instant message. The owner can also select "invite people", which will automatically constructs an email to notify the recipient. Users can either share a single file, or a folder containing multiple files. We also notice there is a feature called "request file", which allows a user to request a file from another user. We test all of these scenarios and record our results in Table 2. As illustrated in the table, it can be seen that in nearly 30% of situations the Dropbox-chosen account does not match with the user-chosen account.

Dropbox Paper. Dropbox *paper* is a paper collaboration service, which allows multiple people to edit the same paper simultaneously. Dropbox *paper* allows users to send an invitation to collaborators, and the owner can specify whether the recipient should have the edit permission or just the comment permission. We test both of these two scenarios and record our results in Table 3. As can be seen from Table 3, when sharing a paper with someone who has two accounts alive from the same browser, no matter which account is the paper shared to, the personal account will always be used to access to the paper.

We also notice another interesting and surprising issue with the Dropbox *paper* feature. When a paper is shared with a business account in the comment mode only, if the business account is active with a personal account from the same browser, the personal account will get the permission of both commenting and editing.

Dropbox Showcase. Dropbox *showcase* is a service that allows users to share a project to other people on a single page. Similarly, Dropbox *showcase* allows

Table 3. Dropbox paper sharing

File sharing	Log-in sequence		Sharing manner	Dropbox-chosen account
User-chosen account	First	Second		
D_B	D_B	$\mathbf{D_P}$	invite people, edit	$\mathbf{D_P}$
D_P	D_B	$\mathbf{D_P}$	invite people, edit	$\mathbf{D_P}$
D_B	D_B	$\mathbf{D_P}$	invite people, comment	$\mathbf{D_P}$
D_P	D_B	$\mathbf{D_P}$	invite people, comment	$\mathbf{D_P}$
D_B	$\mathbf{D_P}$	D_B	invite people, edit	$\mathbf{D_P}$
D_P	$\mathbf{D_P}$	D_B	invite people, edit	$\mathbf{D_P}$
D_B	$\mathbf{D_P}$	D_B	invite people, comment	$\mathbf{D_P}$
D_P	$\mathbf{D_P}$	D_B	invite people, comment	$\mathbf{D_P}$

Table 4. Dropbox showcase sharing

File sharing	Log-in sequence		Sharing manner	Dropbox-chosen account
User-chosen account	First	Second		
D_B	$\mathbf{D_B}$	D_P	invite people	$\mathbf{D_B}$
D_P	$\mathbf{D_B}$	D_P	invite people	$\mathbf{D_B}$
D_B	$\mathbf{D_B}$	D_P	link	$\mathbf{D_B}$
D_P	$\mathbf{D_B}$	D_P	link	$\mathbf{D_B}$
D_B	D_P	$\mathbf{D_B}$	invite people	$\mathbf{D_B}$
D_P	D_P	$\mathbf{D_B}$	invite people	$\mathbf{D_B}$
D_B	D_P	$\mathbf{D_B}$	link	$\mathbf{D_B}$
D_P	D_P	$\mathbf{D_B}$	link	$\mathbf{D_B}$

users to either send an invitation to other people, or send a link to other people. For both cases, the recipient can make comments about the shared project. We test both scenarios and record our results in Table 4.

The main insights we gain from this set of experiment is, when we share a showcase with someone who has two accounts (one business and one personal account) alive from the same browser, the *Dropbox-chosen* account is always the last active account. In other words, when the recipient opens the showcase, the last active account will always be used to open the showcase - and when we were performing the experiments for Table 4, the last active account was the business account.

Privacy Implications. For all the three main services Dropbox provides, as we can see, there is always a decent chance (30% to 50%) that the Dropbox-chosen account is not the user-chosen account. This could lead to some privacy leakage issue. Next we will describe an example in which this privacy leakage issue could hurt Dropbox users. Let us suppose user Bob wants to share a business file with his co-worker Alice. Bob creates a link, and sends this link to Alice via email. Alice has two Dropbox accounts signed in the same browser. The link goes to her business account email box, and she tries to open it, but Dropbox does not know it is opened from her business account email box. So a Dropbox-chosen account will be used, which at this moment could happen to be her personal account. So the file will be opened from her personal account, and she does not realize this. After viewing the file, she writes a comment about this file - and this comment will be visible to everybody in the business group - meaning that everybody would see Alice's personal account and its profile picture. This could lead to two problems. First, Alice would be embarrassed if her personal profile picture is an inappropriate picture. Second, Alice might be violating the company's policy and be punished for using her personal account to access business resources. Yet in her defense, she does not expect any of her personal account's information to be exposed to her colleagues or business partners, and she does not have any intention to access business resources with her personal account. The whole procedure happens without her knowledge.

6   Defense

The root cause of all the problems we have identified in the multiple sign-in process is due to the shortcomings in current cookies mechanism. When a shared link is opened in a browser where multiple accounts have signed-in, there is insufficient context information in the cookies about the accounts. Specifically, if the link is clicked inside one account (e.g., *Gmail*), the server side has to open the *default account* (e.g. Google-chosen or Dropbox-chosen) because the current cookie mechanism lacks the account information. This could be solved by enhancing servers with new cookies containing accounts information. However, if a link is clicked outside web browsers, the browsers will not be able to know which account should be used to open this link. For instance, a user simply copies and pastes a Google *Drive* link to the browser's address bar. In this case, the server side has no idea on which account is the "correct" account. Therefore, it would open the link with a *default account*, which might not be the user's intended account. As a result, we argue that this account selection procedure must be in some way explicitly delegated to users.

6.1   Server Side Defense

Ideally, such a delegation mechanism should be implemented by the service providers, i.e., Google, Dropbox, etc. We have reported the issues we found to Google. After reading our report, the corresponding security team at Google told us that our finding is surprising, but instead of fixing the security issues, they stressed that the capability-based access control should not be used to share a document if the document is very confidential. We do not agree with Google, as no existing research or literature has shown that the capability-based

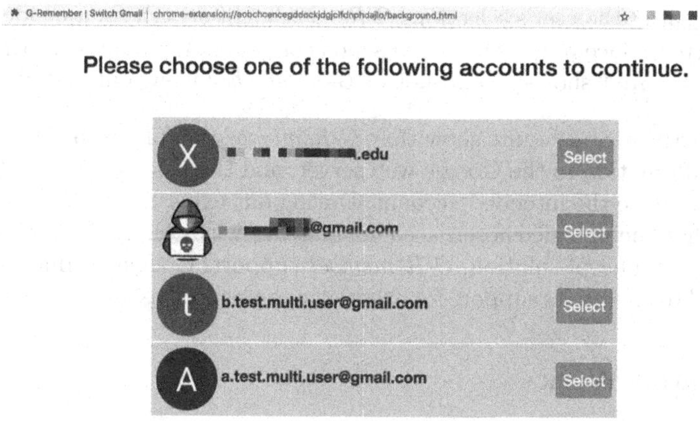

Fig. 1. A snapshot of G-Remember.

access control is less secure than the ACL based access control. As we have stated before, the security issues do not manifest just because of the capability-based access control, they arise when both the multiple sign-in feature and the capability-based access control are used.

6.2 Client Side Defense

Since the server side is out of our control, we consider to demonstrate that the issue could also be mitigated from the client side, even though that is not ideal. We propose a proof-of-concept solution for Google products by allowing end-users to make the decision on which account should further proceed upon opening links without context information. We call our solution *G-Remember*, which is a browser extension, and is implemented with JavaScripts+HTML+JSON. *G-Remember* collects all accounts' information, intercepts URLs, and reproduces the link sent to remote server by adding some user input (account choice). As a result, *G-Remember* enables the user to choose the appropriate account. Specifically, *G-Remember* consists of four parts.

- First, *G-Remember* collects the account information by recording a unique identifier (e.g., session index), the profile picture, as well as the email address. The unique identifier works as a trusted parameter for verifying accounts' identities. The email address and the profile picture will be presented to the user for account selection. All of these pieces of information are automatically collected while the user signs in.
- When a link is opened, *G-Remember* intercepts the HTTP request, extracts and analyzes the URL information to determine the target service and product. This function is accomplished by keyword and structure matching.
- After figuring out the target product, *G-Remember* will display a customized web page with all of the accounts' details (e.g., picture and email address from step one) included, and ask the user to select one account to proceed.

- Finally, after the user's selection, *G-Remember* inserts the unique identifier in the correct place in the URL, and sends corresponding request to the remote server. Figure 1 shows a snapshot of *G-Remember* using our tested emails.

Our experimental results show that *G-Remember* enables web clients to send context information to the Google web server, and the Google server is therefore able to recognize the intended account. During our experiments, we consistently observe that the Google-chosen account matches with the user-chosen account. As a proof-of-concept solution, *G-Remember* supports Google products only, but it is trivial to extend its support for other companies such as Dropbox's products.

7   Related Work

To the best of our knowledge, we are the first to study cookie issues in the context of multiple accounts. Our work is related to web security, especially cookies related security issues.

Cookies enable web servers to store the states of clients, and thus they are widely used by first-party and third-party websites [14]. Previous large-scale measurements [8,11] found that cookies in practice are much more sophisticated than the standard. Ill-managed cookies could be exploited by attackers to obtain private data or track users. As a result, cookies have attracted numerous attention. Sivakorn et al. [16] presented a comprehensive study on the HTTP cookie hijacking attack. They showed that such attacks not only disclose private and sensitive information, but also can gain access to protected account functionality. Historiographer [9] demonstrates that the web search history of Google users could be reconstructed from the personalized suggestions. Englehardt et al. [10] showed that third-party cookies could be used as unique identifiers to track users even with different IP addresses. Even worse, cookies are prone to be leaked due to cross-site scripting (XSS) attacks [15]. To mitigate the risk of client side scripts accessing cookies, HTTP-only cookies are introduced. Unfortunately, Zhou et al. [17] demonstrated that such a mechanism cannot completely eliminate XSS vulnerabilities. Cookies are also widely used as fingerprinting to track users [6,7]. Mendoza et al. [13] studied the inconsistencies between mobile and desktop HTTP security response, and showed that the inconsistencies on the same website can cause various vulnerabilities. Our work also studies the fragility in existing cookies design. However, we focus on the scenarios of multiple-accounts, which have not been studied in previous work.

8   Conclusion

In this paper we study the multiple sign-in feature in several web applications, including Google, Dropbox, Yahoo and Postman. We identify four different models used by web applications to implement the multiple sign-in feature, and report various security, privacy, and usability concerns regarding its implementation in Google and Dropbox applications. We investigate the root cause and present a proof-of-concept client solution to alleviate these concerns. Until the service providers fix the problems on the server side, we recommend users to be cautious when using those web services that provide the multiple sign-in feature.

References

1. Access two gmail accounts at once in the same browser. https://gmail.googleblog.com/2010/08/access-two-gmail-accounts-at-once-in.html
2. File with 1.4 billion hacked and leaked passwords found on the dark web. https://www.forbes.com/sites/leemathews/2017/12/11/billion-hacked-passwords-dark-web/#1d2ef9ec21f2
3. Hold security recovers 272 million stolen credentials from a collector. https://holdsecurity.com/news/the_collector_breach/
4. Sessionbox. https://sessionbox.io/discover
5. Twitter advising all 330 million users to change passwords after bug exposed them in plain text. https://www.theverge.com/2018/5/3/17316684/twitter-password-bug-security-flaw-exposed-change-now
6. Acar, G., Eubank, C., Englehardt, S., Juarez, M., Narayanan, A., Diaz, C.: The web never forgets: persistent tracking mechanisms in the wild. In: Proceedings of the 2014 ACM SIGSAC Conference on Computer and Communications Security, pp. 674–689. ACM (2014)
7. Acar, G., et al.: FPDetective: dusting the web for fingerprinters. In: Proceedings of the 2013 ACM SIGSAC Conference on Computer and Communications Security, pp. 1129–1140. ACM (2013)
8. Cahn, A., Alfeld, S., Barford, P., Muthukrishnan, S.: An empirical study of web cookies. In: Proceedings of the 25th International Conference on World Wide Web, pp. 891–901. International World Wide Web Conferences Steering Committee (2016)
9. Castelluccia, C., De Cristofaro, E., Perito, D.: Private Information disclosure from web searches. In: Atallah, M.J., Hopper, N.J. (eds.) PETS 2010. LNCS, vol. 6205, pp. 38–55. Springer, Heidelberg (2010). https://doi.org/10.1007/978-3-642-14527-8_3
10. Englehardt, S., et al.: Cookies that give you away: the surveillance implications of web tracking. In: Proceedings of the 24th International Conference on World Wide Web (WWW) (2015)
11. Gonzalez, R., et al.: The cookie recipe: untangling the use of cookies in the wild. In: 2017 IEEE Network Traffic Measurement and Analysis Conference (2017)
12. Levy, H.M.: Capability-Based Computer Systems. Digital Press, Bedford (2014)
13. Mendoza, A., Chinprutthiwong, P., Gu, G.: Uncovering HTTP header inconsistencies and the impact on desktop/mobile websites. In: Proceedings of the 2018 World Wide Web Conference on World Wide Web (WWW) (2018)
14. Roesner, F., Kohno, T., Wetherall, D.: Detecting and defending against third-party tracking on the web. In: Proceedings of the 9th USENIX conference on Networked Systems Design and Implementation (NSDI) (2012)
15. Singh, K., Moshchuk, A., Wang, H.J., Lee, W.: On the incoherencies in web browser access control policies. In: 2010 IEEE Symposium on Security and Privacy (SP) (2010)
16. Sivakorn, S., Polakis, J., Keromytis. A.D.: Cookie hijacking in the wild: security and privacy implications. BlackHat (2016)
17. Zhou, Y., Evans, D.: Why aren't http-only cookies more widely deployed. In: Proceedings of 4th Web 2.0 Security and Privacy (2010)

Authenticated LSM Trees
with Minimal Trust

Yuzhe Tang[⊠], Kai Li, and Ju Chen

Syracuse University, New York, USA
ytang100@syr.edu

Abstract. In the age of user-generated contents, the workloads imposed on information-security infrastructures become increasingly write intensive. However, existing security protocols, specifically authenticated data structures (ADSs), are historically designed based on update-in-place data structures and incur overhead when serving write-intensive workloads.

In this work, we present LPAD (Log-structured Persistent Authenticated Directory), a new ADS protocol designed uniquely based on the log-structure merge trees (LSM trees) which recently gain popularity in the design of modern storage systems. On the write path, LPAD supports streaming, non-interactive updates with constant proof from trusted data owners. On the read path, LPAD supports point queries over the dynamic dataset with a polynomial proof. The key to enable this efficiency is a verifiable reorganization operation, called verifiable merge, in LPAD. Verifiable merge is secured by the execution in an enclave of trusted execution environments (TEE). To minimize the trusted computing base (TCB), LPAD places the code related to verifiable merge in enclave, and nothing else. Our implementation of LPAD on Google LevelDB codebase and on Intel SGX shows that the TCB is reduced by 20 times: The enclave size of LPAD is one thousand code lines out of more than twenty thousands code lines of a vanilla LevelDB. Under the YCSB workloads, LPAD improves the performance by an order of magnitude comparing with existing ADSs.

Keywords: Storage security · Query authentication · Key-value stores · LSM trees · TEE

1 Introduction

In the age of cloud computing, outsourcing data storage to the cloud is a common practice (e.g., Dropbox [6], Google drive [9], etc). When using the cloud storage to host security-critical infrastructures (e.g., Bitcoin like cryptocurrencies [2,3, 7,18], Google's certificate transparency schemes [4,5,38], etc.), the lack of trust to the public clouds is real and becomes increasingly pressing, in the presence of the constant cloud-security incidents. It calls for security hardening of untrusted

© ICST Institute for Computer Sciences, Social Informatics and Telecommunications Engineering 2019
Published by Springer Nature Switzerland AG 2019. All Rights Reserved
S. Chen et al. (Eds.): SecureComm 2019, LNICST 305, pp. 454–471, 2019.
https://doi.org/10.1007/978-3-030-37231-6_27

cloud storage. In particular, the authenticity of data storage is a fundamental security property critical to many information-security applications. To protect the data authenticity, a common approach is to instantiate an authenticated data structure (ADS) protocol with an untrusted cloud provider and trusted clients.

Many emerging security applications feature a write-intensive workload. For instance, in cryptocurrency, transactions are constantly generated. A public key directory (for certificate transparency) features an intensive stream of certificate-registration and revocation requests. To serve the write-intensive workload with data authenticity, existing ADS protocols present an ill-suited solution. Because most existing ADS protocols [30,34,36,40–43,49,52–54] are designed based on update-in-place data structures, which incur multiple rounds of communications for serving an update (i.e., interactive update), incurring high overhead in write-intensive workloads.

In this work, we propose LPAD,[1] an authenticated data structure designed uniquely based on the log-structured merge tree (LSM tree) [39]. An LSM tree is an external-memory data structure that optimizes the write performance and is widely adopted in many modern storage systems such as Google LevelDB [11]/Big-table [27], Apache HBase [12], Apache Cassandra [10], etc. With the LSM tree's append-only write design, the LPAD supports streaming, non-interactive data updates from cloud clients. To support verifiable merge operation in an LSM tree, we assume a trusted third-party (TTP) in formulating the LPAD protocol. We believe this assumption is necessary, otherwise the protocol construction will require expensive protocols such as verifiable computations (VC) [22,23,45] – the state-of-the-art VC systems [25,44,46,50] cause multiple orders of magnitude performance slowdown comparing to an unsecured system (without VC).

This work aims at building a real LPAD system with minimal third-party trust. We propose to build the LPAD system by leveraging Intel SGX [15] which supports a trusted "enclave" on an otherwise untrusted platform. The proposed system design runs minimal functions inside SGX enclave, that is, the merge operation and timestamp management. Other than this, majority of the codebase of an LSM data store runs outside the enclave. By this means, it is promising to minimize the trusted computing base (TCB) in the enclave, which renders the system amenable to formal program verification. To authenticate the data storage outside the enclave, we design a digest structure that is aligned well with the LSM tree. The LPAD digest structure is implemented by co-locating the digests (Merkle trees [33]) with the data index, which is promising to save disk seeks when retrieving the query proof.

We evaluate our LPAD protocol and systems in terms of (1) security, (2) minimal TCB and (3) performance overhead. We analyze the protocol security by reducing the query authenticity to the hardness of finding collision in cryptographic hashes. We build a functional LPAD system based on Google Lev-

---

[1] LPAD stands for Log-structured Persistent Authenticated Dictionary which follows the naming of a common ADS protocol, PAD [20,32].

eIDB [11] and SGX SDK. In our LPAD implementation, the TCB size, namely the lines of code running in enclave, is reduced to 4.4% of the entire codebase. We evaluate the performance of our LPAD prototype extensively: Under the common YCSB workloads that are write intensive, LPAD improves the performance by an order of magnitude comparing existing update-in-place ADS.

In summary, the contributions of this work are:

New ADS protocol: This work addresses the authenticated storage of data updates in emerging security scenarios. We identify the performance problem of all existing ADS protocols: The update-in-place data structures existing ADSs rely on cause significant performance slowdown on the write path. To the best of our knowledge, we are the first to propose a log-structured ADS protocol, named LPAD, that allows for non-interactive updates from clients.

New system design: We materialize LPAD with a functional system built on Google LevelDB and Intel SGX. The system design of LPAD reduces the TCB size in enclave. This is done by placing only the computation-oriented code routine inside the enclave. The system design of LPAD also collocates the digests with data, saving data-retrieve overhead.

2   Preliminaries

This section presents the preliminaries of related techniques to this work.

2.1   LSM Trees and Write-Intensive Workloads

A log-structured merge tree (LSM) is designed to be a middle ground between classic B+tree like data structures that are read-optimized and the temporal log structures that are write-optimized. An LSM tree only causes sequential IO for writes, thus preserving write locality similarly to the pure log-structured storage. It avoids the full-disk scan per read by decomposing the storage into several sorted runs, each of which can be indexed and randomly accessed in sublinear time.

Target Workloads: The targeted workload of LSM tree is write-intensive workloads which become popular in serving user-generated contents in modern applications. The target workloads feature (1) an intensive stream of updates on individual data records and (2) data reads that result in random data accesses. In addition, (3) our workloads are issued from security-sensitive scenarios where the data integrity, membership and freshness needs to be guaranteed. Such application scenarios include Bitcoin-alike cryptocurrencies, data-transparency schemes, etc.

2.2   Authenticated Data Structures

An authenticated data structure (ADS) is a protocol that allows a data owner to outsource the data storage to a third-party host which will be queried later by data users. In a public-key setting, the data owner holding the secret key can initially sign and later update the dataset, and the user trusting the owner's public key can verify the query result (assuming an external PKI). An ADS protocol can be thought of as an extended digital signature scheme where the message is a dataset and new algorithms are added to support data-read/write queries. While there is recent ADS research [43, 49, 54] to support expressive queries and various data structures, in this work we consider the most foundational form of ADS, that is, an authenticated dictionary supporting set-membership queries [20].

Existing ADS constructions [34, 48] are mainly based on update-in-place data structures. In the case of a Merkle tree, for instance, an update-in-place ADS requires the data owner (keeping a simple digest/signature) to issue read query first, modify the Merkle authentication proof, and then generate a new signature before writing it to the host. Variants of update-in-place ADSes are proposed, such as replicated ADSes [34, 54] and cached ADSes [31]; they improve the update efficiency at the expense of a larger owner state. Update-in-place ADS constructions have been used to implement system prototypes, such as consistency-verified storage [35] and authenticated databases [34].

2.3   Intel Software Guard eXtension (SGX)

Intel SGX is a security-oriented x86-64 ISA extension on the Intel Skylake CPU, released in 2016. SGX provides a "security-isolated world" for trustworthy program execution on an otherwise untrusted hardware platform. At the hardware level, the SGX secure world includes a tamper-proof SGX CPU which automatically encrypts memory pages (in the so-called enclave region) upon cache-line write-back. Instructions executed outside the SGX secure world that attempt to read/write enclave pages only get to see the ciphertext and cannot succeed. SGX's trusted software includes only unprivileged program and excludes any OS kernel code, by explicitly prohibiting system services (e.g., system calls) inside an enclave.

To use the technology, a client initializes an enclave by uploading the in-enclave program and uses SGX's seal and attestation mechanism [21] to verify the correct setup of the execution environment (e.g., by a digest of enclave memory content). During the program execution, the enclave is entered and exited proactively (by SGX instructions, e.g., EENTER and EEXIT) or passively (by interrupts or traps). These world-switch events trigger the context saving/loading in both hardware and software levels. Comparing with prior TEE solutions [1, 14, 17, 19], SGX uniquely support multi-core concurrent execution, dynamic paging, and interrupted execution.

3   System Overview and Motivation

In this section, we present the system architecture in terms of target applications and trust model. We also present our motivating observation, that is, placing existing update-in-place ADS construction over log-structured storage results in inefficiency.

3.1   System Model and Security Goals

We consider the common cloud-storage scenario that cloud customers outsource their data storage to a third-party cloud platform. The cloud instance runs over an SGX machine and exposes an enclave to the customer. The server runs application and storage services. It persists data to its storage media through a key-value store. In this work, we consider the LSM tree based key-value stores exposing a standard PUT/GET interface (will be elaborated soon). The use of LSM-based key-value store allows the system to ingest an intense stream of data writes, featured in our target applications.

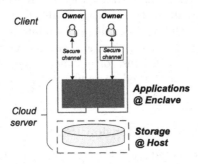

Fig. 1. System trust model: The box with solid lines (in green) means the trusted domain including the enclave and owners. The box with dotted lines (in red) means the untrusted host domain. (Color figure online)

The enclave is trusted by the cloud customer and we assume the standard techniques to establish such trust (e.g., software attestation mechanism [21] and key-exchange protocols [33]). The communication channel between the customer and the server enclave is thus secured by standard TLS protocols. In our system model, we assume the enclave and cloud customer are securely connected. Figure 1 illustrates the system architecture.

In the system, the enclave runs the server-side applications, and the host outside the enclave runs an LSM-tree based key-value store. The two interact through a standard key-value store API: Given key k, value v, timestamp ts, a write operation $\text{PUT}(k, v)$ returns an acknowledgment about committed timestamp ts, and a read operation $\text{GET}(k, ts_q)$ returns result record $\langle k, v, ts \rangle$ where ts_q denotes the timestamp at the invocation time of GET and ts denotes the timestamp of record returned. Formally,

$$ts := \text{PUT}(k, v)$$
$$\langle k, v, ts \rangle := \text{GET}(k, ts_q) \tag{1}$$

Timestamp Management: In our scheme, timestamp is managed inside enclave and is backed by a trusted storage service (e.g., TPM chip) to defend roll-back attacks by the untrusted host. Upon PUT/GET requests, the timestamps are managed in the following manner: (1) For each PUT operation issued by the application, the enclave serializes the operation and monotonically increases the current timestamp to assign a unique timestamp for the operation. (2) For each GET operation issued by the application, it simply retrieves the current timestamp and uses it as t_q in the GET request. (3) The timestamp is periodically "flushed" to the trusted storage. The "flush" of timestamp counter can be set at a fixed rate or be coupled with the "flush" operation in the underlying LPAD.

Given a read operation, there are several properties associated: (1) Result integrity is about whether the result of a read, say $\langle k, v, ts \rangle$, is a valid data record (meaning the one written by a legitimate write before). The result integrity can be protected by a simple use of message authentication code (MAC), and it is not our main security goal. (2) Result membership is about whether a read result is fresh and complete in the dataset stored in the key-value store. The freshness states whether the result $\langle k, v, ts \rangle$ has the largest timestamp (or is the latest) among all records of the queried key k and with a timestamp smaller than ts_q. The completeness prevents a legitimate result from being omitted. The result membership in freshness and completeness can be authenticated using the LPAD scheme.

Threat Model: The trust boundary in our system occurs between the enclave and the server host. The server host includes (1) hardware devices except for the SGX processor, and (2) software that is loaded and is executed in the untrusted memory, including the privileged operating system. The adversary can control the server host software stack and subvert the storage systems there by forging operation results (will be described next). The adversary in this work is assumed not to compromise the SGX hardware which is tamper resistant. In addition, this work does not address the following attacks: denial-of-service attacks, proven deletion under Sybil attacks, SGX side-channel attacks [51], design flaws or enclave program security.

A query-forging adversary can modify the result of a data read (or a write) returned from the untrusted server host. Given a read query, the adversary can present an incorrect result. Specifically, she can present a non-exist data record (breaking the result integrity), present a properly signed but stale result to the enclave (breaking the freshness), or present an empty result while omitting a matching record in the dataset (breaking the completeness).

Security Goals: The security goal in this work is that the enclave issuing PUT/GET requests can verify the freshness of the query results. If the untrusted host forges any query results, the verification algorithm in the enclave cannot pass. Note that in this work, we don't address the mitigation of query-forging attack, that is, when the forging occurs, the enclave cannot recover the honest result from the forged result.

4   LPAD Protocol: Scheme and Constructions

In this section, we define the standard LPAD scheme. An LPAD is an ADS scheme tailored to the LSM tree structure. We first present a model of an LSM tree before describing the LPAD scheme and security.

4.1   Design Motivation

To motivate our LPAD protocol, we present a strawman design that layers the update-in-place ADS over an LSM-tree based store.

When placing an update-in-place ADS over an LSM tree, an immediate problem is that the authentication data has a different structure from the actual data. The structure mismatch creates extra engineering difficulty and performance overhead. As the motivation of our work, we conduct a performance study and show the slowdown. We consider an update-in-place ADS built on top of an imaginary binary search tree, which is mapped to the input domain of the underlying LSM store (e.g., through the encoding of in-order tree traversal). Each tree node is mapped to a key-value record in the LSM store. By this means, each read (write) is translated to a series of index-node lookups and the final data transfer. The performance result of this strawman comparing the ideal case (an LSM tree without any ADS) is illustrated in Fig. 2a. It shows that with the presence of an update-in-place ADS, it adds a significant amount of overhead to the write performance. In addition, in the target workload featuring an intensive stream of writes, the slowdown is up to several orders of magnitudes.

4.2   Model of LSM Tree

An LSM tree represents a dataset m by a series of so-called levels, $l_0, l_1 ... l_{q-1}$. A level l_i is a list of ordered data records $l_i = b_1 b_2 ... b_j ....$ An LSM tree supports the basic data reads and writes, where a write only updates the first level l_0. A read may iterate through all levels to find a match. An LSM tree supports the MERGE operation that merges two adjacent levels (e.g., l_i and l_{i+1}) into one level. In the LSM tree, the first level l_0 resides in memory and all immutable levels $l_{\geq 1}$ reside on disk. Note this simple structure ensures writes are clustered into sequential storage access (Table 1).

Table 1. Notations

b	Key-value record	m	Dataset
n	Security parameter	ts	Timestamp
a	Answer	π	Proof
l	LSM-tree level	q	Number of levels

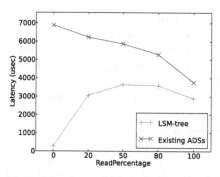

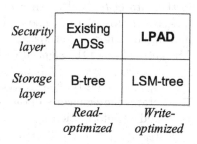

(a) Performance mismatch between data-level LSM tree and security-level ADSs

(b) Comparing the LPAD design with existing ADS: This figure considers random-read access and excludes the pure log-based design (e.g., log-structured file systems and hash-chain).

Fig. 2. Performance of update-in-place ADS over LSM and the design of LPAD

4.3   LPAD Scheme and Security

LPAD extends an ADS scheme with new algorithms to handle the MERGE operation interactively. Formally, consider a set-membership predicate: Given dataset m and record b, a set-membership predicate is $0, 1 := P(m, b)$ where $0/1$ represent non-membership/membership of the record in dataset m. The scheme of an LPAD is the following:

LPAD scheme Π^{LPAD} consists of eight probabilistic polynomial-time (PPT) algorithms (GEN, SETUP, QUERY, VRFY, UPDATE, REFRESH, MERGE, SIGMERGE), where the first six are defined in a standard ADS scheme, and the last two are new algorithms in LPAD. Specifically, SETUP signs the initial dataset (m), (QUERY,VRFY) forms an interactive[a] sub-protocol for point-read (record b), and (UPDATE,REFRESH) forms an interactive point-write sub-protocol. The pair of new algorithms, (MERGE,SIGMERGE), interactively merge the levels.

For simplicity, consider the three-party ADS model[b] where a data owner writes to a server host and clients read ADS from the server. The owner holding secret key sk keeps a full copy of dataset m.

- $pk, sk \leftarrow \text{GEN}(1^n)$: A pair of public/private keys are generated with security parameter n.
- $s \leftarrow \text{SETUP}_{sk}(m)$: Owner signs the initial dataset m using secret key sk.
- $\pi, a \leftarrow \text{QUERY}_{pk,P(\cdot,\cdot)}(m, b)$: The host processes a set-membership query on record b against dataset m using public key pk. It returns the answer a of set-membership relation $P(\cdot, \cdot)$ and a proof π.
- $1, 0 := \text{VRFY}_{pk}(\pi, a)$: The client receiving proof π and answer a verifies using public key pk whether the answer is authentic. 1 means the authentic answer.

- $l'_0, s'_0, upd \leftarrow \text{UPDATE}_{sk}(b, l_0)$: The owner adds a new record b to level-zero in the dataset l_0. It also generates update information upd.
- $l'_0, s'_0 := \text{REFRESH}_{pk}(b, l_0, upd)$: The host receiving a new record to add b and update information upd (resulted from Algorithm UPDATE or SIG-MERGE) refreshes the signature of level zero to be s'_0 using upd.
- $\varnothing, s'_i, l'_{i+1}, s'_{i+1}, upd := \text{SIGMERGE}_{sk}(l_i, s_i, l_{i+1}, s_{i+1})$: The owner merges two adjacent levels (l_i, l_{i+1}) in the prior state to posterior state $(\varnothing, l'_{i+1})$. It generates the signatures of the two levels in the posterior state (s'_i, s'_{i+1}) with update information upd.
- $\varnothing, s'_i, l'_{i+1}, s'_{i+1} := \text{MERGE}_{pk}(l_i, s_i, l_{i+1}, s_{i+1}, upd)$: The host merges two adjacent levels (l_i, l_{i+1}) to posterior state $(\varnothing, l'_{i+1})$ using public key pk and update information upd.

---

[a] Here, interactive means that the two algorithms (QUERY and VRFY) can be called multiple times.

[b] The extension from the three-party model to the two-party model is straightforward and can be found in related work [43].

The correctness of LPAD scheme is straightforward and similar to that of ADS [43]; informally, the correctness can be stated by that given any state resulted from calling UPDATE/REFRESH and MERGE/SIGMERGE, and given any correct QUERY on the state, running the verification algorithm (VRFY) will return 1. The security of LPAD scheme is defined in a game where an adversary can access public key pk (i.e. freely access VRFY, MERGE, REFRESH).

4.4   LPAD Construction by a Forest of Merkle Trees

This subsection presents a basic construction of LPAD and next subsection presents a read-optimized construction.

The basic LPAD construction authenticates each level by a standard ADS such as a Merkle tree. While this paper considers Merkle tree for construction, we stress that the LPAD is a paradigm that can work with other per-level ADS primitives (e.g., multi-set hash [28]). Concretely, $\text{GEN}(1^n)$ runs the standard public-key generation algorithm, and $\text{SETUP}_{sk}(m)$ signs the initial dataset m using secret key sk before the owner uploads the digest to the server. On the read path, the untrusted server runs $\pi, a \leftarrow \text{QUERY}_{pk, P(\cdot, \cdot)}(m, b)$ that prepares a query proof by including the membership proof for the level that contains the answer and more importantly the non-membership proofs for the levels that don't contain the answer. Then the client receiving proof π and answer a verifies the answer integrity by running $1, 0 := \text{VRFY}_{pk}(\pi, a)$, which further runs the verification algorithms of the per-level ADS against corresponding per-level proofs. It only accepts when *all* per-level verification accept.

On the write path, the trusted owner updates the remote dataset by running the UPDATE algorithm of the first-level ADS, namely $l'_0, s'_0, upd \leftarrow \text{UPDATE}_{sk}(b, l_0)$. Then, the untrusted server refreshes the dataset based on the owner's update by running the first-level ADS's REFRESH algorithm, namely $m'_0, s'_0 := \text{REFRESH}_{pk}(b, m_0, upd)$.

Asynchronously, the server and owner interactively run algorithms to merge two adjacent levels: The owner locally updates the two adjacent levels (l_i, l_{i+1}) to posterior state $(\varnothing, l'_{i+1})$, with signatures and update information *upd*. The server then merges two adjacent levels (m_i, m_{i+1}) to $(\varnothing, m'_{i+1})$ and simply updates their signatures using update information *upd*. The SIGMERGE(l_i, l_{i+1}) is constructed by the owner retrieving from the host the two input levels, l_i and l_{i+1}, and linearly scanning them. This straightforward construction with linear cost may not be feasible in the traditional setting, but is practical in the case with TEE where the server is co-located with the enclave owner.

The correctness of LPAD construction is straightforward and we omit it in this and subsequent constructions.

Security Analysis: The basic LPAD construction is secure as long as the per-level ADS constructions are secure. Because our security proof is based on the reduction to the security of per-level ADS. That is, if LPAD is insecure, it means at least one of per-level ADSes is insecure. Briefly, our formal security proof under the LPAD-forging game relies on the idea that MERGE can be "simulated" by a series of UPDATEs.

5   LPAD Systems

In this section, we present the engineering of LPAD protocol when building a functional storage system on Intel SGX. We build the system based on Google LevelDB [11], which is a representative and widely adopted storage system based on the LSM trees. In this paper, we use the term "LevelDB" to represent a broad class of log-structured key-value stores, such as Apache HBase [12], Apache Cassandra [10], Facebook RocksDB [8].

5.1   System Design and Implementation

System Overview. Our LPAD schemes are built on public key cryptography. When instantiating the scheme on SGX, we naturally place the secret key inside the enclave. Note that we assumed a secure key-management component in enclave such as sgx-kms [26]. In addition, all LPAD algorithms that access the secret key are run inside enclave. Algorithms with the public key are run by the untrusted host, except for the VRFY algorithm whose return value is security critical.

Therefore, our system runs the following LPAD algorithms in enclave: (1) The algorithms involving secret keys, that is, GEN, SETUP, UPDATE, SIGMERGE (recall the LPAD scheme in Sect. 4) are executed in an enclave. (2) The verification algorithm (i.e. VRFY) is placed in an enclave as the verification result is critical to the protocol security.

In particular, to support SIGMERGE, it runs a clone of MERGE computation inside enclave. The data buffered in memory is placed outside the enclave but we allow the in-enclave MERGE computation to directly access the buffer outside enclave. The data buffer is placed outside enclave, because it is accessed by the enclave for once (i.e. no locality) and placing it in enclave does not save boundary-crossing overhead. During the MERGE, the inputs are read from the disk to buffer and enclave, and are authenticated in a deferred fashion by reconstructing the entire Merkle tree of the levels. By the end of MERGE, the newly generated level is signed by the enclave. Details about implementing verifiable MERGE is presented in Sect. 5.

Digest Structures. In LPAD, the data storage is hosted in the untrusted world and it entails to authenticate the data outside the enclave by building a digest structure. We design and implement a digest structure that is aligned well with the data layout in an LSM store, aiming to minimize the imposed IO overhead.

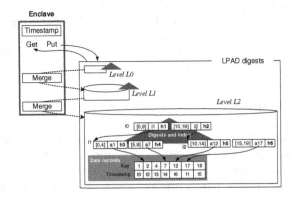

Fig. 3. LPAD system architecture with digest structures

The LPAD digest structure consists of Merkle trees built over the LSM tree dataset. Each Merkle tree digests an LSM-tree level. The data records are digested in their original order, that is, sorted first by data keys and then by timestamps. In an LSM store, data records are stored in a data file where records are indexed to facilitate the data lookup. The LPAD Merkle tree is stored by being embedded in the index. That is, each pointer in a tree index is augmented to store the hash of the Merkle tree.

An Example: In Fig. 3, there is an LSM tree with three levels. For the third level, it contains a list of key-value records, sorted first their data keys and then by timestamps. There exist an index structure that facilitates the lookup of a data key in the level. The index is a three-node B tree (of nodes $i0, i1, i2$). Each index node contains multiple entries, each with a data-key range and a pointer to the child index node. For instance, the index node $i1$ has an entry $([0,4], a1)$, which is used to direct a search with data key in $[0,4]$ to the data block starting with record $\langle 1, t0 \rangle$. LPAD system augments each index entry with a Merkle-tree hash. For instance, the index entry $([0,4], a1)$ is augmented with hash $h3$ where

$h3 = H(\langle 1, t0 \rangle \| \langle 2, t2 \rangle \| \langle 4, t3 \rangle)$. In the LPAD Merkle tree over level l_2, the Merkle tree is constructed by $h1 = H(h3 \| h4)$ and $h2 = H(h5 \| h6)$.

In LPAD system, the storage of LPAD Merkle trees is co-located with the index in an LSM store. One of the benefits for this design is that the co-located data and digest storage can reduce the data-access cost. That is, when storing the Merkle trees in a separate file, retrieving the Merkle proof involves multiple random accesses on disk, incurring expensive disk seeks. In our co-located digest storage, the random-access to retrieve proof is piggybacked in the data access path, namely, the seek to look up the index is also used to prepare the hashes in a LPAD proof, saving extra seeks.

MERGE **Implementation.** Our system runs three functionalities in enclave for verified MERGE: (1) the computation of MERGE, (2) the authentication of input data that comes into the enclave in a streaming fashion, (3) the signing of the output data. The code of these three functions run inside the enclave and the data buffer resides outside the enclave. More specifically, given multiple files at consecutive levels as input, the verified MERGE inside enclave loads the data files into data buffers outside enclave, merge-sort the data records, reconstructs the Merkle root hashes for all input files, and builds a Merkle tree over the merged output stream of records. If the reconstructed Merkle root hashes are identical to what are stored in enclave, the enclave make effective of this MERGE operation by updating the digest of the relevant levels with the reconstructed Merkle hash.

5.2 Security Analysis

In our system in SGX, an invariant is that on both write and read paths, *the in-enclave algorithm of LPAD (i.e. UPDATE and VRFY) occurs after the outside-enclave algorithm (i.e. REFRESH and QUERY)*. This invariant, with the promise of fully serialized execution,[2] allows the enclave to construct the execution order (of reads and writes) from the order these in-enclave algorithms are called. This execution order further allows to fully specify the execution history, based on which the membership can be authenticated by LPAD (e.g., freshness assumes the temporal order among reads/writes).

Concretely, we consider the freshness attack that the adversary from the untrusted host presents a correct but stale read result. The freshness property requires that a read result $\langle k, v, ts \rangle = \text{GET}(k, ts_q)$ is fresh as of timestamp ts_q. By definition, it can be authenticated by the membership of result record $\langle k, v, ts \rangle$ and the non-membership of a virtual record $\langle k, v', ts' \rangle$ that is "fresher" and with $ts' \in [ts, ts_q]$. Both the membership and non-membership can be further authenticated by the LPAD scheme underneath. Based on freshness authentication, any stale result returned from the untrusted host can be easily detected (by the failure of VRFY). Here, special notes should be taken that under the above invariant (i.e. in-enclave algorithms occur after the untrusted LPAD algorithms), the untrusted host is given the chance to store the data no older than the digest

---

[2] The untrusted host can break the promise of serialized execution, but will eventually be detected through the in-enclave checks.

in enclave, and thus any deviation from the (non)-membership proven by the digest can be attributed to the misbehavior of the untrusted host.

The freshness attack can be extended to different forms: (1) The completeness attack is a special form of freshness attack where the untrusted host omits the result and falsely returns an empty result. In this case, the non-membership authentication (for the empty result) will not pass. (2) The forking attack [37] works by the untrusted host presenting different views to different reads. As our enclave under LPAD protocol fully specifies the operation history (without ambiguity), there is always only one legitimate result that can be authenticated, thus eliminating the forking vulnerability. Note that we do not consider concurrency attacks.

6   Evaluation

In this section, we evaluate LPAD system with the goal of answering the following questions:

- What is the trusted code size (Sect. 6.1)?
- What is the performance of LPAD under IO-intensive workloads (Sect. 6.2)?

6.1   Implementation and Enclave Code Size

Original LevelDB Codebase: The codebase of LevelDB consists of several code modules. Their profiles are the following: (F1) A skip list that is accessed by reads and writes on level l_0 consists of $1.3K$ lines of code. (F2) A write-ahead log (WAL) that is accessed by a write at level l_0 consists of $1K$ LoC to persist writes and recover state. (F3) LRU data cache and Bloom filter that are accessed by reads on levels $l_{\geq 1}$ consists of $1K$ LoC. (F4) Merge computation for compaction consists of $0.2K$ LoC. (F5) Thread management code for compaction ($<0.1K$ LoC), (F6) Application-specific IO handling, e.g., for file parsing, file meta-data management, etc., consists of $4.7K$ LoC, and F7) miscellaneous utility code, e.g., for computing regular hash, consists of $4K$ LoC.

Code Modification of LevelDB: The system implementation is based on the codebase of LevelDB with the following changes: 1. We add a program to hook our in-enclave program to the LevelDB running in the untrusted host. 2. We add a program to store and serve the Merkle trees for QUERY on the untrusted host; several LevelDB utilities are reused for the Merkle-tree persistence. 3. We modify the LevelDB codebase to make each PUT return its timestamp. The change is not significant and does not cause overhead.

For evaluating the trusted code size, we prepare a baseline realizing Haven-style partitioning. In particular, our baseline is based on the latest systems-level support in enclave, Panoply [47]. Comparing with Haven [24], Panoply considers the application logic is partitioned to several modules, with each loaded in a container with Panoply's rich systems interface (e.g., thread management). Despite its rich in-enclave functionalities and minimized systems-level TCB, we stress Panoply is not application partitioning scheme and cannot specify how to partition LevelDB. Thus, in our baseline, we map the entire codebase of LevelDB into enclave.

Recall that the LPAD places inside the enclave trusted LPAD algorithms (SIGMERGE, UPDATE, VRFY) and requires the enclave to include the code for Merkle proof and SHA computation. Additionally, the enclave runs some glue code generated by Intel SGX SDK [16]. The total number of code lines in enclave is around 900. Comparing with the baseline approach, trust-minimized partitioning reduces the application-level trusted code size by 20 times.

The result of enclave code size is presented in Table 2.

Table 2. Trusted code size with LPAD partitioning strategies

Partitioning scheme	Trusted code size (LoC)
LPAD	891
The Haven [24] approach (LevelDB in enclave)	~20000

6.2 Performance Evaluation

In this section, we present the performance of LPAD under Yahoo Cloud Serving Benchmark (YCSB) [29] which is a standard benchmark suite. We evaluate the performance under IO-intensive workloads. We start by describing the common experiment setup.

Experiment Setup: We did all the experiments on two laptops with an Intel 8-core i7-6820HK CPU of 2.70 GHz and 8 MB cache, 32 GB Ram and 1TB Disk. This is one of the Skylake CPUs with SGX features.

We used the YCSB benchmark suite [29] that provides a workload generator and a multi-threaded execution platform for evaluating the performance of generic key-value stores. We leverage the LevelDB-YCSB adapter based on online projects.[3] In our experiment, we run the YCSB workload driver on one machine and the storage system on another machine; the two machines are connected in a high-speed LAN network.

We use two datasets in this experiment: The large dataset contains 200 million records (which is 24 GB without compression under 100-byte values), and the small dataset contains 1 million records (140 MB without compression). The large dataset is intended to capture the IO-intensive workload where the working set is larger than memory and IO is constantly triggered during data serving. The small dataset captures the memory intensive workloads with the working set fully residing on memory; in this case memory references (or cache misses) are the bottleneck. Both datasets are generated with uniformly distributed keys,

---

[3] https://github.com/jtsui/ycsb-leveldb.

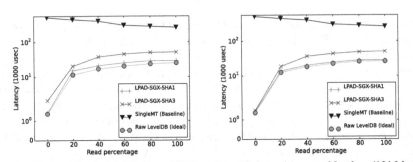

(a) IO-intensive workloads (116-byte records, SingleMT stands for the base-line approach of a single Merkle tree for authentication)

(b) IO-intensive workloads (1016-byte records)

Fig. 4. LPAD-SGX performance

each key-value record contains a 16-byte key and a value that can take a size of 100 or 1000 bytes.[4] We used the SHA3 hash algorithm from the Crypto++ library [13].

IO-Intensive Workload. In the experiment, we varied the read percentage from 0% (that is, a write-only workload), 20%, 40%, 60%, 80% to 100% and we tested 1 million queries. We consider both SHA1 and SHA3 algorithms. We vary record size (116 bytes and 1016 bytes). Our experiments are conducted with MERGE turned on and in a single thread. Each experiment is run at least three times. We report the latency per operation.

We compare the performance of our LPAD-SGX system against two base-lines: (1) The first is a raw LevelDB instance running in the untrusted world. This is an unsecured solution, but its performance is ideal. We name this baseline by "Raw LevelDB (Ideal)". (2) The second baseline is a LevelDB protected by a single Merkle tree, which represents most existing work in the ADS literature. This baseline is named by "SingleMT (Baseline)".

The performance result under the IO-intensive workload is presented in Fig. 4a and b. For both 1016-byte and 116-byte record sizes, the LPAD-SGX scheme matches well with the write-optimized characteristics of the original LevelDB – their latency increases as the workload becomes more read intensive. By contrast, the baseline of a single Merkle tree exhibits a read-optimized behavior. More over, with any read-write ratio, the LPAD-SGX systems' slowdown comparing the ideal performance is at most $2X$, which is much smaller than the $500X$ slowdown of the SingleMT baseline (the single Merkle tree). By using SHA1 instead of SHA3, the LPAD-SGX system further reduces the slowdown

---

[4] Note the smaller size a value is (e.g., 100 byte), the more challenging to serve for a storage system as small writes cause more random access IO.

to 36% for the 116-byte records and 12% for the 1016-byte records. This result confirms the benefit of matching security protocol with the underlying storage system.

7 Conclusion

This work presents **LPAD**, an ADS protocol designed based on LSM trees to address the efficiency under write-intensive workloads. A functional system is built based on **LPAD** that is on top of Google LevelDB with Intel SGX. The system design of **LPAD** features three salient properties: (1) It supports a small enclave program by having around one thousand in-enclave code lines out of more than twenty thousands code lines of LevelDB. (2) It guarantees query authenticity in terms of data integrity and membership. (3) The performance slowdown of **LPAD** is less than 12%.

Acknowledgement. Yuzhe Tang's work is supported by National Science Foundation under Grant CNS1815814 and a gift from Intel.

References

1. ARM TrustZone. https://www.arm.com/products/security-on-arm/trustzone
2. Bitcoin core. https://bitcoin.org/en/bitcoin-core/
3. Bitcoin. https://bitcoin.org/en/
4. Certificate transparency
5. Certificate transparency, the internet standards
6. Dropbox. http://www.dropbox.com
7. Ethereum project. https://www.ethereum.org/
8. Facebook RocksDB. http://rocksdb.org/
9. Google drive. https://www.google.com/drive/
10. http://cassandra.apache.org/
11. http://code.google.com/p/leveldb/
12. http://hbase.apache.org/
13. http://www.cryptopp.com/benchmarks.html
14. IBM SCPU. http://www-03.ibm.com/security/cryptocards/
15. Intel corp. software guard extensions programming reference, no. 329298–002 (2014)
16. Intel software guard extensions (Intel SGX) SDK
    plus .1em minus .1em
17. Intel TXT. http://www.intel.com/technology/security/downloads/
    trustedexecoverview.pdf
18. Litecoin. https://litecoin.org/
19. TPM. http://www.trustedcomputinggroup.org/tpm-main-specification/
20. Anagnostopoulos, A., Goodrich, M.T., Tamassia, R.: Persistent authenticated dictionaries and their applications. In: Davida, G.I., Frankel, Y. (eds.) ISC 2001. LNCS, vol. 2200, pp. 379–393. Springer, Heidelberg (2001). https://doi.org/10.1007/3-540-45439-X_26
21. Anati, I., Gueron, S., Johnson, S.P., Scarlata, V.R.: Innovative technology for CPU based attestation and sealing (2013)

22. Arora, S., Lund, C., Motwani, R., Sudan, M., Szegedy, M.: Proof verification and the hardness of approximation problems. J. ACM **45**(3), 501–555 (1998)
23. Arora, S., Safra, S.: Probabilistic checking of proofs: a new characterization of NP. J. ACM **45**(1), 70–122 (1998)
24. Baumann, A., Peinado, M., Hunt, G.C.: Shielding applications from an untrusted cloud with haven. In: 11th USENIX Symposium on Operating Systems Design and Implementation, OSDI 2014, Broomfield, CO, USA, 6–8 October 2014, pp. 267–283 (2014)
25. Braun, B., Feldman, A.J., Ren, Z., Setty, S.T.V., Blumberg, A.J., Walfish, M.: Verifying computations with state. In: Kaminsky, M., Dahlin, M., (eds.) ACM SIGOPS 24th Symposium on Operating Systems Principles, SOSP 2013, Farmington, PA, USA, 3–6 November 2013, pp. 341–357. ACM (2013)
26. Chakrabarti, S., Baker, B., Vij, M.: Intel SGX enabled key manager service with openstack barbican. CoRR, abs/1712.07694 (2017)
27. Chang, F., et al.: Bigtable: a distributed storage system for structured data (awarded best paper!). In OSDI, pp. 205–218 (2006)
28. Clarke, D., Devadas, S., van Dijk, M., Gassend, B., Suh, G.E.: Incremental multiset hash functions and their application to memory integrity checking. In: Laih, C.-S. (ed.) ASIACRYPT 2003. LNCS, vol. 2894, pp. 188–207. Springer, Heidelberg (2003). https://doi.org/10.1007/978-3-540-40061-5_12
29. Cooper, B.F., Silberstein, A., Tam, E., Ramakrishnan, R., Sears, R.: Benchmarking cloud serving systems with YCSB. In: SoCC, pp. 143–154 (2010)
30. Devanbu, P., Gertz, M., Martel, C., Stubblebine, S.G.: Authentic data publication over the internet. J. Comput. Secur. **11**, 2003 (2003)
31. Elbaz, R., Champagne, D., Gebotys, C.H., Lee, R.B., Potlapally, N.R., Torres, L.: Hardware mechanisms for memory authentication: a survey of existing techniques and engines. Trans. Comput. Sci. **4**, 1–22 (2009)
32. Goodrich, M.T., Tamassia, R., Schwerin, A.: Implementation of an authenticated dictionary with skip lists and commutative hashing. In: Proceedings of DARPA Information Survivability Conference & Exposition II, DISCEX 2001, vol. 2, pp. 68–82. IEEE (2001)
33. Katz, J., Lindell, Y.: Introduction to Modern Cryptography. Chapman and Hall/CRC Press, Boca Raton (2007)
34. Li, F., Hadjieleftheriou, M., Kollios, G., Reyzin, L.: Dynamic authenticated index structures for outsourced databases. In: SIGMOD Conference, pp. 121–132 (2006)
35. Li, J., Krohn, M.N., Mazières, D., Shasha, D.: Secure untrusted data repository (SUNDR). In: OSDI, pp. 121–136 (2004)
36. Martel, C.U., Nuckolls, G., Devanbu, P.T., Gertz, M., Kwong, A., Stubblebine, S.G.: A general model for authenticated data structures. Algorithmica **39**(1), 21–41 (2004)
37. Mazières, D., Shasha, D.: Building secure file systems out of Byantine storage. In: Proceedings of the Twenty-First Annual ACM Symposium on Principles of Distributed Computing, PODC 2002, Monterey, California, USA, 21–24 July 2002, pp. 108–117 (2002)
38. Melara, M.S., Blankstein, A., Bonneau, J., Felten, E.W., Freedman, M.J.: CONIKS: bringing key transparency to end users. In: Jung, J., Holz, T., (eds.) 24th USENIX Security Symposium, USENIX Security 2015, Washington, D.C., USA, 12–14 August 2015, pp. 383–398. USENIX Association (2015)
39. O'Neil, P.E., Cheng, E., Gawlick, D., O'Neil, E.J.: The log-structured merge-tree (LSM-TREE). Acta Inf. **33**(4), 351–385 (1996)

40. Pang, H., Tan, K.-L.: Authenticating query results in edge computing. In: Proceedings of the 20th International Conference on Data Engineering, ICDE 2004, Washington, DC, USA, p. 560. IEEE Computer Society (2004)
41. Papadopoulos, S., Yang, Y., Papadias, D.: CADS: continuous authentication on data streams. In: VLDB, pp. 135–146 (2007)
42. Papamanthou, C., Tamassia, R., Triandopoulos, N.: Authenticated hash tables. In: Ning, P., Syverson, P.F., Jha, S., (eds.) Proceedings of the 2008 ACM Conference on Computer and Communications Security, CCS 2008, Alexandria, Virginia, USA, 27–31 October 2008, pp. 437–448. ACM (2008)
43. Papamanthou, C., Tamassia, R., Triandopoulos, N.: Authenticated hash tables based on cryptographic accumulators. Algorithmica 74(2), 664–712 (2016)
44. Parno, B., Howell, J., Gentry, C., Raykova, M.: Pinocchio: nearly practical verifiable computation. In: 2013 IEEE Symposium on Security and Privacy, SP 2013, Berkeley, CA, USA, 19–22 May 2013, pp. 238–252. IEEE Computer Society (2013)
45. Rubinfeld, R., Shapira, A.: Sublinear time algorithms. SIAM J. Discrete Math. 25(4), 1562–1588 (2011)
46. Setty, S.T.V., Braun, B., Vu, V., Blumberg, A.J., Parno, B., Walfish, M.: Resolving the conflict between generality and plausibility in verified computation. In: Eighth Eurosys Conference, EuroSys 2013, Prague, Czech Republic, 14–17 April 2013, pp. 71–84 (2013)
47. Shinde, S., Tien, D.L., Tople, S., Saxena, P.: Panoply: Low-TCB Linux applications with SGX enclaves. In: 24th Annual Network and Distributed System Security Symposium, NDSS 2017, San Diego, California, USA, 26 February–1 March 2017 (2017)
48. Stefanov, E., van Dijk, M., Juels, A., Oprea, A.: Iris: a scalable cloud file system with efficient integrity checks. In: ACSAC, pp. 229–238 (2012)
49. Tamassia, R.: Authenticated data structures. In: Di Battista, G., Zwick, U. (eds.) ESA 2003. LNCS, vol. 2832, pp. 2–5. Springer, Heidelberg (2003). https://doi.org/10.1007/978-3-540-39658-1_2
50. Wahby, R.S., Setty, S.T.V., Ren, Z., Blumberg, A.J., Walfish, M.: Efficient RAM and control flow in verifiable outsourced computation. In: 22nd Annual Network and Distributed System Security Symposium, NDSS 2015, San Diego, California, USA, 8–11 February 2014 (2015)
51. Xu, Y., Cui, W., Peinado, M.: Controlled-channel attacks: deterministic side channels for untrusted operating systems. In: 2015 IEEE Symposium on Security and Privacy, SP 2015, San Jose, CA, USA, 17–21 May 2015, pp. 640–656. IEEE Computer Society (2015)
52. Yang, Y., Papadias, D., Papadopoulos, S., Kalnis, P.: Authenticated join processing in outsourced databases. In: Çetintemel, U., Zdonik, S.B., Kossmann, D., Tatbul, N. (eds.) Proceedings of the ACM SIGMOD International Conference on Management of Data, SIGMOD 2009, Providence, Rhode Island, USA, 29 June–2 July 2009, pp. 5–18. ACM (2009)
53. Yang, Y., Papadopoulos, S., Papadias, D., Kollios, G.: Authenticated indexing for outsourced spatial databases. VLDB J. 18(3), 631–648 (2009)
54. Zhang, Y., Katz, J., Papamanthou, C.: IntegriDB: verifiable SQL for outsourced databases. In: Ray, I., Li, N., Kruegel, C. (eds.) Proceedings of the 22nd ACM SIGSAC Conference on Computer and Communications Security, Denver, CO, USA, 12–16 October 2015, pages 1480–1491. ACM (2015)

Modern Family: A Revocable Hybrid Encryption Scheme Based on Attribute-Based Encryption, Symmetric Searchable Encryption and SGX

Alexandros Bakas[(✉)] and Antonis Michalas

Tampere University, Tampere, Finland
{alexandros.bakas,antonios.michalas}@tuni.fi

Abstract. Secure cloud storage is considered as one of the most important issues that both businesses and end-users take into account before moving their private data to the cloud. Lately, we have seen some interesting approaches that are based either on the promising concept of Symmetric Searchable Encryption (SSE) or on the well-studied field of Attribute-Based Encryption (ABE). In this paper, we propose a hybrid encryption scheme that combines both SSE and ABE by utilizing the advantages of both these techniques. In contrast to many approaches, we design a revocation mechanism that is completely separated from the ABE scheme and solely based on the functionality offered by SGX.

Keywords: Access control · Attribute-based encryption · Cloud security · Hybrid encryption · Policies · Storage protection · Symmetric searchable encryption

1 Introduction

Cloud computing plays a significant role in our daily routine. From casual internet users, to big corporations, the cloud has become an integral part of our lives. However, using services that are hosted and controlled by third parties raises several security and privacy concerns. For example, in [12] it is stated that there has been a 300% increase in Microsoft cloud-based user's account attacks over the past couple of years. However, when considering a cloud-based environment, cyber-attacks performed by remote adversaries is only a part of the problem. More precisely, when we design cloud services we also need to take into consideration cases where the actual cloud service provider (CSP) acts maliciously.

To overcome this, both academia and big industrial players have started looking on how to build cloud-based services that will utilize Symmetric Searchable Encryption (SSE) [4,7]. In such a scheme, whenever a user wishes to access her files, she can search directly over the encrypted data for specific keywords. Unfortunately, revocation cannot be implemented efficiently since sharing an

© ICST Institute for Computer Sciences, Social Informatics and Telecommunications Engineering 2019
Published by Springer Nature Switzerland AG 2019. All Rights Reserved
S. Chen et al. (Eds.): SecureComm 2019, LNICST 305, pp. 472–486, 2019.
https://doi.org/10.1007/978-3-030-37231-6_28

encrypted file implies sharing the encryption key. As a result, if a data owner wishes to revoke a user, then all files that are encrypted with the same key must be decrypted and then re-encrypted under a fresh key. Another promising technique that fits cloud-based services is Attribute-Based Encryption (ABE). In ABE schemes, all files are encrypted under a master public key but in contrast to traditional public key encryption, the generated ciphertext is bounded by a policy. Each user has a distinct secret key which is associated with specific attributes. This way a user's secret key can decrypt a ciphertext if and only if the her attributes satisfy the policy bound to the ciphertext. However, using an asymmetric encryption scheme to store data is rather inefficient.

Contribution: We propose a hybrid encryption scheme that combines SSE and ABE in a way that reduces the problem of multi-user data sharing to that of a single-user. We use the ABE scheme as a sharing mechanism and not as a revocation one to achieve better efficiency. To deal with the problem of revocation, we utilize the functionality offered by SGX. Furthermore, this work extends the protocol presented in [11].

Organization: In Sect. 2, we present important works that have been published and address the problem of secure cloud storage, data sharing and revocation. In Sect. 3, we define our system model while in Sect. 4, we present the cryptographic tools needed for the construction of our scheme. In Sect. 5, we give a formal construction of our scheme which is followed by the security analysis in Sect. 6. Finally, Sect. 7 concludes the paper.

2   Related Work

In [13] authors present a revocable hybrid encryption scheme while at the same time a key-rotation mechanism is used to prevent key-scrapping attacks. The authors use Optimal Asymmetric Encryption Padding (OAEP) as an All-or-Nothing-Transformation (AONT) [2] to prevent revoked users from accessing stored data. This is due to the fact that reversing OAEP, requires to the entire output. Thus, changing random bits, renders the reversion infeasible. Hence, to decrypt a file, the changed bits need to be stored. However, this implies that with each re-encryption, the size of the ciphertext grows. Thus, decrypting a file that has been re-encrypted multiple times is an expensive operation. Moreover, to achieve better efficiency, authors suggest that the AONT could be applied by the server. However, this implies the existence of a fully trusted server.

A promising idea is presented in [5], where the authors present a protocol based on functional encryption, with the main functionalities running in isolated environments. The decryption of a file, and the application of a function f on the decrypted file both occur in SGX enclaves. Moreover, all enclaves can attest to each other and exchange data over secure communication channels. In our construction, even though we use the same hardware principles, we build a hybrid encryption scheme by combining SSE and ABE.

In [9] authors present a revocable ciphertext-policy attribute-based encryption scheme. The revocation mechanism is offered by a revocation list that is attached to the resulted ciphertexts. To avoid maintaining long revocation lists, a policy through which users' keys expire after a certain period of time is enforced. As a result, the revocation list only includes keys that have been revoked before the expiration date. Another Hybrid encryption scheme is presented in [6], in which authors propose a scheme based on SSE and ABE. In the proposed scheme, data owners encrypt their files using SSE, but the resulted indexes are encrypted under ABE. This way, users can locally generate search tokens based on their attributes, that are then sent to the cloud. However promising, their scheme is static and as a result can only have very limited applications in real-life scenarios. Moreover, authors do not provide a revocation mechanism – a problem of paramount importance in cloud-based services.

In our construction, we overcome these issues by designing an efficient revocation mechanism that is utilizing the SGX functionality and it is separated from the ABE scheme.

3   Architecture

In this section, we introduce the system model by explicitly describing the main entities that participate in our protocol as well as their capabilities. The system model of our work is built on top of the model presented in [10] and it is enhanced with some important additions.

Cloud Service Provider (CSP): We consider a cloud computing environment similar to the one described in [14,15]. Moreover, the CSP must support SGX since core entities will be running in a trusted execution environment offered by SGX.

Master Authority (MS): MS is responsible for setting up all the necessary public parameters for the proper run of the involved protocols. MS is responsible for generating and distributing ABE keys to the registered users. Finally, MS is SGX-enabled and is running in an enclave called the Master Enclave.

Key Tray (KT): KT is a key storage that stores ciphertexts of the symmetric keys that have been generated by various users and are needed to decrypt data. Registered users can directly contact KT and request access to the stored ciphertexts. KT is also SGX-enabled and runs in an enclave called the KT Enclave.

Revocation Authority (REV): REV is responsible for maintaining a revocation list (*rl*) with the unique identifiers of the revoked users. Similar to MS and KT, REV is also SGX-enabled and is running in an enclave called the Revocation Enclave. Finally, for the security of the stored revocation list, it is important to mention that *rl* is generated by the enclave (i.e. in an isolated environment) and never leaves its perimeter. Therefore, there is no need to encrypt *rl*.

SGX: Below we provide a brief presentation of the main SGX functionalities needed for our construction. A more detailed description can be found in [3,5]

Isolation: Enclaves are located in a hardware guarded area of memory and they compromise a total memory of 128 MB (only 90 MB can be used by software).

Intel SGX is based on memory isolation built into the processor itself along with strong cryptography. The processor tracks which parts of memory belong to which enclave, and ensures that *only* enclaves can access their own memory.

Attestation: One of the core contributions of SGX is the support for attestation between enclaves of the same (local attestation) and different platforms (remote attestation). In the case of local attestation, an enclave enc_i can verify another enclave enc_j as well as the program/software running in the latter. This is achieved through a report generated by enc_j containing information about the enclave itself and the program running in it. This report is signed with a secret key sk_{rpt} which is the same for all enclaves of the same platform. In remote attestation, enclaves of different platforms can attest each other through a signed quote. This is a report similar to the one used in local attestation. The difference is that instead of using sk_{rpt} to sign it, a special private key provided by Intel is used. Thus, verifying these quotes requires contacting Intel's Attestation Server.

Sealing: Every SGX processor comes with a Root Seal Key with which, data is encrypted when stored in untrusted memory. Sealed data can be recovered even after an enclave is destroyed and rebooted on the same platform.

4   Cryptographic Primitives

In this section, we give a formal definition for the two main encryption schemes that the paper is based on. We proceed with the definition of a CP-ABE and SSE schemes as described in [1] and [7] respectively.

Definition 1 (Ciphertext-Policy ABE). *A revocable CP-ABE scheme is a tuple of the following five algorithms:*

- CPABE.Setup *is a probabilistic algorithm that takes as input a security parameter λ and outputs a master public key* MPK *and a master secret key* MSK. *We denote this by* $(MPK, MSK) \leftarrow Setup(1^\lambda)$.
- CPABE.Gen *is a probabilistic algorithm that takes as input a master secret key, a set of attributes $\mathcal{A}$ and the unique identifier of a user and outputs a secret key which is bind both to the corresponding list of attributes and the user. We denote this by* $(sk_{\mathcal{A},u_i}) \leftarrow Gen(MSK, \mathcal{A}, u_i)$.
- CPABE.Enc *is a probabilistic algorithm that takes as input a master public key, a message m and a policy $P \in \mathcal{P}$. After a proper run, the algorithm outputs a ciphertext c_P which is associated to the policy P. We denote this by* $c_P \leftarrow Enc(MPK, m, P)$.
- CPABE.Dec *is a deterministic algorithm that takes as input a user's secret key and a ciphertext and outputs the original message m iff the set of attributes $\mathcal{A}$ that are associated with the underlying secret key satisfies the policy P that is associated with c_p. We denote this by* $Dec(sk_{\mathcal{A},u_i}, c_P) \rightarrow m$.

Definition 2 (Dynamic Index-based SSE). *A dynamic index-based symmetric searchable encryption scheme is a tuple of nine polynomial algorithms* $SSE = (Gen, Enc, SearchToken, AddToken, DeleteToken, Search, Add, Delete, Dec):$

- SSE.Gen *is a probabilistic key-generation algorithm that takes as input a security parameter* λ *and outputs a secret key* K.
- SSE.Enc *is a probabilistic algorithm that takes as input a secret key* K *and a collection of files* **f** *and outputs an encrypted index* γ *and a sequence of ciphertexts* **c**.
- SSE.SearchToken *is a (possibly probabilistic) algorithm that takes as input a secret key* K *and a keyword* w *and outputs a search token* $\tau_s(w)$.
- SSE.AddToken *is a (possibly probabilistic) algorithm that takes as input a secret key* K *and a file* f *and outputs an add token* $\tau_a(f)$ *and a ciphertext* c_f.
- SSE.DeleteToken *is a (possibly probabilistic) algorithm that takes as input a secret key* K *and a file* f *and outputs a delete token* $\tau_d(f)$.
- SSE.Search *is a deterministic algorithm that takes as input an encrypted index* γ, *a sequence of ciphertexts* **c** *and a search token* $\tau_s(w)$ *and outputs a sequence of file identifiers* $\mathbf{I}_w \subset \mathbf{c}$.
- SSE.Add *is a deterministic algorithm that takes as input an encrypted index* γ, *a sequence of ciphertexts* **c**, *an add token* $\tau_a(f)$ *and a ciphertext* c_f *and outputs a new encrypted index* γ' *and a new sequence of ciphertexts* **c**$'$.
- SSE.Delete *is a deterministic algorithm that takes as input an encrypted index* γ, *a sequence of ciphertexts* **c** *and a delete token* $\tau_d(f)$ *and outputs a new encrypted index* γ' *and a new sequence of ciphertexts* **c**$'$.
- SSE.Dec *is a deterministic algorithm that takes as input a secret key* K *and a ciphertext* c *and outputs a file* f.

The security of an SSE scheme is based on the existence of a simulator that is given as input information leaked during the execution of the protocol. In particular to define the security of SSE we make use of the leakage functions $\mathcal{L}_{in}, \mathcal{L}_s, \mathcal{L}_a, \mathcal{L}_d$ associated to index creation, search, add and delete operations [4].

5   Modern Family (MF)

In this section, we present Modern Family (MF) – the core of this paper's contribution. We start by giving an overview of the SGX hardware functionalities used by the communicating parties as defined in [5]. and we continue with a formal construction.

Hardware:

- **HW.Setup(1^λ)**: Takes as input a security parameter λ and produces the secret key $\mathsf{sk_{rpt}}$[1] used to MAC the reports.
- **HW.Load(Q)**: Takes as input a program Q. An enclave enc_i is created in which Q will be loaded. Moreover a handle $\mathsf{hdl_{enc}}$ is created that will be used as an identifier for the enclave.
- **HW.Run(hdl, in)**: Takes as input a handle hdl and some input in. It runs the program in the enclave specified by hdl with in as input.

---

[1] $\mathsf{sk_{rpt}}$ is shared with every enclave on the same platform.

– **HW.Run&Report**(hdl, *in*): Takes as input a handle hdl and some input *in*. It will output a report that is verifiable by any other enclave on the same platform. The report contains information about the underlying enclave signed with sk_{rpt}.

– **HW.ReportVerifiy**(hdl′, rpt): Takes as input a handle hdl′ and a report rpt. Uses sk_{rpt} generated by HW.Setup to verify the MAC of the report.

5.1 Formal Construction

MF is divided into a *Setup phase* and four main phases; *Initialization, Key Sharing, Editing* and *Revocation*. During the *Setup phase*, all the necessary enclaves are initialized by running the MF.Setup algorithm. In the rest of the phases, the user is interacting with the enclaves by running one of the following algorithms: MF.ABEUserKey, MF.Store, MF.KTStore, MF.KeyShare, MF.Search, MF.Update, MF.Delete and MF.Revoke as described below.

Setup Phase: In this phase MF.Setup runs. Each entity receives a public/private key pair (pk, sk) for a CCA2 secure public cryptosystem PKE. In addition to that, the entities running in enclaves generate a signing and a verification key pair. Finally, MS runs CPABE.Setup to acquire the master public/private key pair (MPK, MSK). An enclave is initialized as follows:

MF.Setup(*"initialize"*, 1^λ): Each enclave is initialized by generating a public/private and signing/verification key pairs. To do so, the program $\mathbf{Q_{ID}^{init}}$ is loaded:

$\mathbf{Q_{ID}^{init}}$
- On input (*"initialize"*, 1^λ):
    1. Run (pk, sk) ← PKE.KeyGen(1^λ).
    2. Output pk.
    Run hdl ← HW.Load(Q_{ID}^{init}).

Additionally, during the setup phase, the MS enclave loads a program $\mathbf{Q_{MS}^{Setup}}$ that outputs the master public/private key pair (MPK, MSK):

$\mathbf{Q_{MS}^{Setup}}$
- On input (*"initialize"*, 1^λ):
    1. Run (MPK, MSK) ← PKE.KeyGen(1^λ).
    2. Output MPK.
    Run hdl_{MS} ← HW.Load(Q_{MS}^{Setup}).

Initialization Phase: As a first step, a user u_i contacts the MS enclave and requests a secret CP-ABE key. Upon reception, MS authenticates u_i and checks if the user is eligible for receiving such a key. If so, MS generates a CP-ABE key $sk_{\mathcal{A},u_i}$, encrypts it under pk_i and sends it back to u_i. This is done by running the program $\mathbf{Q_{MS}^{SKey}}$ in the MS enclave as shown below:

MF.ABEUserKey("$KeyRequest$", MSK, u_i, $cred_i$, $\mathcal{A}$): The master enclave program $\mathbf{Q}_{MS}^{SKey}$ for generating users' ABE keys is defined as follows:

$\mathbf{Q}_{MS}^{SKey}$

- On input ("$KeyRequest$", MSK, u_i, $cred_i$, $\mathcal{A}$):
    1. Verify that u_i is registered. If not, output $\bot$.
    2. Use MSK and compute $sk_{\mathcal{A},u_i}$.
    3. Compute and output $c = \mathsf{PKE.Enc}(pk_i, sk_{\mathcal{A},u_i})$.
  Run $c \leftarrow \mathsf{HW.Run}(hdl_{MS}, ($"KeyRequest", MSK, i, $cred_i$, $\mathcal{A}))$.

After u_i successfully received $sk_{\mathcal{A},u_i}$ she can start using the CSP to store files remotely. To do so, she first sends a store request $StoreReq$ to the CSP. Specifically, u_i sends $m_{req} = \langle r_1, \mathsf{E}_{pk_{CSP}}(cred_i), StoreReq, H(r_1||cred_i||StoreReq)\rangle$ where r_i is a random number. The CSP authenticates u_i as legitimate and sends back an authorization $Auth$ as $m_{ver} = \langle r_2, (Auth), \sigma_{CSP}(H(r_2||u_i||Auth))\rangle$. At this point, u_i generates a symmetric key K_i to encrypt her files and sends $m_{store} = \langle r_3, \mathsf{E}_{pk_{CSP}}(\gamma_i), \mathbf{c}_i, H(r_3||\gamma_i||c_i)\rangle$ to the CSP.

MF.Store("$Store$", m_{req}): The CSP enclave program $\mathbf{Q}_{CSP}^{Store}$ that is responsible for storing encrypted files is defined as follows:

$\mathbf{Q}_{CSP}^{Store}$

- On input ("$StoreReq$", m_{req}):
    1. Open m_{req}; verify the message[a]; if the verification fails, output $\bot$.
    2. Compute and output $m_{ver} = \langle r_2, (Auth), \sigma_{CSP}(H(r_2||u_i||Auth))\rangle$.
  Run $m_{ver} \leftarrow \mathsf{HW.Run}(hdl_{CSP}, ($"StoreReq", $m_4))$.
- On input ("$store$", m_{store}):
    1. Open m_{store}; verify the message; if the verification fails, output $\bot$.
    2. Store (c_i, γ_i).
  Run $\mathsf{HW.Run}(hdl_{CSP}, ($"store", $m_{store}))$.

---

[a] By this, we mean that the entity receiving the message verifies the freshness and the integrity of the message and it can also authenticate the sender.

Initialization phase concludes with MF.KTStore where u_i encrypts K_i under MPK to get $c_P^{\mathsf{K}_i}$ and sends $m_{keystore} = \left\langle \mathsf{E}_{pk_{KT}}(r_4), c_P^{\mathsf{K}_i}, \sigma_i\left(H\left(r_4||c_P^{\mathsf{K}_i}\right)\right)\right\rangle$ to KT. Upon reception, KT generates a random number r_{K_i} that is stored next to $c_P^{\mathsf{K}_i}$.
MF.KTStore("$store$", $m_{keystore}$): The KT enclave program $\mathbf{Q}_{KT}^{Store}$ that stores a symmetric key K_i encrypted with MPK is defined as follows:

$\mathbf{Q_{KT}^{Store}}$

- On input (*"store"*, $m_{keystore}$):
  1. Open $m_{keystore}$; verify the message. If the verification fails, output $\perp$.
  2. Generate a random number r_{K_i}.
  3. Compute $c = \mathsf{PKE.Enc}(\mathsf{pk}_{u_i}, r_{K_i})$.
  4. Store $\left(c_p^{K_i}, c\right)$.

  Run $\left(c_p^{K_i}, c\right) \leftarrow \mathsf{HW.Run}(\mathsf{hdl}_{KT}, ("store", m_{keystore}))$.

Key Sharing Phase: This phase begins with u_j executing MF.KeyShare to prove that is not revoked. To this end, u_j sends $m_{verReq} = \langle r_5, \mathsf{E}_{\mathsf{pk}_{REV}}(u_j), \sigma_j(r_5||u_j) \rangle$ to REV. Upon reception, REV verifies the message and checks whether $u_j \in rl$ or not. Assuming that $u_j \notin rl$ (i.e. she has not been revoked), REV replies with $m_{token} = \langle r_6, \mathsf{E}_{\mathsf{pk}_{KT}}(u_j), \mathsf{E}_{\mathsf{pk}_{KT}}(\tau_{KS}), \sigma_{REV}(H(r_6||u_j||\tau_{KS})) \rangle$. The user then simply forwards m_{token} to KT who verifies it. After the verification is complete KT sends $m_{key} = \langle (\mathsf{E}_{\mathsf{pk}_{CSP}}(u_j, t)), c_p^{K_i}, \sigma_{KT}(H(u_j||t)) \rangle$ back to u_j, where t is a timestamp declaring the time that u_j accessed $c_p^{K_i}$. If u_j already received K_i in the past, KT will only send back the first and last components of m_{key}.
MF.KeyShare(*"share"*, m_4): REV and KT enclave programs ($\mathbf{Q_{REV}^{Ver}}$, $\mathbf{Q_{KT}^{Share}}$) that are responsible for sharing $c_p^{K_i}$ are defined as follows:

$\mathbf{Q_{REV}^{Ver}}$

- On input (*"share"*, m_{verReq}):
  1. Open m_{verReq}; verify the message; if the verification fails, output $\perp$.
  2. Check if $u_j \in rl$; if so, output $\perp$.
  3. Generate τ_{KS}.
  4. Compute and output m_{token}.

  Run $m_{token} \leftarrow \mathsf{HW.Run}(\mathsf{hdl}_{REV}, ("share", m_{verReq}))$.

$\mathbf{Q_{KT}^{share}}$

- On input (*"share"*, m_{token}):
  1. Open m_{token}; verify the message; if the verification fails, output $\perp$.
  2. Decrypt $\mathsf{PKE.Enc}(\mathsf{pk}_{KT}, u_j)$ and $\mathsf{PKE.Enc}(\mathsf{pk}_{KT}, \tau_{KS})$.
  3. Compute and output m_{key}.

  Run $m_{key} \leftarrow \mathsf{HW.Run}(\mathsf{hdl}_{KT}, ("share", m_{ver}))$.

User u_j can now run MF.Search to access certain files that are stored in the CSP. To do so, she locally runs SSE.SearchToken to generate $\tau_s(w)$ and then sends $m_{search} = \langle \mathsf{E}_{\mathsf{pk}_{CSP}}(u_j, t, \tau_s(w)), \sigma_i(H(u_j||t||\tau_s(w))), \sigma_{KT}(H(u_j||t)) \rangle$ to the CSP[2]. Upon reception, CSP runs SSE.Search.
MF.Search(*"search"*, m_{search},): The CSP enclave program $\mathbf{Q_{CSP}^{Search}}$ that is responsible for searching over the encrypted data is defined as follows:

---

[2] The user simply forwards the components of m_{key} to the CSP along with a search token $\tau_s(w)$.

Q_{CSP}^{Search}

- On input ("*search*", m_{search}):
    1. Open m_{search}; verify the message; if the verification fails, output $\perp$.
    2. Run SSE.Search($\gamma_i, c_i, \tau_s(w)$) $\rightarrow \mathbf{I_w}$
    3. Output $\mathbf{I}_w$.
    Run HW.Run(hdl$_{CSP}$, ("*search*", m_{search}), which internally runs SSE.Search $\rightarrow \mathbf{I}_w$.

Editing Phase: In this phase[3], registered users can add files to the database and data owners can also delete files. To do so, u_i executes MF.Update and MF.Delete. To update the database, u_i first generates an add token by running $(\tau_a(f), c_f) \leftarrow$ SSE.AddToken(K_i, f). This token is sent to the CSP via $m_{add} = \langle E_{pk_{CSP}}(u_i, t, \tau_\alpha(f), c_i, \gamma_i), \sigma_i\left(H(u_i||t||\tau_{\alpha(f)}||c_i||\gamma_i)\right), \sigma_{KT}(u_i||t)\rangle$. Finally, the CSP verifies the message and its freshness and executes SSE.Add($\gamma_i, c_i, \tau_\alpha(f), c_f$) $\rightarrow (\gamma_i', c_i')$.

MF.Update("*update*", m_{add}): The CSP enclave program Q_{CSP}^{Up} for adding files to the database is defined as follows:

Q_{CSP}^{Up}

- On input ("*update*", m_{add}):
    1. Verify the message. If the verification fails, output $\perp$.
    2. Run SSE.Add($\gamma_i, c_i, \tau_\alpha(f), c_f$) $\rightarrow (\gamma_i', c_i')$.
    Run HW.Run(hld$_{CSP}$, ("*update*", m_{add}), which internally runs SSE.Add($\gamma_i, c_i, \tau_\alpha(f), c_f$) $\rightarrow (\gamma_i', c_i')$.

Deletion of a file is a more complicated task. This is due to the fact that we only allow the data owner to delete files. To achieve this, u_i needs to prove her ownership over K_i. This can be done by requesting the random number r_{K_i} from KT. After u_i receives r_{K_i}, she signs it, runs $\tau_d \leftarrow$ SSE.DeleteToken(K_i, f) and replies to KT with: $m_{delete} = \langle E_{pk_{CSP}}(u_i, t, \tau_d(f), \gamma_i'), \sigma_i(H(u_i||\tau_d(f)||\gamma_i'||r_{K_i})\rangle$. KT verifies the message and is convinced that u_i is the owner of K_i. Finally, KT generates a report (rpt) containing the delete token. This is sent to the CSP who proceeds with the deletion of the specified files.

MF.Delete("*request*", $\sigma_i(u_i||t), c_p^{K_i}$): The enclave programs $Q_{CSP}^{Del}, Q_{KT}^{Del}$ that are responsible for deleting files from the database are defined as follows:

Q_{KT}^{Del}

- On input ("*request*", $\sigma_i(u_i||t), c_p^{K_i}$):
    1. Verify the signature. If the verification fails, output $\perp$.
    2. Get r_{K_i} and compute $c = $ PKE.Enc(pk$_{u_i}, r_{K_i}$).
    3. Output c.
    Run $c \leftarrow$ HW.Run(hdl$_{KT}$, ("*request*", $\sigma_i(u_i||t), c_p^{K_i}$).
- On input ("*delete*", m_{delete}):
    1. Open m_{delete}; verify the message and authenticate u_i as the owner of K_i. If the verification or the authentication fail, output $\perp$.
    2. Generate and output rpt.
    Run HW.Run(hdl$_{KT}$, ("*delete*", m_{delete}) and then
    rpt $\leftarrow$ HW.RunReport(hdl$_{KT}$, ("*delete*", m_{delete})).

---
[3] One could completely ignore the *Editing Phase* and the result would be a static MF.

Q_{CSP}^{Del}

- On input (*"delete"*, rpt):
  1. Verify rpt. If the verification fails, output $\perp$.
  2. Run SSE.Delete($\gamma_i', c_i', \tau_d(f)$) $\rightarrow$ (γ_i'', c_i'').
  Run HW.Run(hdl$_{CSP}$, (*"delete"*, rpt)) who will internally run HW.ReportVerify (hdl$_{CSP}$, rpt) and SSE.Delete($\gamma_i, c_i, \tau_d(f)$) $\rightarrow$ (γ_i'', c_i'').

Revocation Phase: To successfully run MF.Revoke, u_i first needs to prove ownership over K_i by following the same steps as in MF.Delete. When u_i signs r_{K_i}, she sends $m_{revoke} = \left\langle r_{10}, E_{pk_{KT}}\left(u_i, u_j, c_P^{K_i}\right), \sigma_i\left(H(u_i||u_j||c_P^{K_i}||r_{K_i})\right)\right\rangle$ to KT. Now that KT is convinced that u_i is the owner of K_i, it generates rpt containing u_j's identity, which is then sent to REV, who adds u_j to rl.

MF.Revoke(*"request"*, $\sigma_i(u_i||t), c_p^{K_i}$): The enclave programs $\mathbf{Q_{KT}^{Rev}}, \mathbf{Q_{REV}^{Rev}}$ that are responsible for revoking users are defined as follows:

Q_{KT}^{Rev}

- On input (*"request"*, $\sigma_i(u_i||t), c_p^{K_i}$):
  1. Verify the signature. If the verification fails, output $\perp$.
  2. Get r_{K_i} and compute $c = PKE.Enc(pk_{u_i}, r_{K_i})$.
  3. Output c.
  Run $c \leftarrow$ HW.Run(hdl$_{KT}$, (*"request"*, $u_i, c_p^{K_i}$)).
- On input (*"revoke"*, m_{revoke}):
  1. Open m_{revoke}; verify the message and authenticate u_i as the owner of K_i. If the verification or the authentication fails, output $\perp$.
  2. Generate $r_{K_i'}$ and replace it with r_{K_i}.
  3. Generate and output rpt.
  Run HW.Run(hdl$_{KT}$, (*"revoke"*, m_{revoke})) and then
  rpt $\leftarrow$ HW.RunReport(hdl$_{KT}$, (*"revoke"*, m_{report})).

Q_{REV}^{Rev}

- On input (*"revoke"*, rpt):
  1. Veirfy rpt. If the verification fails, output $\perp$.
  2. Add u_j to the revocation list rl.
  Run HW.Run(hdl$_{REV}$, (*"revoke"*, rpt)) who will internally run HW.Report Verify (hdl$_{REV}$, report).

---

6 Security Analysis

We construct a simulator S that simulates the algorithms of the real protocol in such a way that any polynomial time adversary $\mathcal{ADV}$ will not be able to distinguish between the real protocol and S. S intercepts $\mathcal{ADV}$'s communication with the real protocol and replies with simulated outputs.

Definition 3 (*Sim-Security*). *We consider the following experiments. In the real experiment, all algorithms run as defined in our construction while in the ideal one, S intercepts $\mathcal{ADV}$'s queries and replies with simulated responses.*

Real Experiment		Ideal Experiment	
1. $\mathbf{EXP}_{MF}^{real}(1^\lambda)$:		1. $\mathbf{EXP}_{MF}^{ideal}(1^\lambda)$:	
2. $(\text{MPK}, \text{MSK}) \leftarrow \text{MF.Setup}(1^\lambda)$		2. $(\text{MPK}) \leftarrow \mathcal{S}(1^\lambda)$	
3. $\text{sk}_{\mathcal{A},u_i} \leftarrow \mathcal{ADV}^{\text{MF.ABEUserKey}(\text{MSK},\mathcal{A})}$		3. $\text{sk}_{\mathcal{A},u_i} \leftarrow \mathcal{ADV}^{\mathcal{S}(1^\lambda)}$	
4. $ct \leftarrow \text{CPABE.Enc}(\text{mpk}, m)$		4. $ct \leftarrow \mathcal{S}(1^\lambda, 1^{|m|})$	
5. $(\gamma, c) \leftarrow \mathcal{ADV}^{\text{SSE.Enc}(\text{K},\mathbf{f})}$		5. $(\gamma, c) \leftarrow \mathcal{ADV}^{\mathcal{S}(\mathcal{L}_{in}(\mathbf{f}))}$	
6. $\text{MF.Search}(\text{``search''}, m_s) \rightarrow \mathbf{I_w}$		6. $\mathcal{S}(\text{``search''}, m_s) \rightarrow \mathbf{I_w}$	
7. $\text{MF.Update}(\text{``update''}, m_{add}) \rightarrow (\gamma', c')$		7. $\mathcal{S}(\text{``update''}, m_{add}) \rightarrow (\gamma', c')$	
8. $\text{MF.Delete}(\text{``delete''}, m_{delete}) \rightarrow (\gamma', c')$		8. $\mathcal{S}(\text{``delete''}, m_{delete}) \rightarrow (\gamma', c')$	
9. Output b		9. Output b'	

We say that MF is sim-secure if for all PPT adversaries $\mathcal{ADV}$:

$$\mathbf{EXP}_{MF}^{real}(1^\lambda) \approx \mathbf{EXP}_{MF}^{ideal}(1^\lambda)$$

Everything $\mathcal{ADV}$ observes in the real experiment can be simulated by $\mathcal{S}$. Moreover, we use an IND-CCA2 public key encryption scheme. If $\mathcal{ADV}$ can distinguish between real and ideal answers, she can also break the IND-CCA2 security. Finally, we let $\mathcal{ADV}$ can load different programs in the enclaves and record the output. This assumption significantly strengthens $\mathcal{ADV}$ since we need to ensure that only honest attested programs will be executed in the enclaves.

Theorem 1. *Assuming that* PKE *is an IND-CCA2 secure public key cryptosystem and* Sign *is an EUF-CMA secure signature scheme then MF is a sim-secure protocol according to Definition 3.*

Proof. We start by defining the algorithms used by the simulator. Then, we will replace them with the real algorithms. Finally, the help of a Hybrid Argument we will prove that the two distributions are indistinguishable.

– MF.Setup*: Will only generate MPK that will be given to $\mathcal{ADV}$.
– MF.ABEUserKey*: Will generate a random key to be sent to the adversary. That is, when $\mathcal{ADV}$ makes a key generation query, $\mathcal{S}$ will simulate CPABE.KeyGen and it will output $\text{sk}_{\mathcal{A},u_i}^*$. This key is a random string that has the same length as the output of the real MF.ABEUserKey*. The key will be given to $\mathcal{ADV}$.
– MF.KeyShare*: In the ideal experiment, after $\mathcal{ADV}$ requests a secret key, $\mathcal{S}$ will encrypt a sequence of bits based on $\mathcal{L}_{in}$, under MPK. The ciphertext will be returned to $\mathcal{ADV}$.
– MF.Search*: When $\mathcal{ADV}$ generates a search token $\tau_s(w)$, $\mathcal{S}$ gets as input the leakage function $\mathcal{L}_s$ and outputs a simulated response. When $\mathcal{ADV}$ makes a search query, $\mathcal{S}$ will once again generate a simulated $\mathbf{I_w^*}$ which will be sent back to her.
– MF.Update*: When $\mathcal{ADV}$ generates an add token $\tau_\alpha(f)$, $\mathcal{S}$ gets as input the leakage function $\mathcal{L}_a$ and outputs a simulated response. $\mathcal{S}$ will simulate the add token, the ciphertext to be added to the database and will also update the encrypted index.
– MF.Delete*: When $\mathcal{S}$ generates a delete token, $\mathcal{S}$ gets as input the leakage function $\mathcal{L}_d$ and outputs a simulated response. Apart from $\tau_d(f)$, $\mathcal{S}$ will also update the encrypted index.

– MF.Revoke*: The system does not revoke any user.

In the pre-processing phase, $\mathcal{S}$ runs HW.Setup(1^λ), just as in the real experiment, in order to acquire $\mathsf{sk_{rpt}}$. Moreover, the challenger $\mathcal{C}$ generates a symmetric key K_i, that will be needed in order to reply to search, add and delete queries. We will now use a hybrid argument to prove that $\mathcal{ADV}$ cannot distinguish between the real and the ideal experiments.

| **Hybrid 0** | MF runs normally.

| **Hybrid 1** | Everything runs like in Hybrid 0, but we replace MF.Setup with MF.Setup*.

These algorithms are identical from $\mathcal{ADV}$'s perspective and as a result the hybrids are indistinguishable.

| **Hybrid 2** | Everything runs like in Hybrid 1, but MF.ABEUserKey* runs instead of MF.ABEUserKey.

Hybrid 2 is indistinguishable from Hybrid 1 because nothing changes from $\mathcal{ADV}$'s point of view.

After Hybrid 2, we have ensured that $\mathcal{ADV}$ has followed all the required steps in order to ask for K_i. We are now ready to replace MF.KeyShare with MF.KeyShare*.

| **Hybrid 3** | Like Hybrid 2, but MF.KeyShare* runs instead of MF.KeyShare. Also, the algorithm outputs $\perp$ if HW.Run is queried with ($\mathsf{hdl_{KT}}$, ("*share*", m_{token})) but $\mathcal{ADV}$ never contacts REV.

Lemma 1. *Hybrid 3 is indistinguishable from Hybrid 2.*

Proof. Replacing the two algorithms, does not change from $\mathcal{ADV}$'s perspective. If $\mathcal{ADV}$ can generate m_{token}, then she can forge REV's signature. Given the security of the signature scheme, this can only happen with negligible probability. So $\mathcal{ADV}$ can distinguish between the Hybrids with negligible probability.   □

At this point, $\mathcal{ADV}$ has received what she thinks is a valid K_i. The simulator now gets access to all leakage functions $\mathcal{L}$ from the SSE scheme.

| **Hybrid 4** | Like Hybrid 3, but when HW.Run is queried with ($\mathsf{hdl_{CSP}}$, ("*search*", m_{search})), $\mathcal{S}$ is given the leakage function $\mathcal{L}_\mathcal{S}$ and generates $\mathbf{I_w^*}$ which is then sent to the user.

Lemma 2. *Hybrid 4 is indistinguishable from Hybrid 3.*

Proof. Assuming the $\mathcal{L}_i$ − security of the SSE scheme, the token sent by $\mathcal{ADV}$ to the CSP, as part of m_{search}, is generated by $\mathcal{S}$ with $\mathcal{L}_s$ as input. As a result when $\mathcal{S}$ receives m_{search}, it will generate a sequence of file identifiers $\mathbf{I_w^*}$ that will be send back to $\mathcal{ADV}$. $\mathcal{ADV}$ cannot distinguish between the real and the ideal experiment since she receives a sequence of files corresponding to a search token that was also simulated by $\mathcal{S}$. Moreover, if $\mathcal{ADV}$ manages to generate m_{search} without having contacted KT earlier, then she can also forge KT's signature. However, this can only happen with negligible probability, and as a result $\mathcal{ADV}$ can only distinguish between hybrids 4 and 3 with negligible probability.   □

Hybrid 5 Like Hybrid 4, but when HW.Run is queried with $(\mathsf{hdl}_{\mathsf{CSP}}, (\text{"}update\text{"}, m_{add}))$, $\mathcal{S}$ is given the leakage function $\mathcal{L}_a$ and tricks $\mathcal{ADV}$ into thinking that she updated the database.

Lemma 3. *Hybrid 5 is indistinguishable form Hybrid 4.*

Proof. By assuming the $\mathcal{L}_i$ − security of the SSE scheme, we know that $\mathcal{ADV}$ will not be able to distinguish between the real add token and the simulated one. Moreover, similar to the previous Hybrid, if $\mathcal{ADV}$ can generate m_{add} without having contacted KT, then she can also forge KT's signature – which can only happen with negligible probability. Hence, $\mathcal{ADV}$ can only distinguish between hybrids 5 and 4 with negligible probability.   □

Hybrid 6 Like Hybrid 5, but when HW.Run is queried with $(\mathsf{hdl}_{\mathsf{KT}}, (\text{"}delete\text{"}, m_{del}))$, $\mathcal{S}$ is given the leakage function $\mathcal{L}_d$ and tricks $\mathcal{ADV}$ into thinking that she deleted a certain file from the database. Moreover, $\mathcal{S}$ outputs $\perp$, if ReportVerify is queried with $(\mathsf{hdl}_{\mathsf{CSP}}, \mathsf{rpt})$ for a report that was not generated by executing HW.RunReport$(\mathsf{hdl}_{\mathsf{KT}}, (\text{"}delete\text{"}, m_{delete}))$.

Proof. By assuming the $\mathcal{L}_i$ − security of the SSE scheme, we know that $\mathcal{ADV}$ will not be able to distinguish between the real delete token and the simulated one. Moreover, if $\mathcal{ADV}$ can query HW.ReportVerify with $(\mathsf{hdl}_{\mathsf{CSP}}, \mathsf{rpt})$, for a rpt that was not generated by KT, then $\mathcal{ADV}$ can produce a valid MAC which can only happen with negligible probability since she does not know $\mathsf{sk}_{\mathsf{rpt}}$. Thus, $\mathcal{ADV}$ can only distinguish between Hybrids 5 and 6 with negligible probability.   □

Hybrid 7 Like Hybrid 6 but instead of MF.Revoke, $\mathcal{S}$ executes MF.Revoke*.

The hybrids are indistinguishable since no one can access the content of the revocation list and as a result nothing changes from $\mathcal{ADV}$'s point of view.

With this Hybrid our proof is complete. We managed to replace the expected outputs with simulated responses in a way that $\mathcal{ADV}$ cannot distinguish between the real and the ideal experiment.   □

6.1   SGX Security

Recent works [3,8,16,17] have shown that SGX is vulnerable to software attacks. However, according to [5], these attacks can be prevented if the programs running in the enclaves are data-obvious. Thus, leakage can be avoided if the programs do not have memory access patterns or control flow branches that depend on the values of sensitive data. In our construction, no sensitive data are used by the enclaves. KT acts as a storage space for the symmetric keys and does not perform any computation on them. Hence, all the $c_p^{K_i}$ are data-obvious. Moreover, rl is stored in plaintext and every entry in the list is padded to achieve same length.

7   Conclusion

In this paper, we proposed MF, a hybrid encryption scheme that combines *both* SSE and ABE in a way that the main advantages of each encryption technique are used. The proposed scheme enables clients to search over encrypted data by using an SSE scheme, while the symmetric key required for the decryption is protected via a Ciphertext-Policy Attribute-Based Encryption scheme. Moreover, our construction supports the revocation of users by utilizing the functionality provided by SGX. In contrast to recent works, the revocation mechanism has been separated from the actual ABE scheme and is exclusively based on the utilization of trusted SGX enclaves.

References

1. Bethencourt, J., Sahai, A., Waters, B.: Ciphertext-policy attribute-based encryption. In: Proceedings of the 2007 IEEE Symposium on Security and Privacy, SP 2007, pp. 321–334. IEEE Computer Society, Washington, DC (2007)
2. Boyko, V.: On the security properties of OAEP as an all-or-nothing transform. In: Wiener, M. (ed.) CRYPTO 1999. LNCS, vol. 1666, pp. 503–518. Springer, Heidelberg (1999). https://doi.org/10.1007/3-540-48405-1_32
3. Costan, V., Devadas, S.: Intel SGX explained. Cryptology ePrint Archive, Report 2016/086 (2016). https://eprint.iacr.org/2016/086
4. Dowsley, R., Michalas, A., Nagel, M., Paladi, N.: A survey on design andimplementation of protected searchable data in the cloud. Comput. Sci. Rev. **26**, 17–30 (2017)
5. Fisch, B., Vinayagamurthy, D., Boneh, D., Gorbunov, S.: Iron: functional encryption using Intel SGX. In: Proceedings of the 2017 ACM SIGSAC Conference on Computer and Communications Security, CCS 2017, pp. 765–782. ACM (2017)
6. Guo, W., Dong, X., Cao, Z., Shen, J.: Efficient attribute-based searchable encryption on cloud storage. J. Phys. Conf. Ser. **1087**, 052001 (2018)
7. Kamara, S., Papamanthou, C., Roeder, T.: Dynamic searchable symmetric encryption, pp. 965–976 (2012)
8. Lee, S., Shih, M., Gera, P., Kim, T., Kim, H., Peinado, M.: Inferring fine-grained control flow inside SGX enclaves with branch shadowing. In: 26th USENIX Security Symposium, BC, Canada, 16–18 August 2017, pp. 557–574 (2017)
9. Liu, J.K., Yuen, T.H., Zhang, P., Liang, K.: Time-based direct revocable ciphertext-policy attribute-based encryption with short revocation list. Cryptology ePrint Archive, Report 2018/330 (2018). https://eprint.iacr.org/2018/330
10. Michalas, A.: Sharing in the rain: secure and efficient data sharing for the cloud. In: Proceedings of the 11th IEEE International Conference for Internet Technology and Secured Transactions (ICITST-2016). IEEE (2016)
11. Michalas, A.: The lord of the shares: combining attribute-based encryption and searchable encryption for flexible data sharing. In: Proceedings of the 34th ACM/SIGAPP Symposium on Applied Computing, SAC 2019, pp. 146–155. ACM, New York (2019). https://doi.org/10.1145/3297280.3297297, http://doi.acm.org/10.1145/3297280.3297297
12. Microsoft: Microsoft Security Intelligence Report (2017)
13. Myers, S., Shull, A.: Practical revocation and key rotation. In: Smart, N.P. (ed.) CT-RSA 2018. LNCS, vol. 10808, pp. 157–178. Springer, Cham (2018). https://doi.org/10.1007/978-3-319-76953-0_9

14. Paladi, N., Gehrmann, C., Michalas, A.: Providing user security guarantees in public infrastructure clouds. IEEE Trans. Cloud Comput. **5**(3), 405–419 (2017). https://doi.org/10.1109/TCC.2016.2525991
15. Paladi, N., Michalas, A., Gehrmann, C.: Domain based storage protection with secure access control for the cloud. In: Proceedings of the 2014 International Workshop on Security in Cloud Computing. ASIACCS 2014. ACM, New York(2014)
16. Weichbrodt, N., Kurmus, A., Pietzuch, P., Kapitza, R.: AsyncShock: exploiting synchronisation bugs in Intel SGX enclaves. In: Askoxylakis, I., Ioannidis, S., Katsikas, S., Meadows, C. (eds.) ESORICS 2016. LNCS, vol. 9878, pp. 440–457. Springer, Cham (2016). https://doi.org/10.1007/978-3-319-45744-4_22
17. Xu, Y., Cui, W., Peinado, M.: Controlled-channel attacks: deterministic side channels for untrusted operating systems. In: Proceedings of the 36th IEEE Symposium on Security and Privacy (Oakland). IEEE, May 2015

ATCS Workshop

A Nature-Inspired Framework
for Optimal Mining of Attribute-Based
Access Control Policies

Masoud Narouei[(⊠)] and Hassan Takabi

Department of Computer Science and Engineering, University of North Texas,
Denton, TX, USA
Masoudnarouei@my.unt.edu, Takabi@unt.edu

Abstract. Even though attribute-based access control (ABAC) has
been applied to address authorization in areas such as cloud and internet of things, implementing ABAC policies can become complex due
to the high expressiveness of ABAC specifications. In order to semi-
automate this process, several policy mining approaches have been proposed that mostly derive ABAC policies from access request logs. These
approaches, however, do not take into account the existing ABAC policies
and attempt to define all policies from scratch, which is not acceptable
for an enterprise that already has an implemented ABAC system. Given
basic assumptions on how access control configurations are generated,
we first provide a formal definition of ABAC policy mining with minimal
perturbation that fulfills the requirements that enterprises typically have.
We then present an effective and efficient methodology based on particle
swarm optimization algorithm for addressing the ABAC policy mining
and ABAC policy mining with minimal perturbation problems. Experimental results demonstrate that the proposed methodology is able to
generate much less complex policies than previous works using the same
realistic case studies. Furthermore, we perform experiments on how to
find an ABAC state as similar as possible to both the existing state and
the optimal state.

Keywords: Access control policy · Attribute-based access control ·
Policy engineering · Particle swarm optimization

1 Introduction

In attribute-based access control (ABAC), a subject's request to perform an
operation on an object is granted or denied based on the attributes of the subject,
attributes of the object, environmental conditions, and a set of policies that are
specified in terms of those attributes and conditions [10]. The key difference
between ABAC and the other models of access control such as role-based access
control (RBAC) is the concept of policies, which express a complex Boolean rule
set and can evaluate many different attributes. For example, a subject is assigned

© ICST Institute for Computer Sciences, Social Informatics and Telecommunications Engineering 2019
Published by Springer Nature Switzerland AG 2019. All Rights Reserved
S. Chen et al. (Eds.): SecureComm 2019, LNICST 305, pp. 489–506, 2019.
https://doi.org/10.1007/978-3-030-37231-6_29

a set of attributes upon being employed by the organization (e.g., James, B is a lecturer in the computer science department). An object is also assigned a set of attributes upon being introduced to the system (e.g., a laboratory with cloud service capabilities). The administrator then creates an ABAC rule using the attributes of subject and object to control the set of operations that the subject is allowed to perform on that object (e.g., all lecturers in the computer science department can access cloud service capabilities). Migrating to ABAC simplifies system implementation, in which hundreds of roles can be replaced by just a few ABAC policies. While this enables flexibility in large enterprises [10], implementing ABAC policies can become complex due to the existence of an attribute management infrastructure and high expressiveness of ABAC specifications. To reduce the complexity of policy specification, several policy mining approaches have been proposed [13,25]. While these approaches aim to semi-automate the construction of ABAC policies from available access control information such as access logs, they do not take into account the existing ABAC policies and attempt to define all policies from scratch, which is not acceptable for an enterprise that already has an implemented ABAC system. Once an ABAC model is in place, system maintenance becomes important as the system requires regular updates to meet the new access requirements. For example, employees may leave or move to a different department within the enterprise, new resources may be added that need new permissions, some permission needs to be updated to comply with new regulations, etc. Adopting a completely distinct ABAC system and redefining policies may cause disruptions that prevent the enterprise from functioning properly. In fact, migrating to a new set of policies should cause as few disruption as possible. We aim to address this issue by looking for a new set of ABAC policies that are as similar as possible to both the existing ABAC state (current set of policies) and the optimal ABAC state (set of policies that cover all old and new permission requirements).

We first provide a formal definition of ABAC policy mining with minimal perturbation and then present a nature-inspired algorithm based on particle swarm optimization (PSO) for solving the ABAC policy mining and ABAC policy mining with minimal perturbation problems. Furthermore, we propose a global optimization function (GOF) and perform experiments to facilitate migrating to a new ABAC state with the goal of minimizing possible disruptions to the system. This methodology can also be helpful for organizations that want to adopt an already implemented ABAC from a different organization. To the best of our knowledge, there is no work in the literature that addresses how to update an ABAC state with minimal perturbation and this is the first report on doing so. The contributions of this paper are hence three-fold:

- We provide a formal definition of ABAC policy mining with minimal perturbation.
- We propose a nature-inspired mechanism based on PSO algorithm in order to effectively and efficiently mine ABAC policies.
- We propose a methodology to find a new ABAC state as close as possible to both the current ABAC state and the optimal state.

The rest of the paper is organized as follows: An overview of the previous litera-ture is presented in Sect. 2. We formalize the problem of mining ABAC policies with minimal perturbation in Sect. 3, followed by the explanation of the algo-rithm and its components in Sect. 4. The experiments, results, and discussions are then presented in Sect. 5. Section 6 concludes the paper.

2   Related Work

The problem of mining ABAC policies from logs was first investigated in [25]. The authors presented an algorithm that iterates over tuples in a user-permission relation extracted from the logs, uses selected tuples as seeds for constructing candidate rules, and attempts to generalize each candidate rule to cover addi-tional tuples in the user-permission relation. Medvet *et al.* proposed a multi-objective evolutionary approach based on genetic operators for learning ABAC policies [13]. Using an iterative process, they executed an evolutionary search, where all the rules in the population were updated based on genetic operators (mutation and crossover). Iyer and Masoumzadeh proposed another algorithm based on concepts adopted from the PRISM rule mining algorithm to mine ABAC policies that may contain both positive and negative authorization rules [11]. Most recently, Cotrini *et al.* proposed Rhapsody, an ABAC mining algo-rithm that mines a rule if and only if the rule covers a significant number of requests, its reliability is above a given threshold, and there is no equivalent shorter rule [4]. The proposed algorithm avoids mining overly-permissive rules by using reliability, a new rule quality measure, to guide the mining of rules.

Das *et al.* investigated the problem of policy adaptation for ABAC. They defined the policy adaptation as the problem of assigning proper values to subject attributes with respect to a given set of desired accesses [5], and presented a migration path in which an organization adapts to the ABAC policy of another organization with which it enters into a collaboration for data sharing.

Regarding measuring the goodness of RBAC state, literature has provided some reports. Zhang *et al.* proposed a heuristic algorithm for role mining, which modeled an RBAC state as a graph and considered the role mining problem as a graph optimization problem [27]. Their algorithm starts with an initial RBAC state and iteratively improves the system using pairs of roles such that merging or splitting the two roles will result in a graph with a lower cost. Vaidya *et al.* defined the minimal perturbation as the "problem of discovering an optimal set of roles from existing user permissions that are similar to the currently deployed roles" [22]. They proposed a heuristic solution based on previously developed FastMiner algorithm [23] and computed the similarity or distance between two roles as well as between two sets of roles using the Jaccard Coefficient. Takabi *et al.* proposed StateMiner, a heuristic solution to find an RBAC state as similar as possible to both the existing RBAC state and the optimal state. They formally defined the problem of mining a role hierarchy with minimal perturbation and introduced two measures: a measure for goodness of an RBAC state and a measure for minimal perturbation [21].

While mining ABAC policies from natural language documents have not been extensively investigated in the literature, there have been some reports that discuss extracting ABAC policies from natural language documents. Narouei *et al.* proposed two methodologies based on recurrent neural networks [15] and a combination of multiple natural language processing techniques [14] in order to identify access control policy (ACP) sentences from non-ACP sentences. Then, they used semantic role labeling (SRL) technique to extract access control policy elements (subject, object, action) from ACP policy sentences [16,17]. Most recently, Das *et al.* discussed a hybrid approach toward policy engineering that used entropy and frequency to construct an ABAC policy [6]. An essential step towards automatically converting ACP sentences to ABAC policies is the extraction of attributes and environment conditions from policy documents. Das *et al.* presented an ABAC policy mining algorithm that considered the environmental attributes and their associated values while forming the rules [7]. They used Gini impurity to form the rules, which helped minimize the number of rules in the generated policy. Narouei *et al.* proposed a top-down policy engineering framework for ABAC where they briefly discussed attribute extraction and how to represent an ABAC policy using the extracted subject, object, and environmental attributes [15]. Then, Alohaly *et al.* [1] proposed the first evaluated effort, leveraging natural language processing (NLP), relation extraction (RE) and machine learning (ML) techniques to automate the attributes extraction task of the ABAC policy authoring lifecycle [3].

3   The Problem of ABAC Policy Mining with Minimal Perturbation

In this section, we provide a formal definition of ABAC policy mining with minimal perturbation and introduce two measures: a measure of goodness and a measure of perturbation for an ABAC state. We consider the same ABAC policy language described in [26] and further considered in [13]. In this language, U refers to the set of users, R refers to the set of resources, O refers to the set of operations, A_u is the set of user attributes, A_r is the set of resource attributes, d_u is the user attribute data, d_r is the resource attribute data, UAE is the user attribute expression, and RAE is the resource attribute expression. More information about the policy languages can be found in the original report [26].

3.1   Policy Mining Problem

The input to the problem of mining ABAC policies with minimal perturbation is a set of users U, a set of resources R, a set of operations O, attribute data $ATT = \langle A_u, A_r, d_u, d_r \rangle$, a current ABAC configuration $\pi = \langle U, R, O, A_u, A_r, d_u, d_r, Rules \rangle$, a user-permission relation $\rho' = \langle U', R', O', UPR' \rangle$ indicating the new permission requirements, and depending on its availability, top-down information ($TDI = \langle A'_u, A'_r, d'_u, d'_r \rangle$). TDI is the information about the new users and resources such as their attributes, and can includes, for instance, department, affiliations, or location of the users. We infer that UPR' can be expressed as $UPR' \subseteq U' \times R' \times O'$, where U' can include some members of U and potentially introduces new members. R' and O' are defined similarly. We define $U'' = U \cup U'$, where U'' is the union of both U and U', similarly, $R'' = R \cup R'$, $O'' = O \cup O'$, $A_u'' = A_u \cup A_u'$, $A_r'' = A_r \cup A_r'$, $d_u'' = d_u \cup d_u'$, and $d_r'' = d_r \cup d_r'$.

Definition 1 (ABAC Policy Mining Problem). Given an existing ABAC state $\pi = \langle U, R, O, Au, Ar, du, dr, Rules \rangle$, find a new ABAC state $\gamma = \langle U'', R'', O'', Au'', Ar'', du'', dr'', Rules'' \rangle$ that is consistent with user-permission relation ρ' accompanied by TDI and is as close as possible to the existing ABAC state π. $Rules''$ is a new set of ABAC policies that includes $Rules$ and possibly introduces new rules to support the new user-permission relation configurations ρ'. The ABAC state is consistent with ρ' if every user in π has the same set of authorized permissions as in γ.

3.2 A Measure for Goodness of an ABAC State

Given an existing ABAC state π, a user-permission relation ρ', and possibly TDI, many ABAC states may be consistent with π that cover ρ'. We need to have a measurement of how good an ABAC state is in order to select among them. [26] used weighted structural complexity (WSC) as the policy quality metric in order to measure the quality of mined ABAC policies. WSC is described as the weighted sum of the number of elements in the policy. Formally, [26] described WSC as Eq. 1:

$$WSC(e) = \sum_{a \in attr_1(e)} |e(a)| + \sum_{a \in attr_m(e), a \in e(a)} |s|$$

$$WSC(\langle e_u, e_r, O, c \rangle) = w_1 WSC(e_u) + w_2 WSC(e_r) + w_3|O| + w_4|c| \tag{1}$$

where $|s|$ is the cardinality of set s. We adopt the same definition of WSC for an ABAC policy, which is defined as the sum of the WSC of all the rules in that policy, to measure the goodness of an ABAC state. For the experiments, we used the same weights ($w_i = 1$); however, these weights can be adjusted based on specific needs.

3.3 A Measure for Minimal Perturbation.

In order to evaluate whether the new ABAC state is as close as possible to the initial ABAC state, we need to measure perturbation. In other words, we need to measure how similar the new ABAC policies are to the initial ABAC policies. In the following sections, we will define a similarity measure for policies that will consider both syntactic and semantic similarities.

Syntactic Similarity. Measures the fraction of conditions, constraints, and actions that rules or policies have in common. Xu and Stoller described syntactic similarity of rule sets $Rules1$ and $Rules2$ as the average, over rules ρ in $Rules1$, of the syntactic similarity between ρ and the most similar rule in $Rules2$ [26]. They further defined syntactic similarity of policies π_1 and π_2 ($Syn(\pi_1, \pi_2)$) as the maximum of the syntactic similarities of the sets of rules in the policies, considered in both orders. We adopt the same definition for syntactic similarity with the assumption that $Rules1$ is the larger rule set.

Semantic Similarity. We adopt the same definition of semantic similarity of two policies as described in [26], which aims to measure the fraction of requests that both policies accept. First, we define accepted requests of rule r_1, $accepted(r_1)$, as the number of requests that are accepted by rule r_1. Then we expand this definition to the accepted requests of policy π_1, $accepted(\pi_1)$ as the number of requests that are accepted by all rules in policy π_1, as presented in Eq. 2:

For any policy π_1, we define accepted requests of π_1 as

$$accepted(\pi_1) = \sum_{i \in \pi_1} accepted(r_i) \tag{2}$$

Using Eq. 2, we define the semantic similarity of policies π_1 and π_2 as Eq. 3:

$$Sem(\pi_1, \pi_2) = \left| \frac{accepted(\pi_1) \cap accepted(\pi_2)}{accepted(\pi_1) \cup accepted(\pi_2)} \right| \tag{3}$$

Policy Similarity. We define the similarity between policies as follows:

Definition 2 (Policy Similarity). For any two policies π_1 and π_2, their similarity is defined as Eq. 4:

$$sim(\pi_1, \pi_2) = w_1 \times Syn(\pi_1, \pi_2) + w_2 \times Sem(\pi_1, \pi_2) \tag{4}$$

where Syn is the syntactic similarity of policies and $w_1 + w_2 = 1$. We consider the weights as $w_1 = w_2 = 1/2$ for the experiments, giving equal weights to both syntactic and semantic similarities. However, these weights could be adjusted based on the requirements. When two policies are identical with regards to all conditions, constraints, and actions, their similarity is 1, and when two policies have mutually exclusive conditions, constraints, and actions, their similarity is 0.

Global Optimization Function. Takabi et al. defined the global optimization function (GOF) for RBAC with the goal of (1) minimizing the WSC of the resulting RBAC state, and (2) maximizing the similarity between identified roles and the existing roles [21]. We expand their definition for the problem of mining ABAC policies with minimal perturbation as follows:

Definition 3 (Global Optimization Function). Given a weighted structural complexity, wsc, of an ABAC state, a new weighted structural complexity of an updated ABAC state, wsc', and a similarity measure, sim, between two policies $\pi_{current}$ (current ABAC state) and π_{new} (updated ABAC state), GOF is defined as Eq. 5:

$$
\begin{aligned}
&GOF(wsc, wsc', sim(\pi_{current}, \pi_{new})) \\
&= (1 - wf) \times (wsc/wsc') + wf \times sim(\pi_{current}, \pi_{new})
\end{aligned}
\tag{5}
$$

where $wf \in [0,1]$ is a user defined weighting factor for similarity. As the new ABAC state is the result of updating the initial ABAC state with some new rules that cover new permission requirements, we tend to minimize the ratio of wsc'/wsc. In this formula, if the $wf = 0$, $GOF(wsc, sim) = wsc/wsc'$, which means the only important issue is the ratio of weighted structural complexities. In other words, we do not care about how similar the new ABAC state is compared to the initial one. Also, choosing $wf = 1$ yields $GOF(wsc, sim) = sim$, which means we only care about the similarity of the new ABAC model to the initial one. Choosing the proper wf can also control the level of over-assignments[1] and under-assignments[2] introduced to the system. The higher the wf, the higher the emphasize is on choosing similar rules. This will reduce the chances of introducing new over-assignments and under-assignments as the new rules will have many elements in common with the current rules and hence there will be less perturbation. We will analyze this issue in future works. Finally, we define the problem of mining ABAC policies with minimal perturbation as follows:

Definition 4 (The problem of Mining ABAC Policies with Minimal Perturbation). Given an existing ABAC state $\pi = \langle U, R, O, Au, Ar, du, dr, Rules \rangle$, and a user-permission relation $\rho' = \langle U', R', O', UPR' \rangle$ accompanied by $TDI = \langle A'_u, A'_r, d'_u, d'_r \rangle$, find a new ABAC state $\gamma = \langle U'', R'', O'', Au'', Ar'', du'', dr'', Rules'' \rangle$ consistent with UPR' such that it maximizes $GOF(wsc, wsc', sim(\pi_{current}, \pi_{new}))$.

Our goal is to maximize the GOF so that we can find an updated ABAC state as close as possible to the existing one and the optimal one. In other words, an updated ABAC state that does not introduce many over-assignment and under assignments.

4 Methodology

In its most basic terms, optimization is a mathematical discipline that concerns with finding the best solution, if it is possible, from all feasible solutions. Many real-world problems such as policy mining [3] have various solutions and sometimes

---

[1] An over-assignment is when a permission is inappropriately granted to a user.

[2] An under-assignment is when a user lacks a permission that he or she should be granted.

[3] Identifying a set of policies that can satisfy a number of requests.

an infinite number of solutions may be possible. For such problems, optimization can be achieved by finding the best solution from an infinite number of solutions in terms of some performance measure [2]. While mathematical optimization techniques such as linear programming and dynamic programming have been successful in addressing optimizations problems with few variables, they often fail (or reach local optimum) in solving NP-hard problems with large number of variables and non-linear objective functions [12]. To overcome these issues, evolutionary-based algorithms have been proposed for finding near-optimum solutions [8]. There are two major categories of optimization problems, namely discrete optimization and continuous optimization. In a continuous optimization problem, the variables used are required to be continuous variables (i.e. chosen from a set of real values between which there are no gaps). In discrete optimization, on the other hand, some or all of the variables used are restricted to be discrete variables (i.e. assume only a discrete set of values, such as the integers). As policy mining problem is restricted to a finite set of users, resources, and operations, it is categorized as a discrete optimization problem.

Medvet *et al.* proposed an evolutionary approach based on genetic algorithm (GA) for learning ABAC policies from sets of authorized and denied access requests [13]. They presented an incremental strategy for learning a policy by learning single rules, each one focused on a subset of requests. Their methodology used genetic operators (mutation and crossover) and was able to deal with complex case studies. However, in a discrete optimization setting, it has been shown that PSO algorithm generally outperforms most other algorithms (e.g. GA) in terms of success rate, solution quality [8], and processing time [18]. A particle in PSO is analogous to a chromosome in GA. However, as opposed to GA, the evolutionary process in PSO is not solely based on creating new solutions, but rather modifying the existing solutions to become a more desirable solution set. In other words, each particle only evolves its social behavior and accordingly its movement towards the desired destination [19].

In this paper, we propose a heuristic method based on PSO algorithm to solve the policy mining problem. In PSO, each solution simulates a 'bird' in the flock and is called a particle. As a flock of birds search for food, each bird communicates with the other birds and locates the bird that is closest to the food. Then, the bird moves towards that bird using a velocity that depends on its current location. This process repeats until the flock reaches the desired destination (food). Similarly, each particle moves in the problem search space looking for the closest position to the optimal solution, and over time adjusts its position according to its own experience (i.e. the best position it reached in the past) as well as other particles. Hence, each particle utilizes both social interaction or global search (i.e. the experience of other particles around it) as well as local search (i.e., its self-experience), attempting to balance both exploration and exploitation.

Throughout the search process, each particle considers the following three variables in an n-dimensional space:

- *Current position:* $X_i = (x_{i1}, x_{i2}, ..., x_{in})$
- *Best previous position:* $P_{Best} = (p_{i1}, p_{i2}, ..., p_{in})$
- *Velocity:* $V_i = (v_{i1}, v_{i2}, ..., v_{in})$

where the velocity for particle i, V_i, represents the distance that the particle needs to travel in order to get to the new desired location. In each iteration, each particle updates its velocity according to the Eq. 6:

$$New\ V_i = \omega \times current\ V_i + C_1 \times rand() \times (P_{Best} - X_i)$$
$$+ C_2 \times rand() \times (G_{Best} - X_i) \tag{6}$$

where G_{Best} represents the global search elements, the position of the best particle among the entire population. c_1 and c_2 are positive constant parameters that control the maximum step size the particle can do (usually $c_1 = c_2 = 1$), and $rand()$ is a random functions with a range of $[0, 1]$. The inertia weight, ω, is a user-specified parameter proposed by Shi and Eberhart [19] that controls, alongside c_1 and c_2, the impact of the previous history of velocities on the current velocity. ω is intended to balance the global search and the local search, where a larger ω puts more weight towards exploration (searching new area) while a smaller ω prefers exploitation (fine-tuning the current search area). ω alongside c_1 and c_2 are generally called "learning factors" and can be updated throughout the circulation of the algorithm.

Using the new velocity V_i, particle i adjusts its position using Eq. 7:

$$New\ X_i = current\ X_i + New\ V_i \tag{7}$$

This process repeats until a stopping criteria is satisfied. Throughout the process, the performance of each particle is calculated based on a fitness function, which is usually proportional to the cost function associated with the problem [20].

4.1 A Particle Swarm Optimization Algorithm for ABAC Policy Mining

Similar to [13], we adopt a divide-and-conquer strategy [9] in order to build an ABAC policy. Given a problem instance $\pi = \langle U, R, O, Au, Ar, du, dr \rangle$ and a number of input requests $UP = U \times R \times O$ in the form of $\langle user, resource, operation \rangle$, our methodology first attempts to create an initial population of particles based on the requests in UP, where each particle is a rule accepting each request in UP. Considering the following request in UP from one of the case-studies considered in this research[4]:

- $u = \langle uid = stu4, position = applicant \rangle$
- $r = \langle rid = app5, student = stu4, type = application \rangle$
- $o = \langle checkStatus \rangle$

---

[4] *University* case-study.

The corresponding rule ρ generated from this request will be:

$$\rho = \langle \{position = applicant\} \wedge \{student = stu4 \wedge type = application\},$$
$$\{checkStatus\}, \{\}\rangle.$$

We execute the PSO algorithm, where at each iteration, each particle attempts to update its position based a new updated Velocity V. When all the population have updated their positions (end of a cycle), we rank all particles according to the number of requests from UP that they accept (the fitness function). We then pick the particle ρ that accepts the highest number of requests, and add it to the set of new ABAC policies. Finally, we exclude all the requests that ρ accepts from the UP and repeat the process on the new smaller set of UP. This process continues until there is no more requests remaining in UP. The overall process is illustrated in Algorithm 1.

There are two versions of the POS algorithm based on the neighborhood topology used to exchange experience among particles: $Global_{Best}$ and $Local_{Best}$. In the $Global_{Best}$ model, the neighborhood of the particle is the entire swarm. In the $Local_{Best}$ model, however, a swarm is divided into overlapping neighborhoods of particles and each particle looks at its own neighborhood to find its neighborhood best particle [24]. In order to take advantage of both topologies, we incorporated both in the velocity function. Instead of updating the velocity based on all three parameters (global best, local best, previous best) using the adjustable weighs in the original formula (Eq. 6), we randomly pick one of the parameters and update the velocity based on it. Note that to update using the $Local_{Best}$ parameter, we chose a neighbourhood of 12 rules around the current rule. We verified experimentally that variations in this neighbourhood value do not cause significant difference in the results. Finally, we introduce a new parameter called $requestLimit$. This parameter ensures the quality of the final policy as after each iteration, for a rule to be chosen, it has to at least satisfy a minimum $requestLimit$ number of requests.

The details of the velocity algorithm are illustrated in Algorithm 2. Note that we used the $randomsubset()$ function instead of adding/removing all the elements that are difference between two rules r and y. This is because few of the rules contained a large number of some elements such as operations (due to random generation of some rules) and adding all those elements to the updated rule would lead to more generalized rules (rules that accept over-assignments).

5   Experiments

The evaluation consists of two independent experiments. We first compare the performance of the proposed PSO algorithm with the GA, proposed by [13], with respect to mining ABAC policies. We then analyze the framework, described in Sect. 3, in updating an ABAC model using a new set of permission requirements. For the experiments, we used the case studies introduced in [25]. We considered

Algorithm 1. Particle Swarm Optimization

```
1: procedure PSO (toAcceptRequests)
2:     Population ← InitPopu(toAcceptRequests)          → Initialize Population
3:     Rules ← []
4:     for all x ∈ Population do          → Initialize parameters
5:         x ← initParameters()          → fitness, previous best rule, etc.
6:     end for
7:     gbr ← GetGlobalBest(Population)          → Find global best particle
8:     while toAcceptRequests.isEmpty() do
9:         toRemoveRequests ← []
10:        for all r ∈ Population do
11:            Choice ← Random(3)          → Randomly pick how to update velocity
12:            if Choice = GlobalBest then          → IF pick is based on global best
13:                V_r = velocity(r, gbr);
14:            else if Choice = LocalBest then          → IF pick is local best
15:                LocalRules ← []
16:                shift ← 6          → Initialize local neighbourhood
17:                minIndex ← r_index − shift
18:                maxIndex ← r_index + shift
19:                LocalRules ← Population[minIndex : maxIndex]
20:                lbr ← GetLocalBest(LocalRules)          → Find local best particle
21:                V_r = velocity(r, lbr);
22:            else if Choice = PreviousBest then          → IF pick is Previous best
23:                V_r = velocity(r, r_pbr);
24:            else
25:                V_r = 0;          → Do not update
26:            end if
27:            r′ = r + V_r          → Update the rule based on the new velocity
28:            if r′! = r then          → IF the rule is updated
29:                if r′ > r′_pbr then          → IF new rule is better than previous best:
30:                    r′_pbr ← r′          → replace previous best with the new rule
31:                end if
32:                if r′ > gbr then          → IF new rule is better than the global best:
33:                    gbr ← r′          → replace global best with the new rule
34:                end if
35:                Population.remove(r)          → Remove the old rule
36:                Population.add(r′)          → Add the new rule to the population
37:            end if
38:        end for
39:        newRule = FindBestRule(Population)          → Find the best rule
40:        toRemoveRequests ← SatisfyRequests(newRule)          → Get all
       requests that are satisfied by the new rule
41:        if toRemoveRequests.size() ≥ requestLimit then
42:            toAcceptRequests.removeAll(toRemoveRequests)
43:            rules.add(newRule)
44:        end if
45:    end while
46:    return rules
47: end procedure
```

Algorithm 2. Velocity

1: **procedure** VELOCITY(R,Y)   → y is the rule by which x will be updated
2:     $Component \leftarrow Random()$ → Randomly pick a component of the rule to update: e.g. operation, constraint, UAE, RAE
3:         **if** $Component = operation$ **then**   → IF pick is operation
4:             $O_1 \leftarrow Ops(r) - Ops(y)$
5:             $O_2 \leftarrow Ops(y) - Ops(r)$
6:             **if** $O_1 > 0$ **then**   → IF the current rule has elements in difference
7:                 $Ops(r) \leftarrow Ops(r) - randomSubset(O_1)$ → remove a random subset of the elements in difference
8:             **else if** $O_2 > 0$ **then**   → IF updating rule has elements in difference
9:                 $Ops(r) \leftarrow Ops(r) + randomSubset(O_2)$ → add a random subset of elements in difference to the rule
10:             **else**
11:                 $Ops(r).add(Random(ops))$ → add a random operation to the rule
12:             **end if**
13:         **else if** $Component = constraint$ **then**   → IF pick is constraint
14:             ...   → Similar to operation
15:         **else if** $Component = UAE$ **then**   → IF pick is user attribute expression
16:             $uae_1 \leftarrow UAE(r) - UAE(y)$
17:             $uae_2 \leftarrow UAE(y) - UAE(r)$
18:             **if** $uae_1 > 0$ **then**
19:                 $UAE(r) \leftarrow UAE(r) - randomSubset(uae_1)$
20:             **else if** $uae_2 > 0$ **then**
21:                 $UAE(r) \leftarrow UAE(r) + randomSubset(uae_2)$
22:             **else**
23:                 $UAE(r).add(Random(uae))$ → add a random user attribute
24:             **end if**
25:         **else if** $Component = RAE$ **then**
26:             ...   → Similar to UAE
27:         **end if**
28: **end procedure**

---

four hand-crafted policies and one of the synthetic (i.e., pseudo randomly generated) policies. Each case study includes a set of users U, a set of resources R, a set of operations O, a set of user attributes A_U, a set of resource attributes A_R, and a set of rules P_0. The hand-crafted policies contain a few instances of each type of user and resource. For example, there are two academic departments, several students, a few faculty, etc. in the *University* case study. On the other hand, synthetic policies include a much larger number of users and resources. The details of each case study is presented in Table 1. Note that for the *University* synthetic case study, there are 11 operations listed, instead of 9. We added two random operations to this case study because in the second experiment, we wanted to generate new permission requirements that have not been seen by the system. In this table, S_A represents the portions of requests (from all possible requests, i.e., $S = U * R * O$) that are accepted by P_0 and S_D represents the portions that are rejected by P_0.

Table 1. Details of hand-crafted and synthetic case studies. $|P_0|$ is the number of manually written rules and UP is the total number of generated requests.

Case study	$|P_0|$	$|U|$	$|R|$	$|O|$	$|A_U|$	$|A_R|$	$|S_A|$	S_D	UP	$WSC(P_0)$
Healthcare	9	21	16	3	6	7	51	957	1008	33
Online video	6	12	13	1	3	3	78	78	156	20
Project mgmt	11	19	40	7	8	6	189	5131	5320	49
University	10	22	34	9	6	5	168	6564	9732	37
University (synthetic)	10	168	315	11	6	5	3633	575022	578655	37

5.1 Comparison of PSO Performance with the State of the Art

In order to have a direct comparison with the most recent work [13], we executed our approach on the same four hand-crafted case studies that they used (see Table 1). For the synthetic case studies, since [13] used a smaller random sample ($|S_D| = 5|S_A|$) of these policies, we were not able to compare our methodology as generating a new random sample will not yield the same samples that they used. To perform the experiments, we used the same population size ($n_{pop} = 100$) and repeated the experiments three times to make sure the results are consistent. Throughout the experiments, we also verified that a value of $requestlimit = 15$ (see Sect. 4.1) yields the highest quality rules. The experimental results are presented in Table 2. All of the experiments were performed on a 2 GHz Intel Core i7 PC with 8 GB of physical memory. The results are presented with respect to $\frac{WSC(P_0)}{WSC(P)}$, where $WSC(P_0)$ refers to the WSC of the original policies (presented in Table 1) and $WSC(P)$ refers to the WSC of the generated policies. A value greater than one indicates that the generated policies are less complex than the original policies. The table also presents the number of rules generated, the total evaluations (the total number of times the rules were updated and new rules created), and the execution time. Similar to [13], our approach was able to generate policies without special attributes rid and uid as these attributes make policies less general. Overall, our methodology was able to produce a smaller set of policies that are much less complex and redundant than the baseline and [13], using fewer number of evaluations and a faster execution time. One reasons for the better performance of PSO especially in terms of less number of evaluations and faster performance is because in PSO, rules are updated based on global, local, and previous best rules, which make the rules lean towards the better rules. In comparison, in the genetic algorithm, each rule goes through a mutation or a crossover operation with another randomly chosen rule, which means more cycles of evaluation is needed to find more favorable rules. Compared to the genetic algorithm, our approach has fewer parameters to tune (only population size and requestlimit). In order to analyze the effects of using different values for n_{pop}, we performed experiments with respect to $\frac{WSC(P_0)}{WSC(P)}$ using varying values of n_{pop} (100, 200, ..., 2000). The results are presented in Fig. 1 where Green depicts the performance on the *University* case study while blue is on the *healthcare*. While [13]

mentioned that reasonable variations in parameters do not cause significant variations in their results, it is clear that our methodology tends to achieve much higher
performances using larger population sizes.

Table 2. Comparison with genetic methodology.

Case study	n_{eval}	$\dfrac{WSC(P_0)}{WSC(G)}$	$\dfrac{WSC(P_0)}{WSC(P)}$	Rules(G)	Rules(P)	Evals(G)	Evals(P)	Time(G)	Time(P)
Healthcare	500	1.07	1.375	11	4	5536	3101	1.2	0.172
	2500	1.18		9		19776		4	
	5000	1.18		9		22691		5.3	
Online video	500	1	1.82	6	2	2768	310	0.6	0.067
	2500	1		6		5215		0.8	
	5000	1		6		7715		1.1	
Project mgmt	500	0.96	1.26	13	10	6646	8622	3.5	0.397
	2500	1.06		11		24368		14.7	
	5000	1.06		11		27791		22.2	
University	500	0.95	1.02	10	9	5904	6706	3.1	0.318
	2500	0.98		10		22846		14.1	
	5000	1		10		26487		21.8	

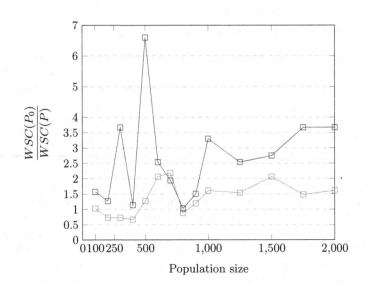

Fig. 1. Trade-off between population size and $\dfrac{WSC(P_0)}{WSC(P)}$. Green is the performance on
the *University* case study while blue is the performance on the *healthcare* case study
(Color figure online)

5.2   Updating an ABAC Model

As motioned in Sect. 1, an ABAC system requires regular updates to meet the new access requirements. Adopting a completely new ABAC system and redefining all policies from scratch may cause disruptions that prevent the enterprise from functioning properly. So the goal is to search for a new set of policies that are as similar as possible to both the existing ABAC state and the optimal ABAC state. For this experiment, we considered both hand-crafted and synthetic policies of the *University* case study. This case study has a larger number of hand-crafted rules and more variety of users, resources, and operations. We considered the hand-crafted policies as the current ABAC state and then generated random permission requirements using the synthetic policies, which serve as the new updates introduced to the system. While the original case study includes nine operations, we manually added two new random operations to this set in order to come up with unique permission requirements, not seen by the current ABAC model. To generate the new permission requirements, we first considered all possible requests from synthetic *University* case study, i.e., $S' = U' \times R' \times O'$, divided into $|S_A|'$ and $|S_D|'$. We excluded from this set, all those requests that are accepted by the current ABAC state, respectively. Out of the remaining $\sim$500K requests, we randomly picked 50K requests as the new updates (UP'). Instead of creating a new population solely based on UP', we first initialized the population based on the current policies in the initial ABAC state. Even though the current ABAC state has only nine rules, that will help convey the current settings and organizational structures to the new policies, which will help create rules that are more similar to the current rules. We then added new random rules based on requests in UP' to create an initial population of size $n_{pop} = 500$. We chose 500 as according to the Fig. 1, a population of 500 resulted in the highest value of the $\dfrac{WSC(P_0)}{WSC(P)}$ for *University* case study.

We executed the PSO algorithm and each time a new rule was generated, we added it to the initial ABAC model and calculated the perturbation using GOF. If the new ABAC model did not perturb more than a pre-specified threshold, we continued with more iterations until we exceeded the threshold or all the new permission requirements were covered. Evaluation results are presented in Table 3. As the Table 3 illustrates, defining the proper value for GOF plays the key role in generating a new ABAC state that is as similar as possible to both current ABAC state and optimal ABAC state. A lower GOF value means we are covering more permission requirements. However, this leads to generating an ABAC state that is not very similar to the current state, potentially introducing more overhead (over-assignments) to the system. A higher value, however, leads to covering fewer permission requirements, but, resulting in a more stable ABAC state. GOF can be used as a measure for automated/manual policy mining as we can run the algorithm as long as it does not exceed the threshold. Once the new ABAC state hit the threshold, we can resume rule generation manually with a much smaller set of requests to satisfy.

Table 3. GOF values while updating an ABAC state. *ABAC* is size of the final ABAC, *WSC* is the WSC of the final ABAC, *Accepted RQ* is the number of accepted requests, and *Remaining RQs* is the number of remaining requests.

ABAC	WSC	Accepted RQ	Remaining RQs	Syntactic	Semantic	GOF
11	40.0	3600	46400	0.888	0.0445	0.696
12	43.0	3585	42815	0.866	0.0228	0.653
13	48.0	2350	40465	0.838	0.0173	0.599
14	53.0	3600	36865	0.818	0.0126	0.557
15	58.0	1880	34985	0.797	0.0110	0.521
16	63.0	1500	33485	0.784	0.0100	0.492
17	66.0	2425	31060	0.768	0.0087	0.474
18	70.0	3380	27680	0.753	0.0074	0.455
19	87.0	16553	11127	0.733	0.0043	0.397
20	91.0	1000	10127	0.721	0.0041	0.385
21	94.0	1000	9127	0.711	0.0040	0.376
22	98.0	1250	7877	0.702	0.0039	0.365
23	100.0	940	6937	0.693	0.0038	0.359
24	102.0	625	6312	0.686	0.0038	0.354
25	104.0	225	6087	0.683	0.0038	0.349
26	108.0	1106	4981	0.676	0.0037	0.341
27	110.0	656	4325	0.670	0.0036	0.337
28	120.0	3875	450	0.658	0.0033	0.319
29	126.0	450	0	0.648	0.0033	0.309

6   Conclusion and Future Work

In this paper, we focused on ABAC policy mining problem in scenarios that there is already an ABAC system in place. We first defined the problem of mining ABAC policies with minimal perturbation and then presented an effective and efficient methodology based on PSO algorithm for solving the policy mining task. Our methodology was able to produce a smaller set of policies that are less complex than the baseline and related works, using a fewer number of evaluations and faster execution time. Furthermore, we presented global optimization function and experimentally presented how to find an ABAC state as similar as possible to both the existing state and the optimal state. A limitation of our current solution is the sole use of support as the fitness function, which does not account for over-assignments and under-assignments. In the future, we plan on incorporating new metrics to address the over-assignments and under-assignments introduced using our methodology.

References

1. Alohaly, M., Takabi, H., Blanco, E.: A deep learning approach for extracting attributes of ABAC policies. In: Proceedings of the 23nd ACM on Symposium on Access Control Models and Technologies, pp. 137–148. ACM (2018)
2. Antoniou, A., Lu, W.S.: The optimization problem. In: Antoniou, A., Lu, W.S. (eds.) Practical Optimization, pp. 1–26. Springer, Boston (2007). https://doi.org/10.1007/978-0-387-71107-2_1
3. Brossard, D., Gebel, G., Berg, M.: A systematic approach to implementing ABAC. In: Proceedings of the 2nd ACM Workshop on Attribute-Based Access Control, pp. 53–59. ACM (2017)
4. Cotrini, C., Weghorn, T., Basin, D.: Mining ABAC rules from sparse logs. In: 2018 IEEE European Symposium on Security and Privacy (EuroS&P), pp. 31–46. IEEE (2018)
5. Das, S., Sural, S., Vaidya, J., Atluri, V.: Policy adaptation in attribute-based access control for inter-organizational collaboration. In: 2017 IEEE 3rd International Conference on Collaboration and Internet Computing (CIC), pp. 136–145. IEEE (2017)
6. Das, S., Sural, S., Vaidya, J., Atluri, V.: Hype: a hybrid approach toward policy engineering in attribute-based access control. IEEE Lett. Comput. Soc. 1(2), 25–29 (2018)
7. Das, S., Sural, S., Vaidya, J., Atluri, V.: Using Gini impurity to mine attribute-based access control policies with environment attributes. In: Proceedings of the 23nd ACM on Symposium on Access Control Models and Technologies, pp. 213–215. ACM (2018)
8. Elbeltagi, E., Hegazy, T., Grierson, D.: Comparison among five evolutionary-based optimization algorithms. Adv. Eng. Inform. 19(1), 43–53 (2005)
9. Fürnkranz, J.: Separate-and-conquer rule learning. Artif. Intell. Rev. 13(1), 3–54 (1999)
10. Hu, V.C., et al.: Guide toattribute based access control (ABAC) definition and considerations (draft). NIST Spec. Publ. 800(162) (2013)
11. Iyer, P., Masoumzadeh, A.: Mining positive and negative attribute-based access control policy rules. In: Proceedings of the 23nd ACM on Symposium on Access Control Models and Technologies, pp. 161–172. ACM (2018)
12. Løvbjerg, M.: Improving particle swarm optimization by hybridization of stochastic search heuristics and self-organized criticality (2002)
13. Medvet, E., Bartoli, A., Carminati, B., Ferrari, E.: Evolutionary inference of attribute-based access control policies. In: Gaspar-Cunha, A., Henggeler Antunes, C., Coello, C.C. (eds.) EMO 2015. LNCS, vol. 9018, pp. 351–365. Springer, Cham (2015). https://doi.org/10.1007/978-3-319-15934-8_24
14. Narouei, M., Khanpour, H., Takabi, H.: Identification of access control policy sentences from natural language policy documents. In: Livraga, G., Zhu, S. (eds.) DBSec 2017. LNCS, vol. 10359, pp. 82–100. Springer, Cham (2017). https://doi.org/10.1007/978-3-319-61176-1_5
15. Narouei, M., Khanpour, H., Takabi, H., Parde, N., Nielsen, R.: Towards a top-down policy engineering framework for attribute-based access control. In: Proceedings of the 22nd ACM on Symposium on Access Control Models and Technologies, pp. 103–114. ACM (2017)
16. Narouei, M., Takabi, H.: Automatic top-down role engineering framework using natural language processing techniques. In: Akram, R.N., Jajodia, S. (eds.) WISTP 2015. LNCS, vol. 9311, pp. 137–152. Springer, Cham (2015). https://doi.org/10.1007/978-3-319-24018-3_9

17. Narouei, M., Takabi, H.: Towards an automatic top-down role engineering approach using natural language processing techniques. In: Proceedings of the 20th ACM Symposium on Access Control Models and Technologies, pp. 157–160. ACM (2015)
18. Salman, A., Ahmad, I., Al-Madani, S.: Particle swarm optimization for task assignment problem. Microprocess. Microsyst. **26**(8), 363–371 (2002)
19. Shi, Y., Eberhart, R.: A modified particle swarm optimizer. In: The 1998 IEEE International Conference on Evolutionary Computation Proceedings. IEEE World Congress on Computational Intelligence, pp. 69–73. IEEE (1998)
20. Shi, Y., Eberhart, R.C.: Empirical study of particle swarm optimization. In: Proceedings of the 1999 congress on Evolutionary computation, CEC 99, vol. 3, pp. 1945–1950. IEEE (1999)
21. Takabi, H., Joshi, J.B.: StateMiner: an efficient similarity-based approach for optimal mining of role hierarchy. In: Proceedings of the 15th ACM Symposium on Access Control Models and Technologies, pp. 55–64. ACM (2010)
22. Vaidya, J., Atluri, V., Guo, Q., Adam, N.: Migrating to optimal RBAC with minimal perturbation. In: Proceedings of the 13th ACM Symposium on Access Control Models and Technologies, pp. 11–20. ACM (2008)
23. Vaidya, J., Atluri, V., Warner, J.: RoleMiner: mining roles using subset enumeration. In: Proceedings of the 13th ACM Conference on Computer and Communications Security, pp. 144–153. ACM (2006)
24. Wenbiao, Z., Yan, Z., Zhigang, M.: A link-load balanced low energy mapping and routing for NoC. In: Lee, Y.-H., Kim, H.-N., Kim, J., Park, Y., Yang, L.T., Kim, S.W. (eds.) ICESS 2007. LNCS, vol. 4523, pp. 59–66. Springer, Heidelberg (2007). https://doi.org/10.1007/978-3-540-72685-2_6
25. Xu, Z., Stoller, S.D.: Mining attribute-based access control policies from logs. In: Atluri, V., Pernul, G. (eds.) DBSec 2014. LNCS, vol. 8566, pp. 276–291. Springer, Heidelberg (2014). https://doi.org/10.1007/978-3-662-43936-4_18
26. Xu, Z., Stoller, S.D.: Mining attribute-based access control policies. IEEE Trans. Dependable Secur. Comput. **12**(5), 533–545 (2015)
27. Zhang, D., Ramamohanarao, K., Ebringer, T.: Role engineering using graph optimisation. In: Proceedings of the 12th ACM Symposium on Access Control Models and Technologies, pp. 139–144. ACM (2007)

Author Index

Printed in the United States
By Bookmasters